OLD ORAIBI

A Study of the Hopi Indians of Third Mesa

Mischa Titiev

OLD ORAIBI
A STUDY OF THE HOPI INDIANS OF THIRD MESA

THE PUEBLO OF OLD ORAIBI.

OLD ORAIBI
A STUDY OF THE HOPI INDIANS OF THIRD MESA

MISCHA TITIEV

FOREWORD BY RICHARD FORD

UNIVERSITY OF NEW MEXICO PRESS

ALBUQUERQUE

Library of Congress Cataloging-in-Publication Data
Titiev, Misha, 1901–1978
    Old Oraibi: a study of the Hopi Indians of Third Mesa / Mischa
Titiev; foreword by Richard Ford.—University of New Mexico Press
ed.
    p. cm.
    Originally published: Cambridge, Mass. : Peabody Museum of
American Archaeology and Ethnology, Harvard University, 1944.
(Papers of the Peabody Museum of American Archaeology and
Ethnology, Harvard University ; vol. 22, no. 1).
    Includes bibliographical references and index.
    ISBN 0–8263–1344–2
    1. Hopi Indians —Social life and customs.   2. Hopi Indians-
-Religion and mythology. I. Title.
    E99.H7T5 1992
    973 .04974—dc20   92–3702
                                               CIP

Old Oraibi: A Study of the Hopi Indians of Third Mesa, Papers of
the Peabody Museum of American Archaeology and Ethnology, Harvard
University, vol. 22, no.1, was originally published in 1944.
This volume contains the complete text and illustrations of the
first edition.

University of New Mexico Press edition, 1992.

FOREWORD TO 1992 EDITION

I

IN 1932 it was unusually arid on the Hopi Mesas of north central Arizona. By contrast, New England, Mischa Titiev's adopted home, was lush and not the parched landscape that greeted him when he first visited the Hopi pueblos with Dr. Leslie White and his classmates under the auspices of the Laboratory of Anthropology summer field program. But he instantly liked the country and the people, who, until his arrival, had been impersonally portrayed to him on the pages of anthropological texts. Titiev was well-prepared by his Harvard professors to study a Pueblo and his own openness and warmth led to instant friendships that the Hopi and Titiev sustained throughout the anthropologist's professional career.

Mischa Titiev was born in Krementchug, Russia, on September 11, 1901, and he became a naturalized citizen of the United States in 1912. He graduated from Boston Latin School in 1919 and from Harvard University in 1923. He continued his graduate education at Harvard in anthropology, and he received his master of arts degree in 1924 and his doctorate in 1935. He financed part of his advanced education by tutoring at the Manter Hall School in Cambridge, Massachusetts. Mischa Titiev died on August 17, 1978.

Even in the 1930s a field experience was required for a dissertation in anthropology. Titiev selected the Hopi town of Oraibi for his study. He began his research at Hopi, under White's direction, with fellow students, Fred Eggan, Edward Kennard, Jesse Spirer, and George Devereux—a distinguished group that now reads as a who's who in midcentury American ethnology. In the summer of 1932 Titiev lived with his fellow students at Kykotsmovi and walked to Oraibi on the mesa above. A more extended sojourn ran from August 1933 to March 1934, while he resided in Oraibi. To say the least, his stay in Oraibi was quite eventful. Titiev organized a softball team of townsmen and was an avid participant. He developed friendships with many artists, and even though his means were strapped by the Depression, he purchased their paintings, katcina dolls, and other handicrafts to help them meet their basic needs.

Unlike many anthropologist who seek knowledge of other cultures only to leave their dissertation field site forever, Titiev returned to Hopi in the summers of 1937 and 1940 before *Old Oraibi* was published, and then frequently thereafter until 1973. He traveled widely and published significant anthropological articles and monographs about the Araucanians in Chile (1949, 1951), and the Japanese in Peru and Okayama, Japan (1954). Oraibi, however, always drew him back, even when his debilitating illness would have kept others homebound.

Following the completion of his doctorate, Titiev became an assistant museum curator and junior archaeologist with the National Park Service at historic Williamsburg (1935–1936). In 1936 he moved to Ann Arbor as an instructor of anthropology at the University of Michigan. He was promoted at Michigan to assistant professor in 1939, associate professor in 1944, and professor in 1954. He was awarded emeritus status in 1970. In the midst of his active scholarly career, he served the government in World War II as a member of the Office of Strategic Services, with assignments in India and China. In 1954 he had a Fulbright at the Australian National University.

His publications and professional honors acknowledge his contribution to theories of kinship and social anthropology, to ethnography in North America, especially Pueblo culture, and also to an interest in culture change as witnessed in the Japanese of Peru and Japan and the Araucanian Indians of Chile. He was a fellow of the American Anthropological Association, the secretary-treasurer of its Central States branch (1939–40), and treasurer of the Michigan Academy of Science, Arts, and Letters

(1943–44). He was a member of numerous distinguished learned societies.

Mischa Titiev married Estelle Berman in 1935. She and their son, Robert, accompanied him on his many travels. Oraibi, however, was their home away from home. Mischa and Estelle were married a second time at Oraibi in 1937. When they weren't among the Hopi and other demands limited Mischa's time for correspondence, Estelle's letters kept Hopi friends informed. Don C. Talayesva, who was dubbed Sun Chief by Leo Simmons in the book of the same title, was Titiev's teacher at Hopi (Simmons 1942: 307, 373) and in 1941 visited the Titiev family in Ann Arbor. After Mischa's death, Estelle maintained contact with Hopi families and with Fred Eggan, who, until his death in 1991, was assisting the Hopi as an expert witness for several legal cases.

Titiev's relations with the Hopi were special. When he returned to Oraibi in 1933, he rented a room from Don, and his sister, Inez, cooked for the anthropologist. Don maintained that "I was careful to teach him [Titiev] how to behave in the Hopi way" (Simmons 1942:309). Mischa's popularity in Oraibi extended to the children as well.

> My little boy loved Mischa, too. I [Don] told him that if he would obey us I would give him a complete cowboy outfit for Christmas. He kept reminding us of this, saying, "Daddy, you said that you would get me a cowboy suit." I always replied, "Yes, if you keep obeying us." Mischa helped me order the suit from Sears Roebuck. (Simmons 1942:309)

Titiev was adopted into the Sun Clan and became Don's younger brother. The esteem between Mischa and Don, however, was even deeper.

> I think he was the best-liked white man that had ever been to Oraibi. Some of the women even let him name their babies. I was sad when he left [1934] and was very gentle to his little dog which stayed with me. One of the finest things "Misch" ever did for me was to order medicine to treat my sore eyes. We were like real brothers. (Simmons 1942:311–12)

II

Titiev changed the name of the very much diminished village of Oraibi to Old Oraibi in order to distinguish it from Kykotsmovi, or New Oraibi, a growing community at the intersection of two important wagon roads below Third Mesa. The name has become familiar to anthropologists.

Old Oraibi is unlike any ethnographic monograph written about the Pueblos before 1944. Instead of the usual static chapter headings of culture traits that characterized most ethnographic publications about American Indians, Titiev wrote a dynamic study to capture the web of social relations and ceremonial obligations that a Hopi had to negotiate in daily life. For him descriptions of cultural categories were meaningless because each Hopi was defined by many social expectations; every social encounter required a different response. *Old Oraibi* is in part a study of Hopi social relationships in the everyday world, and in part a cultural history of Oraibi as seen through the experience of its oldest residents.

For readers seeking a conventional ethnography, *Old Oraibi* will be a disappointment. When Titiev studied with these venerable people, the community was still recovering from the famous social split of 1906. The ceremonial performances had been fragmented and ritual positions were lost with the exodus of religious specialists. Titiev explored the impact of this event on village life in the 1930s against a cultural reconstruction of religious life before the turn of the century. Many problems of social integration remained unresolved in Oraibi in 1933–34, but they could not be understood without a comprehensive understanding of critical issues of Hopi social structure. Part One of *Old Oraibi* investigates social relationships as experienced by Titiev's Hopi friends. In Part Two Titiev changes temporal perspectives and examines Hopi ceremonialism as he witnessed it and as his friends remembered it from four decades earlier.

Titiev was preceded by several others who observed Oraibi first-hand. The Reverend Henry R. Voth, who was a Mennonite missionary fluent in the Hopi language, published numerous articles and monographs about their ceremonies at the turn of the century. Early anthropologists such as Jesse W. Fewkes and Titiev's contemporary, Elsie Clews Parsons, had been there before him as well. The other Hopi villages had also been studied by anthropologists, so Titiev saw no reason to write a traditional village study. His objective was to illuminate more fully major problems in Hopi ethnography—social structure, personal relationships, the famous split of 1906, and the religious institutions that solidified the pueblo.

Titiev was a behaviorist and approached Oraibi with a scientific perspective. He analyzed personal observations, interviews in translation, and census data to produce an exceptional monograph. In preparing his study of Hopi ceremonialism, A.W. Geertz said:

> Titiev's anthropological work is the most reliable scientific report available. It is an in-depth view of the Hopi, coordinated by a holistic theory of Hopi society and religious organization. Together with his diary, one can gain insight into the Hopi in their everyday way of life. (Geertz and Lomatuway'ma 1987:10)

Titiev's field methods were sophisticated by contemporary standards. His observations were astute and as thorough as possible for an ethnologist doing fieldwork at Hopi in the 1930s. Few others were permitted to reside in a mesatop village at that time, and others were unprepared for a lack of running water, indoor lavatories, or general privacy. The absence of amenities never bothered Mischa. (This is reflected in his diary from his stay in Oraibi in 1933–34 [Titiev 1972]; the document is a splendid supplement to *Old Oraibi*.) Beyond the general method of participation-observation, Titiev used a census of the residents in Oraibi at the time of the famous split of 1906 and a work- activity schedule of his male neighbors twenty-seven years later. These have been invaluable for later researchers (e.g., Whitely 1988a, Kennard 1979).

The household census enabled Titiev to investigate many anthropological quandaries of Hopi social relations and kinship structure. For one, the question of cross-cousin marriage in the matrimonial Hopi villages was an unresolved question. Some evidence noted by earlier anthropologists suggested its existence but others published emphatic denials. Titiev demonstrated that 10 percent of the men in Oraibi had married their fathers' clanswomen and even more had mistresses from this group of relatives. Even the behavior of cross-cousin men and women impressed upon him that this marriage practice probably was more prevalent in the past. Titiev's study resolved the issue.

His work on clans and phratries was a contribution to still another problem for interpreting Hopi social organization. He demonstrated that clans drew from plant, animal, and supernatural personages for names, and that these were indeed regarded as ancestors. His door-to-door census again demonstrated that clans belonged to certain unnamed phratries. But the origin of phratries remained in contention. Titiev argued that new clans in a phratry arose from lineage segmentation from a clan . However, his close friend and fellow student of Hopi culture, Fred Eggan, disagreed by suggesting that clans were related in phratries according to ancestral subsistence similarities and their different origin myths argued against an ancient union (Eggan 1950:81). Their work on this subject is complementary.

Titiev's work settled further arguments about the order of closeness of relatives and the extension of kinship terms. His census records and observations of social behavior enabled him to show nine categories of relations regulated by incest and the possibility of marriage to distant relatives. At the time his delineation of these relationships became the basis for understanding Hopi social structure, even in the face of changing demographic and residency patterns.

His investigations of the most inclusive social category—the village—revealed important insights. He exposed the fragility of Hopi political activities and the internal forces that resisted concerted action or obedience to a village chief. His comprehensive reconstruction of the famous split of 1906 portrayed a social conflict far more complex than a simple rivalry of Hostiles vs. Conservatives over acculturation pressures, which is how historians and the government presented it. Instead his assessment suggested that clan disputes in a single phratry led to a disruption of the ceremonial calendar for the village and ultimately to a division of the village. Furthermore he regarded this as a lesson for archaeologists who sought to explain the abandonment of prehistoric sites as a response to environmental problems rather than to sociological causes. Titiev, however, did not have the last word about the split, as will be explained below.

In Part Two Titiev described what Eggan (1950:90) called "the only adequate interpretation of Hopi ceremonials." Titiev presented the organizing concepts of Hopi ceremonies and the role of the katcina cult in the ceremonial calendar. Many of his ceremonial descriptions remain the best we have for any Hopi village.

Titiev demonstrated the centrality of the Soyal ceremony for linking tribal initiation to the sequence of solar rites that would follow through the year. He recognized that the split prevented him from ever witnessing all the ceremonies and at best they would have to be communicated verbally by informants. Thus this section of his study is well documented with comparative information by earlier observers in Oraibi (Voth) and the other Hopi villages. Titiev provided a rich corpus of ceremonial information.

One particular contribution of *Old Oraibi* that has often been ignored but must be reassessed for its value to understanding intervillage relations, is his detailed discussion of Oraibi warfare and Momtcit rituals that surround the warriors' society and the *real* warriors, or those who have slain enemies. It is doubtful that we will ever again have a more thorough description of the rituals surrounding Hopi raiding.

While conceding the inherent value of *Old Oraibi*, two of the original reviewers had some criticisms of the study. Goldfrank (1945:301) wanted an introduction of detailed environmental and historical information to account for the social and ceremonial complexity at Oraibi. Goggin (1945:112) concluded that it was "the most complete account of a Hopi town to date" but that it lacked details of material culture. And many readers today may notice an absence of symbolic analysis. But in retrospect these are minor

wishes compared to the prodigious detail, insightful interpretations, and original and still unique observations of Hopi daily life and ceremonial activity contained in *Old Oraibi*.

III

The value of any ethnographic study is its utility for succeeding generations of scholars. *Old Oraibi* has passed this test many times. Book after book published since 1944 depends upon it for most details of Hopi society. This generalization is emphatically underscored by the articles on Hopi in Volume 9 of the *Handbook of North American Indians* (Ortiz 1979). Without Titiev's published works on Oraibi as a basic reference, these chapters would be impoverished.

Titiev's presentation of Hopi ceremonial organization was written to explain the belief system and ritual activities at Oraibi. However his work has been extended by later writers to all the Hopi villages. His detailed analysis certainly served as the baseline for Frigout's (1979) overview of "Hopi Ceremonial Organization"; Hieb's (1979) discussion of "Hopi World View" begins by accepting Titiev's analysis of the Hopi universe as fundamental to understanding the belief system of any knowledgeable Hopi. Likewise Geertz and Lomatuway'ma (1987) and Lofton (1991) introduce new ideas to interpret Hopi ceremonialism and religious behavior, but they depend upon Titiev as an accepted authority, as their numerous footnotes attest. Even archaeological studies of the origin and development of the katcina culture are dependent upon Titiev's research and functional interpretations (Adams 1991). Indeed Titiev would be delighted to learn of the extent to which *Old Oraibi* is used by archaeologists because he professed that to understand a culture in its natural setting, archaeology and ethnology must be complementary.

While his extensive discussion of the split at Oraibi in 1906 has long influenced all studies of Hopi, it has become the subject for continuing detailed research in the past twenty years. Bradfield (1971) has reopened the question of environmental degradation as a primary cause of the split. He views the social tensions described by Titiev as exacerbated by the erosion of arable land along Oraibi Wash. But while Bradfield's environmental assessment may provide useful background information, it unfortunately lacks chronological validity and fails to address the social account of the split as Titiev attempted to do. One must turn to Whitely to discover an exciting and relevant overview reassessment of the social dimension and cultural logic of the split. Whitely goes beyond Titiev and sees the split as predicted by Hopi prophesy. He sees the split as a deliberate action to challenge the existing leadership and to create a new social order at Hotevilla and Bacavi (Whitely 1988a, b). Titiev's interpretation of the split introduced an anthropological appreciation of the divisive nature of the social order, but he could not pursue a study of the split until he understood the fundamental social structure—lineage, clan and phratry —of Oraibi society. Whitely has challenged Titiev's failure to appreciate the fluidity of the social organization and has delved into the split from the stand point of the Hopi who left rather than those who remained when Titiev was in Oraibi a half century earlier. The split is fundamental to understanding Hopi social process and probably history, as Titiev knew. Beginning with Titiev and now with Whitely's comprehensive reassessment of the split, we have a greater appreciation of Hopi society.

Old Oraibi contains still more ethnographic insights that are benefiting the Hopi in their struggle against an often antagonistic world. As the styles of anthropology change, *Old Oraibi* will be read differently or for different purposes. Today it remains a remarkable contribution about a single Hopi village, and an indispensable document to aid all Hopi in their almost constant battle to maintain their culture and their natural resources. Its descriptions of the sacredness of water and the economic activities of Oraibi are useful for legal disputes to preserve Hopi water rights and land base, and to demonstrate the importance of herding in Hopi economic life. Without *Old Oraibi* and the witness statements Titiev recorded, we would lack the authentication required to assist the Hopi in litigation. Similarly, the reprinting of *Old Oraibi* will be useful to younger Hopi as they seek the details of their past. Some will be angered that glimpses of the esoteric side of their culture are again available. But they should also note that the efficacy of the ceremonies, rituals, and sacred activities remain unrevealed because the secret prayers and rituals' deliberations are not part of the study's structural and functional descriptions. When *Old Oraibi* was first published, it helped outsiders appreciate and understand the Hopi; today it promises to help anthropologists, historians, and the Hopi people preserve a culture threatened by avaricious corporations and unenlightened governmental polices. Mischa Titiev would only have wanted *Old Oraibi* to serve the Hopi people well.

RICHARD I. FORD
University of Michigan
Ann Arbor

ix

REFERENCES CITED

ADAMS, E. CHARLES
  1991 *The Origin and Development of the
     Pueblo Katsina Cult.* Tucson:
     The University of Arizona Press.

BRADFIELD, MAITLAND
  1971 *The Changing Pattern of Hopi Agri-
     culture.* London Royal Anthropological
     Institute Occasional Paper No. 30.

EGGAN, FRED
  1950 *Social Organization of the Western
     Pueblos.* Chicago: University of
     Chicago Press.

FRIGOUT, ARLETTE
  1979 Hopi Ceremonial Organization. In
     Alfonso Ortiz, ed., *Southwest,
     Handbook of North American
     Indians* 9:564–576.

GEERTZ, ARMIN and
MICHAEL LOMATUWAY'MA
  1987 *Children of Cottonwood, Piety and
     Ceremonialism in Hopi Indian
     Puppetry.* Lincoln: University of
     Nebraska Press.

GOGGIN, JOHN M.
  1945 Book Review: Old Oraibi. *American
     Journal of Science* 243 (Feb): 112.

GOLDFRANK, ESTER S.
  1945 Book review: Old Oraibi. *American
     Anthropologist* 47(2): 300–301.

HEIB, LOUIS A.
  1979 Hopi World View. In Alfonso Ortiz, ed.,
     *Southwest, Handbook of North American
     Indian* 9:577–580.

KENNARD, EDWARD A.
  1979 Hopi Economy and Subsistence. In
     Alfonso Ortiz, ed., *Southwest, Handbook of
     North American Indians* 9:554–563.

LOFTON, JOHN D.
  1991 *Religion and Hopi Life in the
     Twentieth Century.* Bloomington:
     Indiana University Press.

ORTIZ, ALFONSO, ed.
  1979 *Southwest. Handbook of North American
     Indians* Vol. 9. Washington: Smithsonian
     Institution.

SIMMONS, LEO W.
  1942 *Sun Chief, the Autobiography of a Hopi
     Indian.* New Haven: Yale University Press.

TITIEV, MISCHA
  1944 *Old Oraibi, A Study of the Hopi Indians
     of Third Mesa.* Cambridge: Papers of the
     Peabody Museum of American
     Archaeology and Ethnology,
     Harvard University, Vol. 22 no. 1.

  1949 *Social Singing among the Mapuche.*
     Ann Arbor: Anthropological Papers,
     Museum of Anthropology.
     University of Michigan No. 2.

  1951 *Araucanian Culture in Transition.* Ann
     Arbor: Occasional Contributions
     from the Museum of Anthropology
     of the University of Michigan No. 15.

  1954 *Chinese Elements in Japanese
     Culture.* Canberra: Australian
     National University.

  1972 *The Hopi Indians of Old Oraibi.* Ann
     Arbor: University of Michigan Press.

WHITELY, PETER
  1988a *Deliberate Acts.* Tucson:
     The University of Arizona Press.

  1988b *Bacavi, Journey to Reed Springs.*
     Flagstaff: Northland Press.

TO
THE MEMORY OF MY FATHER

MISCHA TITIEV WITH DON C. TALAYESVA, THIRD MESA, ca. 1950

PREFACE

BY FAR the greater part of the data presented in this monograph was obtained in the course of two visits to the Hopi Indians of Oraibi, Arizona. The first trip was made during the summer of 1932, as a member of the field party in ethnology which was led by Professor Leslie A. White, of the University of Michigan, and which was financed and sponsored by the Laboratory of Anthropology, Santa Fe, New Mexico. The second visit was of much greater duration, beginning on the first of August, 1933, and terminating at the end of March, 1934. The extended stay was made possible by a generous grant from the Division of Anthropology at Harvard University, and the Laboratory of Anthropology served as field headquarters. Since then I have twice revisited Oraibi, in the summers of 1937 and 1940, in order to freshen my contacts with Hopi culture.

The researches conducted by Professor White in 1932 fell into two divisions. While Dr. White, assisted principally by Kennard and Spirer, was investigating clans, lineages, and related phenomena, Eggan and the writer devoted themselves primarily to a study of the kinship system and the behavior of kindred toward each other. The material secured by all the members of the party was interchanged, and the results of the expedition's work are incorporated within the present volume. On my second visit I was permitted to live in the old pueblo of Oraibi on top of Third Mesa, and to participate to a considerable extent in the everyday life of the village. At this time I followed up the previous study of Hopi social organization, and undertook an intensive investigation of Hopi religion. In writing out my notes it has been impossible to segregate the material secured on the two field trips, so that it is to be understood that this monograph embodies a report of the work accomplished by the Laboratory of Anthropology's party in ethnology for 1932.

It is with a feeling of sincere appreciation that I wish to acknowledge my indebtedness to the entire staff of the Division of Anthropology at Harvard University during the years that I studied there. More particularly, I am grateful to Professors Tozzer and Hooton for their continued support of my project, and especially to the late Professor Roland B. Dixon, under whose guidance a good deal of my field work was done, and with whose help my material was first written out.

I am likewise indebted to the Laboratory of Anthropology and to its former director, Jesse L. Nusbaum, for the award of a scholarship in the summer of 1932, and for the additional help I received in the following two years.

To Professor Leslie A. White I owe thanks for a sound introduction to practical field work, and for many useful suggestions regarding my subsequent investigations. From my fellow students at Oraibi in 1932—Fred Eggan, Ed Kennard and Jess Spirer—I have received various aids from time to time, notably from Dr. Eggan, some of whose work has run parallel with my own, and who has always offered me his unstinted help and co-operation and has given me the benefit of a penetrating criticism of my manuscript.

While I was in the field, the late Dr. Elsie Clews Parsons[1] was editing the "Hopi Journal of Alexander M. Stephen," an invaluable sourcebook for all students of the Hopi. Although it had not yet been released, Dr. Parsons very kindly supplied me with a full set of galley-proofs. These I used throughout my extended stay at Oraibi, and they proved to be of immeasurable help in my work. In addition, Dr. Parsons has put a number of other publications and articles at my disposal and has sent me a host of fruitful suggestions both for field investigation and with regard to the handling of data after they were gathered. Dr. Parsons has very graciously taken the trouble to criticize a typescript of a good part of my manuscript, and a large number of her comments have been included in the final text.

I should like to take this opportunity also to

[1] While this manuscript was in the hands of the printer, the author was saddened by news of the untimely death of Dr. Elsie Clews Parsons. With her passing, American anthropologists have been deprived of a brilliant and versatile colleague, and students of Pueblo culture have lost one of their most forceful leaders.

Dr. Parsons' death followed by only a short time the decease of Benjamin L. Whorf, whose intensive study of the Hopi language was being eagerly awaited. The loss of these outstanding scholars will be keenly felt, especially by those anthropologists who are studying the cultures, past and present, of the Southwest.

express my thanks to Professor Clyde Kluckhohn for his helpful advice in regard to the arrangement of my material; to Professor W. L. Warner, particularly for his aid in the analysis of the kinship data; to Mr. and Mrs. Fletcher Corrigan, whose pleasant home at Oraibi furnished a most welcome relaxation from anthropological pursuits; to Mr. Lorenzo Hubbell, for his never-failing courtesy whenever I visited his trading post; to Mrs. Charis Denison Crockett, who gave me the notes she had gathered at Oraibi in the summer of 1933; to Miss Donna K. Miles, Miss Helen Gleason and her staff at the Dictaphone Station at the University of Michigan, for having typed the entire manuscript; and to my wife for her help in the tedious work of checking references and making final revisions.

MISCHA TITIEV

January 6, 1941

CONTENTS

PART THREE: MISCELLANY

PART FOUR: APPENDIX

LIST OF FIGURES

LIST OF PLATES

LIST OF CHARTS

LIST OF TABLES

INTRODUCTION

INTRODUCTION

THE HOPI Indians, a tribe speaking a Sho-shonean language, are located in the Little Colorado drainage, about 70 miles north of Winslow, Arizona.[1] They are the westernmost representatives of the Pueblo pattern of culture, and archaeological evidence has indicated that they are probably the direct descendants of some of the earliest tribes which settled in the South-west. Owing in part to geographical isolation, and in part to their stubborn resistance to outside influences, the Hopi have managed to preserve so great a part of their aboriginal culture that they afford a particularly attractive subject for ethnological investigation.

According to unofficial estimates based on the 1940 census, the Hopi number about 3000 individuals, who occupy eleven towns in northeastern Arizona. As one enters their reservation from the direction of Keam's Canyon, until recently the most practicable approach, the easternmost of three inhabited mesas comes first into view. For this reason, it has long been known as First or East Mesa. On its summit are perched the Tewa village of Hano and the Hopi town of Walpi, with its "suburb" of Sichumovi. A journey of a scant dozen miles further west brings one to the Second or Middle Mesa, on which are located the pueblos of Mishongnovi, Chimopovy, and Shipaulovi; and about 10 miles off to the northwest one encounters Third Mesa, at whose foot lies the town of New Oraibi and on whose summit from south to north are situated the pueblos of Old Oraibi, Bakavi, and Hotevilla. Forty miles westward, in the direction of the Grand Canyon, one finds the last of the Hopi villages, Moenkopi, a farming colony of Old Oraibi.

The present work is concerned principally with the inhabitants of the old pueblo of Oraibi, which was the only town on Third Mesa until 1906. As a result of successive divisions which began in that year, most of the previous inhabitants of Old Oraibi have since moved into the recently-founded villages of Hotevilla, Bakavi, and New Oraibi,[2] or else have settled permanently at the Moenkopi colony. Consequently, a study of Old Oraibi's former populace, which is the central aim of this undertaking, is basic to an understanding of all the Third Mesa towns.

Among the chief objectives of Part One have been a full description of the social organization of Oraibi as it functioned prior to the split of 1906, an analysis of the factors leading to that schism, a discussion of the dynamics of the pueblo's disintegration, and a study of the dispersal of the original population to new habitations. On the basis of these findings an analogy has been drawn with prehistoric Pueblo collapses, and an attempt has been made to interpret the latter in the light of the historic break-up of Oraibi.

Part Two is devoted to a description and analysis of Hopi ceremonialism. When all the major rituals are systematically arranged on the basis of their underlying aims, a coherent picture of the entire religion emerges. It then becomes plain that the religious beliefs and practices of the Hopi have been devised to serve as a supernatural buttress to support the weakest points of their social organization.

In order to prevent the main threads of the discussion from being lost in a sea of detail, several aspects of Hopi culture have been only briefly summarized in Parts One and Two. These are treated more fully either in the miscellaneous section that comprises Part Three, or in the Appendix.

Owing to a lack of linguistic training, I have made no attempt to record native terms precisely, but I have tried to make my approximations as accurate as possible.[3] During my stay at Old Oraibi, I acquired a sufficient knowledge of spoken

---

[1] The Hopi territory was known as Tusayan in former times, and the people were mistakenly called the Moqui or Moki. See Fewkes, 1907, p. 560.

[2] Throughout this monograph the names Oraibi and Old Oraibi will be used interchangeably to designate the ancient pueblo on Third Mesa. On the other hand, the recently-established village below the Mesa will invariably

be called New Oraibi.

[3] The fullest Hopi glossary available at this date has been compiled by Dr. Parsons, with the help of Benjamin L. Whorf. It occurs in Parsons, 1936b, pp. 1198–1326.

Both Mr. Whorf and Dr. Kennard have made studies of Hopi vocabulary and grammar, and it is to be hoped that their material will soon be published.

Hopi to serve as a control over informants, but for the most part I was unable to dispense with interpreters. However, there were enough English-speaking natives on hand to make this drawback relatively unimportant.

Throughout the course of my work I have endeavored to make available as much fresh material as I had been able to gather in the field; but at the same time, I have included digests of the literature published by many other investigators. Instead of keeping the two sets of data apart, however, I have tried to weld them together, in order to present the reader with a single yet comprehensive picture of Hopi life. Wherever possible I have attempted to interpret as well as to describe the phenomena under consideration, but unless otherwise stated, the responsibility for all interpretations must rest with me.

Inasmuch as my field work was done primarily at Oraibi, it follows that my account of Hopi culture applies to that village in particular and to Third Mesa in general; but whenever material was available I have indicated the chief resemblances and differences that are to be found at the other Mesas. A comparative study reveals that on the whole the Third Mesa situation may be regarded as typical of the entire tribe.

As the manuscript began to take shape, the question of making comparisons with other Pueblo groups arose. At the suggestion of the late Professor Dixon, I decided to concentrate entirely on the Hopi, with a view to interpreting each segment of their culture in relation to the whole. To achieve this goal, I have found it necessary to refrain from making comparisons with other Pueblo tribes, lest a tendency develop to explain Hopi customs in terms of non-Hopi patterns of behavior. While a comparative Pueblo study would unquestionably have been interesting and informative, I feel that the method of concentration followed in this volume has provided a deeper insight and has given me a fuller grasp of the dynamics of Hopi culture than could otherwise have been obtained.

Everyone who has worked among the Pueblo Indians realizes only too well how averse they are to revealing the details of their manner of life. This attitude on the part of native informants makes it virtually impossible to secure a complete record of any Pueblo tribe. Nevertheless, it is hoped that the present monograph has succeeded in filling some of the gaps in our knowledge of the Hopi and in clarifying some of the obscure points regarding their culture.

PART ONE

KINSHIP AND SOCIAL ORGANIZATION

Chapter I

THE KINSHIP SYSTEM

T HE FIRST petulant wail of a normally born Hopi infant has immediate significance primarily for two women. To the mother it means a welcome relief from the pain and labor of a solitary childbirth, for custom decrees that a Hopi woman shall engineer her own delivery as best she can at the time of the child's actual birth; and to the maternal grandmother it announces that she is now free to enter the delivery room, to sever and tie the umbilical cord, and to make mother and child as comfortable as possible. Soon after the baby is born several other women may be summoned. Chief among these are women from the child's father's clan, particularly the father's mother or the father's sister, who washes the tiny infant's head and forthwith assumes the role of master of ceremonies during the twenty-day lying-in period which terminates with the baby's naming rites and a general feast.[1]

From the outset the task of inducting a baby into the social sphere of which it is to be a part rests with women. Under ordinary circumstances no medicine men hover anxiously over a laboring woman, nor do Hopi fathers fidget eternally in waiting rooms of maternity wards. On the contrary, immediately following the birth of a child its father does not wait to be shooed away or to be brusquely ordered about by bustling women. Instead, under pretext of better observing the forty day period of continence imposed on recent parents, he retires to the seclusion of the kiva where days are less harassing and nights far more serene than in a household sheltering a new-born-babe.[2]

Not for some years, regardless of a baby's sex, is the predominance of women in ordering its adjustment to life relaxed. As a consequence of the Hopi custom of having daughters remain for life in their mother's household, and through the agencies of matrilineal descent and strict matrilocal residence,[3] a newly-born child automatically becomes a member of a household group among whom it comes to distinguish its maternal grandparents, its parents, its mother's sisters with their husbands and children, its mother's unmarried brothers, its married sisters with their husbands and children, and its unmarried brothers and sisters. It is in the company of these relatives that the growing child eats, sleeps and plays, and it is among them that it first becomes cognizant of those ties of kinship which in later life are to be extended to other relatives.[4]

We have but to make a diagram of the relatives with whom a child shares common residence in a matrilocal, matrilineal society, and the basic nature of the household group comes clearly to to light (chart I). In the first place, by comparison with the total kinship system as shown on chart II, we find all but three of the Hopi terms for consanguineous relatives represented on the household diagram. Only the terms for child, grandchild, and father's sister are missing. Thus, in so far as terminology is concerned, most of the essential features of the whole system are incorporated within the limits of the household. In the second place, it will be seen that all the members of the household, except for men who have moved in by virtue of marriage, belong to the same clan. Accordingly, from the child's point of view, his first concept of clan ties is not general but is confined to those members of the clan who live in his household. Finally, the basic feature of this grouping is the fact that a mature woman, her daughters, and, occasionally, her granddaughters, occupy a common residence through life and bring up their children under the same roof.

---

[1] Accounts of Hopi natal customs may be found in Voth, 1905a; Owens, 1892; Beaglehole, E., and P., 1935, pp. 30–38; and Parsons, 1921c, pp. 98–102.

A general treatment of Hopi rites of passage in chronological order occurs in Beaglehole, E., 1937, pp. 72–77.

[2] In reality men often take advantage of this period for indulging in extra-marital affairs.

[3] Linton, 1936, pp. 163–165, makes an excellent point when he insists that the terms matrilocal and patrilocal are relative, and that it is essential for writers to explain in each instance the degrees of distance and separation that are involved.

Among the Hopi, matrilocal residence normally implies a change of households within the same village. Only in exceptional cases does a man move very far from his natal household. See also Titiev, 1943c.

[4] I am indebted to Dr. Fred Eggan for having first called my attention to the great importance of the household among the Hopi. This unit is also discussed in Beaglehole, E., 1937, p. 5; and Beaglehole, P., 1935, pp. 41–54.

Viewed in this aspect the women of a household in a matrilineal, matrilocal society constitute, with their offspring, a distinct segment of a lineage.

marry, and men from other groups move in at marriage. Because household membership is subject to numerical fluctuation its composition can-

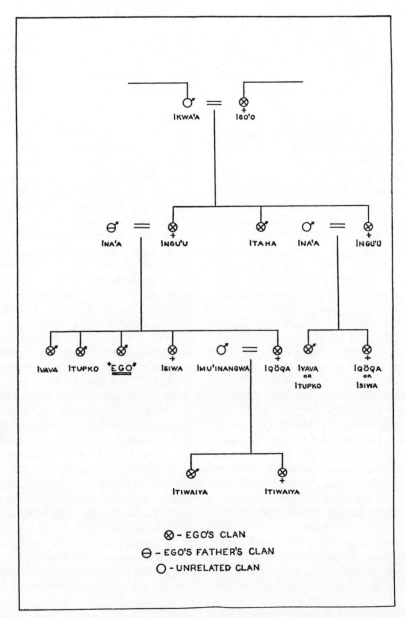

CHART I. A HOUSEHOLD GROUP.

The composition of the household group combines elements of fixity and mobility. The women have a status which is fixed and gives permanency to the entire structure, but the masculine element is often in a state of flux since men born within the household move out when they

not be rigidly delimited nor precisely defined. In fact, although for purposes of analysis the household group may be treated as a distinctive part of the kinship system, it should be made clear that there is no native term for this grouping, and that the Hopi do not recognize it as an independent

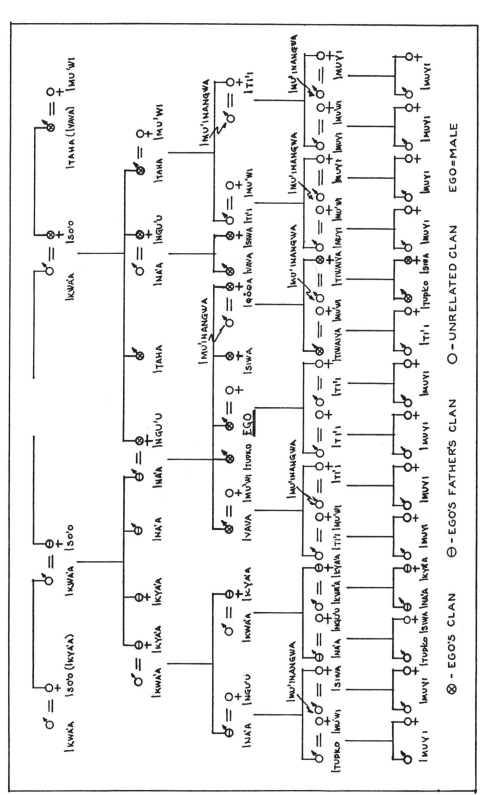

CHART II. THE HOPI KINSHIP SYSTEM.

kinship unit. At the same time there is no denying the important part the household plays in their scheme of existence.[5] So strong is an individual's attachment to the household of his birth that when a married man refers to "his house," he generally means not his wife's house where he is now living, but his mother's house where he was brought up.[6]

Women too feel the pull of the natal household. I knew an Oraibi woman who had long

he means siblings whose mothers were sisters. So close are the ties of sisters that it is not impossible to find middle-aged individuals failing to distinguish their mothers from their mothers' sisters, a confusion brought about by the triple factors of common residence, the application of exactly the same kinship term to the mother and the mother's sisters, and the use of identical terms for their offspring.

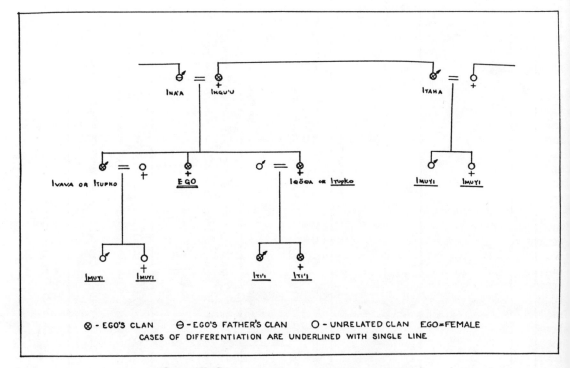

CHART III. SEX DIFFERENCES IN KINSHIP TERMINOLOGY.

resided at Walpi with her First Mesa husband in violation of the custom of matrilocal residence, but she had returned to her mother's house for the birth of each of her three children. "She always comes home to have her babies," I was told.

It is because of the strong feeling for household ties that the Hopi, without recognizing this group of kindred terminologically as a separate unit, nevertheless make a distinction between these relatives and general clanmates. A person feels closer to his mother's sisters and their children than to the offspring of other women in his clan; and almost invariably, when a Hopi refers in English to his "clan brothers" or "clan sisters,"

As a consequence of this system, a natural thing for a Hopi woman to do in the event of a sister's death is to adopt the children of the deceased, an act that implies no change either in residence or terminology, and that scarcely affects the tenor of household life.

As a Hopi infant begins to grow up he becomes increasingly aware of relationships outside his own household group. These center primarily about the father's natal household where a child is a frequent and a welcome visitor. Here he meets his paternal grandparents, his father's unmarried brothers, his father's unmarried sisters, and his father's married sisters together with

[5] Compare Parsons, 1939, p. 5.
[6] Compare Voth, 1903b, p. 13, footnote 1; and Tozzer,

1928, p. 173, where he speaks of a husband as a "privileged boarder in the house of his wife and her relatives."

their husbands, daughters, and unwed sons. It should be remembered that the women of the father's household play extremely important parts in a baby's birth and naming rites. During these ceremonies they inaugurate a fond and continuously active interest in the child which later develops into one of the most affectionate relationships in Hopi life.

Kinship ties with the father's household, complementing those with his own group, soon enable a child to understand without conscious effort his proper position in the complete kinship pattern. And now, having shown the orientation of an infant, we may take up our discussion from an adult point of view.

The Hopi system of reckoning relationships is classificatory and of the bifurcate-merging or Crow type[7] (chart II). The father and the father's brothers are grouped together, and the mother's sisters are classed with the mother; but father's sister and mother's brother are set clearly apart. This method of designating kindred classes together parallels cousins and differentiates cross cousins.

In a system bifurcated according to sex, there must be some differences in the terminologies employed by a male and a female ego; for a Hopi woman's sister's children are grouped with her own and her brother's children are set apart (chart III), whereas the reverse is true of a man's siblings' children. Again, where a man calls his mother's brother's children *iti'i*, a woman terms her mother's brother's children *imuyi*.[8] These usages are explained in rule 4 for men and rule 6 for women given below. There is an additional instance of sex differentiation in Hopi terminology which is not inherent in the Crow system. A man calls his younger sister by a special term, *isiwa*, but a woman designates her younger sister as *itupko*, the term used by both sexes for the younger brother. I do not know the reason for this usage.

The role of the matrilineal clan in the total kinship system is simple and clearly defined. We have already noted that the closest feeling of relationship known to a Hopi is with those members of his lineage and clan who live in his household. From this nucleus kinship ties reach out toward nonresident members of the lineage, and from them to the entire clan. The basis of the extension, as shown by the terminology and as reflected in the behavior, is the sole principle that all men and women of the same generation and clan are actually or theoretically brothers and sisters to each other. With this as an axiom, six other rules of reckoning kindred follow as corollaries.[9]

1. Ego ♂ or ♀ : All men and women in one's own generation and clan are brothers (*itupko*, *ivava*), and sisters (*isiwa*, *iqöqa*).[10]

2. Ego ♂ and ♀ : All men and women in one's father's generation and clan are father's brothers (*ina'a*), and father's sisters (*ikya'a*).

3. Ego ♂ or ♀ : All men and women of the same generation, whose fathers are in the same clan, are brothers and sisters.[11]

4. Ego ♂ : All children of men in one's own clan are brother's children (*iti'i*).

5. Ego ♂ : All children of women of one's own clan are sister's children (*itiwaiya*).

6. Ego ♀ : All children of men in one's own clan are brother's children (*imuyi*).

7. Ego ♀ : All children of women of one's own clan are sister's children (*iti'i*).

Even these few simple rules of clan relationships may be still further condensed after the principles involved are thoroughly understood. For all practical purposes the entire situation may be summed up in a brief formula: A newly-born baby is automatically a member of its mother's clan, and a child of its father's clan.[12]

Perhaps the most puzzling feature of the Hopi kinship system to an outsider is the utter disregard of generation levels in the terminology. A little analysis soon reveals that this disregard,

---

[7] Lowie, 1937, pp. 84–86.

[8] The prefix "i" in Hopi means "my." Since Hopi kinship terms never stand alone a speaker changes the possessive prefix as his meaning changes. For purposes of simplification we shall arbitrarily use the possessive form of the first person singular in all instances. The Hopi suffix "m" indicates the plural. Comparative data on the use of kinship terms may be found in Parsons, 1936b, pp. 1042–1052.

[9] These rules should be checked by reference to charts II and III.

[10] Where there is a marked age discrepancy ego may "raise" a clan brother or sister to his mother's generation

level and so call the older person mother's brother (*itaha*) or mother's sister (*ingu'u*).

[11] The operation of this rule was neatly illustrated one day when I was teasing an Oraibi girl named Duwayauonim (Shifting Sand), daughter of a Sand clansman, regarding marriage to a Hotevilla man named Pongyayesva (Standing Altar). "I can't marry him," said the girl. She then went on to explain that Standing Altar was a Sand clan name (Hopi altars are set in sand), which indicated that Pongyayesva was the son of a Sand clansman and therefore a brother to her and ineligible for marriage.

[12] Compare Parsons, 1925, p. 15, footnote 12.

far from being random and chaotic, is based on fixed principles of clan relationship.[13] Practically all the instances of the violation of generation lines in naming relatives are listed below, and consultation of the appropriate rules on page 11 shows that every case is clearly explicable in terms of clan kinship ties.

EXAMPLES FROM CHART II

Ego ♂ or ♀ : Father's sister's son (*ina'a*)
Father's sister's daughter (*ikya'a*)
(See Rule 2)

Father's sister's son's son (*itupko*)
Father's sister's son's daughter (*isiwa*)
(See Rule 3)

Father's sister's daughter's son (*ina'a*)
Father's sister's daughter's daughter (*ikya'a*)
(See Rule 2)

Ego ♂   Mother's brother's son (*iti'i*)
Mother's brother's daughter (*iti'i*)
(See Rule 4)

Sister's son's son (*iti'i*)
Sister's son's daughter (*iti'i*)
(See Rule 4)

Sister's daughter's son (*itupko*)
Sister's daughter's daughter (*isiwa*)
(See Rule 1)

EXAMPLES FROM CHART III

Ego ♀   Brother's son (*imuyi*)
Brother's daughter (*imuyi*)
(See Rule 6)

Mother's brother's son (*imuyi*)
Mother's brother's daughter (*imuyi*)
(See Rule 6)

So far we have been concerned only with relatives by consanguinity. Let us now turn to a brief discussion of relationships by marriage. The Hopi employ only two generic terms for relatives-in-law. (See chart II.) All men who marry women of ego's generation and below are called *imu'inangwa;* and all women, regardless of generation, who marry into ego's clan are termed *imu'wi.* While the term for relative-in-law is almost never employed in the vocative when speaking to males, the opposite is true in the case of females. From the moment a bride enters on the first step of the long wedding ritual, she is invariably addressed as *imu'wi* by the groom's relatives and often by unrelated villagers. Even a boy's mistress may sometimes be called *imu'wi* by

his clanmates. It is a feature of the Hopi system that the two terms of affinity are non-reciprocal. Thus, a man or a woman is called relative-in-law by the mate's relatives, but husband and wife, apart from sex differences in terminology, customarily employ the same terms for each other's kindred.

In some instances relatives by marriage are addressed by terms of consanguinity, and in these cases the terms are reciprocal. Men who marry women in the generations above ego are called father (*ina'a*) or grandfather (*ikwa'a*) as the case may be, and all men who marry women standing in an *ikya'a* relationship to ego are invariably addressed by the regular term for grandfather.

The Hopi extend kinship terminology beyond clan limits by virtue of the fact that each clan is an integral part of a larger exogamic unit, or phratry.[14] Since all the clans in any given phratry stand in a brother-sister relationship to each other, kinship extensions to the phratry involve no new principles. It is merely a matter of substituting the term phratry for clan throughout the preceding discussion and the same factors continue to operate intact.

Utter ignorance of infant hygiene and dietetics often serves to bring about still another extension of kinship. Nearly every Hopi infant seems destined to pass through at least one serious illness before it reaches adolescence. In such a case the frantic mother generally gives the child to be adopted by some specially qualified individual, such as a medicine man. If the baby survives it finds itself provided with an adoptive father, and as it grows up it is taught to employ exactly the same terminology for the doctor father's clan and phratry that it uses for its own paternal relatives. Since this type of adoption does not mean that the child is expected to move out of the mother's household, it is quite possible for an individual to have more than one doctor father.

There is one other form of extending kinship which, far from being optional, is a universal requisite. Every Hopi youngster begins his ceremonial career by being inducted into the Katcina cult. As a child nears the customary initiation age the parents look about for some worthwhile neighbor to serve as its ceremonial father.[15] A

---

[13] Failure to recognize this principle in actual operation has led to serious confusion in the interpretation of at least one aspect of Hopi religion. For a discussion of this point, see Titiev, 1937b.

[14] Throughout this monograph the word phratry is used

only in the narrow sense of an exogamic unit consisting of two or more clans. Among some students of the Hopi the term phratry is not accepted as applicable. This problem will be discussed in a later chapter.

[15] In the case of a girl a ceremonial mother is chosen.

good deal of care is exercised in making a decision, as the parents are eager to provide for their child a man who will be both loving and helpful. Yet, ceremonial parents may not be chosen either from the novice's own or his father's phratry. When we asked the reason for this discrimination against one's closest relatives, we were told that it is better to choose ceremonial kindred from unrelated clans "because it brings more people to you." In other words, kinship ties are extended *in toto* to the ceremonial father's clan and phratry, and in native theory it is an advantage to have connections with as many groups as possible.

Through the agency of wholesale kinship extension a Hopi generally finds himself related, exclusive of relatives acquired through marriage, to his own, his father's, his doctor father's, and his ceremonial father's phratries, thus furnishing him early in life with specific relationship ties in four of the nine phratries on Third Mesa.[16] The importance of this feature will become more apparent when we analyze the integrative and disintegrative aspects of Hopi society.

Kinship extensions on so vast a scale not only foster large numbers of relatives, but also permit individuals to stand in a variety of relationships to each other.[17] For example, there was a Sun clansman at Oraibi whose father was a Bear, and whose ceremonial father was of the Masau'u clan. At the same time, the Village chief was a Bear, his true father was Masau'u, and his ceremonial father was of the Sun clan. Accordingly, the following relationships existed between the chief and his subject:

Bear clan connection—subject calls chief father, rule 2.[18]

Masau'u clan connection—subject calls chief older brother, rule 3.

Sun clan connection—subject calls chief child, rule 4.

In such cases there is no fixed order of preference for the use of one term rather than another,

but it is customary for terms based on relationships within one's own clan to take precedence over those based on the father's or the ceremonial father's clan. Furthermore, in the particular instance cited above, the subject was considerably younger than the chief, hence I was told that it was more fitting for the subject to employ the term for father in addressing the chief.

In a society where an individual often extends kinship terminology to more than half his fellow villagers, it is inconceivable that so large a host of relatives as must be included under each term should all rate on a par. Distinctions of some sort must be made or felt even when they are hidden from view by classificatory phrasing which serves, superficially, to amalgamate rather than to differentiate kindred.[19] Such distinctions as are made between relatives addressed by identical terms cannot be ascertained precisely, but in a general way it may be said that a Hopi feels attached to his relatives in the following order:

1. Limited family, consisting of own parents, brothers, and sisters.[20]
2. Mother's sisters and their children.
3. Other members of own household.
4. Other members of own clan.
5. Father's household.
6. Other members of own phratry.
7. Other members of father's clan-phratry.
8. Ceremonial father's clan-phratry.
9. Doctor father's clan-phratry.

This list was compiled on the basis of such bits of evidence as the fact that in many instances a Hopi will say that he is related to all the members of his clan, but "only a little bit related" to the other members of his phratry. And yet identical sets of kinship terms are applied to both groups of relatives. Another example of this kind of discrimination was brought to light on one occasion when the Oraibi chief was cross-examining me in great detail on my dealings with a Hopi stranger for whom I had once arranged a ride to Moenkopi.

[16] Extensions of kinship are not restricted to the confines of one's own village but are freely made on a clan-phratry basis throughout the entire tribe. On the same basis, kinship may be extended to any tribe known to the Hopi. In fact, this may be carried to such an extent that where a foreign tribe has a clan which does not occur among the Hopi, the name may be equated on a rationalistic basis with some one of the Hopi clans. Thus a Hopi woman from the Masau'u clan once called a Navaho Wood clanswoman "sister," because, as she explained it, the Hopi Masau'u clan is related to the Cedar clan and

this is related to Wood. (A similar case is described in Parsons, 1923c, p. 207.) Since such far-fetched extensions come into play only rarely, we shall limit our discussion to village and mesa relationships which are ever present in the consciousness of the native.

[17] On this point compare Lowie, 1929a, p. 369.
[18] These rules are from p. 11.
[19] Compare Lowie, 1915, p. 230.
[20] After marriage, spouse and children become part of one's limited family.

It seems that the man was demented, and in a violent outburst against a set of Katcina dancers, he had linked my name with his cause. Surprised and upset by so unfortunate a turn of events, I tried to take refuge in the kinship system. Though I knew that the chief was childless, I protested that I had granted the stranger a favor only because he had represented himself as a son of the chief. At this the chief exclaimed testily, "Oh yes, in a ceremonial way he is my son, but he's not my real son,"—a rare critical distinction on the part of the chief and forced from him only by the stress of emotion.

A still more striking proof that degrees of relationship are implicitly recognized by the community is found in the rules governing exogamy. Within the first seven degrees on our list marriage is forbidden, although with the fifth and seventh (father's household and clan-phratry) it is only theoretically forbidden but actually tolerated; but with the eighth and ninth it is freely permitted.

In conclusion, it appears fairly evident that despite their wide use of classificatory terminology, the Hopi are fully conscious of varying degrees of relationship even among those relatives who are classed under a single term.[21]

[21] Lowie, 1915, p. 230, has already noted that "the linguistic grouping of different relatives under the same category does not blind the users of such a terminology to the differences in the relationships."

CHAPTER II

THE RECIPROCAL BEHAVIOR OF KINDRED[1]

NEARLY all modern ethnologists make it a part of their field work to ferret out information on kinship systems. Some regard the search as an end in itself and publish relationship patterns as isolated parts of their studies; others content themselves with giving lists of kinship terms from which the reader may, with a good deal of weary labor, puzzle out the system for himself; only a few attempt to analyze the basic structure of a kinship system and to relate it, wherever possible, to other ethnological phenomena in the tribe under consideration. It cannot be denied that kinship data have but limited worth when regarded as ends in themselves. To treat them thus is to speak the words of a language without knowing their meanings. It seems highly desirable, therefore, that after describing and ranking the various groupings of kindred, we should proceed to an examination of the values that the natives impute to their terms of relationship.

Among the Hopi every kinship term carries with it a set of rights, privileges, duties, and obligations, which are reflected in the behavior of kindred; and in turn, the behavior pattern serves to endow each term with a fixed value in the minds of the natives. This is shown by the fact that despite its wide application kinship terminology is never carelessly employed. On the contrary, whenever relatives quarrel they generally make heated proclamations renouncing the use of the appropriate kinship terms for each other. One of these quarrels at Oraibi involved Inez, my housekeeper. It so happened that for a number

of reasons Inez had come to despise the woman who had served as her ceremonial mother. To tease her I would sometimes refer to this woman as "her mother," whereupon Inez would invariably flare up and exclaim, "I told you that I don't call her 'mother' any more!" Such examples could be multiplied indefinitely.

That relationship terms connote definite values can be readily established, nor is it hard to show that these values find expression in the behavior pattern. In order to vitalize the kinship system, then, it becomes necessary to examine in some detail the rights and duties inherent in each term of relationship.[2] Among the Hopi an individual's adjustment to his household group (chart I) forms the nucleus of his attitudes towards most of his relatives. This is true even today, despite the modern tendency for married daughters to leave their natal households and to move into houses of their own. It may be that this change of custom will in the future alter the present feeling for household kindred, but as late as 1934 the Hopi of Oraibi still felt their closest ties to be with those of their kindred who would have lived together under the old system of matrilocal residence. Accordingly, we shall begin with a consideration of the reciprocal behavior of those relatives who comprise the household group.

HUSBAND ⟵⟶ WIFE[3]

The term for wife is *inuma* when used by outsiders, and *iwuhti* (my woman) or *sowuhti* (old woman) when used by a husband. The customary term for husband is *igonya*, but there is a rarely

---

[1] A good deal of the material for this chapter was collected in conjunction with Dr. Fred Eggan while we were both members of the field party at Oraibi in 1932, which was supervised by Dr. Leslie A. White, and which was financed by the Laboratory of Anthropology at Santa Fe, New Mexico. Some of this material may be found in Eggan, 1933.

This section and the ones immediately following have had the great advantage of numerous suggestions from Dr. E. C. Parsons. For these the author is truly grateful, although it has been impossible to acknowledge each item separately.

[2] In the preceding chapter it was shown that it is often possible for two people to stand in a variety of relationships to each other. Where feasible the behavior attendant

on each connection is carried out. For instance, my principal interpreter, Don Talayesva, was the ceremonial father of a girl named Elizabeth, and as a father he made her the customary present of a Katcina doll during the Powamu ceremony. Elizabeth belonged to the Greasewood clan from which Don's own ceremonial father had been chosen. She was, therefore, through the operation of rule 2 above, a father's sister (*ikya'a*) to Don, and in this capacity she brought him food when he danced as a clown.

[3] Many of the behavior patterns treated from this point on may be compared with Second Mesa customs by consulting Beaglehole, E., 1937, and with First Mesa by consulting Parsons, 1936b, pp. L–LI, 1065–1066, *et passim*.

For comparative Pueblo data, see Parsons, 1939, pp. 57–60.

used alternative, *ivusingwa* (my sleeping partner). When there are children in the family teknonymy is fairly common on the part of either parent, but this practice is rapidly fading out in favor of American names. Hopi personal names are not applied to each other by a married couple.

In former times the custom of matrilocal residence was probably universally observed with the possible exception of inter-mesa marriages where a wife went to live in her husband's village. More recently, all brides of Moenkopi men have gone there to live.

Matrilocal residence in the old days meant that a groom moved into his wife's house and thus became a member of her household group. Under present conditions there is an increasing tendency for young couples to build houses for themselves. In such cases the heavier work of cutting and hauling stones and beams is done by the husband while such light tasks as plastering and thatching are performed by the wife. Nevertheless, all houses belong to women and are transmitted only to female heirs. Similarly, all household utensils belong to the women, although in some instances the men help to fashion them. On the other hand, men own such distinctively masculine objects as farming tools and harness.

In labor there is a marked sex dichotomy. Generally speaking, women fetch water, chop wood, prepare meals, tend the children, wash clothes, keep the house in repair, make plaques or baskets, and cultivate small garden patches which are situated near springs. The men do the farming, herd sheep, haul wood, weave blankets, rugs and wearing apparel, and make moccasins.

Since all land, theoretically, is held by clans, it is felt, in this matrilineal society, to be the property of women. Similarly, all crops raised by married men belong to the wives whose land they cultivate. Likewise, although the Hopi women never herd sheep, they may inherit or acquire shares in flocks which the men look after.

Women play relatively minor parts in the religious life of the village, but they participate by washing and dressing the husband's hair on all ceremonial occasions and by bringing food to Katcina dancers at the noon rest period. During many observances the women are required to prepare special foods which must be brought to the kiva in prescribed vessels at definite times and the sacred cornmeal which is used in a rituals must be ground by women. Wives also share in the excitement of a dance day by keeping open house for friends and relatives and dressing themselves and their children in holiday attire.

There is a four-day tabu on sexual relations between husband and wife for all common participants in ceremonies, and a sixteen-day tabu for officers. Sex activities are generally lapsed during menstruation but may be resumed without special ritual at the conclusion of the period. For a primitive people the Hopi show an exceptional disregard for "contagion" and have no fear of menstrual blood. No tabus are imposed on menstruating women, who may even participate at will in the dances of women's societies.[4]

It is thought best to abstain from sexual activity during pregnancy, and a woman who bears children annually is likened to a beast. Partly to prevent such occurrences, and partly for other reasons, there is a ban on sexual intercourse for forty days after the birth of a child.[5] During this period the husband moves out of the house and sleeps in his kiva. Over-frequent child-bearing is checked in rare cases by the use of an emmenagogue administered by medicine men, but more commonly women suffer many miscarriages due to utter disregard for pre-natal care and to the continuance of difficult physical tasks.

The nature of the bond between husband and wife varies widely with the characters of the individuals concerned. Some couples are devoted and loyal, others quarrelsome and jealous. Very often one finds a strange brusqueness even on the part of happily married men towards their wives. Sometimes, they will leave the house abruptly in the morning without a word regarding their plans for the day. Again, although they may take their wives with them to view a dance at another village, they will rarely make visits together, and they invariably sit apart while the dance is in progress. Except in unusual cases where unanimity of opinion is essential, husband and wife are free to follow individual notions to such an extent that there are many instances of a Hopi turning Christian while the mate remains true to the native belief.[6] Rarely does a man take it on himself to make a decision for his wife or vice versa.

---

[4] Compare Beaglehole, E., and P., 1935, p. 45.

[5] On Second Mesa, the tabu is said to last twenty-five days. Compare Beaglehole, E., and P., 1935, p. 38.

[6] It must not be thought that conversion to Christianity is taken lightly. The history of Oraibi shows that such a step is very seriously regarded.

On the whole, the marriage situation is in keeping with the general Hopi emphasis on individual freedom. There is no compulsion in the choice of a mate, and there is no restriction on divorce. When a separation takes place the objects owned by the couple are divided along the lines of ownership discussed above. Young children invariably remain with the mother, but older children may follow either parent.

In analyzing the husband-wife reciprocal it is extremely important to consider their relative positions in the household. The man is an outsider whose warmest ties, apart from wife and children, are with his own household.[7] Still, he must work his wife's land, help build her house, and in many ways contribute to the support of her entire household. In direct contrast the wife, at marriage, suffers no severance of kin and home ties, and every improvement in her condition is a gain for her household and clan. Small wonder, then, that every girl is expected to marry, and that her brothers should be especially active in guiding her conduct to prevent divorce.

Nevertheless, as our discussion of "Courtship, Marriage, and Divorce" will demonstrate, divorce is of frequent occurrence. Its effect is minimized through the mechanism of the household which is so ordered that it takes up the shocks that result from the breakdown of individual families. So secure and firmly embedded is the position of a woman in her household group, that a change of husband has little or no effect on the larger unit.

FATHER ⟷ SON[8]

ina'a ⟷ *iti'i*

ina'a is applied to: Father, father's brother, father's sister's son, mother's father's brother's son, mother's father's sister's son, all men belonging to the father's clan, all sons of an *ikya'a*, all husbands of an *ingu'u*.)

iti'i is applied to: Son, daughter, brother's children [male speaking], children of men in own clan [male speaking], children of sister's sons [male speaking], children of women of own clan [female speaking], sister's children [female speaking].)

A Hopi father has no special duties of any sort at the time of a son's birth. He bestows no gifts, makes no offerings, and goes through no ceremony of any kind. He is not allowed to be in the room when the child is born, and he spends very little time at home for the first forty days of the baby's life. Of course he kills a sheep and provides food for the son's naming feast on the twentieth day following his birth, but on the whole a father's greatest interest in his son does not manifest itself until the child is nearly of age to enter the Katcina cult.

In choosing ceremonial parents, a father consults his wife, and between them they decide on the man they consider most fit to aid their son in later life.[9] Only the real father has a voice in picking his son's ceremonial father. This is also true in the event that a child's illness warrants his being given in adoption to a doctor father.

While a son is still a baby all Katcina secrets are carefully guarded from him, and whenever a father is dancing as a Katcina he will conceal his identity from the child but will manage to bring him various gifts as if they were sent by the gods. When the proper time comes for the boy to go through the Katcina initiation, both his ceremonial father and his real father make him gourd rattles and bows and arrows. It sometimes happens that a boy's own father is acting as the Katcina who whips initiates, but in such cases the father must show no partiality for his son.

Sex dichotomy in labor tends to make the bond between father and son very close, as the greater part of a boy's instruction in farming and herding is received from his father. Almost as soon as a boy can walk he begins to accompany his father into the fields or to the sheep corral. Here, at first, he spends most of his time in play, but as he grows older the father begins to give him

---

[7] The attraction a man feels for his own household is clearly evident on feast days. Everywhere one sees men going to dine with their mothers and sisters while their wives remain at home. Racing customs also show how adherence to clan and household ties tends to loosen the marital bond. When races are held by clans, husbands and wives affiliate themselves solely with their own groups.

[8] It is impossible in every instance to differentiate between the various personages to whom a single term is applied. Accordingly, the material on reciprocal behavior

has been presented here from a general point of view for each degree of relationship. Wherever special cases require a distinction as, let us say, between one type of father and another, we shall call attention to the fact in our discussion.

[9] For a boy a ceremonial father is chosen and this man's sister, or some other woman from his clan, serves as the ceremonial mother. For a girl the ceremonial mother is first chosen and her brother, or some man from her clan, acts as the girl's ceremonial father.

definite lessons in husbandry and will often spend part of the noon rest period in what may be called moral teachings. A father tries to impress on his son the need of being thrifty, energetic, and unafraid of inclement weather.

From the time of his Katcina initiation (which took place at ten to twelve years of age in former times, but which now takes place between the ages of seven and ten), until marriage removes him to another sphere of activities, a boy is most intimate with his father. During this period a father teaches his son how to dance and takes great pride in the lad's early Katcina performances; he sets aside a few head of sheep from his flock as the special property of his son; and he allows the boy to try his own hand in the management of a small plot of land. Gradually, as decreasing vigor forces the father to do less and less active work the son takes on himself increasingly greater burdens, but Hopi fathers must be aged and feeble indeed before they begin to think of retiring.

One outstanding feature of the father-son reciprocal is the amount of mutual consideration they show for each other's welfare. Rarely does a father exercise his right of punishing a son, and I have often seen a man, cut to the quick by his son's misbehavior, remain calm without a show of exasperation.[10] Even when the occasion absolutely demands that a father take disciplinary action, he will strive hard "not to hurt the little boy's feelings." On the other hand, in the event that some catastrophe such as blindness overtakes the father, a son will often delay his marriage in order that he may not deprive the household of his services. This is especially true if the father lacks married daughters.

When a son is contemplating marriage the father may give advice and pass judgment on the girl's qualifications, but his opinion is by no means final. At the time of a son's wedding the father will make him a special pair of moccasins and will generally give him as his portion about a third of his flock and a good share of his other property.

At death a man is buried by a son if one is available. For performing this office a son gets a somewhat better preference or a larger share of the father's property. Whether or not th dying man expresses a wish respecting his burier or the division of the inheritance, the sons usu ally come to a peaceful agreement in suc matters.

Although the status of classificatory fathers i not limited merely to an identity of terminology it would be idle to expect that they should bestow as much love and attention on a "son" as does th true father. As a rule they are friendly, ofte bring gifts, and sometimes volunteer instruction With the father's brother, especially, a boy i apt to develop close ties, but there are instance where other sociological fathers come to b preferred.

In striking contrast to the affection and tender ness of true fathers is the case of a man who too every possible advantage of his nine year ol step-son. Although this man had so many partner that he was called upon to tend their joint flock o sheep only about once a week, he would keep th lad out of school, if his herding turn fell on weekday, in order that he might remain idl while the boy went out to herd. A climax cam when the herding day fell on a Saturday on whicl a neighboring village was giving an interestin; dance. Nearly the entire population of Oraib including the step-father, planned to see th dance, and it was really pathetic to see the littl fellow, smiling and waving cheerfully to th dance-bound groups that passed him. Every on commented on such disgraceful behavior toward a step-son, but there was nothing that could b done about it.

Not all step-fathers behave so as to be regarde with aversion. When a young man named Luke who was destined soon to die of tuberculosis, wa too sick to sow beans at Powamu, he preferre to ask his step-father to do the planting for him although his true father was living and they wer on the best of terms with each other. This ma have been due to the fact that Luke's own fathe had divorced his mother and was married to an other woman and living in a different household Actually, when Luke died a short time later, h was buried by his real father.

Finally, in a classificatory system, where gen eration lines may be completely disregarded, i

---

[10] The rarity of punishment which is bestowed on children by their parents is due partly to the fact that the mother's brother is the acknowledged disciplinarian of the family, and partly to the attitude that even young children's individuality must not be curbed. Thus whe a child's whims oppose the father's judgment, the parer uses no coercion whatever, merely saying, "It's up t him."

often happens that a man has "fathers" who are much younger than himself. Under such circumstances the Hopi make a very simple and effective adjustment by reversing the reciprocal behavior, so that the mature "son" acts as a father to his youthful "parent."

MOTHER ⟷ SON

ingu'u ⟷ iti'i

(*ingu'u* is applied to: Mother, mother's sister, mother's mother's sister's daughter, any elderly woman in one's own clan, any wife of an *ina'a*.)

(*iti'i*—See under Father ⟷ Son.)

Whereas the division of labor tends to force a son very close to his father it serves to pull him somewhat apart from his mother. This does not mean that there is a weakening of affection, but it does imply that a mother's influence over her son is greatest in the early years of his life.

Hopi mothers are notoriously over-indulgent towards their children. I have often seen them deny themselves even a taste of some particular dainty at meals in order that a child may have more for himself; and I have seen little boys, old enough to know better, strike their mothers viciously while their parents assumed an air of indifference in order that those present might not note how badly they were hurt physically and mentally. Mothers often scold and threaten punishment, but only rarely do they make good their threats.

As a boy outgrows his childish fits of temper he begins more and more to appreciate his mother's position in the household and to rely on her advice. At this stage she generally encourages him not to be lazy, to go with his father and uncles into the fields, and to comport himself in a manner befitting a good Hopi.

When the time comes for a son's initiation into the Katcina cult, the mother helps choose his ceremonial father,[11] and after the ceremony she brings food to the home of her child's sponsor. When a boy is old enough to go into his Tribal Initiation, the mother makes special cakes for his ceremonial father.

A mother's word counts heavily but is not necessarily final in a man's choice of a bride. During the actual wedding ritual a mother plays a very active part, and when a son goes into housekeeping she gives him various useful gifts and helps carry water to his new residence.

Even after marriage, when a man has left his mother's household and has gone from a subordinate position in his family of orientation to a more dominant one in his family of procreation, he does not feel that he has severed his ties with his natal home.[12] He is always welcome to drop into his mother's house for meals, to bring friends there for entertainment, and to leave harness, tools, or other equipment in the mother's house if it happens to be more conveniently located than his wife's. Furthermore, if a mother becomes a widow her sons are expected to raise crops for her even if they happen to be married and primarily occupied in working their wives' farms. It is regarded as highly disgraceful for married sons to neglect a widowed mother.[13]

The birth of children to a married son again brings his mother into prominence, for it is she who first washes and cares for the tiny infant, and it is she who conducts the ceremonies that lead up to the naming rites on the twentieth day. On that occasion she takes charge of the proceedings and is the first of many eligible women to bestow a name referring to her clan on the baby.

If a man's mother happens to be the head woman of her clan a greater amount of respect than usual is accorded her; for not only does she have a good deal to say in regard to clan affairs and clan ceremonies, but she is also very influential in helping her brother, who is the head man of the clan, choose and train the ablest of her sons to be his successor.

Apart from his real mother a man's closest ties are with the mother's sister who usually stands ready to adopt him in the event of the mother's death. If she lives apart, a man always feels as free in her home as he does in his own mother's house. I knew an Oraibi man who became greatly excited, and who sent all sorts of vehement demands to Washington for redress against a man

[11] According to a statement by Stephen in Parsons, 1936b, p. 957, footnote 2, a woman on First Mesa chooses a ceremonial father for her child while she is still pregnant. This custom was unknown at Oraibi.
[12] When the tubercular Luke, who was mentioned above, was returned to Oraibi in an incurable condition, he begged to be taken to his mother's rather than to his wife's home. This was particularly notable because he was

very fond of his wife and her family, and she tended him faithfully until his death.
[13] A noteworthy exception was the case of Sakwapa whose adult sons flatly refused to farm for her. Sakwapa had been notoriously licentious throughout her life and was constantly at odds with her family. In 1934 she was the only Hopi woman at Oraibi who had to do the greater part of her own farming.

who had assaulted his mother's sister, long resident at Walpi.

Ceremonial mothers too are often regarded with a great deal of affection, and they take quite seriously any rupture that may occur in their dealings with a "son." Because he suspected his ceremonial mother of having spread malicious gossip about him, Don Talayesva had come to hate her most heartily. One day, unaware of her "son's" presence in a house, she came in and was treated to so hateful and persistent a glare from Don that she promptly burst into tears and withdrew. Needless to say, Don never calls this woman "mother."

Once in a while it happens that a real mother and son fail to get along. In one case that came to my attention each did what was possible to hurt the other's feelings.[14] When the son's wife became pregnant his mother circulated a rumor that her son had been cuckolded. In retaliation, the wife accused her mother-in-law of having bewitched and killed a baby born to her the previous year. In spite of this quarrel the mother let it be known that she would feel badly hurt if she were not chosen to wash the child at its birth. Actually, her son asked a clan sister to perform this office, but disregarding so deliberate a snub the mother showed up on the twentieth day and exercised her privilege of bestowing a name on the baby.

As an example of the weight that relationship terms carry, we have the case of Genevieve and Alma, two sisters aged eleven and thirteen. An older sister to this pair had a three year old son who was being taught to call them "mother." To Genevieve and Alma, who were receiving American schooling, this sounded incongruous, and I heard them pleading that their sister's son should call them "sister" or "aunt" but not "mother."

FATHER ⟷ DAUGHTER

ina'a ⟷ *iti'i*

(For the application of these terms see under Father ⟷ Son)

There is a feeling among the Hopi that a father is closer to a son while a mother is more bound up with her daughters. As a result, a father's reciprocal behavior towards his daughter is rather limited in its scope. In a general way a father is expected to aid in a girl's upbringing and to help

shape her character, but he has few specific instructions to impart. Young daughters are usually very affectionately regarded by their fathers, and it is a revelation to watch a fond parent lower rather than raise his voice when it becomes necessary to chide an obstreperous child.[15]

Through the early years of a girl's life her father presents her with gifts from time to time (such as Katcina dolls at Powamu), helps choose her Katcina mother, and contributes his judgment to her choice of a mate. In the wedding ceremony the father plays only a small part, but in addition to contributing sheep and other supplies for her wedding feast he generally supervises the manufacture of her wedding garments.

There is no undue attempt made to hurry a girl into marriage, but a father is generally happy when his daughter weds because the addition of another worker to the household serves to lighten his own labors. Inez's mother used to call her "no good," because Inez was twenty-six and unmarried, and Inez freely admitted that her father was getting pretty old and that she ought to marry partly for his sake. The mythology of the Hopi contains many stories of girls who refuse all suitors and who ultimately go through a series of strange adventures with supernatural beings.[16]

Owing to the prevalence of divorce a daughter is often forced into the care of a step-father. (With a boy a step-father's influence terminates at marriage. In a girl's case there is no break in the relationship unless the mother goes through another divorce.) Under ordinary circumstances, a step-father functions very much as does a true father.

MOTHER ⟷ DAUGHTER

ingu'u ⟷ *iti'i*

(For the application of these terms see under Mother ⟷ Son)

This is one of the warmest bonds in the whole scheme of Hopi relationships. Many ties serve to unite the mother and daughter, and these persist through life. It is up to the mother, primarily, to pick a girl's ceremonial mother, to decide on the need for a doctor father, and to choose which of the women's societies she wants her daughter to join.

Early in life a girl is taught by her mother to grind corn, to plaster houses, to make *piki* bread

---

[14] The woman was Sakwapa, see p. 19, footnote 13.
[15] Compare Parsons, 1925, p. 9.

[16] This theme occurs in stories nos. 14, 16, 31, and 36 in Voth, 1905b, and in Titiev, 1939a.

and other foods, and to carry and take care of her younger brothers and sisters. A mother also gives a daughter lessons in weaving (Third Mesa) or coiling (Second Mesa) baskets and plaques of *siva'api*. In former times girls were taught to make pottery, but this is now restricted to First Mesa.

Mothers teach their daughters the conventional standards of behavior towards strangers, relatives, and prospective mates. A woman thus tries to guide her daughter's choice of a husband and to prepare her properly for the rôle of wife. When a girl reaches puberty her mother teaches her how to take care of herself during menstruation, but at Oraibi the first period is given no special recognition. On First and Second Mesas there is, or was, a regular ritual at this time.[17] A mother plays a central part in the marriage of her daughter and is expected to give the girl much sound advice on the eve of the wedding. Again, when the daughter begins to bear children, it is her mother who attends her during and after her confinements.

Despite occasional quarrels a good deal of affection is usually involved in the relationships of mother and daughter. Not long ago a white visitor to Oraibi took a picture of a young woman, intending to give her an enlarged copy on his next trip. Unfortunately, the woman died before the visitor returned to the village so he presented her mother with the photograph. The poor woman took it gratefully, but next day she returned in tears and begged the man to take back his gift, because the picture reminded her too vividly of her bereavement.[18]

Girls generally exhibit a good deal of respect as well as love for their mothers. Sometimes a daughter will allow her mother's judgment to influence her choice or rejection of a mate, and rarely does an unmarried girl dare to act in opposition to a direct order from her mother. One day Inez was eager to accompany a friend on a walk to New Oraibi, but her mother pointed out that it was the day before a feast and there was a good deal of cooking to be done, so Inez did not go.

Many a time Inez had her mind made up to do one thing or another only to have her mother cancel her plans.

Despite the control exercised by a mother a daughter's individuality is by no means completely stifled. One young woman in her twenties decided to turn Christian despite the fact that her parents were orthodox. After the conversion the mother showed so much resentment that the girl promptly went off to Moenkopi to live with other relatives.

Ceremonial mothers too play significant parts in a girl's training, but the mother's sisters come closer to approximating the mother's position since they share the same household. In the event that a girl's mother has died, the mother's sisters carry out all the functions of the true mother.

OLDER BROTHER ⟷ YOUNGER BROTHER

ivava ⟷ *itupko*

(*ivava* is applied to: Older brother, alternative for mother's mother's brother, slightly older males in one's own clan, sons of an *ina'a* if older than ego.)

(*itupko* is applied to: Younger brother, slightly younger male in own clan, sons of *ina'a* who are younger than ego.)

Under ordinary conditions this bond is very close and all brothers aid each other whenever possible. In most cases the older brother helps to teach and train the younger, but this situation may be reversed as the Hopi feel that the one with the best understanding ought to be obeyed by the others.[19] The preference for ability rather than age is best brought out in the transmission of ceremonial offices where the oldest of the eligible brothers is by no means assured of being chosen to succeed his maternal uncle. The choice of the present Village chief was based entirely on his personal qualifications and was made with utter disregard for the principle of seniority.

Older brothers often tease the younger, but this is seldom overdone. Quarrels between brothers are comparatively rare and generally blow

[17] For First Mesa procedure, consult Parsons, 1936b, pp. 139–143. For Second Mesa, see Beaglehole, E., and P., 1935, pp. 44–45. On Third Mesa there was a corresponding ritual which is described in the article, "Adolescence Rites for Girls," in Part Three.

[18] Dr. Parsons has called my attention to the fact that this episode was not merely a display of personal feelings. No Pueblo Indian of the older generation wants a picture of a deceased relative.

[19] Brothers seldom attempt to hamper each other's individuality. The Oraibi chief was a staunch adherent to the Hopi religion; on the other hand his brother, Charles Frederick, was a zealous Christian. When the latter attempted to convert the chief he was severely criticized by the villagers for trying to influence his brother's mind.

over pretty quickly. Still, there are instances where real or classificatory brothers "cut out" each other in a rivalry for the same woman. When this happens the defeated man may sulk and grumble, but never does he plan to take revenge on his brother.

Co-operation among brothers is extremely common. Since most Hopi are too poor to own wagons individually all the brothers in a family generally combine to purchase one wagon. It takes no little skill in management for them to plan their turns in using the wagon for hauling wood or farm produce, as it must be remembered that once married, all the brothers live in separate households and sometimes even in different villages. Nevertheless, they manage to get their carting done somehow without conflict. Horses too are often jointly owned and brothers co-operate in tending and using them.

The care of sheep demands a pooling of resources, for only by taking turns at herding combined flocks can the men arrange to have enough free days for farming. Nowadays, with many opportunities open for earning ready money by working on government projects, it is the custom for brothers to rotate their jobs, each one herding extra days while the others are employed.

There is no definite rule of precedence in regard to marriage, but not infrequently a younger brother marries first because the elder feels a greater responsibility for helping the father, especially if he be old, sick, or without sons-in-law. Although it is by no means urged, it often happens, and it is considered a good idea, that brothers marry two sisters or two girls of the same clan. The former practice allows continued co-operation on the part of the brothers who find themselves again members of one household, and it serves to eliminate much of the friction between sisters-in-law.[20] Two brothers, clan or real, who have married sisters call each other by a special term, *imu'inangsinwa*.

On the death of a father all the brothers expect an equal share of the patrimony with the exception of the one who actually performed the burial. Older brothers sometimes anticipate and actually claim a disproportionate share, but the feeling is that this is not justified.

Apart from his true brother, a man's closest ties are with his mother's sister's son, a blood relative with whom he shares common residence,

clanship, and kinship terminology. Accordingly, it was no surprise when I overheard a man lecturing his mother's sister's son for carrying on an irregular affair with a married woman.

With the father's brother's son the bond is far less close, and in all cases of classificatory kindred who are unrelated by blood, the degree of intimacy depends entirely on the nature of the persons concerned.

An unusual application of the term for older brother, *ivava*, came to my attention when I heard it used by a three year old boy in addressing his mother's mother's mother's husband. He also used the older sister term for his maternal great-grandmother. Whether this is established usage or an individual habit could not be determined.

OLDER AND YOUNGER BROTHER ⟵⟶
OLDER AND YOUNGER SISTER

ivava, itupko ⟵⟶ *iqöqa, isiwa*
(For the application of terms for
brother see above.)

(*iqöqa* is applied to: Older sister, somewhat older woman of own clan.)

(*isiwa* is applied to: Younger sister [male speaking], somewhat younger women of own clan [male speaking].)

Hopi freedom from tabus in social intercourse and general behavior is nowhere more clearly brought out than in the analysis of this reciprocal. There is absolutely no avoidance prescribed either for youngsters, adolescents, or mature persons, so that brothers and sisters may communicate freely at all times even during menstruation periods.

Boys play freely with their sisters until about the age of ten when labor dichotomy serves to bring about a separation. Even in adult life, sometimes, a sister will go into the fields with her brother to prepare meals for him while he is harvesting, and in some instances, girls will help with such difficult tasks as sheep shearing although this is specifically a man's job. Another link that often binds a brother and sister is ceremonial parenthood of the same boy or girl. If a woman is chosen to sponsor a girl she calls on one of her brothers to be her "daughter's" ceremonial father, and if a man is asked to take charge of a boy's initiation he invites one of his sisters to serve as "mother." Thus a brother and sister may unite in the mutual care of a ceremonial child.

[20] In a personal communication, Dr. Parsons informed   me that she had noted several such marriages at Laguna.

Brothers and sisters frequently tease each other, but there is usually so much affection between them that no offense is taken. Sisters take great pride in their brothers' achievements and do what they can to make a success of such ceremonies as their brothers engage in, by providing food or other essentials. Girls resent slurs on their brothers to such an extent that they will refuse their friendship to all who fail to get along with them. Thus Inez refused to carry gifts to a woman whom her brother disliked, and both of Don's sisters were angry with me for inviting a young couple to dine, because they accused the woman's mother of having said nasty things about their brother.

Boys too are not remiss when it comes to expressing fondness for their sisters. In one case an Americanized Hopi who had a steady government position took out a life insurance policy for his sister. In another case, when a white friend wrote to Don that he was contemplating several days' stay at Oraibi, Don urged his sister to earn a few dollars by accommodating him, although the sister claimed that she couldn't look after a white man and begged that the task be entrusted to some one else.

In the days of strict matrilocal residence a married woman actually remained with her mother, so that when a man visited his mother's household he incidentally called on his sister. Nowadays, when so many girls move to their own homes at marriage, a man feels just as free to drop into his sister's house and to bring guests there as he does at his mother's place of residence. On feast days a man takes his friends on a round of visits which seldom fail to include his mother's and his sisters' houses. Likewise if, on account of a mother's death, or for some other reason, an unmarried man must vacate his natal household, he generally goes to live with a married sister.

If there is a considerable age difference a man often stands somewhat in the position of a father to a younger sister, and in many respects an elder sister acts as a mother by encouraging an immature brother to learn masculine occupations and to avoid idleness. At the time of his Katcina initiation a boy's sisters help the mother to make *piki* bread, and when a youth is married his mother and his sisters wash the bride's hair, give her a ceremonial bath, and prepare large quantities of *piki*. Like his mother too a man's sister helps

intending and naming his new-born children.

In view of the prevailing *laissez-faire* attitude of the Hopi, it is surprising how much weight brothers and sisters give to each other's advice regarding the choice of mates. I knew a girl who had her mother's permission to receive a young fellow's attentions, but who hesitated to let him court her openly because her brothers objected to him. Conversely, an Oraibi man angrily decided to remain a bachelor for the reason that his sister found fault with every girl he wanted to marry.

The strong affection existing between brothers and sisters and the great influence they exert on each other are the basis for two of the most important kinship bonds among the Hopi. When brothers and sisters marry and have children they become to each other's offspring, respectively, mother's brother and father's sister. Throughout the forthcoming discussion of the status of the latter relatives, sight must never be lost of the significant fact that their influence on each other's offspring is a direct continuation and extension of the lifelong attachment between brothers and sisters.

There is a current belief among the Hopi that boys have more tractable dispositions and better tempers than girls. When a boy has a fight with someone he "doesn't mean it" and soon gets over his anger, but when a girl quarrels she nurses her resentment for a long time afterwards. In fact, it is said that an angry girl may, out of self pity or to spite her parents, decide to die. In such an event she turns her face to the west and refuses to heed the good advice of parents, uncles or medicine men. After a time, even fear and late repentance are of no avail and, despite all efforts to save her, the girl withers away and dies. This type of wilful suicide is called *qövisti* and is carefully distinguished from other self inflicted deaths. Instances of girls dying *qövisti* are freely cited.[21]

Not all girls are said to be endowed with the capacity to become *qövisti* and some readily admit that they have tried it and failed, while others are pointed out as having latent tendencies in that direction. The symptoms are moodiness, sullen silence, and stubbornness. Men are by nature incapable of going *qövisti* as they want to live as long as possible. A native theorist told me that girls were subject to this phenomenon, because

[21] Further details of this custom are given in Kennard, 1937, p. 495. Compare the folk tale in Parsons, 1926, p. 211.

they put too high a value on themselves. As prospective mothers on whom the perpetuation of the clan depends, they become so vain (*qwivi*) that they disregard the instructions of their brothers and maternal uncles. Men and women alike are ever ready to admit the temperamental differences between the sexes, and a young woman once told me naïvely that one of the men in the village was "as mean as a girl."

OLDER SISTER ⟵⟶ YOUNGER SISTER

iqöqa ⟵⟶ *itupko*

(For the application of *iqöqa* see above. The term *itupko* is the general term for younger brother but is also used by females for the younger sister.)

On the whole, an older sister is but slightly differentiated from a younger sister unless there is a wide age discrepancy. In such an event the elder helps instruct the younger and looks after her somewhat in the fashion of a mother. Indeed, where the age difference warrants it, a girl tends to call a much older woman in her own clan "mother" rather than "sister." An older sister helps her mother bake *piki* and prepare a feast at the time of a junior's entrance to the Katcina, Marau or other women's societies, and at marriage. There is no feeling of impropriety if a younger sister is the first to marry.

In many tasks sisters co-operate, and when corn grinding activities are in full swing soon after harvest, sisters always help each other whether they occupy the same house or live apart. Community of interests and occupations tends to bring sisters very close to each other, but in some cases a good deal of bickering goes on between them. Two of the chief's "daughters" (actually his wife's sister's children), were notoriously quarrelsome, and the only time I saw the chief exert any personal authority was when he ordered the younger to exercise more care in supervising her children's activities in order to eliminate the main source of trouble.

If a mother dies without having made disposition of the house ownership, sisters are very apt to compete for possession, and sometimes a defeated sister will move out and build a house for herself.[22] Usually, such disputes are left to the parties concerned, but in some instances an older brother or maternal uncle will attempt to make a settlement of the matter at issue. Other household property left by a woman is shared equally among

the daughters, but ownership means the privilege of use rather than actual possession, so that the objects are not removed from the maternal household, and daughters who reside elsewhere must come here to use the things they inherited from the mother. This is particularly true of ceremonial paraphernalia which may be kept in a clan house even when it is no longer occupied. In such instances, the members of the ceremony will come to the abandoned house regularly, but the paraphernalia are almost never removed.

Sometimes an older sister carries a good deal of authority with a younger. A most striking example was the case of a Hotevilla a girl who, though unmarried, became pregnant. Normal procedure called for the girl to marry the man who was responsible for her condition. On this occasion the girl's sister announced that she did not want a marriage to take place because she disliked the man's character, and although it is somewhat harder for a girl with a bastard to find a good husband later on, the sister's decision prevailed and no marriage was arranged.

We have already called attention to the firm position held by women in the structure of the household. This gives rise to a feeling of solidarity between sisters that is well exemplified by a seemingly insignificant detail. It was noted that whenever a man, whether a husband, relative, or friend, did a favor for any woman in a household her sisters and mother invariably thanked him in common, even though the courtesy in no way directly affected them. Let a man bring in an armful of wood for a woman and all her sisters who are present at the time automatically respond with, "*Askwali*" (Thank you), even though none of the sisters is living with the woman concerned.

The feeling of being one with her sisters is most clearly brought out by the prevalence of the custom of adoption. Although it is comparatively rare in a woman's lifetime, it frequently occurs in case of her death that her children are adopted by her sister. Here, again, it is the organization of the household that makes this an easy and simple move as adoption implies no change in the reciprocal behavior of the adoptive mother and children, no change of residence, and no change in terminology. (Cf. page 10.) Once more, then, we see how it is that the household functions to steady the social structure, in spite of dis-

---

[22] Older daughters usually expect to get more of their mother's possessions than do their younger sisters, but there is no fixed rule of seniority in the inheritance customs.

turbances brought about by death, or in some cases by repeated divorces which tend to wreck the limited family.

Under these conditions it is not surprising that children adopted by a mother's sister should be completely absorbed into their adoptive families.[23] On one occasion the Oraibi chief gave us his mother's sister's name when we inquired for his mother, and the more we demanded to know if he were naming his real mother, the more he insisted that he was. As a youngster he had been adopted by his mother's sister and had come to regard her, and her only, as his real parent.

In a similar connection, Don and his wife had adopted the latter's sister's young son, partly because their own children had all died in infancy, and partly because the boy's mother, Barbara, leads a hectic marital existence. By another husband Barbara has a daughter named Madge, and Don's adopted son always refers to Barbara not as his mother but by the teknonymic phrase, "the mother of Madge."

It is primarily through the medium of women that clan relationships are extended to other villages and even to other tribes. The feeling is that all women of a given clan have the same blood and so are sisters. Thus when some Zuñi visitors came to Oraibi they stayed with a "clan sister," and even Christian Hopi from other villages will not hesitate to call on their orthodox Hopi clan sisters.

The eight behavior patterns treated up to this point comprise the so-called primary reciprocals between members of the immediate family. Although, theoretically, the Hopi family does not exist alone, its members form the core of the household group of which it is an integral part. The relatives who combine with the family to form the household will be considered next.

MOTHER'S BROTHER ⟷ SISTER'S SON, DAUGHTER

itaha ⟷ *itiwaiya*

(*itaha* is applied to: Mother's brother, mother's mother's sister's son, alternative for mother's mother's brother, elderly men in own clan.)

(*itiwaiya* is applied to: Sister's children of either sex [male speaking], younger children of women of own clan [male speaking].)

Since the father's brother is classed with the father, a Hopi who uses the English term "uncle" always means the mother's brother. Throughout this monograph the use of "uncle," if unqualified, should be taken to indicate the maternal uncle.

The position of the mother's brother in the household helps us understand why he should be the disciplinarian *par excellence*. He is the only male member of the mother's generation who is in ego's own lineage and clan; and his close link with ego's mother, as was brought out in the study of the brother-sister reciprocal, gives him an additional claim to authority. If, as sometimes happens, he is also the head man of the clan, then he is indeed a person to command respect.

To a boy, his uncle's prestige is still further enhanced by the fact that from him the lad hopes to inherit ceremonial and clan offices. It is the custom for a man who holds a ritual chieftainship to select and train his own successor. Usually he picks the most capable of his sisters' sons[24] and personally teaches him the necessary sacred lore. This is most often done by having the nephew accompany his uncle into the fields, where cooperation in farming or sheepherding tends to foster a bond of intimacy between them, and where there is sufficient privacy to permit lengthy discussions of ceremonial secrets.

Apart from the need of training the nephew who is to succeed him in office, a large share of the practical care of his sister's children also falls to the mother's brother. This is especially true when there are widowed, divorced, or unmarried sisters in a household. Hence, an uncle is all the more careful to supervise rigidly the upbringing of his sister's sons in order that they may grow up to be reliable workers who will help him provide for the needs of the household. In addition to more conventional methods of instruction, uncles pour water on boys who like to lie abed of mornings, subject lazy youngsters to long runs, and force their nephews to roll in snow or to take cold dips in the springs to make them hardy and brave.

On ceremonial occasions such as Katcina and other society initiations, an *itaha* has no special duties, but at the time an *itiwaiya*, especially a girl, is being married, he takes a very important part. He is the main one to be consulted in the

<hr/>

[23] Numerous examples of adoption by sisters could be given for Third Mesa, and Dr. Parsons, in a personal communication, has noted a First Mesa situation at Walpi where Honi, the Crier-chief, began by calling

Shalako, his mother's sister, his mother.
[24] Stephen reports that on First Mesa a successor is chosen prescriptively from among a man's eldest sister's sons. Parsons, 1936b, p. 951. This is not so at Oraibi.

choice of a mate and his advice is seldom neglected. He can be counted on to contribute something to the nuptial feast, to do his share in the
preparation of the wedding garments and moccasins, and to give the young couple a long harangue
at the conclusion of the rites on their mutual
duties as man and wife. When a sister's daughter
has been married and is bringing her husband into
the household to live, it is the maternal uncle who
makes the formal speech of welcome.

No doubt there is an element of harshness in the
itaha's behavior when he is punishing an *itiwaiya*
or making him run errands, but this reciprocal is
by no means devoid of affection. An uncle de-
lights in narrating clan legends or other stories,
and he often brings live rabbits or other pets to
his nephew or niece. At one time, when a woman
and her husband had gone off to the fields during
harvest, her *itaha* moved into her house in order
that he and his wife might the better look after
the children who were left to his care. On another occasion, a little girl less than ten years
old voluntarily gave up a trip to a Butterfly dance
at a neighboring village in order that she might
stay home and keep house for her mother's unmarried brother. Children frequently accompany
their uncles and play or picnic while the latter attend to their farming duties.

At marriage, of course, an *itaha* moves into his
wife's household, but he is always welcome at
the home of an *itiwaiya*. An aged uncle from
Hotevilla, related by phratry and not by direct
clan ties to Irene, wife of Don, invariably made
her house his headquarters on visits to Oraibi and
was always courteously received. One day he
showed up with some trifle that he wished to
trade and although neither Irene nor her sister had
any need for it, they made an exchange which
highly pleased the old fellow.

The mother's mother's brother may be called
either *ivava* or *itaha*. In other words, one has the
choice of calling an older male in one's own clan
either "older brother" or "maternal uncle." This
relative is usually accorded even more respect
than the mother's brother, and he is sometimes
considered a sterner disciplinarian. His authority
is great and his teachings are generally followed.

There are instances of an *itaha* who is thoroughly disliked by his sister's children, and I was
told several times of uncles who had been accused of bewitching their relatives. However, this

[24a] See Titiev, 1943a, p. 550, footnote 3.

must not be given too much weight as the Hopi
pattern of witchcraft beliefs includes the tenet
that all witches must be related to their victims.[24]

GRANDFATHER ⟷ GRANDCHILD
ikwa'a ⟷ *imuyi*

(*ikwa'a* is applied to: Father's father, father's
father's brother, father's mother's brother,
mother's father, mother's father's brother, all
husbands of an *iso'o*, all husbands of an *ikya'a*, as a
mark of respect to any aged man.)

(*imuyi* is applied to: Children's children, any
child of *iti'i*, children of men of own clan [female
speaking], brother's children [female speaking].)

Although the maternal grandfather, who lives
in ego's household, comes into much more frequent contact with a grandchild than does the
paternal grandfather, we have combined the two
here because such differences as exist in their behavior are of degree rather than kind.

The outstanding feature of this reciprocal is
the warmth of attachment. Rarely does a grandfather chide a grandchild under any conditions.
Once, when I had a particular dainty which the
Village chief liked I sent some to him by his
granddaughter. On the way the greedy youngster
gobbled it all up. When I expressed regret that
the chief had been deprived of a share, my housekeeper remarked that it really didn't matter as
the chief would have given it all to the grand-
daughter anyway.

When a grandchild is ill the grandfather may
try his hand at using a "family remedy" or he
may summon a medicine man. In either case he
always shows a good deal of concern and will stay
out of a dance if his mind is troubled by a grandchild's illness.

A maternal grandfather likes to sleep with a
grandson and takes great delight in teaching him
songs and in telling him stories. Grandfathers on
both sides supplement a father's and uncle's
teachings with instructions in farming, herding,
and hunting. A good deal of teasing and jesting is
permitted in this relationship.

GRANDMOTHER ⟷ GRANDCHILD
iso'o ⟷ *imuyi*

(*iso'o* is applied to: Mother's mother, mother's
mother's sister, mother's father's sister, father's
mother, father's mother's sister, father's father's

sister, any wife of an *ikwa'a*, as a mark of respect to very old women.)

(For *imuyi*, see the preceding page.)

Although our discussion of these relatives is meant to include both the paternal and the maternal grandmother it is based primarily on observations of the behavior of the latter and applies only in modified form to the former.

Grandmothers are felt to be more kind and indulgent than mothers, and when a mother becomes irritated and loses patience with a fretting child, the grandmother often consoles and soothes it. On the other hand there are times when a grandmother feels called upon to discipline a grandchild, and one of the favorite punishments is to pour water on the naughty youngster. Very rarely, however, does a woman exercise the privilege of chastening a grandchild unless they live in the same household.

An *iso'o* teaches her *imuyi* Hopi songs and legends, takes an active part in the grandchild's training, and helps a mother with all the duties pertaining to her children's initiations into ceremonies, or to their marriages. She is generally very much beloved, and I knew a little girl who used to keep track of her grandfather's herding dates so that while he was spending the night at his sheep camp she could come over from her own house to sleep with her grandmother.

A good deal depends on the age and energy of a grandmother. If she is comparatively youthful and active she functions as the head of the household and plays a very prominent part in all matters concerning the family and clan, but if she is old and feeble she may command respect but will rarely be consulted. While the grandmother is able to carry on in normal fashion her position helps the household maintain its stability in the face of "brittle monogamy." Even if she has been living in a separate house, a divorced daughter can always find refuge at her mother's house for herself and her children. Likewise, if a girl has a bastard which may embarrass her in the quest of a husband, the grandmother can always be counted on to look after the child.

Although it was not observed on Third Mesa, we were told that on First Mesa there is a joking relationship between grandmother and grand-daughter which generally takes the form of the older woman teasing the grandchild for being in love with the grandfather.

This brings to a close our survey of the relationships existing among the consanguineous relatives in the household. There is a strong feeling that this group comprises one's closest kin and that, except for marital connections, the whole range of a Hopi's social activities could be restricted to this circle. From a cold, practical point of view this may be true, but how much zest and emotional response would a Hopi lose if he were deprived of his relationships with the father's sister! It is all very well to speak of the tenderness one feels for one's mother, grandmother, or other relatives, but the greatest thrill of a Hopi's life comes from his dealings with his beloved *ikya'a*.

FATHER'S SISTER ⟷ BROTHER'S DAUGHTER

ikya'a ⟷ *imuyi*

(*ikya'a* is applied to: Father's sister,[25] as an alternative for father's father's sister, all women in the father's clan.)

(For *imuyi* see above.)

In taking up this reciprocal we must again call attention to the fact that because of the very intimate bond existing between brothers and sisters, it is only natural that a good deal of interest and affection should be found in a woman's behavior towards her brother's children.

With a girl an *ikya'a* is somewhat less concerned than with a boy, but even with girls her relations are pleasant and enduring. The paternal aunts arrive as soon as possible after a child is born to one of their brothers, and there is often a friendly rivalry to see which will be the first to wash the baby and earn the right to play the leading rôle throughout the lying-in period and at the naming rites.[26]

When a brother's daughter reaches the time of her initial Powamu celebration, during the first February after her birth, her aunts all prepare tiny plaques for her as gifts. With each succeeding year the size of the plaque is increased until the girl reaches her Katcina initiation. In return for these presents, the baby's mother gives each aunt as much cornmeal as the gift plaque can hold.

---

[25] The term "aunt" applies only to the paternal aunt.

[26] Each Hopi infant thus receives a number of names, but in the course of time only one name "sticks" and the others tend to be forgotten. Ordinarily, the name which "sticks" is one which the child's parents habitually employ. Compare Parsons, 1921c, p. 101.

A girl's *ikya'a* is active during all the ceremonial phases on which her niece enters, and is particularly concerned in the preparations for the wedding of an *imuyi*. In later life paternal aunts and their nieces often help each other in the performance of such household tasks as replastering a house or carrying water, and Inez, who was fairly deft with a needle, was always ready to sew a dress for her old *ikya'a*.

Under certain conditions a girl will prefer to take shelter with an aunt rather than with some relative from her own clan. When a girl named Tilly became pregnant illegally for a second time, she was ashamed to be seen in that condition in her own village so she came to reside with an *ikya'a* at Oraibi. She remained there until the day of her delivery, but returned home to be confined.

The terminology employed in connection with the father's sister shows a very strong tendency to equate her with the grandmother. An *ikya'a* calls her brother's child by the regular term for grandchild, and her husband is called grandfather. Furthermore, one of the grandmothers, the father's father's sister may be addressed alternatively as *ikya'a*, particularly if she happens to be fairly young. Lowie has made an interesting contribution towards an understanding of this phenomenon,[27] but no complete explanation has yet been reached.

FATHER'S SISTER ⟷ BROTHER'S SON

ikya'a ⟷ *imuyi*

(For the application of these terms see the preceding page.)

Almost from the moment of a boy's birth his *ikya'a* begin to treat him with affectionate regard. They help care for him, they name him in some fashion that refers to their own clan, and they make him feel everlastingly welcome in their homes. As soon as possible a boy begins to pay back their favors by bringing them gifts, by giving them a good share of the rabbits that he kills when hunting, and by bringing them salt whenever he goes on salt-gathering expeditions.[28]

As a lad grows up a paternal aunt soon has a chance to give public expression to her fondness for him by choosing him as her partner in a Buffalo or Butterfly dance. It is a custom on these occasions for the favored *imuyi* to express his appreciation by presenting his *ikya'a* with a gift which she in turn repays at a later date. Here too as in the case of several sisters expressing thanks for a favor rendered to one of their number, several *ikya'a* often contribute items to help the one concerned repay their *imuyi* in handsome style.

A boy's aunts never fail to reiterate their love for their nephew. They side with him when he opposes their husbands in a jesting relationship, they express jealousy of all his sweethearts, and during his marriage rites they attack his bride and the women of his household for having taken their nephew from them.

Whenever a man performs as a clown all his aunts, whether real or ceremonial, bring him gifts of food, and a good deal of the sexual byplay in which clowns indulge is directed towards their aunts. Indeed, there are so many instances of implied or actual sexual intercourse between a man and his father's clanswomen, that there is a possibility that in former times a man may have been expected to marry his father's sister's daughter, or some other woman addressed as *ikya'a*.[29]

On First Mesa the father's eldest sister comes and washes the body of a dead man and gives him a new name.[30] This custom seems to have been unknown at Oraibi.

Having concluded an examination of the reciprocals existing between kindred by consanguinity, we come now to a brief discussion of the status of relatives by affinity.

MALE RELATIVE-IN-LAW

imu'inangwa

(This is the generic term employed for all men marrying women in or below ego's generation level. The term is non-reciprocal.)

When a man moves into his wife's household at marriage he begins to share in the responsibility of conducting that household. If he is a good worker and of a pleasant disposition he soon comes to be regarded with a great deal of warmth and affection. In fact, there is a marked tendency to call one's own sister's husband by the term for

---

[27] Lowie, 1929a, p. 383.
[28] Titiev, 1937a, p. 255.

[29] This whole question has been dealt with in some detail in Titiev, 1938b.
[30] Parsons, 1925, p. 75; and Parsons, 1936b, p. 827.

brother. *Imu'inangwa* is rarely employed in direct address, and in ceremonial smoking the term for brother-in-law is never used. If no other relationship between the smokers exists, the term for partner, *imu'inangsinwa*, is used.

A man often co-operates with his brother-in-law at harvest or in the care of horses or in sheep-herding, especially if the latter has completely identified himself with his wife's group. The more harmonious his relations with the wife's household, the more a brother-in-law comes to be regarded as a real brother.

FEMALE RELATIVE-IN-LAW
imu'wi

(*imu'wi* is applied to all women marrying men of one's own clan.)

This is the one relative in addressing whom teknonymy is most rigidly prescribed. As soon as she comes to the groom's house to begin the first stage of the wedding ceremony, her personal name must never be used by any member of the prospective husband's clan. By an extension of this idea a boy's clanmates often call his sweetheart *imu'wi*, as if anticipating a wedding.

In keeping with their somewhat belligerent love for a brother's son, a man's *ikya'a* profess hatred for their *imu'wi* who is threatening to oust them in the affections of an *imuyi*. Actually, an *imu'wi* is very affectionately regarded by her relatives-in-law, in spite of the fact that at marriage she is robbing them of a worker. Whenever her brother's duties took him out of the village, Inez always made it a point to get me to invite "imu'wi" to dine with us rather than have her eat by herself.

The esteem in which a female relative-in-law is held—which incidentally provided an example of how terms, as such, carry weight—was illustrated during a mud fight which I witnessed while an Oraibi pair was being married. It happened that one of the attacking *ikya'a*, who was casting all sorts of aspersions on the defending mother of the groom, was *imu'wi* to the women in the household where the wedding was being performed. She climaxed her verbal assault by singing out, " . . . and I'll never let you call me *imu'wi* any more!"

Another example of the strong feeling for relatives-in-law was forced on my attention in regard to a Second Mesa woman who had divorced a Sun clansman and married a Parrot man. This woman was residing at Oraibi in violation of matrilocal residence customs, and when her first child was born after her second marriage the Sun clanswomen, realizing that she lacked relatives at Third Mesa, very kindly helped her through her confinement. This aroused the deep resentment of the Parrot women, who let it be known far and wide that they feared lest the Sun clan again start calling the divorced woman *imu'wi*.

In exchange for all the courtesies rendered her at the time of marriage and afterwards by her husband's people, an *imu'wi* may always be counted on to do her full share whenever a woman of her husband's household or clan is going through the long wedding ceremony.

FATHER'S SISTER'S HUSBAND
ikwa'a

(This term is applied to all men who marry women of the father's clan.)

It is only with his wife's brother's son, *imuyi*, that this relative stands in a position apart from that of an ordinary relative-in-law. Between these two there exists a joking relationship which grows out of a man's fondness for his paternal aunt. Thus a lad will tell his *ikya'a* that her husband is no good and that he can look after her and satisfy all her wants, and the aunt will reply in kind. The *ikwa'a* will retort that the *imuyi* is lazy and never kills any rabbits for his *ikya'a*, and that he lacks the courage to go on the dangerous salt expedition to fetch salt for his aunt. In all such exchanges the aunt always sides with her nephew against her husband. Not only is this joking relationship formalized, but it is also considered an inalienable right, so that a middle-aged man reported disgustedly that one of his *imuyi* had resented his jests, but that he intended to keep them up just the same because that was the Hopi way. In some respects the joking relationship between an *ikwa'a* and an *imuyi* may reflect a real rivalry between them for the love of the former's wife.[31] On the whole, *ikwa'a* are usually on good terms with their wives' nephews, and they often help each other with farming or other duties. Many a time an *imuyi* will bring a gift for his *ikya'a* and leave it with express orders that his "no good *ikwa'a*" was to get none of it, but such remarks are never misunderstood and never taken seriously.

[31] Titiev, 1938b.

CHAPTER III

COURTSHIP, MARRIAGE, AND DIVORCE

ALTHOUGH knowledge of a people's patterns of sexual behavior is essential for an understanding of their social organization, no complete report has yet been made of so important an aspect of Hopi life, and many of the partial accounts are inaccurate and misleading. This situation is due in part to inadequate observation, and in part to the attempts of the natives to keep hidden the true nature of their sex habits. It is not hard to understand the Hopi desire for secrecy in regard to this subject. In the closing years of the past century their contacts with government agents and school teachers soon taught them that violations of the American code would be severely punished. It did not take them long to realize that in all clashes between the two systems of morals it would be the native divergences from American patterns that would invariably be judged at fault. Accordingly, as they became more familiar with the white man's professed standard of morality, they tended to develop a tacit understanding among themselves that in the presence of strangers there was to be no discussion of sexual irregularities.[1] Consequently, the data on Hopi sexual behavior are incomplete and often faulty. This is particularly true of the period from adolescence to marriage. Recent investigations, however, have begun to fill in some of the gaps in our knowledge of this subject.

In the preceding chapter it was pointed out that among the Hopi there is no avoidance prescribed between brothers and sisters. Similarly, there is a marked freedom from tabus in regard to social intercourse between all persons, whether or not related and whether or not of the same sex. It is true that men and women are sometimes segregated in public, as the seating arrangement during night dances in the kivas clearly indicates;[2] and it cannot be denied that a dichotomy of the sexes exists in occupational and religious matters; but on the whole, the "condition of affairs in a Hopi village is such that young people have ample opportunity of becoming thoroughly acquainted. . . . So the Hopi mingle with one another from childhood; they grow together into manhood or womanhood; they meet and learn to love or to hate one another."[3]

Hopi children develop an early awareness of sexual matters. Babies are soothed by stroking their genital organs; affairs of sex are freely discussed in the presence of youngsters; parents make little effort to conceal their marital relations even though they sleep only a few feet from growing children;[4] little boys are taught all manner of obscene remarks and actions when they serve as clowns; and adult women during clown performances do not hesitate to simulate copulation with pre-adolescent boys.[5]

Altogether, youngsters of either sex are under so little constraint in matters of sex that it is not surprising to find that pre-marital affairs are taken for granted and readily condoned. As soon as a girl has attained her maturity she undergoes an adolescence ritual,[6] after which she begins to sleep either further removed than formerly from her parents or in an adjoining room. When boys reach the ages of twelve or thirteen, there is no formal recognition of their attainment of puberty, but they soon begin to spend their nights in the kivas rather than at home. Facilitated by this sleeping arrangement, there has developed a custom which, today, forms the preliminary step to marriage in the vast majority of cases.

The boys who sleep in the kivas, freed from parental supervision, may prowl about by night

[1] Beaglehole, E., and P., 1935, p. 47, has noted that while the Hopi pattern of courtship appears puritanical, it "does not reveal the volcano below the surface."

A flood of new light has been thrown on this subject recently by the publication of "Sun Chief," edited by Dr. Leo W. Simmons.

[2] During the series of night dances held each winter in the kivas, married women and young children sit on the raised floor south of the entrance ladder, men and boys sit along the east and north benches, and unmarried girls occupy the west bench, generally sitting with their faces

averted or covered with shawls, and making a great show of modesty in public.

[3] Voth, 1900, p. 238.

[4] All these items were gathered at Oraibi but similar data are given in Beaglehole, E., and P., 1935, pp. 39–41. Other details may be found under the title "A Few Sex Practices" in Part Three.

[5] Parsons, 1936b, p. 366.

[6] This ritual, which will be described in Part Three, "Adolescence Rites for Girls," is no longer observed in Oraibi.

to their hearts' content. Wrapping blankets about their bodies and across their faces so that their identities may not be readily observed, the young men go to call on the girls of their choice, sometimes by pre-arrangement, and sometimes on the mere chance of getting a favorable reception. Cautiously a lover proceeds to the home of his sweetheart, and taking care not to arouse the other sleepers in the household, he makes his way to the girl's side.

"Who is it?" she whispers when she becomes aware of his presence.

"It is I," replies the caller, for it is customary that he shall not give his name but shall allow himself to be recognized by his voice. If he proves acceptable to his mistress, as most often is the case, the young man spends the remainder of the night with her, generally departing before daybreak to avoid detection.

This custom is called *dumaiya*, and is now widespread in all the Hopi villages.[7] It goes on with the connivance of the elders although it has probably never received open sanction. In spite of some effort to preserve secrecy on the part of the young people it generally comes about that a girl's lovers become known to her parents and to the community at large. Either some villager, observing a boy going *dumaiya*, tracks him to his sweetheart's home; or the loving pair is betrayed by a jealous rival who finds that some earlier caller has been received with favor; or the housemates catch the lovers in the act. In any event it happens only rarely that an affair can long be carried on in secret.

Exposure, however, leads to no punishment stronger than a call-down unless a lover is considered unworthy of the girl he visits. It is at this point, rather than when marriage is being contemplated, that parents and other relatives are most apt to pass judgment on a girl's choice of potential mates. If a boy is lazy, if he is a poor farmer, if he lacks the few essentials necessary to the support of a wife, or if he is of a mean or quarrelsome disposition, a girl will be urged to cease receiving his attentions. If, on the other hand, a lover is diligent and in fair circumstances, no objection will be raised to his visits. Similar considerations affect the decision of a boy's relatives regarding the girls to whom he pays court.

Thus it comes about that most girls of marriageable age generally manage to have several lovers, any one of whom is more or less acceptable as a prospective husband to her and to her family. Since contraceptives are rarely or never employed, it usually befalls that before very long a girl finds herself pregnant by one or another of her sweethearts. Unless she has been devoting herself quite regularly to one man, she is now free to name her favorite lover as the father of her child. Ordinarily, since the girl's relatives have already passed judgment, and since the average boy seeks out only such girls as he would be willing to marry in the event of pregnancy, there is no difficulty in arranging a match. And yet, no matter to whom a girl attributes the paternity of her child, the women of the village invariably respond, "She had her big belly for so-and-so, but she picked the wrong man."

Not always is Hopi courtship so clandestine a procedure. In former times there existed the pleasant custom of holding a sort of picnic on the day following a Katcina dance or after the public performance of one of the more important rituals. This was called *oveknaiya* and was arranged without the observance of any special formality.[8] In anticipation of the coming festivity the boys would rest during the day in order to appear at their best in the evening. Then they would dress in velvet shirts and knee trousers, don all their beads and other finery, smear red ochre (*suta*) on their faces, pick out their most resplendent head bands, and tie fine, downy, eagle feathers

[7] While this monograph was in manuscript the word *dumaiya* appeared in print for the first time in Beaglehole, E., and P., 1935, p. 62. On page 41 of the same work there is another reference to the same habit. Prior to 1935 the only observer to have noted this custom was Curtis, 1922, p. 37. Curtis' account is incomplete and garbled. He writes in part, "The Youth now attempts to enter by stealth the house of his beloved. If he succeeds he awakens her and she calls to her parents, who seize the young man if he has remained, or, if he has run away, take steps to ascertain his identity." The lack of frankness on the part of Curtis' informants is perfectly obvious. Why should the lover "attempt to enter by stealth," if his purpose is merely to rouse the girl and have her call to her parents? The inconsistency is apparent.

[8] The first informant to mention this custom to me at Oraibi used the word *ovekniwa*, which Fewkes uses in the sense of holiday, to describe the tenth day's (i.e., the day following the public dance) activities in the Snake ceremony. Other informants used the term *oveknaiya*, which Parsons, 1923b, p. 168, lists as the tenth day of that ceremony, and which she translates as "to take a walk, but used only in this post-ceremony sense, and meaning to be on mere pleasure bent." Dr. Parsons seems to have had an intimation of the deeper significance of *oveknaiya* as appears from the comment she appended to her journalist's all too meager account of this custom, in Parsons, 1925, p. 56, footnote 107.

(*qwavuhu*) in the hair. For their part, the girls too were eager to appear at their best. After spending the early part of the day in making *somiviki*,[9] they would dress carefully in white moccasins and wrapped leggings, *manta*, and ceremonial blanket (*atu'u*), numerous strands of beads, and hair done up in the butterfly wing fashion required of unmarried women.[10]

At Oraibi, the boys would leave first in the late afternoon for Talaudöka (Getting Light Point), the customary meeting place, which is situated on the road to Hotevilla. On the way they would scatter to hunt rabbits, combining into small groups as they approached the chosen spot and singing Katcina songs as they drew near. Meantime, just before sunset, the girls would start out carrying bundles of *somiviki* and accompanied by their little sisters to serve as messengers in summoning to their sides the boys of whom they were most fond.

At the picnic ground the boys prepared the rabbits they had killed and the girls spread out the *somiviki* and other dainties which they had brought with them. The little girl messengers bustled about as their elder sisters directed, and in a short while the gathering was divided into small congenial groups. Sometimes no proposals of any sort were made at this time, sometimes pairs of lovers slipped off by themselves for sexual indulgence, sometimes arrangements were made for a *dumaiya* visit to be paid late at night, and sometimes overtures to marriage were carried out.

In the event that a girl had fixed on some youth as being most desirable for her husband, she would prepare along with the other foods carried to an *oveknaiya* meeting, a large loaf of *qömi*, fashioned from a dough of sweet cornmeal. If the man of her choice responded to the invitation she sent him, she would hand him the *qömi*, a proceeding that is equivalent to a formal proposal of marriage. As any girl was apt to spring this surprise on a lad she liked, the boys were careful

to accept picnic invitations only from girls at whose hands they would be willing to receive a gift of *qömi*.[11] Since marriage proposals rendered during *oveknaiya* were usually made without any definite agreement having been reached beforehand, the groom's relatives may have had no opportunity to pass judgment on the match. Accordingly, when a boy came home with a loaf of *qömi*, he notified his parents, and they called a consultation in which the lad's oldest maternal uncle, who is generally an influential figure in the clan, played the most important part in deciding whether or not a marriage should take place.

Somehow, although my informants did not think it was due to interference by white people, the *oveknaiya* custom has tended to die out in all the Hopi villages. For a time it was carried on in modified form by having boys and girls meet for a song-fest on the evening after a dance, but it soon degenerated into a mere preliminary to *dumaiya* meetings and was given up.[12] Nowadays, the younger people always speak of *oveknaiya* as a sort of out-of-door *dumaiya* procedure.[13]

There were two or three other occasions when maidens had an opportunity to make marriage proposals by means of *qömi* presentations. Perhaps the most favorable time, other than at *oveknaiya*, was during the Powamu night dance, popularly called the Bean dance. This performance takes place in a dimly lighted kiva, with recently initiated youngsters ranged along the east banquette, and unmarried girls seated against the west wall. Generally, there are few mature men in the audience as every male adult is expected to participate in the dance.

As the dancers conclude their performance and begin to file out of the kiva, they must pass the bench where sit the unmarried girls, each of whom has brought with her a large bundle of *somiviki*, from which she gives a few packets to every performer as he goes by. Sometimes a girl may prepare a large loaf of *qömi* which she hands in lieu of *somiviki* to her sweetheart. This action

[9] Nequatewa, 1933, p. 42, calls this food "maiden's cake." It is frequently mentioned in accounts of Hopi courting. Beaglehole, E., 1937, p. 64, describes the manner of its preparation.

[10] See "Adolescence Rites for Girls" in Part Three.

[11] The Hopi show a good deal of wisdom and tact in trying to forestall situations in which a boy might be forced publicly to reject a girl's proposal.

[12] The custom known as *ñötiwa* (p. 126), when men run through the village with presents which the women seize, may likewise have been a preliminary to sexual affairs.

Nowadays at New Oraibi, and perhaps elsewhere, when young people gather in the evenings girls may snatch money or trinkets from boys who pursue and make love to them.

[13] During one of my interviews on this subject the inpreter, who was too young to have participated in *oveknaiya*, professed envy towards his uncle who was supplying the details to me, and soon a friendly argument began as to whether the old-timers had had more fun at *oveknaiya* than the young fellows have with the greater prevalence of *dumaiya*.

may or may not be observed by the kiva audience, but in either case the dancer has no choice but to take the *qömi* lest he offend the giver. He is not doomed, however, to enter on an engagement which may be distasteful to him, for in the event that he does not care to marry the girl he gives her *qömi* on the sly to the father of the Katcinas, or else he unobstrusively throws it away. In such an event, he sees to it that the girl soon learns that her *qömi* has been rejected and that consequently her offer of marriage has not been taken. If, on the other hand, the boy keeps the *qömi*, he brings it to his parents and arrangements for a match go on as usual.

In former times there was still another event which sometimes culminated in marriage proposals. This occurred in the spring during a festival called Nevenwehe which will be described in Part II. It was a happy, outdoor procession, with numerous stops during which the girls exchanged *somiviki* for various green plants that the boys had picked. At the last stopping place where a food exchange took place, a young woman might tender a loaf of *qömi* in place of the customary *somiviki*. Here, as at the Bean dance, the loaf was taken without fail, but the true intent of the recipient was not made known until later.[14]

We come now to another form of courtship, one that has most frequently been described as universal among the Hopi, and which is usually mentioned in folk tales. It is the only form of wooing about which the natives talk freely to outsiders. In former times it was often advantageous to have girls grind corn during the night in a chamber somewhat removed from the parents' sleeping quarters. Here would come the amorous swain to exchange courtesies, to propose marriage, and to suggest that each get the consent of his family. This pattern is quite in keeping with what the Hopi know is most highly regarded by the teachers, government agents, and missionaries with whom they come into contact. While I have no doubt that such formal romances did, on rare occasions, take place, I have still less doubt that nine times out of ten the talk during night corn-grinding was concerned with arrangements for *dumaiya*.

To summarize the situation up to the eve of marriage, we find the sex life of the Hopi beginning early in adolescence for both sexes, with youngsters soon learning the trick of visiting girls by night, with the choice of lovers supervised in varying degrees by parents and other relatives, and with pre-marital pregnancy carrying no particular stigma and almost invariably resulting in marriage. Virginity, while recognized, is not requisite for marriage,[15] and a girl who has borne a bastard, though slightly less desirable, is by no means out of the running,[16] especially if the child is being brought up by its grandparents. No compulsion is exercised in the choice of mates, but the clan head has great influence and the maternal uncle's advice is often heeded.

Even if no girl has ever proffered him *qömi* or charged him with the paternity of a child, a Hopi youth comes in time to be sated with visiting a number of girls and begins to consider marrying some one of the village maidens, usually one of his mistresses.[17] Apart from the customary factors of temperament and economic condition, the prospective groom is expected to meet several other requirements. Of these, the foremost involves the custom of exogamy. In no sense does the clan-phratry reveal itself more in the light of an extended family than when we find all marriages within this unit branded as incest. In all the hundreds of marriage combinations (see

[14] Nequatewa, 1933, p. 49, mentions another occasion when an exchange of foods constitutes an offer of marriage. At Second Mesa *somiviki* might be given to favored boys during rabbit hunts held at the conclusion of adolescence rites for girls. Beaglehole, E., 1936, p. 13, also refers to this custom.
Although Oraibi informants told of rabbit hunting at the close of girls' adolescence rites, no reference was made to courtship.

[15] There is an illuminating note in Voth, 1900, p. 240, footnote 1, in which he says that in all the weddings he saw at Oraibi the bride's hair was taken down before she left her house for the ceremony. According to Nequatewa, 1933, p. 50, note 4 B, this signifies on Second Mesa that the bride is not a virgin. If the same interpretation applies at Oraibi, it would mean that none of the girls whom Voth

saw being married was a virgin.
[16] That a girl who has had a pre-marital bastard may still be eagerly sought in marriage, is illustrated in Titiev, 1939a. Such a child is called a stolen baby, that is, " 'stolen' from his father's people." Parsons, 1939, p. 43.
[17] When a boy forsakes a mistress to marry some other girl trouble is apt to result. In one instance a jealous woman came to her lover's house while he was in process of being married. The relatives of the legitimate bride withdrew her and allowed the mistress to complete the ceremony and to claim the groom.
In another case a sweetheart, without consulting her lover, came to his house and began the wedding rites. Although he went through with the complete ceremony, he did not follow her to her house at the conclusion of the ritual and so was automatically divorced.

PHRATRY	CLAN	NO. OF INDIVIDUALS	NOT RE-MARRIED	RE-MARRIED 1	RE-MARRIED 2	RE-MARRIED 3	RE-MARRIED 4,5,6	RE-MARRIED BUT NOT DIVORCED	DIVORCED 1	DIVORCED 2	DIVORCED 3	DIVORCED 4	DIVORCED 5	DIVORCED BUT NOT RE-MARRIED	TOTAL DIVORCED
I	RABBIT	26	14	5	5	1	1[4]	3	6	4	0	1	0	2	11
	KATCINA	7	4	2	0	1	0	1	2	0	1	0	0	1	3
	PARROT	15	5	5	3	2	0	4	2	4	0	0	0	0	6
II	BEAR	12	11	1	0	0	0	0	3	0	0	0	0	2	3
	SPIDER	14	8	3	2	0	1[4]	1	3	1	1	0	0	0	5
III	SAND	31	20	6	4	0	1[4]	2	5	3	1	0	0	0	9
	LIZARD	28	15	7	5	0	1[4]	3	9	1	1	0	0	1	11
	SNAKE	7	5	0	1	0	1[4]	0	1	0	1	0	0	0	2
IV	SUN	22	12	7	2	1	0	3	3	3	1	0	0	0	7
	EAGLE	9	3	1	3	1	1	2	0	3	0	0	1	0	4
V	GREASE WOOD	37	20	13	3	1	0	8	9	3	0	0	0	3	12
	REED	15	8	2	2	2	1[6]	1	3	2	1	0	1	1	7
	BOW	9	6	2	1	0	0	1	2	1	0	0	0	1	3
VI	MASAU'U	17	10	5	0	2	0	2	4	0	1	0	0	0	5
	REAL COYOTE	20	13	5	1	1	0	3	2	3	0	0	0	1	5
	WATER COYOTE	26	14	8	4	0	0	5	6	2	0	0	0	1	8
	KOKOP	12	6	4	1	1	0	1	2	3	0	0	0	0	5
	CEDAR	2	1	1	0	0	0	0	0	1	0	0	0	0	1
	LE	6	3	1	0	2	0	0	2	1	0	1	0	1	4
VII	REAL BADGER	23	14	4	3	1	1[5]	3	3	1	1	0	1	0	6
	GRAY BADGER	23	15	5	2	1	0	1	6	0	1	0	0	0	7
	NAVAHO BADGER	3	1	1	0	1	0	0	3	0	0	0	0	1	3
	BUTTERFLY	3	1	1	1	0	0	1	1	0	0	0	0	0	1
VIII	PIKYAS	21	11	3	7	0	0	1	7	3	1	0	0	2	11
	PATKI	20	10	2	6	1	1[4]	2	3	3	0	1	1	0	8
	SIVA'AP	2	2	0	0	0	0	0	0	0	0	0	0	0	0
IX	CRANE	4	3	1	0	0	0	1	0	0	0	0	0	0	0
	SQUASH	4	3	1	0	0	0	0	1	0	0	0	0	0	1
	CHICKEN HAWK	5	3	1	0	0	1[4]	1	1	0	0	0	0	0	1
	TOTALS	423	241	97	56	19	10	50	89	42	11	3	4	17	149

INDIVIDUALS —— 423

NOT RE-MARRIED — 241

RE-MARRIED —— 182

DIVORCED —— 149

DIVORCE PERCENTAGE } —— 35%

RE-MARRIED —— 182

RE-MARRIED NO DIVORCE } —— 50 / 132

DIVORCED BUT NOT RE-MARRIED } — 17

TOTAL DIVORCED — 149

CHART IV. ORAIBI MARRIAGES (MALE).

PHRATRY	CLAN	NO. OF INDIVIDUALS	NOT RE-MARRIED	RE-MARRIED 1	RE-MARRIED 2	RE-MARRIED 3	RE-MARRIED 4,5,6,7,8	RE-MARRIED BUT NOT DIVORCED	DIVORCED 1	DIVORCED 2	DIVORCED 3	DIVORCED 4	DIVORCED 5,6,7,8	DIVORCED BUT NOT RE-MARRIED	TOTAL DIVORCED
I	RABBIT	32	19	8	4	0	1[4]	1	9	2	0	0	1[5]	0	12
	KATCINA	5	4	1	0	0	0	0	1	0	0	0	0	0	1
	PARROT	14	5	6	2	1	0	2	5	2	0	0	0	0	7
	CROW	2	1	0	0	0	1[4]	0	0	0	1	0	0	0	1
II	BEAR	7	5	0	1	0	1[7]	0	1	0	0	0	1[7]	0	2
	SPIDER	14	10	3	1	0	0	1	3	0	0	0	0	0	3
III	SAND	27	15	6	3	2	1[4]	1	6	2	3	0	0	0	11
	LIZARD	28	19	3	4	1	1[4]	1	6	2	2	0	0	2	10
	SNAKE	2	1	1	0	0	0	1	0	0	0	0	0	0	0
IV	SUN	22	11	7	1	2	1[4]	0	9	1	0	1	0	0	11
	EAGLE	10	7	2	1	0	0	1	2	0	0	0	0	0	2
V	GREASEWOOD	35	21	9	3	0	2[5,4]	4	4	4	0	2	0	0	10
	REED	32	22	4	3	2	1[5]	1	5	3	1	1	0	1	10
	BOW	7	5	1	0	0	1[5]	1	0	0	0	0	1[6]	0	1
VI	MASAU'U	28	18	6	4	0	0	3	4	3	0	0	0	0	7
	REAL COYOTE	25	16	5	1	2	1[8]	3	2	3	1	0	1[8]	1	7
	WATER COYOTE	22	15	4	2	1	0	1	4	1	1	0	0	0	6
	KOKOP	7	3	1	2	1	0	0	2	2	0	0	0	0	4
	LE	5	3	1	1	0	0	0	2	1	0	0	0	1	3
VII	REAL BADGER	15	9	4	2	0	0	0	6	1	0	0	0	1	7
	GRAY BADGER	6	3	0	1	1	1[5]	1	1	0	0	0	1[5]	0	2
	NAVAHO BADGER	7	6	1	0	0	0	0	1	0	0	0	0	0	1
	BUTTERFLY	1	1	0	0	0	0	0	0	0	0	0	0	0	0
VIII	PIKYAS	23	12	4	4	2	1[4]	1	3	6	0	1	0	0	10
	PATKI	16	12	4	0	0	0	1	2	1	0	0	0	0	3
	SIVA'AP	1	1	0	0	0	0	0	0	0	0	0	0	0	0
IX	CRANE	2	1	0	0	0	1[6]	0	0	0	0	1	0	0	1
	SQUASH	3	3	0	0	0	0	0	0	0	0	0	0	0	0
	CHICKENHAWK	5	4	1	0	0	0	0	1	0	0	0	0	0	1
	TOTALS	403	252	82	40	15	14	24	79	34	9	6	5	6	133

INDIVIDUALS —— 403
NOT RE-MARRIED — 252
RE-MARRIED —— 151
DIVORCED —— 133
DIVORCE PERCENTAGE } —— 33%

RE-MARRIED —— 151
RE-MARRIED, NO DIVORCE } —— 24
                            127
DIVORCED BUT NOT RE-MARRIED } —— 6
TOTAL DIVORCED — 133

CHART V. ORAIBI MARRIAGES (FEMALE).

charts IV and V), which were recorded at Oraibi, there were only three instances of clan endogamy. In one case a Sun clan couple, in another a Coyote pair, and in the third two members of the Pikyas clan were the offenders. In none of these instances could direct ties of blood be established, and some extenuating factor was invoked to explain each divergence. The Coyote couple were Christian missionaries and felt themselves unaffected by Hopi custom, the Sun couple met off the reservation and claimed to have married without inquiring about their clan affiliations, and the Pikyas pair consisted of a Third Mesa woman who married a Mishongnovi man from Second Mesa. Nevertheless, despite these "explanations" all three marriages were recognized to be illegal, and the natives felt that they were not instances of typical Hopi unions.

The rule of exogamy is extended in theory to the father's phratry as well as to one's own, but here there is far more tolerance of violations. Out of all the marriages at Oraibi in the last half century, of which I tried to collect a complete list, I recorded 37 cases of men marrying women of the father's phratry and of these, 16 were unions with women of the father's own clan. I also secured data on 19 women marrying males from the phratry of the father, including two instances of marriage with men of the father's actual clan. In view of the fact that these figures are based not on the full number of marriages recorded but rather on the comparatively smaller group of marriages of people whose fathers' clans could be ascertained, it is clear that insofar as recent times are concerned, matings with members of the father's clan and phratry are readily condoned.[18]

There remains for consideration one other restriction in the choice of a mate. It is considered improper for a man, formerly married but now single through death or divorce, to court a girl

who has never yet been wedded; and it is equally wrong for a youth who has never been married to seek the hand of a widow or a divorcée. This custom serves, to some extent, as an age grading factor,[19] and its violation is punished in the afterlife by forcing the offender to carry a heavily loaded basket (hoapu) on the journey from the grave to the home of the dead. Those who enter matrimony for the first time with partners who have had previous mates are the victims of this supernatural judgment and are popularly referred to as "basket-carriers" (hoap-iqwilta).[20] Since the general trend of Hopi religion is decidedly nonethical, only witches being punished in the other world, the tabu against marriages of hitherto unwed individuals with those who have had previous marital experience cannot be lightly regarded. It is impossible to say how the idea first arose, but we may suggest an interpretation based on the way in which it works.

To some extent the "basket-carrier" code helps to preserve the stability of marriages as it discourages boys from seducing married women, and girls from seeking the attentions of wedded men. In this way a considerable portion of the populace is eliminated as a possible source of contention between husbands and wives. Furthermore, it may well be that marriages between boys and girls of about equal age and sex experience are thought to be more enduring than unions between unequally matched couples. I hesitate to say that the wavering nature of Hopi marriages was the cause which led to the "basket-carrier" tabu as a partial check on adultery, but the fact remains that bachelors rarely "cut out" married men.

In spite of tabus, forbidden marriages do occur. I have listed ten males who must "carry baskets" in the after-life, and no less than thirty women who are doomed to the same fate. I do not know

[18] A full discussion of this aspect of the marital situation involves the complicated problem of cross-cousin marriage. See Titiev, 1938b, p. 110.
[19] Marital conditions are expressed among the Hopi as follows:
Unmarried male is called a boy (tiyo).
Bachelor of long standing is called (siwahova).
Married male is called a man (taka).
Unmarried female, regardless of age, is called a girl (mana).
Spinstress of long standing is called (siwahopmana).
Married female is called a woman (wuhti).
Divorced man, or widower, is called a cow man (wukas-taka).
Divorced woman, or widow, is called cow woman

(wukaswuhti).
Age grading notions are suggested in the terminology inasmuch as a male remains a "boy" until marriage makes him a "man"; and a female is a "girl" until marriage converts her to a "woman."
[20] It is a previous mate who fashions a basket for an offending boy or girl, and while the offender carries it on his back, the ex-mate loads it with lumps of gravel (kalavi). Any children born of such a forbidden union must accompany the offending parent to the Underworld, lingering along the path to the home of the dead and subsisting entirely on piñon gum.
Other notions related to this custom may be found in Beaglehole, E., and P., 1935, pp. 46–47; and in Voth, 1905b, pp. 110, 111.

whether or not clan affiliations have any bearing on the tendency to violate this custom, but the ten men belong to various clans, whereas six of the women are from the Sun clan and six others from the phratry containing the Coyote clan.

In contrast to the dearth of information regarding Hopi courtship methods, we possess several good accounts of the nuptial rites.[21] Consequently, we shall limit ourselves to a brief summary of the main events. Once a marriage has been decided upon, usually with the consent of the relatives on both sides, the girl prepares a quantity of cornmeal which she bears late in the evening or early in the morning to the home of the groom, where she is to be made welcome throughout the duration of the rites. From this time on she is addressed as "*imu'wi*" by all her husband's clanspeople and generally by every one in the village. Not until she returns to her own mother's home will her personal name be used again by neighbors and friends.

The first three days of her temporary patrilocal residence constitute a probationary period during which she spends most of her time in semi-seclusion, busily grinding corn from morning to night. On the other hand, no test is demanded of the groom, who goes about his daily routine in normal fashion. At some time during the probationary period, the boy's paternal aunts prepare an attack on his house to "punish" the bride for "stealing" their sweetheart, and to get revenge on the groom's mothers and sisters for having allowed their nephew to court another woman.[22] First they make an announcement of impending trouble, and then they appear in a body armed with water and mud and ready for battle. (See pl. II a.) Not content with smearing each other with mud and casting all manner of recriminations at each other, the attacking aunts often carry away whatever they can snatch from the household that is sheltering the bride. When possible, the aunts snip a lock of hair from the head of either the groom's mother or father.[23] In spite of the

seeming ferocity of the attack, an air of good nature prevails throughout, and recompense is later made for all damage inflicted during the combat.

Early in the morning of the fourth day there occurs the culminating rite of the wedding. The mothers of the bridal pair, with the help of other female relatives, wash the heads of the newlyweds in one basin. During this process the hair of the bride and groom is mingled or actually knotted to symbolize the act of union. At this point, when their nephew is in the very act of being lost to them forever, his paternal aunts make a final show of resentment by trying to force the couple apart, or by obtruding their own heads into the receptacle in place of the bride's. As soon as the hair dries the couple go together to the east edge of the mesa to pray to the sun; and on their return the bride makes *piki* for her mother-in-law before the wedding breakfast is served.

From this time on the pair may sleep together as man and wife,[24] but the rites are by no means concluded. It is still necessary to make the bride's wedding garments, and until her whole outfit is ready she continues to remain in her husband's home and to do the major part of the cooking for his people. *Tcukuviki*[25] and *somiviki* are the foods that she usually prepares on alternate days.

The task of spinning and carding wool, as well as the actual weaving of the nuptial costume, is not left only to the groom and his immediate relatives. Every man in the pueblo is invited to participate, and people often come from other villages to show their good-will towards a family by helping to fashion the garments for *imu'wi*. On stated occasions devoted to various parts of the work, the groom's family holds a feast to which the public is invited, but which only those who are actually sharing in the labor are expected to attend. A number of relatives supply the necessary mutton and corn for these meals.

For several weeks in most cases, and even for

---

[21] For First Mesa consult Parsons, 1921a; Parsons, 1925, pp. 32–38; and Parsons, 1936b, pp. 997–1001, *et passim*.
For Second Mesa see Nequatewa, 1933; Beaglehole, E., and P., 1935, pp. 50–59; and Beaglehole, E., 1937, pp. 75–77. For Third Mesa consult Voth, 1900.
[22] A possible interpretation of this phase of the wedding, in terms of cross-cousin marriage, is offered in Titiev, 1938b, pp. 109–110.
[23] Dr. Parsons, in a personal communication, has suggested that in ceremonials, cutting hair is a substitute for taking a head. (See pl. II b.)

[24] Parsons, 1921a, p. 264, expresses suprise because an informant forgot to mention the day when a married couple may sleep together. "He forgot that," she comments, "because, I presume, it was the ceremonial that was of significance, not the personal relationship." In the light of more recent observations, a more likely interpretation would be that "He forgot that," because in all probability the couple had long been in the habit of sleeping together.
[25] Nequatewa, 1933, p. 49, note E, calls this food "Bride's cake."

a longer period in many instances, the bride remains with her mother-in-law. At last, when all is ready, she dresses in her newly-made wedding finery and, just at daybreak, returns to her own house carrying a duplicate outfit wrapped in a reed case and resting across her outstretched arms.[26] When she is received by her mother the long, elaborate ritual is considered at an end. The groom does not accompany the bride at this time but appears at her home during the course of the day. A final, mutual exchange of food gifts between the husband's and wife's households constitutes the concluding episode of the performance.

There was little conformity in the opinions of various informants regarding the nuptials of a "basket-carrier." The whole question is tied up with the need of possessing various parts of the bridal outfit in order to make a proper entry to the other world after death.[27] This is more of a necessity for a woman than for a man, so the feeling seems to prevail that a girl is entitled to a set of wedding clothes and should go through with the rites even if she is marrying a "*taka.*" On the other hand, it was fairly well agreed that no ceremony need be performed when a male "basket-carrier" weds, as his bride already possesses the essential garments. For Second Mesa, Nequatewa reports that a ritual is performed for maidens marrying widowers and for youths marrying widows. With characteristic Hopi reticence on such matters, he makes no mention of the attitude towards remarriages on the part of divorced people.

The need for wedding garments in the after-life makes their acquisition extremely important, and is one of the compelling motives towards marriage. It sometimes happens, therefore, that a girl, usually a mistress, will make an attempt to "trap" a boy by going to his house in bridal fashion and inaugurating the rites without having come to an understanding with the prospective groom.[28] When such a contingency arises the boy may flatly refuse to go through with the ceremony. In this event his relatives would weave a Hopi dress for the girl as a partial recompense

for the gifts she brings and in payment for the favors the lad has received at her hands. More often a youth would grudgingly go through the full nuptial rites with an insistent mistress, but when they were terminated he would not follow to take up residence at her home, and it would then be understood that the pair were free to re-wed in the fashion of any divorced couple.

Another custom relating to marriage is based on the supernatural value attributed to the wedding costume. Once instituted, the full rites must be carried to their termination regardless of what may occur to interrupt the proceedings. I was told of several instances where a groom died during the probationary period, early in the ceremony, while the bride was grinding corn at his house. Nevertheless, the girl continued carrying out her part of the ritual to the very end.

That the occurrence of pre-marital pregnancy occasions no lasting disgrace among the Hopi is shown by the formal recognition of children who may be born before the completion of the rites. Far from trying to hush up such matters, the groom's relatives and friends add to the regular bridal outfit a miniature wedding robe in the case of a girl baby or a black and white blanket (*pisalhöya*) for a boy child. Then when the mother, dressed in her nuptial garments, proceeds from the groom's home to her own, the child is proudly carried along, resplendent in its newly made wrappings.

Marriage is practically universal for women. I found no spinstresses mentioned in any of my interviews along this line of investigation, but in 1934 I knew of three eligible girls at Oraibi who were not yet married although they were well along in their twenties. Two were being courted and will probably wed in due time, but the third is shy and unpopular and may actually live to be an "old maid." Bachelors, on the other hand, are somewhat more common, although still very much in the minority. Of sixteen unmarried men from various clans about half had failed to marry because of family objections to all the girls they courted; and the other half had found it impossible to get mates because of some peculiarity

---

[26] Only in the event that a marriage terminates in December, the dangerous month when spirits of all sorts abound, is there apt to be a long delay in a bride's return home. Brides whose rites are concluded in that month must wait for the next moon before they leave for home.

The length of time requisite for the completion of the wedding outfit helps to explain why Hopi unions generally

take place in the months between harvest and planting. At any other time the men are too busy in the fields to help in the spinning and weaving.

[27] Compare Nequatewa, 1933, p. 49; and Beaglehole, P., 1935, p. 48.

[28] Nequatewa, 1933, p. 50, gives an account of "trapping" on Second Mesa.

such as defective speech or singular appearance. Although albinos of either sex are found in each village, I knew of only one bachelor whose failure to marry was attributed to albinism.

That there should be a preponderance of bachelors over spinsters is to be expected from the structure of Hopi society. The marriage of a girl is an economic gain to her household; the wedding of a boy is a direct loss to his natal group.[29] Therefore, brothers and uncles insist, insofar as they are able, that girls get married; but there is far less pressure brought to bear on a boy, and in some instances he is even dissuaded from marriage by various members of his household. Although the economic aspect is not the only one considered in passing judgment on proposed marriages, it certainly is one of the most important factors. That is why, from the Hopi point of view, it is regarded as senseless to demand chastity of girls, inasmuch as pre-marital affairs often serve as preliminaries to desirable marriages.

Turning next to the question of the permanency of Hopi marriages, the data for Oraibi indicate surprising instability. As is shown on charts IV and V, about 34% of the 826 men and women whose marital records were studied, had figured in anywhere from one to eight divorces. In recognition of the fact that these statistics contradict a current belief that divorce is "comparatively rare" among the Hopi,[30] an account is here given of the procedure by which the data were gathered.

As part of a study of the perplexing clan-phratry situation, a house to house census of Old Oraibi as of 1900–1905 was undertaken, during the progress of which questions were asked regarding the clan, ceremonial affiliations, marriages, divorces, and remarriages of each individual who was mentioned. The results were later tabulated on index cards, so that in the end there were available case histories of 826 Oraibi inhabitants whose marital records are summarized in charts IV and V. A transcript of a page taken

almost verbatim from my field notes will serve to illustrate specifically the form in which the raw data on marriage were obtained.

Qötcnimka married Talasyauoma who died, then Kuwanventiwa (div), then Kuwanve'ima (div), then Piqösa.

Kuwanve'ima was first married to Tcocwusnim (div),[31] then to Qötcnimka (div), then to Siwingyaunim (died), then to Puhumana.[32]

Tcocwusnim, after her divorce then married Piphongva.

Piphongva was first married to Sihepnim (div), and then to Tcocwusnim.

Sihepnim, after her divorce married Siheptiwa (div), stayed single for a while and then again married Siheptiwa.

Siheptiwa was first married to Pongyayesnim (died), then to Qömayonsi (div), then to Sihepnim whom he divorced and later remarried.

Qömayonsi was first married to Sikyaletstiwa who died, then to Siheptiwa (div), then to a First Mesa man (div), then to a Zuñi residing at Walpi, and then to various Walpi men.

Siwingyaunim was first married to Kuwanve'ima (div), then to Kuwanventiwa.

Kuwanventiwa, after his first divorce, was married to Qötcnimka (div), then to Masakwapnim (div), then to Tangakvenka (div), then he stayed single.

Masakwapnim was first married to Sakhongva (div), then to Kuwanve'ima (div), then to Sikyaletcioma.

There are many gaps in the records owing to the fact that in the beginning my informants[33] deliberately withheld divorce data, some of which were revealed in later interviews, and some of which never came to light. Other gaps resulted from the inability of informants to remember the complete marital histories of individuals long dead or long removed from the village. In all likelihood, had it been possible to obtain more exact information, the incidence of divorce

---

[29] A confirmation of this viewpoint is found in the figures in charts IV and V relating to people who did not remarry after having been divorced. In this category we find 17 men but only 6 women.

[30] Murdock, 1934, p. 344. One of the most extravagant statements ever made on the subject of Pueblo morals occurs in Lummis, 1892, p. 326. "The Pueblo was a prehistoric monogam and punished unfaithfulness with death"; wrote Lummis, "and it is doubtful if any American community can show a less percentage of loose women."

[31] Observance of the tabu against "basket-carrying" marriages is indicated by the fact that almost invariably both parties in a remarriage have had previous matrimonial experiences.

[32] As later evidence revealed, this woman had been five times married and four times divorced.

[33] Work on the census, during which a great deal of valuable material was gathered incidentally, was done primarily with Chief Tawaqwaptiwa and Don Talayesva, both of whom were middle-aged.

would have been considerably higher than 34%.[34]

One of the most significant aspects of the distribution of divorces and remarriages, as shown on charts IV and V, is the evenness with which it is spread throughout the population. There is so little concentration by clan, phratry, or sex that the figures cited must be interpreted as affecting the entire pueblo. Such evidence forces us to conclude that marriages at Old Oraibi are essentially unstable, and that Hopi monogamy is of a very brittle order indeed.

Whether or not similar conditions exist in the other Hopi towns cannot be satisfactorily determined in the absence of comparative statistics. Mrs. Beaglehole, on the basis of an analysis of 23 marriages at Second Mesa, came to the conclusion that "there is no reason to believe that estrangements occurred frequently."[35] However, Mrs. Beaglehole worked with only a single informant, and her data are admittedly "not conclusive."[36] On the other hand, Dr. Kennard and Dr. Eggan, both of whom investigated Second Mesa towns have often assured me that marital conditions there are closely comparable to those at Third Mesa, and it is our consensus that the situation at Oraibi may well be regarded as typical of the entire tribe.

The instability of Hopi marriages may be considered as a concomitant of the divorce customs. These are so lax that they present no bar to the easy dissolution of marital bonds. Separation may take place at the desire of either party without a semblance of formality. Either a dissatisfied woman asks her husband to leave her house or a disgruntled man withdraws from his wife's residence and returns to his natal household. No official cognizance is taken of a divorce, and no announcement is made to the villagers. Word simply spreads about that a given couple has separated. Possessions are divided according to the lines of ownership indicated in the preceding chapter, and young children remain with the mother, while the older offspring may follow either parent. People contemplating divorce may consult various relatives, but family consent is by no means essential. Ordinarily, a husband offers no

resistance when asked for a divorce by his wife, but in the event that he proves stubborn her brothers and uncles may come to her aid.

The most common grounds for separation are stinginess, laziness, violence of temper, and above all, adultery. It is noteworthy that the economic habits of the Hopi make possible a great deal of infidelity. Most men herd sheep in conjunction with two or more partners, and each one usually tends the flocks for two successive days, spending the intervening night at a sheep camp. At the height of the farming season too men often find it convenient to sleep in field huts, and on nights when a husband is known to be out of the village, his wife is very apt to receive a *dumaiya* visit, particularly from a widower or a husband who is free from his own wife's vigilance, as in the case of the forty-day period following a woman's confinement.

If a widower or a divorced man gets into the habit of making regular *dumaiya* calls on one woman every time the occasion permits, it soon becomes an open secret that he is "cutting out" the husband. A quarrel then ensues, and if the lovers insist on carrying on their affair a divorce usually follows, in which case the lover simply moves into the place formerly occupied by the cast-off husband. No lasting disgrace is attached to such proceedings and the whole matter is soon taken for granted.[37]

The lack of any formal procedure relative to divorce makes it very hard, in many instances, to differentiate temporary separations from actual divorces. For example, a man may find himself being "cut out" so regularly that he leaves his wife and takes up residence with some other woman. Ordinarily, this is to be construed as a second marriage, but, on the other hand, it may turn out that if his first wife's love affair was only temporary the husband will return to her as soon as she is ready to receive him. I was given no less than 16 instances of couples who had separated, engaged on independent sex careers, and then returned to each other again. In many other cases, where the intervening separations were not of long duration, it was hard to tell whether to

---

[34] Informants often admitted that in particular cases they had described persons as married only once because they could not recall the names of their other marriage partners. As a sort of rough corrective, I have omitted from the figures given above, about 40 young people whose marriages were of such recent date as to preclude the possibility of divorce.

[35] Beaglehole, P., 1935, p. 41.

[36] Beaglehole, P., 1935, p. 41.

[37] The most frequently divorced Hopi female, a notoriously loose woman who had made no less than eight "official" changes of husbands, was often a subject of jest but was never ostracized, not even by the family of the Village chief. Furthermore, even after she was well launched on her divorce record, her family once objected to one of her lovers as unworthy and they did not wed.

record them as infidelities or as divorces and re-marriages.[38]

Inasmuch as frequently broken marriage bonds exert a profound effect on social organization, it was pertinent to our study to determine whether this state of affairs was a recent development or an old characteristic of Hopi society. Accordingly, Don's father, a man of about seventy-five years of age, was asked to describe the marriage careers of several people who had died long ago, and who were remembered only vaguely by younger informants. With the matrimonial adventures of one couple as a point of departure, the old man began a recital of names and experiences which covered six pages written on both sides before a halt was called. The following selection is representative and is given in almost the exact form in which the material was recorded.

Siwihongniwa was first married to Hongya-vatca who died, then to Qömawuhti (div), then to Sikyakwapnim.

Sikyakwapnim was first married to Suyusi who died, then to Masauyauoma (div), then to Kuktiwa (div), and then to Siwihongniwa.

Masauyauoma was first married to Honyes-nim (div), then to Yoiwainim (div), then to Qaiyowuhti (div), then he again married Honyesnim.

Kuktiwa was first married to Sikyahongka, but he didn't like her as she was older than he was. He "happened to talk to her" and that's how she got him for a husband, but they were soon divorced. (A few moments later the informant explained that Kuktiwa might have freed himself from this woman except for the fact that "having got into her" he was forced to agree to her demand for marriage "or something would happen to him.") Kuktiwa, after divorcing Sikyahongka then married Siwinya who died, then Sikyakwapnim (div), then Simeya (died), then Honanmana.

Honyesnim was first married to Masauyau-oma (div), then to Talahongi (div), then to a Walpi man (div), and then back to Masauyau-oma.

Yoiwainim was first married to Sikyamö-niwa (div), then to Masauyauoma (div), then back to Sikyamöniwa again.

Qaiyowuhti was first married to Masan-gainiwa (div), then to Masauyauoma (div), then to Qwatcakwa (div), then to Kyachong-niwa (div), then to a Walpi man (div), then to Kuwanvikwaiya (div), after which she did not re-wed.

The close analogy between this information regarding nineteenth century inhabitants of Oraibi, and that pertaining to residents of about the years 1900–1905, gives ample justification for the conclusion that loose marriage ties and frequent adultery are long-standing Hopi traits. That this has not been more clearly brought out in the writings of former students of the Hopi is due in part to Victorian conventions. Thus, in the accepted style of their day, Fewkes and Stephen frequently translate *mana* (unmarried female) as "virgin," whereas the Hopi word for a true maiden is *kapukupu* (not opened), an awkward periphrasis which is almost never used in ordinary speech.[39] Again, Fewkes did not hesitate to delete descriptions of obscene behavior, so that his works cannot be relied upon to give a proper insight into the morals of the Hopi of his time.[40]

It is true that Stephen's nature was more robust, and that he lacked the squeamishness of some of his contemporaries, but, unfortunately, he did not attempt to make a systematic collection of sociological data. Nevertheless, by reading somewhat between the lines of his journal, one gets a glimpse of conditions that tally well with the observations made in this chapter. Thus we learn from Stephen of little boys taught to sing songs on such topics as "*luwa* (vulva), *kwashi* (penis), and *chova* (sex desire)"; of the Yayatu society whose members were equally

---

[38] A passage in Parsons, 1936b, p. 766, points to a similar state of affairs over half a century ago. "Sikyapiki," records Stephen, "has a wife in Shipaulovi . . . but she is inclined to cohabit with other men. Hence . . . he married another wife at Tewa and goes over there occasionally and lives with the Tewa wife."

Dr. Parsons, in her capacity as editor, appends a footnote suggesting that this may be an instance of Navajo influence or that "possibly the Pueblos were not the strict monogamists they were said to be, at the coming of the Spaniards."

Rather than resort to the possibility of Navaho borrow-ing or to a possible change in marriage regulations, I should be inclined to interpret Stephen's entry regarding Sikyapiki's wives as an instance of that wavering sort of divorce and remarriage which I found so common at Oraibi. This seems to indicate the probability that loose marriage and frequent divorce were already established features of Hopi society as early as 1892.

[39] Parsons, 1939, p. 44, also uses virgin where previously unmarried person is really meant.

[40] Fewkes, 1892a, p. 48. In describing clowns Fewkes writes that they indulged in "many obscenities which cannot be mentioned in this place."

"keen to bugger a man or ravish a woman or maid"; of male clowns whose behavior was lewd and filthy in the extreme; but which was nevertheless matched by the antics of women performers; and of a jealous husband who went so far as to strike a faithless wife a blow which "brought the blood."[41] Indeed, Dr. Parsons has noted that Stephen's journal contains "several references to remarriage . . . which suggest that separation and remarriage were not at all uncommon."[42]

Insofar as we can reconstruct the situation from the information given by my oldest informant and from the hints contained in Stephen's writings, there seems to have been little change in Hopi standards during the last fifty years. This conclusion is supported by the earliest reference to Hopi morality that I have been able to find. In 1655, while the Hopi were protesting the murder of an Oraibi man at the hands of Father Salvador de Guerra, they "also testified that several other persons, especially boys and girls guilty of immoral conduct, had been whipped and tarred with hot turpentine."[43] Similarly, in a letter sent to Major Powell in 1884, J. H. Sullivan writes, "Their notions of the marital relations between husband and wife are not as good as they should be, as they are often broken up, frequently from merely the incompatibility of tempers, the only cause of separation."[44] Since this was the state of affairs in 1884, we may be sure that the "brittle monogamy" of the Hopi goes back to a time when they were relatively uninfluenced by American contacts.

The laxness of Hopi sexual behavior over a period of many generations must unquestionably have had a detrimental effect on their family life and must have been a disturbing factor in their social organization. That they have long recognized these facts is plainly evident in their folklore, and we may turn to the tales collected in the latter years of the past century for corroboration of some of the material here presented, and for verification of the hypothesis that these conditions are not of suspiciously recent origin. Many of the myths express a good deal of concern over immorality which is judged, according to Hopi

standards, by the prevalence of adultery and violations of the "basket-carrier" code. Such behavior is constantly condemned as evil, and there are frequent laments over the dissensions that are thus caused among married people. The opening story in Voth's collection of tales strikes the keynote. It describes the conduct of a newly-created man and woman, whose relationships towards each other were supposed to set the pattern of wedded life for all time. It turned out that this couple failed to get along smoothly,"and that is the reason," remarks the narrator, "why there are so many contentions between the men and their wives."[45]

On one point practically all the versions of the Emergence story are agreed, and that is that the exodus from the Underworld took place largely because people were misbehaving to such an extent that their leaders decided to make a radical change in the hope of bettering conditions. Thus an Oraibi myth reports that prior to the Emergence "the people began to live the way we are living now, in constant contentions. . . . They became very bad. They would take away the wives of the chiefs."[46] It is important to note how the teller of this tale has drawn a parallel between the setting of the ancient story and a contemporary background of strife and misbehavior.[47]

We have but to consider an almost identical tone in a myth recorded by Stephen on First Mesa to realize that we are dealing with a tribal rather than a local or a village situation. "In the Underworld," begins this tale, "all the people were fools.[48] . . . Youths copulated with the wives of the elder men, and the elder men deflowered virgins."[49] The full intent of this passage is lost if we regard it only as a general condemnation of sexual indulgence. Actually, the speaker is branding people as "fools" because married men and women are having illegal relations with unmarried girls and boys, in violation of the "basket-carrier" tabu.

Such far-reaching proofs of marital instability make it self-evident that the limited family of father, mother, and children, often has but little

[41] Parsons, 1936b, pp. 275; 330–331; 366; 1001; 1008.
[42] Parsons, 1936b, p. 1065, footnote 1.
[43] Scholes, 1937, p. 154.
[44] Sullivan, 1884, p. 101.
[45] Voth, 1905b, p. 4.
[46] Voth, 1905b, p. 16.
[47] Compare Curtis, 1922, p. 10. "About the year 1862 came the third successive season of crop failure, which the

Hopi attributed to the evil ways of the people, especially as regards adultery."
[48] "Fools" is a poor translation of the Hopi term *ka-hopi* which Stephen's informant used in telling this story. Literally, *ka-hopi* means un-Hopi, that is, improper, evil, restless. It is often used to designate those who over-indulge in sexual activities.
[49] Stephen, 1929, p. 3.

permanency in the structure of Hopi society. Some other agency must function to give the necessary stability to the social fabric and to absorb the victims of repeated family breakups. It is in this connection that the full significance of the household unit is most clearly revealed.

We have previously noted that whereas the position of men in a household is in a constant state of flux, the status of women is marked by its permanence. Theoretically, a woman lives from birth to death under the same roof with her mothers, sisters, and daughters. If she is not the actual owner of her house, she is at least a life tenant there. According to Hopi custom she is also entitled to a share of her clan's land and its usufruct.[50] This land is worked by her father, her unmarried maternal uncles, her bachelor brothers, her husband, her unmarried sons, and her sisters' husbands, all of whom contribute directly or indirectly to her support. Under such a system a woman's material welfare depends very little on her husband, and the only economic deterrent to divorce is the fact that the men of her household may object to a separation which will rob them of a co-worker.[51]

On the care of her children too a woman's marital condition has little practical bearing.

Thanks to the joint principles of matrilineal descent and matrilocal residence, all children are automatically as firmly ensconced in their natal household groups as are their mothers.

From the standpoint of material considerations, divorce is of as little moment to men as to women. A divorced man can always find refuge in a mother's or a sister's household until he decides to take up a new residence in the home of another wife.

As long as there is a constant operation of the household system it makes comparatively little difference in Hopi society whether marriages endure or not. The strength and durability of the household unit is scarcely affected by the collapse of limited families, and it is for this reason that the social structure of the Hopi has been unshaken by the widespread prevalence of such disturbing factors as adultery and divorce.[52]

In bringing this chapter to a close, it would be misleading if nothing were said of marriages which are characterized by affection and permanency. Where a man's marital experience is happy, he tends more and more to identify himself with his wife's group; and not infrequently, a married man remains devoted to his wife's household even at the expense of allegiance to his own clan.

[50] Beaglehole, E., 1937, p. 10.

[51] With the modern trend for girls to move into separate houses at marriage a wife has greater economic need of a husband. Forde, 1931, p. 382, quotes a story from Aitken regarding a First Mesa divorcée who had hired a young clansman to work for her. This plan did not work out well and one of her relatives advised the woman to make things up with her husband. " 'One of your own people might be willing to plant for you,' " she was advised, " 'but only a husband will give you meat and clothes.' "

It is my belief that had she continued to live in her natal household after marriage, she would have been less dependent on her husband.

[52] Linton, 1936, p. 164, makes an analysis of a similar social system among the Iroquois which may be compared with the above.

Chapter IV

HOUSEHOLDS, LINEAGES, AND THE CLAN-PHRATRY PROBLEM

WHEN investigators among the Hopi first began to solicit sociologic information, they were given long lists of seemingly totemic names which the natives applied to groups of kindred that appeared to be clans. In time it was found that these putative clans were somehow arranged into larger unnamed units which were assumed to be phratries. There were numerous legends to account for the clustering of clans into larger groups, but all of them were based on one pattern which may be briefly summarized.

In the days when the Hopi still lived in the Underworld, clan divisions already existed. Hardly had the people emerged to the present surface of the earth than the groups split up for various reasons and traveled widely throughout the Southwest in small units of one or two clans each. This movement was not a continuous trek, but was broken up by periods of settlement at a number of places, the locations of which are indicated by ruins. While traveling, some of the clans formed "partnerships," or experienced adventures with certain plants and animals with whom they established a vague sort of totemic relationship. "The legends indicate a long period of extensive migrations in separate communities; the groups [coming] . . . to Tusayan at different times and from different directions. . . ."[1] Ultimately, one group arrived first at each of the present pueblo sites. In due time other clans came on the scene, being admitted to the village after a period of probation, or upon demonstrating a ceremony capable of producing rain and other benefits. As more and more clans arrived and were admitted, the present composition of the Hopi towns was brought about.

In the hope that exhaustive research into the complete repertoire of migration myths would serve the double purpose of explaining the social situation, and of illuminating the archaeological problems of the area, Stephen and Fewkes plunged into the task of recording clan legends as narrated by the best available informants. "While engaged in collecting the migration legends of different Hopi clans," writes Fewkes,

"the author has consulted, when possible, the clan chiefs . . . [for] the collector of the unrecorded history of Walpi soon recognizes that it is best not to give too much weight to stories of clans to which the informant does not belong."[2]

Despite his care and accuracy in gathering data, Fewkes found himself baffled at every turn in the matter of interpreting his material. There were at least three points that he might have had reason to hope his researches would settle: (1) the directions from which the various clans at Walpi had originally approached the village, (2) the order in which the clans had arrived, and (3) the manner in which the clan-phratry grouping had been formed. Unfortunately, he was unable to settle any one of these problems, for we find him pointing out that "There is so much obscurity in the information derived from legends in regard to the direction whence the family groups came to Tusayan that this testimony should not be given too much weight," and that "the legend of the sequence of the advent of the . . . people in Tusayan are also obscure."[3] With respect to the clan-phratry combinations, he wrote, "Each of the . . . nyû-mû(s) [phratries] or peoples contains several gentes [clans], a knowledge of which has an important bearing on Tusayan kinships. As the determination of these groups is difficult the classification is often obscure."[4]

Nearly half a century has elapsed since ethnologists were first mired in the Hopi clan muddle, yet the situation is still full of perplexities. For the most part anthropologists have now abandoned as futile the quest of the proper directional or sequential approach of the various clans, but the problem of what constitutes a Hopi clan or phratry is still being actively pursued. Some of the difficulties are purely terminological, and these will be considered first. The Hopi are divided into a number of comparatively small unilateral exogamous units which, in turn, are grouped into larger exogamic divisions. In the usage of most of the older anthropologists the smaller group is called a clan and the larger phratry. Parsons and others, however, prefer to

[1] Mindeleff, V., 1891, p. 17.
[2] Fewkes, 1900c, p. 579.

[3] Fewkes, 1894a, pp. 405, 406.
[4] Fewkes, 1894a, pp. 405, 406.

44

call the smaller unit a maternal family or lineage, and the larger one a clan.[5] In the opinion of Dr. Parsons it is "unwise" to speak of phratries among the Hopi.[6]

It seems to me that a review of the characteristics of the two units involved in the discussion supports the clan-phratry designation as those terms are commonly used today. The smaller division of Hopi society is an unilateral matrilineal group of kindred which is totemically named and exogamous. This accords with Lowie's definition of a matrilineal clan as an unilateral grouping of kindred comprising "a female ancestor with her children and the children of her female descendants through females";[7] and with the fuller description given by Goldenweiser, "A clan . . . comprises individuals partly related by blood and partly conceived as so related; it is hereditary . . . it is unilateral . . . without including them in the definition, two additional features must be added, for completeness: a clan almost always has a name, and more often than not it is exogamous. . . . "[8]

Unless one disagrees with the definitions of Lowie and Goldenweiser, there can be no serious objection to calling the smaller exogamic unit of the Hopi a clan. On the other hand, there are valid objections to Parsons' use of maternal family or lineage as descriptive of this unit. According to Goldenweiser, "The difference between a maternal family and a clan . . . consists in the fact that whereas in a clan . . . some or even many persons are not related by blood, though assumed to be so related, in a maternal family all the component individuals are connected by genealogically traceable ties of blood relationship."[9] If we accept Goldenweiser's definition of the term maternal family, as I believe Dr. Parsons does,[10] there are two urgent reasons why it should not be used with reference to the Hopi. In the first place, it is notoriously difficult to secure from Hopi informants reliable lists of "individuals [who] are connected by genealogically traceable ties of blood relationship"; and

in the second place, as Lowie's data show, the units which Parsons designates as maternal families or lineages may actually contain from one to five "distinct matrilineal lineages, i.e., lineages between which . . . informants fail to discover any bond of blood-kinship. . . . "[11]

Until a new set of definitions comes to be generally accepted among anthropologists, there is no reason why the smaller exogamic units of the Hopi should not be called clans. On the other hand, utter confusion must follow if we call a group of kindred "a lineage" only to discover that it may comprise as many as five lineages.[12]

When we turn to the larger divisions of Hopi society we find that they consist of unnamed, exogamic units, each of which contains two or more clans. These units I have termed phratries on the basis of Lowie's definition that "a phratry . . . is simply a union, possibly very loose yet recognized by the natives, of two or more clans."[13] Furthermore, as Linton has indicated, "The various clans within a society may have special functions with regard to each other . . . [and] may also emphasize this social relationship by an extension of their marriage rules, putting members of the other clan on the same basis as those of their own. . . . Such groupings of closely affiliated clans are known as *phratries*."[14] Linton's description too applies very well to the unit of Hopi society which I propose to call a phratry. Dr. Parsons, on the contrary, prefers to call this unit a clan.

There is a serious objection to Parsons' usage, inasmuch as both Goldenweiser[15] and Linton[16] regard possession of a name as a customary feature of a clan; but on Third Mesa, at least, the larger exogamic unit *invariably lacks a name*.[17] Nor would it do to follow Parsons' practice of arbitrarily calling the larger group by the name of one of its constituent branches. To do this at Third Mesa would force us to call the exogamic unit comprising both Bear and Spider, for example, either the Bear clan or the Spider clan. Such a practice is directly opposed to native cus-

[5] Parsons, 1925, p. 15, footnote 11; Parsons, 1936b, pp. xxii–xxiv, *et passim;* and Beaglehole, E., 1937, pp. 8, 9.
[6] Parsons, 1939, p. 60.
[7] Lowie, 1920, p. 112.
[8] Goldenweiser, 1937, p. 304.
[9] Goldenweiser, 1937, p. 361.
[10] Parsons, 1936b, p. xxxiv.
[11] Lowie, 1929b, p. 330. Also compare White's data from Third Mesa, table 2, p. 49.
[12] The author has discussed many aspects of this prob-

lem in Titiev, 1943c.
[13] Lowie, 1934, p. 262.
[14] Linton, 1936, p. 207.
[15] Goldenweiser, 1937, p. 304.
[16] Linton, 1936, p. 198.
[17] Parsons, 1933, pp. 79, 80, gives lists of First Mesa groups in which the larger exogamic unit is named for one of its constituent smaller divisions. This is *contrary* to Third Mesa practice and was found not to prevail on Second Mesa by Dr. E. A. Kennard.

tom, for Bear and Spider are kept apart meticulously; they resent even the theoretical implication that they are descended from a common ancestress; and neither would tolerate being called by the other's name.[18]

In the long run there does not seem to be any justification for departing from the current use of the terms clan and phratry in describing Hopi kinship groupings, and it may be that the reader is wondering why so much effort has been expended in confirming what ought to be anthropological truisms. The answer is bound up with the fact that all recent investigators have found that the natives frequently exhibit a strong feeling for some lesser grouping of kindred contained within the clan. It is unfortunate that the Hopi do not define this inner core, and that they even lack a distinctive name for it. Accordingly, to outsiders the lesser grouping appears vague and nebulous, but all field workers who have had personal experience with the Hopi are convinced of its reality and importance. As Lowie puts it, "Whenever the statement is made that a certain office or ceremonial privilege belongs to a clan, concrete data always show that transmission is, above all, within the narrow circle of actual blood-kin and only secondarily extends to unrelated clansmen."[19] Parsons has come to the conclusion, and Lowie inclines to agree with her, that offices and privileges are held *"not in the clan as a whole, but in a maternal family or lineage in the clan."*[20] (Italics in the original.)

Here the matter of terminological confusion must be reckoned with, because Parsons and Lowie are employing the same term to describe two entirely different groups of kindred. Lowie's use of lineage refers to "a narrow circle of actual blood-kin"; but as Parsons uses the term lineage it is the equivalent of Lowie's clan which may contain as many as five distinct lineages. And to make matters worse, it may be repeated that Hopi genealogies are generally so untrustworthy that it is virtually impossible to get accurate lists of supposed blood relatives.

Nevertheless, in spite of the native tendency to confuse lines of descent, there still persists among ethnologists a feeling that within the clan there

is a smaller, distinct unit of consanguineous kin which functions actively, among other things, in the control and hereditary transmission of ceremonial offices and paraphernalia. It is my belief that much of the uncertainty regarding the identity of this unit is cleared away if we recognize that Lowie's "narrow circle of actual blood-kin" is none other than that segment of a matrilineal lineage which I have termed a household (chart I). It is partly because this unit has no distinctive native name, and partly because the traditional household system is tending to break down, that the true significance of the rôle played by the household kindred in Hopi society has become obscured. However, if we examine its theoretical position, its true nature comes plainly to light, and the relationship of the household to other units of kindred becomes readily understandable.

To avoid wandering afield at the outset, let us repeat that "the basic feature of this grouping is the fact that a mature woman, her daughters, and, occasionally, her granddaughters, occupy a common residence through life and bring up their children under the same roof.[21] (See page 7.) It should be noted that this description of a household group conforms equally well to what some anthropologists call a matrilineal lineage, and that it is also the equivalent of a matrilineal clan in the restricted sense of "a female ancestor with her children and the children of her female descendants through females."[22] Since the members of a household, lineage, and clan may conform conceptually to a single definition, it may be postulated that there was a stage in the development of Hopi social organization when a nascent, unnamed clan comprised a single lineage whose members resided in one household. Plotted in diagrammatic form, this arrangement of kindred would appear as shown in Situation A below.

Hypothetically, Situation A shows the appearance of a household group in its pristine form, while the original ancestress is alive, and the interrelationships of all the members are clearly remembered. Judged on the basis of its present attributes, this unit of kindred owned and occupied its own house, probably owned its own land, and possibly owned a fetish which entitled it to a

[18] As a matter of fact Old Oraibi was wrecked because of the opposition of the Spider people to the Bear group. See pp. 73–95.
[19] Lowie, 1929b, p. 330.
[20] Parsons, 1933, p. 23.
[21] It is to be understood, of course, that sons move out at

marriage and husbands move in. For purposes of simplification, married sons and relatives by affinity will not be considered in the ensuing discussion. Compare the following discussion with the hypothesis developed in Titiev 1943c, Section VI.
[22] Lowie, 1920, p. 112.

strong measure of control over any ceremony involving its use.[23] The custodianship of the fetish would pertain to the original ancestress; and her brother, possibly, her son, would be the officer in charge of the ceremony. Trusteeship of the fetish would be transmitted from mother to daughter, and the office of ceremonial chief would pass from an incumbent to his sister's son, possibly to his younger brother, in order that both of these privileges should be retained within the household group. They would thus circulate within a "narrow circle of blood-kin."

With the passage of time the pristine structure of the household tends to be altered. This may best be explained by the fact that under favorable circumstances a household group tends to expand until the original house becomes overcrowded. When this happens a younger daughter, let us say woman #3 on the diagram of Situation A, may move into new rooms, contiguous to her parental home, or she may build a new house adjacent or close to her mother's.[24] As Dr. Parsons has so aptly phrased it, "The house groups are a kind of reproduction by budding."[25] Thus the original membership of the household becomes

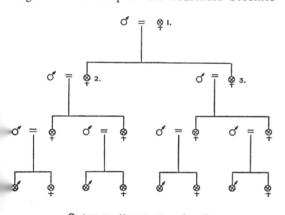

FIG. 1. SITUATION A.

egmented into two units, one still residing in the quarters of the original ancestress, the other living in the new home of woman #3. In due time, when the ancestress dies, her elder daughter, woman #2 in Situation A, will become head of the original house. We will then have the condition pictured as Situation B.

Situation B shows two households whose essential nuclei consist of members of the same clan. Since the house headed by woman #2 was formerly the original home of the group, it is still known as *the* clan house, and it is here that all ceremonial objects pertaining to the clan are

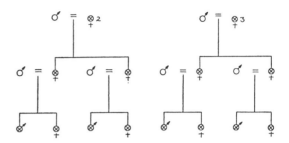

FIG. 2. SITUATION B.

stored. Indeed, "except at the proper ceremonial time there is always the greatest reluctance to remove a fetish, which is sometimes left behind, but looked after, in an otherwise abandoned house."[26] This house too serves as the meeting place for all gatherings called to discuss clan affairs, and even if it is no longer inhabited, *the* clan house continues to be regarded in many ways as the original home of the first ancestress of the entire clan.[27]

As long as informants recall that women #2 and #3 are real sisters, it can be demonstrated genealogically that they and their descendants belong to one and the same lineage as well as to the same clan. In such a case each of their households may properly be said to comprise a distinct segment of a lineage. Nevertheless, it must not be thought that the two households are equivalent in the minds of the natives, for woman #2 resides in *the* clan house, and as an elder daughter she has probably succeeded to the female leadership of the clan, while her sons have become the holders of, or the principal heirs to, the clan's male offices. In this way the clan members residing in *the* clan house continue to be set apart from their fellows and still comprise "the narrow circle of actual blood-kin" within a clan, referred to by Lowie and Parsons, among whom there circulate various items of tangible and intangible property.

Let us now examine Situation B as it would ap-

[23] For a discussion of this complex of traits, consult rong, 1927. For additional material see Parsons, 1936a.
[24] Mindeleff, C., 1900, p. 647.

[25] Parsons, 1939, p. 6.   [26] Parsons, 1939, p. 480.
[27] Parsons, 1933, p. 24; Parsons, 1936b, pp. xxxv–xxxvi; and Parsons, 1925, p. 77, footnote 125.

pear to people who had forgotten that women #2 and #3 were sisters, and daughters of the same mother. Under such circumstances, informants would describe Situation B as representing two sets of clanspeople who comprised two different households and who belonged to two distinct lineages. Hence, when a contemporary investigator decides that a particular Hopi clan consists of one or several lineages his decision may frequently be shown to depend on nothing more significant than the memories of his informants.[28]

To recapitulate the relationship of household, lineage, and clan, it may be postulated that a household group such as we have been discussing may come into being in a society where women own houses, where descent is matrilineal, and where marital residence is permanently matrilocal.[29] At the time of its origin a household formed by such a combination of factors would be equivalent to a matrilineal lineage and commensurate with a nascent matrilineal clan (Situation A). If, however, the original household later expanded by budding into two or more household groups[30] (Situation B), the latter would appear either as members of the same lineage and clan while the genealogical record was clear; or as two or more separate lineages of the same clan, if the lines of descent were obscured or forgotten. With the passage of centuries from the time that the postulated pristine situation prevailed, all three possibilities have emerged at Oraibi. Today one can find instances of one clan containing a single lineage and a solitary household;[31] of one clan containing a single lineage but several households;[32] or of one clan containing what seem to be several lineages whose members are scattered among a number of households.[33] In all likelihood, similar conditions exist at each of the large Hopi towns.

Turning now from general and theoretical considerations to the specific problem of clans and phratries at Third Mesa, we are faced at once with a number of fresh perplexities. These arise from the Hopi custom of calling the same group of kindred by a variety of names, or of ascribing a particular individual to two or more differently named units. Why there should be a multiplicity of designations for Hopi clans is a matter for conjecture, but as far back as 1917 Professor Kroeber noted that there seemed to be more names than there were clans.[34] This over-abundance of names is brought to light whenever an investigator compares a list of putative clan titles with a record of the names of clans which are actually represented by one or more lineages. Thus, for example, Lowie gives a list of 29 names of clans for Mishongnovi on Second Mesa, but only 13 of these are found to have actual representation in the village.[35]

A similar situation was discovered by Professor Leslie A. White during a study of clanship at Oraibi in 1932. When a composite list of all the purported clan names mentioned by 5 informants was compiled, it was found to contain a total of 65 names, grouped into 9 exogamous divisions as shown in table 1.

It took very little checking to show that this list contained more names than existent clans, so Dr. White, assisted principally by Kennard and Spirer, began to assemble a large amount of genealogical data with the two-fold purpose of determining which of the names were actually associated with clans, and of ascertaining how many lineages were contained in each clan. As the data were being analyzed a large number of discrepancies were found inasmuch as informants frequently assigned a particular individual to different lineages or clans, or else they ascribed

[28] In addition to faulty memories there are of course several other factors that affect the number of lineages in a clan. Multiple lineages may result from adoption by means of inter-pueblo marriages, or through the coalescence of originally distinct lineages. On the other hand, a clan once possessed of several lineages may be reduced to one by the extinction of the others. There may also be cases of clans which have never had more than their original lineages.

[29] Compare Professor Lowie's comments on sib origins in Lowie, 1919, especially, pp. 38–40; Lowie, 1920, pp. 157–162; and Titiev, 1943c, Section IV.

[30] The budding of a household into *two* groups as shown in Situation B has been demonstrated purely as a matter of convenience. The actual number of potential subdivisions would depend on the number of daughters born to woman #1.

For a discussion of the growth of kinship units by a process of segmentation, see Morgan, 1909, p. 88; and Lowie, 1920, pp. 130–131; and Titiev, 1943c, Section VI

The question of how the same process may account for the development of Hopi phratries will be discussed towards the close of this chapter.

[31] This is illustrated by the Crane clan whose hous occurs on the fifth street on chart VII. Lowie foun seven clans at Mishongnovi "which coincide with singl lineages." Lowie, 1929b, p. 330.

[32] See the Squash clan on the sixth street on chart VI

[33] The various Coyote households on chart VII exem plify this situation.

[34] Kroeber, 1917, p. 136; and Parsons, 1936b, p 1067–1068.

[35] Lowie, 1929b, p. 330 and p. 332.

TABLE 1. COMPOSITE LIST OF CLAN NAMES AT ORAIBI.

I	V
Jack Rabbit	Greasewood
Cottontail Rabbit	Reed
Tobacco	Road Runner
Pipe	Bow
Katcina	Arrow
Spruce	
Parrot	**VI**
Crow	Masau'u
	Fire
	Elder War Twin
II	Coyote
Bear	Fox
Bear's Eye-ball	Kokop
Bear's Bones	Kwan
Spider	Yucca
Bluebird	Samoa[36]
Carrying-strap	Cedar
	Pinion
III	**VII**
Sand	Badger
Earth	Butterfly
Lizard	Porcupine
Snake	
Burrowing Owl	**VIII**
Prairie Dog	Pikyas
Clay	Corn
Horned Toad	Patki
	Rain-Cloud-Thunder-
IV	Lightning-Rainbow
	Frog-Tadpole
Sun	Snow
Moon	Siva'ap
Star	
Sun's Forehead	**IX**
Eagle	Chicken Hawk
Hawk (2 kinds)	Crane
Turkey	Squash
	Duck

varying clan names to the same group of kindred. In this dilemma Dr. White was forced to weigh the evidence for each disputed case, and to adopt the viewpoint of whichever informant seemed to be the most reliable. When the tangled lines of descent were finally arranged on the most accurate basis possible,[37] it was found that only 31 clan names appeared to have actual representation at Oraibi.[38] Since 10 of these seemed to be only

"other names" for certain units, Dr. White concluded tentatively that there were only 21 distinct clans, and that these contained a total of 39 lineages distributed as shown below:

TABLE 2. CLANS AND LINEAGES AT ORAIBI, 1932.

PHRATRY[39]	NAME OR NAMES OF CLANS	NUMBER OF LINEAGES
I	Rabbit–(Tobacco)	4
	Parrot	1
	Katcina–(Crow)	1
	Parrot or (Katcina–Crow)	1
II	Bear	3
	Spider	2
III	Sand	1
	Lizard–(Snake)	3
IV	Sun	2
	Eagle	1
V	Greasewood	2
	Bow	1
	Reed	2
VI	Hovahkop–(Kwan–Masau'u–Kokop)	1
	Water Coyote	2
	Man Coyote	3
VII	Badger	4
	Butterfly	1
VIII	Pikyas	1
	Patki	2
IX	Crane–(Pumpkin–Chicken Hawk)	1

A study of table 2 instantly raises a number of questions. In Phratry I, for example, is it really justifiable to separate Katcina–(Crow) from Parrot or (Katcina–Crow)? And in Phratry VI, can one assume with any degree of assurance that Hovahkop–(Kwan–Masau'u–Kokop) are merely four names for one and the same lineage? In the latter case, data which were subsequently gathered at Oraibi tended more and more to separate Masau'u and Kokop into two distinct lines of descent. Without going into greater detail at the moment, the fact remains that Dr. White's list is highly tentative despite the great care with which it was compiled. One thing was clearly demonstrated by the summer's work at Oraibi in 1932, and that was that the genealogical approach alone would not solve the problem of Hopi lineages, clans, and phratries.

---

[36] Samoa is identified as yucca baccata torr., in Hough, 898, p. 143.

[37] Owing to difficulties of publication the lineage diagrams are not included with this monograph. Copies are available for consultation at the Laboratory of Anthropology at Santa Fe, New Mexico, and at the Peabody Museum, Cambridge, Massachusetts.

[38] Although the data were gathered at Oraibi, the material covers residents of that pueblo prior to the split of

1906. Accordingly, this discussion applies rather to the inhabitants of Third Mesa than to the meager population of present-day Old Oraibi.

[39] The term phratry is my own designation, not necessarily that of Dr. White. As the phratries at Oraibi are unnamed, they have been numbered, and the same numbers will be used throughout the present work. This arrangement was adopted only for convenience in making references. The order of the phratries is purely arbitrary.

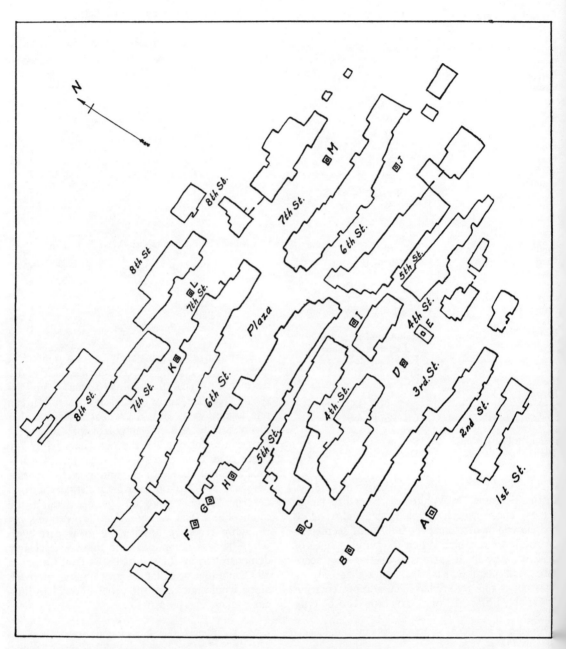

FIG. 3. HOUSE AND STREET PLAN OF OLD ORAIBI. KIVAS ARE INDICATED BY DOUBLE SQUARES.

As an outgrowth of this conviction, the writer decided early in the course of a second visit to Oraibi to abandon the genealogical approach and to undertake a fresh study of the entire problem through a detailed analysis of the composition of Oraibi's household groups as of the early twentieth century, prior to the 1906 division of the village. Since much of the pueblo had fallen into ruins by 1933–1934, the household study was made on the basis of a plan of Oraibi streets and houses which Alexander M. Stephen had used in the course of a somewhat similar inquiry made half a century ago.[40]

As the first step in the new attack, a number of informants were asked to identify all *the* clan houses on fig. 3, that is, houses in which fetishes and other sacred objects pertaining to the clans were stored. A total of 31 such houses were named, and these are listed in the first column of chart VI. To verify this list a different approach was used. An elderly informant, not previously consulted, was asked to name the *heads* of as many clans as he could. In an effort to avoid guiding his answers, all the 65 putative clan names from table I were read to the old man one at a time. In response to many of them he merely shook his head, but in 30 instances he gave the names of clan leaders. Their clans appear in the third column of chart VI, and examination reveals that they agree very closely with the names of clan houses in column one. It seems reasonably certain therefore that at the turn of the century Oraibi's inhabitants had been divided into about 30 clan units.

In the belief that the household survey was yielding more fruitful results than the genealogical method, it was then decided to secure more detailed information on the composition of households by making a house to house census on the basis of Stephen's plan of Oraibi.[41] As the work progressed over a period of many weeks, numerous questions were asked about each individual, but in order to get entirely spontaneous and undirected replies with respect to clan affiliations, a conscientious effort was made to abstain from any query other than "What clan?" on every occasion that a personal name was given. As most people were mentioned in several contexts at varying phases of the work, it was felt that the census material afforded a rare opportunity for checking the accuracy and consistency with which informants assigned the populace to particular clans.

When the raw material obtained in this way was tabulated and analyzed, it was found that 880 individuals had been discussed, and that they were distributed among 30 clans as shown in the fourth column of chart VI. It was highly gratifying to find that the names of these clans tallied very closely with those in the first and third columns which had been previously ascertained by other methods, thus strengthening the conclusion that Oraibi once held about 30 clans. The census data revealed a high degree of consistency on the part of informants, for it was found that 863 individuals had invariably been assigned to the same clan each time that their names were mentioned. In only 17 instances had discrepancies as to a person's clan ties occurred, and in not a single instance were phratry affiliations confused.[42]

Material from the census served to throw light on still another aspect of the clan-phratry problem, namely the relative stability of these units at Oraibi over comparatively long periods of time. Information on this topic was found by making a comparison of the 1933–1934 census with Stephen's census which had been made about fifty years earlier. As it happened, Dr. Fred Eggan had once inserted the names of various

[40] The plan used by Stephen is published in Mindeleff, V., 1891, plate xxxvi. A copy of this plan, showing the arrangement of all the houses, but with no clue to their clan affiliations, had been used by Lyndon L. Hargrave during his tree ring studies at Oraibi. Similar copies were furnished me through the courtesy of Dr. Harold S. Colton of the Museum of Northern Arizona, and these provide the basis for the simplified diagram shown in fig. 3.

[41] An attempt to limit the census to the population at Oraibi during the years 1900–1905 was not entirely successful, but in a general way that is the period covered. In gathering the material Chief Tawaqwaptiwa of Oraibi, who assumed office at about the time in question, served as the principal informant. Don Talayesva acted as interpreter and secondary informant.

All original notes pertaining to this census are stored at the Peabody Museum, Cambridge, Mass., where they are available for consultation.

[42] To avoid the inclusion of doubtful material the 17 uncertain cases do not appear in the final tally of Oraibi's population as given on chart VI. It is interesting to note that 15 of the discrepant instances pertain to men and only 2 to women. This is to be expected in a household system in which the men fluctuate but the women remain fixed for life.

Of the 17 doubtful cases, 3 each are from Phratries I and VI, 4 from Phratry III, 2 from Phratry V, and 5 from Phratry VIII. This is in accord with those phratries which appear least certain in White's list (table 2). For further details consult Titiev, 1934, p. 91.

PHRATRY	① CLAN HOUSES	② HOPI NAME	③ CLAN HEAD	④ PRESENT HOUSE CENSUS	⑤ STEPHENS' HOUSE CENSUS	⑥ PRESENT CENSUS NO. OF HOUSEHOLDS	⑦ STEPHENS CENSUS NO. OF HOUSEHOLDS	⑧ PRESENT CENSUS POPULATION FEMALE	⑨ MALE	⑩ TOTAL
I	RABBIT	TAPNYAM	RABBIT	RABBIT	RABBIT	13	12	33	28	61
	KATCINA	KATCINYAM	KATCINA	KATCINA	KATCINA	2	1	5	6	11
	PARROT	KYACNYAM	PARROT	PARROT	PARROT	5	10	16	15	31
	CROW	ANGWUCNYAM	CROW	CROW		1	0	2	0	2
II	BEAR	HONNYAM	BEAR	BEAR	BEAR	5	5	6	13	19
	SPIDER	KOKYANGNYAM	SPIDER	SPIDER	SPIDER	3	2	16	15	31
III	SAND	DUWANYAM	SAND	SAND	SAND	9	8	28	31	59
	LIZARD	KUKUTCNYAM	LIZARD	LIZARD	LIZARD	4	14	28	30	58
	SNAKE	TCUNYAM	SNAKE	SNAKE	SNAKE	2	1	2	4	6
	SUN	TAWANYAM	SUN	SUN	SUN	9	8	24	23	47
IV	GRAY HAWK	MASIKWAINYAM								
	EAGLE	KWANYAM	EAGLE	EAGLE	EAGLE	6	6	12	9	21
V	GREASEWOOD	TEPNYAM	GREASE WOOD	GREASE WOOD		14	0	37	36	73
	REED	BAKAPNYAM	REED	REED	REED	7	24	32	17	49
	BOW	AWOTNYAM	BOW	BOW	BOW	4	4	7	8	15
VI	MASAU'U	MASNYAM	MASAU'U	MASAU'U		7	0	29	19	48
	REAL COYOTE	ISNYAM	REAL COYOTE	REAL COYOTE	COYOTE	10	16	24	22	46
	WATER COYOTE	PA-ISNYAM	WATER COYOTE	WATER COYOTE		10		27	30	57
	KOKOP	KOKOPNYAM	KOKOP	KOKOP		3	0	8	14	22
	MILLET	LENYAM	LE	LE		1	0	5	6	11
	AGAVE	KWANNYAM			KWAN	0	1			
		HONYAM	CEDAR	CEDAR				0	2	2
					BURROWING OWL	0	9			
VII	REAL BADGER	BASHONANYAM	REAL BADGER	REAL BADGER		5		14	23	37
	GRAY BADGER	MASIHONANYAM	GRAY BADGER	GRAY BADGER	BADGER	3	11	6	27	33
	NAVAHO BADGER	TASAPHONANYAM	NAVAHO BADGER	NAVAHO BADGER		3		7	4	11
	BUTTERFLY	POLINYAM	BUTTERFLY	BUTTERFLY		1	0	2	3	5
					MOTH	0	1			
VIII	YOUNG CORN	PIKYASNYAM	PIKYAS	PIKYAS	PIKYAS	7	9	25	20	45
	WATER-HOUSE?	PATKINYAM	PATKI	PATKI		7	0	17	19	36
	RABBIT BRUSH	SIVA'APNYAM	SIVA'AP	SIVAAP		1	0	1	2	3
IX	CHICKEN HAWK	KELNYAM	CHICKEN HAWK	CHICKEN HAWK	CHICKEN HAWK	2	1	5	5	10
	CRANE	ATOKNYAM	CRANE	CRANE	CRANE	1	1	1	4	5
	SQUASH	PATGNYAM	SQUASH	SQUASH	SQUASH	2	1	3	6	9
	TOTALS 31		30	30	21	147	145	422	441	863

CHART VI. CLAN AND PHRATRY DIVISIONS AT ORAIBI.

households, ascertained from Stephen's published data,[43] on a blank outline plan of Oraibi such as I had used in the 1933–1934 census. Thanks to the named diagram which Dr. Eggan kindly put at my disposal, a reasonably accurate comparison of my findings with those of Stephen was made possible. This was done by casting the two sets of data independently into similar forms, as shown in chart VII. Out of 136 houses that were capable of exact comparison, 88 or 65% had been given identical clan names, a satisfactory degree of correspondence when it is considered that fifty years had elapsed between the two investigations. With respect to phratry affiliations, a still higher degree of conformity was found, for 117 houses or 86% were assigned to the same phratries in the two censuses.[44] This seems to indicate once more that phratry lines are more clearly distinguished than clan ties, and that phratry groups remain stable over reasonably long periods of time.[45]

On the basis of all the available evidence, a final tabulation of live clans and phratries on Third Mesa would appear as shown in table 3.[46]

Even if it is conceded that we have now achieved a definitive list of all the Third Mesa clans that have living representatives, there still remain for consideration the problems of why there should be multiple appellations for certain clans; how the phratry system arose; why individuals are assigned sometimes to one clan and sometimes to another; and why the natives are more accurate in keeping phratry rather than clan lines distinct.

With respect to the multiplicity of names for certain clans, native informants generally offer several stereotyped explanations. One of these is taken directly from Hopi folk-lore and tells how the clans in the course of their wanderings after

the Emergence, encountered a variety of objects from which they took their names. A brief specimen, dealing with the Tobacco people of First Mesa, will suffice to illustrate the pattern.

"After they came out they found a weed which they pulled up. They knew it was tobacco, and so they called themselves Tobacco people. . . . They went on and they found a rabbit sitting. They named themselves Rabbit."[47]

TABLE 3. FINAL LIST OF THIRD MESA CLANS
AND PHRATRIES.

Phratry I	Phratry VI
Rabbit	Masau'u
Katcina	Real (Man) Coyote
Parrot–(Crow)	Water Coyote
	Kokop
Phratry II	Le[48]
Bear	Cedar (Kwan)
Spider	
	Phratry VII
Phratry III	Real Badger
Sand	Gray Badger
Snake	Navaho Badger
Lizard	Butterfly
Phratry IV	**Phratry VIII**
Sun	Pikyas
Eagle	Patki
	Siva'ap[49]
Phratry V	**Phratry IX**
Greasewood	Chicken Hawk
Bow	Crane
Reed	Squash

Such explanatory tales are obviously re-interpretations or rationalizations, and instead of explaining the existing situation they merely re-affirm and sanction it. Equally unconvincing is the suggestion that multiple names have arisen from the absorption of a dwindling or dying clan by a more thriving unit. It need not be denied that such

[43] Stephen's data were published in Mindeleff, V., 1891, pp. 104–108, plates xxxvi, xxxvii.

[44] The cluster of houses on the western end of the fourth street (chart VII) is somewhat confused in Mindeleff, V., 1891, plate xxvii. If these houses are thrown out of the reckoning, we would have 85 identically named clan houses out of 126 for a score of nearly 68%; and the phratry figures would be 112 similarities out of 126, a 90% agreement in the two studies.

[45] Since 88 houses were assigned to the same clans, whereas 117 were put in the same phratries, there are 29 cases in which clan ties were confused while phratry lines were kept clear. These clan discrepancies are distributed as follows: 3 in Phratry I, 11 in Phratry V, 11 in Phratry VI, 1 in Phratry VII, and 3 in Phratry VIII. The 11 discrepancies in Phratry V are due to consistent

use of Reed by Stephen in cases where my informants used Greasewood. The single disagreement in Phratry VII is terminological, Stephen using Moth instead of Butterfly.

A fuller discussion of variant items is given in Titiev, 1934, pp. 90–98.

[46] Comparative lists for the other Mesas may be found in Lowie, 1929b, p. 332; and Parsons, 1936b, pp. 1068–1073.

[47] Parsons, 1933, p. 28. Although this quotation refers to First Mesa, similar tales are told on Second and Third Mesas.

[48] Le (Lehu) is identified as Indian millet in Whiting, 1939, p. 105.

[49] Siva'ap is listed as Rabbitbrush in Whiting, 1939, p. 108.

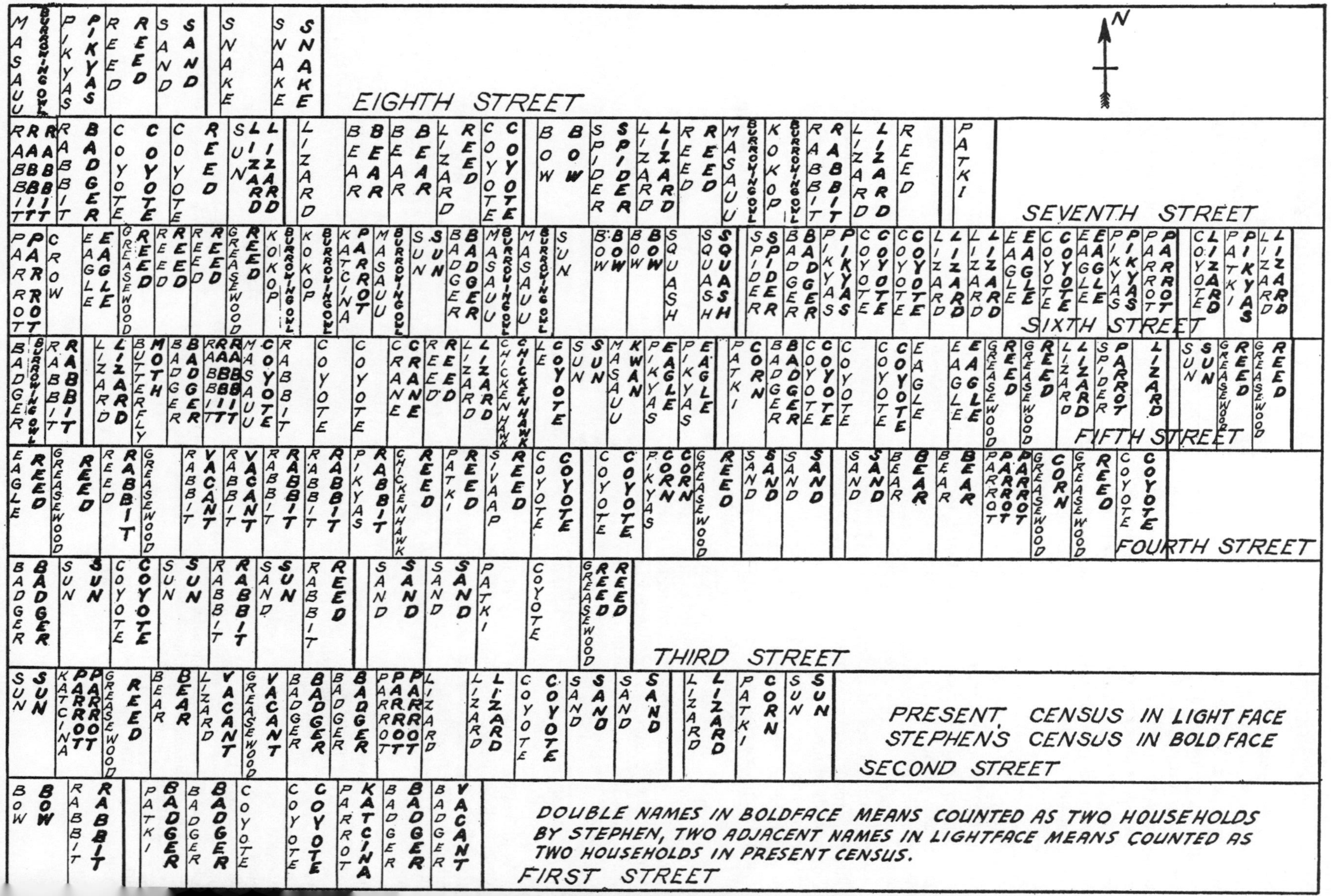

EIGHTH STREET

SEVENTH STREET

SIXTH STREET

FIFTH STREET

FOURTH STREET

THIRD STREET

SECOND STREET

FIRST STREET

PRESENT CENSUS IN LIGHT FACE
STEPHEN'S CENSUS IN BOLD FACE

DOUBLE NAMES IN BOLDFACE MEANS COUNTED AS TWO HOUSEHOLDS BY STEPHEN, TWO ADJACENT NAMES IN LIGHTFACE MEANS COUNTED AS TWO HOUSEHOLDS IN PRESENT CENSUS.

fusions have sometimes occurred, but this explanation assumes a rapid rate of extinction for Hopi clans, an assumption that I consider highly fallacious. Indeed, when Stephen made his house survey at Oraibi about the year 1886, he recorded only 21 clans, but half a century later a census of the same population showed 9 additional clans and only one doubtful case of extinction.[50] This affords a direct contrast to Lowie's findings at Mishongnovi, where 13 clans are listed as having living representation and 9 are specifically referred to as "extinct."[51] I believe that the answer to the contradiction may be found in the nature of the data on which the opposed statements are based. Stephen and the present author had the advantage of dealing solely with an actual population, but Lowie was recording information not only on contemporary conditions at the villages he visited, but also on their historical backgrounds.[52] Accordingly, there was no way of telling whether Lowie's informants were dealing with clan names or with actual clans—two very different things among the Hopi. As a matter of fact, almost any native can supply an inquirer with a prodigious list of clan names—witness the 59 names in table 1—but if one tries to find representatives of these "clans" he is calmly told that they have become extinct. No doubt Hopi clans have died out from time to time, but never with the rapidity that modern informants kill them off!

There are several more plausible suggestions that have been offered to account for the plurality of clan names. For example, since the Hopi conduct an elaborate ritual calendar, it is likely that clans have sometimes combined for the better performance of ceremonials.[53] In such cases, if their identities were to have become merged while their names were retained, we would ultimately have a clan with two or more designations. Another way in which the same result might have been achieved is through the adoption by one clan of members of another, as when Lowie

reports the last Coyote man at Mishongnovi to have joined the Quoquop (Kokop) clan.[54] Kroeber's suggestion of "a tendency toward polarity within what is really one clan,"[55] may also have some bearing on the point at issue. It may explain, for example, the association of Moon and Star names with the Sun clan in Phratry IV. Then too there is an observable inclination for each village to include names that occur at other pueblos. Although there are no Bluebird people at Oraibi, this name is sometimes given with Bear and Spider by analogy with Second Mesa.[56]

There remains one other approach to the problem of clan combinations and multiple names, and that is through a study of what may tentatively be called Hopi totemism.[57] The great majority of names on any clan list are those of plants, animals, or supernatural personages. These eponyms the Hopi call *wuya* or *n'atöla*, terms which seem to refer to ancestors or ancients. Some of them are represented by masks, figurines, or fetishes of various sorts,[58] others have no tangible representation; but in either case there is a strong feeling of empathy and kinship between each group and its *wuya*.[59] Those *wuya* which are in the form of physical objects are stored in *the* clan houses and are so sacred that they are regarded as the "heart" of a clan.[60] So closely linked in native belief are the two concepts, that the myths "explaining" the origins of clan *wuya* and clan names are frequently the same. An excellent example is found in the story of the Coyote people of First Mesa.

After they came out, they came to a place where a man was sitting by the roadside. The man said, " . . . I am your uncle, but they call me Coyote.". . . They went along with him. They came to a good place where there were cedar trees. They said it was a good thing for them to have that name in their clan. . . . They built a fire. . . . They said they would have Fire in their clan. . . . They saw a tall man standing by the trail. . . . Then he said he called himself Masawa. So they called him their uncle. . . .

[50] See columns 4 and 5 of chart VI. The doubtful case refers to Kwan. Other clans mentioned by Stephen which do not occur on my list should not be considered extinct, because they represent only differences in nomenclature.

[51] Lowie, 1929b, p. 330, gives the living clans. The 9 "extinct" clans mentioned are Raven–(Crow), Spider, Bear's-eye, Tobacco, Cottontail, Squash, Crane, Wild Turkey, and Sand. Lowie, 1929b, pp. 333–334.

[52] Kroeber, 1917, p. 135, calls attention to this drawback in the study of Hopi clans.

[53] Lowie, 1929b, p. 310; and Parsons, 1936b, p. xxxiii.

[54] Lowie, 1929b, p. 320. Also, see Parsons, 1939, p. 16, footnote*.

[55] Kroeber, 1917, p. 142.

[56] Compare Parsons, 1921b, p. 214.

[57] Lowie, 1929b, pp. 337, 338, has a brief section called "Totemism," but most Hopi students neglect this topic almost entirely. See Parsons, 1939, p. 56 and footnote*. I deeply regret that circumstances prevented me from studying this subject more fully while I was in the field.

[58] Parsons, 1933, pp. 37, 66, *et passim*.

[59] Parsons, 1933, p. 21.

[60] Strong, 1927, p. 50; and Parsons, 1933, p. 36.

Here they got his name.[61] (Parsons reports that "An image of Masawa . . . is kept in a Coyote clan house at Walpi.")[62]

As this narrative indicates, and as may be gathered from other sources, it is likely that each clan has one primary and several secondary *wuya*.[63] Since clan names are derived from their *wuya*, a plurality of *wuya* would account for a multiplicity of names.[64] Thus an informant may give several names for the same clan, depending on which of its associated *wuya* was uppermost in his mind at a given time.[65]

We are now in a position to take up the question of how the various clans came to be grouped into the larger exogamic units which I call phratries. As Professor Lowie has stated the problem, "Where such lesser and greater units coexist, the question inevitably arises as to their relationship. It is conceivable that the greater evolved from an original sib by subdivision. . . . It is equally conceivable that social groups once distinct should have come to unite. . . . "[66] In the past it has been the second alternative that has been almost universally employed to account for the origin of Hopi phratries. Only Forde seems to have noticed that most of the supposed mergers occurred between clans that were already in the same exogamous group, and that consequently there was a logical fallacy involved in the use of clan fusions to explain the formation of phratries. ". . . Merging," wrote Forde, ". . . is not haphazard. . . . Merging appears to follow pre-existing linkages."[67] If merging follows "pre-existing linkages," it can scarcely be used to account for the origin of the linkages.

Far more plausible with respect to the Hopi

is Lewis H. Morgan's suggestion that phratries arise from the segmentation of clans.[68] Following this line of reasoning, we may now put forward a more likely hypothesis to account for the development of Hopi phratries.[69] Where possible we shall support our position with specific instances taken from existing sources and our own observations in the field. It should be kept in mind that since we are proposing a new nomenclature for some of the segments of Hopi kindred, the designations quoted from the literature will not always accord with our terms and, therefore, the definitions of these terms should be carefully noted.

Essentially, Hopi phratries may be said to arise from the continuation of those cleavages which begin with the segmentation of an original household as previously described (p. 47). At first, it may be assumed, an off-shoot unit continues to venerate the ancestral *wuya* which has remained in *the* clan house. It is highly probable, however, that in the course of time the derivative household will acquire a fetish of its own, either by taking some minor object from the parental home, or as a bold innovation. Such a step would lead the derived household to adopt a new name, thus producing a situation in which directly related lineages come to be known by different titles.[70] That such a contingency has already been recognized by Hopi theorists is plainly evidenced in some of Lowie's findings. At Walpi he was told that "The Cloud-Corn people do not represent two originally distinct clans that have become joined, but *one* clan with two names; the same applies to the Charcoal-Coyote people."[71] And in a footnote Lowie adds, "This is the native conception of the matter as repeatedly impressed

[61] Parsons, 1933, p. 30. Although the quotation is from a First Mesa story, similar tales are current on all the Mesas.   [62] Parsons, 1933, p. 31.

[63] Parsons, 1936b, p. 1078; and Parsons, 1939, p. 60 footnote †. The same idea is suggested by the divergent symbols pictured as pertaining to the Corn clan in Colton, M. R. F., and H. S., 1931, p. 34.

[64] Even one *wuya* may yield several names each of which bears some reference, direct or indirect, to the characteristics of the eponym. "Thus," according to Mindeleff, C., 1900, p. 647, "in the Corn clan . . . there grew up subclans claiming connection with the root, stem, leaves, blossom, pollen, etc."
Compare Voth, 1915, p. 74, *et passim*.

[65] In most instances an unprompted informant will first name the major *wuya* of a clan, but if pressed for complete lists of clans, he will probably name all the *wuya* of which he can think. Compare Parsons, 1936b, p. xxxv.

[66] Lowie, 1920, p. 130.   [67] Forde, 1931, p. 375.

[68] Morgan, 1909, p. 88; and Titiev, 1943c, Section VI.

[69] While this report was still in manuscript, Dr. Parsons published an hypothetical reconstruction of Hopi kinship groups which closely parallels the postulated development here presented. The many agreements in these independently achieved reconstructions are surprisingly close in view of the different approaches employed. See Parsons, 1939, pp. 1088, 1089. Another type of reconstruction is made by Steward, 1937, pp. 101, 102.

[70] Parsons, 1937, p. 562, has also stated the opinion that owing to the multiple names possessed by a clan, "a woman leaving the maternal house may take for herself and her descendants another of the lineage names of the clan (rare practise)."

[71] Lowie, 1929b, p. 309. This statement supports our belief that Hopi phratries arise from segmentation rather than from merging.

on me *on the First Mesa.*"[72] (Italics in the original.)

Sometimes too a segment of a lineage may adopt a new name without an attendant change of *wuya*. Such instances usually arise when there is a violent quarrel among relatives, as a result of which one group decides to change its name. Lowie reports such a case from Mishongnovi. "An old Parrot man said he could not explain why the Parrot and Kachina people belong together, but made an obscure remark about a quarrel and consequent division."[73] Far from considering such a statement as obscure, I regard it as highly illuminating, because it establishes a motive for the separation of one set of relatives into two differently named units. Nor should it be thought that such occurrences are rare and belong only to ancient times, for a similar case was brought to light at Oraibi in the summer of 1932. While Eggan and the writer were collecting genealogies under the supervision of Dr. White, we came across an old woman named Sakwapa who claimed to be of the Yellow Fox clan. When her lineage was collated with other data gathered at the same pueblo, however, it was found that all the other informants were unanimous in assigning her to the Coyote clan; and Dr. White, quite rightly, placed her in that clan on his charts.[74] Nevertheless, as often as she was cross-examined on the subject, Sakwapa persisted in calling herself Yellow Fox, although she freely admitted her kinship with Coyote and the other clans in Phratry VI. It later developed that Sakwapa was a notorious character whose entire life had been marked by dissension, for it was she whose eight divorces established the record at Oraibi (see chart V); whose loose behavior even in her old age had made her the laughing stock of the village (p. 40, note 37); and whose quarrels with her sons were so violent that they absolutely refused to farm for her (p. 19, note 13). No wonder Sakwapa insisted on a separate category for herself!

Another example of the same procedure was noted by Beaglehole at Second Mesa. Here a Sun's Forehead woman quarreled with her clanmates "and started calling herself and her children Reed clan people."[75] An unusual feature of this episode is to be found in the fact that in this case the "stolen" name was taken from a phratry to which the "thief" did not belong.[76]

To return to the main thread of our hypothesis, we have already shown (pp. 46–48) that an original household may start out as the equivalent of one matrilineal lineage and clan, and that if it expands in size it may then become segmented into two households which later develop into two apparently distinct lineages within the same clan. Inasmuch as the two households have never been allowed to intermarry, we may safely postulate that the resultant lineages remain exogamous. At a later stage each of the recently separated lineages is apt to acquire a new *wuya*, or a new name, or both.[77] When this happens each lineage may properly be spoken of as a matrilineal clan, inasmuch as it comprises a totemically named, exogamous group of unilateral kindred, whose members claim at least theoretical descent from a common ancestress.

As more and more such clans arise among the progeny of the first ancestress and her daughters,[78] the ties that originally held them together become obscured, if not obliterated, and the related clans form a new unit which may be called a phratry, and which consists of two or more clans.[79] The phratry itself has no name and is rather colorless in nature, because among its constituent clans each gives allegiance primarily to its own name group and worships its own *wuya* above all others. Nevertheless, the common origin of all the clans making up a phratry is reflected in their continued interest in each other's *wuya* and ceremonies,[80] in their right to use each other's stocks of names, and above all, in the ceaseless

---

[72] Lowie, 1929b, p. 309, note 2. At Mishongnovi, according to Lowie, these clans were considered to be distinct units. [73] Lowie, 1929b, p. 333.

[74] All informants agreed that Yellow Fox was one of the *wuya* of the Coyote clan.

[75] Beaglehole, P., 1935, p. 51.

[76] A similar episode regarding the "theft" of a name was reported to me at Oraibi. The wife of a Pikyas man gave her baby to the Crane clan to be named because all her children who had been named in conventional fashion by Pikyas women had died in infancy. The Crane women called the child Cucuzruya (Little Tail), a Duck name which had previously belonged only to Pikyas and the

other clans in Phratry VIII. After its "theft" by the Crane people, Duck names came to be used by the clans in Phratry IX.

[77] Parsons, 1936b, p. xxxiv, has written, "... a lineage grown large might split, and take different names."

[78] Thus Stephen listed only 21 clans in his house census of Oraibi, whereas fifty years later, I recorded 30 for the same populace. See columns 6 and 7 on chart VI.

[79] Parsons, 1933, p. 74, speaks of "The Hopi tendency towards the phratry." Since then she has come to the conclusion that the Hopi have no phratries.

[80] Compare Parsons, 1936b, p. xxxv.

exercise of exogamic regulations among all phratry mates.[81]

The foregoing discussion suggests one reason for the Hopi habit of ascribing an individual sometimes to one clan and sometimes to another. It is clear that the segmentation process is a continuous, dynamic force, potentially capable of springing into action whenever conditions are favorable.[82] Any lineage within a clan may be transmuted into a clan by the acquisition of a *wuya*, and a name of its own. When a new clan has just arisen, there must be a period of uncertainty during which informants may designate its members sometimes by the old name of its parental clan and sometimes by its new name. Thus when the Sun's Forehead woman, as reported by Beaglehole at Shipaulovi, broke with her clan, "and started calling herself and children Reed clan people," there must have been a time when an investigator would have found this group referred to sometimes as Sun's Forehead and sometimes as Reed.

One other point remains to be discussed. If the phratry is an unnamed unit, and the clan has a name, why should natives rarely err in assigning people to their proper phratries, but make frequent mistakes with regard to clan membership? For one thing, since exogamy prevails throughout the phratry, exact lines of demarcation between related clans are of little moment in that respect. Then again, we must recall that each member clan shares in the ownership of all *wuya* and names associated with its entire phratry. In Phratry VII, for example, it is perfectly proper for a Badger clanswoman to give a Butterfly name to a child born to a male member of her clan.[83] It may well be that joint phratry ownership of all member clans' *wuya* enables the Hopi to keep phratry divisions more distinct than clan lines. Specifically, at Oraibi it is far easier to remember all the *wuya* associated with each of 9 phratries, than to keep in mind the particular ownership of certain *wuya* among each of 30 different clans.

In bringing this chapter to a close, I propose the following classification and description of Hopi kinship divisions:

1. HOUSEHOLD—the smallest distinct unit of Hopi society. It consists basically of an exogamous group of kindred, demonstrably related through matrilineal descent from the same ancestress, and sharing a common residence. Sometimes a single household may be identical with a matrilineal lineage, but more often it is only a segment of a lineage. The household incorporates the limited family through the agency of matrilocal residence,[84] and in many ways, such as in the inheritance of ceremonial offices, it is the most important social unit of all.[85] However, it is not distinguished by name, and it owns no *wuya* in its own right.

2. LINEAGE—an exogamic, unilateral group of matrilineal kindred, demonstrably descended from a common ancestress. Since such demonstrations cannot always be made among the modern Hopi, and since the lineage lacks both name and *wuya* and may be scattered over several households, it is the vaguest of the Hopi divisions. Its importance lies primarily in its theoretical implications as a nascent clan, and in the tendency for inheritance to follow the lineage pattern.

3. CLAN—a totemically named, exogamous, unilateral aggregation of matrilineal kindred, comprising one or more lineages all of which are supposedly descended from one ancestress. Each clan has at least one *wuya* stored in *the* clan house. If this *wuya* forms the nucleus of a pueblo ritual, the controlling clan furnishes the officers who conduct the ceremony. It is the only kinship group for which there is a native term,[86] and since land is held in the name of the clan, this unit is the cornerstone of Hopi society.

4. PHRATRY[87]—a nameless division of kindred made up of two or more clans which share certain privileges, mainly ceremonial, in common. The outstanding features of the phratry are that it delimits the greatest extension of kinship terms based on any given relationship, and that it marks the largest exogamic unit recognized by the Hopi.

[81] The use of brother-sister terms for phratry mates also implies a recognition of common descent.

[82] For a discussion of the instability of Hopi social units, see Parsons, 1921b, p. 209, and p. 215.

[83] Similarly, in a list of totemic signatures appended to a government petition, published in Fewkes, 1894a, pp. 409, 410, a Kokop clansman identified himself by making a picture of Masau'u.

[84] Attention is drawn once more to the fact that the masculine consanguineous members of a household are

not permanent residents because after marriage they move into their wives' households. On the other hand, in practice if not in theory, each household includes a number of affinal relatives who are the spouses of its female members.

[85] Compare Parsons, 1939, p. 5.

[86] The terms for clanspeople are *wungwa* in the singular and *nyamu* in the plural.

[87] In a recent work Dr. Parsons speaks of these Hopi units as "pseudo-phratries." Parsons, 1939, p. 988.

Chapter V

THE AMORPHOUS HOPI STATE

MUCH HAS BEEN written about the Hopi
... but little has been said about their
political organization and their common law."[1]
This comment, published by Dr. Colton in
1934, is equally valid today, chiefly because
the Hopi "state" is so unobstrusive that its outlines can scarcely be discerned in the general
social structure. The term "Hopi theocracy"[2]
which has been used in the past fails to give an
accurate picture of the Hopi scheme of government because of the special nature of their priest-
hood. Formerly, it was the custom among ethnologists to call all participants in every ceremony
"priests,"[3] but since every mature man normally
participates in at least one ceremony a year, it is
obviously absurd to speak of the entire adult male
population of the tribe as priests.[4] Even the officers and leaders of ceremonial observances can
scarcely be termed priests, for not one of them
devotes himself exclusively or even primarily to
the performance of religious exercises, no one of
them wears distinctive garb throughout the year,
and none is sanctified in the eyes of the populace.
Instead, as one ritual succeeds another in the
ceremonial cycle, various leaders conduct particular rites and then resume lay lives for the
balance of the year.[5] Such an arrangement can
scarcely provide the framework for a theocracy
in the ordinary sense of the word. At the same
time it must be admitted that the sacred and the
civil are inextricably commingled in the political
structure, for pueblo officials are invariably leaders in one ceremony or another, and all have
mythological sanctions for their positions.

Dr. Parsons frequently refers to the Hopi
system of leadership as an hierarchy, but she
notes "that the principle of hierarchy is more developed or conspicuous at Zuni than among the
Hopi."[6] According to her account of the workings of the hierarchy on First Mesa, when the
members meet in council each man declaims in the
order of precedence. But the order of precedence
is anything but fixed, for two variant lists of
thirteen Walpi chiefs agree only in the first two
and the final positions, whereas the ten officers in
between are ranked haphazardly.[7] Certainly,
where these circumstances prevail, the term
hierarchy in the sense of a regularly graded pro-
gression of offices cannot be applied.[8]

The problem of whether or not Hopi chiefs
can be ranked in a fixed order, however, is far
less important than the question of their law-
making functions. On First Mesa, it is reported,
"The chiefs meet and make rules for Walpi and
Sichumovi";[9] but a description of the proceedings
reveals nothing of a legislative nature. Instead,
the Town chief urges the people to live properly,
the other chiefs repeat his words, and the War
chief adds a threat of punishment for disobedience.

At Oraibi too there is no evidence of a law-
making body, but non-legislative assemblies at
which the chiefs talked about the Hopi way of
life were held on various occasions. The most important of these assemblages, known as Monglavaiyi (Chiefs' Talk),[10] occurred annually at the
conclusion of the Soyal, the major rite performed
at Third Mesa. Participating in the Chiefs' Talk
were the officers who had just brought the Soyal
to a close. The Village chief (Kikmongwi) of
Oraibi spoke first, and was followed in order by
the head man of the Parrot clan; the Pikyas clan
chief; the Tobacco chief (Pipmongwi), normally

---

[1] Colton, H. S., 1934, p. 21.
[2] Parsons, 1933, p. 53.
[3] This usage is found in the works of Fewkes and Voth.
[4] Compare Parsons, 1939, p. 132, footnote †. Fewkes
was also aware that the term priest had been loosely used
and calls "for more exactness in this particular." Fewkes
and Stephen, 1892b, p. 190, footnote 3.
[5] In 1890 A. M. Stephen wrote, "The priests and chiefs
are not privileged persons. . . . They engage in the same
labors and lead precisely the same life as the other vil-

lagers. . . ." Donaldson, 1893, p. 17.
[6] Parsons, 1933, p. 77; and Parsons, 1936b, p. 145.
[7] Parsons, 1933, pp. 53, 54.
[8] It may be that Dr. Parsons employs the term hierarchy
without the connotation of a fixed series of ranks, as the
references she has indexed under "Hierarchy" in Parsons,
1936b, generally deal with gatherings of chiefs in which
the question of precedence plays no part whatsoever.
[9] Parsons, 1933, p. 55.
[10] Compare Colton, H. S., 1934, p. 22.

the head of the Rabbit clan; the Crier chief (Tca'akmongwi),[11] usually leader of the Greasewood clan; and the War chief (Kaletaka), who may be from the Badger or the Coyote clan. In every respect these men are the most important officials in the pueblo "and seem to take the position of assistant chiefs to the head chief,"[12] but except for the Village chief and the War chief, their administrative and political functions are limited primarily to their own clans.

The importance of the Soyal officers is verified in the minds of the natives by mythological sanctions. The Village chief has in his possession a sacred stone said to have been brought from the Underworld by Matcito, legendary founder of Oraibi. This stone is supposed to have been kept in the custody of the Bear clan from the beginning and is zealously shielded from profane observation because its markings are believed to convey Matcito's intentions regarding the control of Oraibi's lands. In a most unusual burst of confidence, Chief Tawaqwaptiwa once allowed me to examine this important relic.[13] It is a rectangular block of greyish-white, smooth-grained stone, about 16 inches long, 8 inches wide, and one and a half inches thick, splotched here and there with irregular red dots which the chief[14] interprets as points of land. On both sides there are lightly incised markings which are explained in the following way.

One surface is covered with miscellaneous symbols, including a row of eight little scratches, said to stand for the eight-day period during which the Soyal is observed; cloud and lightning emblems in a random arrangement; an unidentified Katcina figure; two or three sets of bear claws; an old age crook; a poorly executed serpent, said to represent the Little Colorado river; and eight circles, arranged in two parallel rows, which the chief explains as thunder (?) because the sound of a thunder clap is like that of a number of ob-

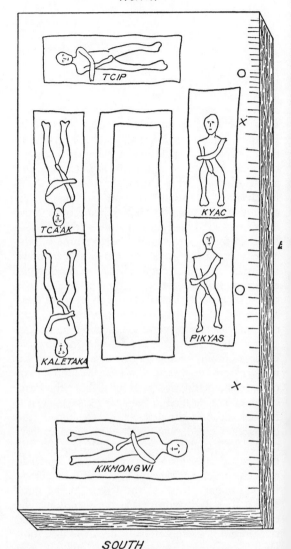

NORTH

SOUTH

FIG. 4. ORAIBI'S SACRED STONE.

[11] Care must be exercised to differentiate the Village Crier chief from men who call out secular announcements. The real Tca'akmongwi cries out only on the most important occasions and addresses himself primarily to the Cloud people, although the villagers are free to listen if they choose.

[12] Voth, 1901, p. 102, footnote 6. The list of officers here published omits the Pikyas clan chief, but in another publication, Dorsey and Voth, 1901, p. 12, a Pikyas leader is included. Recently, the importance of this official has increased, because he serves as the Oraibi chief's "lieutenant" in charge of the growing colony at Moenkopi.

Parsons, et al., 1922, p. 290, has a list of Oraibi chiefs

which omits the Pikyas man but adds a Medicine chief from the Badger clan. I was unable to verify the additional chief's position, or to determine if he were a separate officer.

[13] It was exciting to think that perhaps I was enjoying the privilege of viewing the very stone which the Hopi refused to let Cushing see in 1883. During Cushing's troubled visit to Oraibi in that year, a Hopi speaker referred to "the stone which our ancients made that we might not forget their words." Parsons, et al., 1922, p. 266. My description is tentative as I was never shown the stone again.

[14] When chief is used as a noun without any modifier in this chapter, it refers only to the Village chief.

jects being struck in succession. Along the edge of one of the long sides of the relic there runs a series of little lines which were not interpreted; and along the other edge there is a succession of conventional cloud and rain symbols to indicate that in Matcito's lifetime there was always plenty of rain. The pictures on the other surface of the stone tell a connected story (see fig. 4). A double rectangle in the center is supposed to represent the Oraibi domain. About this are grouped six figures which depict the Soyal officers. Reading from the bottom in a counterclockwise circuit, they refer to the Village, Pikyas, Parrot, Tobacco, Crier, and War chiefs. Each figure stands with the left hand across the chest and the right extended downwards to cover the genitalia. This posture is said to indicate that the chiefs are claiming the land enclosed within the central rectangles. Along the edge representing the east, there is a line of small scratches, interspersed with occasional circles or crosses, which depicts the proper Hopi path that the chiefs are supposed to travel. The War chief brings up the rear to make sure that no one turns aside from the correct road.

At each Soyal celebration the sacred stone is brought from its repository, the officers examine it closely and then reaffirm their rights to hold office and their claims to the land. After this comes the Monglavaiyi (Chiefs' Talk), at which the Village chief's speech is echoed by the other leaders. Ordinarily, the event occurs early on the morning of the closing day of the Soyal, and the speech tells the populace of the prayers made during the recently-concluded rites and ends with a prayer for good crops and long lives.[15] Whether or not such meetings may rightly be called political may be a matter of opinion, but the intimate connection of pueblo leadership with land control is clearly demonstrated. It is from this viewpoint that we shall now approach the question of Hopi government.

In the matter of land ownership, as with every important aspect of their culture, the Hopi "explain" the existing state of affairs by referring to their mythology. A composite summary of several myths is needed for an understanding of the connection between the authority of the chiefs and their claims to the land.

For some time prior to their Emergence from the Underworld, people had been hearing footsteps above them, but when they reached the surface of the earth it was cold and dark, and nothing could be seen. In due time they noticed a distant light and sent a messenger who returned with the welcome news that he had discovered "a field in which corn, watermelons, beans, etc., were planted. All around this field a fire was burning . . . by which the ground was kept warm so that the plants could grow."[16] Nearby the messenger found a man whose handsome appearance contrasted strangely with the grotesque death's head mask that stood by his side. At once the messenger realized that "it was Skeleton (Masauwuu) whom they had heard walking about from the other world."[17] The deity proved kindly disposed, fed the courier and sent him to fetch all his companions. Here they built a large fire, warmed themselves, and "Skeleton gave them roasting ears, and watermelons, melons, squashes, etc., and they ate and refreshed themselves. Some of the plants were very small yet, others still larger, so that they always had food."[18]

In time the people left Masau'u and set out on the wanderings that were ultimately to bring them to their present settlements. For a while the Bear people settled at Chimopovy but "they all had heard that Skeleton was living where Oraibi now is, and so they all traveled on towards Oraibi."[19] The Bear clan leader, Matcito, asked Masau'u to give him some land and to be the chief of his people, but "Skeleton replied, 'No, I shall not be chief, You shall be chief here. . . . I shall give you a piece of land and then you live here.'"[20] Hereupon he stepped off a large tract of land which he allotted to Matcito. Soon other clans began to arrive, each seeking permission to dwell at Oraibi and each offering in exchange to perform a beneficial ceremony for Matcito. If the trial performance proved pleasing to the chief he would say, "'Very well, you participate in our cult and help us with the ceremonies,' and then he would give them their fields according to the way they came. And that way their fields were all distributed."[21]

Thus do we find the myths "explaining" how present conditions arose, for at Oraibi the leader of the Bear clan is the Village chief and the theoretical owner of all the village lands, and all the other clans hold land only on condition of good behavior and the proper observance of ceremonies.[22] For himself the Bear leader was said

[15] See Colton, H. S., 1934, p. 22; and Parsons, 1933, p. 55.
[16] Voth, 1905b, p. 12.
[17] Voth, 1905b, p. 12.
[18] Voth, 1905b, p. 13. Other versions ascribe the origin of plants to various deities or leaders, but black corn and squash always belong to Masau'u.
[19] Voth, 1905b, p. 23. In other renditions of this story

Matcito seeks out Oraibi only after quarreling with his brother at Chimopovy, Hargrave, 1932, p. 3.
In First Mesa legends the Bear chief overthrew Masau'u and thus won the land. Parsons, 1936b, p. 814.
[20] Voth, 1905b, p. 23.
[21] Voth, 1905b, p. 24.
[22] One of the present sources of contention between

to have selected a large tract of land southwest of the village, traversed by the Oraibi wash, which was so shallow in those days that its flood waters were a great boon to the nearby fields. (See fig. 5, plot marked Bear.) The western limit of his holdings was marked with a boundary stone

aided him in the performance of the Soyal ceremony, and to have enough left over to reward the other officers and men who participated in that rite.[24]

Just west of the chief's holdings is another vast plot given over to the Patki clan. When the Bear

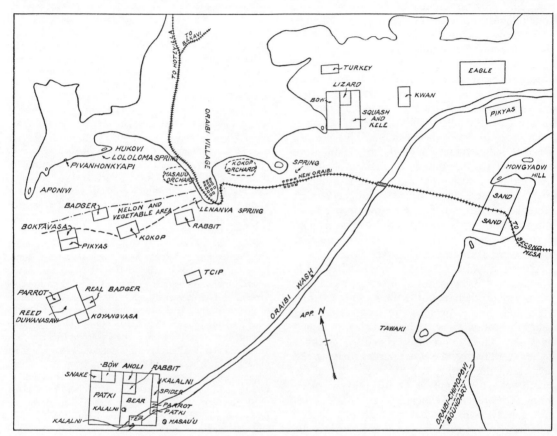

FIG. 5. ORAIBI LAND HOLDINGS.

(kalalni owa) on which a Bear claw was carved. A similar stone, marked with the head of Masau'u, commemorated that deity's original claim to the entire domain,[23] and boundaries and shrines (pahoki) were erected at the south and northeast corners. So great a piece of land was reserved for the Village chief that he was able to allot some of it to the War chief (Kaletaka) who

chief or his delegate impersonates the Eototo Katcina on great ceremonial occasions, the Patki head man plays the part of the Aholi, second in importance.[25] Together they make the rounds of the village on the morning of the Bean dance during Powamu, and Aholi opens the main cistern of the village. It is for this service, as well as for his part in the Soyal, his function as Sun Watcher,

Old and New Oraibi is that when the latter lapsed their ceremonies they did not give up their lands.

[23] Compare Parsons, 1936b, p. 390, footnote 1, p. 637.

[24] These special plots of ground are supposed to be held by Soyal officers only during their terms of active service.

Disputes often arise when retiring officers refuse to cede their lands to their successors. Compare Parsons, 1939 p. 863, and consult "The Pikyas-Patki Conflict" in Part Three.

[25] See Voth, 1901, pp. 110–115.

and his ownership of the Gray Flute ceremony that the Patki leader gets so huge a share of land.[26] Apart from the lands allotted to the Patki clan, the individual who impersonates the Aholi Katcina gets the special plot marked Aholi in the northwest corner of the Bear holdings. Others to share the Village chief's land are the Greasewood (Tep) clan, from which is chosen the important Crier chief; the Rabbit (Tap) clan, which supplies the Tobacco chief; and the Spider (Kokyang) clan, which helps with the Soyal and controls such important ceremonies as the Blue Flute, Antelope, and Momtcit.[27] The Parrot (Kyac) clan, too has a piece of the chief's land because it furnishes one of the main Soyal officers; and the small Patki plot just south of the Parrot lands goes to that member of the Patki clan who dances with stalks and leaves representing crops, during the Antelope rites which precede the public dance of the Snake society.

Here and there, on the basis of various traditions, other clans were allotted land as they arrived at Oraibi, but even those clans which had no legendary claims to particular plots were not left landless.[28] A large triangular stretch of ground near the Oraibi wash was known as "free land," on which any resident, with the chief's consent, was permitted to lay out a farm. Anyone who was a good citizen generally received ready permission, and the tests of good citizenship were frequent participation in Katcina dances, particularly the Homegoing (Niman) dance; readiness to haul wood to the kivas in preparation for important winter rituals such as the Soyal; promptness in responding to calls for communal work, such as the cleaning of springs, or farming for the chief; and willingness occasionally to take the responsibility of sponsoring a dance.[29]

The religious character of chieftainship at Oraibi is exemplified by the merging of the office of Village chief with leadership in the Soyal. Generally speaking, both offices are held by the head of the Bear clan, and they are transmitted together according to the customary pattern of inheritance.[30] As a ruling Village chief grows old he selects a successor from among his brothers or his sisters' sons, usually picking not the eldest eligible relative but the best qualified.[31] The prospective heir then begins to accompany the chief to his fields or to his sheep camp, and there he receives secret instructions regarding his future duties.[32] In this way the people become aware of the chief's choice of a successor, so that when the incumbent dies the succession is more or less automatically determined. If the Village chief should die without having trained an heir, the members of the Bear clan, assisted by the Soyal chiefs and, sometimes by the heads of other clans, hold a series of meetings to choose a Bear clansman for the vacant offices.[33]

Once chosen, the new Village chief begins to function immediately, but some time may elapse before his ceremonial induction to office occurs. This takes the form of a "baptism," performed by

[26] Note that at the present time the head of the Pikyas clan, which is in the same phratry with Patki, plays the rôle formerly assigned to the Patki chief. It is partly because both leaders claim the land here described that there is so much antagonism between the two clans today. See "The Pikyas-Patki Conflict" in Part Three.

[27] It is important to notice, in conjunction with the following chapter, how small a proportion of the Bear land holdings is given over to the Spider people, a "sister" clan in the same phratry. It must be admitted that the Spider land is not very large when we consider that they control three major ceremonies and act as singers in the Soyal. It was their grievance in regard to land distribution that was one of the underlying factors in the civil "war" that led to the split of 1906.

[28] The land held by all the Oraibi clans is shown in fig. 5. The exact boundaries are uncertain despite the fact that the Oraibi chief was my principal informant on this question. He did not give me perfectly reliable data in all instances, and he frequently omitted important material. For example, the diagram fails to show the lands held by the chiefs of the four branches of the Wuwutcim (Tribal Initiation) ritual. Compare Colton, H. S., 1934, p. 23.

[29] It is characteristic of Hopi society that in spite of the great need for having these duties carried out, there is no mechanism to compel their performance.

[30] The tangible sign of chieftainship in a society is possession of its most sacred fetish, known as a *tiponi*. For the Village chieftainship at Oraibi there is no special *tiponi*, but a new Village chief becomes the recipient of the Soyal *tiponi*. On First Mesa it is the Flute society's *tiponi* whose possession marks the Village chief. Parsons, 1936b, p. xxxvi and p. 70.

In 1920 Dr. Parsons listed the Oraibi Town chief and the Winter Solstice (Soyal) chief as separate officers. This was due to the fact that the Village chief had delegated a well-known Sun clansman (brother-in-law of a former chief) to serve in his stead. Parsons, *et al.*, 1922, p. 290. Hopi officials frequently "rest" in this way, and take such opportunities to further the training of a successor.

[31] Compare Parsons, 1939, p. 107. Note that in either case the heir is a member of the chief's natal household group.

[32] Compare Parsons, 1939, pp. 154, 155.

[33] An account of the actual selection of a Village chief at Walpi occurs in Parsons, 1936b, p. 951, *et passim*, and in Parsons, 1939, p. 155.

the Agave (Kwan) chief at the time of that society's New Year celebration known as Yasang-lalwa (Year Making).[34] The object of the "baptism," according to Chief Tawaqwaptiwa, is to fit the new leader for his position in the other world, thus putting him into close contact with the Cloud People (spirits of the dead), who control rain. At the close of the rites the Kwan head advises the chief and "gives him a good road to follow." "Now I make you a chief," he says, "and now I give you a good path to lead us to the Sun. Now you are our father. Look forward for the good and not for the bad, and see that things go rightly so that we may have good crops and long life."

Although the Village chief receives no badge of office to be publicly displayed at this time, he later comes into possession of a symbol of authority called a *mongkoho* (chief's stick).[35] Since it is very sacred, being considered a direct inheritance from Matcito, he appears with it only during the performance of the Soyal and Wuwutcim ceremonies. Another sign of office, known as chief's markings, consists of a heavy coating of clay, applied in the form of crescents under the right eye and on the eyelid, and of circles an inch in diameter that run across the left shoulder and arm and down the left leg. The Village chief is painted in this fashion only on the most important ritual occasions, and when he lies in death just prior to his burial.

Similar insignia of high office pertain to all the Soyal chiefs, except the War chief, and to the leaders of the Al, Singers, and Kwan[36] societies. Even ordinary members in these societies are loosely known as "chiefs";[37] and they too employ chiefs' markings and carry chiefs' sticks, but the latter lack the sanctity of great antiquity, for they are made for the members by their ceremonial fathers at the time of their initiations, and are buried with them at death.

Thus we find rather a large body of men to whom the term chief might properly apply, but only two of them possess political functions that concern the entire pueblo. Outstanding in this regard is the Village chief, primarily by virtue of his stewardship of all the pueblo's lands. It is not surprising, therefore, that his authority most frequently manifests itself in the settlement of land disputes. In most instances he is called upon either to render decisions regarding title to a given plot of ground, or to award damages for the destruction of crops by livestock. In cases of the latter type, it is customary for the chief to rule in favor of the landowner on the theory that farm products are more essential to the Hopi than livestock. Where the damage is small, as much corn as a man can readily carry is considered a fair recompense.

A general feeling seems to prevail that no other contentions should be aired before the Village chief. He is regarded as the father of the people,[38] and it is considered highly improper to worry him with petty grievances. On his part too the chief maintains a paternal attitude towards his subjects. His thoughts are always concerned with their welfare, and the people look to him to lead them on a path of good life. To his prayers they attribute the success or failure of their crops, and so

---

[34] Voth, 1912b, p. 115, contains a description of a New Year ceremony in which, unfortunately, no "baptism" was performed. These "baptisms" take place only at the time of the first Wuwutcim initiation following a chief's entrance into office. As initiations are held not oftener than once in four or five years, it may happen that a new chief serves for a considerable period of time without completing the entire ritual of accession.

The Kwan society is conceptually closely linked with death and the after-life and plays a key part in the Wuwutcim rituals. The Kwan leader "baptizes" not only the Village chief but also the other Soyal leaders, with the exception of the War chief who is "baptized" by the chief of the Kokop clan.

Stephen fails to mention "baptism" by the Kwan society at the time of a new Town chief's accession to office at Walpi, but this may be due to the fact that Stephen died in 1894, before the next Wuwutcim initiation was held. Note that the new Walpi Town chief was "to be confirmed" during the Wuwutcim ceremonials. Parsons, 1936b, p. 426, footnote 1.

[35] I do not know whether the Village chief receives his *mongkoho* at the same time that he is given the *tiponi* of the Soyal society. A number of *mongkoho* are pictured in Dorsey and Voth, 1901, plate xi. For First Mesa usage regarding chiefs' sticks, see Parsons, 1936b, p. 27, *et passim*.

[36] In keeping with their relationship to Masau'u, the god of death, who does things by opposites, the Kwan men have chiefs' markings under the left eye and on the right shoulder, arm, and leg, in reverse fashion from the practice of the other groups.

[37] Voth has noted that at Oraibi the term Village chief (*Kikmongwi*) may be applied generally to various relatives of the chief. Voth, 1901, p. 102, footnote 6.

Regarding the general use of chiefs' sticks, see Dorsey and Voth, 1901, p. 26, footnote *. According to these authors, all chiefs' sticks are sacred and are buried with the owners.

[38] Compare the following statement from a First Mesa source, "We all help because the Town chief is our Father. We all help him because we all like our Father and Mother." Parsons, 1925, p. 114.

great is his responsibility for the health and welfare of his subjects,[39] that no matter how little part he plays in the active business of governing, the cares of the Village chief are by no means light. Formerly, when he returned home after a lengthy absence, he was expected to smoke and pray even before he ate or drank, and it was customary for him to remain awake long after the entire village was asleep.[40] He would smoke and meditate while the War chief made his final rounds for the night, and he would retire only after he had received a report that all was well.

To provide the chief with a much needed "rest" from time to time, the sponsor of a formal ceremony, a Katcina dance, or a communal task, is expected to assume the duties of the Village leader,[41] taking over the nightly vigils and holding himself responsible for the state of the weather during the four days following the termination of his enterprise. It is a matter of great importance, accordingly, to allow no one to serve as sponsor unless he has a good "heart" (character), and an untroubled mind.[42]

Many of the community enterprises performed by the inhabitants of a pueblo are intended to show the people's regard for their Village chief, and to a lesser extent, for other high officers.[43] Any person, preferably a public-minded commoner rather than an official, may seek permission to sponsor such an activity.[44] He chooses a time when the pressure of private needs is not too great, and if his request is granted, he asks the Crier chief to make the necessary announcements. In the past, communal tasks were carried out with so pleasant an admixture of ceremonialism and entertainment, that work parties were regarded as pleasant social activities and no one considered it a hardship to relieve chiefs of a large share of their farming duties.[45]

On the whole, the Village chief is looked upon rather as a guide and an adviser than an executive; and as an interpreter of Hopi tradition rather than as a legislator. A chief's word is respected and his opinion usually sought on any vital matter, but there is virtually no provision for his active participation in government. No compulsion is brought to bear on those who do not care to consult the chief on matters that do not come directly under his personal supervision, and he lacks the power to enforce such decisions as he may render. A man may dance Katcina or not as he sees fit; he may join a secret society or not as he pleases; participation in community work is largely voluntary; and there is scarcely an activity that is not optional rather than compulsory. Even if the head of a very important ceremony were to allow it to lapse, there is little to hinder him and no mechanism to punish him. The policy of the "state" is one of nearly complete *laissez-faire*, and the phrase "*Pi um i*" ("It's up to you") may well be the motto of Hopi society.

The great emphasis on individual freedom of behavior is checked by a fear of non-conformity. "It's up to you" is balanced by "People say it isn't right." So marked is the dread of running afoul of public opinion among the Hopi, living as they do in closely grouped communities where privacy is out of the question, that only a man of exceptional character dares to depart from conventional modes of behavior in any important respects.[46]

Despite Hopi docility in most matters, there must have been occasions, even before the present disintegration of Pueblo culture began, when it was necessary for the welfare of the group that some sort of punishment be inflicted on those who misbehaved. To the War chief was given the duty of maintaining discipline, and he was the nearest approach to a policeman in each Hopi town. He had the right of scolding miscreants, of boxing

---

[39] This idea is directly expressed by several First Mesa men who "attribute continued drought to the discordant thoughts and speeches of Lololamai and other Oraibi chiefs and elders." Parsons, 1936b, p. 437, footnote 1.

Another statement conveying the same idea is found in Parsons, 1925, p. 101, where rheumatism is attributed to the incontinence of the Powamu chief. The pattern of behavior for the Village chief applies on a lesser scale to all other chiefs. In times of trouble, chiefs are often accused of witchcraft. Compare Parsons, 1939, p. 154.

[40] The same custom is found at First Mesa. "The Town chief and the man next to him . . . have to stay up all night and smoke to ask for snow and rain, in order to have more crops next year." Parsons, 1925, p. 115.

[41] A similar notion prevailed on Second Mesa as is shown by Sikyapiki's speech in Parsons, 1936b, p. 728.

[42] Compare Kennard, 1937, p. 492. The custom of having participants in ceremonies remain awake throughout the night preceding a public performance, may indicate that they are sharing the nightly vigil with the sponsor of their ceremony. Because of its responsibilities, the office of sponsor is never regarded lightly.

[43] Similar customs are mentioned in Parsons, 1939, p. 158.

[44] See Colton, H. S., 1934, p. 24.

[45] Compare Parsons, 1925, pp. 112–115; and Beaglehole, E., 1937, pp. 29–31.

[46] "Fear of witchcraft, fear of ridicule, fear of public opinion! Apprehensiveness is a noticeable Pueblo trait." Parsons, 1939, p. 67. For the influence of witchcraft beliefs on Hopi life, see Titiev, 1943a.

their ears, and, perhaps, of thrashing them.[47] The basis of his authority lay in his military leadership, for to those who misbehaved he would say, "Very well, you think you are showing yourself to be a brave man by acting this way. Well, in the next battle you can show what a man you are by taking my place at the head of the warriors, and fighting as I do." Since the War chief led his men into action with no other weapon than a stone axe,[48] his threat was not lightly regarded. With the abandonment of native warfare, the power of the War chief has diminished until his position today is entirely devoted to ceremonial observances.

At one time, informants reported, the War chief's duty of preserving order was supplemented by several Katcina impersonations of a disciplinary or punitive character. For example, if it were known that some one were behaving improperly, a man might dress in the costume of Tcaveyo,[49] an armed giant Katcina. In this guise he would visit the law-breaker and order him to mend his ways, challenging him to a fight in the event that he refused to reform. Of course no Hopi was expected to strike a Katcina, but if any one were rash enough to try it, the impersonator of Tcaveyo would not hesitate to use whatever weapon he was carrying.

Other Katcinas helped to regulate village working parties.[50] When such an enterprise was announced, several men usually volunteered to appear as disciplinary Katcinas, and as soon as they were in costume they would run through the pueblo rounding up workers, putting tools in the hands of the dilatory, and making sure that the work began promptly. Unlike most Katcinas, they were permitted to speak (in the disguised, choked-up voices that mark the speech of the Koyemsi), in order to allow them to give orders in their capacity as supervisors. Sometimes, in a spirit of fun, a man would taunt the Katcinas with

being lazy and would offer his tool for an imper sonator to use. Thereupon the Katcina woul work feverishly for a few moments, to the vas amusement of the crowd, before returning the implement to his critic.

Only rarely did anyone seriously challenge the authority of the Katcinas, but there was one occa sion during the cleaning of a spring at Oraib when a conflict occurred between a Yongaktcina a Katcina armed with a cactus whip,[51] and Qöyan gainiwa, of the Badger clan, an important figure who was War chief of the village[52] and who had recently been appointed "Judge" of the pueblo by the superintendent of the Hopi reservation Resenting the commands of the insignifican young man whom he knew to be playing the part of the Yongaktcina, Qöyangainiwa scorn fully refused to take orders and went so far as to strike the Katcina in the shins with a shovel At this the Yongaktcina brought his cactus whip into action, and with the help of the other Kat cinas who were on duty, subjected the offender to a severe flogging. Then the Yongaktcina ordered Qöyangainiwa to leave the work party and to return to the village, but the stubborn old man refused and called out to his fellow workers asking them if they really wanted him to go Thereupon the Village chief, who was present in the unofficial capacity of an ordinary helper,[53] cried, "I want you to go home! You ought to know better than to strike a Katcina."[54] Qöyan gainiwa then withdrew without further commen and work was resumed.

Up to this point it has been shown that a few executive and judicial functions are carried out by the Village chief and the War chief, supplemented by disciplinary Katcinas; but there seems to be no machinery for the making of laws, and so called council meetings appear to be more fre quently deliberative than legislative.[55] In this

---

[47] Beaglehole, E., and P., 1935, p. 59; Parsons, 1925, p. 85, footnote 134; and Parsons, 1933, pp. 55, 56, provide comparative data.

[48] Described in Beaglehole, E., and P., 1935, p. 20.

[49] For a description of this Katcina, see Fewkes, 1903, p. 75 and plate xiii; and the references under Chavaiyo in Parsons, 1936b, p. 1138.

[50] Compare Colton, H. S., 1934, p. 24.

[51] The name Yongaktcina is compounded of the word for cactus (*yonga*) and Katcina. Whiting, 1939, p. 110, identifies the plant as Prickly pear.

[52] He is pictured in ceremonial regalia in Dorsey and Voth, 1901, plate x.

[53] The chief was acting as an ordinary helper because the sponsor of the work party was supposed to be Village chief *pro tempore*.

[54] This remark carried all the more weight because Qöyangainiwa was not only a pueblo official, but also an officer in the Badger clan which is in charge of the Katcina cult for half the year.

[55] It may well be that legislative functions were formerly more pronounced, for in 1776 Escalante wrote to Murillo that "the reduction of that rebellious province [Tusayan] has become more difficult because the principal men ... promulgated by common agreement for midable penalties ... against those who ... were proved

way the Hopi situation conforms closely to Lowie's analysis of primitive governments. "The legislative function . . . seems strangely curtailed. . . . All the exigencies of normal social intercourse are covered by customary law, and the business of such governmental machinery as exists is rather to exact obedience to traditional usage than to create new precedents."[56]

Among the Hopi the tasks of fitting individuals into their proper social spheres and of exacting "obedience to traditional usage," are left primarily to the household and the clan. Each household is responsible for training and controlling its members, and conducts its affairs with very little interference from the outside. Related households share in the administration of their clan's activities, but the larger units of Hopi society lack all semblance of political organization. The phratries exist only as extended kinship and ceremonial units, and the political framework of the pueblo itself is extraordinarily weak.

Under such conditions it is not surprising that petty quarreling and bickering have long been rife among the people and have been a constant source of grief to the chiefs. This state of affairs is reflected in numerous myths. "A long time ago, the people were living below," one story begins. "There were a great many of them, but they were often quarreling with one another. . . . So the chiefs, who were worried and angry over this, had a council and concluded that they would try to find another place to live."[57] Nor does the narrator find any difference between ancient and modern conditions. "In the under-world the people had been very bad, there being many sorcerers and dangerous people, just like there are in the villages to-day. . . ."[58]

Like the myths, the rituals also reflect the contentious nature of Hopi society. During the preliminary preparations for the Snake ceremony, to cite but one instance, the leaders repeat a set formula, ". . . Now then, therefore, sixteen days after tomorrow then these Snakes and Antelopes, if they have a good heart, will celebrate . . . this (ceremony). Hence from now we must not live at variance with each other (and be troubled)."[59] Similar prayers for social unity and "a peaceful spirit within the pueblo,"[60] are so fervently and frequently repeated as to suggest that harmony is a rare attribute of pueblo life. In spite of this, it is likely that most of the dissensions are petty and that only infrequently do they threaten the stability of the social structure. On the whole, "the unwritten laws of customary usage" are generally obeyed, and the authority of the chiefs is seldom questioned and rarely challenged.

Each Village chief's jurisdiction is strictly limited to his own pueblo; there is no recurrent occasion when all the Village chiefs meet together; and there is no such thing as a tribal council. Politically speaking, the Hopi can hardly be called a tribe,[61] and apart from their participation in the Pueblo revolt of 1680, there is no record of a co-operative action embracing all the Hopi towns. Mention is sometimes made of inter-pueblo assemblies of Village chiefs, but if the detailed description of a gathering which took place at Mishongnovi in August, 1933,[62] is at all typical, it is evident that very little of a political or administrative nature is involved in these meetings. All that happened at Mishongnovi was that each chief spoke disparagingly of his own ability to lead his subjects, yet deep in his heart, each felt that he alone was following the proper Hopi path and that the others were responsible for all the ills of the tribe. These are old, old accusations, identical in form with those that were current more than fifty years ago. In 1893 Stephen heard the elders of First Mesa say, "the clouds passed this side of Oraibi, rain falling only on East and Middle Mesas. Cloud had no ear for the Oraibi, he hates discord."[63] And on a visit to Second Mesa an old man told Stephen that " 'Cloud does not care for the Walpi ceremony, but me,' patting himself on the breast, 'the Clouds desire, love.' Then he went on to say that at Walpi there was no unison, while here

---

to have been talking . . . with the fathers in matters of religion." Thomas, 1932, p. 160. Also, consult Parsons, 1936b, p. 951.

[56] Lowie, 1920, p. 358.   [57] Voth, 1905b, p. 10.

[58] Voth, 1905b, p. 11. Other myths contain nearly identical passages.

[59] Voth, 1903a, p. 277.

[60] Parsons, 1936b, p. 107, footnote 1.

[61] Parsons, 1939, p. 10; Lowie, 1920, p. 387; Colton, H. S., 1934, p. 21. In recent years attempts have been made by some of the younger men as well as by the Office of Indian Affairs to organize the Hopi on a tribal basis. There has been little success to date.

[62] See "An Inter-pueblo Council of Chiefs," in the Appendix.

[63] Parsons, 1936b, p. 437, footnote 1.

at Shipaulovi it was wholly peace and love, etc. And in evidence . . . he cited the heavy rain showers that have fallen here. . . ."[64]

So runs the tale over and over again. Within each village the lack of a strong central authority permits the growth of factions and leads to schisms; and between pueblo and pueblo there is an attitude of jealousy, suspicion, and subdued hostility. Never has any town been entirely free from strife, and never has a leader arisen to mould the autonomous villages into a co-ordinated unit worthy of being called a tribe. Whatever other talents they may possess, the Hopi do not have the gift of statecraft.

[64] Parsons, 1936b, p. 744.

CHAPTER VI

THE DISINTEGRATION OF ORAIBI

FROM a practical point of view, the social structure of every Hopi town is made up of a number of matrilineal clans, each comprising one or more closely related households. Despite a nominal allegiance to the Village chief, each clan is to a large extent autonomous, choosing its own officers and transacting its own affairs with a good deal of independence. Since a clan owns land, houses, gardens, and water rights, it is virtually a self-sufficient unit. Only the rule of exogamy and the custom of matrilocal residence force it to co-operate with other groups. Even so, its solidarity is scarcely disturbed by marriages, for a married woman retains an unaltered status in her household and clan, and a married man preserves many ties with his natal group even after he has shifted his residence to an affinal household. Furthermore, the clan absorbs the limited or biological family through the agency of its constituent households, and in many ways it forms so cohesive a group of kindred that it tends to resist assimilation into larger units.[1] Thus we find that the phratry elects no officers and has neither political nor economic functions, and that the pueblo is characterized by a decentralized and essentially non-legislative type of government. In short, Hopi society consists of a number of closely-knit matrilineal clans which are loosely combined into phratries and villages.

Such a social system rests on unstable foundations, for the more firmly people adhere to clan lines, the weaker must be their village ties. A Hopi pueblo is like an object with a thin outer shell which holds together a number of firm, distinct segments—should the shell be cracked, the segments would fall apart. Theoretically, the Hopi towns are in constant potential danger of dividing into their component parts, but in practice there are several factors that strongly counteract the tendency to disintegration. In the first place, the enforcement of exogamic regulations inevitably leads to the formation of new bonds which must cut across clan ties; and in the second place the proper performance of rituals demands co-operation, for even if a clan "owns" a given rite, it depends on outside groups to supply secondary leaders and common members.[2] Still, the separatistic quality of Hopi clans is a force to be reckoned with, for it exerts a steady pressure on phratry and village links and provides an ever-present threat of ultimate collapse. That such breakdowns have frequently taken place in the past can be readily established by the archaeological record in the Southwest which seems to indicate that "long before the advent of the Conquistadores the habit of town splitting must have developed."[3] It is impossible at this date to establish all the sociologic implications of prehistoric pueblo divisions, but it so happens that Oraibi affords a contemporary illustration of the same process, and a study of Oraibi's disintegration should throw considerable light on the more ancient splits.[4]

Oraibi was founded prior to 1150 A.D., and Hargrave regards it as "the oldest inhabited town in the United States, sharing with Acoma, in New Mexico, the distinction of occupying the same site since its discovery by Europeans in 1540."[5] It is first mentioned in history when Luxan speaks of the arrival of Espejo's expedition in 1583 at "the pueblo of Olalla [Oraibi][6] which is the largest in the province."[7] Two centuries later, in 1782, Father Morfi declared that Oraibi "is like the capital of the province the largest and best arranged of all. . . ."[8] Even as late as 1906 Oraibi was still "the largest and most important of the villages of the Hopi,"[9] with a population of over 600 inhabitants distributed

---

[1] Although, theoretically, Hopi phratries originated by a process of clan segmentation, they have the appearance nowadays of combinations of related clans.

[2] Any complete list of participants in a major ritual bears out this statement. For example, in the Oraibi Soyal of 1899, the leaders came from 7 clans other than the Bear which "owns" the ceremony, and the common members were from 9 clans in all. Dorsey and Voth, 1901,

pp. 12, 13.

[3] Parsons, et al., 1922, p. 283.

[4] This point is elaborated in the next chapter.

[5] Hargrave, 1932, p. 1.

[6] Olalla is identified as Oraibi in Hodge, 1910, p. 143.

[7] Luxan, 1929, p. 102.

[8] Thomas, 1932, p. 108.

[9] Hodge, 1910, p. 142.

among nearly 150 households,[10] but in that year a civil "war" led to the secession of half its populace, and by 1933 it had dwindled to a ghostly settlement of 112 men, women, and children, occupying about 25 houses in the midst of over a hundred ruined dwellings. Within the span of a single generation the Hopi "capital" had been reduced to a dying village, a modern instance of a pueblo that fell apart when its outer shell was cracked. In this case, as perhaps in many others, it was the impact of foreign culture that struck the fatal blow.

Hopi contacts with white men fall into two major divisions, those with the Spaniards from 1540 to 1823, and those with Americans from 1834 to the present.[11] Spanish influence begins with the famous visit of Don Pedro de Tovar, a member of Coronado's expedition, who appeared before the startled Hopi in 1540. As Don Tovar and his party were the first white men ever seen by the natives, it is no wonder that the Indians hurriedly armed themselves, but after a brief skirmish they offered no resistance to the invaders and promptly sued for peace.[12] Reports of the strangers' arrival must have spread rapidly throughout the Hopi towns, for later in the same year, Cardenas "was well received when he reached Tusayan and was entertained by the natives. . . ."[13] Whether motivated by fear or out of genuine friendship, the Indians remained well disposed to their Spanish visitors for several years, so that when Espejo reached the Hopi in April, 1583, he was greeted with food and requests for peace.[14] At the same time, the seeds of future conflict may well have been sown on this occasion, for the Spaniards seem to have taken some Hopi women with them when they left.[15]

Fifteen years later, in November 1598, the Hopi formally surrendered to Juan de Oñate in the name of the king of Spain, and within a short time an "intensive effort to Christianize the Hopi

was begun . . . with the appointment of missionaries and the construction of mission buildings."[16] Here was an undoubted cause of strife, for while some of the Hopi became nominal Christians in the first half of the seventeenth century, there were many others who were bitterly antagonistic towards the priests. Judged on the basis of the general situation that prevailed throughout the Southwest, there must have been a great "number of complaints concerning the harsh discipline enforced by the clergy on their wards and the moral laxness of an unfortunately large number of the mission priests."[17] More specifically, to show how this general state of affairs affected Oraibi, it is only necessary to cite one notorious instance of priestly misbehavior.

According to France V. Scholes, the "friars often resorted to the imposition of physical punishment . . . [but] the most flagrant case on record during the entire seventeenth century occurred in 1655. In the summer of that year several Indian captains from the Hopi pueblos appeared before Custodian Ibargaray . . . to denounce the actions of their priest, Friar Salvador de Guerra. . . . Several Indians were summoned to testify, and they told a harrowing tale. They stated that an Oraibi Indian named Juan Cuna had been discovered in some act of idolatry. In the presence of the entire pueblo, Father Guerra gave him such a severe beating that 'he was bathed in blood.' Then, inside the church, the friar administered a second beating, following which he took burning turpentine and larded the Indian's body from head to feet. Soon after receiving this brutal punishment the Indian died. The Indians also testified that several other persons . . . had been whipped and tarred with hot turpentine."[18]

In the light of such an episode it is not difficult to understand why the Hopi, who had previously refused to participate in an earlier rebellion, did not refrain from joining wholeheartedly in the

[10] See columns 6 and 7 on chart VI (p. 52) for the number of households, and p. 88, for the 1906 population figures.

[11] During the period between 1823 and 1834, the Hopi were left almost entirely to themselves.

[12] Winship, 1896, p. 488. For a chronological account of Hopi-Spanish contacts, consult Bartlett, 1934.

[13] Winship, 1896, p. 489.

[14] Luxan, 1929, p. 96.

[15] During a visit to Acoma soon after leaving the Hopi, the Spaniards quarreled with the Acoma Indians over

"a Hopi woman belonging to Barreto, who had escaped from him. . . ." Luxan, 1929, p. 37 and p. 112.

[16] Hargrave, 1932, p. 5.

[17] Scholes, 1936, p. 22.

[18] Scholes, 1937, pp. 144, 145. I am indebted to Dr White for this reference.

During his trial Father Guerra admitted occasionally beating and larding with turpentine a number of villagers. He was removed from office and ordered taken to Mexico City for further hearings, but Scholes was unable to learn anything more about his case.

Pueblo Revolt of 1680.[19] As their share in the uprising they killed all four of the missionaries who were stationed among them.[20]

Although the reconquest of the territory by De Vargas in 1692 did not extend as far as Oraibi, the inhabitants of that pueblo seem to have been divided on the issue of renewing friendship with the Spaniards. On the one hand, the Oraibi chief, Espeleta, was ready to make peace with Governor Cubero in 1700, on condition that he be permitted to continue his "pueblo rites and pagan ceremonies";[21] on the other hand, when the pueblo of Awatovi agreed, in the same year, to receive a baptizing friar, it "was attacked by Oraibi and other Hopi, sacked, and abandoned. . . ."[22] These related events have led Dr. Parsons to infer, with a good deal of probability, that in 1700 "there were two parties at Oraibi, a pro-Spanish or at least a conciliatory one . . . and a stiff-necked one. . . ."[23] For many years contentions between the rival factions must have prevailed, for in 1741, reports Escalante, "God . . . allowed a grave discord over the election of a chief at Oraibe. On this account the pueblo was divided into two parties, who took arms against one another."[24] Very likely the anti-Spanish group predominated as Fathers Escalante and Garces were unsuccessful in their efforts to convert the Hopi between 1774 and 1776. In those days, as at present, the village leaders seem to have exerted little or no compulsion on their followers, for when the crop failures of 1778 and 1780 had reduced the people to starvation and had led some of them to request help from the Spaniards, the Oraibi chief adopted the customary Hopi policy of *laissez faire*. For himself, he told Governor Anza on September 23, 1780, "he had resolved to die in the same manner with those who remained with him."[25] As for those who wished to follow

the Governor and to become Christians, "On his part," the chief said, "neither in the present nor in the future would they be impeded."[26] Despite the lack of official constraint, only a few families left Oraibi, and from that day until the end of the Spanish period in 1823, occasional missionaries came to preach "but none was allowed to live in Hopiland."[27]

Nearly three centuries had now elapsed since the Hopi had first seen a white man, and during this period there was ample time for stories dealing with the early Spaniards to have taken on a mythological coloring.[28] Many legends gathered in the late nineteenth century contain episodes dealing with Bahana (White Man), who had come to be regarded as a contemporary of the first Hopi to have emerged from the Underworld.[29] In several origin tales Bahana is described as an elder brother to the Hopi, who, after a short period of wandering together, had departed for the east promising to return at some future date when the Hopi had need of him.[30] How Bahana was to be identified, and whether or not he was to be welcomed, were lively topics of debate in the closing decades of the past century.[31]

During the period of nominal Mexican control, 1823–1848, the Hopi were rarely visited by white men, but the first of their contacts with Americans which took place in 1834 was of such a nature that it could not have failed to antagonize them. Several trappers who had wantonly plundered some Hopi gardens fired into a crowd of natives that had gathered in protest and killed about 15 or 20 of them.[32] Small wonder if the effects of this act were felt throughout the Hopi towns and provided the basis for a hostile attitude towards all Americans.

At Oraibi, Talaiyauoma, who was Village chief from 1825 (?) to 1850 (?),[33] was probably the

---

[19] Hackett, 1911, p. 130.

[20] For details of Hopi participation see Bartlett, 1934, pp. 56, 57.

[21] Bloom, 1931, p. 197, footnote 37.

[22] Parsons, 1939, p. 862. For further details on the destruction of Awatovi, see Fewkes, 1893; and Brew, 1937.

[23] Parsons, 1939, p. 862, footnote *.

[24] Thomas, 1932, p. 159. The date is given on p. 160.

[25] Thomas, 1932, p. 234.   [26] Thomas, 1932, p. 234.

[27] Parsons, 1939, p. 862.

[28] The speed with which recent events can be woven into Hopi mythology is well brought out in Nequatewa, 1938. In 1898 Dr. Fewkes left Walpi because of a smallpox epidemic. Less than forty years later a vivid tale was being told that he had been frightened off by a nocturnal

visit from Masau'u, the Hopi god of death.

[29] Mrs. Colton and other students of the Hopi believe that the Bahana myth antedates the Spanish coming. Nequatewa, 1936, p. 105, note 14. In the opinion of the writer there is insufficient evidence for such a belief.

Bahana is now a general term for all white men except Mexicans, who are called Castillas.

[30] Voth, 1905b, pp. 11, 15, *et passim*; Cushing, 1923, p. 169; and Wallis, 1936, pp. 11, 12.

[31] Nequatewa, 1936, p. 50.

[32] Bartlett, 1936, p. 34. This episode is described in Victor, 1871, p. 153.

[33] My informant on the subject of nineteenth century Oraibi chiefs was the present Village leader, Tawaqwaptiwa. All dates followed by question marks are approxi-

head of the pueblo when the fracas with the trappers took place. Talaiyauoma was a member of
the Squash clan, but he held the Village chieftainship by virtue of the fact that his father was a
Bear clansman.[34] He is described as a hot-tem-
pered individual, so we may be sure that he deeply
resented the killing of his tribespeople by Americans. He was succeeded by Nakwaiyamptiwa, of
the Bear clan, who held office from 1850(?) to
1865(?). The new leader was an albino who was
nicknamed Qötctaka (literally, white man, but
not to be confused with Bahana). Only a few details are known about Nakwaiyamptiwa, but he
was probably anti-American, for in 1858 Lieutenant Ives "found the Oraibi chief surly and
unfriendly."[35] He is supposed to have been a good
chief and a good rain-maker. During a plague of
prairie dogs one fall he is said to have called for
a Masau Katcina dance,[36] which caused a veritable
cloudburst that drowned all the prairie dogs.
Nakwaiyamptiwa never married, "because in
those days 'ladies' did not like albinos." He had
trained Talahöniwa, presumably one of his sisters'
sons, to succeed him, but the latter died some
time before Nakwaiyamptiwa's own death about
1865. Since he left no acknowledged heir, the
choice of Nakwaiyamptiwa's successor lay between two youthful brothers from the Bear clan,
Sakhongyoma and Lololoma. Both were considered too young to hold the Village chieftainship,
so their father, Kuyingwu of the Water Coyote
clan, served as regent and temporary head of the
Soyal ceremony from 1865(?) to about 1880.

While Kuyingwu was acting Village chief of
Oraibi, the Hopi suffered dreadfully from drought
and famine, particularly between 1866 and 1868.[37]
It was while they were still troubled by hard
times that the Moqui [Hopi] Pueblo Agency was
established by the government of the United
States in 1870. Apparently, Kuyingwu was bitterly antagonistic to Americans, for under date
of November 15, 1871, the Special Agent for
Moqui Pueblo Indians reported, "My reception

by these people was of a cordial character, apart
from the Oreybes, who manifested much hostility to me, saying they did not wish to have
anything to do with the Government, and, I
regret to say, a portion of them continue to be
hostile. I also found the relation between the six
villages and the Oreybes was not of a friendly
character. . . . The chiefs [of the other towns]
said they had no unkind feeling toward the Oreybes, but the chief of the Oreybes was angry with
them because they were friends to the white man
and the Government. . . . Early in August I
visited the Moquis with a view of taking the
census . . . and was successful apart from the
Oreybes, the chief utterly refusing me the privilege."[38] In 1873 Oraibi is reported to have shown
a somewhat more tolerant attitude towards Americans, but even as late as 1878 the villagers still
refused to permit a census to be taken.

It was in an atmosphere of marked opposition
to American influence, then, that Kuyingwu's
sons, Sakhongyoma and Lololoma, grew to maturity. At first, as their father's regency drew to
an end, the brothers held the chieftainship alter-
nately, but by 1880 Lololoma, the younger of the
two, had come to be recognized as Village chief
of Oraibi, although Sakhongyoma continued to
perform the Soyal ceremony on his behalf.[39] At
the start of his rule, Lololoma continued his
father's anti-American policy,[40] but not long
after 1880 he completely changed his attitude,
thus taking the first direct step towards the ultimate disintegration of the Hopi "capital."

Lololoma's conversion to Americanism occurred early in the Eighteen Eighties. At that
time the Navaho were a constant source of worry
to the Hopi as they kept filtering into the latter's
reservation. To discuss ways and means of stopping the Navaho, a party of Hopi chiefs was taken
to Washington by Thomas Keam, one of the
first traders to become established on Hopi territory. Lololoma was a member of Keam's group
and took part in a conference with the President

mations which were made on the basis of the data he
provided.

[34] Although Village chiefs should be from the Bear clan,
it is not unusual for fathers or sons of Bear men to hold
office under special circumstances, as in the case of
Kuyingwu whose story follows.

[35] Donaldson, 1893, p. 29.

[36] Masau Katcina, representing the god of death who
does things by opposites, is the only Katcina that may appear in the fall.

[37] Donaldson, 1893, pp. 19 and 42.

[38] Crothers, 1872, p. 704. The writer of the report was
W. D. Crothers, United States Special Agent for Moqui
Pueblo Indians, Arizona territory.

[39] Although the Village chief is theoretically chief of
the Soyal, the latter office is often filled by a close relative. See p. 63, footnote 30.

[40] A missionary school had opened at Keam's Canyon
soon after 1875, according to Nequatewa, 1936, p. 60.
That Lololoma opposed the opening of this school appears
from the statement he made to Julian Scott which is
quoted on the following page.

of the United States.[41] While they were in Washington, the Hopi chiefs "were asked to try to bring their people down off their mesas and advised to get them to spread about and form other small communities in the country nearby,"[42] as a means of checking the Navaho spread.[43]

The trip to Washington made so deep and so favorable an impression on Lololoma that it caused him to reverse completely his former attitude towards Americans and their culture. While discussing the education of Oraibi children with Special Agent Julian Scott, Lololoma admitted "that he had been opposed to the school until his visit to Washington, when he saw . . . so many wonderful things which . . . grew out of the system of education existing among the white people, [that] he had changed his mind and would use all his influence in the future in persuading his people to send their children to school."[44] Lololoma is also thought to have promised the President that he would permit the establishment of a Protestant mission at Oraibi, and the Mennonite sect was the first in the field.[45] From this time on the acceptance of American schooling and conversion to Christianity became closely linked concepts in Hopi thought.

Lololoma's change of policy immediately caused a violent reaction among his people. Some of them favored the new attitude, but a large part of Oraibi's populace was ultra-conservative and vigorously condemned the Village chief's change of heart. In the ensuing struggle those who favored Lololoma's point of view came to be known as Progressives or Friendlies, while those who opposed it were called Conservatives or Hostiles. The Friendlies were led, of course, by Lololoma, but the opposition soon found a worthy leader in the person of Lomahongyoma, head man of the Spider clan, who was nicknamed "Uncle Joe" by government agents. Lomahonygoma was anything but an upstart who rashly defied his tra-

ditional Village chief. On the contrary, he had long been an important figure at Oraibi and was in a strong position to challenge Lololoma's authority.

Lomahongyoma was the son of Leonim of the Spider clan by a Sun clansman. He had been chosen head of the Spider clan which is in the same phratry as the Bear, thus making the rival leaders "brothers." Furthermore, Lomahongyoma was married to Qötcyamka of the Water Coyote clan, to which Lololoma's father, Kuyingwu, had belonged. Thus Qötcyamka was paternal aunt (*ikya'a*) to Lololoma, which made her husband Lomahongyoma the "grandfather" (*ikwa'a*) of his arch rival.[46] Apart from kinship connections with the Village chief's family, Lomahongyoma was also an important religious officer. He had been initiated into the Wuwutcim at Blue Flute kiva (Sakwalenvi), which automatically qualified him for Soyal membership, and in that ceremony he held an important post as a singer of sacred songs. He was also the chief of the highly regarded Blue Flute ceremony, and the head of the Blue Flute kiva in which the Soyal was performed. Finally, he was a member of the Warrior society (Mutcwimi), of which his own mother's brother, Talai'ima, was chief.[47]

His position in the community plainly shows that Lomahongyoma was no unworthy opponent to Lololoma, and it is not surprising that he should have threatened to usurp the chieftainship as soon as the Conservative faction had rallied about him. In the conflict that followed, each side sought to justify its stand and to prove the "holiness" of its cause by citing Hopi mythology. Lololoma's version ran along the following lines.[48]

In the Underworld so much trouble was caused by the Spider and the Bow clans which were "partners" in mischief-making,[49] that Matcito, the Bear clan chief, decided to order an Emergence. He planned to lead only his good followers to the surface of the earth, but some of the bad

[41] Probably President Arthur, who was in office from 1881 to 1885.

[42] Nequatewa, 1936, p. 109, note 47.

[43] The rights of the Hopi to their territory "were tacitly recognized by President Arthur in his proclamation of December 16, 1882, when he threw about them the protection of a reservation to keep off white people and the Navajos." Donaldson, 1893, p. 9.

[44] Donaldson, 1893, p. 56.

[45] According to Parsons a Moravian mission was established at Oraibi some time after 1870. Parsons, 1939, p. 62. My informants dated the event closer to 1880.

[46] There is a touch of irony in this situation, for a man and his paternal aunt's husband are supposed to enjoy a

joking relationship.

[47] The biographical material used throughout this chapter is taken from notes obtained during the census of Oraibi, as described on p. 51.

[48] The version given here is condensed from an account supplied by Tawaqwaptiwa, who had been chosen and trained for the Village chieftainship by Lololoma. As the Bear chiefs tell it, the story is full of pointed references, not found in other versions, that color the narrative and support the Friendlies' position. For a more conventional rendition see Voth, 1905b, pp. 10–15.

[49] The Bow clan is frequently called "crazy" at Oraibi, and at least two of its members were actually psychopathic.

people (witches) also climbed out. Soon the young daughter of the Bear chief died, and it was found that she had been killed by Spider Woman, ancestress (*wuya*) of the Spider clan. Matcito was going to punish Spider Woman but she showed him that his daughter had returned happily to the Underworld so he let her go.[50]

After journeying for some time, Matcito drew on the ground a line running to the east with two forked branches, one pointing north and the other south. "I am going to walk on the path to the south," announced Matcito. "You, Spider Woman, must go to the north. I have no power to feed my people or to bring rain. I have only the Watchmen Brothers [Little War Twins], the Katcinas and the Soyal ceremony. I think more people will follow you because you can bring rain and make the crops grow. You know how to protect your people from sickness— I have nothing."[51]

Now the choice was with the people and a few prepared to go with Matcito but most of them went with the Spider Woman who had the Blue Flute ceremony which is supposed to bring a warm sun for the crops. As she was leaving, Spider Woman said, "I am going to the north to Kawestima[52] where it is always cold. For a number of years we shall travel apart, but some day we shall come together again. Whenever we meet I will draw your people away from you and you will have no followers— you will be worthless."

Among those who had emerged with the Hopi was a White Man, Bahana [Montezuma], who had exceptional qualities and who looked upon the Hopi as "younger brothers." When Spider Woman had finished it was Bahana's turn to speak. "Now I will leave you and travel east," he said, "but I will turn to watch you, Matcito, and I will keep my ears open. If there is any trouble with the Spider Woman, I'll keep watch and help you. You, chief, turn to the east and watch me. We came from the same home—we are not friends but brothers. If Spider Woman makes trouble [witchcraft] I shall return and cut off her head."

Then Bahana departed for the east, Matcito started south, and the Spider Woman traveled to the north. In time Matcito settled at Oraibi and Spider Woman stopped at Kawestima, near the Colorado river. During the first year her crops were very good, in the second year they began to fail, and in the third and fourth years she had no harvest at all. Then Spider Woman admitted her failure and advised her followers to rejoin Matcito. So they searched for his settlement and finally came to Oraibi

and asked to be admitted. The Spider clan leader said, "I'll make a kiva for you and help you at Soyal. When you make *nakwakwosi* (prayer-feathers) for the Six Directions (the four cardinal points, zenith and nadir), I'll distribute them. I'll fetch the things you need in the ceremony, and I'll help you to erect the altars. At *totokya* (food providing, usually the final day devoted to secret exercises in the kiva), I'll collect the corn to be 'blessed' and I'll carry the offerings to Lehu spring and pray for your people. I'll be your helper and messenger, and you can just sit here and not do hard work while you are performing the Soyal."[53]

The Spider chief also offered to sing during the Soyal, to perform his Blue Flute ceremony, and to hold the winter observances of the Blue Flute in his kiva. But despite his fair words and good promises he still had in his heart the idea of stirring up future trouble which he had received from the Spider Woman. Matcito too knew what his destiny was, but he accepted the offers of the Spider leader and allowed his clan to settle at Oraibi.

Just as the Friendly leaders took a fatalistic view of the prospect of future trouble, so too did the Hostiles accept their rôle of dissenters and rebels, even to the point of admitting that they were destined to be beheaded by Bahana.[54] In only two basic respects did their legends differ from those of their rivals. In the first place, they did not admit that they were witches but imputed witchcraft to their opponents. In the second place, they made a major issue of the need for properly identifying the true Bahana before agreeing to accept his wa y of life. According to the Conservative accounts, as Bahana was about to leave the Hopi soon after the Emergence, each party "took a stone upon which there were some marks and figures, and that fitted together."[55] When the true Bahana returned, argued the Hostiles, he would be able to converse with his younger brother in Hopi, and he would produce a stone to match the one held by the Hopi. On both counts, Lololoma was accused of having made an erroneous identification of his American friends as Bahanas. "These white men are no the true Bohanna, who will come some day and who will know the Hopi language,"[56] insiste

---

[50] Most of the origin tales do not attribute the first death to Spider Woman. In fact, another account of this episode blames the first death on the nephew of Matcito, the Bear chief. Voth, 1905b, p. 12.

[51] There is a triple motive for stressing Matcito's humbleness. The gods are more apt to help a poor man, humility is a great Hopi virtue, and unusual ability is the mark of a witch. See Titiev, 1943a, p. 553.

[52] Described as "a ruin in a canyon near Navajo Mountain," in Nequatewa, 1936, p. 65. Note the contrast of

Matcito with Spider Woman who openly makes boast throughout her speech.

[53] The promises attributed to the Spider chief ar only a catalogue of the duties he performed at Oraib Throughout the narrative the present situation is ratior alized.

[54] Compare Cushing, 1923, pp. 169, 170.

[55] Voth, 1905b, p. 21. Compare p. 60.

[56] Crane, 1926, p. 167. The speaker was Yokioma the Kokop clan who later succeeded Lomahongyoma leader of the Conservatives.

one of the outstanding Hostiles. Again and again he reminded his supporters that "the Bahana who established the school was not their true brother who had come up from the underworld with them. If he was, he would have shown the Hopis his written tradition to compare with their tradition."[57] And to emphasize his position, the same exponent of Conservative beliefs stoutly maintained that if the Hopi did submit to the teachings of a false Bahana, the mythical water serpent, Palulokong, would punish them by sending a flood to end the world.[58]

To stress only the expressed differences in mythological interpretation between the contending parties would be to give a distorted view of the situation. In reality there was a strong sociological aspect to the quarrel between the Bear and the Spider leaders. The Spider people regarded themselves as peers of the Bears because the two clans were "partners" in the same phratry, yet the highest office in the village was held only by the Bear clan and the Spiders were not eligible to be Village chiefs. Then too the Spider people had a grievance in another respect. The Bear clan owned only one major ritual, the Soyal, but the Spiders controlled the Blue Flute and the Antelope ceremonies, besides helping with the Soyal and sharing in the control of the important Warrior society. Nevertheless, the Bears were owners of the entire Oraibi domain, while the Spider clan was allotted only a small piece of land in spite of its ceremonial importance.[59]

Analysis reveals, therefore, that Lololoma's receptiveness to American influence provided a *casus belli*, but that the primary division of the village resulted from the splitting of the weak phratry tie that had held two strong clans together.[60]

As the conflict gained headway, the Spider clan received its strongest support from the Kokop clan.[61] According to their traditions, the Kokop people were the most aggressive and warlike of the Hopi clans. They were in the same phratry as the Masau'u and Coyote clans (Phratry VI), and they claimed as their ancients (*wuya*) both Masau'u and the Little War Twins. They were supposed to have been refused admittance to Oraibi by Matcito, until a threat of invasion forced him to call on them for help.[62] For having repelled the invaders, Matcito permitted the Kokop clan to live in Oraibi on condition that they continue to serve him as warriors. With them they brought the Warrior society (Momtcit), whose control they shared with the Spider clan, thus linking the two groups. In addition, there were numerous personal ties between the leading men of the two clans. Lomahongyoma, the Spider chief, had a favorite uncle (own mother's brother), Talai'ima, head of the Warrior society, with whose son he used to herd sheep.[63] This uncle was married to a Kokop woman named Pongyamönim. Then too one of Lomahongyoma's own nephews (sister's son), Humiwai'ima, also a Warrior society chief, was likewise married to a Kokop woman, who was called Duveyesnim.

Of the Kokop men to join the Spider clan's cause, one of the most important was Patupha. He was a member of the Warrior society and the last survivor of the now extinct real Medicine society (Pocwimi). Patupha was regarded even by his enemies as an outstanding shaman, and his power was greatly feared. He was very active on the Conservative side, but he died before matters came to a head in 1906. His place was taken by his younger brother, Yokioma.[64] This Kokop leader belonged to the Warrior and the Antelope

[57] Nequatewa, 1936, p. 62.

[58] As Yokioma said to Crane, 1926, p. 188, "Suppose I should willingly accept the ways of the Bohannas. Immediately the Great Snake would turn over, and the Sea would rush in, and we would all be drowned. You too. I am therefore protecting *you*." Compare Wallis, 1936, p. 12.

[59] See p. 63, footnote 27, and fig. 5, p. 62.

[60] A similar diagnosis of the situation is found in Leupp, 1906, p. 124. "It is believed by not a few persons who know these Indians well," wrote Leupp, "that their division grew wholly out of the internal political dissensions of the tribe; that one of the factions conceived the device of declaring itself friendly to the United States Government, not because it felt so especially, but because it believed that by such a declaration it could win the favor

of the Government and obtain an invincible ally in its struggle with the other faction. . . . I, for one, cherish no illusions as to the meaning of the professions of good will on the part of the Friendly faction."

[61] The word Kokop has been variously translated as Firewood, Cedarwood, Charcoal, etc. All of these are incorrect, and it is far better to leave the word untranslated.

[62] Some legends say that the Kokop clan deliberately invited the enemy to attack Oraibi, in order to compel Matcito to use their services as warriors.

[63] Lomahongyoma herded sheep in partnership with his brother, Lomayestiwa, and Talangainiwa, a Kokop who was the son of Talai'ima.

[64] I cannot determine whether Yokioma was a full brother of Patupha, a half-brother, or a clan brother. Be-

societies, both of which had Spider chiefs. It was his niece, Duveyesnim, who was married to Lomahongyoma's nephew, Humiwai'ima; and his own son, Qötchongva, of the Sun clan, was married to Lomahongyoma's niece, Kuwanwunka. The close ceremonial and family ties between the two men help to explain why Yokioma gradually replaced Lomahongyoma as the major figure in the Conservative party.

So quickly did the schism between Hostiles and Friendlies spread after Lololoma's return from Washington early in the Eighteen Eighties, that when Cushing arrived at Oraibi in 1883, he found the village already divided into two antagonistic camps. "Opposed to these officials of the regulative system of the Oraibis [that is, the traditional chiefs]," wrote Cushing, "are certain men who, by virtue of their claimed heredity and craft, are supposed to have possession of superhuman powers or magic, the sorcerer priests of the tribe. . . . [65] By means of a reckless effrontery unparalleled by anything I have else known of other Indians, they in council boldly attack the regular chiefs. . . . They go so far as to threaten the life of the highest priest-chief of the tribe, if this incumbent . . . be so bold as uncomprisingly to oppose their aims. . . . So great is their power that their leader assumes all the title . . . of the highest priest-chief of the tribe . . . tracing his descent from the mythic grandmothers of the human race—the Spider and the Bat."[66]

There can be no doubt that Cushing is referring to the faction led by "Uncle Joe" Lomahongyoma, although he does not mention the latter by name. These people openly insulted Lololoma and prevented him from trading with Cushing; they reviled Cushing and reiterated their hatred for "Washington and his American children";[67] they made frequent allusions to such mythological elements as demands that Washington send soldiers "to kill the Oraibi and sit on their heads";[68]

and they spoke of ancient markings recorded on magic stones.[69]

From Cushing's narrative it appears that the Conservatives were the stronger group in 1883. They had already convinced themselves that Americans were not true Bahanas, and they had reached the point of repudiating every aspect of American culture. Accordingly, when a government school was opened at Keam's Canyon in 1887,[70] they refused to send their youngsters, and even as late as 1889 it was noted by Fewkes that most of the pupils were from East Mesa and that "few children were obtained from Oraibi."[71] To remedy the situation quotas were established for each of the Hopi towns, but the Oraibi people stubbornly refused to conform. In November, 1890, Mr. Keam went with a party of officials to Third Mesa to explain the idea of the quota to the villagers, but Lololoma "replied that he understood what the nature of the business was, but that the bad element in the town was working against him."[72] Keam asked to have the ringleaders pointed out, and Lololoma sent the officials to a kiva where they found and arrested a badly frightened Hopi who was supposedly one of the principal medicine men of the tribe.[73] As he was being led away, the party encountered his brother (Yokioma?) and promptly took him into custody, too. Lololoma's betrayal of their chiefs aroused the Conservatives to such a pitch that they imprisoned him in a kiva, from which unfortunate predicament he was rescued in December, 1890, by United States troops under Lieutenant Grierson.[74]

By now the Hostiles were bolder and more defiant than ever. In the spring of 1891 when the government sent a party of surveyors to survey the Hopi reservation with a view to allotting the land in severalty, all the Village chiefs were opposed to the scheme, but it remained for the Oraibi people to pull up most of the surveyors'

cause Yokioma was leader of the Hostiles when they were expelled from Oraibi in 1906, many recent Hopi informants are inclined to regard him as having led the Conservatives from the first. Note, however, that Dorsey and Voth, 1901, p. 9, speak of Lomahongyoma's leadership in 1901, but fail throughout their discussion to mention Yokioma.

[65] As a descendant of the Spider Woman, Lomahongyoma was credited with being able to do "wonderful" things by magic.
[66] Parsons, et al., 1922, pp. 258, 259.
[67] Parsons, et al., 1922, p. 263.
[68] Parsons, et al., 1922, p. 264.

[69] Parsons, et al., 1922, p. 266. Cf. Cushing, 1923, p. 170.
[70] Donaldson, 1893, p. 36. According to Fewkes, the school was not firmly established until 1889.
It is of the utmost significance that the school was opened soon after a petition had been signed in 1886 by several leading men from First and Second Mesas, but no signatures were obtained from Third Mesa. See Atkins, 1886, p. lxxx.
[71] Parsons, et al., 1922, p. 273.
[72] Donaldson, 1893, p. 57.
[73] The medicine man referred to here is probably Patupha of the Kokop clan.
[74] Donaldson, 1893, p. 37.

akes as soon as the men had left.[75] At about the me time some of the Oraibi children who had en taken to the school at Keam's Canyon ran vay and returned home. These and "various her irritations led to the issuing of an order in 391 to arrest several of the chiefs of Oraibi who d become outspoken."[76]

The duty of making the arrests fell to First ieutenant L. M. Brett. On June 21, 1891, he d a small party of six cavalry men, "the school acher, the agent, and an interpreter," to raibi.[77] As he was approaching the pueblo, ololoma met him, "warning him not to enter the llage . . . as most of the men, under the influ- nce and direction of their medicine man, were in ms and fortified to resist his command. . . . ieutenant Brett arrested some of the recalcitrants 1 the plain at the foot of the mesa, and placing 1e of the prisoners alongside of each of his men cended the mesa. . . ."[78] In the main plaza he und himself confronted by a large force of arriors, stationed on the housetops and armed with bows and arrows and old firearms, some f which may have dated back to the Conquest."[79] efore the lieutenant knew what to expect, the lopi began to make a formal, ceremonial decla- tion of war. To this end they had "dressed ree of their number to represent the three War- ds. . . . The first two, arrayed in prescribed ostumes, appeared in the plaza. . . . The last ientioned, or the Little War-god, did not appear 1 public. . . ."[80] The proceedings began when A man, clothed to represent [Kokyangwuhti, 1e Spider Woman] . . . approached the force rawn up on the plaza and advised them to leave, ating that trouble would result if they did not o so. The next personification to approach rep- esented the God of Death, clothed to represent Iasawuh. He wore a black mask painted with ots and carried various objects, among which as a bowl filled with a liquid medicine that had en prepared for the occasion, and as he passed ong the line of soldiers he sprinkled them all ith this medicine, using for this purpose a ather. He peremptorily ordered the soldiers to

leave the pueblo before the appearance of the Little War God, when hostilities would immedi- ately begin. . . . This Little War God is the leader of the warriors in their war parties and is known by his knitted cap with a rounded point somewhat resembling a German helmet. His shield is adorned with a figure of the sun and he wears various symbols of war and is decorated with feathers painted red."[81]

Elsewhere, in discussing the same episode, Fewkes ventures the opinion that still another figure, in addition to the Little War God, had also been dressed up and was ready to emerge. This impersonation stood for a curious "bird-like animal, with one long and a small singular ap- pendage to the neck on the upper side. The name Kūa-tu-ku-ě [Kwatoko][82] has been given me for the personage which it represents, and those with whom I have spoken about it have sometimes con- cealed information with a shudder, as if it was a terrible being. . . ."[83]

Luckily for all concerned, the theatrical decla- ration of war was not carried through to the be- ginning of actual hostilities, and Lieutenant Brett and his little band wisely withdrew without forc- ing an issue. A short time later, on July 16, 1891, Lieutenant Colonel Corbin went with a much larger force to carry out the arrest order. Keam accompanied the soldiers, and on the way they "met a courier . . . who informed us that the bad Oraibis had threatened to kill La-lo-la-my on sight of the troops and were prepared to fight."[84] However, Keam sent a message urging the Hos- tiles to surrender, and when Corbin's command arrived at Oraibi they had little trouble in arrest- ing the wanted men. Corbin urged the Hopi to obey Lololoma as their legal chief, and "fired the Hotchkiss guns to show what would have hap- pened if they resisted. In the excitement one Hos- tile jumped off the mesa and escaped."[85] The prisoners were taken to Fort Wingate, and it seems that leaders from both factions were ar- rested, for Patupha "was taken by the soldiers to Wingate,"[86] and Lololoma was a prisoner at the fort in November, 1891.[87]

[75] Parsons, et al., 1922, p. 274.
[76] Parsons, et al., 1922, p. 274.
[77] Parsons, et al., 1922, p. 275. General McCook's re- ort says that there were ten soldiers in the party. onaldson, 1893, p. 38.
[78] General McCook, in Donaldson, 1893, p. 38.
[79] Parsons, et al., 1922, p. 275.
[80] Fewkes, 1902b, pp. 493, 494.

[81] Parsons, et al., 1922, pp. 275, 276.
[82] For references to Kwatoko, see Parsons, 1939, p. 178, et passim. This creature is pictured in Parsons, 1936b, pp. 1013, 1025, 1026.
[83] Fewkes, 1892b, pp. 14, 15.
[84] Donaldson, 1893, p. 37.
[85] Donaldson, 1893, p. 37.   [86] Parsons, 1936b, p. 723.
[87] Donaldson, 1893, p. 16.

Thus ends the story of one of the most exciting and dramatic incidents in Oraibi's history, as told by a number of non-Hopi participants. To the natives within the pueblo the same series of events had a somewhat different connotation, and it is highly illuminating to compare the foregoing account with the Hopi version.

As Chief Tawaqwaptiwa relates it,[88] the rumor that troops were coming to Oraibi stirred the Hostiles into action. Gathering near the Wiklavi kiva,[89] they made an attempt to murder Lololoma before the soldiers arrived.[90] One man, Qötcyauoma, a Water Coyote,[91] pointed a gun at the Village chief, but when Lololoma stood facing him without fear, his adversary failed to shoot.[92] Then Lololoma said, "Well, you're the one that's going to kill me. Well, go ahead and shoot." Still no shot was forthcoming. Four times the chief dared him to fire, getting more insistent with each challenge. Meantime, the troops had appeared and were awaiting Qötcyauoma's shot before they opened fire on the Hostiles.[93] When Qötcyauoma failed to carry out the threatened assassination, a white soldier fired in the air "to show that there was to be no shooting."[94]

Just as the echoes faded, a low moaning cry, characteristic of Masau'u, was heard coming from the Kokop clan house.[95] "Come out, Masau'u, don't be a coward," cried Lololoma, "I'm not afraid of you." At this Patupha came out, dressed in complete Masau'u costume. In full view of the white soldiers he made a sweeping gesture as if embracing something, to indicate that he owned all the surrounding land; and then, pointing to the troops, he motioned away from his chest to show that none of it belonged to them. Then he went back into the house, but soon reappeared with a plaque containing *piki* bread and prayer-feathers. He waved the tray in four rotating motions "to show that the attack on the Hopi had failed, and that bad thoughts were to leave the minds of the people." Then he went to the shrine north of the village where Masau'u impersonators usually undress, and here he took off his costume and deposited prayer-offerings before returning to *the* Kokop house where he cleaned up and washed off the blood which is poured on Masau'u's hood.

Meantime, within *the* Kokop house, a number of other impersonators had been prepared to emerge had the attack not failed. After Masau'u had appeared, a woman named Sinimka was supposed to come out with a gourd full of ashes.[96] This she was to dash on the ground, scattering the ashes and so weakening the enemy that they would be helpless to resist being clubbed to death. Then the elder of the Little War Twins (Pukonghöya), impersonated by Talasyestiwa of the Lizard clan,[97] was to have made his appearance, and after him the Hostile leader, Lomahongyoma, stood ready to enact the part of his *wuya*, the Spider Woman. He carried medicine for making the hearts of his followers "swollen and insane" in order that they might the more easily be led to attack their fellow villagers. The Little War Twin (Palungahöya), played by Puhuwaitiwa,[98]

---

[88] It must be borne in mind that Tawaqwaptiwa, an adolescent youth at the time of the disturbance, was destined to succeed his uncle Lololoma as Village chief and was obviously prejudiced in favor of the Friendlies. Then again, in our interviews in 1934 he was describing events that had transpired over forty years ago, and it is only natural that his story should contain several factual errors. On the whole it is surprisingly accurate when compared with the printed accounts.

[89] This is the kiva in which the Warrior society, owned jointly by Kokop and Spider, normally met. It is near *the* Kokop clan house, and seems to have been a center of Hostile activities.

[90] In 1906 the Hostiles were again accused of plotting to murder the Friendly chief. Leupp, 1906, p. 129.

[91] Qötcyauoma, a clan brother of Lomahongyoma's wife, belonged to Phratry VI which contains the Kokop clan. He was in exactly the same three ceremonies as Lomahongyoma. He was the War chief of the latter's Blue Flute society, and a member of the Warrior society, and of the Wuwutcim at Blue Flute kiva.

[92] Nequatewa, 1936, p. 71, tells almost an identical story—with the emphasis reversed. He makes Yokioma

the hero and Tawaqwaptiwa the dastard who dares not shoot.

[93] The nearest non-Hopi parallel to this recital is given in Donaldson, 1893, p. 16.

[94] This cryptic phrase may refer to Corbin's firing the Hotchkiss guns as a warning.

[95] It is important to remember that Masau'u is a *wuya* of the Kokops.

[96] Sinimka was from the Pikyas clan, most of which sided with Lololoma, but her father was a Cedar clansman and a phratry brother of Kokop. It was through his influence that she was led to join the Hostiles. Details of her costume were not known, but the ashes she carried were potent war medicine for which the Kokop people had long been noted. Compare p. 155.

[97] He was married to Kuwanyonsi, sister's daughter of Lomahongyoma, and he was in the Al and Snake societies, both of which are partially military in character.

[98] Puhuwaitiwa was a Snake, or possibly a Lizard clansman. He was in Lomahongyoma's Blue Flute ceremony and had also entered the Wuwutcim at Blue Flute kiva (Sakwalenvi) of which Lomahongyoma was the head.

as next in line; and finally, as Fewkes had
[gu]essed, there was an impersonation of the dread
[K]watoko, a powerful war-bird that lives in the
[sk]y and has the reputation of being a fierce killer.
[A]fter a slaughter," the Hopi say, "Kwatoko is
[su]pposed to come out and feast on the dead."
[T]his part was played by an Eagle clansman
[na]med Qötcnöva.[99]
At the same time that the special actors were
[w]aiting their turns to emerge, all the Kokop
[cl]ansmen were crowded into their clan house.
[So]me of them went out of the back door to throw
[me]al at the sun in order to "kill" it, i.e. make it
[da]rk so that they might fight in darkness. (How-
[ev]er, Tawaqwaptiwa says that they were really
[pr]aying to the sun for the power to kill Lolo-
[lo]ma.) They were dressed for war, with bands
[of] knotted yucca leaves about their foreheads,[100]
[an]d all had war symbols drawn on their cheeks
[an]d noses with specular iron. To the townspeople
[w]ho had sided with Lololoma the Kokop men
[ca]lled out, "Now the world is going to end, and
[if] you want to be saved come to *the* Kokop house
[an]d join our side!"[101] But the Progressives re-
[pl]ied, "It is better for us to stay by our chief even
[if] we die."
In spite of the elaborate preparations for war
[th]at the Kokop clan had made, only the Masau'u
[im]personator actually appeared in public, and
[w]hen he found that Qötcyauoma had failed to
[ca]rry out his part in the shooting of Lololoma, he
[si]gnalled peace by waving the tray of *piki* bread.
[W]ere it not for that action, the other characters
[w]ould have come forth as planned, and war and
[de]struction would have followed, for the Hos-
[til]es had arranged that after the death of the Vil-
[la]ge chief they would make a mass attack on his
[su]pporters and gain possession of the pueblo.
By dressing as Masau'u with the intent of de-

claring war against his own fellows, Patupha had
done a great wrong, and people often came to
reproach him, crying for sorrow over the trouble
he had caused them. Then he fell sick, and his
cheeks puffed up until his eyes were closed. This
was the "whipping" punishment that came to
him for his actions, even though he had tried to
escape the consequences by performing a discharming rite with the tray of *piki*.[102]
As is to be expected, the turbulent events of
the summer of 1891 caused the rift between
Progressives and Conservatives to grow wider
and wider, until the latter finally seceded from
Lololoma's jurisdiction "and soon after began to
recognize Lomahongyoma as leader."[103] Since the
Hostiles claimed the greater following, Lomahongyoma argued that he, and not Lololoma, was
the actual Village chief; and in the course of
numerous long arguments with his rival he contended that *he* owned the Oraibi lands because of
his position as head of the Spider clan.[104] To this
claim Lololoma retorted, "You had a piece of
land for acting as my servant in the Soyal, and
when you quit that job the land became mine and
not yours." "That is not so," insisted Lomahongyoma, "it belongs to me. I own all these
fields, not you. I've got it all and you've got
nothing. That is why I ought to stand at the head
of the people instead of you."[105] Not content
with debating the issue, Lomahongyoma actually
went so far as to select a good field for himself on
Bear clan territory, and this he cultivated until
his expulsion in 1906.
On the basis of his ceremonial qualifications
too Lomahongyoma began to contend with
Lololoma for the Village chief's position. He
compared the Blue Flute ritual with the Soyal,
rating his ceremony above the Soyal.[106] In the
face of these threats to his supremacy there was

[99] It was appropriate for an Eagle man to impersonate
[K]watoko, as "powerful" birds are *wuyam* of the Eagle
[cla]n. Qötcnöva was married to the daughter of Yokioma's
[m]other.
[100] Only Kokop warriors were supposed to wear yucca
[hea]dbands.
[101] This refers to the tradition that if the Hopi accepted
[a f]alse Bahana, the mythical water serpent would send a
[flo]od to end the world.
[102] Each secret society has an ailment which it inflicts
[on] those who betray its secrets or break its rules. This is
[kn]own as its whip, and those who have been in contact
[wi]th sacred objects must discharm themselves lest they
[inc]ur the whipping disease. The chief is merely following
[a c]onventional pattern in closing a story of ritual action
[wi]th an account of discharming. See Parsons, 1939, pp.

457–460.
[103] Dorsey and Voth, 1901, p. 9; and Parsons, *et al.*,
1922, p. 284.
[104] Lomahongyoma claimed to have been promised the
Oraibi territory by his *wuya*, Spider Woman. The statements in quotation marks are taken literally from interviews with Tawaqwaptiwa.
Later, when Yokioma replaced Lomahongyoma as the
leading Conservative, he too claimed to control Oraibi's
land by virtue of his *wuya*, Masau'u, who was the first
owner of Oraibi.
[105] According to Tawaqwaptiwa, such vain and boast-
ful talk was good proof that Lomahongyoma was a
genuine descendent of Spider Woman, and a trouble
maker (witch) like his ancestress. Cf. Leupp, 1906, p. 130.
[106] Lomahongyoma's claims of superiority for the Blue

very little that Lololoma could do. So amorphous is the Hopi "state" that even at this juncture, when his leadership was being openly threatened, there was no mechanism for punishing rebels and no means of carrying out the hereditary Village chief's wishes. In no way is the weakness of a Hopi pueblo's social structure better revealed than in the picture of Lololoma's helplessness when confronted by an outspoken rebel who refused, for the nonce, to be guided by "traditional usage."

As matters now stood, the rival parties were so bitter towards each other that they would not co-operate in one another's ceremonies.[107] Worse still, neither side would permit its opponents to use any of its sacred objects, thus endangering the entire ceremonial cycle of the village.[108] A climax was reached in December, 1896, when Lololoma prepared to hold the Soyal services as usual in Sakwalenvi (Blue Flute kiva), of which the Spider chief was the head. As Lololoma started down the ladder he found the way blocked by his arch rival. "Now I don't think you'll have your Soyal here," said Lomahongyoma. "This is my kiva and not yours. Now take your things and move somewhere else to make your offerings." Lololoma had no alternative, for clan privileges are so incontrovertible that under no condition may they be transcended. Accordingly, Lololoma made no protest, but withdrew to a kiva where he was sure of being made welcome. He transferred his sacred materials to Circle kiva (Pongovi) which was owned by the Water Coyote clan and of which his own father, Kuyingwu, was the head.[109]

Emboldened by his success in driving Lololoma out of his kiva, Lomahongyoma then took a daring step towards establishing himself firmly as Village chief. He decided to hold a Soyal ceremony of his own. Apart from the lack of traditional sanctions, there was nothing to stand in his way. For years he had participated in Lolo-

loma's Soyal, as a singer he knew all the songs and prayers, and as an officer he had been present throughout the esoteric parts of the ritual and had grown familiar with the altars, fetishes and other paraphernalia employed. Thanks to his thorough knowledge of the procedure, he had only to manufacture duplicate ritual objects to be ready for his first Soyal. The fact that his properties were of recent, secular origin, was more or less neutralized by the circumstance that *his* performance was being held at the traditional kiva (Sakwalenvi), which was the recognized "home" of the ceremony.

As soon as Lomahongyoma had proclaimed himself a Soyal chief, all officers and men who had ever been initiated into that ritual were faced with the choice of attending the orthodox services held by the Bear chief at Pongovi, or of taking part in Lomahongyoma's usurped performance at Sakwalenvi. On the basis of his choice each participant gave positive proof of his affiliation with one side or the other. In this way party lines were sharply drawn, the cleavage between Hostiles and Friendlies was made evident to all the pueblo, and the disintegration of Oraibi received a tremendous impetus.

During the winter of 1897 every Soyal member at Oraibi had to make a final decision. When the competing leaders checked over their followers it was found that of the six major traditional officers,[110] three had remained with Lololoma and three had gone over to Lomahongyoma. On this score honors were even and each side was obliged to appoint three substitute officers, but Lomahongyoma seems to have had a larger following of ordinary members. When Soyal time came, the principal positions in the rival ceremonies were filled as shown in table 4.

To indicate the sociological trends of Oraibi partition, it may be well to analyze as fully as data permit the kin and clan relationships of the men listed in table 4, and to explain the motives

Flute ceremony were said to have been made with a view to winning over his opponent's followers, just as Spider Woman's promises had lured many people away from Matcito. To make such claims openly is believed to be a sign of witchcraft.

[107] Compare Dorsey and Voth, 1901, p. 10; and Fewkes, 1895a, p. 280.

[108] See Voth, 1912b, p. 113, footnote 2.

[109] On the death of Kuyingwu, leadership of the Pongovi kiva passed to his son-in-law, Talaskwaptiwa, a Sun clansman who had married Lololoma's sister, Pongyanumsi. Through this relationship Talaskwaptiwa was oc-

casionally permitted to act as head of the Soyal, see Parsons, *et al.*, 1922, p. 290, table 2. Talaskwaptiwa renamed the kiva Tawaovi (Place of the Sun) in honor of his own clan. At his death the kiva was repaired by his brother Qöyayeptiwa, who served as its head until he died in 1934. His successor was Talayesva, his sister's son, who is the present kiva chief. Ever since it has housed the Soyal, it has been known as Chief kiva.

[110] By "traditional officers" are meant those leaders who had served in the Village chief's Soyal during the period that the ceremony was undisputedly in the control of the Village chief.

for their choice of sides wherever possible.

Talaskwaptiwa (Sun clan) was married to Lololoma's sister, Pongyanumsi (Bear clan), and alternated as orthodox Soyal chief with Sakhongyoma, Lololoma's elder brother.[111]

TABLE 4. OFFICERS IN THE RIVAL SOYALS, 1897.[112]

POSITION	BEAR CLAN SOYAL	SPIDER CLAN SOYAL
Soyal chief	Talaskwaptiwa	(Lomahongyoma)[113]
Parrot chief	(Sikyamöniwa)	Lomanaksu
Pikyas chief	Ye'siwa	(Sikyaheptiwa)
Tobacco chief	(Tangakve'ima)	Lomayaktiwa
Crier chief	(Lomankwai'ima)	Talaswungniwa
War chief	Qöyangainiwa	(Masangöntiwa)

Sikyamöniwa (Parrot clan) joined the Bear side because his wife, Yowainim, was sister to Tanaknimptiwa (Masau'u clan), who was the father of Lololoma's acknowledged successor, Tawaqwaptiwa.

Ye'siwa (Pikyas clan) remained orthodox, partly because he was head of the Moenkopi colony which was generally faithful to the Oraibi chief, and partly because his wife, Nuvayonsi (Water Coyote clan), was a clan sister of Lololoma's father.[114]

Tangakve'ima took office in the Bear Soyal because his daughter Nuvayamsi (Lizard clan) was married to Lololoma's own son, Tangakhöniwa (Masau'u clan).

Lomankwai'ima (Greasewood clan) favored the Bear faction because he was the father of Tawaqwaptiwa's wife, Nasingönsi (Parrot clan).

Qöyangainiwa (Real Badger clan) stayed in the traditional Soyal because he was married to Lololoma's wife's sister.[115]

Lomahongyoma, of course, was the founder of the Spider clan's Soyal and had made himself its chief.

Lomanaksu (Parrot clan) had entered the Wuwutcim, and subsequently the Soyal at Sakwalenvi kiva. He seems to have become a Hostile out of genuine convictions, for he deserted Lololoma's ceremony in spite of the fact that he was Lololoma's ceremonial (Wuwutcim) father and had given him a Parrot clan name meaning "good," which refers to the pretty feathers of the parrot.[116]

Sikyaheptiwa (Pikyas clan) was made a new officer by Lomahongyoma for reasons which I could not determine. Actually, one would have expected to find him in the opposing camp as his wife, Qötcavatca (Sun clan), became the mistress and later the wife of Yokioma. However, this incident may have occurred after his conversion to the Hostiles.

Lomayaktiwa (Rabbit clan) was closely related to two Conservative leaders through his wife, Masangyamka (Kokop clan). One of her mother's brothers was Patupha, and another was Yokioma.

Talaswungniwa (Greasewood clan) had been initiated into the Wuwutcim at Sakwalenvi and was also a member of Lomahongyoma's Blue Flute ceremony. He seems to have gone over to the Hostiles for ceremonial rather than familial reasons.

Masangöntiwa (Snake clan) had no kinship ties with the Conservative heads, but he was chosen War chief because he was an important religious leader in his own right. He had entered the Wuwutcim at Sakwalenvi, he was a member of Momtcit, and he was chief of the Snake society. I do not know why he was a Hostile.

A check of the Soyal chiefs appointed in 1897 shows that Lololoma's new officers were all related to him, an indication that most of his following was drawn from his relatives. On the other hand, Lomahongyoma's appointment of two substitute leaders who were not related to him indicates that his support was more general. Table 4 also reveals how ceremonial ties serve to cross-cut clan lines, for the Parrot, Pikyas, Rabbit, and Greasewood clans all contributed chiefs to each of the contending factions.

Despite the seriousness of their rivalry, both

[111] See p. 80, footnote 109, and p. 72.
[112] The discussion of the ceremonial split in Dorsey and Voth, 1901, p. 11, is somewhat confusing. It begins with the statement that before 1900 the Soyal had always been held in Sakwalenvi, but later it says that in 1897 the Conservatives had held an independent celebration there with an improvised altar. The latter statement is the more accurate.
For comparative lists of Soyal officers, see Dorsey and Voth, 1901, p. 12; and Parsons, et al., 1922, p. 290. Parsons' lists are incomplete.

[113] Names of newly appointed substitute officers are given in parentheses.
[114] Yesiwa later divorced Nuvayonsi.
[115] Dorsey and Voth, 1901, p. 13.
[116] Lomanaksu's case requires a little further comment. A review of all the evidence suggests that he was originally a Friendly, not only because he was Lololoma's ceremonial father, but also because he served as Lakon chief in the Progressive cycle of rites. At a later time, he shifted to the Conservatives and allowed the Lakon ceremony to lapse at Oraibi.

sides lived up to the Hopi ideal of peacefulness and the two Soyals were conducted concurrently without open conflict. One incident, however, reveals the underlying bitterness that was generated in the struggle. On the eighth day (*totokya*) of the ceremony, it is customary for messengers to collect corn from every household and to bring it to the kiva to be "blessed" during the night. When Lololoma's men made the rounds of the village they took particular care to avoid antagonizing anyone by calling indiscriminately at the houses of Conservatives and Progressives alike. Lomahongyoma, on the contrary, sent his messengers only to the homes of Hostiles, and yet they collected more corn than did their opponents. Lololoma's people were greatly distressed and his older brother, Sakhongyoma, felt so bad that he began to cry. At this, Tawaqwaptiwa, who was then a forceful young man, said, "Stop crying, my uncle. You are the one who has been telling us that this was destined to be, and you know that we can't avoid it now that the time has come. So there is no use in crying and feeling upset." Thereupon the old man stopped crying and resumed his prayers and ritual duties.

The success of his Soyal performance encouraged Lomahongyoma to build up a complete cycle of ceremonies. As a nucleus he used those orthodox fetishes, altars, and sacred goods which legitimately belonged to members of his party,[117] but to these he added improvised paraphernalia as needed. If the traditional chieftainship of a ritual belonged to one of his followers, he was kept in office; if not, Lomahongyoma appointed a substitute.[118] So speedily was the program pushed forward, that when the time came for the Powamu celebration in the winter of 1898, the Hostiles were ready to duplicate the Friendlies' performance. However, there was a discrepancy in the selection of dates, for Lololoma held his ceremony first and Lomahongyoma's was given somewhat later. Inasmuch as the preceding Tribal Initiation rites had been held in the abbreviated, non-initiatory form, Lololoma's Powamu was also short and non-initiatory;[119] but Lomahongyoma conducted his Powamu in the extended form, in order that no time should be lost in initiating the children of his supporters into *his* Katcina cult.[120] The Bear chief's observances were held in Hotcitcivi kiva, the traditional home of Powamu, but Lomahongyoma was denied the use of this kiva so his performance was given in his own kiva, Sakwalenvi.

Throughout the summer of 1898 Katcina dances were held by both sides, and in mid-summer two Homegoing (Niman) rituals were performed. Lomahongyoma's came first and used Coyote (Is) kiva as a base, and Lololoma's followed with Hawiovi as its center. Later in the summer, when the Snake ritual was to be held, it was found that all the main officers were in the Hostile party. They gave the ceremony in traditional style from Rattlesnake (Tcu) kiva, with the customary co-operation of the Antelope society, most of whose men were also Conservatives. There was no rival celebration, as Lololoma refused to violate orthodox procedure by staging a substitute performance.[121]

The next fall, in November 1899, when it was time to perform the Tribal Initiation, Lololoma's men staged their rites a little in advance of Lomahongyoma's celebration, and for the first time an open quarrel took place between the rival groups. The Friendlies at Hawiovi kiva had just terminated their rites and were "resting" for four days, when the Conservatives tried to enter and use the same kiva because it was the regular home of the ceremony. The Conservatives won

---

[117] Possession of a society's most sacred fetish is the tangible sign of chieftainship, but once an individual has taken office he is regarded as the owner of the fetish, and may dispose of it as he likes. The accompanying rites are held entirely at his pleasure.

[118] Insofar as possible, Lomahongyoma tried to have his substitutions conform to traditional ideas by selecting men from the same clans or phratries which had always owned the offices in question.

[119] All major rituals at Oraibi may be given in short or extended forms, and the performance of the Tribal Initiation controls the form of most of the rites that follow.

Nequatewa, 1936, pp. 64, 65, relates a similar story of ceremonial dualism during the 1906 Powamu at Shungopovi. There too the Hostile faction selected a later date

and trouble arose when they refused to conceal their kiva-grown bean plants from the other party's uninitiated children. No such trouble was reported for Oraibi.

[120] Children enter the Katcina cult in years when the Powamu is given in its initiatory form. Lomahongyoma made a shrewd move when he held his Powamu in the extended form, because he thus secured firmly on his side all the children who were initiated under his auspices.

[121] Since the Snake ceremony alternates with the Flute no Flute rites were scheduled for the summer of 1898. When the Flute ceremony fell due the next year, the Blue Flutes were with Lomahongyoma and the Gray Flute were on Lololoma's side. Instead of performing jointly as is ordinarily done, each society gave an independent performance.

their point by driving out the Friendlies, but when they tried the same tactics at Singers' (Tao) kiva,[122] Lololoma's followers pulled up the kiva ladder and denied them entrance. The Hostiles then withdrew to a new kiva, Kiacsuckiva (Parrot Tail) which had recently been built by a Conservative member of the Tao society.

In December, 1899, two Soyal performances were held again, and from then until 1906 two separate ceremonial cycles were conducted annually. Table 5 lists the principal officers on both sides.

TABLE 5. CEREMONIAL OFFICERS AT ORAIBI, ABOUT 1899–1906.

CEREMONY	LOLOLOMA	LOMAHONGYOMA
Soyal	Sakhongyoma (Bear) Talaskwaptiwa (Sun)[123]	(Lomahongyoma)[124] (Spider)
Powamu	Si'ima (Badger) Qömahöniwa (Badger)	(Napkuiva) (Rabbit)
Kwan	Nasingyamptiwa (Masau'u) Lomaleohtiwa (Masau'u)	(Sikyave'ima) (Reed)
Al	Tanakhongniwa (Bow) Nasiwaitiwa (Bow)	Qötcventiwa (Bow)[125]
Wuwutcim	Talasnöngtiwa (Kele)	(Pitcangwu) (Crane)
Tao	Talangnakyoma (Katcina or Parrot) Masawistiwa (Katcina or Parrot)	(Napkuiva)[126] (Rabbit)
Snake	Kuktiwa (Snake)	Masangöntiwa[127] (Snake)
Antelope	......	Masaiyamptiwa (Spider) Duvengötiwa (Spider)
Blue Flute	......	Masaiyamptiwa (Spider) Lomahongyoma (Spider)
Gray Flute	Kelyamptiwa (Pikyas or Patki) Lomahongva (Patki)	......
Marau	Qötcnumsi (Lizard) Kuwanvikwaiya (Lizard)	......
Oaqöl	Qöyangösi (Sand) Kelnimptiwa (Sand)	......
Lakon	Kuwanyamka (Parrot) Lomanaksu (Parrot)[128]	......

[122] The Tao, Al, Kwan, and Wuwutcim societies are known jointly as Wuwutcim and hold their rites concurrently. Their combined performances make up the Tribal Initiation.

About a decade after the Hostiles had attempted to murder him and to declare war on the United States troops, Lololoma died. To succeed him he had selected and trained Tawaqwaptiwa, one of his sisters' sons. (See pl. II c.). It is the opinion of some of the old Hopi that Tawaqwaptiwa was chosen in preference to his older brothers because he was young and impetuous, and Lololoma evidently had hoped that he would be energetic enough to bring matters to a head and so end the incessant bickering at Oraibi.[129] Tawaqwaptiwa became Village chief in 1901 or 1902;[130] and coincidentally, Lomahongyoma began to take a less active part in the direction of Hostile affairs, while Yokioma (Kokop) came forward as the head of the Conservatives. Yokioma's policy was one of vigorous opposition to the introduction of American ideas, and he insisted that the Kokop clan would never submit to "the new ways taught by these white men of the Government."[131]

With the advent on both sides of forceful and uncompromising leaders, it was not long before a major crisis occurred. To swell their ranks, the Conservatives had invited a Hostile faction from Second Mesa to migrate to Oraibi. Led by Tawahongniwa, of the Bluebird clan,[132] a party of about

[123] Where two names are given for the same office it means that the two men alternated as chiefs.

[124] The personal names in parentheses are those of non-traditional chiefs.

[125] The real Al paraphernalia were said to have been retained by the Progressives, but parts were later transferred to the Hostiles.

[126] Napkuiva seems to have held two important offices under Lomahongyoma. He was Powamu chief as well as the Tao leader.

[127] Both Kuktiwa and Masangöntiwa had traditional claims to the Snake chieftainship. The orthodox Snake materials were used for a time by Masangöntiwa, but were later given back to the other side. The ceremony was then abandoned at Oraibi and the paraphernalia were later turned over to Puhunimptiwa, of the Lizard clan, who revived the Snake ritual at Hotevilla. See p. 209.

[128] In table 4, Lomanaksu is given as a member of the Hostile Soyal, but here he is listed as a Friendly. See p. 81, footnote 116. In all likelihood Lomanaksu had served in the Friendly cycle of rites for several years before he joined the Conservatives.

[129] Crane, 1926, pp. 86, 87, describes Tawaqwaptiwa as "The most negatively contentious savage and unreconstructed rebel . . . in the Oraibi community."

[130] Nequatewa, 1936, p. 108, footnote 41, says, "Lololoma died some time after the smallpox epidemic about 1901."

[131] Crane, 1926, p. 166.

[132] Tawahongniwa was a Shipaulovi Hostile who had moved to Chimopovy and joined the Conservative party

thirty people came from Chimopovy and settled at Oraibi in the fall of 1904.[133] Tawaqwaptiwa tried to refuse them admittance, but Lomahongyoma, his brother Lomayestiwa, and perhaps Yokioma,[134] disregarded his commands and brought the Second Mesa settlers into the village. Lomahongyoma even went so far in carrying out his pretensions to Oraibi's chieftainship as to give the new arrivals permission to build houses within the pueblo, and to assign them farms on land claimed by the Bear clan.[135] Inasmuch as the year 1904 had been marked by a severe drought, Tawaqwaptiwa protested that the influx of additional householders would cause increased food and water shortages,[136] but the Hostiles paid no attention to him as they no longer recognized him as Village chief.

Throughout 1905 Tawaqwaptiwa made several unsuccessful attempts to send the Chimopovy people back to Second Mesa, and in 1906 he went to Keam's Canyon to make an official complaint to the Superintendent, Mr. Theodore G. Lemmon. Mr. Lemmon agreed to help Tawaqwaptiwa and authorized him to tear down the houses and destroy the crops of the immigrants,[137] but this he dared not do. Instead, he called a meeting of his followers and they agreed that another attempt should be made to drive the Chimopovy group out of Oraibi. Although no action was taken at the time, the incident served to heighten the ever-rising tension in the village.

The first serious clash occurred in the summer of 1906, while the Conservatives were celebrating their Homegoing (Niman) dance. The Hemis Katcina was being impersonated, and as the dancers were going down one of the village streets they were stopped by Loma'asniwa, a Friendly from the Sand clan who frequently served as father of the Katcinas for his party. He made a speech accusing the Hostile faction of misbehaving, but then stepped aside and allowed the

Katcinas to file into the plaza for the final dance formation of the day's performance. Tawaqwaptiwa, who preferred not to watch the ceremonies of his enemies, was at his mother's house when the Katcinas were stopped. A short time later he was visited by Sakhongniwa (Katcina clan) and Sikyayestiwa (Greasewood clan), two of his supporters, who urged him to lead another stand against Lomahongyoma's dancers. At first the chief refused to sanction such a move, but later he consented grudgingly, as he feared that the same agitators who were now on his side might later turn against him.

Tawaqwaptiwa was still in an uncertain frame of mind when he and his advisers approached the dance plaza. As the Katcinas began to move towards the shrine where they usually disrobed after a Niman performance, Loma'asniwa said to the chief, "Now block them up! Step in front of them! We don't have to hurt the Katcinas, but let's block them up!" Thus did his followers wait for Tawaqwaptiwa to make the first hostile move, although he had not originated the plan and was not in full sympathy with it. Nevertheless, he stepped into the path of the dancers, and Loma'asniwa called out to the Conservative officers in the performance, "Now we don't think we will let you take your Katcina friends to their real home (shrine). You will have to find another place for sending your Katcinas home."

To this, one of the Hostile leaders replied, "We must go to the right place to send our Katcinas home."

"No," countered Loma'asniwa, "We won't let you take your Katcinas to their real home. You'll have to find another place." Thereupon the opposing Katcina father turned and led the dancers to another shrine—one not traditionally associated with the Homegoing dance. Then insults were exchanged by onlookers from the two factions, and in the midst of the quarrelling,

---

there a few years before he came to Oraibi. On Second Mesa, the Bluebird clan is in the same phratry as Bear and Spider. Third Mesa has no Bluebird people but ascribes that clan, in theory, to Phratry II which consists of the Bear and Spider clans.

[133] The leaders of the Chimopovy group were, in addition to Tawahongniwa, his four sons, Humiyesva, Lomawuna, "Washington" Talayamptiwa, and "Rutherford" Duvewai'ima, all of the Sun's Forehead clan; Sikyayamptiwa of the Eagle clan; and Talawisyoma of the Carrying-Strap clan of Second Mesa which is in the Bear-Spider-Bluebird phratry. See Nequatewa, 1936, p. 111, note 49.

Nequatewa, 1936, pp. 64, 65, gives the year 1906 as

the date of the Chimopovy migration, but Oraibi informants agreed on 1904. Leupp, 1906, p. 129, wrote in that year that the migration had occurred "A good while ago. . . ." Hence 1904 is probably the correct date.

[134] See Nequatewa, 1936, p. 65.

[135] See p. 61.

[136] Tawaqwaptiwa is supported on this point by the statement in Leupp, 1906, p. 129.

[137] Since Tawaqwaptiwa was personally relating this episode, it is hard to tell exactly what advice he received from Mr. Lemmon. Tawaqwaptiwa seriously believed that Lemmon had promised him government aid in expelling the Hostiles, but in a later conference Leupp disillusioned him. See Leupp, 1906, p. 127.

the chief returned home, greatly disturbed because he had taken the advice of his hot-headed followers.

A few days later the Progressives staged their Homegoing dance, and although there was no interference on the part of the Conservatives, the subdued enmity of the two parties was so great that each side felt that a climax would quickly be reached; and from then on regular meetings were held to prepare for the coming test of strength. Tawaqwaptiwa believed that since the Snake dance was soon to be performed, it would not do to start a disturbance in the presence of white visitors, so he selected the third day after the ceremony for the long-deferred attempt to expel the Chimopovy group. In anticipation of the struggle, he sent word to his Moenkopi colony, nearly all of which was on his side, urging the men to come to Oraibi in time to help him.

In 1906 only the Hostiles were celebrating the Snake rites, and in order to gain time they delayed the date from the usual period late in August to September 5,[138] thus making September 8 the fateful day on which open hostilities were supposed to break out.[139] On the night of September 6, both sides held meetings and laid plans for the coming encounter. The Hostiles met at the house of Nakwave'ima[140] (Eagle clan), and Tawaqwaptiwa wrapped himself in a blanket and went to spy on them. He managed to get near enough to overhear some of the speakers, but the house was so crowded that he could not identify all those who were present. Among the leaders he recognized Yokioma and Nakwave'ima, Tawahongniwa and his associates from Chimopovy, and two other Oraibi men, Nakwayauoma[141] (Gray Badger clan) and Qöyahöniwa (Sand clan). Tawaq-

waptiwa did not hear Lomahongyoma's voice, and it may be that he was not present at the meeting.[142]

Somehow, Tawaqwaptiwa does not know in what way, the Hostiles were well informed of his plans for trying to expel their Second Mesa allies, for he heard them advising each other to remain seated so that the first overt move would have to be made by the Progressives. Tawaqwaptiwa also overheard Nakwave'ima cautioning his hearers not to lay violent hands on the Oraibi chief. "Our plan is not to hurt anyone," Nakwave'ima was saying. "If some one from their side goes crazy and kills a person it's their fault, but we don't mean to kill anyone. But let us take our weapons so that we can defend ourselves if necessary."[143]

At this point Tawaqwaptiwa, fearing detection, returned to his own house. Here his own supporters had assembled, including the Moenkopi men who had responded to his call for help. The chief reported what he had heard at the Hostile gathering, and he too advised that there be no bloodshed and as little physical violence as possible. Several other men then spoke to the same effect, and all present agreed to keep their tempers under control and refrain from murder. Just then a Government official[144] arrived at the house and after a brief conference with Tawaqwaptiwa, he suggested that Yokioma be approached peacefully and asked to leave Oraibi without making a disturbance.[145] The official warned that if there were violence the troops would be sent "to wipe out both sides."

All night long the two factions deliberated, and by morning the Progressives had decided on their plan of action—they would start to drive

---

[138] Forrest, 1929, p. 281, helps fix the exact date. In 1906 Forrest heard that the Snake dance was postponed "on account of factional differences," and that it would be given on September 5. He himself saw the foot race on that day.

[139] Something must have gone wrong with the original plan, for Leupp, 1906, pp. 128, 129, specifically gives September 7 as the day on which the conflict ultimately took place.

[140] Nakwave'ima was very active in the Hostile cause, partly because his daughter, Nakwayesnim (Sand), was married to Lomahongyoma's sister's son, Poliwuhioma (Spider). Thus Nakwave'ima and Poliwuhioma had married into the same Sand household and lived together in two of the adjacent Sand houses shown on chart VII.

[141] Nakwayauoma was a Conservative although he was the husband of Tawaqwaptiwa's sister, Talashongsi (Bear).

[142] Despite his position as leader of the Hostiles, Lomahongyoma seems to have tried to avoid an issue that might have resulted in a forced exodus from Oraibi.

[143] It is interesting to note that so pacific are the Hopi by tradition that even in reporting the words of his worst enemies Tawaqwaptiwa admitted that they were trying as hard as his own side to avoid shedding blood.

Nevertheless, according to Leupp, 1906, p. 129, both sides planned to use arms until dissuaded by Government employees.

[144] Tawaqwaptiwa could not recall the name of his visitor, but it was probably Leupp, Leupp, 1906, p. 129.

[145] This is the first time that the chief's narrative indicated a desire to expel Yokioma and the Oraibi Hostiles as well as the Chimopovy settlers. For a comparative account of this series of events see Nequatewa, 1936, pp. 66–68, et passim; and also Parsons, 1939, pp. 1134–1136.

out the Chimopovy group and if the Hostiles interfered they would turn on them and force them to leave for the north, for Kawestima, where the ancestors of the Spider clan had left the Spider Woman when they went to seek out the Bear clan's settlement at Oraibi. Immediately after breakfast, Chief Tawaqwaptiwa led his followers to the home of Nakwave'ima.[146] His men urged him to refrain from active participation,[147] and with this understanding they marched into the house and ordered the Chimopovy group to leave Oraibi and to return to Second Mesa. The Hostiles refused to budge, tenaciously remaining seated as they had agreed to do during the previous night's discussion. After some argument, the Friendlies seized one or two of the Chimopovy men and began to evict them forcibly. In the scuffle some of the Conservatives tried to aid their friends, whereupon their opponents shouted, "They're helping the Chimopovy people, now we can drive them all to Kawestima." A man named Sikyahongva then grabbed Yokioma "and just slung him out of the door,"[148] after which a general scrimmage followed. For several hours the rough and tumble lasted, and by late afternoon on September 7, 1906, the two sides found themselves facing each other on the level ground just outside the northwest corner of the pueblo. Yokioma shouted to his followers, and both sides paused to hear what he had to say. With his big toe trailing in the sand, the Hostile leader drew a line running east and west. To the north of it, facing south towards Oraibi, he grouped his own men, while the Friendlies clustered together south of the line with their backs to the village. Then Yokioma announced the manner

in which Oraibi's fate was finally to be settled.

"If your men," he said to Tawaqwaptiwa, "are strong enough to push us away from the village and to pass me over the line, it will be done. But if we pass you over the line, it will not be done, and we will have to live here."[149] Without more ado, Yokioma placed himself on the line, facing Oraibi; beside him stood Tawahongniwa, leader of the Chimopovy party; and behind them their followers were ranged ready to push them towards the pueblo. Face to face with Yokioma stood Humihongniwa of the Water Coyote clan,[150] and behind him there lined up all the men on the Progressive side. Humihongniwa placed his hands on Yokioma's shoulders, and the struggle was on. With his own people at his back shoving him towards the village, and with the enemy in front pushing him away from Oraibi, poor Yokioma was badly mauled. Forward and back went the opposing groups until at last Yokioma was conclusively forced well over the line, towards the north, away from the town.[151] Oraibi's fate was decided; the Hostiles would leave the village! As soon as he could speak, Yokioma said, "Well, it has to be this way. Now that you have passed me over this line, it is done."[152] The victorious Tawaqwaptiwa gave his defeated rivals permission to take food, bedding and whatever personal belongings they could carry with them, and towards sundown Yokioma began his exodus, walking slowly towards the north with his people.

That night the Hostiles made camp at Hotevilla, a place seven miles north of Oraibi, where there were known to be excellent springs. Had they followed their legendary beliefs literally,

---

[146] Some informants said that the skirmish began at Yokioma's house. For a comparative account of the succeeding events, see Leupp, 1906, pp. 129, 130.

[147] Tawaqwaptiwa claims that his men were trying to shield him from violence, but his opponents argue that he was afraid to take an active part. See Nequatewa, 1936, p. 66.

[148] Nequatewa, 1936, p. 66.

[149] The line drawn by Yokioma was supposed to represent the Colorado river, and the position of his men indicated that if they were pushed away from the direction of Oraibi, they would go north to Kawestima near the Colorado river.

The manner of action decided on by Yokioma was a form of divination to determine whether the moment had come when the Spider Woman's descendants were to draw the Bear chief's followers away from Oraibi.

[150] Humihongniwa was one of the Moenkopi men who had answered the chief's call for help. The Water Coyote

clan is one of the military clans as it is in the same phratry as Kokop and shares with it the ownership of Masau'u and the Little War Twins as *wuya*. Thus two phratry brothers faced each other as Oraibi literally split into halves. Tawaqwaptiwa was again asked to stay out of violent action.

[151] Some say that Yokioma was forced over the line four times, but this is a conventional number in all rites and tales and cannot be taken as specific.

[152] Near the scene of the conflict a memorial of the event is inscribed on a flat rock. It shows a figure of Masau'u (*wuya* of Yokioma's Kokop clan), several bear's claw designs to indicate Tawaqwaptiwa's clan, and a line running roughly east and west. The legend reads, "Well it have to be this way now that when you pass me over this line it will be DONE." It is dated September 8, 1906.

At Oraibi the inscription is said to have been made by Silena (Masau'u clan), but it is ascribed to Poli (Payestiwa) in Nequatewa, 1936, pp. 108, 109, note 46.

they would have moved far to the north of this point in due time, but the leaders evidently decided to make a permanent settlement here, and Hotevilla became the site of a Conservative pueblo which now overshadows its parent village in every respect.

A short time after the split troops arrived at Oraibi,[153] and after finding out the details of the late conflict they proceeded to Hotevilla, taking Coin Humiventiwa (Greasewood clan) as an interpreter and guide.[154] Coin identified the Chimopovy people at Hotevilla and the soldiers rounded them up and dispatched them to Second Mesa without any show of resistance. Yokioma and several other Hostile leaders were taken off to jail, thus depriving the newly-founded settlement of many able-bodied men at a time when their help was desperately needed.[155] While the Conservatives were in distress, working feverishly to build shelters before winter came,[156] the Progressives celebrated their victory at Oraibi by holding a Butterfly dance "which had the significance of an earlier scalp dance that used to be performed after a successful raid, and in which the songs ridiculed the Hotevilla folk as though they were defeated enemies."[157]

The splitting of Oraibi into halves affords a unique opportunity for an inspection of the inner workings of a pueblo's social organization, and a study of the kin, clan, and ceremonial affiliations of the members of both factions should reveal the strong and the weak aspects of Hopi society, and should throw into sharp contrast the units that survived and those that collapsed as Oraibi disintegrated. To understand the dynamics of the situation we must now examine Oraibi's partition in detail.

Numerically, the Friendlies and Hostiles were about equal.[158] Counting together all the people ever attributed to one party or the other by various informants, we find that Lololoma and Tawaqwaptiwa had on their side 201 men and 190 women, or 391 followers in all;[159] whereas

TABLE 6. FRIENDLIES AND HOSTILES AT ORAIBI, 1906.

Phratry	Clan	Friendlies			Hostiles		
		♂	♀	Total	♂	♀	Total
I	Rabbit	17	14	31	6	12	18
	Katcina	4	4	8	0	0	0
	Parrot	7	6	13	7	8	15
II	Bear	6	2	8	1	1	2
	Spider	0	0	0	11	12	23
III	Sand	7	5	12	19	11	30
	Snake	2	1	3	2	0	2
	Lizard	11	6	17	12	9	21
IV	Sun	14	13	27	8	5	13
	Eagle	2	1	3	6	5	11
V	Greasewood	17	9	26	11	15	26
	Bow	6	2	8	1	0	1
	Reed	3	10	13	10	13	23
VI	Masau'u	14	23	37	0	0	0
	Real Coyote	13	13	26	4	4	8
	Water Coyote	8	8	16	14	15	29
	Kokop	0	0	0	7	7	14
	Le	0	0	0	6	3	9
	Cedar	0	0	0	0	0	0
VII	Real Badger	9	4	13	9	4	13
	Gray Badger	5	0	5	12	3	15
	Navaho Badger	0	6	6	1	1	2
	Butterfly	0	1	1	1	0	1
VIII	Pikyas	9	12	21	7	0	7
	Patki	11	6	17	4	4	8
	Siva'ap	2	1	3	0	0	0
IX	Chicken Hawk	3	4	7	1	0	1
	Crane	1	1	2	1	0	1
	Squash	1	0	1	3	2	5
	Totals	172	152	324	164	134	298

[153] Nequatewa, 1936, p. 110, footnote 50.

[154] According to Third Mesa informants, Coin used to act as interpreter for Lololoma. He is now living at New Oraibi where he serves as Crier chief, an office traditionally held in his clan (Greasewood).

[155] Compare Nequatewa, 1936, p. 111, notes 53, 54.

[156] In order to help the expelled faction, the Indian Agent at Keam's Canyon urged the Oraibi chief and his followers to permit the Hostiles to remove some of their belongings under carefully stipulated regulations. The terms of this arrangement are given in the Appendix, under the heading "Statement and Agreement."

[157] Quoted directly from an interview with Otto Loma-

vitu (Rabbit clan), one of the most fluent English-speaking, Christian Hopi at New Oraibi. The dance is mentioned in Nequatewa, 1936, p. 72.

[158] The raw figures which are used throughout this part of the discussion were obtained in the course of the census of Oraibi that has already been described on p. 51. Concerning each individual, questions were asked regarding Hostile or Friendly sympathies and action taken in 1906. All the statistics are approximate.

[159] The Oraibi Friendlies' figures include their Moenkopi supporters throughout the present analysis, as Moenkopi co-operated closely with Oraibi's chief, and the entire colony was Friendly.

Lomahongyoma and Yokioma counted 208 men and 179 women, a total of 387 adherents.[160] Before their struggle reached a climax the Friendlies lost 67, and the Hostiles 89 members through death. Consequently, when the two sides faced each other on September 7, 1906, there were 324 Progressives opposed to 298 Conservatives. These were distributed by clans as given in table 6.[161]

Even a hasty glance at table 6 shows at once that the split did not proceed entirely along clan lines, since each side drew followers from nearly every group in the village. Only those clans with which the main leaders were affiliated tended to act as units. Thus we find that 8 out of the 10 Bear people had joined the cause led by their clansmen Lololoma and Tawaqwaptiwa; that the Masau'u clan to which Lololoma's wife, Nakwavenka, and their seven children belonged, was entirely Friendly; and that the Katcina clan was completely Progressive through its close tie with the Parrot clan to which Tawawqaptiwa's wife, Nasingönsi, belonged.[162] Similarly, all of Lomahongyoma's Spider people and all of Yokioma's Kokop clanmates are to be found among the Conservatives; and the Water Coyote clan of which Lomahongyoma's wife, Qötcyamka, was a member, also favored the Hostiles by 29 to 16.[163] Hence, five of the principal clans involved in Oraibi's partition were Bear and Masau'u versus Spider, Kokop, and Water Coyote. A significant line of cleavage is revealed when we note their phratry bonds, for Bear opposed Spider from within Phratry II; and Masau'u, opposed Kokop and Water Coyote from within Phratry VI. Here then is a convincing demonstration of the weakness of phratry ties in Hopi society.

A question regarding clan lines comes next to mind. If the clans are such firmly bound, cohesive groups as has been previously suggested, why did so few of them act as units? The answer is found

TABLE 7. MOENKOPI FRIENDLIES, 1906.[164]

Phratry	Clan	Men	Women	Total
I	Rabbit	3	3	6
	Katcina	0	0	0
	Parrot	2	1	3
II	Bear	0	0	0
	Spider	0	0	0
III	Sand	0	0	0
	Snake	0	0	0
	Lizard	3	4	7
IV	Sun	1	4	5
	Eagle	2	0	2
V	Greasewood	4	2	6
	Bow	0	0	0
	Reed	2	7	9
VI	Masau'u	2	1	3
	Real Coyote	2	5	7
	Water Coyote	5	4	9
	Kokop	0	0	0
	Le	0	0	0
	Cedar	0	0	0
VII	Real Badger	0	0	0
	Gray Badger	2	0	2
	Navaho Badger	0	0	0
	Butterfly	0	0	0
VIII	Pikyas	5	5	10
	Patki	2	0	2
	Siva'ap	0	0	0
IX	Chicken Hawk	0	0	0
	Crane	0	0	0
	Squash	0	0	0
	Totals	35	36	71

to lie primarily in the workings of exogamy and matrilocal residence which disperse the male members of a clan among numerous unrelated households. It follows inevitably that in the case

---

[160] The data on Hostiles at Oraibi do not include the Chimopovy settlers who lived there temporarily. Informants at work on the census did not regard them as part of Oraibi's population.

[161] Moenkopi statistics are incorporated with those of Oraibi's Friendlies. For a separate study of Moenkopi affiliations, see table 7.

[162] It would have been closer to expectations if the Parrot clan were undivided, but, as we have shown on p. 81, even Lololoma's ceremonial father, Lomanaksu (Parrot), threw in his lot with the Hostiles. Nevertheless, Katcina is very close to Parrot, and the two are not infrequently confused.

[163] The Water Coyote group was divided because some of its members were Hostiles through the influence of Lomahongyoma's wife, but others supported the Friendlies through relationship with Kuyingwu, Lololoma's father.

Yokioma's wife had no influence in swaying her clanmates as did the spouses of the other leaders, because at the height of the trouble he was giving up his first wife Kuwankwapnim (Greasewood), and carrying on an intrigue with his second, Qötcavatca (Sun).

[164] This table deals only with Friendlies who had already moved to Oraibi's Moenkopi colony prior to the split in 1906.

of all permanent marriages, intimate bonds develop among husband, wife, and children. Accordingly, there are times when a man's theoretical attachment to his mother's (natal) household is really very much subordinated to his genuine interest in the members of his wife's household. It is in such cases that clan lines are over-ridden and clan cohesion notably weakened. Indeed, the situation at Oraibi shows a strong tendency for households (including male relatives by affinity) to remain together at the expense of clan solidarity. Out of 131 households for which data could be obtained, 61 were entirely Friendly, 48 were completely Hostile, and only 22 were divided.[165]

A further examination of household behavior during Oraibi's segmentation helps to illuminate the problem at hand. What may be called the typical condition was one in which a household contained several married daughters, all of whose husbands remained loyal to their wives and either stayed at Oraibi or moved to Hotevilla with their marital groups. For example, Yokioma's brother Kuiwisa (Kokop) lived with his wife Humikwapnim (Greasewood) in the fourth house from the west on the Sixth Street (chart VII). They had three married daughters, all of whose husbands, from the Gray Badger, Real Coyote, and Water Coyote clans, respectively, accompanied them when the household left for Hotevilla. On the other hand, Honapsi, a Friendly Navaho Badger woman who occupied the fourth house from the west on the First Street (chart VII), remained at Oraibi with her five married daughters and their husbands from the Patki, Mishongnovi Katcina, Rabbit, Parrot, and Masau'u clans.[166] Sometimes the typical condition was reversed

if a husband happened to have affiliations that drew him with exceptional strength to one faction or the other. In such cases a wife was apt to follow her husband's lead. Thus the brothers of Kuwannimptiwa (Sand), a prominent member of the Hostiles, were living with Reed and Pikyas wives, respectively, and apparently induced their wives' households to accompany them to Hotevilla. More outstanding still, is the case of Talashongsi, a Bear clanswoman closely related to Lololoma and Tawaqwaptiwa, who nevertheless followed her Conservative husband to Hotevilla. In the last analysis, so much more binding did household ties prove when compared with clan bonds, that there were only four instances in which married couples were separated on September 7, 1906, because they belonged to opposite parties.[167]

In view of the fact that certain clans "own" particular ceremonies, it is impossible to understand Oraibi's cleavage without examining the ceremonial aspects of the schism. In charts VIII and IX, therefore, we have tabulated the ceremonies to which all the members of the two parties belonged.[168] From a general comparison it appears that the Conservatives were the more devoted to religious observances, for the 208 male Hostiles held 319 ceremonial memberships, whereas 201 Friendly men held only 219.[169] More specifically, the affiliations in the Tribal Initiation help to show the division between the parties. Only Progressive men entered the Wuwutcim at Tawaovi, the kiva to which Lololoma took his Soyal ceremony after he was expelled from the Blue Flute kiva; and for the rest the Friendlies tended to go into the Wuwutcim at Hano kiva whose chief, Talasnimptiwa (Squash), was on their side.[170] The Hostiles, as is to be expected,

---

[165] Moenkopi households are included in the Friendly count, but the Hostile figures do not include the Chimopovy people. Note that data are available for only 131 of the 147 households listed on chart VI.

[166] Only the youngest daughter, Sivensi, did not live in her mother's house.

[167] One example illustrates the way in which nonmarital ties may operate to sever the bonds between a husband and wife even when they are in love with each other. Kiaro, a Sand woman, was a Hostile as were her mother and her brother, especially the latter who was married to a Kokop woman. Kiaro's husband was Qötcyamptiwa (Water Coyote) who was a Progressive because his father was chief at Tawaovi kiva in which the Friendlies celebrated their Soyal. Informants delight in telling how Qötcyamptiwa called in his wife for a last marital bout before letting her leave Oraibi on the day of

the split. Subsequently, each married another partner.

[168] Charts VIII and IX are based on the largest followings ever attributed to either faction, whether or not the individuals were alive in 1906. Moenkopi data are incorporated with Oraibi Friendlies' material, but the Hostile figures do not include the Chimopovy contingent. A separate study of Moenkopi's membership in Oraibi's ceremonies is given in chart X.

[169] It should not be forgotten that the Hopi permit a person to join several societies so that the totals of ceremonial affiliations exceed those of party membership.

The women's ceremonial statistics will not be analyzed because their societies are relatively unimportant. Note that their ceremonial ties show no division into party lines.

[170] Nine Friendlies joined the Wuwutcim at Hano kiva, as opposed to two Hostiles.

CHART VIII. CEREMONIAL AFFILIATIONS OF ORAIBI FRIENDLIES.

Phratry	Clan	Wuwtcim Tcu	Wuwtcim Hano	Wuwtcim Sakwalenvi	Wuwtcim Hawiovi	Wuwtcim Tawaovi	Snake	Antelope	Blue Flute	Gray Flute	Powamu	Momtcit	Kwan	IV	Tao	Miscellaneous (Men)	Maran	Oaqöl	Lakon	Powamu (W)	Miscellaneous (Women)
I	Rabbit		1	1	4	3	2			3	5	1	1	1	1	{1 Tob. Chief / 1 Oaqöl}	4	8	4	4	1 Gray Flute
	Katcina										3				3		1		1		1 Soyal
	Parrot			3	1	1					5	2	1		3	1 Oaqöl	3	3	4	3	
II	Bear					4	2	1*		2							2		1		2 Soyal
	Spider		3																		
III	Sand				4		2		1	1	2	2	1	1	1	3 Oaqöl	2	5	1		1 Snake
	Snake	1			1	1	2					2	1		1	3 Marau	1	1			1 Soyal
	Lizard																				
IV	Sun		1		2	6	4			1	1	1	1		1		4	2	1		
	Eagle			1														1			
V	Greasewood		1		4		2			1	1	1		2		1 Oaqöl	3	4	2	1	
	Bow			2	2		1		2		1	1		2			2	3			
	Reed				1												2				
VI	Masau'u		1	2	3		2			1	2	6	4			1 Soyal War Chief	5	15	6		1 Soyal
	Real Coyote			2	5					3			2				6	6	4		
	Water Coyote				1												2	1	1		
	Kokop																				
	Le																				
	Cedar																				
VII	Real Badger			3	1						8	1	1	3	1		1	3	1	2	
	Gray Badger				1						3										
	Navaho Badger																				
	Butterfly			1	3	1	1	1		2							4	2	1	1	
VIII	Pikyas	1	1	1	1	1	1		1†	5	1			1	1		5	6	4		1 Soyal
	Patki				1					2				2			3	2	2		2 Gray Flute
	Siva'ap																	1	1		
IX	Chicken Hawk		1				1			1			1				1	2	4		4 Gray Flute
	Crane									1								1	1		
	Squash									1											
	Totals	2	9	16	35	20	20	2	4	24	32	17	13	12	12	11	51	67	39	11	14

* Chief Tawaqwaptiwa joined the Antelope society as a young man, but later allowed his membership to lapse.

† After the split, this individual switched to Gray Flute.

Phratry	Clan	Wuwtcim Tcu	Wuwtcim Hano	Wuwtcim Sakwalenyi	Wuwtcim Hawiovi	Wuwtcim Tawovi	Snake	Antelope	Blue Flute	Gray Flute	Powamu	Momtcit	Kwan	IV	Tao	Miscellaneous (Men)	Marau	Oaqöl	Lakon	Powamu (W)	Miscellaneous (Women)
I	Rabbit	1		2			1	1	1		2	2		1	1	{1 Masau'u, 1 Katcina Chief}	4	6	5	1	1 Antelope
	Katcina	1														2 Lakon					
	Parrot	1		2	1			2	2		4			2	1		4	3	4	2	1 Soyal
II	Bear						1		1								4				10 B. Flute, 1 Soyal
	Spider			9			1	4	12			6		1	1						
III	Sand	2		3	3		2	1	1		1	4	3	6	2		4	11	4		1 Snake, 1 Antelope
	Snake	4		1			12		1			1	4	1			4	2			
	Lizard																				
IV	Sun										1		1	5	1		1	1	1		
	Eagle			4	1			2				2	2	1	2		3	2			
V	Greasewood	2		2					1		1		1	1	1		3	10	3		1 Blue Flute
	Bow	3		3	2		3		1	1*		3		1	1		16	6	5		
	Reed								3												
VI	Masau'u	3		3	1		8	2	1		1	1	1	2	2		9	1	12		
	Real Coyote	4		1	6		1		1			1		1	2		3	9			
	Water Coyote	1	1	1	1			1	3			6		2							
	Kokop	1			2			1				1									
	Le																				
	Cedar																				
VII	Real Badger	2		2	1		1	1	2		6	1	3	1	8	1 Marau	2	1	1	3	
	Gray Badger	2		2			1		2		15			6		1 Lakon	1	1	1	2	
	Navaho Badger										1							1			
	Butterfly			1																	
VIII	Pikyas	1	1	1			1	1	1			1	2	4				7	6	1	1 Antelope
	Patki	1					1							1				3		1	
	Siva'ap																				
IX	Chicken Hawk	2		2														1	1		
	Crane				1			1	1												
	Squash				1												1			1	
	Totals	31	2	37	20	0	32	14	42	1	32	29	16	36	21	6	55	65	44	10	17

(Men)   (Women)

* This individual had probably joined the Gray Flute prior to the split of 1906.

CHART IX. CEREMONIAL AFFILIATIONS OF ORAIBI HOSTILES.

		(Men)											(Women)*		
Phratry	Clan	Wuwutcim Hano	Wutuwcim Sakwalenvi	Wuwutcim Hawiovi	Wuwutcim Tawaovi	Snake	Gray Flute	Powamu	Momtcit	Kwan	Al	Tao	Marau	Oaqöl	Lakon
I	Rabbit			2						1			3	3	2
	Katcina											1	1		
III	Sand												1	3	
	Lizard			1	3	1	2		1			1	2	1	1
IV	Sun			1	2								5	2	1
V	Greasewood	2		6	3		1							1	
	Reed	1		1		1					1		5	3	
VI	Masau'u		1	2		1	1		1	1			2	6	2
	Real Coyote		1	3				1	2				1	3	1
	Water Coyote	2		4	2	1		1					3	2	1
VII	Real Badger		1					1					1	1	
VIII	Pikyas	1	1	1	3						1		5	5	2
	Patki			1			3		1			2	1	1	1
IX	Crane													1	1
	Totals	6	4	22	13	4	7	3	5	2	2	4	30	32	12

* 3 Katcina and 2 Real Badger women were in Powamu.

CHART X. MOENKOPI MEMBERS OF ORAIBI CEREMONIES.

showed a strong inclination for going into the Wuwutcim at Sakwalenvi which was owned by Lomahongyoma;[171] and as a second preference they joined the Wuwutcim at Tcu (Rattlesnake) kiva, whose head man, Masangöntiwa (Snake clan), acted as Snake society chief in the Conservative ceremonial cycle. Membership in several other ceremonies also shows a clear dichotomy. The Gray Flute had 24 Progressives to one Conservative because its chief, Lomahongva (Patki), was a staunch Friendly; but in the Blue Flute, Antelope, and Momtcit societies, which were owned entirely or in part by the Spider people, Hostiles predominated in the proportions of 42 to 4, 14 to 2, and 29 to 17, respectively.

Ceremonial bonds cross-cut clan ties as can be readily demonstrated by a study of the Flute societies, with the Gray Flute representing the Progressives and the Blue Flute standing for the Conservatives. The membership of the Gray Flute was made up of men from 13 different clans, and the Blue Flutes were drawn from 15 clans, with the Rabbit, Bear, Greasewood, and Patki clans contributing members to each of the rival ceremonies.[172]

If I may be permitted to add to the statistical data the impressions gained in the field and in the frequent handling of the raw material, I should say that the division of Oraibi proceeded somewhat as follows. First, the chiefs of the Bear and Spider clans, finding their phratry affiliations too weak to hold them together in the face of disputes over land and other strong differences of opinion, began a struggle for the control of the pueblo. Second, the members of their own clans quickly sided with their leaders. Third, the men of the conflicting clans brought into their respective parties their wives and children, thus emphasizing household ties and beginning to break up clan cohesion. The most important results of this step were to link the Masau'u clan with the Bear through the influence of Lololoma's wife; and to join the Water Coyote and the Spider clans on the basis of Lomahongyoma's marriage to a Water Coyote woman. Another notable consequence of conjugal fidelity was the addition of the Kokop clan to the Conservative faction.[173] Fourth, the women of the five leading clans in the struggle generally induced their husbands and other household relatives to join

[171] Sixteen Progressives are listed as belonging to the Wuwutcim at Sakwalenvi. In most cases this implies that they had joined prior to the start of Oraibi's schism. Sometimes these men transferred to another kiva, and sometimes they gave the ceremony up.

[172] The Flute membership lists again indicate the tendency for phratries to divide. In Phratry VI, 3 Real Coy- otes and one Masau'u are Gray Flute; and 11 Water Coyotes and 2 Kokops are Blue Flute. Also, in Phratry VII, 2 Real Badgers are Gray Flute while 2 Gray Badgers and 2 Navaho Badgers are Blue Flute. See charts VI and IX for these and similar cases.

[173] Lomahongyoma's uncle and nephew, both of whom were Spider men, were married to Kokop wives.

their cause, thus breaking down clan ties still more. Fifth, those men who were not closely related to the leaders either through descent or marriage made their choice of sides on the basis of their most cherished ceremonial connections; for, with the establishment by the Hostiles of a full ceremonial cycle to rival that of the Friendlies, all the villagers were forced to declare themselves unequivocally on one side or the other. Sixth, when this stage was reached the original clash between Hostiles and Friendlies resolved itself into a struggle between the participants in the Spider-led ceremonies and those in the Bear-controlled rituals. Seventh, wives and unmarried children tended to follow the leads of husbands and fathers. Eighth, after the entire populace had been divided, a climax occurred when the Friendlies expelled the Hostiles from Oraibi on September 7, 1906.[174]

Not long after they had celebrated their victory over the Conservatives, the Progressives were called upon to demonstrate their receptiveness to Americanism in a somewhat startling manner. Word came to Oraibi that Tawaqwaptiwa was to be deprived of his chieftainship temporarily, until he had gone to school and acquired a knowledge of the English language and American customs.[175] Arrangements were made to take the chief and Frank Siemptiwa, with their wives, and about twenty children, to Sherman Institute at Riverside, California. Tawaqwaptiwa, who was then in his thirties, did not relish the idea of going to school and protested that his recently torn village had not yet had time to readjust itself, but his complaints went unheeded and he was taken to Riverside in October 1906. In his absence, it was decreed by Francis E. Leupp, Commissioner of Indian Affairs, that Oraibi was to be "governed by a commission consisting of the teacher in charge of the day school, who shall preside, the old judge who represents the friendly faction[176]

... and a judge chosen from the hostile faction. . . ."[177] Leupp's arrangement was nominally accepted by Tawaqwaptiwa, but before leaving for California he put his brother, Bert Fredericks (Sakwaitiwa), in charge, and friction soon developed between "Judge" Qöyangainiwa and Bert Fredericks.

Meantime the Hostiles were in great distress at Hotevilla. Not only were they short-handed, but they were faced with a shortage of food that was bound to last for nearly a year, until they had sown and harvested their first crops.[178] To make matters worse, their chiefs soon began to quarrel. Yokioma boldly insisted on continuing without abatement his program of resistance to Americans and Hopi Progressives, but Lomahongyoma argued that they ought to attempt a reconciliation with the Friendlies. At this juncture a new leader arose in the person of Kuwannimptiwa (Sand clan), whose wife Qömamönim (Spider) was Lomahongyoma's niece, and whose father Nawungni'ima (Katcina) had served as Katcina chief for the Hostiles. Kuwannimptiwa supported Lomahongyoma's stand against Yokioma, and at last they resolved to take advantage of Tawaqwaptiwa's enforced absence at school to try to return to their old homes in Oraibi. With a small party of moderate Conservatives they left Hotevilla late in the fall of 1906 and reoccupied their former residences. The Friendlies mocked and jeered them, but they did their best to lead normal lives in spite of the taunts of their neighbors.

When the news of Lomahongyoma's return reached Tawaqwaptiwa in California, he was greatly incensed and prepared to order him and his followers driven out at once. The government authorities intervened, however, on the grounds that Tawaqwaptiwa was temporarily out of office, and coerced him into signing a document offering peace to the returned Hostiles on

---

[174] These eight steps may be regarded as a general summary of events, but the chronological implications should not be given too much emphasis. Then too it should not be forgotten that many people joined one side or the other because they favored or resented the introduction of American elements of culture, rather than on account of kin, clan or ceremonial connections.

The comparative weights of various kinship ties should be compared with the ratings on p. 13.

[175] Leupp, 1907, p. 85.

[176] The old judge was Qöyangainiwa (Badger), Village War chief, and the same man whose quarrel with a Katcina was described on p. 66.

[177] Leupp, 1907, p. 86.

[178] The day after the expulsion of the Hostiles, Tawaqwaptiwa signed an agreement with Superintendent Lemmon to the effect that he would permit his opponents to remove their property and to harvest their crops. See "Statement and Agreement" in the Appendix. Leupp, 1907, pp. 88, 89, relates that the Hostiles were moderately comfortable at Hotevilla, but Nequatewa, 1936, p. 76, and other Conservative sympathizers, insist that Tawaqwaptiwa deprived his opponents of their crops and failed to live up to his agreement.

For the later course of events at Hotevilla, see "The Rise of Hotevilla," in Part Three.

TABLE 8. MOVEMENTS FROM ORAIBI TO MOEN-
KOPI AND NEW ORAIBI AFTER 1906.

Phra-try	Clan	Moenkopi		New Oraibi	
		Men	Women	Men	Women
I	Rabbit	1	1	7	6
	Katcina	1	3	3	1
	Parrot	0	0	2	1
II	Bear	0	0	2	0
	Spider	0	0	0	0
III	Sand	0	2	1	1
	Snake	0	0	1	1
	Lizard	2	0	2	1
IV	Sun	2	3	3	3
	Eagle	0	0	0	0
V	Greasewood	7	1	4	0
	Bow	1	0	2	0
	Reed	1	0	0	1
VI	Masau'u	2	7	6	8
	Real Coyote	5	2	2	3
	Water Coyote	2	4	1	0
	Kokop	0	0	0	0
	Le	0	0	0	0
	Cedar	0	0	0	0
VII	Real Badger	2	1	4	2
	Gray Badger	0	0	1	0
	Navaho Badger	0	0	0	6
	Butterfly	0	0	0	1
VIII	Pikyas	3	5	1	0
	Patki	1	1	4	5
	Siva'ap	0	0	2	0
IX	Chicken Hawk	0	0	2	3
	Crane	0	1	0	0
	Squash	0	0	1	0
	Totals	30	31	51	43

condition that Lomahongyoma "stay out of the Flute ceremony."[179] Tawaqwaptiwa's capitulation had little effect at home, for his brother, Bert Fredericks, took the lead in hounding Lomahongyoma's party and finally drove them out of Oraibi once more, in October, 1907. Again they turned north on Third Mesa, but this time they stopped at another place known for its springs, Bakavi, about a mile southeast of Hotevilla. Kuwannimptiwa now took charge,[180] and realizing how little chance his group had of surviving the coming winter without help, he shrewdly professed a great love of Americans and thus secured government aid in the construction of a small but well-built pueblo, of which he became the undisputed Village chief.[181]

Upon Tawaqwaptiwa's return to Oraibi about 1910 he exhibited a quality of character which served to irritate his people and to cause them to drift away from the pueblo. From all accounts he seems to have been quarrelsome, stubborn, vindictive, and unusually licentious.[182] When some of the villagers began to adopt American ways and to entertain the notion of accepting Christianity, Tawaqwaptiwa decided that such behavior was contrary to the teachings of his "uncles" and decreed that all converts must leave Oraibi.[183] The result was a slow stream of emigrants moving to Kikötcmovi at the southern foot of Third Mesa. In due time the Christian Hopi were followed by others who favored increased Americanization without conversion, and by still others who sought only to escape from Tawaqwaptiwa and the atmosphere of incessant bickering that had come to mark life at Old Oraibi. By 1911 there were so many settlers at Kikötcmovi that it began to take on the appearance of an independent village and came to be known as New Oraibi (see table 8). The inhabitants of New Oraibi are the most

[179] This document is given as "Letter from Sherman Institute" in the Appendix. Tawaqwaptiwa maintains that he flatly refused to sign until threatened with the complete loss of his chieftainship. For the official version of the episode, reference may be made to Leupp, 1907, pp. 90, 91.

[180] Evidently, Lomahongyoma was now a dispirited old man who had hoped to be allowed to die peacefully in his native village. At no time does Lomahongyoma appear to have favored a split which might have caused him to leave Oraibi.

[181] Crane, 1926, p. 87, writes ". . . but for the prompt assistance of the Government Agent, the whole lot . . . would have perished." Compare Nequatewa, 1936, pp. 75, 76. For the original composition of Bakavi's populace,

see "Clan and Ceremonial groups at Bakavi in 1907" in table 10; and for later developments consult "The Ceremonial Cycle at Bakavi" in Part Three.

[182] Nequatewa, 1936, pp. 74, 75, reports that Tawaqwaptiwa molested the women who had returned from Hotevilla, but this is impossible as he was at Sherman Institute while they were at Oraibi. Nevertheless, by Tawaqwaptiwa's own admission, he was very "powerful" with the "ladies" in his younger days.

[183] I could not determine just how this decree was made nor how it was enforced. It certainly did not originate in a piece of formal legislation, and its enforcement was probably never challenged in open defiance. Consult table 8, "Movements from Oraibi to Moenkopi and New Oraibi after 1906."

Americanized Hopi at Third Mesa, and because of the comparatively large number of Christians among them, the villagers have limited their ceremonial life to minor rituals such as Katcina dances and Buffalo or Butterfly dances.

Another population movement away from Old Oraibi was in the direction of Moenkopi. To this ancient farming colony came those villagers who preferred to live apart from Tawaqwaptiwa without severing their ties with the mother pueblo (table 8). In secular matters the Moenkopi colonists are led by the Oraibi chief's "lieutenant," Frank Siemptiwa (Pikyas). As for their ritual life, they have built three kivas from which they stage Katcina dances and other minor rites,[184] but for major ceremonies such as the Soyal or the Powamu they come to Oraibi and participate in that village's ceremonial cycle.

Since 1906, when it lost half its inhabitants in one great exodus to Hotevilla, Oraibi's population has been steadily diminishing as a consequence of the drifts to Bakavi, New Oraibi, and Moenkopi. In November, 1933, a count of the populace showed that only 112 individuals, counting tiny babies, were still living in the village.[185] Some of these were close relatives of Tawaqwaptiwa or his wife, a few had stayed on because of genuine loyalty to their traditional Village chief, and the rest had remained through sheer inertia. Until 1935 there was an attempt to maintain the Soyal and a partial cycle of rites, but gradually more and more ceremonies were allowed to lapse. According to Tawaqwaptiwa, the time is quickly approaching when he will lose his entire following

[184] The Moenkopi kivas are Kuwanovi, Istiya, and Kawaiovi.

and will remain alone at Oraibi with his ceremony (Soyal). All other rites, dances, and prayers will be given up, and there will come a great famine,

TABLE 9. POPULATION OF ORAIBI, 1933.

Phratry	Clan	Male	Female	Total
I	Rabbit	5	8	13
	Parrot	7	12	19
II*	Bear	4	2	6
III	Sand	6	1	7
IV	Sun	4	7	11
V	Greasewood	6	8	14
	Bow	1	0	1
	Reed	0	1	1
VI	Masau'u	2	8	10
	Real Coyote	4	1	5
VII	Real Badger	2	0	2
	Gray Badger	3	4	7
VIII	Pikyas	4	8	12
	Patki	1	0	1
	Totals	49	60	109

* A Carrying-strap woman and two children from Chimopovy were living at Oraibi in 1933. They belong in Phratry II, but are not included in the Bear figures.

after which the full ceremonial calendar will be revived. Such does Tawaqwaptiwa regard Old Oraibi's destiny to be, and complacently he awaits its fulfillment.

[185] See table 9, "Population of Oraibi, 1933."

CHAPTER VII

ORAIBI ETHNOLOGY AND PUEBLO ARCHAEOLOGY

IN OUR preceding chapter we went into the record of Oraibi's disintegration in considerable detail because the situation seemed to provide a good opportunity for a study of cultural dynamics in a contemporary primitive society. At the same time, there is a strong likelihood that the events of the past few decades at Oraibi may throw light on an archaeological problem of long standing. All students of the Southwest have been puzzled by the quick abandonment, not long after their original construction, of some of the large communal villages that mark the Great Period of Pueblo development. In my opinion the recent history of Oraibi contains the clue to the solution of the prehistoric puzzle.

Today when we visit Hotevilla, Bakavi, Moenkopi, and New Oraibi, we are in a position to know a good deal about their origins, and we are fully aware that all four towns are direct offshoots of the old pueblo of Oraibi which is now fast crumbling into ruin. If we are to appreciate how this knowledge may serve to interpret an ancient state of affairs, we must shift our perspective and try to view the situation as it would appear four or five centuries from now if all the towns were deserted and all written documents pertaining to the split of 1906 were lost.

The archaeologist of the future, let us assume, will some day unearth on the southeastern extremity of a mesa in Arizona, the remains of a large, ruined village (Old Oraibi). His evidence will clearly indicate that it once supported a thriving population, and that the period of occupancy came to an abrupt close in the twentieth century after several hundred years of continuous habitation; but in the archaeological record there would be no hint of the reason for the town's abandonment. If our investigator were to extend his field of operations northward for about six or seven miles along the top of the same mesa, he would come upon a pair of pueblos, side by side within a mile of each other (Hotevilla and Bakavi); were he to search the southern foot of the mesa he would discover still another town site (New Oraibi); and if his reconnaissances took him about forty miles westward along the plains he would locate a fourth abandoned town (Moen-

kopi). When they had been completely excavated and their contents studied, all four of these pueblos would prove to be smaller and later than the great village on the southeastern end of the mesa top; all would yield signs of having been founded nearly simultaneously; all would supply abundant skeletal and material data to assure the archaeologist that they had been inhabited by very closely related peoples; and all would show an undoubted connection with the large town nearby.

So far our future investigator would have but little trouble in piecing together his evidence, but what of the facts that lie beyond the reach of his spade? What would he know of the true reasons for the abandonment of the archaic large pueblo and the foundation of the four scattered, more recent, smaller towns? Would he not be forced to invoke as explanations the old triumvirate of pressure from nomadic enemies, unfavorable climatic changes, and devastating plagues?

This, in brief, is the position in which modern archaeologists sometimes find themselves as they examine the Pueblo ruins throughout the Southwest. In this area one of the most puzzling phenomena is the degree of mobility exhibited by its ancient inhabitants. As Dr. Kidder has phrased it, "For some reason, not yet clearly understood, the Pueblos ancient and modern were very prone to shift from one dwelling place to another, and a site once abandoned was seldom reoccupied. Although their houses were of the most permanent construction, and their agricultural life should have tended to render them solidly sedentary, they moved about to a surprising extent."[1] Dr. Parsons too has discussed the problem of Pueblo mobility. "Although attached to their houses or town," she has recently written, "the Pueblos are far from being absolutely sedentary peoples. They have the house or town living habit, but they . . . will move from house to house, new or old, quite freely. . . . This is true today and must have been so in the past, according to historical and archaeological records. The very great number of ruins in the Pueblo territory . . . can only be accounted for as the result of semi-nomadism. The early Pueblos were nomads in

[1] A. V. Kidder, in his Introduction to Guthe, 1925, p. 3

96

rms not of days or seasons but of decades or enturies."[2] Generally speaking, the main explanation advanced by analysts of this peculiar Pueblo "nomadism" is that their settlements were constantly being disrupted by enemies, drought, or pestilence.

Another puzzling feature of the prehistory of the Southwest is the quick collapse of the Great Period in the San Juan drainage within a comparatively short time of its inception. It is the consensus of American archaeologists that the so-called "classic phase" of the Great Period in that area began about 900 A.D. and ended between 1200 and 1350.[3] As Kidder diagnoses this condition, "It seems ordained that periods of high achievement shall be followed by years of slackening and even atrophy. So it was with the Pueblos. The years between about 1100 A.D. and the Spanish invasions of 1540 were evidently a time of tribulation. The formerly prosperous communities of the North and the South were abandoned, the population shrank, the arts degenerated. . . . What brought about this decline is not surely known, droughts, inter-tribal wars, pestilences, inbreeding, may all have been in part responsible; but its principal cause was probably the ever-increasing attacks of nomadic enemies."[4] Once more Dr. Parsons' viewpoint accords very closely with Dr. Kidder's. In her opinion, "Tree records show that from 1276 to 1299 there was a severe drought in the Southwest which contributed to the abandonment of the great pueblos in the North and a movement southward. . . ."[5] In addition to drought, Dr. Parsons has suggested that many villages may have been deserted in the past on account of "War or dread of war,"[6] "Internal feud,"[7] or "Famine."[8]

Leaving aside "Internal feud" for the moment, it is hard to accept the conventional diagnoses as thorough or definitive. With regard to the influence of war, for example, we find Kidder's suggestion that it was "the principal cause" of Pueblo desertions, contradicted by Roberts' postulate, on the basis of present indications, "that a constantly augmented pressure from the wilder, more nomadic Indians of the borderlands forced

the Pueblos in self-defense, to gather in populous centers."[9] In this case of disagreement between doctors, logic seems to favor Roberts' position; for while it was probably a great advantage for the Pueblos to have congregated for purposes of defense, it would have been an undoubted disadvantage for them to have scattered under hostile pressure. Nor can we readily assume that the Pueblos were actually forced to disperse because they were driven out of their large centers by enemies, for Kidder himself has pointed out that "Apparently the roaming tribes seldom waged definite wars against the Pueblos, nor did they often carry out organized attacks on their towns."[10]

There are equally fundamental difficulties in the way of accepting drought and pestilence as explanations for the abandonment of the great pueblos. As a matter of fact these "explanations" have come to have as little meaning in archaeological reports as that comfortless phrase "ceremonial significance." With regard to the part played by drought, I can do no better than to quote the words of Dr. Roberts. "The theory is frequently advanced," he has written, "that the abandonment of the outlying districts may be attributed wholly to a progressive and intensive desiccation of the entire region. It would seem, however, that there had been no catastrophic climatic change in the area since the days when the Pueblos attained their fullest development. Hence, such natural phenomena should be considered only in the light of a contributing factor."[11]

The effects of pestilence have likewise been greatly over-emphasized in the past, for there is abundant historical evidence to show that the Hopi, for instance, have stubbornly clung to their villages in spite of epidemics that have several times threatened them with extinction. In 1780 Governor Anza found their territory in such a wretched condition from "hunger and pestilence" that he reported the Hopi tribe to be "in the last stages of its extermination."[12] Still, he could persuade only a few families to forsake their homes, and most of the chiefs begged Anza "not to force any of their people to abandon their pueblos, as most of them desired to end their lives there. . . ."[13]

[2] Parsons, 1939, p. 14 and footnote †.
[3] Roberts, 1930, p. 11.
[4] A. V. Kidder in his Introduction to Guthe, 1925, pp. 10.
[5] Parsons, 1939, p. 1026.
[6] Parsons, 1939, p. 14.
[7] Parsons, 1939, p. 15.
[8] Parsons, 1939, p. 16.

[9] Roberts, 1930, p. 5.
[10] Kidder, 1924, p. 43.
[11] Roberts, 1930, p. 6.
However, it must be admitted that scarcity of water was undoubtedly one of the major factors in the abandonment of the northern pueblos during the great drought of 1276 to 1299.   [12] Thomas, 1932, p. 237.
[13] Thomas, 1932, p. 232.

Again and again in more recent times have the Hopi been ravaged by smallpox and other diseases, but there is not a single instance on record of their having abandoned a pueblo on that account. Indeed, when Leo Crane was superintendent of the Hopi Reservation, he complained that it was impossible to check the smallpox epidemic of 1898 because the Hopi rejected help and preferred "to die unassisted by aliens."[14]

To deny that war, drought, and disease were the motivating causes of the speedy decay of the Pueblos, is not to deny that all three have played very important contributory parts; but if we are to make any progress towards the final solution of our problem we must stop relying on standard "explanations" and seek in all directions for particular and perhaps more valid interpretations.[15] On the basis of a study of Third Mesa's recent history, it seems to me that the phenomena of Pueblo mobility and Pueblo decline are interrelated, that both are caused by the same sets of factors, and that they may be more fruitfully studied as sociological rather than ecological problems. This is by no means an original suggestion, for long ago Dr. Parsons noted a direct connection between Pueblo social organization and the termination of the Great Period. Writing in 1922 Dr. Parsons called attention to the disintegration of Oraibi as "an instance of that process of tribal or town division which has probably been a character of Pueblo Indian life for centuries. The Oraibi split was a consequence of friction from contact with white culture. . . . *But, if Southwestern ruins say anything, long before the advent of the Conquistadores the habit of town splitting must have developed.*"[16] (The italics are mine.)

Dr. Roberts has expressed a similar opinion. In speaking of enemy pressure as one factor in the ultimate collapse of the Great Period, he says, "The outside enemies were probably aided by factional strife within the villages and by discord between the various centers. There likely was little co-operation between communities, and concerted defensive measures probably were lacking."[17]

There is excellent authority, then, for treating our problem as a sociological one, and in order to focus attention on the main issue it may be well to phrase it as a direct question. "What is the particular aspect of their social organization that led the Pueblo Indians to abandon their large villages and to move into smaller communities?" The answer seems to be inherent in the manner in which Pueblo society developed.

At an early stage the ancestors of the Pueblo groups appear to have lived "for a protracted period of time in small communities scattered throughout the region. In the northern part of the area, the culture nucleus, the dwelling was mainly of the form called single clan or unit structures."[18] This terminology, first employed by Prudden,[19] Fewkes,[20] and other scholars, implies an early recognition of a connection between sociology and ecology in the Southwest, a subject which has received its fullest treatment to date in a recent article by Dr. Steward. In Steward's judgment, "It is difficult to reconcile the division of the early villages into small house clusters with any other social unit than unilateral lineage or band."[21] A discussion of the exact nature of the social groups which resided in the little settlements of the early Pueblo period is irrelevant to our present argument, but it is important to stress the fact that at one time the Pueblo peoples were living in small, probably autonomous, villages within which the social system seems to have been dominated by units no larger than the clan. Later on, perhaps under the pressure of enemy raids, the small communities found it to their advantage to gather into large towns. This step brings us to the crux of the entire problem, and I venture the opinion that while the material culture of the Pueblos gradually became adjusted to an enlarged scale, their social organization failed to keep pace with it.[22] As Steward puts it, "During the growth of communal houses, which begins in Pueblo II, the formerly separated small groups are amalgamated, *but do not lose their social and ceremonial integrity.*"[23] (Italics are mine.)

[14] Crane, 1926, p. 150.

[15] Bryan, 1941, pp. 238–242, likewise expresses dissatisfaction with current explanations and advances the hypothesis that arroyo cutting has had much to do with bringing the Great Period in the San Juan to a close.

[16] Parsons, *et al.*, 1922, p. 283.

[17] Roberts, 1932, p. 11.

[18] Roberts, 1932, p. 10.

[19] Prudden, 1903, pp. 234, 235, *et passim*. See also Prudden, 1914, p. 34.

[20] Fewkes, 1917b, p. 411.

[21] Steward, 1937, p. 99.

[22] A material instance of Pueblo unwillingness to adapt themselves to new conditions is the retention of underground structures for religious chambers. Consult Roberts 1932, p. 9.

[23] Steward, 1937, p. 96. Compare the idea of coalescence without loss of integrity which Fewkes discusses in regard to the growth of Hopi religion. Fewkes, 1879d p. 145.

There, I believe, we have the heart of the whole matter, for the huge pueblos failed to endure precisely because they continued to operate with social structures that were best adapted to small communities. As the chapter on "The Amorphous Hopi State" has shown, the preservation of powerful clan ties prevented the development of strong, central, village administrations; and the fact that the lesser social units successfully retained their integrity is ample proof that the pueblos were never welded into homogeneous wholes. Consequently, the large towns were constantly faced with the possibility of internal division. That the potentiality was not invariably realized is due to the joint action of exogamy and ceremonial co-operation which developed cross-ties strong enough to bind villages together for varying lengths of time. When, however, exceptionally powerful disruptive forces manifested themselves, the pueblos could not withstand their shock and ultimately collapsed in the manner of Oraibi. Their inhabitants then disbanded and went off to found numerous smaller settlements which were more congenial to their way of life. That is why the period of Pueblo decline "stands out distinctly as one which saw innumerable small bands tramping hither and yon in search of a suitable place in which to begin anew."[24]

Thus does one set of sociological factors serve to account for the abandonment of the great pueblos, the large number of Pueblo ruins, and the puzzling phenomenon of Pueblo mobility. By analogy with what took place on Third Mesa, when Hotevilla, Bakavi, Moenkopi, and New Oraibi were founded as the result of intra-village quarrels that have drained Old Oraibi of virtually its entire populace,[25] it is highly probable that the Great Period of the Pueblos in the San Juan district was quickly terminated not so much by the operation of external forces as by internal disintegration arising from a weakly-knit social structure.[26]

---

[24] Roberts, 1930, p. 6.

[25] Although Oraibi is the only example here cited, its experience has been duplicated at other Hopi villages. On First Mesa, according to Fewkes, 1894a, p. 414, and Parsons, 1936b, pp. 943–944, the "suburb" of Sitcumovi was supposed to have been established by malcontents from Walpi; and on Second Mesa, it is reported by Hargrave, 1930, p. 3, that the little town of Shipaulovi was founded by a dissentient group from Chimopovy soon after 1680.

[26] In Parsons, et al., 1922, p. 283, Fewkes expresses the opinion that divisions such as Oraibi's "Probably occurred in pueblo migration history again and again . . . ." For a summary of non-Hopi town splits, consult Parsons, 1939, p. 15.

Dr. White has drawn my attention to the fact that in virtually all the historic feuds one of the major factors was a dispute over the acceptance of foreign cultural influences. However, there is no reason to believe that other sociologic causes may not have been equally effective in bringing about schisms in prehistoric times.

PART TWO

HOPI CEREMONIALISM

CHAPTER VIII

THE BASIC PATTERN AND UNDERLYING CONCEPTS OF HOPI CEREMONIES

THE BASIC PATTERN

'N EVERY Hopi pueblo the populace is organized into a number of secret societies, each which is responsible for the conduct of a single remony (*wimi*);[1] and a particular clan has arge of each society and its associated ritual. iis means that care of the essential sacred maials and selection of officers are the duty and ivilege of the controlling clan.[2] There is a posiility that at one stage of Hopi cultural developent the entire membership of a religious society as drawn from the proprietary clan, but in odern times it has been customary for ordinary rticipants, as well as minor officials, to be seted from any clan in a village.[3]

As a rule, the head man of a clan is the chief of group's society and holds the most important ject pertaining to the performance of his rites. iis is a fetish (*tiponi*) consisting of an ear of rn, feathers, and a variety of outer wrappings.[4] is called the "mother" or the "heart" of a remony, and its possession marks a society's in leader. The *tiponi* is highly venerated,[5] and ien not in use it is secreted in *the* clan house in stody of the clan's head woman. Altar parts, tted gourds, and other paraphernalia are someies entrusted to secondary officials and may be red in their clan houses.

There is a fixed time of the year during which ociety is expected to celebrate the observances trusted to its care. The opening dates of some uals are determined by the sun's position on the rizon at daybreak; others are announced when a certain moon appears; and a few begin when a given number of days have elapsed after the completion of the preceding ritual.[6] Those leaders whose ceremonies are dated by solar observation are notified at the proper times by the Village Sun Watcher,[7] but other society chiefs must determine their own starting dates.

A few important rites are conducted in the main houses of the clans in charge, but it is far more customary to have the members of a society assemble in a kiva for their observances. Hopi kivas are rectangular ceremonial chambers built underground and oriented approximately north and south. They are entered through a hatchway in the roof, by means of a stout ladder that projects a few feet beyond the opening and comes to rest almost in the center of the room beneath.[8] The floor is built on two levels, the area south of the ladder being raised several inches above the northern portion. As a rule the raised southern part of the floor space is smaller and is reserved for spectators and ritual activities of slight importance, while the lower or main floor is somewhat larger and is the scene of the more significant performances. The kiva ladder rests on the upraised section, near its juncture with the lower level. On the main floor, just north of the ladder's base, there is a small scooped-out fireplace;[9] and along the east, north, and west sides there run stone banquettes about two feet high. These appear solid but are actually hollow, and are used to conceal sacred objects from profane view. In the middle of the main floor there is a small cavity,

---

As some writers employ the term "*wimi*" it may mean ier ceremony or ceremonial object. Sometimes two or re societies combine to perform a single rite, but in h cases the members of the co-operating groups are t distinct.

Consult "The Ritual Calendar at Oraibi," in the Apdix, for a list of ceremonies and their controlling clans.

This point of view is discussed in Fewkes, 1898b, p. .

Fewkes suggests that "the *tiponi* was originally a rve ear of seed-corn kept with reverential care as a resort if all other seed failed." Fewkes, 1901b, p. , footnote 1.

[5] According to Parsons, 1936b, p. 781, each chief was supposed to have had a *tiponi* in the Underworld prior to the Emergence.

[6] The time schedule of the major rites is given in "The Ritual Calendar at Oraibi," in the Appendix.

[7] For a discussion of the Hopi calendar and of the duties of the Sun Watcher, consult Titiev, 1938c, pp. 39, 40, and fig. 1 on p. 41; and Parsons, 1939, pp. 493, 497, *et passim*.

[8] A full account of kiva construction and arrangement occurs in Mindeleff, V., 1891, p. 111 ff.

[9] In recent years cast iron stoves have replaced the oldfashioned fireplaces in most kivas.

representing the *sipapu*,[10] which is hidden with a wooden plug when not in use.

Kivas are owned by the clans whose members took the initiative in building them. In the event that a kiva has fallen into disuse, its ownership may be transferred to whatever clan is most instrumental in its repair. A kiva is named at its dedication in some fashion that refers to its controlling clan; and not infrequently the head man of the clan, who is generally leader of his group's ceremony, is at the same time chief of the kiva in which his society meets.[11] A kiva chief has several ritual duties attendant on his office, such as acting as father of the Katcinas on certain occasions, smoking formally with messengers who come to announce impending ceremonies, and sponsoring the Niman (Homegoing) dance in the years when that obligation, which rotates annually, falls to his kiva. In addition, he is leader of many secular pursuits which are performed by kiva units, including communal hunts and cotton-spinning bees, and it is up to him to see that the chamber is kept in good repair and is well stocked with firewood during the winter months. Stephen makes reference to a system of dual leadership at Walpi,[12] but this does not seem to have been practiced regularly on Third Mesa. However, a kiva head, like any other dignitary, might choose and train a successor, and this man would serve as an assistant as long as the actual incumbent remained active. This may be the custom to which Stephen refers.

Except on special occasions, such as on nights when there are to be Katcina dances or when the women's ceremonies are going on, females are barred from the kivas, but boys begin to frequent these chambers as soon as they have passed their Katcina initiations. Usually, a boy associates himself with the kiva to which his ceremonial Katcina father belongs, but in later life he transfers his allegiance to that kiva which houses hi particular branch of the Tribal Initiation rites.

All major rituals that are performed in kiva are of nine days' duration. Sometimes, howeve as in years when new members are admitted to th Tribal Initiation ceremony, some observances ar held over a period of 17 days. These extended per formances generally begin with a brief prelim nary meeting known as Paholawu (Prayer-stick making), which usually occurs eight days befor the main rites begin. At this time the society' officers come together for a formal smoke, t prepare prayer-feathers and other offerings,[13] an to arrange for the public announcement of the ceremony. Ordinarily, these gatherings take plac in the controlling clan's house, but occasionall they occur in a kiva. At their conclusion some c the prayer-objects are placed at designated shrine by special messengers, and others are turned ove to the town's Crier chief (Tca'akmongwi), wh deposits them at the following daybreak in shrine on the housetop from which he makes a announcement of the impending observances.[14]

When the eight intervening days have gone by the leaders go to the kiva which houses their cere mony and erect a standard (*na'atsi*) south of th entrance hatch, or suspend one from a rung of th kiva ladder, thus giving notice that a secre society is in session. From this time on, none b members of the appropriate group may enter th kiva,[15] and all participants must observe tabus c salt, fat, and sexual indulgence.

The first day of nine-day performances is calle Yungya'a (Entering), and is generally so unin portant that only rarely does the full membersh of a society assemble. The next eight days ma be divided for convenience into halves, with th latter period usually the more significant. Th days of the first half are known only by ordin numbers, but all the days in the second half a

---

[10] The *sipapu* is supposedly the opening through which mankind first climbed out upon the earth. See Parsons, 1939, pp. 309, 310, *et passim*.

[11] For a list of kivas and information regarding their owners and the ceremonies which they house, see "Oraibi Kivas Prior to 1900," and "Kivas and Their Associated Shrines," in the Appendix. The question of kiva ownership is also discussed in Parsons, 1936b, p. xliii.

[12] Parsons, 1936b, p. 210.

[13] For details of prayer-offering manufacture see Voth, 1903a, pp. 274–281; Parsons, 1936b, p. 30, *et passim*; Solberg, 1906, pp. 49–63; and Fewkes, 1897a, pp. 196–199.

[14] The town Crier chief is the one who serves in the

Soyal. He is an important religious officer, known as t "mouth of the Village chief," who announces the Soy; Tribal Initiation, Niman, Snake, Flute, Marau, Oaqöl, a Lakon ceremonies, as well as communal enterprises a planting parties for chiefs. At Oraibi he calls out from t Kele clan house, sometimes speaking in a low voice show that he is addressing the Cloud People rather than t villagers. This official is not to be confused with lay crie who announce bartering and other secular functions. Cor pare Fewkes, 1895a, p. 275.

[15] Those who trespass on a kiva where secret rites a being held are forced to join the society in charge. Cor pare Parsons, 1939, p. 113, footnote *, *et passim*.

specially designated. The nomenclature for the nine days is as follows:

First day...........Yungya'a (Entering)
Second day.........Suctala (First day)[16]
Third day..........Löctala (Second day)
Fourth day.........Paictala (Third day)
Fifth day..........Nalöctala (Fourth day)
Sixth day..........Suckahimu'u (Once not anything)[17]
Seventh day........Piktotokya (Piki providing)[18]
Eighth day.........Totokya (Food[?] providing)[19]
Ninth day..........Tikive (Dance day)[20]

As a rule, the first seven days of the above schedule are given over entirely to esoteric, kiva ritual; the eighth day sometimes combines public activities with private; and the ninth day is generally featured by a public exhibition, commonly called a dance. Despite the zeal with which the various societies guard their rites from each other, there is very little difference of procedure among them, and although the order in which particular acts are performed may vary widely they all tend to conform to a regular pattern.[21]

The greater part of the secret ritual in the kivas is devoted to smoking, singing, and praying to the accompaniment of shell or gourd rattles, and the manufacture of offerings. These are deposited at appropriate shrines, and each society usually delegates one or two of its members to make four decreasing circuits around the village on successive days, during which prayer-objects are put down at a number of sacred places. Sometimes living actors impersonate cultus figures, and each society's repertoire never fails to include the erection of altars (*pongya*), the making of sand paintings, and the preparation of medicine-water (*nakuyi*).

Hopi altars are made in two parts: a reredos consisting of a series of slabs affixed to an upright frame, and a group of objects set out on the floor before it. The reredos is comprised of "a number of wooden slats and clay tiles or flat stones,"[22] on which are painted symbolic or realistic representations of maize, rainclouds, lightning, heavenly bodies, sacred animals, and cultus heroes. It is set vertically with its base resting on the kiva floor, and in front of it are placed *tiponis*, effigies of sky and earth gods and of cult patrons, and "a medicine bowl around which are radially arranged certain objects.... This bowl ... is placed on a low pile of sand, upon which are drawn six radiating lines of sacred meal representing the six directions.... On each of these lines of meal is an ear of corn corresponding to the direction with which it is associated ... viz., north, yellow; west, blue or green; south, red; east, white; above, black; below, speckled."[23] Various other objects such as bird feathers, aspergills (*makwanpi*), bits of crystal, small stone animal figures (*tohopkom*), and vari-colored pebbles are also arranged in the six directions.

The making of medicine is a co-operative activity. While the officers of the society are busy with the actual concoction, other members sing sacred songs and rattle or beat the floor in order to notify the people in the Underworld of what is taking place. For this purpose, the *sipapu* is usually uncovered at such times. The water which forms the base of the preparation is fetched from a special spring in a netted gourd (*mongwikuru*). As it is being poured into the medicine bowl, various items are picked up from the six-direction altar and dropped into it at stated intervals during an accompanying song cycle. Sometimes a ray of light is reflected into the mixture with a crystal;[24] sometimes smoke is blown into it;[25] and almost invariably some one kneels and whistles into the liquid with an instrument made of eagle or turkey bone (*totoq'pi*).[26]

In fashioning a sand mosaic it is customary for one of the society's chiefs to take charge, al-

[16] Owing to the fact that in native opinion the rites begin on the day after the initial assembly, the Hopi count runs a day behind ours. See Voth, 1901, p. 84, footnote *.

[17] The meaning of this designation has never been satisfactorily explained.

[18] Stephen names this day *komoktotokya* (wood carrying sleeps). Parsons, 1936b, p. 162.

[19] Although Stephen calls this day *totokya*, as did Voth's and my own informants on Third Mesa, he translates it "sleeps." Parsons, 1936b, p. 162.

[20] Pigumnovi (Porridgefeast) is one way that Stephen terms this day. Parsons, 1936b, p. 162.

[21] Compare Parsons, 1939, pp. 476–478.

[22] Fewkes, 1901b, p. 216.

[23] Fewkes, 1901b, p. 215.

[24] Reflecting sunlight into the water may be interpreted as a prayer for fertility. There are several myths which describe how women become impregnated when a sun ray falls on the vulva. See Stephen, 1929, p. 13, *et passim*.

[25] Blowing smoke into water is interpreted as a direct appeal to the home of the Clouds.

[26] Blowing on a bone whistle is a means of summoning the deities. One of the Hopi myths tells how a man who sought help from the gods blew on a bone whistle and "immediately a great noise was heard and a small man entered the room. This was Cotukvnangwuu, the Star and Cloud deity, living in the sky." Voth, 1905b, p. 127.

though he may be assisted by one or two other men. As a rule the painting is laid out in freehand but mechanical aids are occasionally used. The maker sifts some fine dry sand to the thickness of about half an inch as a field, and on this he drops lines of vari-colored sands or pulverized earth by letting them trickle in a fine stream between the thumb and forefinger.[27] The subjects portrayed are similar to those depicted on the reredos of an altar.

The kiva rites generally culminate on the eighth day, during which the altars are dismantled and the sand paintings effaced. The next day, practically the full membership of the society appears in public, often brilliantly costumed, for an exhibition which is popularly called a dance, although this term is not a very apt description of some of the performances. After the dance is over, celebrants who must continue to observe prohibitions on fat, salt, and sexual indulgence for four more days, sleep in the kiva to avoid temptation, and then resume normal secular lives.

Initiation into any secret society is open to all who are of the proper sex and age, and in some cases it is even possible for women to join men's organizations and for males to enroll in the women's ceremonies. To enter a society, a candidate must choose a ceremonial father or mother from among the members of the group. The novice (kelehöya, little chicken hawk) receives an ear of corn and sometimes a head scratcher. Early in the performance he enters the kiva with his sponsor and observes the esoteric rites for the first time. On or about the fourth day his head is washed in yucca suds and he is given a new name by his ritual parent. Members of a clan which control a ceremony are expected to join that society, but there is no compulsion in the matter.

Nearly every one of the secret societies has a particular form of illness which it controls. This is called its "whip" (wuvata) and is inherent in the sacred paraphernalia employed by an order.[28] The "whip" afflicts all who trespass on ceremonial secrets, but it may also affect persons and things that come into contact with religious objects even in legitimate ways. Hence, all celebrants must discharm themselves to prevent being stricken by their society's ailment. This rite, called navotciwa, consists of waving a pinch of ashes, held in the left hand, counter-clockwise over the person or object to be purified.[29] Navotciwa may also be accompanied by a discharming song. Ritual of this sort is always performed at the conclusion of a ceremony before the performers may mingle with their fellows without danger to themselves or others.

There is a Hopi, and general Pueblo belief that whatever causes a disease may also cure it.[30] Accordingly, a sufferer from the ailment controlled by a society may call upon its head man, or any other member, to give him relief. This is generally done by waving ashes over the patient while the society's discharming song is being sung. As a rule, the sick person then joins the order which cured him, either permanently or for a period of years.

Although every ceremony is supposed to bring benefits to the entire pueblo,[31] no noticeable effort is made to compel eligible members to attend the services. Participation must be entirely voluntary because of the Hopi belief that only those who know their minds to be good (untroubled) are fit to have their prayers heard by the gods. Similarly, although the omission of a scheduled rite is sadly regarded, there is nothing to prevent a chief from refusing to carry out his ceremony. If he has taught his duties to a successor, a leader may decide to "rest" for a few years, but if he has failed to train an heir before retiring, his observance may be permanently dropped from the calendar. There is always the chance, however, that in the future some ambitious member of the controlling clan may attempt to revive the performance.[32] In that case he must persuade the head woman in charge of the paraphernalia to allow him their use, and he must get a former member of the society to teach him the ritual. Before a long-lapsed ceremony may be re-introduced to the town's cycle, the Village chief must give his consent, but he has no authority to prevent the

---

[27] Voth, 1903a, p. 303, describes this process.

[28] Compare Dorsey and Voth, 1901, p. 109, footnote 2. Dr. Parsons discusses the curative aspect of Hopi religion in Parsons, 1933, pp. 9–20. For a list of "whips" see "Major Ceremonies at Oraibi" in the Appendix.

[29] See Parsons, 1939, pp. 457–460. Emesis is another means of purification.

[30] Parsons, 1923b, p. 163.

[31] The notion is often extended to cover the entire trib[e] and even all mankind.

[32] There is a good deal of hesitancy in offering to assum[e] a chieftainship, not only because of the responsibility in[-] volved, but also because the Hopi believe that a forward o[r] aggressive person is a witch. Cf. Titiev, 1943a, p. 55[3]

rmination of any rite which is not controlled by s own clan.[33]

Members of both sexes are launched in their eremonial careers before reaching the age of ten y being initiated into the tribe's Katcina cult. few years later all boys and girls are expected take another step in religious participation by ining one or more of several secret societies. At is stage it is customary for a girl to seek admission to the Marau, Lakon, or Oaqöl ceremonies, all of which are conducted by women. here is very little distinction among them, and a rl may ultimately join one, two, or all three, as e chooses. Ordinarily, this marks the extent to hich women may participate in formal esoteric ligious exercises, but properly qualified females ay be asked to fill special offices in the men's tuals. On the other hand, boys who have passed eir Katcina initiations generally join the Blue lute, Gray Flute, Snake, or Antelope societies.

boy's selection is greatly influenced by the filiations of the ceremonial father who put him to the Katcina cycle, for a ceremonial parent xes to have his "son" join his own group. However, no compulson is brought to bear on a candidate, and a young man may either refuse to go to any additional ceremony, or else he may ercise his own preference by the simple expedint of selecting another ceremonial father from e group he elects to join. There is no restriction garding the number of societies that a boy may oose; but on achieving adolescence a youth is pected to enter still another order by going rough the Tribal Initiation, after which he may tomatically reach the climax of his ceremonial reer by being admitted to the Soyal observances.

THE UNDERLYING CONCEPTS

The most fundamental concept of Hopi religion a belief in the continuity of life after death. This int is stressed in a variety of ways and is early manifested in the mythology. Nearly all e origin myths agree that the first death on rth occurred in the family of the chief who led e Emergence. When the murderer, a witch who related to the chief, is threatened with punish-

ment, he protests that the victim is unharmed and has merely returned to the Underworld from which mankind had just come forth. When the people look down they see that the dead person appears to be normal and happy, whereupon the witch says, " 'That is the way it will be. If anyone dies, he will go down there . . .'."[34] At first, according to a First Mesa tale, it was even understood that the dead would have the privilege of returning to earth, but Coyote changed things by throwing a large flat stone over the *sipapu*. "All the people were angry at Coyote for this and drove him away, because only for his action people who died would have been able to revive and walk around on this world four days after death."[35]

Thus do the myths tend to minimize the distinction between the living and the dead, and in a similar vein, other "legends indicate that the deceased Hopi plant and harvest, that the dead have ceremonies and altars, . . . [and] that the customs of those who occupy the abode of the dead resemble those living on earth."[36] So little division is there thought to be between the quick and the dead that it is widely believed that many people die (i.e., become unconscious) and visit the other world, only to be returned to life (consciousness) if their time has not yet come.[37] Quite often, persons who have had these experiences "remember what they saw while they were dead," and the Hopi regard their accounts as accurate descriptions of conditions in the realm of the dead.[38]

In general, these stories verify the notion that the behavior of the deceased is a replica of life on earth, with one essential difference. Human beings consume material food, but the dead eat "only the odor or soul of the food."[39] On this distinction there is based another of the most fundamental concepts of Hopi religion. Because they eat only what may be called the "essence" of food, the dead "are not heavy. And that is the reason why the clouds into which the dead are transformed are not heavy and can float in the air."[40] The expressed relationship between clouds and the dead is a basic point in Hopi doctrine, since it is primarily in the guise of rain-bearing clouds that

[33] Examples of lapsed and revived ceremonies may be und in Chapter Six, and in "The Rise of Hotevilla" in rt Three.
[34] Voth, 1905b, p. 12. In other myths the details vary t the story's main outline is the same.
[35] Stephen, 1929, p. 9.
[36] Fewkes, 1923, p. 490.

[37] Voth, 1905b, pp. 114–119; Titiev, 1941.
[38] Titiev, 1937a, p. 246.
[39] Voth, 1905b, p. 116. Note too that Masau'u, the god of the dead, also inhales only the "steam" of food.
[40] Voth, 1905b, p. 116. Compare Parsons, 1925, p. 77, footnote 124. "The dead have to go up to become clouds."

the deceased are potential benefactors to the living. As some of the inhabitants of the Underworld explain to a young man who pays them a temporary visit, "We . . . shall work for you here, too. We shall send you rain and crops. You must wrap up the women when they die, in the owa [sic] (wedding garment), and tie the big knotted belt about them,[41] because these owas are not tightly woven and when the Skeletons move along on them through the sky as clouds, the thin rain drops through these owas and the big raindrops fall from the fringes of the big belt."[42]

Another notion that must be grasped in order to understand Hopi religion is the equation of the dead not only with clouds but also with Katcinas.[43] As Fewkes expresses it, "The relation between the living and the dead is apparently not severed by death, but the 'breath-bodies' of those that have passed on revisit the pueblo and are represented by masked personations called Katcinas which are past members of living clans. . . . These personations of the dead, or Katcinas, return to the earth and take part in the pageants, also called Katcinas. . . ."[44] More recently, Dr. Kennard has written that Kachina refers "to the masked and painted impersonation, to the spiritual being impersonated, to the clouds, and to the dead."[45]

Further proof of the identity of clouds, Katcinas, and the dead is found in the burial practices. When a corpse is being prepared for the grave, a cotton mask is put on the face of the deceased "with the idea of making the body (breath body) light. . . ."[46] Parsons comments that the wearing of the mask "plainly identifies the dead with the Kachina,"[47] and Kennard calls the cotton covering a "cloud mask."[48] When a burial is concluded, reports Stephen, "They say or imply, 'You are no longer a Hopi, you are changed (nihti, grown into) a kachina, you are Cloud (Omauüh).'"[49]

We may now sum up briefly the underlying concepts on which most of the religious structure of the Hopi is based. The dead return to the Underworld through the same sipapu whence mankind first climbed to the earth's surface. There they carry on an existence which is nearly identical with that of the living. On some occasions they may revisit their former homes in the form of clouds or Katcinas, bringing rain and other benefits to those who are still alive.[50]

[41] Compare the emphasis laid on a woman's need of acquiring a set of wedding garments, p. 38.

[42] Voth, 1905b, p. 117.

[43] Although the dead are commonly equated with Katcinas, not all the Katcinas are necessarily spirits of deceased humans. Hopi Katcinas may also represent animals such as the bear or the humming bird, heavenly bodies such as stars, and a host of other beings both animate and inanimate. There is no fixed limit to the number of Katcina types, and new ones are freely added from time to time.

[44] Fewkes, 1923, p. 486. Compare Voth, 1912a, p. 35, footnote 1.

[45] Earle and Kennard, 1938, p. 1.

[46] Parsons, 1936b, p. 825.

[47] Parsons, 1936b, p. 825, footnote 1. In the same note Dr. Parsons qualifies her statement respecting the identity of the dead and Katcinas by declaring that such equations are customary at Zuñi "but unusual among the Hopi." I cannot agree with Dr. Parsons, for my Third Mesa informants repeatedly made statements identical with Kennard's remark, "It is generally believed that the spirits of the dead go to the west where they become Kachinas and return to the village as clouds." Earle and Kennard, 1938, p. 2.

[48] Earle and Kennard, 1938, p. 2.

[49] Parsons, 1936b, p. 826. Also compare Parsons, 1925, p. 75, footnote 121, where the face of a corpse is said to be covered with cotton, "so that the dead may become a white cloud. . . ."

[50] Although the spirits of the deceased are frequently regarded as benefactors, it must be realized that the Hopi, like so many primitive peoples, have an ambivalent attitude towards their dead. In some contexts they are loved and venerated, but in others they are greatly feared.

CHAPTER IX

THE KATCINA CULT

INTRODUCTORY

IN KEEPING with the rationalizing tendency of their culture the Hopi consider their Katcina cult to have been in existence since the beginning of life on earth. Chief Tawaqwaptiwa relates an origin myth which states that when the Hopi left the Underworld they brought with them a large number of living spiritual beings known as Katcinas, whose songs and dances constantly procured many benefits for the people. The Katcinas accompanied the Hopi in their early wanderings until they made a settlement at Casa Grande.[1] Here they suffered a violent attack from the Mexicans, during which all the Katcinas were killed and returned to their homes in the Underworld.[2] The surviving Hopi, eager to retain every possible contact with their powerful benefactors, shared among themselves the masks, costumes, and other articles formerly used by the deities; and developed the custom of dressing in the sacred garments in order to impersonate the gods.

Ordinarily, Katcina impersonations take the form of group dances. A number of men secretly rehearse songs and steps for some days prior to public exhibition, and then perform from daybreak to sunset with intervals of rest interspersed between dances. All the performers are elaborately costumed, and each wears a mask that covers his face and head. It is the mask, rather than any other part of the costume, that translates a man into a god in Hopi belief. Katcina masks are usually manufactured by their owners and are re-decorated each time a different style of Katcina is to be represented.[3] There is almost no limit to the number of variations and innovations permitted, except for a few special types known as Chief (Mon) Katcinas, whose masks are permanent and never duplicated.[4] These belong to particular clans, in most instances, and are regarded as ancestors (wuya). Unlike ordinary Katcinas, Chief Katcinas may be impersonated only on particular occasions by men chosen by the proprietary clan.

Admission to the Katcina cult is universal for the entire tribe. The adult attitude towards an impersonator is that from the moment he dons his mask, he is invested with the attributes of the particular spirit or deity he is representing. Accordingly, he is regarded as sacred, but he is more commonly called a friend than a god. Little children, on the other hand, are taught to believe that the Katcinas whom they see are actually supernatural visitants. Naturally, such a pretense cannot be kept up with youngsters approaching adolescence, so it is customary to initiate boys and girls into the cult when they are about ten years old.[5]

There is an open and a closed season for Katcina performances, as the spirits are supposed to be free for visiting the upper realms during one half of the year, and to be confined to their Underworld homes during the other half.[6] The open period runs approximately from the winter to the summer solstice, and all Katcina activities, with a single exception,[7] must be held within the traditional time limits.

Theoretically, all the Katcinas "belong" to the Village chief, but in practice two clans co-operate in the conduct of the annual cycle. The Badger clan is in charge from the termination of the preceding season in late summer until the Powamu performance in February; and from that point until the open season ends with the Niman (Homegoing) dance soon after the summer solstice, it is the Katcina clan that is in charge of the

---

Compare Bandelier, 1892, p. 322. "There is a decided inclination toward attributing . . . [Casa Grande] to some section of the Moki [Hopi] tribe . . . ."

Note that the Katcinas returned to the Underworld where the spirits of deceased humans also make their homes. This establishes another close link between the dead and the Katcinas.

For an account of Katcina costume, see Parsons, 1939, 730–736; and Earle and Kennard, 1938, pp. 7–11. Pictures of costumed Katcinas, drawn by native artists,

are reproduced in Fewkes, 1903. Illustrations by a modern artist are to be found in Earle and Kennard, 1938.

[4] Consult Earle and Kennard, 1938, p. 4.

[5] Formerly, the age of Katcina initiation was between 10 and 12. Today it is between 7 and 10. Entry to the cult occurs in conjunction with the Powamu ceremony.

[6] This point is elaborated and interpreted on p. 175.

[7] Only the Masau Katcina, representing the god of death, may appear in the closed season. See p. 174.

cult. In the following pages we shall describe in chronological sequence all the Katcina events that occur in the yearly cycle.

THE SOYAL KATCINA

The honor of opening the season falls annually to the Soyal Katcina, one of the Chief Katcinas, who is generally impersonated by the Soyal chief.[8] Because it is believed that the "locked up" Katcinas rest and sleep at their Underworld homes, on mountain tops, or in springs, the impersonator of the first Katcina to arrive at the village attempts to express by his behavior the sluggishness that results from excessive sleep. It is always on an afternoon in late November, on the day following the termination of the Wuwutcim rites, and sixteen days before the start of the Winter Solstice (Soyal) ceremony, that the villagers see walking along the southwest trail into the pueblo, a solitary Katcina who is supposed to have come from the home (shrine) of Matcito, the legendary founder of Oraibi.[9] He gives the appearance of a weary old man, and his gait is slow and uncertain. For the most part, the Soyal Katcina is dressed in the conventional garb worn by ordinary Katcina impersonators, but in addition, he wears an old cotton shirt with faded designs that are almost obliterated, over which there hangs a sort of cloth poncho, probably a Wuwutcim garment. About his throat there is wrapped a shabby fox pelt. In his right hand he carries a gourd rattle, and in his left he holds four prayer-sticks and a large sack full of sacred cornmeal. Thus equipped, the Soyal Katcina totters towards the dance plaza where he pauses to execute a brief dance, performing with the feeble motions of an aged man, and singing spasmodically in a low voice as though it were too great an exertion for him to sing and dance at the same time.[10]

The Katcina then stumbles along to the Chief kiva, where the Soyal rites are soon to be observed. Here he deposits the four prayer-sticks south of the hatch, after which he again sings and dances awkwardly, to the vast amusement of the onlookers. This done, he makes his way north of the kiva, and with a liberal handful of meal he makes a road from the ladder towards the north. Then he sprinkles paths from the hatch towards the west, south, and east, the customary ritual circuit. This action symbolizes the opening of the kiva for the arrival of Katcinas from any direction, and at its conclusion, the Soyal Katcina takes up a position a few paces from the southeast corner of the kiva. At this point of the performance the Village chief emerges,[11] bearing a little tray of cornmeal and prayer-feathers (nakwakwosi) with breath lines attached. The chief gives the Katcina the tray of offerings and takes from him his rattles and the remainder of his sacred meal. Then the chief makes a cornmeal path to the southeast for the Katcina, and the impersonator sets out in that direction to the end of the street, turns west on the next street, and so completes a circuit which brings him back to Matcito's shrine.

THE MASTOP KATCINAS[12]

Although the season is now declared open, it is some time before the Katcinas return in force. In fact, the next impersonations are limited to two Mastop performers who appear on the afternoon of the eighth day of the Soyal. They come rushing into the village from the northwest, making antic gestures as they go, and signifying in pantomime

---

[8] It should be remembered that at Oraibi the Soyal chief is usually the Village chief as well. In 1933 Chief Tawaqwaptiwa, who normally impersonates the Soyal Katcina, decided to rest and entrusted the impersonation to Myron Poliqwaptiwa of the Parrot clan, his wife's sister's son. In the absence of heirs from the Bear clan, and because his own wife is barren, Tawaqwaptiwa is grooming Myron for the Soyal and Village chieftainships.

[9] The following account is based on personal observations made in 1933. In that year the Soyal Katcina arrived on November 26. For comparative material, see Parsons, 1936b, p. 3, footnote 5; Earle and Kennard, 1938, pp. 15, 16, and plate 1; and Dorsey and Voth, 1901, plates 5, 6.

Note that the Soyal Katcina does not appear at this time on First Mesa. Parsons, 1936b, pp. 3, 4. This may be due to the fact that at Walpi the Bear clan head is not the Village chief, and consequently not the most important figure in the town. However, Stephen refers in other contexts to

a dance by "Shoyal kachina, youth and maiden. . . ." Parsons, 1936b, pp. 28 and 37.

[10] The low singing is not only "in character," but also has a practical value, as the Soyal Katcina's songs are too sacred to be heard by the spectators.

[11] If the Village chief were impersonating the Soyal Katcina, he would designate another official to receive him.

[12] The name Mastop may be derived from a combination of the words Masau'u and totop (fly). The meaning of the name could not be determined.

The present description is based on my observation of the Oraibi performance that occurred on December 1, 1933. Comparative accounts may be found in Dorsey and Voth, 1901, p. 45 and plates 23–25; and in Earle and Kennard, 1938, p. 16 and plate II.

According to Parsons, 1936b, p. 4, the Mastop Katcinas do not appear on First Mesa.

at they are being consumed with sexual desire. Then they reach the Chief kiva, where the Soyal es are in progress, they stop to consult each her with regard to the satisfaction of their ints. Suddenly, they pretend to have become vare of the near presence of women among the ectators. At once they dash madly towards a oup of female onlookers, and in turn, the Mas-p Katcinas place their hands on the shoulders each of the women, and by making little jumps th both feet, indicate the act of copulation. hen they return to the vicinity of the kiva, en-ge in another consultation, and once more rush lter-skelter to "copulate" with another cluster women. They continue to act in this fashion til they have had "intercourse" with all or most the women in the audience. Although they sert several comic touches into their byplay, eir behavior is regarded as a serious fertility e. Even women who are by nature very timid d shy, submit readily to the public "embraces" these performers; and females of any age, from bes in arms to great-grandmothers, are included the Mastop activities.[13]

As soon as the Mastop Katcinas have finished eir performance, there emerge from the Chief va four Soyal celebrants bearing sacred objects. hey make a ceremonial circuit four times ound the kiva, and then move off to deposit eir offerings at Flute spring (Lenva). The astop impersonators mimic the Soyal men, and en descend into the kiva for a brief rite, after hich they are dismissed and return to their shrine disrobe.

THE QÖQÖQLOM KATCINAS[14]

On the day after the Mastop appearance, the st day of the Soyal observance, there occurs the öqöqlom performance, the first dance of the

season by a group of Katcina personators. Although they are masked and are considered to be real Katcinas, they wear a motley costume of native and "white" garments, and they inject an element of comedy into their behavior. The primary purpose of the Qöqöqlom is to supplement the work of the Soyal Katcina in "opening" the kivas. While most of the performers sing and dance, one or two of their number are delgated to "open" various kivas by sprinkling meal in the cardinal directions from the kiva hatch. Nearly all the Katcinas interrupt their dance to co-operate in opening the Powamu kiva.[15]

Whereas the Soyal Katcina and the Mastop impersonations are highly specialized and seem to be linked with the Soyal rites rather than with the general scheme of Katcina organization, the Qöqöqlom have a definite place in the Katcina cycle. This is shown by the fact that the kiva sponsorship for the Qöqöqlom rotates annually in a fixed sequence, and the same kiva which has charge of the opening group dance in December is likewise entrusted with the responsibility for the concluding Katcina performance during the following summer.[16] Furthermore, the officer who serves as the father of the Qöqöqlom Katcinas during their dance, is the chief of the Powamu society, a position customarily held by the head of the Badger clan, who is in charge of the first half of the Katcina season.

ANNOUNCING THE NIMAN DANCE

At the conclusion of the Qöqöqlom dance, the Katcina season is considered fully open, and it is permissible for dance groups to impersonate any of the ordinary Katcina types they may select. Before the first public dance takes place, however, it is necessary for the kiva that is to stage the Homegoing (Niman) dance at midsummer to

---

[13] There is a noteworthy distinction between the sexual y of the Mastop and of ordinary clowns. The latter gen-lly make sport with eligible women, and bashful specta-s run from their "embraces"; but the Mastop per-mers pretend to fertilize even their own mothers and sis-s among the onlookers, and no one seeks to avoid them.
[14] The name of these Katcinas is supposed to refer to les on mesa tops (qöqlöm) in which water is caught. The formance given at Oraibi on December 20, 1933, is scribed in Part Three. Compare Dorsey and Voth, 1901, 58 and plates XXXI–XXXIV; Fewkes, 1903, plate XIV; and Earle and Kennard, 1938, p. 16 and plate

Parsons, 1936b, p. 4, points out that no Qöqöqlom tcinas are impersonated at First Mesa.

[15] Dorsey and Voth, 1901, p. 58, report that they "open" all the kivas that have participated in the Soyal. The main rites are held at the Powamu kiva, a center of the Katcina cult.
[16] Rotation of kiva sponsorship implies only that each kiva in turn is expected to guarantee the proper performance of the dance by supplying from its membership all the necessary officers. In reality, it is one member of the kiva who is chosen to be the sponsor, and it is he who is responsible for the weather, etc. The sponsor may be only a common kiva man whose offer to serve has been approved by the kiva chief.

The order of kiva rotation at Oraibi has been so badly disturbed since the schism that began about 1883, that informants were unable to agree on the correct sequence.

give a preview of that performance. This takes place on the third night following the termination of the Soyal, while the members of that ceremony are still observing ritual tabus and sleeping in their kivas.[17] In anticipation of the event, the man who has been chosen to sponsor the Niman composes or has composed for him one of the songs that is to be used during the dance next summer. He then notifies the men whom he has selected to serve as officers during the Home-going rites, and on the proper evening they as-semble in his kiva for a preliminary smoke. While this is in progress, a number of volunteers drop in, and as soon as the formal smoke has ended, the sponsor teaches the song to the entire assemblage. When it has been mastered by all present, the men dress in their Katcina costumes but do not mask. After a short rehearsal of the dance steps and gestures, the group visits each kiva, where it performs to the tune it has just learned. As the dancers are about to leave, the sponsor pauses by the ladder and announces that he is the one who will "put up" the Homegoing dance at the customary time.[18]

THE FIRST GROUP OF NIGHT DANCES

It is usually early in the January Moon (Pa-muya) that the last of the introductory Katcina rites is concluded. From now on the cycle of dances gets into full swing, and the entire month is one of gay activity. Owing to the uncertainty of the weather at this season of the year, Katcina performances are given in kivas rather than in the village plaza. Dances are held at night, each group appearing as an independent unit and making the rounds of all the kivas in the pueblo.

The organization of night Katcina dances is very informal. Any well-behaved man or woman may ask the Village chief's permission to sponsor a performance, and if the date chosen is suitable,[19] the chief readily gives his assent. The word is

then spread about, and the head of each kiva chooses the type of Katcina to be impersonated by his group, supervises the composition and learning of songs, overlooks the preparation of masks and costumes, and selects the officers to take charge of the dancers. These officers are temporary officials, being named only in con-junction with a single performance. They consist of a father of the Katcinas who sprinkles (feeds) the dancers with cornmeal and shouts directions and encouragement from time to time, a leader of the male Katcinas who signals the start and finish of each song and who gives out the tune, and a leader of the "female" impersonations (played, however, by men) who starts the song for those taking women's parts. In addition, one man is designated to attend the fire in each kiva. Usually, each kiva unit learns only two songs, and two or three days' notice is considered ample time for getting ready the entire performance.[20] Inasmuch as uninitiated youngsters are debarred from at-tendance at the night dances, the performers often are careless about the complete concealment of their identities, and those who act as "fe-male" Katcinas sometimes appear in everyday clothes.[21]

The day of a dance is always full of excitement and pleasant activity. Each kiva group is eager to outdo its rivals, and all day long one may observe men hurrying here and there with bits of dance regalia concealed under their shirts, or wrapped in blankets, or otherwise hidden from the curious eyes of the uninitiated. Late in the afternoon, each group holds an independent rehearsal in its own kiva, and the muffled sounds of singing and danc-ing arouse a pleasurable glow of anticipation in all the inhabitants of the village. At last, towards sunset, the rehearsal comes to a close and the men hurry home to their suppers. Not long after-wards, the performers re-assemble in their kivas to paint up and dress. Then they take their masks

[17] In 1933, the Niman was officially announced on December 23. The writer observed the entire procedure.
[18] Further details of this step in the Katcina cycle will be given in connection with the account of the Niman dance, p. 227. The brief preview indicates to the ob-servers the identities of the sponsor and some of his officers, and the type of Katcina selected for next summer's Niman. Stephen tells of a similar rite at Walpi's Soyal, in Parsons, 1936b, p. 49.
[19] Formerly, the Oraibi Snake-Antelope and Flute societies, as well as the Marau and Lakon groups, used to hold winter observances in January, as a supplement to their summer and fall performances. During the operation

of this system, sponsors of night dances tried to time their celebrations to coincide with the conclusion of each of the winter ceremonies, although these were unrelated to the Katcina cult.
[20] If a village has many active kivas each group prepare only a single song. Theoretically, new songs must b composed for each Katcina performance, but occasionall a group finds itself forced, through lack of time or lack c composers, to use old tunes.
[21] This was observed at Hotevilla in the winter of 1933 1934. The inhabitants of the pueblo are so conservative tha dancers rely on them to observe implicitly the tabu again bringing uninitiated but observant children into the kiva

in hand and withdraw to some previously selected private house where they attend to the last details of makeup and costuming, and where they hold a final dress rehearsal before they issue forth as "real" Katcinas to perform in public.[22]

As soon as the kivas have been vacated by the dancers, the spectators begin to file in. Down the ladder come unmarried boys and girls, women, frequently with infants on their backs, old men, Hopi visitors from other villages, Navahos and white people. Most of the villagers resort to the kiva to which their nearest kin belong, but at these performances all are welcome and guests are hospitably received in all the kivas. On the banquette running along the west wall sit the unmarried girls in old-fashioned costumes and gay shawls; men and boys occupy the benches on the east and north; and married women and infants make themselves comfortable on the raised platform south of the ladder. The father of the Katcinas sits just in front of the raised section near the ladder's base, and west of the fireplace crouches the fire-tender.[23] While the chattering audience is awaiting the arrival of the performers, the father generally keeps up a line of good-natured banter with those about him. Soon the sound of bells and rattles—sometimes too the beat of a drum—announces the approach of the dancers. With shouts and hoots they draw near, while the father of the Katcinas and some of the spectators call out loudly, inviting them to enter.

When he arrives at the kiva hatch the leader of the group shakes his gourd rattle, peers down at the crowd (which thus becomes aware of the type of impersonation it is about to witness), and engages in dialogue with the Katcina father. He speaks in a choked, disguised voice, and usually announces that he has just come to the village from the shrine where his type of Katcina is supposed to reside. After exchanging a few jests he yields to the repeated requests to enter, and one after another the Katcinas come down the ladder, passing to the east side as they step down to the main floor, and making the characteristic call of their impersonation as they take up their dance positions.[24]

The father of the Katcinas now rises to his feet, thanks the dancers for having come, and starting at the head of the line, begins to sprinkle each man with sacred cornmeal which he carries in a little pouch. When he reaches the leader, who always stands in the middle of the line, he pauses for a moment and calls out, "All right! Now, sing! May you sing with happy hearts!" At this the leader signals by shaking his gourd rattle, and the dance begins while the father continues sprinkling down to the end of the line. From time to time, while the dance is in progress, the father shouts encouragement and thanks, and at stated intervals he again sprinkles the performers with meal. When the performance concludes, the Katcinas generally distribute gifts among the spectators and then begin to file out, taking care to approach the ladder from the west side. If the dance is pleasing, as it generally is, either the father, or some one of the spectators, may demand one or more encores by the simple expedient of heading off the first man who reaches the ladder and guiding him around it instead of permitting him to clamber up. His mates then follow him around the ladder and back to the main floor, where the dance is repeated.

The schedule of the evening's activities is so arranged that each group makes two rounds of all the kivas, singing and dancing to one song the first time and to another the second.[25] Care is taken to begin the first round, and to wind up the concluding round, at the home kiva. Between these two performances it matters little in what order the other kivas are visited, but the Hopi are excellent showmen and they do not like to have any unit perform twice in succession in any of the kivas. When a group reaches its home kiva on its second round, the audience realizes that the night's activities are being brought to a close, and as soon as the last dance has ended and the Katcinas have withdrawn, the spectators hurry home and the dancers return to the empty kiva to undress and wash up.

During the next four days the performers must remain continent, but otherwise they behave in normal fashion. Most families hold a feast of mut-

---

[22] On one occasion, during my stay at Oraibi, I was honored by having the Katcinas use my house as their dressing room. Never was I more impressed with the dramatic quality of these performances. The atmosphere was exactly like that which prevails back-stage just prior to the curtain's rising.

[23] In former times (and even to-day at Hotevilla), a skillful fire-tender was essential to the success of a dance as the same open fire served to give light as well as heat.

[24] Compare Dr. Kennard's account in Earle and Kennard, 1938, pp. 17, 18.

[25] As has been previously noted, on a night when many kivas participate only one performance is given by each.

ton stew, *piki*, and *pikami* on the morning after a dance, but there is less emphasis on feasting and visiting than one finds during out-of-door Katcina performances in the spring and summer.[26]

At frequent intervals throughout the month of January the Hopi hold night Katcina dances, play gambling games for men and women, and stage Buffalo dances.[27] As the moon wanes, the people say, "Pretty soon it will be Powa-muya (February), and then our fun will stop,"—a reference to the fact that with the commencement of the Powamu ritual all other dance performances must be suspended.[28]

THE POWAMU CEREMONY[29]

As soon as the February moon is seen by the head of the Powamu society, he assembles the officers and some of the members of that organization for a preliminary rite called Powalawu, which he performs in conjunction with the Katcina chief, eight days prior to the regular Powamu observance.[30] The primary purpose of the Powalawu is the preparation of prayer-offerings, to be used in taking the first steps towards the successful performance of the Powamu.

At daybreak the next morning the Powamu chief begins a round of visits to all the kivas in the village. In each ceremonial chamber he sits west of the fireplace, to the left (north) of the kiva's chief. The kiva head fills and lights a pipe of native tobacco, puffs for a few moments, then passes the pipe to the Powamu chief who finishes it. Both men face the east as they smoke, and they exchange reciprocal terms of relationship as they

pass the pipe.[31] After the smoke is finished the Powamu chief presents the kiva leader with one of the prayer-feathers that had been made on the previous night during the Powalawu, and tells him that he may now begin planting beans. This procedure is repeated at each of the other kivas, and not long after the Powamu chief's departure, each kiva head picks a few sturdy young men to fetch the requisite amount of soil. These men take with them the prayer-offering left by the Powamu chief and partially bury it in the sand before they begin to dig. Then they sprinkle it with sacred meal, and loading their blankets heavily with moist earth, they carry it as unobtrusively as possible to their kivas. Other men fetch quantities of water, containers, and seed beans for planting; every one making an effort to hide these activities from the sight of uninitiated children. Within the kivas, each man fills a large basin or box with earth, plants from 50 to 100 beans not far beneath the surface, and waters his little plot thoroughly. From this time until the culmination of the Powamu ceremony, a blazing fire is kept going night and day in each kiva, and in their spare moments all the members congregate to look after their "crops" and to begin learning the songs which have been composed for the coming Bean dance.

Although each man is actually to have the use of his individual yield, these beans are said to be grown, in theory, for the benefit of the Eototo and Aholi Katcinas.[32] Eototo is the spiritual counterpart of the Village chief who has charge of the Eototo mask and who, alone, may im-

---

[26] According to the Hopi manner of reckoning, the day prior to an out-of-door dance of any kind, is called *totokya* (food providing), and the dance day is called *tikive*. Night dances, however, are always held on *totokya* but the feast occurs on the following day as in other dances.

[27] Buffalo and Butterfly are pleasure dances and have no true connection with the formal ceremonial calendar.

[28] Compare Dr. Parsons' statement in Parsons, 1936b, p. 123.

[29] The fullest and best description of Oraibi's Powamu celebration is given in Voth, 1901. Although I was present at Oraibi during the 1934 performance, I was not allowed to witness the esoteric rites. The summary here given is taken largely from Voth, but is supplemented by interviews with Powamu members.

An excellent study of Powamu on First Mesa occurs in Parsons, 1936b, pp. 155–257. For a comparative study of certain aspects of the Powamu, see Parsons, 1939, pp. 467–476, *et passim*.

[30] Voth, 1901, p. 73, expresses uncertainty as to whether

the Powalawu should be treated as an independent rite or as part of the Powamu. Since he goes on to point out "that other nine-day celebrations are preceded by a short ceremony, that the same leaders officiate in both ceremonies, and, especially, that a close relation seems to exist between the two," I think we are justified in calling the Powalawu a part of the Powamu. Voth's account is given in Voth, 1901, pp. 73–82.

The Powamu differs from most of the major ceremonies in that its officers do not include a War chief (Kaletaka).

[31] On this point see Titiev, 1937b.

[32] Eototo is a Chief Katcina who is identified with the ancestors of the Bear clan, and Aholi is a Chief Katcina who is a *wuya* of the Pikyas clan. These Katcinas are pictured in Earle and Kennard, 1938, plates IV and V.

On First Mesa Eototo pertains to the Cedarwood clan. Parsons, 1936b, p. 437. There is no Aholi Katcina at First Mesa, but Ahul, who is unknown at Oraibi, plays an important part in the Powamu there. Consult Parsons 1936b, pp. 170–173; and Parsons, 1925, p. 46.

personate this Katcina.[33] It is said that the Eototo was first brought to Oraibi by its traditional founder, Matcito. The Aholi Katcina is second in importance at Oraibi, and is portrayed by the Pikyas chief, who is first assistant to the Bear clan leader in the performance of the Soyal.

The Powamu chief, the Village chief (Eototo), and the Pikyas head (Aholi), plant small crops of corn to be artificially sprouted at the same time as the beans. Sometimes the corn is grown in the kivas and sometimes in the homes of various kinswomen of the chiefs in question. While the plants are maturing they must be carefully handled, and certain Katcina impersonations, Patcava Hu, have the duty of inspecting them. If they discover any damaged sprouts they may come in a body and whip the members of the offending kiva. Likewise, men who make a habit of lying down in the kivas at this time may also be thrashed because of the feeling that mimetically the plants will be retarded in their growth.[34] Every one is eager to have a good yield, not only as an indication of a successful farming season to come, but also because a thriving "crop" is a sign that a person has a "good" heart.[35]

During the eight-day period between the introductory Powalawu and the Powamu, kivas may be whitewashed or have minor repairs done on them. At this time too little children of either sex are subjected to very close haircuts which give them a strange appearance. Women everywhere are busy weaving plaques to be distributed as gifts at Powamu, and men spend a good deal of their spare time in the manufacture of Katcina dolls, bows and arrows, and toy rattles. Each night the kiva groups meet to rehearse their Bean dance songs, and from time to time they hold informal Katcina dances, unmasked, uncostumed, and using a miscellany of favorite old songs, in order "to help the beans to grow."[36] When a kiva unit has mastered its Bean dance songs it pays a visit in "undress" to the other kivas so that they may have a preview of this kiva's performance; and in due time, the other kivas reciprocate with similar visits. Each group eagerly discusses the merits of its own showing in comparison with the exhibitions staged by the other kivas, and much rivalry is expressed not only in judging the singing and dancing, but also in comparing the bean sprout yields throughout the village.

At last the eight days following Powalawu come to a close, the Powamu chief erects his standards (na'atsi) at the hatch of the Powamu kiva, and the observance of the secret rites begins; but in the other kivas, for the time being, there is no change of routine. During the first four days the Powamu chief and the Katcina chief frequently meet and smoke in the Powamu kiva, but little else of note occurs except that on the second day the Powamu chief visits the other kivas to smoke and bless the growing beans, and to announce that the Powamu Katcinas will appear for the Bean dance on the night of the eighth day following. On the fifth day some of the more significant observances are carried on, notably the erection of an altar and the singing of sacred songs. In years when youngsters are to be initiated into the Powamu society, the induction takes place on this day. On such occasions the ritual is more elaborate and includes the fashioning of a sand mosaic and the impersonation of the Tcowilawu Katcina, one of the ancients (wuya) of the Badger clan which controls the Powamu ceremony.

Membership in the society is open to children of either sex, and the manner of induction follows the customary pattern of Hopi initiations. After the candidates have witnessed for the first time some of the esoteric ritual, including a vivid dance by the Tcowilawu, they are addressed by the Powamu chief as follows:

You have now seen these things here; you are not to reveal them to anybody when you now go home; even if your own father or mother should ask you, you must not tell them anything; if they ask you about the Chowilawu, tell them there was no fire in the kiva and you could not see him; you will, later, sprinkle the katcinas with cornmeal when they dance; you will sometimes not eat any salt or salted food; if you reveal any of these things the Katcinas will punish you.[37]

---

[33] In the event that the chief wishes to rest from his ceremonial duties, or if he is training a successor, the Eototo may be impersonated by someone whom he delegates to play the part.

[34] Compare Parsons, 1936b, p. 437 and footnote 1.

[35] For a picture of bean plants maturing in a kiva, see Voth, 1901, plate XLVb.

[36] As the dances are done entirely without an audience,

it is on these occasions that recently initiated youngsters receive many lessons in the art of Katcina dancing. The men rehearse a great variety of dances, the spirit is informal, and errors are of little consequence. Therefore, a youngster who would be ashamed and afraid to participate in a formal public dance does not hesitate to take part in these performances.

[37] Voth, 1901, p. 93.

"Those who have gone through this initiation have in the first place become members of the Powamu fraternity (society), and as such the boys and men are entitled to be present at the ceremonies and learn all the secrets of that order. They may, furthermore, act as Katcinas and later as fathers ('naamu') of the Katcinas, i.e., as leaders of the Katcina dances who lead the Katcinas to the plaza, prompt them in their songs, and, above all, sprinkle them with cornmeal and give them prayer offerings at the dances. The girls, and women, may . . . sprinkle the Katcinas with cornmeal . . . and participate in the Powamu ceremonies whenever and wherever the presence of women is proper and necessary."[38]

Admittance to the Powamu, then, includes the right to participate in Katcina performances, and carries with it the further privilege, for boys and men, of acting as Katcina fathers. There still remain for consideration a large body of children who must be initiated into the ordinary Katcina cult, without the right of participation in Powamu observances and without the privilege of serving as Katcina fathers. For these boys and girls there is a separate initiation which takes place in conjunction with the sixth day's rites of the Powamu. In order to avoid admitting outsiders to the Powamu kiva while a secret ceremony is in progress, the plain Katcina initiation is conducted in another kiva.[39] Here some of the Powamu leaders construct two sand paintings and otherwise set the stage for the coming activities, while the men who are to impersonate various Katcinas are busy making up and dressing. Then the Village chief and the officers who assist him in the Soyal come in, wearing ceremonial regalia or carrying the badges of authority known as mongkoho.

When all is in readiness, the candidates are brought into the kiva by their ceremonial parents, and the novitiates whose induction into the Powamu had taken place on the preceding day are also on hand to witness but not to take an active part in the proceedings.[40] After a few preliminaries the Katcina initiates hear a long recital by the Powamu chief, in the guise of Muyingwa, the main god of germination. He tells them much of the tribe's sacred lore about the Katcinas, describes their homes in the San Francisco mountains and at other shrines, and then takes his departure. Immediately, a member of the Powamu society who has been keeping a lookout while seated on a high roof nearby, stands up in his place as a signal to three Katcina impersonators who promptly head towards the kiva on the run. One of these is dressed as Hahai'i Angwucnasomtaka and the other two are in the garb of the Hu Katcinas.[41] With loud cries and frequent beating on the kiva hatch with the long yucca whips that they carry, they circle the kiva four times, then enter hurriedly and take up positions north of the fireplace. One after another, regardless of sex, the candidates are placed on a sand painting by their ceremonial parents to receive four severe lashes from either of the Hu Katcinas. The boys are naked and hold one hand aloft while they clasp the genital organs with the other to prevent their being struck; the girls wear their dresses and lift both hands high above their heads.[42] When all the initiates have been whipped the Hu Katcinas whip each other and the Hahai'i. Then the Katcina chief dismisses them with gifts of prayer-feathers and cornmeal and they leave the kiva. Thereupon, the Katcina chief warns the neophytes never to betray the secrets they have just learned, on pain of dreadful punishment at the hands of angry Katcinas; and the ceremonial parents take their respective "children" to their homes for an elaborate feast. From now on boys have the privilege of dancing as Katcinas, but they usually do not perform for a year or two after their initiations.[43]

On the following day the Powamu rites are resumed but nothing of great importance transpires.

[38] Voth, 1901, pp. 93, 94.
[39] Voth, 1901, p. 94, states that the Marau kiva was used for Katcina initiations. My informants in 1934 said that Hawiovi was used, even in the days when Oraibi was undivided.
From the published accounts of the Powamu on First Mesa I cannot determine whether or not the rites include a separate Katcina initiation as they do at Oraibi.
[40] Compare Earle and Kennard, 1938, pp. 18–22.
[41] See Voth, 1901, plates LII–LIV, LVI–LVII, LIX, and LXII, LXIII. Also, Earle and Kennard, 1938, plates VI and VII.
[42] Powamu initiates are not whipped on Third Mesa, but according to Parsons, 1933, p. 50 and p. 64, there is a whipping rite for Powamu candidates on First Mesa, where Tüñwüb Katcina does the whipping. This is described in Steward, 1931, pp. 64, 65; in Parsons, 1936b, pp. 200–203; and in Fewkes, 1903, plate VII.
[43] Parsons, 1939, p. 140, footnote *, states that Wuwutcim initiation is "a prerequisite to dancing kachina." I believe that Dr. Parsons is mistaken on this point as I have personally known Katcina performers from several villages who had never been admitted to the Wuwutcim. Furthermore, long after the Wuwutcim had lapsed at Oraibi, new dancers were continually recruited from among recent initiates into the Katcina cult.

The next day, the eighth of the ceremony, a messenger who has been sent to Kisiwu[44] for spruce, returns with his burden and narrates in detail the incidents of his voyage. Somewhat later, the concluding altar rites are performed and the altar is dismantled and stored away. A good deal of time is now devoted to the preparation of masks and other paraphernalia for the ninth day's activities. While the secret observances in the Powamu kiva are drawing to a close, the Chief kiva is the scene of an important dress rehearsal. Here the Bear chief and the Pikyas chief put on the Eototo and Aholi regalia, respectively, and practice the procedure which is to be followed on the morrow in public.[45]

It is long before daybreak that the ninth day's observances begin, and the next twenty-four hours are crowded with events. At about three or four o'clock in the morning, the men rise and hurry quietly to their kivas to "harvest" their bean crops. No ceremony is attached to the act, but care is taken to hide the soil in which the plants were grown and to bring the sprouts secretly into each household, in order that uninitiated youngsters may be led to believe that they were brought by the Katcinas who had raised them at their homes. When the "harvesting" is finished, each man takes a string of yucca and binds a handful of bean shoots to the gifts which he has prepared for his ceremonial children, for his uninitiated offspring, or for favorite relatives such as his paternal aunts. For girls and women Katcina dolls are generally made, while little boys receive toy bows and arrows, miniature gourd and turtle-shell rattles, or little shinny sticks and balls. In each kiva, one or two men then dress in complete Katcina costumes, choosing whatever impersonation they prefer. The other men entrust their gifts to them with specific directions regarding the recipient of each object. Everyone leaves a bunch

of sprouts in the kiva, north of the fireplace, as a reward for the Katcina messengers.[46]

Just at dawn the Village chief, carrying his *mongkoho*, issues from the Chief kiva to make a morning prayer to the Sun (*kuivato*). He is preceded by the Soyal War chief (Kaletaka), and followed by the Soyal Crier chief, each of whom also carries his chief's stick. A few moments later, a strange, subdued singing is heard at the eastern edge of the town, and in the gray light there appears the Hahai'i Angwucnasomtaka, a Katcina mother, impersonated by a male member of the Powamu society.[47] The performer dresses at a distant shrine where the Powamu chief prays over him and makes him a path (by sprinkling meal) towards the village. Chanting "her" song continuously, Hahai'i makes "her" way slowly to the outside of the Powamu kiva, where "she" is blessed with smoke and medicine water by the Powamu officers, and dismissed with prayer-meal and *nakwakwosi*. "Her" performance is said to symbolize a recently-married girl's return to her home at the conclusion of the nuptial rites.

Meantime, the Aholi and the Eototo Katcinas have emerged from the Chief kiva and are approaching the Powamu kiva. Eototo goes first and draws a cornmeal symbol on the ground (ɰ). This is supposed to represent the houses of the village, and Aholi puts his long staff at the juncture of the middle vertical line with the horizontal and slowly revolves it towards him from right to left while he issues a long, drawn-out cry. By this action Aholi indicates that he is embracing the entire pueblo to express the fact that it belongs to him and Eototo.[48] With the latter leading and sprinkling a cornmeal path for his companion, the two Katcinas make their way to a place south of the Powamu kiva where a member of the Bow clan has previously dug a hole to represent a

[44] Kisiwu is one of the most important homes (shrines) of the Katcinas. It is from Kisiwu that the Tcowilawu Katcina is said to come when he appears at the Powamu initiation. Messengers also go to Kisiwu to get spruce for the Homegoing dance, and again they describe the trip in great detail. See pp. 229–231.

[45] Although Dr. Fred Eggan and I were barred from the secret rites in the Powamu kiva, we were allowed to join the activities of the Chief kiva, even to the extent of taking part in the Bean dance. Hence, all the non-esoteric parts of the Powamu were witnessed by the writer.

[46] Each year the men who have finished serving as Katcina messengers name one or two of their kiva mates to play the part during the next Powamu.

[47] This impersonator is supposed to enact the rôle of

Hahai'i for four successive years. He should wear an antique mask, but may fashion a new one if the old mask does not fit him. Hahai'i Angwucnasomtaka is one of several "mothers of all the Katcinas." See Earle and Kennard, 1938, pp. 22, 23, and plate VI.

[48] It is by no means certain that any of the interpretations of specific ritual acts are correct. No informant is entirely trustworthy when the subject deals with sacred matters. Then too it often happens that the true explanation for certain actions is as much a mystery to the performers as it is to us, and they make up "explanations" to answer one's questions.

See Voth, 1901, plates LXIV and LXV. According to Voth, conventional, circular cloud designs are made instead of the straight lines shown above.

water cistern (*patni*). Towards this cavity the Eototo scatters meal from each of the four directions, after which he pours water into the opening from a netted gourd (*mongwikuru*) which he carries. Aholi repeats the performance, and then the Katcinas take turns in rubbing meal on the four sides of the Powamu kiva hatchway, and in pouring water down the hatch to be caught in a basin by a man standing part way down the ladder, out of sight of the spectators. When this rite, which signifies the bringing of much rain, is concluded, the Powamu officials dismiss the Katcinas with rites similar to those performed for Hahai'i.

Instead of going to a shrine where they may disrobe, however, as is usually done at the conclusion of Katcina activities, the Eototo and the Aholi return to the village. In front of the homes of various personages of importance[49] they go through the procedure of symbol drawing and staff waving, and the Eototo makes four cornmeal lines on the walls of the houses and gives each of their owners a bunch of the recently-sprouted corn plants. After this, the Eototo and the Aholi return to the Chief kiva to undress. The rest of the forenoon is devoted primarily to feasting. In the Chief kiva the men partake of a ceremonial meal consisting of "gravy" (*wotaka*), unrolled, flat sheets of *piki*, and boiled beans, brought in special trays and bowls to the kiva by the Village chief's wife and other women relatives of the principal actors.[50] In every household huge vessels of stew made from bean sprouts and corn are prepared, and copious portions are carried to all the kivas.

In the afternoon a great many men dress in a large variety of Katcina costumes and circulate through the village streets, entertaining the populace or handing out gifts which were left over from the morning's distribution. These Katcinas perform no special ceremony and appear without organization, but they are generally led by He'e'e,

another of the "mothers of all the Katcinas." On the last of four rounds which they make about the pueblo, the performers go down into their respective kivas as they pass by, and in this fashion the large crowd of rambling Katcinas melts away. Inside the kivas the men disrobe and prepare for the night showing of the Powamu Katcinas in the Bean dance.

On this occasion too according to Voth, there occurs the So'yoko performance, when a group of bogey Katcinas make a circuit of the village, threatening to carry off little boys and girls who must be ransomed by their parents or other relatives with generous portions of food.[51] Of late the So'yoko appearance at Oraibi, has tended to become detached from the regular ritual calendar, and has been held whenever it was thought desirable to discipline the youngsters; but at First and Second Mesa the bogies appear annually and are directly related to the Powamu.[52]

Late in the evening of this busy ninth day, final preparations are made for the popular Bean dance. All sorts of innovations in costuming are permitted at this time, and the men go about borrowing strange bits of apparel, including "store" dresses and hats and, even, purses and vanity cases. When all is in readiness, the men carry their costumes into their kivas and then hold a final, undress rehearsal in which they practice both of the songs they intend to use later on. After this, the participants sit about in their kivas and rest, but they are forbidden to sleep.[53] At about midnight the Powamu chief visits each of the kivas in turn, and standing by the ladder with his right hand resting on a rung at shoulder height, he makes a formal speech suggesting that the men prepare their paints and dance regalia. A short time later he makes a second round of the kivas, this time telling the dancers to paint up. Soon he makes a third visit, to announce that everyone should dress; and finally, when his own

[49] Voth, 1901, p. 115, reports that Eototo performed at the home of Sakhongyoma, the Eototo impersonator, who was a brother to the Village chief; at the chief's maternal home; at Chief kiva; and at the Pikyas clan house. It should be remembered that Eototo is the ancient of the Bear clan and Aholi of the Pikyas clan.

Because Sakhongyoma used to substitute for the Village chief in performing the Soyal, it seems to me that it is the Soyal chief (not necessarily the Bear clan head) who impersonates Eototo.

[50] Similar meals are prepared by the relatives of the main officers in all important ceremonies, and the foods are made without salt or fat in observance of ritual dietary tabus. The gravy is always eaten first. See Dorsey and

Voth, 1901, plates XII, XIII. The latter is wrongly numbered XVII.

[51] An account of the So'yoko ritual at Oraibi will be found in Part Three. Compare Parsons, 1936b, pp. 224–227; Voth, 1901, p. 118; Earle and Kennard, 1938, plates X and XI; Fewkes, 1923, plates 2 and 7; and Fewkes, 1894d.

[52] When the So'yoko used to be given annually, the sponsorship of the performances rotated in the same order as the Homegoing dance. That is, the same kiva which had charge of the Qöqöqlom and Niman dances also took the responsibility for the Soyoko rites during Powamu.

[53] In 1934, I was surprised to note that the tabu against sleeping was not rigidly enforced.

kiva group is ready, he comes to say that the dance is about to begin. As quickly as possible thereafter, each unit withdraws in order that the spectators may come in to take their places as in ordinary night Katcina dances. Every performer takes up a handful of sacred meal from a tray on the kiva floor, and the men depart in a body to a specific shrine associated with their kiva.[54] Here the meal is breathed upon and thrown to the four directions; then every dancer stretches forth his arm to receive four light taps with a yucca whip (as a sort of re-initiation);[55] and the group gathers around the dance leader for a final trial rendition of the first song.

By now the audience is assembled and includes all the recently-initiated youngsters, both those who went into the full Powamu ceremony and those who were inducted only into the Katcina cult. All the neophytes who are about to witness a night dance for the first time sit motionless on the east banquette with their knees drawn up to their chins, the customary position prescribed at initiations into the Wuwutcim and other cere- monies. The remaining spectators sit in the cus- tomary places. In due time the Powamu Katcinas, who are unmasked for this particular perform- mance, arrive to begin the evening's dancing. Before entering the kiva they throw several ears of baked sweet corn down the hatch, calling out to the initiates to eat, but the children have been instructed by their ceremonial parents that it is wrong for them to leave their places, so they do not stir. Then the dancers enter the kiva while one of their number stands by the hatch and calls down all sorts of jests at the expense of each man as he comes down the ladder. Inasmuch as the performers announce on entering a kiva that they are the real Katcinas, and as they are unmasked, it does not take long for the recent initiates to discover that the Katcina impersona- tors are their relatives and fellow villagers. In

such dramatic fashion is the most important of all Katcina secrets revealed to Hopi children.

The Bean dance moves along at a very fast tempo, and is performed in a style unlike that of any other Katcina dance.[56] When it is over, the dancers file past the west bench where the un- married girls, dressed in old-fashioned Hopi finery and wearing their hair in "butterfly wings," are seated. Most of the men carry gifts which they give to the maidens, in exchange for which each Katcina receives a few packages of somi- viki. This is an occasion when a young woman may offer a loaf of qömi to her sweetheart as a marriage proposal.[57] For the rest, the Bean dance follows the schedule of ordinary night dances, with each group beginning its first round and con- cluding the second in its own kiva. It is almost daybreak when the dancing comes to an end, and the performers gather at their kivas to feast on the somiviki which they have gathered from the spectators in the course of the evening. At the same time, the newly-initiated boys and girls are taken to the homes of their ceremonial mothers where their heads are washed, and they are given new names.

In ordinary years the Powamu rites conclude with the Bean dance, but in years when there has been a full Tribal Initiation during the preceding November, the Powamu is extended by the inclusion of the interesting Patcava per- formance.[58] This begins at twilight of the day following the Katcina initiations. On two succes- sive evenings, He'e'e, one of the "mothers of all the Katcinas,"[59] leads processions of miscel- laneous Katcinas about the village. On the morn- ing of the third day, coincident with the ninth and last day of Powamu, He'e'e makes a circuit of several shrines outside the town, collecting more and more Katcinas at each shrine and bringing them with "her" into the pueblo. This procession is an enactment of the myth told by the Powamu

---

[54] The shrines associated with each of the kivas are dis- cussed in "Kivas and Their Associated Shrines," in the Appendix.

[55] Inasmuch as Dr. Fred Eggan and the writer had never been initiated into the Katcina cult, we were severely whipped across the arms just before we went down into our first kiva for the night. To avoid any sign of discrimi- nation, all our fellow dancers from Chief kiva were also whipped in the same fashion.

[56] Voth, 1901, pp. 120–122; Parsons, 1936b, pp. 231– 235; Earle and Kennard, 1938, p. 25; and Steward, 1931, pp. 71–74; all give descriptions of the Bean dance.

[57] See p. 32.

[58] The summary of Patcava which is here given is based

on the full discussion of the rites in Part Three.

Inasmuch as the Hopi are notorious for irregularities in their day count, the following schedule of Powamu events in 1934 may prove of value for comparative purposes:

Jan. 16 . . . . Concluding Night dance in the kivas.
Jan. 17 . . . . Powalawu.
Jan. 18 . . . . Bean planting begins.
Jan. 21 . . . . Bean planting ends.
Jan. 24 . . . . Standard erected at Powamu kiva.
Feb. 2 . . . . Bean dance.

[59] The fact that there are several "mothers of all the Katcinas" is left unexplained by the Hopi, but the under- lying idea may be an extension of the classificatory princi- ple whereby every individual has many "mothers."

chief when he appeared before the Katcina neo-phytes in the guise of Muyingwa.[60]

The next day the Powamu chief leads four young women called Patcava maidens, and an escort of Katcinas, from a shrine known as Du-wanasavi towards Oraibi. At the outskirts of the town they are stopped by the Village chief, or his representative, in Eototo costume. There then follows a dramatization of the legendery admission of the Badger clan to Oraibi. The Badger leader (Powamu chief) shows Matcito (Eototo) the Patcava maidens who are carrying heavy trays of cornmeal and newly-sprouted bean plants, and promises to raise similar crops for him through the agency of his Powamu ceremony. Thereupon Eototo permits the group to go on, and they proceed into the village.

THE SIGNIFICANCE OF THE POWAMU

In its fullest form the Powamu is a highly complicated set of rites, in which five distinct threads are interwoven. Primarily, it is a ritual designed to promote fertility and germination.[61] For this purpose the entire adult male population engages in the mimetic practice of growing forced crops in the kivas,[62] under the supervision of the Powamu officers; the Powamu chief appears in the rôle of Muyingwa, principal god of germination; and the Patcava maidens carry trayloads of young plants into the village as tangible evidence of the results attendant on the Powamu. Second in importance, is the Powamu's relationship to the Katcina cult. This is evidenced by the privilege, accorded only to its members, of serving as fathers of the Katcinas; by the initiation of children into the Katcina cult as a concomitant of the Powamu observances; and by the impersonation of several Chief Katcinas as well as numerous representations of ordinary types. Third, there is the dramatization of several aspects of Oraibi's mythology as they pertain to the Badger clan which owns the Powamu and controls the first half of the Katcina cycle. To this end we have the impersonation of the Tcowilawu Katcina, a *wuya* of the Badger clan; and the scene in which Eototo

(Matcito) admits the Badger chief to Oraibi exchange for the Powamu. Fourth, the cer mony stresses the importance of pueblo leade such as the Village (Bear) chief, the head of th Pikyas clan, and the Soyal officers. This is dor when these officials appear with their badges authority during the Katcina initiation; whe Eototo and Aholi re-state their claims to Oraib and when the Badger chief is forced to g Eototo's consent before he may bring his follov ers into the pueblo. Fifth, we find many educa tional and training aspects mingled with the r ligious elements. Powamu candidates are warne that they will be punished if they reveal the s ciety's secrets; Katcina initiates are whipped ar warned to be discreet; the So'yoko Katcinas con to discipline uninitiated youngsters; and at the first Bean dance novices are taught not to yie to the temptation of scrambling for sweet corn.

In addition to the five major motives of th Powamu, the ceremony brings out the Bo clan's duty of opening a cistern for the Villag chief, the Katcina clan's co-operation with th Badger in Katcina control, and the connectio of the Powamu with the Tribal Initiation, as result of which initiations into the latter are fo lowed by the addition of the Patcava ceremon to the ritual of the former. Finally, the Powam society cures for rheumatism.

Three days after the conclusion of the Powam a racing season is inaugurated.[63] At the close the first contest, the mothers of recently init ated youngsters bring gifts of *piki* to the cer monial fathers of their children; and women wh had brought babies with them on the night of th Bean dance, are expected to pay for the priv lege by providing food to the kivas where the had been among the spectators.[64]

ANKTIONI, OR REPEAT PERFORM-ANCES: THE SECOND SERIES OF NIGHT DANCES

The Powamu marks the mid-point of the ope Katcina season, in the sense that it terminates th period of Badger control which began when th Badger clan head served as father of the Ka

---

[60] See p. 116.

[61] Voth, 1901, p. 71, footnote *, states that Powamu signifies putting the fields in shape "for the approaching planting season."

[62] Parsons in Parsons, 1936b, p. 156, interprets the growing of beans as "a ceremony for prognostication . . .

for the year's crop. . . ."

[63] Although racing has a marked religious connotatic in many cases, it is not directly related to the Katcir cycle. See Titiev, 1939b.

[64] Only little children, too young to be aware of what going on, may be taken into kivas during dances.

inas at the Qöqöqlom performance.[65] Soon after the close of the Powamu there occurs a transfer of authority to the head of the Katcina clan. This featured by the resumption of night dances in the kivas. These are known as Anktioni (Repeat) from the fact that in former days the first dance in the post-Powamu series was supposedly a repetion of the Bean dance. Although there was some uncertainty among the Hopi men regarding the exact meaning of the term, all informants agreed that it referred to the dances following the Powamu and that it marked the turning point of the Katcina season.[66] Some said Anktioni was "just like the Niman (Homegoing) Dance,"[67] which may have been a reference to the termination of Badger clan authority over the Katcinas; but others said it was a commencement, "like starting a new life again," by which may have been meant the beginning of Katcina clan control.

At any rate, the exact date for inaugurating the Anktioni series is optional with the Katcina chief and is kept secret from the populace in general. When he is ready to call for the first dance, the Katcina chief begins to make a number of nakwakwosi in his kiva. Of course, his kiva mates immediately realize his intent, but they are expected not to release the news prematurely. On the following day, the Katcina leader and one of his clansmen, usually his sister's son, dress in Koyemsi costumes and make their way to the roof of the Kele (Chicken Hawk) clan house where they deposit their offerings at the Village Crier chief's shrine.[68] Then they jump into view, gesticulating wildly and jangling cow-bells while

they announce that the Katcinas are to appear that night. Inasmuch as the performance is to be a duplicate of the Bean dance there is little need of rehearsal, and the element of dramatic surprise, so dear to the Hopi, can be used with telling effectiveness.[69] From the Kele house the Koyemsi announcers descend to the street and run rapidly from kiva to kiva, arousing laughter by telling the men to prepare stews and piki bread, and exchanging repartee with the inmates of the kivas which they visit.

THE WATER SERPENT (PALULOKONG) DANCE[70]

Although the Anktioni at Oraibi in recent times did not begin with an exact repetition of the Bean dance, it was customary for the first series of Repeat night dances to include a rite that was analogous to the Powamu.[71] This was the Water Serpent (Palulokong) dance, in which puppets representing the mythical serpents are manipulated from behind a screen.[72] There is something anomalous about the Water Serpent dance. It is performed as one act in a night series of Katcina dances, its exhibitors take it from kiva to kiva in customary fashion, and it lacks a tiponi, altar, and other attributes of the more formal ceremonies; yet, it requires far more preparation than any ordinary Katcina dance, it employs a great number of religious properties, and it carries a deeper significance and embodies a more elaborate set of rites than any other Katcina performances except the Powamu and the Niman.[73]

[65] See p. 111.
[66] On First Mesa too the connotation if not the translation of Anktioni is clearly the same as at Oraibi. Fewkes and Stephen, 1893, p. 269, footnote 2, refer to 'Uñ-kwa-ti —the second or following dance, i.e., the dance following the 'Powamû.' " Also, Stephen, in Parsons, 1936b, p. 265 and p. 289, speaks of Uñkwati as the second or following dance after Powamu.
In contrast to these statements, Parsons, 1925, p. 53, footnote 88, interprets angkwa as a "term for pouring anything from one vessel to another; referring in this case to the circulation of dancers from kiva to kiva." Dr. Parsons' position is untenable because dancers circulate from kiva to kiva in exactly the same fashion during the pre-Powamu performances, yet the earlier series is never called anktioni or angkwa.
[67] Parsons, 1925, p. 53, footnote 88, reports that the kiva in charge of the post-Powamu series is also responsible for the conduct of that year's Niman observance.
[68] This is on the roof of the Kele clan house.
[69] In 1934 Anktioni was announced at Oraibi on Feb. 3 and performed the next day, 22 days after the Bean

dance. It had been delayed because most of the performers had been working on the roads, and its announcement was greeted with great joy.
[70] Although I observed the entire set of performances, Oraibi's pattern was so deficient as a result of its disintegration, that the present discussion is supplemented by data gathered in numerous interviews.
[71] Fewkes and Stephen often used Uñkwati and Palulokoñti interchangeably. See Fewkes, 1903, p. 40; and Parsons, 1936b, p. 289. At Oraibi the Water Serpent dance was not regarded as synonymous with Anktioni, but it was considered the most characteristic exhibition of the series.
[72] At Oraibi the Water Serpent dance was performed only in those years when some individual saw fit to sponsor it, but at Walpi it seems to have held a fixed place in the annual calendar of ceremonies. See Parsons, 1936b, p. 288.
[73] The following discussion of Palulokong at Oraibi is derived from interviews, particularly with Tawaqwaptiwa. Comparative data may be found in Fewkes and Stephen, 1893; Parsons, 1936b, pp. 287–324, et passim; and Fewkes, 1900d, pp. 605–629.
[74] Parsons, 1936b, p. 288, calls attention to the hybrid

At Oraibi anyone was privileged to ask the Village chief for permission to stage a Palulokong dance during the Anktioni series. If no objection was found, the proposer's kiva prepared to sponsor the observance.[74] In anticipation of the coming rites, each kiva devotes a day or two to the planting of beans (as at Powamu), and the members of the officiating kiva plant corn as well. Again, as during the Powamu period, kivas may be re-plastered, and care has to be taken lest the growing plants be damaged.[75] When the leaves of the corn plants begin to open, the sponsor announces the fifth day following as the date of the dance. He communicates the news to the head of his kiva and to the dance leaders at a ritual smoke, but the other kivas get no official notification. Then the sponsor goes to the shrine at Katcinwala to fetch the Palulokong images,[76] which are deposited on the kiva floor and smoked over by the officials. At the Oraibi performances four serpent effigies were generally used. These were a big male (Palavono) with a red belly, black head, and black stripes on the back and sides; a big female (Qötcavono); with white belly; and two "children" (timatu) of undetermined sex, with white bellies like the "mother."[77]

That night, a Powamu society man from the sponsor's kiva dresses as He'e'e Katcina and appears at Oraibi rock when the after-glow fades from the sky. As in the Powamu ceremony, "she" leads "her" children around the kivas, but

two warrior Katcinas, Wyakote, are on watch at the officiating kiva to keep "her" from approaching too closely while a secret rehearsal is in progress. As at Powamu He'e'e makes three repetitions of this performance and on the morning of the dance "she" appears four times at a distant shrine, Patangwocdöka, from which point "she" returns to Oraibi by a circuitous route, being joined here and there by a variety of impersonators.[78] He'e'e leads "her" entourage into "her" kiva for a lunch of bean sprout stew, and then makes several rounds of the village kivas. On the last circuit the Katcinas drop out at their respective kivas as they are reached, and the itinerary is so arranged that He'e'e's own kiva is the last to be approached, and "she" is accompanied only by "her" own kiva mates when "she" enters the kiva with "her" remaining followers. Almost immediately afterwards, the corn plants are "harvested," fastened into a number of small conical "hills" of mud, and distributed equally among all the kivas. They are kept secreted in baskets until the public exhibition begins.

Towards evening the dance sponsor, the kiva chief, the four men chosen to manipulate the serpent figures, and several Katcina impersonators from the officiating kiva, prepare to carry the images on a pilgrimage to Oraibi's main spring, Lenva (Flute spring).[79] This group is swelled by the addition of four Chief (Mon) Katcinas from the Powamu kiva[80] who lead the procession to

---

character of the Water Serpent rites when she speaks of them as midway between a dance and a ceremony.

[74] Stephen says that Añkwati or Palülükoñti is given by whichever kiva most wishes it. Parsons, 1936b, p. 333.

[75] On one occasion, the boys and girls who were plastering the Kwan kiva at Oraibi accidentally broke a vessel containing bean plants. Several Powamu society men of the Badger clan, on hearing the news, decided to dress as Patcava Hu Katcinas (see p. 116) and to whip the members of the offending kiva; but the latter objected on the grounds that only Powamu "crops" belonged to the Badgers, since they "owned" the Powamu but not the Palulokong ceremony. A council of chiefs was then called to decide the issue. The participants were Lololoma, Village chief; Tanakwai'ima (Gray Badger), chief of the Kwan kiva where the accident had occurred; and Masatöniwa (Sand) who was sponsoring the dance and was therefore Village chief pro tempore. In this capacity Masatöniwa was asked to give his opinion first. ●ie cried because dissension was threatening the success of the rites for which he was responsible, and then decided to avoid further trouble among the performers by ruling against the whipping. Lololoma and Tanakwai'ima concurred in the decision. This incident shows the close association of the Powamu

and the Palulokong in the minds of the natives.

[76] The Oraibi images belong to no particular clan, and I could not determine whether or not the other properties belonged to specific clans. Water Serpent paraphernalia on First Mesa appear to be owned by certain clans, but here too there is some confusion regarding the details. Parsons, 1936b, p. 288 and footnote 3.

[77] Fewkes and Stephen, 1893, p. 276, describe a performance with six serpent figures. Bourke was told of an exhibition with seven serpents. Bourke, 1884, p. 84.

[78] The re-enactment of the He'e'e circuits is striking evidence of the analogy between Powamu and Palulokong observances. Earlier writers do not seem to have stressed the connection, although they did hint at it. In the text accompanying Voth, 1901, plate LXVII b, there occurs the statement that circulating Katcinas perform "on such occasions as this [Powamu], the Balölökong ceremony etc." Fewkes and Stephen, 1883, p. 273, point out the same parallel.

[79] The Walpi rites are performed at Sun spring (Tawapa). They are described in Parsons, 1936b, pp 319–322.

[80] Compare the duties of the Mon Katcinas in the Patcava procession during the Powamu, p. 224.

d from the spring, and by four members of the
lue Flute society who come from the Blue Flute
iva (Sakwalenvi) in full regalia, including their
struments. The observances at the spring are
pen only to officers and special performers,
hile the ordinary Katcinas and the villagers are
ept from intruding by the two Wyakote guards.
he main features of the ritual are the singing of
acred songs, the deposit of prayer-offerings, a
ormal smoke, the blowing of flutes on the sur-
ace of the water,[81] and the dipping of the heads
nd tails of the effigies in the pond.

While these rites are being enacted, the spec-
tors file into the empty kivas as on the occasion
f any night dance. As soon as the ceremonial
 the spring comes to a close, the procession
arts back led by the Mon Katcinas who are
ollowed, in order, by the Flute men, the serpent
andlers, the other officers and the Katcinas, all
f whom make their appropriate calls. One of the
en from the sponsor's kiva impersonates a
oyemsi and serves as a drummer, the sound of
s drum being said to represent the voice of the
alulokong.

As usual, the first exhibition is held in the
onsor's kiva. Before the images are brought
own, all the lights are covered with blankets.
hen, in the darkness, the serpent screen (house)
 speedily erected; a number of the mud cones
ontaining corn plants are set in line before it; the
ffigies are placed in position; the four Mon
atcinas range themselves on the west banquette
nd begin a special set of songs; the Flute men
and along the east wall as they start to play;
nd the remaining Katcinas deploy before the
creen where they rattle accompaniments to
eir own tunes. A shrill cacophony fills the
arkened kiva for a few moments, and then the
ghts are uncovered, revealing the stage proper-
es and supposedly giving the impression that the

corn plants were sprouted on the kiva floor by
the "power" of the ritual. As the light improves
the activity in the kiva increases. The figures of
sand-pipers, mounted on wheels on top of the
screen, are made to dart forward and back, and
suddenly, from hidden openings in the screen,
serpent heads protrude and begin to squirm and
writhe as "they look about and examine their
'house.'"[82] Gradually, the Palulokongs emerge to
full length with a powerful, trembling motion by
which they are said to signify embracing and
dancing. Then an impersonator in the guise of
Hahai'i, mother of all the Katcinas, holds forth a
plaque full of sacred cornmeal into which each
serpent dips its head as if eating. Next, "she"
offers "her" breasts to each figure which simulates the act of suckling. Finally, as the medley of
songs approaches a climax, the serpents reach forward and knock over the corn plant hills to signify that they are harvesting the crops which
they produce and own.[83]

As soon as the ceremony is over, the lights are
hidden again and the paraphernalia quickly dismantled and carried out. While the group of performers is on its way to the next kiva on its
rounds, the father of the Katcinas picks up the
scattered plants and distributes them among
the spectators.[84] Other kiva units then come
in at intervals to exhibit dances such as are
usually portrayed during the night series before
Powamu.[85]

PUPPET DOLL DANCE

In some way which was never satisfactorily
explained by Oraibi informants, two large puppet dolls representing Shalako maidens have become associated with the Water Serpent dance.
It is not clear whether or not the dolls were
formerly exhibited together with the Palulo-

[81] In Stephen's account of the Walpi Water Serpent
ance he makes frequent reference to "gourd trumpets,"
hich are pictured in Parsons, 1936b, p. 296, fig. 172c, d.
 describing the Tewa performance at Hano, however,
ephen mentions a Flute player, Parsons, 1936b, p. 343.
[82] For a detailed explanation of how the images are made
nd manipulated, see Fewkes and Stephen, 1893, p. 275 ff.,
nd Parsons, 1936b, pp. 291–306.
[83] Fewkes, 1900d, p. 628, interprets the knocking over
f corn plants as a representation of the destructive power
f nature; and Haeberlin, 1916, p. 25, describes the final
 ct of the performance as a portrayal of lightning striking
 cornfield. Third Mesa informants did not accept these
 ggested interpretations, but insisted that the entire

ritual stood for the approach of summer and the coming
of heavy rains; and that it concluded with a symbolic
harvesting. Compare Stephen's comments in Parsons,
1936b, p. 322, to the effect that "knocking the corn stalks
flat on the floor typifies ripeness, abundance, a field
of corn with ears so heavy as to break down the stalks."
[84] Pregnant women are forbidden to attend the Water
Serpent dance lest the fetus swell up, and violators of any
regulations connected with the observances are punished
with swollen stomachs. Compare Parsons, 1936b, p. 288,
footnotes 4, 5; and Fewkes, 1900d, p. 627, footnote 1.
[85] Fewkes, 1903, pp. 40–48, describes three different
performances with serpent effigies which were given in
the course of a single night at Walpi.

kong,[86] but in recent years they have been shown in place of the latter as one of the night dances in the first of the Anktioni series. Even when the puppet dolls are independently exhibited, their performance shows a great many resemblances to the Water Serpent dance.[87] Thus the Puppet Doll dance must be individually sponsored, and not long after its announcement beans and corn are planted in heated kivas and are set into little cones of mud as soon as they have matured. Then, on the afternoon of the public exhibition, He'e'e leads a number of mixed Katcinas about the village, and that night the dance is put on in each of the kivas successively.[88]

As with the Palulokong exhibition, the unit putting on the Puppet Doll dance covers the lights in the kiva, puts up a house (screen), sets the dolls and other objects in position, and begins singing, rattling, and flute playing. When the kiva is again lighted, a screen slightly different from the one in the Water Serpent rites appears to view. As seen by the audience, it has boughs of spruce attached at both ends; a large Shalakmana (Shalako girl) figure made of cottonwood stands at the left; a figure of Muyingwa, god of germination, is portrayed in the center; and a Palhikmana (Water-drinking girl) image is at the right.[89] Cloud and rain designs cover most of the remaining surface of the screen; a sandpiper figure is mounted at the top; and a number of corn plant hillocks are set out on the floor in front. In each corner a Hehe'a Katcina squats close by the screen, and behind it there crouches an impersonator of Sotukinangwu'u, the principal sky deity, who occasionally stands up so that his head and shoulders are clearly visible, and

projects a lightning frame out over the "field" « corn.

The dolls, which are nearly two feet high ar about eight inches in diameter, wear elabora headdresses featuring terraced cloud symbol They stand before open spaces in the curta which represent the doorways of their house and the manipulators cause them to lower ar raise their arms in time to the music, in th fashion of dancers who impersonate female Ka cinas. When the first song concludes, the mario ettes are made to bend over little mealing ston at a forty-five degree angle. They remain in th posture while a second song is sung, and as the move their arms up and down they appear to k grinding corn.[90] At the close of this episode, th father of the Katcinas who is on duty for th night's performances, places tiny brooms in th hands of the puppets, and they seem to sweep th newly-ground meal into little plaques. Then th father picks up two small trays heaped with swee cornmeal, which have been hidden from th audience, and passes them about so that each c the spectators may have a taste. After this th lights are again shielded, and the screen and othe properties are rapidly dismantled and carried ou The rest of the evening is given over to Katcin dances performed by other kiva groups in th conventional manner.

SHALAKO

The supernatural personage known as Shalakc which is one of the characters in the Puppet Dc dance, is also impersonated occasionally by hu man actors during one of the performances a Anktioni.[91] Sometimes it is incorporated in th

---

[86] Stephen describes Shalako maiden figurines as part of the Water Serpent dance equipment. Parsons, 1936b, pp. 334–337.

[87] The present account of the Puppet Doll dance is based on the Hotevilla performance which I witnessed at Anktioni on March 23, 1934. Compare Fewkes, 1900d, pp. 618–619.

[88] I did not discover if a preliminary ritual was held at the spring.

[89] Among the Hopi at Oraibi there is so close a conceptual link between the Shalako and the Palhik girls that they are virtually interchangeable and are known together as Corn Maidens. Compare Fewkes, 1900a, p. 130, footnote 1. For illustrations of the performance, see Fewkes, 1903, plates XXVII and LVI.

[90] A connection between the dolls representing corn-grinding maidens (gnumamantu) and the Water Serpent dance is implied in Parsons, 1925, p. 59.

Sometimes, during a long-haired (Anga) Katcina danc a Hehe'a Katcina will bring in a mealing stone on whic one of the "female" impersonators grinds corn in time t the rhythm of the dance. Fewkes, 1900d, p. 611, describe such a bit of action, and I witnessed a similar scene at night dance in a New Oraibi kiva in 1934. Compare th picture in Fewkes, 1903, plate XXXII.

At corn-grinding parties in real life, the participatir girls are frequently alluded to as Palhik maidens. One c these parties is described by Stephen in Parsons, 1936l pp. 153, 154.

[91] Oraibi informants told two incompatible stories abou the origin of the Oraibi Shalako. Some frankly admitte that it was borrowed from Zuñi, but the daughter of th Bow clan chief claimed that her father's ancestors ha brought it from the Underworld. For a discussion of th Hopi borrowing of Shalako, see Parsons, 1939, pp. 97: 973, and footnotes.

Water Serpent dance,[92] and sometimes it is given separately. Only a member of the Bow clan has the right to sponsor a Shalako dance during the Repeat series,[93] and the paraphernalia must be taken from *the* Bow house where they are stored. Shalako actors are always escorted by other Katcinas, most of which are supposed to belong to the Bow people.

Before entering a kiva for a night performance, Shalako is preceded by a number of Duduknantu, male Katcinas who wear cloud headdresses;[94] and by several "female" Heyaupamamantu (Rain Bringing Girls),[95] who range themselves in a semicircle, facing the ladder. The Duduknantu begin to sing and rattle, and the Heyaupamamantu, though remaining erect, keep time by scraping sheep scapulae against notched sticks.[96] Then, when Shalako comes in to dance, the impersonator stands inside the line, looking south. With this group, there generally appear as guardian Katcinas, Tangiktcina and Sa'viki (Bow clan *wuya*), and two Kokosochöyatu, who wear black body paint interspersed with vari-colored spots.

PALHIK MAIDENS

The Oraibi Palhik ceremony, sometimes referred to as the *gnumamantu* (corn-grinding maidens), seems to have differed from those of the other Hopi villages. The dancers were chosen by the head of the officiating kiva, and men impersonated both male and female Katcinas. They danced in a wide arc, boys alternating with "girls." The latter wore the customary ceremonial garb of women, with white masks and terraced headdresses practically undistinguish-

able from those of Shalako.[97] The men were dressed in the usual Katcina skirts and sashes and carried gourd rattles in their right hands, but their bodies were painted in the manner of Powamu Katcinas in the Bean dance. They had on blossom symbols such as are worn by flute players in the Flute ceremony, and they held flutes in their left hands.[98] Their faces were concealed by blue masks, and to their backs were attached *pavaiyokyasim* (rain water shields) such as are borne by the instrumentalists in the Blue Flute dance.

The Palhik dance was performed to singing and drumming by Koyemsi. It was also customary for the Palhik group to include several men in the costume of the Paiyatamu clowns, who did not, however, engage in comic pranks but merely danced as did the others. I was not informed of any reason for this custom, but I noted that clown heads were incorporated into the terraced cloud design of a Palhik headdress that the Oraibi chief prepared in 1934.

On First and Second Mesas, I was told at Oraibi, the Palhik was generally celebrated in conjunction with the Marau winter offering rites. In this case, the older members of the Marau society and of the men's Wuwutcim acted as singers, while the younger ones did the dancing.[99]

THE HUYAN KATCINA DANCE

Another favorite for Anktioni representation at Oraibi was said to be the Huyan (Barter) Katcina dance.[100] The men who are to participate prepare a large number of dolls with which they run

[92] Fewkes and Stephen, 1893, p. 280, describe a Shalako impersonator who engages in a struggle with the Palulokong effigy during the Water Serpent dance.

[93] Shalako was formerly given in the village plaza in July. The Oraibi impersonator wore a "giant" mask and had his body covered with feathers. He was accompanied by Koyemsi who sang and drummed for him. I could not obtain details of the Oraibi Shalako, but there is an account of the First Mesa observance in Parsons, 1936b, pp. 415–442; and in Hough, 1917.

[94] My main informant on the Shalako night dance was Sakwapa, who is notoriously unreliable. Other informants admitted being unqualified to discuss the ceremony, but Sakwapa claimed knowledge of the rites because she was the daughter of a Bow clansman. Nevertheless, she was unable to explain the meaning of Duduknantu and other details, and her account is obviously incomplete.

[95] Compare the Shalako figures shown in Fewkes, 1897b, p. 296 and plates CVII and CIX.

[96] Usually, those who perform with these implements

kneel as they play.

[97] See Fewkes, 1903, plate LVI.

[98] Palhik performers sometimes carried staffs known as *talavaiya* instead of flutes. In both instances the objects had to be borrowed from Flute society men, although the borrowers were not necessarily members of that ceremony and did not play the instruments.

Another tie between Palhik and Flute observances is found in the statement made by Oraibi men that Palhik was frequently performed in dances that were held on the night when the Flute society finished its winter rites.

Fewkes, 1902b, p. 498, calls attention to resemblances between the Palhik, Shalako, and Flute Maidens.

[99] Parsons, 1923b, p. 171, relates that she was told that some of the Singers at Wuwutcim were imitating the actions of Palhik maidens in the Marau ceremony. Also note that Stephen observed two young women doing a Palhik dance during the Marau ritual in 1893. Parsons, 1936b, p. 932.

[100] I was unable to find any link between the Huyan

ñötiwa[101] in the kivas. The women who succeed in grasping dolls must repay the performers by bringing food to their kiva the next day.[102] Furthermore, if a disappointed woman would like to get a gift, she need only provide a feast and the members of the kiva would be obliged to repay her with a doll as soon as possible.

The Huyan Katcinas are known as "watchmen" and carry long yucca whips with which they lash each other before beginning to dance. They enter a kiva by clambering headfirst down the ladder, and some of them leave feet first. If one of their number falls during the performance, the others may whip him. Those who are to take part in this dance are required to sleep in the kiva for four nights and to observe the ordinary ritual tabus in order "to get strength" for their gymnastic feats.

SUMMARY AND CONCLUSION OF ANKTIONI DANCES

When the end of the Powamu celebration brings to a close the Badger clan leadership of the Katcina cult, there occurs a transfer of this authority to the head of the Katcina clan. Under his auspices there soon begins a cycle of night dances which are known as Anktioni. These repeat several of the ritual features of the Powamu. The nearest resemblances occur in the Water Serpent dance, but the Puppet Doll, Shalako, and Palhik dances also bear some relation to the Powamu. All these performances, as well as the Huyan dance, are incorporated into a pattern of night dances very much like that which had prevailed in January, prior to the start of the Powamu. The head of the Katcina clan inaugurates the series, and from then on, at irregular intervals, various kivas sponsor a succession of night dances, each of which is announced by Koyemsi.[103] It is in the

course of this series that one kiva or another generally chooses for its presentation one of the dances that duplicate some of the aspects of the Powamu.

Although the most significant links occur between Anktioni and Powamu as shown by the forced growing of beans and corn, and the He'e'e circuits during the Water Serpent and the Puppet Doll dances, we must not overlook the connections with other Hopi ceremonies. These are manifested by the participation of Flute men in the Water Serpent and Puppet Doll rites, and by the use of Flute society paraphernalia in the Palhik exhibitions. Then too a bond exists between the Palhik, the Marau, and the Wuwutcim ceremonies.

OUT-OF-DOOR KATCINA DANCES

By the time the Anktioni program is concluded, it is late in March or early April and the weather is generally mild enough to permit the staging of all-day, out-of-door Katcina dances. These are given sporadically until the Homegoing dance is held in mid-summer, after which the Katcinas are "locked up" for the season. Any adult male may ask for a Katcina dance.[104] The Village chief, usually with the help of other leaders, carefully weighs the request and considers the person's character, partly because he is to serve as chief on the day of the performance, and partly because he is held responsible for the state of the weather during the dance and for the following four days. If it is decided that the petitioner's "heart is good," permission is generally granted without more ado. The sponsor then chooses the type of Katcina to be impersonated, selects the officers,[105] arranges to have songs composed, and rounds up as many performers as

---

Katcinas and the Powamu, but it seems to have been an old custom to perform this dance during Anktioni. See Fewkes and Stephen, 1893, p. 271.

[101] The custom of having men dodging in and out among women as they bear gifts aloft, is called *ñötiwa*. This was also done during the Huyan dance at Walpi at Anktioni of 1893. Compare Fewkes and Stephen, 1893, pp. 280–281.

[102] At Walpi the recipients of dolls provided food on the same night. See Fewkes and Stephen, 1893, p. 281. According to Parsons, 1936b, p. 274, the Huyan Katcinas on First Mesa traded figurines with women who desired to bear children.

[103] I was unable to determine the exact number of kivas which were expected to sponsor Anktioni performances, nor could I learn whether or not certain kivas took turns

in various years. At Oraibi in 1934, all three of the active kivas were supposed to call for Anktioni night dances, but the men were so busy working on the roads that they begrudged the time needed for ceremonies, and the third kiva called off the program it had planned to sponsor.

[104] If a woman wishes to sponsor a dance she must get a male relative to act in her behalf. For comparative material on Katcina dance organization, consult Parsons, 1936b, pp. 350–351.

[105] The officers consist of a member of the Powamu society to serve as father of the Katcinas; a good singer to lead the men and another to lead the "women," these two being elder brothers of the Katcinas; the sponsor; and the head of the officiating kiva. Sometimes too a drummer (uncle of the Katcinas) is needed; and a few types of dance call for still another officer, a "side-dancer" (grandfather

possible—his kiva mates forming the nucleus of the group although any initiated man is eligible to take a part. The painting of masks and the preparation of costumes is left entirely to the individual participants. Practice is held in the evenings at the officiating kiva, and it takes but a few rehearsals to perfect the performance.[106]

On the night before the dance all those who are to participate in any way meet in the sponsor's kiva for an all-night session devoted to smoking, praying, and rehearsing. The officers make many prayer-feathers (nakwakwosi), some of which are to be given to the dancers when they are dismissed, while others are to be deposited at a Katcina shrine by the sponsor, just before daybreak. In the early dawn the dancers paint and dress themselves, and with masks in hand they proceed to Qowawaima, a shrine just outside the pueblo limits. The masks are ranged in a line on the ground, the men stand in a column parallel to them, and the first song on the day's program is rehearsed. Then, just as the sun is about to rise, masks are donned and the Katcinas start for the village in single file. At the point where the inhabited houses begin, the father of the Katcinas meets his "children," and by sprinkling cornmeal as he goes, makes a path for the dancers all the way to the plaza.[107]

In the types of dances that are most commonly exhibited, each song is repeated many times.[108] For the first rendition the men line up somewhat in the manner of the figure 7 so that some of them face east and the others north.[109] Then the father gives them a path to their second position which may have them all facing north, or which may bend the line so that some look north and the others west. The third position

generally has the whole line facing south. When the song has been finished for the third time, the father leads the Katcinas to the shrine which they are accustomed to use as a resting place. Here, out of sight of the spectators, the Katcinas unmask, smoke, and relax for a few minutes. Then they rehearse the next song on the program, resume their masks, and return to the plaza as before.

From dawn to sunset the Katcinas perform, the duration of their rest periods depending on the number of songs that they have prepared.[110] After the opening dance they stop for breakfast, and at noon they have a lengthy recess, during which their kinswomen bring them abundant food. The sponsor's family is especially obligated to help feed the performers. At the first, pre-breakfast dance, and at all the afternoon appearances, the Katcinas carry gifts into the plaza. These they place on the ground and leave until they have finished singing in the first position, then they distribute them among the audience before they line up for the second. Most of the presents are from the impersonators themselves, but any non-participant may request a dancer to give out some object for him.

During the afternoon too a number of clowns may appear in the dance plaza. Sometimes they belong to organized clown groups,[111] but at other times they are merely volunteers who give impromptu or hastily arranged programs for the crowd's amusement. The clowns may mimic the dancers or they may act independently without reference to the Katcinas. Hopi clowns frequently perform burlesques and generally indulge in gluttonous and obscene pranks. They are often such excellent actors that the bystanders howl with laughter.[112]

of the Katcinas), who does vigorous and comic steps as a soloist.

[106] This is due to the fact that there are fixed dance routines and song rhythms for each type of impersonation, so that knowledge of the tune pattern carries with it the clues to the proper gestures and steps. This is similar to our own custom, where the form of a tune such as a waltz indicates the dance pattern to be used.

[107] The following account is based on numerous observations throughout the Hopi villages. For comparative material see Parsons, 1936b, pp. 350–463, et passim; and Earle and Kennard, 1938, pp. 29–33. Illustrations of Katcinas in action occur in Fewkes, 1923, plates 1, 4, 6.

[108] Each song rendition is given continuously as follows: two verses and choruses, then two choruses, and, finally, one verse and one chorus. The father of the Katcinas calls out thanks and sprinkles each of the performers with cornmeal at the start of each of these parts.

[109] The best singers are clustered about the leader in the center of the line, the poorest participants being at the extremes. If a sponsor wishes to dance he always stands at the head of the line, regardless of his ability. Furthermore, he must then delegate someone to smoke for him throughout the performance.

The manner in which an outdoor dance starts is the same as for night dances. See p. 113.

[110] Eight or ten different songs are usually rendered in one day, but there may be as many as twelve. Sometimes, so many songs are composed that it takes two days to sing them all.

[111] For details regarding clown groups, see Parsons and Beals, 1934, pp. 492–494, et passim; and Parsons, 1936b, pp. 157, 158.

[112] Many clown performances are described in detail in Parsons, 1936b. See under "Grotesques" in the index to that work.

Towards sundown, when the closing song has been completed, the father of the Katcinas thanks them and passes from man to man giving each one a *nakwakwosi* and cornmeal. Then the men return to Qowawaima to unmask and undress, and as soon as possible they deposit their prayer-offerings at Katcina shrines or in their fields. A four-day period of continence concludes the entire performance.

From time to time throughout the spring and summer, Katcina dances are frequently held. Some are sponsored by people who have just recovered from an illness; others are requested to celebrate special occasions such as a child's birthday. A religious element is invariably present but it is frequently overlaid by the sheer pleasure and entertainment derived from the spectacle by participants and onlookers alike. Every dance day is a holiday, and in each home "open house" is kept, with huge vessels of mutton stew (*nukwivi*), corn, *piki*, and melons and peaches available to all comers. Guests are freely welcomed whether they come of their own accord or whether they have been invited by some member of the household. Men, and women to a lesser extent, call at many houses in the intervals between dances, and it is customary to eat something in each of them. So much enjoyment do the natives get from these occasions, that, as Dr. Kennard says, "No Hopi who can possibly attend misses a Kachina dance."[113]

THE HOMEGOING (NIMAN) DANCE[114]

As the sun approaches the summer solstice point the open season draws to a close and preparations are made for sending the Katcinas home. The rites take the form of a sixteen-day ceremony beginning four days after the summer solstice and culminating about mid-July. The Katcina clan chief, assisted by the head of the Powamu society,[115] are the leading officers of the Homegoing observances. They dispatch

messengers to a distant Katcina shrine, Kisiwu, to fetch quantities of spruce; they attend t the formal smoking and the manufacture c prayer-offerings; they supervise the painting c masks and the preparation of costumes; and the arrange frequent song and dance rehearsals. Th Hemis Katcina is the favorite impersonation fo the Niman, but other types such as the Navah Katcina are occasionally chosen.[116]

Throughout the day of the Homegoing danc the performers file in and out of the plaza i routine fashion, but when the dance ends a num ber of officials appear to bless the dancers wit smoke and medicine-water, and to give ther prayer-feathers and sacred cornmeal. Just befor the Katcinas leave the plaza for the last time c the season, their father makes a long speech c farewell in which he thanks them for past favor and prays for continued help from the Katcina and their Cloud relatives.[117] Next the dancers ar led to a special, hollow shrine not far from th pueblo. A cover is removed and each impersona tor drops some of his offerings into the shrine whereupon the lid is replaced to indicate the clos ing of the open cycle. Then the performers un mask and undress and return to the town a civilians.

Early the following morning additional rite are performed by the Eototo Katcina, the Katcin and the Badger leaders, and other officials. Thes terminate before the hollow shrine, into whic offerings are again placed. This time, when th Katcina chief restores the lid, the Katcina seaso is officially closed; and from that moment n masked impersonations may be given until th Soyal Katcina arrives to inaugurate a ne season.[118] Three days later the chiefs who hav just brought the rites to a close assemble for smoke, during which the retiring sponsor of th Homegoing dance names his successor. The lat ter then carries a Katcina mask to his home kiv as a sign that he has accepted the responsibility and with the stage set for next year's perform ance, the Katcina season is finally concluded.

---

[113] Earle and Kennard, 1938, p. 30.

[114] Observations of this ritual at Hotevilla provide the main basis for this account. Since the Third Mesa procedure has never been fully described, a detailed discussion is included in Part Three. First Mesa data occur in Parsons, 1936b, pp. 493–575. Also compare Earle and Kennard, 1938, pp. 35–38.

[115] Note that the same chiefs, with the emphasis reversed, cooperate in the leadership of the other great Katcina ceremony, the Powamu. This is another expres-

sion of the Badger and Katcina clan partnership in th control of the Katcina cult.

[116] Hemis Katcinas are portrayed in Earle and Kennard 1938, plates XIV and XV.

[117] Kennard has translated the speech in Earle and Ker nard, 1938, pp. 37, 38.

[118] As previously noted, the one exception to this rule i the Masau Katcina (see Part Three), which may appear i the closed season.

SUMMARY AND CONCLUSION

The Homegoing dance rounds out an orderly and well-balanced sequence of Katcina activities. Internal cohesion is provided by such devices as having the same kiva sponsor the opening (Qöqöqlom) and the closing (Niman) dances, the oyoko, and perhaps the midpoint performance of the Anktioni series. External integration with the remainder of the ceremonial calendar is accomplished by linking the first Katcina appearances of the year with the Wuwutcim and Soyal rites, by announcing the Niman arrangements in advance to the Soyal men, by incorporating Katcina initiations within the Powamu, by including Flute society activities in the Water Serpent and Puppet Doll dances, and by duplicating some aspects of the Marau in the Palhik performance.

The active Katcina season falls roughly within the period between the winter and the summer solstices, an arrangement that accords well with Hopi economy as it leaves the late summer and fall free for farming duties. The yearly cycle is divided into approximate halves, which are so arranged that the Badger clan assumes control immediately after the Katcinas are "locked up," and remains in charge through the opening performances, the first series of night dances, and the Powamu. Then the Katcina clan assumes the leadership, and is responsible for the Anktioni observances, which duplicate several Powamu features, the outdoor dances, and the Niman.

A great many factors are woven into the Katcina complex. It is the only universal aspect of Hopi ceremonialism, and admission to its mysteries carries age-grading significance. Only uninitiated children are barred from some degree of participation in the rites, and this practical distinction has its counterpart in Hopi religious beliefs. Thus a child which dies prior to its Katcina initiation is given a distinctive type of burial,[119] and its soul does not return to the Underworld as a Cloud or a Katcina, but returns to its mother's roof, where it hovers among the rafters until it is re-born in her next child.[120] Then again, inasmuch as the Katcinas represent friendly spirits of the dead, their cult may well be regarded, as Fewkes has suggested, as a generalized kind of ancestor worship;[121] and the fact that several particular Katcinas are regarded as clan ancestors (wuya), introduces a totemic aspect into the complex. Furthermore, the identification of Katcinas and Cloud people calls attention to their rain-bringing ability and makes it proper to regard them as fertility gods. It is also important to realize, as Dr. Parsons has pointed out, that the Katcinas have curative functions and that they may inflict a variety of ailments on those who transgress the rules of their cult.[122] Finally, the Katcinas are called upon to help discipline young children and to aid the Village chief in preserving order within the pueblo.

The complexities of their Katcina worship are of little moment to the Hopi. They make no effort to systematize or to classify their beliefs, but are content to regard the Katcinas as a host of benevolent spirits who have the best interests of the Hopi ever at heart. To impersonate them is a pleasure, to observe them a delight. Quite apart from its more formal features, the operation of the Katcina cycle brings more warmth and color into the lives of the Hopi than any other aspect of their culture.

[119] Voth, 1912b, p. 101.
[120] Voth, 1912b, p. 103. If the mother fails to bear another child, the soul of her uninitiated, deceased child ultimately accompanies her spirit to the home of the dead.

[121] Fewkes, 1923. Elsewhere the Katcinas are described as " 'the early dead,' those who died long ago." Fewkes, 1897a, p. 198.
[122] Parsons, 1933, p. 13; and Parsons, 1939, p. 104, *et passim*.

CHAPTER X

TRIBAL INITIATION

INTRODUCTORY

SOON AFTER adolescence, but usually before he has become married, a young man is expected to go through a Tribal Initiation which marks the transition from boyhood to adulthood. This rite is practically universal for the entire male population. It is known collectively as the Wuwutcim, but it is divided into four distinct branches called Singers (Tao), Horns (Al), Agaves (Kwan), and Wuwutcim.[1] Although membership in the Wuwutcim society is by far the most common, adult status may be achieved by joining any one of the divisions.[2] On Third Mesa the Wuwutcim is the central one of the four branches. It is controlled by the Kele (Chicken Hawk) clan, whose head man is considered Tribal Initiation chief; novices are called *kele* or *kelehöyam* (little chicken hawks); and the November moon during which annual observances are held is named Kel-muya.[3] Not every year, however, do the exercises include the induction of new members. It is only when there are a sufficient number of candidates on hand to warrant holding the rites in their lengthened, initiatory form that a full Tribal Initiation occurs.[4] One custom connected with the decision regarding whether or not initiations shall be held, shows that from an internal point of view it is the Kwan rather than the Wuwutcim division that controls the most crucial part of the combined ritual; for unless the Kwans agree to conduct their particular services in the extended form there can be no admissions to the Tribal Initiation;[5] and the Kwans will not perform their full ceremony unless they have at least one candidate to induct into their own society. Many other features of the joint performance attest the power of the Kwan, and their rites are more esoteric and far less communal than those of the Wuwutcim, Al, or Tao.

The Tribal Initiations are the most complicated, and among the most vital of all Hopi ceremonies, and their significance must be understood before one can hope to grasp the essential meaning of Hopi religion. Fewkes and Stephen, who witnessed far more of the observances than any other ethnologist to date, deferred "all attempt at interpretation,"[6] because they fully realized the complexity of the rites. However, thanks to their detailed reports and to the material that has been made available by later investigators, we may now attempt a tentative explana-

---

[1] To avoid confusion the term Wuwutcim will hereafter be used to designate only the specific ceremony of that name, and the collective rites of which it forms a part will be known as the Tribal Initiation. The meaning of the word Wuwutcim is obscure, but Voth in Dorsey and Voth, 1901, p. 10, footnote *, suggests that it implies growing to manhood. However, Voth also notes the resemblance of the term Wuwutcim to *Wowoyom*, which means old men, and which Fewkes, 1902a, p. 15 and footnote 1, translates as "Ancient Being." The popularity of the Wuwutcim branch of the Tribal Initiation is attested by the fact that it required four kivas to accommodate its novices, whereas one kiva each was sufficient to hold the Tao, Al, and Kwan initiates. Most of the candidates are between fifteen and twenty years old.

[2] Parsons, 1923b, p. 181, states that in a sense "initiation into one of the four societies may be considered a tribal initiation."

Candidates to the Tribal Initiation had to be sponsored by ceremonial fathers who were generally, but not necessarily, the same men who had put them into the Katcina and other societies. A youth's sponsor had to be selected from the particular branch which the young man wanted to join.

[3] Owing to the lapse of Tribal Initiations at Oraibi, the writer has never seen even the public portions of the ritual. The present exposition combines observation of a few Tribal Initiation proceedings at Hotevilla, interviews with several men who had gone through the rites, and extensive reading in the published accounts of various investigators. The following works contain most of the available data:

Fewkes, 1900a; Fewkes, 1895b; Fewkes and Stephen, 1892b; Parsons, 1923b; Parsons, 1936b, pp. 957–993; Steward, 1931, pp. 56–59.

[4] Fewkes incorrectly calls the extended Tribal Initiation rites *Nā-ac-nai-ya*, and the shorter, non-initiatory form Wuwuchimti. Fewkes, 1900a, p. 80. Natives call both sets of rites Wuwutcim indiscriminately, and *na'acnaiya* means only head-washing, which is a part of initiation proceedings in all Hopi societies. Compare Parsons, 1936b, p. 957, footnote 1; and Dorsey and Voth, 1901, p. 19, footnote *.

In the opinion of the writer, Fewkes erred in stressing the new-fire, rather than the Tribal Initiation aspect of the ceremonies.

[5] This has not been reported for First or Second Mesas.

[6] Fewkes and Stephen, 1892b, p. 217.

on. To furnish a background for a discussion of
the meaning of the Tribal Initiation, it is first
necessary to provide a chronological summary of
the main events.[7]

CHRONOLOGICAL SUMMARY

The Oraibi performance of the Tribal Initiation starts when the Al (Horn) chief, in his capacity as Sun Watcher (Tawawunitaka), announces that the sun has risen at a point on the
horizon which is known as Dingapi.[8] As soon as
the news has been received, the heads of the four
participating societies hold a formal smoke, during which they make various prayer-offerings
which are handed over to the Tca'akmongwi
(Crier chief). Before sunrise the next morning, he
puts down a road-marker facing northeast and
deposits the other objects in the shrine on the roof
of *the* Kele house from which he proclaims the
coming celebration. Soon after dawn on the
fourth day following, the chiefs enter their respective kivas and erect the *na'atsi* (standards)
which indicate that the rites are under way. In the
Kwan and in the Wuwutcim kivas the officers
conduct altar-making exercises,[9] and the leaders
of all four divisions prepare special offerings of
cotton strings to which are attached a number of
pine-needles.

Late in the afternoon, the members of the
other groups file into the central kiva of the joint
observances,[10] and in the presence of the entire
assemblage, Al and Kwan men kindle two fires
with rotating drills. During this part of the ceremony, the Kwan chief, impersonating Masau'u,
is concealed behind blankets; and when the fire
is brought to a blaze, the pine-needle strings are
thrown into the flames as sacrifices to Masau'u.
At this point, an Al man, wearing the two-horned
headdress of his order, lights a cedar-bark torch
at the new fire and hastens out to touch off fires
at all the other participating kivas. Meantime,

another Al goes out to a shrine from which he
brings back the image of Talautumsi (Dawn
Woman, see pl. III b), a very important deity
whose idol is displayed on various kiva hatches
until the fifth day of the observances.

Then the Tao members, followed by the
Wuwutcim and Al men, leave the kiva, but the
Kwan remain behind to perform a brief, secret
ritual before joining the others at the shrine of
Tuwapongtumsi (Sand-altar Woman), the female counterpart of Masau'u.[11] After a brief
ceremony conducted in honor of the goddess, an
Al officer leads the entire party to a space below
the mesa "said to be one great *sipapû* where the
wise old men live.[12] Patting his foot on the
ground, one of the men in the procession said,
pointing downwards, 'Here, just below here, the
old people dwell. We are now,' he continued,
'praying to them for material prosperity—rain,
health, abundant harvests.' The *nakwakwoci* deposited here are offered to the early Hopi ancestors who once dwelt there, and who are now believed to be Katcinas in the lower world."[13] Then
the sacred area is circled four times, and the men
return to their respective kivas.

The day's rites are now completed, and the
novices go to sleep in the kivas, wrapped in the
same blankets with their "fathers"; but from
time to time throughout the night patrols of Horn
(Al) and Agave (Kwan) men keep hurrying
through the village. Early the next morning, the
Tao (Singers) group, escorted by Al men, performs a dance; but the Kwan engage in a ritual
smoke for which they use a special, very large
pipe called Kwantcongo; and in the evening they
again serve as sentries. The third day's observances open with another morning dance by
the Tao; and in the afternoon, the Wuwutcim
give a public performance in which some of their
members appear disguised as women. Many of
them are padded to simulate pregnancy, and all
resemble "squalid married women,"[14] with phallic

---

[7] To prevent confusion, most of the details of costume,
paraphernalia, etc., will be omitted from the chronological
summary. They may be found in the sources listed above.

[8] For information regarding the duties of the Sun
Watchers at Oraibi, consult Titiev, 1938c, pp. 39, 40.

According to Parsons, 1936b, p. 958, the date for the
start of Walpi's Tribal Initiation is determined by sunset
observations made by the Singers' chief.

[9] Fewkes, 1895b, p. 436, describes the way in which the
altars are erected.

[10] At Oraibi, the Wuwutcim chief uses Hawiovi as the
main kiva of all the combined rites, but at Walpi the center

of the Tribal Initiation is the Chief (Moñ) kiva where
Singers' chief presides. See Fewkes, 1900a, p. 81.

[11] Compare Parsons, 1923b, p. 162, footnote 16.

[12] From the nature of the rites performed at this place,
it may well have been an ancient cemetery.

[13] Fewkes, 1900a, p. 96. As will be shown below, there
is reason to believe that at this time the spirits of the dead
are invited to visit the pueblo.

[14] Fewkes and Stephen, 1892b, p. 200. On Third Mesa
it is customary for men of the Wuwutcim group to taunt
Marau women primarily, as the two societies are said to
be brother and sister. Fewkes, 1900a, p. 98 and p. 124,

emblems depicted on their garments. Throughout the fourth day the village is barred to visitors and the trails are closed and carefully guarded. The Tao and Wuwutcim dance with a strong Al escort, and later the Al men hold a private altar ritual in their own kiva. Simultaneously, in the ceremonial chamber of the Kwan, the men prepare their full costumes, paint up with characteristic warrior markings, and otherwise prepare for the most important and strenuous of their nightly patrols. That same afternoon, the Al and Tao units pray before the figure of Talautumsi which is then being displayed on the Kwan kiva's hatch, and when it grows dark they begin night-long ceremonies. At this point, members of the Horn and Kwan societies start making rapid circuits about the village until, a little after midnight, they are moving at a furious pace just as the kiva observances come to a close.

At sunrise on the fifth day, the image of Talautumsi is returned, with appropriate rites by all the groups, to the shrine where it is customarily kept. In the procession the Horn men serve as the actual bearers of the idol, and while it is being secreted, they scatter "among the cliffs . . . [and bound] constantly back and forth among the crags faithfully imitating mountain sheep."[15] Then all return to their kivas where they purify themselves with emetics before indulging in "a fine feast." In the afternoon, the Singers, naked except for breech clouts, and adorned with or carrying realistic phallic representations, revile the women in a bawdy, rowdy exhibition to which the women retaliate by dousing them liberally with water and urine and by smearing them with filth. Some time later, the Wuwutcim men, likewise featuring a variety of phallic signs, emerge from their kiva and try to outdo their predecessors in obscenity, while the women ply them with refuse and even with human ordure. The next day, the sixth since the Tribal Initiation began, is given over to a few dances, but is featured, primarily, by fuel-gathering and hunting expeditions on the part of the various society groups. For the seventh day little of interest is recorded, except that the Wuwutcim again tease and badger the women as they dance; but on the eighth day, the dances are of a more serious nature, and germination motives are emphasized. There is no bandying with the women and no disorderly conduct of any sort. The Wuwutcim dance with "rosettes" symbolizing blossoms affixed to their foreheads, thus bringing out their character as "Corn Youths,"[16] and the Singers appear with trays full of clay molds, liberally studded with vari-colored kernels of corn. These they carry as they dance in alternating columns with the Horn members, and in the end they distribute the molds to women spectators.

The rites on the ninth (closing) day begin long before dawn. The Kwan men carefully decorate themselves, and in the privacy of their kiva they practice a dance with "a strange knee-bending, high-stepping gesture."[17] Then they begin a long series of chants, concluding with a song that is so secret that although they render it in low, almost inaudible voices, they accompany it with a great uproar in order to make sure that not a syllable is overheard by any save members of their own order. After this, in full costume, they leave their chamber for their last appearance of the ceremony. Meantime, four Horn society men, wearing their helmets reversed, have built huge bonfires in the court, and mimicking the antics of mountain sheep, they bound here and there and occasionally leap over the fires. During this performance, the Wuwutcim and the Tao groups file into the plaza and look on. Then the Kwan unit arrives, and after some preliminary rites their chief sprinkles a broad path of cornmeal "from the west end of the line"[18] as the Kwan men sing. Just as the song is coming to a close the chief obliterates the path by sweeping across it,[19] and when the singing ends the Kwan return to their kiva. They are dismissed soon after and given permission to return to their homes for breakfast.

describes similar procedure and beliefs at First Mesa. On the other hand, Parsons, 1923b, pp. 170, 171, reports that Singers taunt Marau and other society women; and Fewkes, 1900a, p. 127, also indicates a connection between Tao and Marau.

[15] Fewkes and Stephen, 1892b, p. 207.
[16] Several Oraibi informants referred to Wuwutcim men as "Corn Youths." Note too that members of the Marau, sister society of the Wuwutcim, may be known as Palhik or Corn Maidens. Compare p. 125.

[17] Fewkes and Stephen, 1892b, p. 216. This step is reminiscent of the gait adopted by the Masau Katcina performers.
[18] Fewkes and Stephen, 1892b, p. 217.
[19] Fewkes and Stephen, 1892b, p. 217. This bit of ritual suggests that the dead, who had earlier been asked to come to the village (footnote 13, above), are now being dismissed, after which their homeward path is obliterated in order to prevent its use by unwanted visitants from the other world.

Later in the day the Tribal Initiation rites conclude with public dances by the Wuwutcim and the Singers.

INTERPRETATION

The main hints that provide an understanding of the complicated Tribal Initiation are contained in the proceedings during which novices are inducted into the ceremonies; and it is forever to be regretted that on the climactic night of the 1891 observances, Stephen "was barred out from the kiva ceremony through the inadvertence of some of the Horns."[20] In the absence of first hand descriptions by trained observers a complete elucidation is obviously out of the question, but with the help of such information as natives were willing to impart, a partial interpretation may be proposed.[21]

Attention has already been called to the facts that on Third Mesa the Wuwutcim is the most widely attended of the four branches of the Tribal Initiation, and that its name is used to designate the entire body of rites that are performed concurrently. The Wuwutcim is controlled by the Chicken Hawk (Kele) clan, and the initiates are known as *kele* or *kelehöyam*. The fancy that candidates are little chicken hawks is carried out in a number of ways. On the first entrance to their kivas, the neophytes have hawk feathers tied in their hair, and they are seated along the east and south walls of the raised floor, with knees drawn up and hands clasped about the shins.[22] For the first three days they may not step down to the main level of the kiva because "their quills are not strong enough." Whenever they are fed by their ceremonial fathers, bits of food are held out to them and they must move their arms with the motion of flapping wings, and cry out shrilly, "Kelele, kelele!"[23] If a candidate wishes to attract attention, as when he desires to smoke, he must again flap his arms and cry, "*Piiva* (Tobacco), kelele, kelele!" To carry out the baby bird parallel still further, each neophyte is provided by his sponsor with a small wooden scratcher which he uses as a bird does its claws.

During the first few days of the rites, or on some previous occasion, each ceremonial father weaves for his "son" a special poncho-like garment, daubed all over with white clay and wider in front than in back. It is called *kelkwackyavu* (chicken hawk dress), and it is secured with a "chicken hawk belt" (*kelkwewe*) in such fashion that the front part is enclosed but the back is left free. This is so disposed that it gives the effect of a bird's tail, and the entire garment is said to represent the feathers, wings and tail of a hawk. These outfits are given to novices on the fourth day of the Wuwutcim initiation[24] and are worn by them on their first public appearance as members of the society.

The custom of representing the initiates as immature fledglings is directly concerned with the idea that they are undergoing a re-birth. As one informant told Dr. Parsons, the Wuwutcim "is the beginning of life, . . . it is like being born."[25] This notion receives literal expression in many ways during the course of the rites. On the first day of the Tribal Initiation each man who is to sponsor a novice's induction calls for his "child," gives him a "mother" ear of corn (*tcotcmingwu'u*), such as newly-born infants receive, and takes him to the Kwan kiva, regardless of what division he is to join. Here the Singers' society conducts a secret ritual, after which all the candidates (except those who are intended for the Kwan) are carried on the backs of their "fathers" to a shrine where there is a black rock, Kanuovi (Place of the gall-bladder), on which everyone spits. Then the youngsters are led back, supported in the fashion of injured football

---

[20] Parsons, 1936b, p. 977. Later the Kwan chief told Fewkes and Stephen that "he much regretted this," Fewkes and Stephen, 1892b, p. 206. However, I strongly suspect that the ethnologists were deliberately prevented from witnessing one of the most carefully guarded rites of Hopi religion. For one reason or another, Fewkes and Stephen, 1892b, p. 208, footnote 1, "Nearly all of the initiation ceremonies were not observed."

[21] The sketch of initiation procedure which follows is taken from interviews with Oraibi men who had gone through the rites in the fall of 1912. It deals primarily with the Wuwutcim society's performance, which is supposed to set the pattern for the Al and Tao initiations. Admissions to the Kwan, however, are said to be markedly different from the others.

[22] Compare Steward, 1931, p. 58.

[23] Fewkes and Stephen, 1892b, pp. 198, 203, 206, report that First Mesa novices must fast for several days; but at Oraibi ceremonial fathers may bring their "sons" food, provided it is prepared without salt, meat, fat, or the use of blue cornmeal. Blue meal is probably forbidden because blue is the color symbolic of the west where the home of the dead is located, and the novices have not yet been assigned their proper stations in the after-life. Compare Titiev, 1937a, p. 244.

[24] Later, the Wuwutcim garments are generally converted into Katcina G-strings.

[25] Parsons, 1933, p. 51; Parsons, 1939, p. 45 and p. 118.

players being helped off the field. After a brief rite outside the Kwan kiva, they are again taken to their own kivas. These actions were interpreted for me by a Third Mesa informant who said in effect, "The carrying of youngsters on the back means the beginning of life from the Emergence. They are carrying children up from the *sipapu* to the next (this) world. Spitting is a purification—they are getting rid of something bad. Support on the way back is like a child being helped to walk. Then the boy is strong enough to walk alone and is merely led back to his house (kiva)."

A similar series of steps occurs in the First Mesa rites. At first initiates are brought into the Chief kiva like babes in arms;[26] later they are carried like children, wrapped in blankets on the backs of Singers' men;[27] and still later they are allowed to walk, "each holding the blanket of the one preceding him."[28]

From Stephen we learn that Talautumsi (Dawn Woman) is regarded as the mother of the novices.[29] That is why her image is displayed on the main kiva hatch during the first day's activities, just before the neophytes are carried down the ladder like helpless babes.[30] Then her figurine is moved from kiva to kiva to indicate Talautumsi's motherhood of all the initiates; and on the fifth day, when the critical rites of the preceding night are ended, her figurine is returned to its shrine. This indicates that she has been safely delivered of her children. To carry out the allusions to childbirth still further, a blanket is placed over the kiva hatchway "to prevent the rays of the sun from shining upon the three novices. They . . . [are] not allowed to see the sun until after their final initiation."[31] This is exactly in accordance with Hopi practice regarding the exclusion of the sun from newly-born offspring and their mothers.[32]

Various acts in the initiatory proceedings th support Stephen's comment that "Talautumsi the mother of the . . . novices. They are now the depths of the underworld sea;[33] in six da they will be elevated to the surface."[34] It will noted from the foregoing discussion that at Ora as well as at Walpi, the idea of birth is implicit and explicitly linked with the concept of t Emergence. This directly confirms the penetra ing analysis of Washington Matthews, who w the first to recognize the Emergence story as myth of gestation and of birth."[35]

To understand more fully the meaning of t Hopi Tribal Initiation we must recall that n only is the *sipapu* the orifice through which m came forth on earth, but it is also the direct e trance to the Underworld where live the spir of the dead.[36] It is to be expected, therefo that the natal aspects of the Tribal Initiation w be complemented by mortuary features. We tu now to an examination of the rites as part of t Hopi cult of the dead.

Of the four Tribal Initiation societies, t Kwan stands most apart; and the others a taught to regard it with awe and dread. This due to its intimate association with Masau'u, g of death, and keeper of the home of the de (Maski). Indeed, a Kwan is very commonly r ferred to not only as Kwanitaka (Kwan man but also as one of the Maskwakwantu (Masau'u Kwan men).[37] Furthermore, on Third Mesa t control of the Kwan division is in the hands of t Masau'u clan, so that normally, the chief of t Kwan is the head of the Masau'u clan. Accor ingly, he regards Masau'u as his *wuya* and do not fear to impersonate him or to assume h functions, as the leader of the Kwan society mu do throughout the rites.[38] Thus, when fire kindled on the first day of the observances, t Kwan chief is present as the personation

---

[26] Fewkes and Stephen, 1892b, p. 197.
[27] Fewkes and Stephen, 1892b, p. 199.
[28] Fewkes and Stephen, 1892b, p. 199.
[29] Parsons, 1936b, p. 973.
[30] According to Fewkes, 1900a, p. 97, the image of Talautumsi is brought from its shrine only in initiatory years. This idol is pictured in Fewkes, 1924, plate 2, no. 1.
[31] Fewkes and Stephen, 1892b, p. 199.
[32] Voth, 1905a, p. 48 and p. 53.
[33] The original *sipapu* is often called *the* Kiva, and is supposed to be concealed from profane eyes by a "lid" of water. Consult Titiev, 1937a, p. 251. Many bodies of water are regarded as entrances to the Underworld and homes of Katcinas or spirits of the dead. Compare Parsons, 1939, p. 173; and Haeberlin, 1916, p. 21.

[34] Parsons, 1936b, p. 973.
[35] Matthews, 1902, p. 738. In this connection, note t that Al society novices wear helmets depicting half-grov horns, but after their initiation they wear large, full-grov horns. See Fewkes, 1900a, p. 137.
[36] See p. 107.
[37] Compare Nequatewa, 1936, p. 104, footnote 10. A cording to this author, the Kwan fraternity "is regard with great awe by the Hopi, for it is the duty of the priests to look after the dead. They are in charge of t spirit upon its journey from this world into Maski. . .
[38] The patron deity of the Kwan is sometimes referr to as Tokonaka, a god who passes judgment on the sou of the dead. Compare Parsons, 1936b, pp. 826, 827. seems to be characteristic of the Hopi pantheon that o

asau'u, the deity who first taught the Hopi
e use of fire.[39] Hence, the kindling of new-fire,
art from whatever other significance it may
ve, may here be regarded as the dramatization
one aspect of the Emergence story.[40]

Among his other attributes, and in keeping with
death-dealing powers, Masau'u is one of the
in war gods. It is only fitting, therefore, that
society of which he is the patron should be a
rriors' group. Thus we find the Kwan painting
mselves with typical warrior markings and
rrying long lances as part of their equipment.[41]
e must keep clearly in mind the fierce and
eathly" nature of the Kwan society if we are
understand the part it plays in the induction of
vices to the Tribal Initiation.

Attention has been called (p. 130) to the fact
t regardless of how many candidates may be
dy to enter the Horn, Singer, or Wuwutcim
cieties, there can be no admission to the
ibal Initiation at Oraibi unless the Kwan men
nduct their part of the joint ceremony, which
y refuse to do unless they have at least one
plicant for their own order. "Why" it may
asked, "must the other societies wait thus
on the pleasure of the Kwan?" In the answer to
s question lies the key to the entire scheme of
Tribal Initiation.

Let us recall that on the fourth day of the pro-
dings, visitors are barred from the pueblo and
the trails are closed. This night is a night of
stery and terror. People are forced to remain
indoors and are forbidden even to glance outside,
and patrols of Kwans and Horns rush madly
through the village, constantly challenging each
other and maintaining a dreadful din.[42] Concurrently, in the kivas underground, a most esoteric
and awe-inspiring ritual is being performed which
no white observer has ever glimpsed.[43] The reason
for the fear and tension that prevail on this night
is that when the roads to the pueblo are being
barred, one path is deliberately left open—the
path to the northwest where the Maski is located;
for on this night the dead are invited to throng into
the village. During the day the women prepare
large quantities of food for the expected "guests."
Then, towards sundown, feasts are set out and the
doors are left wide open in all the houses on one
side of an imaginary line which divides the village
into halves, and all those who live on that side
of the line vacate their homes and take shelter
with friends or relatives who live on the other
side which is tabu for the dead.[44] To all but Kwan
and Al men the spirits are invisible, and the purpose of the night-long patrol is to make sure that no
witches or other undesired visitants have mingled
with the dead. Very often, it is said, a guard will
challenge a spirit, only to have it "change into a
rock or bush" as he draws near. In such cases, the
sentry prays to the metamorphosed object by
sprinkling it with sacred cornmeal. On the other
hand, if an intruder is actually discovered, the
Horns may beat him severely, and if the Kwan
catch him they have the right to put him to death.[45]

ry may have several names, and I believe that Tokonaka
y be equated with Masau'u. Tokonaka, however, has
been equated with the sky god, Sotukinangwu'u. See
sons, 1936b, p. 336 and footnote 1. Neither equation is
tain. Eggan suggests that Tokonaka is a name for
an men in the other world.

[39] Voth, 1905b, pp. 12, 13, tells how the Hopi lacked
until they met Masau'u (Skeleton). Note that special
rings thrown into the newly-kindled fire are called
a-sau-wuh sacrifices," in Fewkes and Stephen, 1892b,
96.

[40] The association of the new-fire with Masau'u, god
eath, explains why "women and children drew back in
panic from the smoke." Parsons, 1923b, p. 162.

[41] Fewkes and Stephen, 1892b, pp. 202, 203. Note that
wood from which fire drills and Kwan lances are
de is called pilakho and is supposed to be gathered
n bushes that surround the site of the sipapu that marks
entrance to the home of the dead. See Titiev, 1937a,
251 and footnote 11. There is also a connection be-
en the horns worn by Kwan men and salt deposits
r the home of the dead. See Fewkes, 1900a, pp. 117,
; and Titiev, 1937a, p. 253.

[42] Compare the vivid description by Stephen in Parsons,

1936b, p. 977; and the experiences related in Parsons,
1923b, pp. 164, 165.

[43] It was on this night that Fewkes and Stephen were
"inadvertently" barred out of the kivas.

[44] This custom was revealed by an Oraibi man. Inasmuch as it has never been reported for any other Hopi
village, it is not known whether or not it occurs elsewhere;
but a meager statement by Steward suggests that the
custom may have existed on First Mesa—at least insofar
as the women are concerned. "That night," writes
Steward, 1931, p. 58, "all the women in Walpi must leave
the town and find lodging in Sichumovi or Tewa."

It must be remembered that since the dead eat only the
essence or "smell" of food, people are not surprised if they
find their feasts unconsumed on the next day. However, to
give point to the belief that the dead did actually dine in the
houses, informants maintain that the presence of the spirits
serves to frighten dogs and other beasts from eating the
physical remains of the food.

[45] Many legendary tales are told of the hair-raising experiences of Kwan and Al sentries during the night's
patrol. In each story, witches who are caught by the Horns
are violently driven off; but those encountered by the
Kwan are supposed to be pursued and killed. Compare

It is not merely to enjoy a feast that the dead return to their pueblos on this occasion, but more serious business awaits them in the kivas. To perform its part in the ensuing ritual, each spirit is supposed to enter the particular kiva with which it was associated while alive. At some time prior to the arrival of the dead, four of the Kwan men who had been inducted into the society at the preceding Tribal Initiation are delegated secretly to visit the local graveyard and to strip four recently interred corpses of their burial garments. There the four Kwan members dress in the foul-smelling grave-clothes, and soon after, they appear before the startled neophytes in dimly-lighted kivas where they are readily mistaken by the terror-stricken novices for the very dead men whose apparel they wear.[46] What befalls the initiates in the presence of this weird assembly of living Hopi, visible "dead," and unseen spirits, no white man can tell with assurance; but from the general context I think that we may reasonably conjecture that in some manner the novices are ceremonially "killed"[47]—their boyish lives are terminated, and they are re-born as *men*. At the same time, they are introduced to the "society of the dead" and thus made certain of occupying their proper places in the other world; for there are special "homes" to which only the shades of Kwan, Al, Tao, or Wuwutcim men may go.[48]

Having played their part in the rites, the dead are dismissed as the Tribal Initiation draws to a close. Whereas, at the time they were asked to visit the pueblo, a path had been left open to them from the northwest, we now find the Kwan chief making a road back to the Maski, after which [he] obliterates the path[49] to show that the usu[al] separation between the worlds of the living a[nd] the dead is once more in force.

If our analysis is correct, the main aims of t[he] Tribal Initiation are: first, to confer manhood [on] boys; second, to establish co-ordination betwe[en] living and dead members of the societies; a[nd] third, to renew the contacts between the popul[a]tions of this world and the next. The attainme[nt] of these objectives provides the climax of t[he] fourth night's observances. Soon after, before su[n]rise on the fifth day, all the ceremonial fathe[rs] bring quantities of yucca root (*movi*) into t[he] kivas and prepare to wash the heads of the "sons." To begin with, a sponsor washes his ow[n] head; then, whichever of his clansmen happen [to] be present wash theirs; and, finally, the novice[s] head is washed and he is given a new name by h[is] "father."[50] From this time forth the initiate [is] called by his Tribal Initiation or man's nam[e] and his boyhood name is either discarded or [re]tained as a nickname.

Thus does a young man slough off his chi[ld]hood and assume adult status. During the morni[ng] of the fifth day the image of Talautumsi, "moth[er] of the novices," having been "delivered" of h[er] offspring, is returned to its shrine. The scratche[d] emblems of novitiate, are gathered up by t[he] heads of the kivas and deposited with cornme[al] at the shrine of Sowika, a protective deity [of] young children. The neophyte is now present[ed] with his Tribal Initiation garments and appea[rs] with his group in public performances; he need [no]

Fewkes and Stephen, 1892b, p. 201, footnote 1. When this happens, each of the Kwan men concerned is expected to take a part of the corpse and to carry it to a point so far from the village that he dies of exhaustion before he can get back to the pueblo.

These myths indicate both the awe-inspiring, war-like character of the Kwan society, and the marked antipathy of the Hopi to the taking of life.

[46] The episode of the grave-clothes is based partly on interviews with a brother of Tawaqwaptiwa, and partly on a deposition made by a Christian Hopi who was condemning the ceremony. Because such a rite does not conform to prevailing notions of Hopi religion, it may be that some students will be inclined to discredit the sources on which the description depends. Nevertheless, the writer is inclined to accept the veracity of the informants, because in personal conversations with Dr. Eggan regarding the nature of the Tribal Initiation, he had postulated the occurrence of incidents of this sort, long before the present data came to light.

[47] From the behavior of impersonators of Masau'u in other rituals, and from the well-known Hopi belief tha[t a] touch from Masau'u's club causes death, it is my su[g]gestion that the Kwan chief appears at this time in [the] guise of Masau'u, god of death, and simulates the killi[ng] of the tyros by touching them with his club. Comp[are] p. 185, ff. Apparently, this is done soon after midnig[ht] while the patrols of Horns and Agaves are rushing fu[ri]ously around the village. See Parsons, 1936b, p. 977. N[ote] especially that Nequatewa, 1938, p. 25, specifically sta[tes] that at one stage of the Wuwutcim, Masau'u and [the] spirits of the dead are present.

[48] Deceased Kwan go not to the general Underworld [but] to a mountain peak called Kwanivi; the Al go to a la[ke] known as Alosaka; the Singers to Duwanasavi; Wuw[ut]cim to any of the "homes" of Katcinas such as the S[an] Francisco Mountains or the spring at Kisiwu. Possi[bly] only the spirits of Wuwutcim men become Katcinas[.]

[49] Fewkes and Stephen, 1892b, p. 217.

[50] The head-washing feature of the Tribal Initiatio[n is] known as *na'acnaiya*. It was this which led Dr. Fewkes [to] call the entire ceremony by that name.

longer be sheltered from the sun, and he may sleep apart from his sponsor during the remaining nights of the ceremony.[51]

At Oraibi it is clearly the Kwan men, by virtue of their impersonations of Masau'u and the dead, who occupy the key position in the inductory rites, and that is why they are considered the *sine qua non* of the entire Tribal Initiation. Because of its mortuary aspect, the Kwan is the most individualistic and the least popular of the four groups, but the Al has many features in common with it. For example, Horns share the nightly patrols with the Agaves, Al men serve as guards when the Singers and Wuwutcim come out to dance, new-fire is kindled by Horn as well as Kwan members, and it is a Horn who carries it to the other kivas. Furthermore, after the ceremony at the shrine of Tuwapongtumsi, an Al leads the way to the "home" of the departed Hopi to whom, in all likelihood, he extends the invitation which culminates in the arrival of the spirits on the climactic night of the Tribal Initiation.

In many respects, then, the Al society seems to duplicate, along somewhat milder lines, the activities of the Kwan division. This may be accounted for on the ground that whereas the Kwan worship Masau'u, the Horns pray to his "female counterpart," Tuwapongtumsi, known to the Hopi as the wife of Masau'u.[52] By the same token we may understand why the Horns imitate the movements of mountain sheep, for among her other attributes, Tuwapongtumsi is the patron deity of all game animals.[53] The difference between Kwan and Al is that between warriors and hunters; the resemblance rests on their common use of weapons and their death-dealing proclivities.[54]

Not only is the Horn society "milder" than the Agave, but it is also less isolated from the Wuwutcim and Tao groups which are essentially fertility cults. With the latter the Horns are brought into close conjunction by virtue of another aspect of the goddess whom they worship, for Tuwapongtumsi is both the wife of Masau'u and the sister of Muyingwa, the major germination deity. In the latter capacity we find that Tuwapongtumsi is regarded as "the mother of all living things . . . plants suck from her breast a nourishing liquid, it passes up from their roots to their flowers and fruit, and animals and man eat of this vegetation. . . ."[55] Similarly, another supernatural patron of the Horns is Alosaka, whom Fewkes has identified as a sun god, to whom prayers for fertility are addressed.[56]

The character of the Tao (Singers) group is best revealed by an examination of their cultus heroine, Talautumsi (Dawn Woman).[57] By the Hopi she is described as owner "of all the crops," and the goddess of childbirth,[58] and her dual nature is reflected in the observances of the Singers' society. As crop "owners," they set out on their kiva hatch an abundance of melons, corn, and other produce, together with a crook (*nöluchöya*), representing long life. While they sing and pray, the women of the village file past, touch the crook and help themselves to the foods on display.[59] On another occasion, as has previously been related, the Tao distribute to women spectators corn-studded molds of clay which symbolize abundant crops. In their capacity as stimulators of fertility, the Singers carry representations of

---

[51] Actually, novices are not considered to have gone completely through their initiation until a succeeding set of candidates has been taken into the Tribal Initiation. Old Oraibi men who were inducted during the last Tribal Initiation ever held there (in 1912) speak of themselves as "never having graduated." Compare Parsons, 1923b, p. 166.

[52] Compare Parsons' statement in Parsons, 1936b, p. XLI.

[53] At Oraibi Tuwapongtumsi is also known under the names of Tuwapongwuhti (Sand-altar Woman), and Tihuyi Wuhti (Childbirth-water Woman). See Parsons, 1939, p. 178; and Parsons, 1936b, pp. 1006, 261.

[54] Parsons, 1939, p. 134, points out that "Among all Pueblos there is a close conceptual relationship between killing men and killing prey animals, between hunting and warring organizations." In this connection, note that the Bow clan, which has "charge" of all weapons, controls the

Al society at Oraibi.

Fewkes, 1899a, p. 544, notes that the Horn men "perform duties suggestive of those of warriors."

[55] Parsons, 1936b, p. 1313.

[56] Fewkes, 1899a, pp. 539, 544. Voth equates Alosaka with Muyingwa and Tcowilawu. See p. 166, footnote 20.

[57] Fewkes thought that Talautumsi was patron of the Al society, partly because Horn men carried her image to and from its shrine. However, Oraibi men explicitly stated that Talautumsi was goddess of the Singers' society; but at the same time they often designated Tao men as Mumuyingtu, or Muyingwa's men. This discrepancy was not explained.

[58] It is because she is the goddess of childbirth that Talautumsi is considered the "mother" of novices in the Tribal Initiation.

[59] Compare Voth, 1903a, p. 311, footnote 5; and Voth, 1903b, p. 27, footnote 2.

the generative organs, and behave in a manner that plainly brands their society as phallic.[60]

There is still another aspect of the Tao that must not be overlooked. They are called Singers because they are supposed to know the original songs that were sung at the time of the Emergence. For that reason, it is Singers' chief who signals the start of the chanting that immediately precedes the new-fire making[61] which symbolizes Masau'u's gift of fire to the Hopi soon after their appearance on earth. The connection of the Singers with the Emergence story is brought out by the fact that their society is owned by the Parrot clan at Oraibi, which claims Yapa (Mocking Bird) as one of its *wuya*. As one narrator tells it, while the people were climbing out of the lower world, "The Mocking-bird sat close by and sang a great many songs, the songs that are still chanted to the Wūwūchim ceremony."[62] In my opinion, it is the Singers, whose controlling clan regards Mocking Bird as one of its ancients, who chant the Mocking Bird's songs during the Tribal Initiation.

The Wuwutcim society is more nearly allied to the Tao in its basic concepts than to any of the other divisions. It is concerned mainly with prayers for crop increase and general fertility. Although I was unable to determine the patron deity of the Wuwutcim on Third Mesa, it may well be that Muyingwa, or some other germination deity, is the central figure of the cult.[63] The only altar reported for this branch of the Tribal Initiation is said to be a realistic vulva carved from watermelon,[64] and throughout their observances the Wuwutcim give ample evidence of their phallic character. In keeping with the fertility motive, the members of the Wuwutcim are known as Corn Youths and wear blossom symbols which signify good crops.

The societies which combine in the conduct of the Tribal Initiation ceremonies may be said to fall into two divisions. The Kwan and the Al pay homage to the destructive forces of war and the hunt; the Tao and the Wuwutcim venerate the powers of germination and the organs of generation. Together, all four branches unite to dramatize the main elements of the Emergence story, including man's coming to earth and the Hopi encounter with Masau'u. Furthermore, the Hopi have not failed to emphasize the wider significance of their origin tales. As Dr. Fewkes explains, "The earth in their conception always existed, and, following the analogy of growing vegetation, organisms grew out of the earth or were born like animals. The earth to them is not a creator but a mother, the genetrix of lesser gods and animals, and the ancestor or first of the human race."[65] Hence we find the Kwan worshipping Masau'u, who owns all the crops; the Al venerating Tuwapongtumsi, who owns all animals; the Tao praying to Talautumsi, goddess of childbirth; and the Wuwutcim concerning themselves with things germinative and phallic.

With their great love of theatrical effects, the Hopi have based their Tribal Initiation drama on the libretto of the Emergence myth, keeping the rites close to the details of the "script."[66] The atmosphere of the Underworld is reproduced by the presence of the visible and the invisible dead in the initiatory kiva, and the parturitive aspect is brought out in the treatment of candidates as babies who are soon to be born out of "the depths of the underworld sea."[67] Step by step, the Emergence story is unfolded to the novices.[68] The songs of the Tao society tell them how the ancestors (Wuwutcim) clambered up a magically-grown reed, to the accompaniment of the Mocking Bird's (Singers') songs, and with the help o the war gods (Kwan and Al men).[69] Then come

[60] Fewkes and Stephen, 1892b, p. 208; and Parsons, 1936b, pp. 978, 979, *et passim*.

[61] Fewkes and Stephen, 1892b, p. 195.

[62] Voth, 1905b, p. 11.

[63] The Wuwutcim patron at Walpi is Taiowa, son of the Sun and brother of the Marau deity. See Parsons, 1936b, p. 25, footnote 1, pp. 929, 1298, *et passim*.

[64] Compare Parsons, 1923b, p. 171.

[65] Fewkes, 1906a, pp. 350, 351.

A variant explanation of the origin of the world is given by Stephen, 1940, p. 102. Sotukinangwu'u creates a beautiful virgin and later transforms her into the World; vegetation, rocks, springs, etc., arising from various parts of her anatomy.

[66] The responsibility for the following synopsis and in terpretation of the Tribal Initiation is entirely mine. Th story which most nearly parallels the action of the Thir Mesa rites, in my opinion, is in Voth, 1905b, pp. 10–1: Also see p. 61.

[67] Parsons, 1936b, p. 973.

[68] Compare Nequatewa, 1931, p. 2, where it is sai that the Wuwutcim "portrays what happened in tl Underworld before the Hopi people emerged, and wh they did to get out."

[69] Voth, 1905b, p. 11, states that the Little War Twi stood beside the reed; but Stephen, 1929, p. 7, sa Masau'u helped the people come out. War gods are i dicated in either case.

the meeting of the ancestors with Masau'u (impersonated by the Kwan chief), and his gift of fire to the Hopi (indicated by the kindling of new-fire in the presence of the Masau'u impersonator). Finally, the acquisition of agriculture is portrayed by the Singers, who "produce" and distribute "crops" to the populace. When they have seen and heard the details of their tribal origins, the novices are no longer regarded as immature chicken hawk fledglings (*kelehöyam*).

Throughout their induction the tyros are kept under rigid discipline, thus intensifying the pedagogical aspects of the Tribal Initiation, but no less important are the spiritual factors involved. The impersonation of the god of death, the visit of the dead to the village, and the Kwan men, presumably masquerading as vivified corpses, cannot fail to have a powerful effect on neophytes who are being made aware that man is born out of the Underworld and returns there when life is ended on earth. It is to affirm the continuity of life after death that the spirits of the deceased are supposed to be present when the youths are "reborn" as men. The Tribal Initiation bestows spiritual status on those who have passed through its rites and gives to each initiate a specific station in the after-life. This helps explain too why the Kwan leader must "baptize" Village chiefs, and other high officers, before their positions as rulers are assured both in this world and the next;[70] and that is why only those who have been initiated may go on the salt-gathering journey which takes men to the very brink of the home of the dead.[71]

THE MASWIK KATCINA

In a year when novices are inducted into the Tribal Initiation societies, the ceremonial calendar is affected in several instances. The Soyal, in which some of the initiates are to take part for the first time, is held in an extended form; and the Powamu is lengthened by the inclusion of the Patcava rites. In addition, there occurs in the month of May a celebration called Nevenwehe ("Spinach"-gathering), during which the tyros load their Tribal Initiation garments with freshly-plucked blossoms of edible plants.[72] Prior to the activities in the spring, a preliminary rite

known as Maswik Katcina is held during the Soyal to serve notice of the coming observances.

Inasmuch as the *real* Masau'u is to be doubly personated on this occasion, the kiva of either performer may sponsor the event, which takes place on the sixth night of the Soyal.[73] The Katcinas who appear at this time are called Maswik, literally, Masau'u—following-at-the-heel, because they enter a kiva first and are soon followed by the Masau'u actors. The Katcina dancers always include those men from the sponsoring kiva who had been admitted to the Tribal Initiation during the preceding month, as well as volunteers from among their more experienced kiva mates.

All the participants in the Maswik performance first assemble for a ritual smoke, during which the kiva head announces that in the spring, during bean-planting time, Nevenwehe will take place. After this the dancers get into costume, some dressing as males and others as "females." The masculine Maswik goes barefooted and wears Katcina skirt and sash, bandoleer of blue yarn, ankle bands, Hopi belt and fox pelt "tail" at the loins. The mask is not of the helmet type, but covers only the face and allows the hair to hang loose at the back. In the right hand he holds a gourd rattle, and in the left he carries a flute. The Maswik "girls" are also barefooted. They wear anklets, a wedding garment (*ova*), a big belt (*wukokwewe*), and a folded wedding robe across the chest as a bandoleer. The coiffure consists of artificial "butterfly wings," and the mask is of the face type such as most Katcina "girls" generally wear. One eagle plume protrudes upward from the forehead, and a wild blossom, *tcimunsi*, is fastened to the right side of the head. A bell carried in each hand completes the costume.

When all is ready, the Maswik Katcinas go to the first kiva on their circuit and begin to sing and dance. After they have sung two verses and choruses and are about to begin the repetition of two more choruses, the Masau'u impersonators enter. They come down the ladder with their backs to it as if it were a stairway, and they step down to the main floor from the west side, contrary to the customary procedure.[74] Then the Masau'u actors go up to the line of Katcinas and

[70] See pp. 63, 64.
[71] See Titiev, 1937a, p. 244, *et passim*.
[72] Nevenwehe is described on p. 140, ff.
[73] Fewkes describes the Maswik Katcina dance as occurring in conjunction with the Powamu at Walpi. It

closely resembles the Oraibi performance at Soyal. Compare Fewkes, 1903, pp. 36–38; and Fewkes, 1902a, pp. 21–23.
[74] It is Masau'u's nature to do things by opposites. For this episode, compare Fewkes, 1917a, p. 227.

each puts his hands on the shoulders of one of the leaders.[75] Thrusting his head forward, he juts out his chin and utters the peculiar, dismal howl that is the cry of Masau'u. Then the impersonators withdraw to the fireplace, where they receive *nakwakwosi* and meal from the kiva chief, after which they make their exit, again passing to the wrong side of the ladder.[76] While the Masau'u performers are on their way to the shrine where they deposit their prayer-offerings, the Maswik Katcinas finish their dance and proceed to the next kiva. Again, at the appropriate time, the impersonators enter and repeat their performance. In this way the men in the village are informed of the plan to hold Nevenwehe in the spring.

Although, on this occasion, Masau'u is appearing in the rôle of a germination deity rather than as the god of death, it is said that the recently-initiated young men await his arrival with a good deal of apprehension.[77] Sometimes, before approaching the leaders, the impersonators may pretend to rush at the neophytes who shrink back in genuine terror. Even those tyros who are dancing as Maswik Katcinas are afraid of the "deity" whom they precede and fear to venture out of the kiva lest they encounter Masau'u himself.

THE NEVENWEHE RITUAL[78]

About six months later, in the month of May (Hakiton-muya), when the Sun Watcher lets it be known that the sun is at Wukomuzri-uyipi, the people are advised to plant their bean crops.[79] At the same time the older members of the officiating kiva begin to practice for a Maswik Katcina performance that they are soon to exhibit.[80] Then, when the officers decide that the "spinach" blossoms are ripe enough, two

Masau'u performers go into retirement at t Kokop house, and the word circulates th "Masau'u didn't wake up today."[81] On each the four nights following, Masau'u makes d creasingly smaller circuits of the village, and the last night Nevenwehe ritual begins.

As soon as it is dark, the Maswik Katci dancers proceed to the shrine called Boki (D House), where they dress but do not mask. The then make their way to the southwest edge of t mesa to a place known as "Masau'u's hous floor" (Kantupha). Here they begin to dance, a as they reach the chorus, the Masau'u actors arri and go through the same performance as in t winter activities in the kivas. Then the speci impersonators go off to the west, and the Masw Katcinas finish their song and move to anoth part of the mesa, where the previous procedure repeated. This time the Masau'u performe upon leaving the dancers, go the main house the Masau'u clan where the clanspeople are awa ing the arrival of their *wuya*. After smoking her the impersonators go to the house of the Villa chief where they wave their clubs with a tren bling motion four times up and down. Then the clasp the ladder of the house tightly, after whi they walk along the walls, patting them with the palms as they go.[82] Meantime, the Maswik Ka cinas have gone into the Chief kiva to dance, a here the Masau'u actors join them and play the customary parts. When the song ends t Masau'u impersonators go back to the Kok house where they have been staying; and t Katcinas, after disrobing at Boki, return to the own kiva to spend the night in smoking, singin and praying.

The next morning, at sunrise, the Crier chi (Tca'akmongwi) calls out for Nevenwehe fro *the* Kele roof, telling the people to get read

[75] That is, one goes to the leader of the male Katcinas, and the other to the leader of the "females."

[76] According to Fewkes, 1917a, p. 227, Masau'u appears in this performance as a fertility god and simulates the act of planting.

[77] Probably because they still have vivid memories of their encounter with Masau'u during the gruesome proceedings on the fourth night of the Tribal Initiation.

[78] The only published account of this ceremony is an incomplete sketch by Stephen, with a note by Parsons, in Parsons, 1936b, pp. 994, 995. A somewhat similar ritual is reported by Stephen in conjunction with the gathering of wild potatoes at First Mesa, Parsons, 1936b, p. 1035.
The name Nevenwehe is derived from that of a plant called *nepni*, which Fewkes, 1896c, p. 15, identifies as *Stanleya* sp.

The time of the rites is determined by the ripening one variety of *nepni*, which is known as *mu'untcavu*. T latter, recorded by Parsons as *moüntoshap*, is identified Poliomintha incana (Torr) A. Gray, in Parsons, 1936 p. 995. Compare Hough, 1898, p. 143.

[79] Titiev, 1938c, p. 42.

[80] The dance is performed in the spring only by the ol men because the candidates recently admitted to t Tribal Initiation are engaged in picking "spinach."

[81] The *real* Masau'u may be impersonated at Ora only by men from the Masau'u, Kokop, or other clans Phratry VI which claim Masau'u as an ancient. Comp the Masau'u performance at Nevenwehe with his activit during communal harvesting parties, pp. 185–187.

[82] This ritual signifies that Masau'u is imbuing house and its inmates with some of his power.

Nothing of note occurs in the forenoon, but after lunch there is a second announcement, telling the people to gather at the Flute spring, west of the village. The girls dress in *manta*, big belt, ceremonial mantle (*atu'u*), and white buckskin moccasins with wrapped leggings, and have their hair done up in "butterfly wings." They carry a load of *somiviki* with them and are often accompanied by their parents or other relatives burdened with extra supplies of food. The youths are dressed in the old-fashioned Hopi manner, in blue woven shirts (*sakwanapna*), open at the sides but stitched at the armpits, buckskin pants, and moccasins. In their hair they wear eagle "breath" feathers, and they have on many strings of beads.

The girls carry their *somiviki* in wedding robes borrowed from any obliging relative; and the young men fashion their Tribal Initiation garments into sacks and carry other bags full of plants which they have gathered during the last few days.[83] When all have assembled at Flute spring, the Crier chief calls out, "Now boys, give your 'spinach' (*nepni*) to these girls before we go!" At the command, the boys start down the line of maidens, giving to each a few of the plucked blossoms, and receiving, in turn, some packets of *somiviki*. As soon as the exchanges are completed, the Village chief, followed by the Crier and the War chiefs, leads the people to the next stopping-place, where the same performance is to be repeated. As they go the girls proceed in line, but the young men and spectators may walk as they please. At Lololoma's spring the party

pauses for a brief rest, the Crier orders the second exchange, and they then go on to a third and a fourth station. From here, they ascend the mesa by the trail used by Masau'u in his nightly circuits, and pause by the Kwan shrine at Kowanvu for the last stage of the ceremonial trading. Now the boys give their "best" girls their choicest tidbits such as onions or cottonwood gum, and the maidens reciprocate with baked sweet corn or other dainties in addition to *somiviki*.[84]

Up to this point the procession has been preceded along its route by four unmasked, male Maswik Katcinas playing on flutes borrowed from the Blue or Gray Flute societies, and three Maswik "men" who sing and keep time with rattles of dentalium shells. At Kowanvu, the Katcinas take part in the final exchange with the rest of the party, and then hurry to Boki where they meet the other Maswik impersonators. All the Katcinas proceed rapidly to Kantupha where they mask and await the coming of the "spinach-gatherers," who move at a more leisurely pace. Then, as the people come into the village from the north, the Katcinas meet them from the south, playing and singing while the participants disperse to their homes.[85]

Thus does the Nevenwehe in May round out the Tribal Initiation observances that began in November. At that time the songs and rituals of the celebrants held forth the promise of fertility and bountiful crops; now, the generous bestowal of edible plants on the village maidens symbolizes the fruition of their prayers.

[83] The preliminary gathering is done by the young men in small groups at their convenience during the four days preceding the public meeting. Wild onions and cottonwood berries, which are made into a sort of gum, are the most highly prized dainties. The plants are moistened so that they will keep fresh until needed. Uninitiated boys may also take a share in Nevenwehe, but they do not use sacks fashioned from Tribal Initiation garments.

[84] This is another occasion, as during the Bean dance,

when a girl may propose to a lover by giving him a loaf of *qömi*, see p. 119.

[85] Before the rites terminate the Maswik Katcinas perform several more of their customary dances at stated places. They are then dismissed with cornmeal and prayer-offerings, but the Masau'u actors go to the village plaza for a final round of activities similar to those described at the close of a communal harvesting party, pp. 186, 187.

CHAPTER XI

SOLSTITIAL AND SOLAR CEREMONIES

INTRODUCTION

LIKE ALL Hopi ceremonies the Tribal Initiation rites do not stand by themselves but are directly linked to other observances. In this case, members of all four of the Tribal Initiation societies are qualified to take part in the Soyal, but the degree of participation varies considerably. Since it is the Wuwutcim division which is considered the main branch on Third Mesa (p. 130), only Wuwutcim men may help conduct the esoteric portions of the Soyal.[1] In the days when Oraibi's populace was undivided, a further distinction was made because the Wuwutcim was so popular that it required several kivas to take care of all its candidates. Accordingly, only those novices who had been inducted into the Wuwutcim at the Chief kiva were considered eligible for complete participation in the Soyal ceremony.[2]

From many points of view the Soyal is the keystone of Hopi ceremonialism on Third Mesa. Its control lies in the hands of the ruling (Bear) clan, its leader is either the Village chief or a proxy appointed by him, the kiva in which its observances are held is known as the Chief kiva, and its supporting officers comprise the most important men in the pueblo. These include the Parrot chief, who heads the Singers' society; the Pikyas chief, who impersonates the Aholi Katcina (p. 117), and who is in charge of the Moenkopi colony; the Tobacco chief, whose duties in connection with ritual smoking are indispensable in the perform-

ance of all important ceremonies; the Crier chief, who is the highest spiritual officer in the pueblo since he serves as the Village chief's mouthpiece in addressing the Cloud people; and the War chief, whose office embodies both religious and executive functions.[3] These are the officials who hold the Chiefs' Talk (Monglavaiyi) at the close of the Soyal,[4] and they are the ones who supervise the sponsorship of a number of activities that may be in prospect during the coming year. Thus, if a man proposes to take charge of a piki-stone (duma) quarrying expedition, he must first make his plans known at Soyal.[5] If a salt-gathering party is being contemplated, arrangements must be made during the Soyal observances.[6] It is at this time too that the Niman Katcina of the following summer is announced annually;[7] and that the Maswik Katcinas appear in initiatory years of the Tribal Initiation, to indicate that Nevenwehe will be held in the spring.[8] For these reasons the natives have a saying that "everything branches out from the Soyal."

THE SOYAL PERFORMANCE[9]

The determination of the starting time of the Soyal again exemplifies its connection with the Tribal Initiation. On the night that the latter rites come to a close, all the officers and men of the Chief kiva remain awake in anticipation of the coming of the Soyal Katcina on the following morning. Sixteen days after his advent,[10] the

---

[1] Dr. Parsons, 1936b, p. 2, states that "membership in one of the four [Tribal Initiation] societies is the prerequisite" to entering the Soyal at Walpi, but she does not report whether men from all the societies participate to the same extent.

[2] Formerly, it was Sakwalenvi that was Oraibi's Chief kiva. Then it became Pongovi, whose name was later changed to Tawaovi. See p. 80 and footnote 109.

[3] Compare p. 65.

[4] See p. 59.

[5] This is described on p. 197.

[6] Consult Titiev, 1937a, p. 244.

[7] See p. 111.

[8] See p. 139.

[9] In ordinary years the Soyal is celebrated over a period of nine days, but whenever novices are taken into the Tribal Initiation the succeeding Soyal is performed in an

extended form lasting 17 days. On Third Mesa the long observance has never been reported, but Dorsey and Voth, 1901, affords a remarkably full picture of the nine-day rites. This account has been summarized in Parsons, 1939, pp. 556–570.

Inasmuch as I saw only the public portions of the abbreviated performance at Oraibi in 1933, most of the present synopsis of events is taken from Dorsey and Voth, 1901, but the interpretation is based mainly on my interviews with Soyal men.

The First Mesa proceedings are best described by Stephen in Parsons, 1936b, pp. 7–82. Although Stephen witnessed one performance of the extended Soyal at Walpi, most of his notes pertain to the nine-day observances. These are supplemented in part by Fewkes, 1898.

[10] The timing of the Soyal is interwoven with solar observations in the following manner. The Tribal Initia-

[So]yal observances begin with the customary pre-[li]minary smoke during which prayer-offerings are [m]anufactured by the leaders. At daybreak on the [fo]llowing morning, the Crier chief makes an of-[fic]ial announcement of the ceremony, and on the [ne]xt day[11] standards are erected at the Chief kiva [ha]tch.[12] For the first three days very little happens [ex]cept that the chiefs occasionally meet to smoke, [pr]ay, and prepare the offerings and paraphernalia [wh]ich are to be used later on. On the fourth day [an] additional standard, featuring flint spear and [ar]row-heads, is put up at Chief kiva, and the rites [ta]ke on a decidedly militaristic aspect. That after-[no]on the War chief dresses in the costume of [P]ükonghöya, elder of the Little War Twins, and [us]es his shield to ward off the attack of a cele-[br]ant who feigns to stab at him. Then war medi-[cin]e is brewed; some of which the participants [dr]ink and smear on their bodies, and the rest of [wh]ich they carry out of the kiva to rub on their [ho]uses and kin.[13] In the evening several Al and [K]wan men, carrying their chiefs' sticks, keep [gu]ard at the kiva opening as the War chief again [pu]ts on his complete outfit; but this time he [m]erely looks on while another officer dances with [a p]air of hawk's wings, with which he brushes all [th]e spectators on several parts of the body.

The main events of the fifth evening's perform-[an]ce are several elaborate and vigorous Hawk [m]an impersonations, during which the partici-[pa]nts, one after the other, dance in imitation of [th]e actions of a hawk. On this night, two or three [fe]males, relatives of the main Soyal officers, are [pr]esent as Soyalmanam (Soyal maidens) and [da]nce with the Hawk performers. The following [da]y, the sixth since the rites began, is devoted [pri]marily to the preparation of objects necessary [fo]r the erection of the Soyal altar; and the greater [pa]rt of the seventh day is devoted to prayer-stick

making, hundreds of various types being made by the members of all the participating kivas. That same evening, each kiva group also manufactures a number of *hihikwispi* (objects-to-be-breathed-upon), consisting essentially of four corn-husks bound together with several kinds of feathers.

The next morning, cornmeal and pollen are put into each *hihikwispi* and messengers carry them on a round of the village, stopping at each house to let all the inmates breathe upon them. They are then brought back to the kivas and later deposited at the Flute spring. Thus begins the eighth day, a day crowded with ceremonial pursuits. In Chief kiva altars are set in position, and in the afternoon the Soyalmanam again enter and are present when four messengers, clad in Katcina costumes but unmasked, are dispatched to gather bundles of corn from each household. On their way out of the kiva, the men press their bodies against the ladder and simulate the act of copulation before they climb all the way up. Then they go from house to house, collecting from the women vari-colored ears of corn tied with yucca fibre. These bundles are brought into Chief kiva where they are placed beside the altar. At about this time the Mastop Katcinas appear (p. 110), and as they conclude their performance four messengers emerge carrying the *hihikwispi* and other objects which are to be deposited at Flute spring (Lenva).[14]

Later, the War chief repeats the medicine-making rites which were performed on the fourth day, and at night there are more Hawk dances by various impersonators, accompanied by Soyal maidens. These activities continue until well past midnight, so that the ninth day's ritual is continuous with that of the eighth. It is still several hours before dawn when two Kwan men bring to Chief kiva a screen featuring a picture of

[begi]n begins when the sun is seen to rise at Dingapi, a spot [on] the horizon which is so located in relation to the [win]ter solstice point that it permits just enough time to [ela]pse so that the climax of the Soyal may be reached on [or] about December 21. This emphasizes the fact that the [festiv]al is a Winter Solstice celebration.

[1]1 Preliminary meetings are held ordinarily eight days [be]fore the main rites of a ceremony begin, but in the case [of] the Soyal the initial smoke occurs on the day preceding [the] onset of the major activities. Consult Dorsey and Voth, [190]1, p. 14.

[1]2 The main standard is erected at Chief kiva by the [Soy]al head, because it is here that the altars are to be put [up] and that the basic esoteric rites are to be performed. [Ho]wever, standards are also placed in position at the [oth]er kivas which are to take secondary parts in the ob-servances. On this point see Dorsey and Voth, 1901, p. 17 and footnote *.

13 The war medicine is believed to make houses sturdy and people brave and healthy. Its tonic effects are also supposed to be felt by animals, and a man will smear his household pets if he has a surplus of the medicine. So valuable is this rite considered, that members of households which lack Soyal participants make it a point to visit the more fortunate households in order to be included in the medicine smearing.

14 Dorsey and Voth, 1901, pp. 44, 45, report that the messengers had departed for the spring before the arrival of the Mastop Katcinas, but in 1933 the messengers did not go to the spring until after the Mastop performance.

Note that according to Hopi tradition, the Spider clan had promised to act as messengers at Soyal. See p. 74.

Muyingwa, to which a variety of seeds have been affixed. These the Soyal chief, after a brief ritual, scrapes from the screen to a tray; and soon after, the Kwan members take the picture and depart. The stage is now set for "the principal act of the whole ceremony."[15] This consists of a solo dance performed by the Star (elsewhere called the Sun) priest, which was climaxed when he "twirled the sun symbol very fast . . . symbolizing the going and coming of the sun." As he danced, the performer sang a song about Palulokong.[16] Soon after the conclusion of these esoteric rites, the men from the various secondary kivas come to Chief kiva to fetch the *pahos* (prayersticks) which they had made on the seventh day. At the first streak of light in the east, all the Soyal celebrants hurry through the pueblo, delivering prayer-offerings to friends and relatives. Just at sunrise the entire populace, everyone with hair recently washed in yucca suds, hastens to deposit the *pahos* at the requisite shrines. The men, their hair hanging loose at the back and many with bells tied at their waists, run at top speed, hallooing as they go, to the Antelope shrine where they deposit their offerings with prayers for success in the chase. (Pl. III a) The women, some clad in ceremonial garments and a few recent brides in their wedding robes, hurry to put down their prayer-sticks near the shrine of Sowika (pl. III c), patron of children, from whom they request long life and fertility.[17]

Later in the morning the altars are dismantled in the Chief kiva, and the four messengers carry the bundles of corn which had been consecrated during the night's ritual through the village. Each woman carefully identifies and picks out her own parcel, and the ears are stored until spring, when they are planted with the rest of the corn crop. Towards noon, all men who wish to partake in the Qöqöqlom performance report to the sponsoring kiva, and in the afternoon they stage the first group Katcina dance of the season (p. 111).

The next three days are devoted to rabbit hunting by kiva units, and each night the men

sleep in their kivas. On the fourth day the closin rites take place when the Soyal membershi each man clad only in a G-string and carryir a dish of "gravy," goes to the house of one of tl Soyal maidens, on the terrace of which are plac large containers full of water. Several wom splash the men liberally, thus giving them an ou door bath during which they rub off some of the ceremonial paint and throw gifts of melons ar other foods to the crowd. Then the men retu to their kivas to terminate the Soyal celebratic by dining on rabbit stew made from the beas they had killed during the last three days.

THE SIGNIFICANCE OF THE SOYAL RITES

More than any other observance on the cer monial calendar, the Soyal provides for cor munal participation in its rites. Not only is tl entire adult male population, by virtue of membe ship in the Tribal Initiation societies, entitled play a part, but provision is made for includir the women and children as well. When the enti populace is invited to breathe on the *hihikwisp* when bundles of corn are collected from ea household, consecrated and returned; when w medicine is smeared on non-participants in tl esoteric exercises during which it is made; wh the Mastop Katcinas "fertilize" all the females the village; and when the ceremony closes with generous distribution of prayer-sticks among rel tives and friends; we have ample evidence to su port the belief that the Soyal is a communi ritual, and that it is performed for the benefit the entire pueblo.[18]

As befits a ceremony conducted by the highe officers in the village and embracing practical the entire populace, every important motive Hopi religion finds expression in one phase another of the Soyal. The war ritual is f bravery and good health as well as for success fighting enemies; the Hawk impersonations a prayers for fertility and strength;[19] the Mast

---

[15] Dorsey and Voth, 1901, p. 54.

[16] Dorsey and Voth, 1901, p. 55. Palulokong plays a far more important part in the First Mesa observance. See Parsons, 1936b, pp. 15, 16.

[17] In order to have their hair dry before daybreak, non-Soyal members wake up before dawn to wash their heads. To see the entire village hastening to deposit their prayer-sticks makes a never-to-be-forgotten picture.

[18] The Hopi often say that *all* their rites are conducted for

the benefit of the entire village, and even for the good the whole tribe and all mankind, but only the Soyal pr vides so many opportunities for the general public to ta an actual share in the conduct of the ceremony.

[19] In the absence of the myth on which the Soyal pe formance is based, it is impossible to interpret specifica many of its features. This is particularly true of the Hav Man impersonations. Stephen, in Parsons, 1936b, p. I terms him "Kisha tiyo" (Cooper's hawk youth), whi

performance is designed to increase the fruitfulness of women; the scraping of seeds from the picture of Muyingwa is mimetic magic to promote the germination of crops; and the Star (Sun) chief's twirling of a shield is intended to aid the sun in its journey from one solstice point to the other.[20]

The all-inclusive nature of the Soyal is most clearly expressed in the prodigious manufacture of prayer-offerings for practically everything that falls within the range of Hopi culture. Some of the *paho* and *nakwakwosi* are of a totemic nature, as when clansmen make them for their eponyms and *wuya* and hand them over to their clan heads to be deposited at appropriate shrines. On the other hand, every celebrant also makes a vast number of offerings for a whole miscellany of purposes. "They are placed in the houses, tied to the ladders to prevent accident, placed in the chicken houses 'that the hens may lay eggs,' into the beef and sheep corrals, and tied to horses' tails, dogs', goats' and sheeps' necks, etc., 'for increase'; tied to the peach trees as prayer for large crops, deposited in springs for an abundant water supply, and disposed of in many similar ways."[21]

In addition to these, we must consider the nature of the prayer-offerings which the Soyal men distribute in person to their fellow villagers at the close of the kiva rites. These "are of three kinds as far as their object or purpose is concerned. First, the bent *bahos* or *nölöshoya*. These are made for little boys by their fathers . . . as a wish that the boy may thrive, be happy and live long. The second kind are the so-called *makbaho* (hunting *bahos*) which men make for themselves and for others as a wish or prayer for good luck in the chase. . . . The third class, and by far the

largest quantity, are offerings for the dead. A *nakwakwosi* is generally made for one deceased. . . . The Hopi say the dead come afterward from the '*Masski*' (skeleton house) and each one gets his *nakwakwosi*, or rather the soul of it, and if any one finds that for him no offering has been made he is unhappy. The short double *bahos* . . . are said to be made for the dead in general, who are believed to reciprocate the kindness by sending the Hopi good crops of corn, watermelons, squashes, etc. Some claim that these *bahos* are, on this occasion, as usual, made for the cloud deities."[22] Once more, then, we find the dead equated with clouds; and at Soyal as well as at the Tribal Initiation, the dead are thought to revisit the pueblo and to participate in the ceremonies conducted by the living. Thus do the Soyal rites again confirm the Hopi belief in the continuity of life after death.

Despite its catholic nature and the wealth of ideas involved in the Soyal, there is one underlying concept that students agree to be the most fundamental of all. As Dr. Parsons puts it, "The observers on both mesas [First and Third] considered that the dramatization of the Sun's motions or progress was the most significant part of the Winter solstice ceremony. . . ."[23] At Oraibi the dramatization is enacted when the "Star priest" twirls the sun symbol; at Walpi it takes the form of "a mimic assault" in which the bearer of a sun shield dashes vigorously in and out among a group of Singers.[24] His actions represent "the Sun deity beginning his yearly shield-bearing journey, but hesitating whether or not to travel over the Hopi region, and this religious society of Singers thus display or typify their efforts to constrain him to his accustomed path."[25] In other

---

would indicate, Parsons, 1936b, p. 100, that he is a hunting divinity; but Fewkes, 1898a, p. 104, identifies Hawk Man as Kwataka, the dreaded war bird, and Fewkes, 1898a, p. 108, explains his dance with the Soyal maidens as "a dramatization of the fructification of the earth and of imparting virility to the seeds of corn."

There is also a possible connection between the Hawk Man appearance at Soyal and the chicken hawk fledgling behavior of tyros at the Tribal Initiations. In the Walpi Soyal a group of Horn men dance before recently inducted novices and give "a rather pleasing imitation of young birds in a flock. . . ." Parsons, 1936b, p. 16.

[20] Parsons, 1936b, p. 24.
[21] Dorsey and Voth, 1901, p. 57.
[22] Dorsey and Voth, 1901, p. 57 and footnote *.
The belief that at Soyal the dead come to the pueblo to get the "souls" of their prayer-offerings, is very vivid in

the minds of the natives. As is true in most societies, the deceased are regarded with mixed feelings; they are loved —and feared. When the spirits are expected in the village at Tribal Initiation, the pueblo is carefully guarded, people may not venture out, and half the town is tabu to the dead (p. 135). On the other hand, at Soyal there are no limitations of time or place imposed on the souls of the departed, and there are no patrols of Al and Kwan men to make sure that no evil spirits have mingled with the others. Accordingly, the moon in which the Soyal occurs, Kya-muya, is "dangerous." People may not stir abroad at night without taking precautionary measures, and brides whose wedding rites have terminated in this month may not go home until the next moon. Compare Parsons, 1933, p. 58.

[23] Parsons, 1936b, p. 4.
[24] Parsons, 1936b, pp. 22, 23.
[25] Parsons, 1936b, p. 24.

words, the main purpose of the Soyal is to perform compulsive magic at the winter solstice, so that the sun may be induced to start back towards its summer home and thus bring suitably warm weather to permit the Hopi to plant their fields. At the same time, the ceremony aims to ensure plentiful crops and general prosperity and good health for the next season.

OFFERINGS TO THE SUN BY THE FLUTE SOCIETIES[26]

According to Hopi theory the sun is supposed to rise at exactly the same spot on the horizon for four successive days after it reaches either of its solstice points.[27] For this reason the Village chief of Oraibi waits until the fifth day following the close of his Soyal ritual, and then accompanies the Sun Watcher (Horn chief) at daybreak to his lookout at the Buffalo shrine, in order to make sure that the sun has responded to the rites and has actually started on the journey to its summer home.[28] When he is convinced that all is well, the Village chief entrusts the Sun Watcher's job to the Gray Flute chief, whose duty it is to observe the sun's path until the summer solstice is reached.[29]

About a month later, both Flute societies hold brief one-day ceremonies called Tawa Baholawu, Sun Prayer-Offering Making.[30] At Oraibi the Gray Flute (Masilalent) meets in Hawiovi kiva where the members smoke and make a number of *paho* and *nakwakwosi*. Then a six-direction altar is laid out and songs are sung to flute accompaniment. Simultaneously, similar rites are being con-

ducted in the Blue Flute kiva by the society that name (Sakwalalent). Both groups depo their offerings at a shrine which is located at t place on the horizon whence the sun seems to r at the winter solstice. As these observances ta place in January,[31] the open season for Katc performances, dances are customarily schedul to be held that night in all the kivas (p. 112, fo note 19).

About six months later, when the Gray Flu chief, from his position on the roof of *the S* clan house, has determined that the sun is at summer home, the two Flute societies again semble to manufacture offerings.[32] On Thi Mesa the Gray Flute rites are somewhat mc elaborate than those of the Blue Flute at this tin and a great variety of prayer-objects are mac Most of these are placed at the summer solst: shrine on the horizon, but some are placed el where. According to one of my informants, t messenger who bears the offerings to the summ solstice point is expected to spend the night short distance away. The next morning he ca fully observes the manner of the sun's rising, visits the shrine to examine the condition of t offerings, and then returns to report all the det of the journey to his society's chief.[33]

These rites for the sun are held annually Third Mesa,[34] and bear witness to the close cc nection of the Flute societies' activities with t occurrence of the solstices. It seems justifiab therefore, to consider the Flute ceremonies complementary to the Soyal.[35]

---

[26] In all villages holding Flute ceremonies there are, or were at one time, two parallel societies. At Oraibi these carried blue and gray or drab instruments, and wore "moisture tablets" or "sun shields," respectively. Compare Parsons, 1936b, p. 768.

[27] Compare Parsons, 1936b, p. 61.

[28] Nequatewa, 1931, p. 2, states that after Soyal "everyone watches . . . to see if the sun starts back to the north."

[29] Titiev, 1938c, p. 40. According to Voth, 1901, p. 152, footnote 4, the duties of watching the sun are shared by the Flute and Soyal "priests."

[30] Described in Voth, 1912b, pp. 123–128, from which the following account is taken. Similar rites at Walpi are recorded by Stephen in Parsons, 1936b, pp. 107–112; and in Fewkes, 1903, pp. 29, 30.

[31] The date of the observance is determined by the appearance of the new moon following the termination of the Soyal. This is the January moon (Pa-muya), and it is watched for by the chief of the society that is about to conduct the rites. These took place at Oraibi on January 20, 1898; and at Walpi on January 21, 1894.

[32] The summer meetings of the Flute societies were observed by Voth at Oraibi on June 13, 1901. They are dis-

cussed in Voth, 1912b, pp. 129–136. There are no counts of similar observances on First Mesa.

[33] Similar reports are made by messengers during conduct of several other Hopi rituals. They are made detail to provide material for deducing omens. Con Parsons, 1939, p. 285; and Parsons, 1936b, p. 60.

According to Parsons, 1925, p. 95, footnote 147, messenger at the summer solstice proceeds very slowl order to delay the sun's movement towards the wir solstice point.

[34] Although the major rites of the Flute societies are j formed biennially, the prayer-offerings to the sun are m and deposited annually at Oraibi. On First Mesa the mi rituals of the Flute groups are biennial according to I sons, 1936b, p. 101; and Fewkes, 1903, p. 29, note b.

[35] In comparatively recent times, probably since lapse of the Flute rites at Oraibi, the Sun clan has ta over the duty of making prayer-objects for its epon These are smoked over and prayed to for a long sum and good crops. On the next day they are deposited distant shrine.

Fewkes, 1902b, pp. 500–506, describes a closely sim "Winter Sun Prayer-Stick Making" as though it we

THE MAJOR RITES OF THE FLUTE SOCIETIES

In addition to the brief solar observances just described, the two Flute groups conduct elaborate ceremonials biennially in August.[36] Again prayers to the sun play a prominent part, but requests for rain and abundant germination are the dominant themes of the ritual.[37] Unlike the general pattern of Hopi ceremonies, the making of the altar and other esoteric exercises are carried on in the main houses of the controlling clans and not in kivas. For the most part the two societies meet independently, but their main public performances are held jointly.

The first four days are given over to smoking, singing, praying, medicine-making, altar construction, and the manufacture of offerings. The next day, on First Mesa, an Alosaka impersonator leads a procession of celebrants; and on the morrow the *tiponi* of the society is reverently unwrapped and then carefully re-covered. An episode occurs at Walpi on the seventh day which probably does not take place at the other villages. The Flute members, approaching the village after a lengthy circuit, find their trail barred by the Bear and Snake chiefs. After some delay they are allowed to proceed on their promise to bring rain by the regular performance of their ceremony. Soon after, they are stopped by Alosaka, who finally allows them to march into the town.[38]

Before dawn on the morning of the ninth day, a cottonwood shelter (*kisi*) is constructed in the plaza, within which (at Walpi) there sits a Masau'u personator. At sunrise there is a race for men from the plain to the village,[39] and that after-

noon there begin the culminating rites which are popularly known as the Flute dance. Although most of the final acts are open to public view, they are preceded by a secret ceremony for which both societies assemble at the main spring of the village, the Gray Flutes gathering on one side and the Blue Flutes on the other.[40] All the men present engage in a ritual smoke, after which the participants begin to dress and paint, the older performers helping the younger. Soon a runner is dispatched to deposit offerings at a distant shrine, and on his return the members of the two groups take their places in prescribed formations on opposite sides of the spring. Several old men sit close by the water's edge and sing and rattle steadily, while two warriors (*kaletakam*) in full costume keep guard high up on the banks and twirl their "whizzers" from time to time. In a few minutes one man, naked except for a breech clout, enters the spring, and after removing fallen leaves and other surface debris, he takes a lighted pipe and blows four puffs of smoke into the water. He then hands the pipe to one of the men on the shore, wades into the stream about hip high, and makes three partial immersions before plunging completely under the surface. Meantime the singing and rattling continue steadily until, with dramatic suddenness, the songs conclude at the very moment that the man in the spring breaks water and appears to view, holding aloft in either hand a rod to which are attached several netted gourds full of water. All the participants thank him heartily, because his actions symbolize the manner in which the pueblo's main spring supplies the inhabitants with water.

separate rite, but a comparison with Stephen's notes in Parsons, 1936b, pp. 53–60 and pp. 70–82, plainly shows that Fewkes is treating as an independent ceremony what appears to be part of the sixth day's observances of the Walpi Soyal celebration.

As Stephen reports it, certain officers led by a Patki chief, withdraw from Chief kiva on the sixth day of the Soyal and go to make offerings to the sun at a Patki clan house in Walpi. These rites correspond closely to the sun offering ritual which the Flute societies perform at Oraibi. This establishes a conceptual tie between the Flute and the Soyal groups, both of which are deeply concerned with the sun's progress. Note that the Patki clan which leads the sun offering ceremony also owns the Walpi Soyal, while at Oraibi it is the Patki clan that controls the Gray Flute society. At both pueblos Patki men serve as Sun Watchers. Note too that at Oraibi the Soyal and the Village chieftainships are combined, whereas at Walpi the Town chief serves as Flute chief.

[36] The date is supposed to be 16 days after the August

moon (Pa-muya) has been sighted.

[37] My abstract of the Flute ceremonials is a composite of the following reports: Fewkes, 1892a, pp. 108–150; Fewkes, 1894c, pp. 265–287; Fewkes, 1895a, pp. 265–282; Fewkes, 1900b, pp. 957–1011; Parsons, 1936b, pp. 768–817; Parsons, 1939, pp. 703–708, *et passim*.

In addition I have used my own notes taken at public performances on all three Hopi Mesas in 1932 and 1933, and I have included material obtained from interviews and from the observation of part of the esoteric ritual at Toreva Spring during the Mishongnovi performance of 1932.

[38] According to Parsons, 1936b, p. 769, these rites dramatize the arrival of various clans at Walpi, and a struggle for chieftainship. Cf. Stephen, 1929, pp. 9, 10. Note a similar enactment of clan legends at the Oraibi Patcava, p. 225 and footnote 20.

[39] For a description and discussion of these races, see Titiev, 1939b, p. 34.

[40] The following description is based on personal observations made at Toreva Spring in August, 1932.

A few moments later both societies prepare to make a ceremonial procession to the village plaza. The Blue Flutes line up first with their chief in the lead, followed by two young girls and a little boy who stands between them.[41] A few paces behind come the other members, some carrying standards, and all singing, shaking rattles, or playing flutes. The warriors of the society bring up the rear. Several yards further back the Gray Flute society ranges itself in similar fashion. Then the Blue Flute chief advances a short distance and draws three conventional rain and cloud symbols by sprinkling white cornmeal on the ground. Then, in rotation, the girl at the left, the little boy, and the girl at his right, attempt to throw looped rings and a cylinder which they carry on the tips of rods, into the newly-made designs.[42] Regardless of where these objects actually land, the leader picks them up and places one in the center of each of the three cloud symbols. He then advances about thirty feet and makes another set of drawings. Then the three youngsters come forward, pick their objects up on the ends of their rods, march to within a short distance of the second drawing, and again try to throw the cylinder and the rings into the cloud designs. As they advance the rest of the society follows, and by short stages the two groups move slowly to the foot of the mesa, climb to the level top, and proceed in the same fashion to the cottonwood booth which had previously been set up in the plaza. A number of songs are sung here, after which the Blue Flute leader deposits within the shelter his share of the gourds that had been brought up from within the spring. After this the Blue Flute group withdraws to its clan house, whereupon the Gray Flute gourds are deposited within the booth, and that society too goes from the plaza to the house of its controlling clan.

There is one significant variant of the ninth day's proceedings which occurs, insofar as available data go, only on Third Mesa.[43] This com- prises a race for women which takes place soon after noon, prior to the exercises at the spring. All the participants wear their hair in the manner prescribed for corpses and carry nakwakwosi for their recently deceased relatives. Each family or household is expected to have at least one representative, who may or may not be a member of the Flute societies. At Oraibi the women racers used to assemble at Muyovatni, a watering place not far from Lololoma's Spring. They would line the south bank of Muyovatni while the Flute groups occupied the north side. After the latter had rendered several songs to the accompaniment of flutes and rattles, one of the Flute chiefs would wade into the water, and at prescribed intervals he would plunge completely beneath the surface. On the first three occasions the women would throw some of their prayer-feathers into the stream, but at the fourth immersion they would toss in all their remaining offerings.[44] When the chief emerged from his last plunge he would bring up a previously concealed rod (köngnötki), to which were attached netted gourds filled with water. When this ceremony was ended, the women would race back to the pueblo.

INTERPRETATION OF THE FLUTE RITUALS

In spite of myriad variations in the details of procedure at the various Hopi towns, the general scheme of the Flute ceremony seems to be the same throughout the tribe. A cultus hero and heroine are invariably represented in effigy on the altars, and in each pueblo a germination deity is also featured. Everywhere too the closing day's activities include a foot race, a dramatic ritual at a spring, and a procession to a cottonwood bower in the plaza. The performance at the spring enacts the bringing of rain (water) from the very home of the clouds (the spring); and the procession dramatizes the original approach of the pro-

[41] The two girls and the boy must be unmarried. They generally belong to the clan which owns the society.

[42] The looped rings thrown by the girls and the looped cylinder thrown by the boy are called "ducks" by Oraibi informants, an identification which is supported by the fact that they do have duck feathers attached to them. These objects are pictured in Voth, 1912b, plate LVI, nos. 7, 8. Pictures of the entire procession, as well as a comparative account of the ritual may be found in Fewkes, 1900b, pp. 996–1000, and plates LVII–LXIII.

[43] The Third Mesa variant was first observed by the writer at Hotevilla on August 27, 1933. Only part of the procedure, however, was actually witnessed, but it pro- vided a lead for later interviews with Oraibi men who had once belonged to the Gray Flute society. The following account, therefore, pertains to Oraibi, although informants insisted that the Hotevilla practice was essentially the same.

In August, 1937, the women's race was again seen by the writer at Hotevilla. It took place in the early afternoon of the ninth day of the Flute celebration.

[44] While the chief is submerged in the spring he is regarded as being in the actual home of the clouds and Katcinas who are equated with the dead. Hence, this is a particularly appropriate moment for depositing prayer-feathers on behalf of the dead.

prietary clans at the time when they offered to perform their ceremony regularly in exchange for admission to the pueblo. At Walpi this element receives its greatest elaboration, but the same idea is expressed at all the towns. In addition, the Flute rites play an important part in the cult of the dead, a feature which seems to be most prominent at Third Mesa, but which has also been observed elsewhere.[45]

The one aspect of the Flute ceremonies which is probably the most significant of all is the solar. At each village a sun, earth, or sky god plays an important part. At Oraibi it is Sotukinangwu'u; at Mishongnovi it is Muyingwa; at Walpi we find both Muyingwa and Alosaka; and at Shipaulovi it is Taiowa. Furthermore, Voth has recorded a myth which links the Flute rites with the creation of the sun, for it describes how the newly-emerged people made the sun by tossing into the sky a sun symbol such as "is still worn on the back of the flute players in the Flute ceremony."[46] Flute performances are invariably associated with warm weather, for the Hopi believe that the flutes represent the sounds of locusts, who are regarded as harbingers of summer. Accordingly, these instruments are valued highly and are employed in conjunction with other rituals such as the Walpi Soyal and the Oraibi Water Serpent and Maswik Katcina observances.

There is good evidence too for associating the Flute rites with solstice celebrations, despite the occurrence of the main performances in August. In this connection it has been postulated by Fewkes that the Flute dance "may have interesting relations with midsummer sun worship, notwithstanding its date is so tardy for the time of the summer solstice."[47] In support of Fewkes' hypothesis, it has already been shown above that the winter and summer offerings of the Flute societies are made at the actual time of the solstices. Then again, during the major Flute rites at Walpi there is placed on the altar a stone image of Palulokong, "wrapped around with the pine needle prayer-feathers of the last winter solstice ceremony. . . ."[48] Moreover, one bit of ritual has been observed which is reminiscent of the Soyal

climax wherein a sun symbol is twirled to indicate the movements of the sun. On the fourth night of the Walpi Flute ceremony a representation of the sky (*tokpela*) is supended over the altar, and while a number of songs are being sung the "sky" is kept swinging with an eagle feather.[49] The next morning a new standard representing the sun is placed on the kiva roof, and Parsons surmises that this "dramatizes either the placing of the *new sun* [italics mine] in the sky or the emergence from the sunless lower worlds into the sunlight."[50] On the basis of such sun-making and sun-handling activities, it may not be unwarranted to hazard the opinion that the Flute rites complement the Soyal, and that if the Soyal is supposed to start the sun on its journey from its winter to its summer home, it is the Flute performance that sends it on the return trip from its summer to its winter home.

INTRODUCTION TO THE SNAKE-ANTELOPE CEREMONIES

In view of the great importance attached to the Flute observances it is somewhat surprising to find that these rites are not performed each year but are held biennially in alternation with the Snake-Antelope ceremonies. If our interpretation of the Flute performance as a summer solstice ritual is correct, it must be shown that the Snake-Antelope celebration likewise deals with the control of the sun, and that the two sets of rites are so nearly equivalent that they occupy similar positions with reference to the entire structure of Hopi ceremonialism. In this regard it is noteworthy that almost from the beginning of detailed studies of Hopi religion, investigators have tended to equate the two ceremonies in question. As a matter of fact, Fewkes first became aware of the existence of the Flute rites among the Hopi when he learned "from various sources" that the Snake dance "was celebrated without the snakes on certain occasions."[51] Intrigued by the notion of a snake-less Snake dance, Fewkes made it a point to witness one of these performances at Walpi in 1890, and from his published description[52] it is perfectly clear that what he had been

---

[45] Fewkes, 1892a, p. 114, mentions four crooks on the Blue Flute altar at Shipaulovi which he believed "personified dead members of the Flute organization."

[46] Voth, 1905b, p. 14. Note too that when Tiyo, hero of the Snake legend, meets the Sun, he finds him dressed like a flute player in the Flute ceremony. See p. 153.

[47] Fewkes, 1896a, p. 254.

[48] Parsons, 1936b, p. 789.

[49] Parsons, 1936b, p. 794 and fig. 424. In this entry of his journal, Stephen has shown that he meant to get at the exact meaning of the "sky" swinging, but unfortunately there is no indication that he ever inquired further into the matter.

[50] Parsons, 1939, pp. 705, 706.

[51] Fewkes, 1891, p. 129.

[52] Fewkes, 1891.

led to believe was a counterpart of the Snake dance was in reality a performance of the Flute ritual.

While it cannot be denied that most of the resemblances which led Fewkes to consider the two ceremonies as closely related were based on his personal observations and interpretations, nevertheless there are many indications that the natives too incline to regard the two rituals as equivalent. Indeed, as more and more data have been gathered and compared, it has become increasingly evident that Fewkes' early confusion was a natural one, for the "ritual patterns of the Flute ceremony are much the same as those of the Snake-Antelope ceremony."[53] One myth in particular serves to indicate the presence of an association between the two rites in the minds of the Hopi. During a stormy winter the Snakes are snowbound, so they send a messenger to the home of the Locusts for help, because "the locusts sometimes play flutes in a ceremony and that was the reason why it was so nice and warm there."[54] The Locusts visit the Snake kiva (home), and as they play on their instruments the cold weather comes to an end. Apparently, the connection between snakes and locusts rests on their mutual tendency to disappear in the winter and to reappear with the approach of summer. On the basis of the *post hoc ergo propter hoc* fallacy, snakes and locusts are regarded as bringing warm weather with them.

Another conceptual tie between the Snake-Antelope and the Flute rituals may be found in their military nature. Concerning the former, Dr. Parsons has called attention to the "sometime warrior character of the two societies, the Antelopes and the Snakes."[55] As to the latter, Locust, whom the Flute groups represent, is described

in the Emergence myths as a daring figure. He is the first to make his way completely out of the *sipapu*, and his outstanding bravery in defiantly playing his flute while the Cloud chiefs hurl lightning at him wins many favors for those who follow him.[56]

At Oraibi there is still another link between the Flute and the Snake-Antelope ceremonies, for the Spider clan which owns the Blue Flute also owns the Antelope society; and preliminary meetings of the Snake and Antelope officers are held in *the* Spider clan house where both the Blue Flute and the Antelope paraphernalia are stored. From several points of view, therefore, it seems justifiable to regard the annual alternation of the Snake-Antelope and Flute rituals in the Hopi ceremonial calendar as an interchange of equivalent parts.

THE SNAKE-ANTELOPE OBSERVANCES

At each of the five Hopi villages which conduct these performances at the present time,[57] the exercises are carried on jointly by two independent societies, the Snake and the Antelope. In years when the Snake-Antelope rites are to be celebrated the members of the two groups make winter offerings about six months before the date of their major performance in August.[58] The latter begins with a preliminary meeting of the two sets of officers who smoke and make prayer-objects together.[59] Eight days later the secret rites begin independently in the Snake and Antelope kivas, and for the most part the sequence of events follows the customary pattern, except that the Snake men go out on four successive days to hunt snakes to the north, west, south, and east, respec-

[53] Parsons, 1936b, p. 768.
[54] Voth, 1905b, p. 219.
[55] Parsons, 1936b, p. 577.
[56] Stephen, 1929, pp. 5, 7.
[57] The Snake-Antelope rites are held in years ending in even numbers at Hotevilla (replacing Oraibi), Chimopovy, and Shipaulovi. In odd years performances occur at Walpi and Mishongnovi.
[58] Voth, 1903a, p. 272, refers to a nine-day winter ceremony by the Snake society, but no account of such a celebration is to be found in any of the writings on the Hopi.
The question of the proper date for the summer observance is complicated by the fact that the time of the ceremony may be regulated by the condition of the crop, according to Voth, 1903a, p. 274. Theoretically, it should

begin on the fourth day following the close of the Niman. Actually, it generally falls on about the third week in August.
[59] The account of the Snake-Antelope rites is based primarily on Voth, 1903a, but the following works were also consulted: Bourke, 1884; Dorsey and Voth, 1902; Fewkes, 1894b; Fewkes, 1900b; Fewkes, 1897c; Mendelieff, 1886; Parsons, 1936b, pp. 577–767.
Wherever possible the writer has included material gathered in interviews at Oraibi, and into the description of the dance on the ninth day of the observances he has introduced notes taken at performances which he has witnessed at all five of the pueblos that conduct these exercises. Also, see Titiev, 1943b.
Recently a new account of the First Mesa rites has appeared in Stephen, 1940, IV, V, VI.

vely. On each of these mornings the Snake chief visits the Antelope chief in his kiva for a formal smoke, and on the evening of the fifth day the snake group goes in a body to the Antelope kiva where the two societies unite for a joint performance.[60] This is featured by the building of an altar, the making of medicine, and singing and praying, during which an Antelope man and a duly qualified woman are dressed to represent the cultus hero and heroine whose adventures are described in the Snake legend.[61] A similar performance is enacted on the sixth night, but the seventh day is devoted primarily to routine tasks, except that a courier is sent to fill a netted gourd (*mongwikuru*) with water in anticipation of a foot race on the following day.

Before daybreak on the morning of the eighth day, two warriors from the Snake society make several circuits of the Snake and Antelope kivas, whirling their "bull-roarers" and shooting their "lightning frames."[62] Towards dawn they go to the starting place from which there is to be a race back to the village. Here they put down prayer-offerings and send the runners off just as the sun becomes visible to spectators assembled on the mesa's edge.[63] The winner of the race hurries to the Antelope kiva with the gourd of water that had been provided on the day before.

Meanwhile, at about the time that the runners are on their way to the starting line, the remaining members of the Snake and Antelope groups assemble in the latter's kiva and prepare to repeat the observances of the fifth and sixth nights. Just as the race is about to get under way a watcher hastens to notify the people in the Antelope kiva so that the rites may begin at the moment that the race is starting. The songs and prayers are brought to their usual close, however, without regard to the winner's arrival.

It is late in the afternoon before the major activities of the eighth day are resumed. At this time the Antelope men, followed in a few moments by the Snakes, appear in the plaza and make four decreasing circuits in front of a cottonwood booth (*kisi*) that has previously been erected. Directly before the booth there lies a foot-drum,

a log placed over a cavity in the ground. As each man passes the foot-drum he sprinkles it with a pinch of cornmeal and stamps on it with his right foot. When the two groups have completed their circuits they line up facing each other, the Antelopes close by the booth with their backs to it, and the Snake men *vis-à-vis* a short distance away. After a few songs have been rendered in unison by the two societies, one of the Antelope officers and the Snake chief leave their respective lines. As they prepare to dance the Snake chief stands behind the Antelope man, with his left hand resting on the latter's left shoulder. In this position the two men dance to the front of the booth where the Antelope officer kneels to receive from someone concealed within the shelter a cluster of vines and other vegetation. This he holds dangling from his mouth as he and his partner continue their dance in exactly the same fashion as the Snake men (with live snakes instead of vegetation) are going to perform exactly twenty-four hours later. When the Antelope man's dance has ended he places the cluster of vines on the ground, whereupon a Snake member picks it up, and the two societies again make four-fold circuits before returning to their respective kivas.

Before dawn on the ninth (concluding) day of the observances, preparations are made for another race which is to be conducted like that of the preceding day. Soon after, a Badger clansman from the Snake society is dispatched to fetch herbs for brewing an emetic which is to be drunk at the close of the Snake dance. During the course of the day all the captive snakes are "baptized" in yucca suds, and a short time later they are deposited in the cottonwood booth in the plaza. Then the men dress and paint up for the public spectacle which is the most widely publicized rite performed by the Hopi. Once more the two groups perform their circuits, and again they line up facing each other while they sing and sway to the accompaniment of rattles held by the Antelopes. Then the Snake men change to a new formation. While the Antelope society retains its position and continues to sing and rattle, the Snake members pair up, with the rear man resting

---

[60] When novices are admitted to either of these cults, initiations take place on this night. For details of initiation, consult Voth, 1903a, pp. 298–300.

[61] See p. 153 below.

[62] The "bull-roarers" and the "lightning frames" represent thunder and lightning and thus serve to indicate that

the warriors are impersonating Sotukinangwu'u, chief sky god and head of all the warriors.

[63] For details of the race and its significance, see Titiev, 1939b, p. 34. The men who participate in this race need not necessarily be members of the Snake or Antelope societies.

his left hand on the left shoulder of his partner.[64] Several unpaired Snake men stand aside ready to act as gatherers of released reptiles. The paired couples dance towards the booth, before which the front man kneels to receive a snake which he holds between his lips as he continues to dance. After making several circuits in this fashion, the snake carrier places the reptile gently on the ground and continues to move toward the cottonwood shelter where he stoops to receive another snake. Thus the couples come and go until every one of the captured snakes has been danced with and released. As soon as any of the animals has been placed on the ground, it is picked up in a prescribed fashion by one of the gatherers.

When the last snake has been gathered, the Snake chief moves off to one end of the plaza where, with thick lines of cornmeal, he draws a circle and marks it into quadrants. All the snakes are then thrown into the circle, women and girls of the Snake clan throw heaps of meal on the writhing mass, and nearby spectators spit towards the wriggling reptiles.[65] A few seconds later some of the younger Snake performers scoop up as many snakes as they can hold and hurry to deposit them in distant shrines located in the four cardinal directions. Upon their return, all the Snake dancers wash off some of their paint, partake of an emetic, and then prepare to break a day-long fast.

THE MEANING OF THE SNAKE-ANTELOPE RITES

Like all the major Hopi ceremonies, the Snake-Antelope observances are not centered about a single set of ideas. As Fewkes has phrased it, "That the ceremony is a rain-making observance can not be doubted, and the nature of many acts shows that it is likewise tinged with sun worship. To these must now be added corn or seed germination, growth and maturity. . . . I am in-

clined to believe that the Snake dance has tw[o] main purposes, the making of rain, and the growt[h] of corn. . . ."[66] In addition to these element[s] which are more or less common to all Ho[pi] rituals, attention must be called to a mortuar[y] aspect which is emphasized particularly during th[e] construction of altars. At such times a number [of] crooks and sticks are set out, whose meaning ha[s] been explained by Stephen. "The crooks repr[e]sent the wise old men bent with age, the thinki[ng] old men of the society who have died; the lo[ng] prayer-sticks, the younger unbent member[s] dead; those around the Antelope altar, the A[n]telope members; and those at the Snake altar, th[e] old dead Snake members. It is analagous to th[e] placing of a planting stick at the grave."[67] Th[us] we have an indication that in the course of th[e] Snake-Antelope exercises, as was also evident [in] the accounts of the Katcina, Tribal Initiation, an[d] Soyal ceremonies, the spirits of deceased Snal[e] and Antelope men are represented in the kiv[a] and are supposed to join with the living membe[rs] in the performance of the rites. This interpret[a]tion is supported by a passage in a Walpi my[th] which purports to describe the first of all Snal[e] ceremonies. "On the fifth evening of the cer[e]mony,[68] and for three succeeding evenings, lo[w] clouds trailed over To-ko-na-bi, and Snake peop[le] from the underworld came from them, and we[nt] into the kiva(s), and ate only corn pollen f[or] food. . . ."[69]

Another element which is strongly marke[d] particularly in the Snake rites, is the militaristi[c]. Several aspects of this feature have already bee[n] pointed out by Dr. Parsons.[70] For example, th[e] animals which figure most prominently in su[ch] esoteric practices as medicine-making, are Bea[r] Puma (Mountain Lion), and Wolf, all of who[m] give great power to warriors. However, the mo[st] specific evidence of the martial character of th[e] Snake performance is to be found in Voth's d[e]

[64] The one who carries the snake is usually the ceremonial son of the partner who dances behind him. The latter brushes the shoulders of the former with his "snake whip," keeping time to the singing and rattling of the Antelope men. It has been said that the brushing diverts the snake's attention from the carrier, but as a rule the rear man appears unconcerned with the snake except when a large bullsnake attempts to coil about his partner's neck. He may then brush the reptile until it uncoils. For further details of Hopi snake handling, see Titiev, 1943b.

[65] Fewkes, 1902a, p. 19, footnote 1, refers to "a rain of spittle from assembled spectators." Spitting as a means of exorcism or as a purificatory rite is discussed in Parsons, 1939, pp. 460–461, et passim.

[66] Fewkes, 1897c, p. 307. Compare the songs publish[ed] in Stephen, 1940, pp. 209–211.

[67] Parsons, 1936b, p. 709. Bourke, 1884, p. 124, al[so] reports that blackened twigs commemorated the H[opi] dead.

[68] The fifth evening of the ceremony is the night [on] which altars are first put up.

[69] Fewkes, 1894b, p. 116.

[70] Parsons, 1936b, p. 577, et passim. I cannot, howeve[r] accept Dr. Parsons' guess, loc. cit. footnote 3, that ratt[le] snakes were hunted with the purpose of poisoning arrow[s] as I can find no convincing proof that the Hopi ever h[ad] this custom. On this point consult Parsons, 1939, pp. 3[?] footnote *, and p. 1043, footnote ‡.

scription of the proceedings just prior to the public dance on the last day of the rites. As the Snake men were preparing to go into the plaza, spots were painted "with a mixture of a red ochre (cūta) and common clay . . . on [various parts] of the body. . . . Concerning these spots . . . I am told that in former days, when the Hopis were still occasionally at war with other tribes, the warriors who were to leave the village to meet the enemy, would assemble by clan groups north of the village. Here one of the older members of the Kokop . . . clan[71] prepared a clay or paste of pulverized (Pöokong vomisis)[72] and water. . . . As the men . . . filed by him, he would put just such marks on their bodies as the Snakes put on to this day, in memory of those occasions."[73] Furthermore, Voth notes that all members of the Snake society were called warriors (*kaletakam*), and on the basis of all his evidence he concludes that there seems to be "no doubt that a certain relation exists between the Snake ceremony and perhaps certain war ceremonies that may formerly have been in vogue. . . ."[74]

There remains for consideration the solar aspect of the Snake-Antelope rites. This element is related to the military one, inasmuch as Hopi sky gods are generally regarded as warriors, and the Sun is the father of the Little War Twins.[75] A still more fundamental connection is brought to light by an analysis of the Snake legend on which many of the Snake-Antelope ritual practices are based. This story is found on all three Mesas, and the different versions agree quite well on the main outlines of the tale.[76] A youth named Tiyo, eager to learn where the waters of a stream lead, embarks in a water-proof box and ultimately lands at a kiva whose inmates appear sometimes as humans and sometimes as snakes. From among these people he chooses a bride, and from them too he learns the secrets of the Snake cult. Before starting his journey homeward, Tiyo visits a

goddess[77] in whose house he meets the Sun "in the form of a handsome young man, beautifully painted and dressed up as the Flute players at the Flute ceremony are painted and dressed at the present day."[78] Tiyo accepts the Sun's invitation to accompany him on his rounds, and soon after completing this adventure he returns to the Snake people, claims his wife, and departs with her for his home. Here he introduces the Snake ceremony and lives happily until his wife gives birth to a brood of snakes. From this point on the various myths end in divergent ways, but I agree wholeheartedly with Haeberlin when he writes, "In spite of the contradictions of the various versions, I believe that Tiyo is more correctly sun-god or rather that his associations with the sun are unmistakable."[79]

On the whole it seems safe to say that the basic myth of the Snake society gives clear indication of that group's concern with the sun, but it is somewhat more venturesome to assert that the Snake rites may be solstitial in character. Nevertheless, on the basis of the analogies with the Flute ritual which are to be discussed in the succeeding section, there may be considerable support for Fewkes' hypothesis that the Snake observance "is a summer solstitial ceremony highly modified."[80]

ANALOGIES BETWEEN THE FLUTE AND THE SNAKE-ANTELOPE CEREMONIES

In the introduction to the discussion of the Snake-Antelope rites attention was called to the fact that some of the earliest students of Hopi religion were struck by the close resemblances they bore to the Flute rituals. Contemporary ethnologists have also arrived at similar conclusions, as is evidenced by Parsons' recent statement that the "Snake-Antelope ceremony is affiliated conceptually with the Flute. . . ."[81]

---

[71] The Kokop clan is outstanding at Oraibi for its military character. See p. 155.

[72] Pukonghöya is the elder of the Little War Twins, and his vomisis is supposed to be particularly potent war medicine.

[73] Voth, 1903a, p. 334. "These marks . . . were said to make the flesh of the warrior tough and proof against the arrows of the enemy."

[74] Voth, 1903a, p. 344.

[75] Stephen, 1929, p. 11, *seq.*

[76] The summary here given is a composite of versions from all three Mesas. The First Mesa legend is taken from Fewkes, 1894b, p. 106 ff.; the Second Mesa tale is from Dorsey and Voth, 1902, p. 255 ff.; and the Third

Mesa myth is taken from Voth, 1903a, p. 349 ff. Compare Stephen, 1939, pp. 197–204.

[77] In some accounts the goddess is identified as the Spider Woman, but in others she is called Huruing Wuhti (Hard Substance Woman).

[78] Voth, 1903a, p. 350.

[79] Haeberlin, 1916, p. 19.

It will be noted that virtually all the references to the sun pertain to the Snake and not the Antelope society. There is some indication, however, that Tiyo learned the Antelope rites as well as the Snake secrets during the course of his adventures. See Parsons, 1936b, p. 675.

[80] Fewkes, 1895a, p. 282.

[81] Parsons, 1936b, p. 769. Still more recently, in de-

Yet, when Stephen questioned native theorists, he was given two contradictory opinions. On the one hand, Kopeli, the Walpi Snake chief, asserted that "The Flute and Snake societies are not the same. They never were the same, they have no connection."[82] On the other hand, Honi, a Walpi Antelope officer who held many important ceremonial positions; and Sikyapiki, the Snake chief of Shipaulovi, both contended "that long ago the Flute and Snake . . . were the same."[83] Indeed, in answer to a direct question on another occasion, Sikyapiki "distinctly says, 'Flute and Snake-Antelope long ago the same.' "[84]

Despite the conflicting opinions of native religionists, so many close analogies may be pointed out between the two rituals that the evidence overwhelmingly supports those who regard them as being closely linked or equivalent to each other. Even "the winter assembly of the Flute . . . has certain points in common with that of the Antelope-Snake,"[85] as Fewkes has indicated; but the ties between the main summer performances are far more noteworthy. Among them the following similarities may be cited: "The Flute standard corresponds to the Snake standard";[86] the necks of the "lightning snakes" depicted on the sand painting of the Blue Flute society were "surrounded by four black marks corresponding to the necklace of the lightning snakes of the Snake Dance";[87] in the Gray Flute altar "a row of eagle's tail feathers was inserted in such a way as to remind one of a similar row back of the altar in the Snake ceremonials";[88] and balls of clay known as tadpoles "are made in both the Flute and the Snake ceremonies at Walpi."[89] During the first day of the Walpi Flute observances a runner carries offerings to distant points along "the same circuit as taken . . . in the Snake-Antelope ceremony";[90] and the same courier plans "to distribute the prayer-feathers at noon every day, same as Kakaptï [his older brother] did at the Snake-Antelope ceremony. . . ."[91]

Then too many of the details of the public exhibition of the Snake and Antelope groups are identical with those of the closing acts of the Flute observance. The races held at daybreak are started and conducted in exactly the same fashion in both cases; "in all essential features the Flute boys were clothed and decorated in the same manner as the Snake youth in the kiva exercises . . . of the Snake ceremonies";[92] with regard to the Flute girls, "their apparel was identical with that of the . . . Snake Virgin of the Antelopes in the Snake Dance";[93] "the small netted gourds of water which the [Flute] boy and girls carried . . . are the same as those used in the Snake dances";[94] the annulets of flag leaf, thrown by the Flute maidens as they proceed to the plaza, are "identical with similar objects made in the Snake Dance";[95] and "in no public ceremony of the Hopi is the cottonwood kisi introduced except in the Snake and Flute rites, in both of which its construction is identical."[96]

So impressed was Fewkes with the manifest parallels between the two rituals that he inclined to the belief that they showed a "development from a common primitive ceremony, now modified into a Snake Dance, now into a Flute observance, but preserving in common many traditional personages."[97] Although we are not concerned here with the problem of divergence from a common source, the fact that both ceremonies revolve about a similar group of notions is of prime importance to our argument, for it provides the reason why the Snake-Antelope and Flute rites may be interchanged annually without disrupting the ceremonial calendar and without slighting any of the fundamental concepts of Hopi religion. If it be granted that one of the most essential functions of the Flute observances is to send the sun from its summer solstice point towards its winter home, then it follows that the same function may be equally well performed in alternate years by the equivalent Snake-Antelope ritual.

scribing an ancient bowl which depicts Locust and Snake, patrons of the Flute and Snake groups, Dr. Parsons refers to both the latter as if they formed a single unit. "I say *society*, not *societies*," writes Dr. Parsons, "for the bowl is evidence for the theory that a closer relation between the two societies once existed in the social organization than is generally recognized by the townspeople today." Parsons, 1940, p. 542.

[82] Parsons, 1936b, p. 713.
[83] Parsons, 1936b, p. 718.
[84] Parsons, 1936b, p. 767.
[85] Fewkes, 1895a, p. 274, footnote 2.

[86] Fewkes, 1900b, p. 998.
[87] Fewkes, 1892a, p. 115. Fewkes frequently refers to the entire Snake-Antelope ceremony as the Snake dance.
[88] Fewkes, 1892a, p. 120.   [89] Fewkes, 1900b, p. 992
[90] Parsons, 1936b, p. 774.
[91] Parsons, 1936b, p. 775.
[92] Fewkes, 1900b, p. 992.
[93] Fewkes, 1892a, p. 139.
[94] Fewkes, 1900b, p. 1000.
[95] Fewkes, 1892a, p. 131.
[96] Fewkes, 1900b, p. 1005.
[97] Fewkes, 1892a, p. 150.

CHAPTER XII

CUSTOMS AND RITUALS RELATING TO WAR

THE KOKOP CLAN MYTH

OF ALL the clans on Third Mesa, the Kokop is by far the most intimately concerned with war. Accordingly, the myth describing the first settlement of the Kokop clan at Oraibi may well serve as an introduction to a study of Hopi warfare.[1]

The Kokop people are said to have reached Oraibi after they had formerly lived in a home situated far to the northwest.[2] At first Matcito refused to admit them to his pueblo, so they circled to the south of the mesa and made a temporary settlement there. From time to time their leaders beseeched Matcito to allow them to move into the village, offering to be his "hands" (warriors), but the chief remained obdurate. In revenge, the head man of the Kokops secretly sent word to the Chimwava, huge men with gigantic feet, supposedly the worst enemies of the Hopi, inviting them to make a raid on Oraibi.[3] Soon after, the people on the mesa top were horrified to find a large host of the dreaded Chimwava marching upon their town. Matcito gathered his men, but realizing that his forces were inadequate, he remembered the Kokop's promises and sent word that the clan would be allowed to reside in Oraibi if it would help beat off the invaders.

Now it happened that the Kokops claimed Masau'u as one of their ancients,[4] so two of their men immediately began to dress as impersonators of that deity. They put on buckskin kilts, headbands of yucca, and many strings of beads; and bound clusters of plumes (hurunkwa) containing two reeds with breath feathers attached, to their hair.[5] On their faces they drew two oblique black lines, running from under the cheek bones and meeting at the bridge of the nose, and in their hands they carried gourds full of ashes. Thanks to the influence of their ancient, these men were far more powerful than ordinary warriors, and were equipped with special songs for use with the various acts of war such as dressing for action, attacking and scalping.

When the two Masau'u impersonators were ready, the Kokop group reported to Matcito. "I'll go with you," he

said, "and I'll carry my club to protect myself, but I remind you that you may live with me at Oraibi only if you kill the enemy; otherwise you must remain where you are." He then hung his weapon from the crook of his left elbow in the manner of Pukonghöya, and led his men to meet the raiders. The Kokop chief instructed the two Masau'u actors to run in opposite directions, describing wide arcs in back of the enemy lines in such fashion that they would meet at a point directly behind their opponents' center. This they did, and as their paths crossed they threw down their gourds of ashes. Immediately the contents flew up like flames, covering the attackers and making them faint and sluggish.[6] Thereupon the Hopi charged forward and killed large numbers of the enemy, thanks to the great power of the Kokop chief's medicine.[7] The Chimwava retreated far to the north and east until they came to a place called Wiwaovi. Here their leader scratched a line on a rock, and at each end he inserted an inverted arrow. "Now you have killed many of my people," said the enemy chief, "and I've got to bring some of them home, so this will be the end."

As soon as the victory of the Hopi was assured, the Masau'u impersonators spoke to Matcito. "Now we've got to say some things right here before you leave," they began. "Because you took part in fighting the enemy, you beat us with your (Bear) strength. You killed more enemies than we did. Now we cannot go back to Oraibi, but we will always stay here (where the Chimwava chief had drawn the line) and protect you." Then the Masau'u men began to cry. Matcito thanked them for their offer of protection and promised to reward them with prayer-sticks and other offerings. After this, the Hopi started for home, leaving the Masau'u impersonators behind; and sometimes their crying can be heard in the night, and once in a while their footsteps may be seen in the snow. During the Soyal everyone makes prayer-sticks which are deposited at a shrine for their benefit.

On the way back to Oraibi the warriors began to count their dead enemies, each man identifying those whom he had slain. If anyone asked, "Who killed this enemy?" the answer would be, "My ancient (wuya) killed this one"; for in those days it was considered bragging to claim

---

[1] The following tale was narrated by Chief Tawaqwaptiwa of Oraibi, reputedly a descendant of Matcito, whose actions he would naturally tend to glorify at the expense of the Kokops. It must be remembered too that in the disintegration of Oraibi, the Kokop clan played a leading part. Tawaqwaptiwa's partisanship is evidenced throughout the story.

[2] Note that the Spider clan, an ally of the Kokop group is also said to have come from the northwest. See p. 74.

[3] The Chimwava are probably to be identified as the Chemehuevi. Their feet were supposed to be about twenty inches long.

[4] See p. 140, footnote 81.   [5] Compare p. 161.

[6] Compare the threats of the Kokop clan during their conflict with Lololoma, p. 78.

[7] Tawaqwaptiwa carefully explained that the Kokop chief's power to brew so potent a medicine was proof that he was a witch.

credit for slaying an enemy, and those who were bold enough to do so were promptly taken into the *real* warrior society.[8] After the dead men had been scalped the Hopi pecked marks on the ground as tallies,[9] and when these were added up it was found that Matcito alone had forty to his credit, whereas the total of all the others combined was only eighty.

When they reached home, Matcito spoke to the Kokop clansmen. "Now I'll let you come up to my mesa to stay," he said. "You have helped me to drive off my enemies. You know how to make wonderful things for war, as I have just seen with my own eyes. Now I have found out that you are true warriors, so I will give you land south of Oraibi, and there you will guard us just like the two Masau'u men in the north."

Thus does the myth "explain" the warlike nature of the Kokop clan and the manner of its entry to Oraibi. When they settled in the village, the Kokop people are supposed to have brought in with them as their ancients, Masau'u and the Little War Twins, and they are said to have introduced into the pueblo the *real* Warrior society. Moreover, since the Little War Twins are considered to be the grandsons of the Spider Woman, the Kokops also entered into a partnership with the Spider clan, helping them to direct the general Warrior society known as the Momtcit or Mutcwimi.

Between the ordinary Warrior society and the *real* Warrior society a clear distinction was made at Oraibi in the days when active fighting still prevailed among the Indians of the Southwest. The term warrior (*kaletaka*) was applied in the sense of an ordinary warrior to any member of the Momtcit, even if he had never participated in

a battle or killed an enemy. Until about fifty years ago, every able-bodied young man was expected to join the Momtcit society.[10] In contrast to this usage, the term *real* warrior (*bas kaletaka*) was reserved for those who had openly acknowledged killing and scalping an enemy, and who had subsequently gone through an additional rite which will be described below. One reason why the average Hopi was so modest about his prowess in war was because he did not care to become a *real* warrior, partly because of the "dangerous" character of the rite, and partly because, in all likelihood, the *real* warriors always fought in the van.[11] One of the outstanding traits of the Kokop clansmen was that they had no fear of becoming *real* warriors and, accordingly, did not hesitate to take full credit for having slain their enemies.

THE MOMTCIT CEREMONY[12]

Until the cessation of Indian warfare, the Momtcit ceremony was celebrated annually in the Wiklavi kiva of Oraibi, in the fall of the year, not long after the close of the women's Marau ritual which generally occurred in September.[13] The membership was very large as it was open to men of any age or clan (some youngsters joining even before their Katcina initiations), and it was considered advisable for every normal male in the village to enroll.[14] The members were divided into two groups, the regular Momtcit and the Nakyawimi, or Stick-swallowers society.[15] The ritual paraphernalia of both divisions were owned by the Spider and Kokop clans, and the Nakyawimi had no permanent leader, being led each

---

[8] See p. 159, below.

[9] Fewkes, 1902b, p. 482. "The Indians still point out . . . a long score of marks cut in the rock, denoting the number of the dead who fell in one of these fights."

[10] Fewkes, 1902b, p. 484, places the membership at Walpi at about 60.

[11] A third use of the term warrior (*kaletaka*) applies to certain officers in most of the major Hopi ceremonies. While these men may once have been chosen from among the *real* warriors or on the basis of membership in the Momtcit, the office later became entirely ceremonial and was filled by men entirely lacking in military experience. Note too that Voth, 1903a, p. 334, says that all Snake society members are called warriors.

[12] The account of the Oraibi Momtcit was secured from a single informant, the last surviving member of that order in the pueblo. His description is here given with as little change as possible. For a comparison with First Mesa, see Parsons, 1936b, pp. 83–100.

[13] According to Stephen, Parsons, 1936b, p. 85, a war society called Kaletakwimkya met in the Reed clan

house on First Mesa, soon after the Soyal in December. I do not know whether this society is the exact equivalent of the Oraibi Momtcit. However, Dr. Eggan has suggested that since Stephen, Parsons, 1936b, p. 89, lists only 19 members in 1892, he may be referring to a more restricted society than the Momtcit. The difference in time of the performances may also indicate that they are different observances, but it is possible that my aged informant's memory of the date was faulty. Parsons, 1939, p. 867 equates Oraibi's Momtcit with Walpi's Kaletakwimkya.

[14] A practical reason for the popularity of the Momtci was that a man could never tell when he might have to g on the warpath and perform a killing. Such an inciden would qualify him for the *real* Warrior society, whos initiatory rites were somewhat easier for those who a ready belonged to the Momtcit. Compare p. 160.

[15] The name Nakyawimi is based on the word *nas tanpi*, meaning to push into the throat, to swallow. Stephe calls this society Nasosotan and states that there "a Stick-swallowers at Oraibi and they exhibit," but gives no details of the performance either at Oraibi or Walpi. Parsons, 1936b, p. 94.

year by an officer selected by the Momtcit chief. The two units met jointly in the same kiva, but the Nakyawimkyam (Stick-swallower society members) used the main lower floor, and the Mutcwimi (Momtcit society) occupied the raised section south of the ladder. If any one of the Momtcit men stepped down during the progress of the ceremony, except for a formal smoke or on other "official" business, he could be forced to join the stick-swallowers.[16]

The observances opened in customary fashion with a smoke by the officers and the manufacture of prayer-objects, but there was no public announcement of the ceremony's start, and the participants were told by word of mouth when it was time for them to assemble at Wiklavi. Once begun, the rites lasted for two days, the first of which was devoted largely to the setting out of an altar and the making of medicine. The Kokop head officer played the part of Pukonghöya, and the Spider chief impersonated the Spider Woman. These deities, as well as the younger War Twin, Palungahöya, and Masau'u, were also present in effigy on the altars; and in addition, six beasts who represented the four cardinal points plus zenith and nadir were made the recipients of special prayers while the medicine was being mixed. In the ritual order in which they were named, these animals were Mountain Lion for the north, Bear for the west, Wildcat for south, Wolf for east, Kwatoko (Vulture?) for above, and Snake for below.[17] Other gods who were prominent in this cult were Sotukinangwu'u, the main sky deity, who was represented either by a star, a cross or a lightning frame; the Sun; and the Milky Way (Songwuka).[18]

The preparation of the war medicine began early in the afternoon of the first day, with the Pukonghöya impersonator playing the main part. He began by inserting an arrowhead into a plaque filled with water, holding it in place as he sang the required songs. Then he added a pinch of flesh scraped from an enemy scalp, and bits of "hard rock." As he bent close over the bowl, Pukonghöya shouted loudly from time to time to notify the powerful beasts who "owned" the medicine of the proceedings. Whenever he shouted the assemblage would utter a war-cry. When it was finished, a little of the medicine was drunk by all present, and the rest was mixed with gray clay and rubbed on arms, legs, heart, and back. Initiated members were permitted to apply some of the medicine to outsiders in order to make them healthy and brave.[19]

When this rite had been concluded, the members of both groups prepared to hold a "practice" dance outside their kiva. The Momtcit men wore conventional dance kilts and sashes, hanks of blue yarn fastened below the knees and across the body as bandoleers, fringed moccasins of red buckskin, and plume clusters (*hurunkwa*) containing four-inch reeds with eagle breath feathers affixed, which were tied to the hair. The body was daubed with yellow, in the manner of the Wuwutcim men at some of their public appearances; and the face was painted with two short parallel marks called Pukongkuku (Elder War Twin's footsteps), which are warrior symbols. They were drawn vertically on each cheek, first with red ochre (*suta*) and then overlaid with specular iron (*yalaha*).[20] Fox pelts tucked into the sashes at the small of the back completed the costume. No masks or leg rattles were worn.

The Nakyawimkyam were similarly dressed, except that their bodies were painted more in the manner of the Powamu Katcinas in the Bean dance. One leg was smeared with yellow and the other with red; one arm was yellow and the other blue; a red line was run down the middle of the chest; and a curved yellow line was run around one nipple and a similar blue line around the other. A soft eagle feather was fastened to the hair in such fashion that it hung down over the forehead, and warrior markings were made on the cheeks.

When all was in readiness, the Momtcit men would emerge first, singing in a low tone as they came out and chanting louder as they formed a half circle at the west side of their kiva. They joined hands with the fingers imbricated, and at some stages they rocked forward and back, rest-

[16] This appears to be an example of initiation for trespass. See p. 104 and footnote 15.

[17] These animals and their directional order were invariably listed in the same sequence by my informant and seem to have been rigidly fixed in the ritual. The directions are mentioned in the same order in all Hopi ceremonies. Compare Fewkes, 1902b, p. 484. These beasts are also shown in the diagram of a warrior room at Walpi, in Fewkes, 1924, p. 387, fig. 2.

[18] There is a very close similarity between the patron deities of the War societies on First and Third Mesas, except that Big Whirlwind, Halakvu, is not found at Oraibi. Consult Parsons, 1936b, p. 91.

[19] This rite sets the pattern for the medicine-making that occurs at Soyal (p. 143). Compare Dorsey and Voth, 1901, pp. 24, 25; and Fewkes, 1894b, p. 60.

[20] This substance plays an important part in the Soyal at Oraibi as described by Dorsey and Voth, 1901, p. 23.

ing on one foot at a time somewhat as do the Antelope members during the Snake dance; and at other times they moved sideways in a sinistral circuit. Soon there would come from the kiva a Nakyawimkya, carrying in his right hand a cedar stick which he had prepared that morning,[21] and accompanied by the Pukonghöya actor who carried a vessel of recently prepared medicine water. Before stepping down from the kiva hatch both men sprinkled meal to the sun;[22] then the Pukonghöya led the way within the arc formed by the Momtcit group, the Nakya performer dancing after him with a high-stepping, prancing motion. Together they moved in a counter-clockwise circle within the larger Momtcit ring; then they reversed their direction. As soon as their manœuvres had brought them into a position facing north, the Nakya man moistened his stick either with saliva or medicine and "swallowed" it, his companion asperging him until the stick was removed. Again the couple danced as before, and as they faced west, south, and east, successively, the Nakyawimkya "swallowed" his stick repeatedly. Throughout the proceedings the Momtcit society men continued to dance and sing. When the exhibition was over the swallower waved his stick in a discharming motion in all directions, to prevent spectators from being stricken with sore throats. He and Pukonghöya would then return to the kiva, and soon after their departure the Momtcit circle would begin to unwind, one man entering the kiva at a time while the rest continued to sing until their turns came. The order of entry was so arranged that the latest initiates were the last to reach the hatchway. Thus ended the public spectacle, for the rest of the first day's ritual was esoteric.

On his return to the kiva the Nakya soloist put his stick down north of the fireplace, and without removing his paint or costume, smoked a pipe of native tobacco over it. Then he made a *nakwa- wosi* and a *paho*, and deposited these with his stic at the Buffalo shrine. When he had returned ar undressed, the Momtcit men likewise washed t and changed to everyday clothes.

That night the members of both groups r mained awake, the Nakyawimkyam occupyir the main floor and the Momtcit using the raise level. They smoked, checked their paraphernali sang songs,[23] and practiced their performanc independently until the Pleiades were overhea At this time the two units combined for a repet tion of the altar ritual and the manufacture another supply of war medicine. Long befor dawn the two divisions began to paint and dre in order to be ready to start at sunrise, and th time the entire Nakya membership prepared take part. They decorated themselves in the san manner as yesterday's solitary performer, exce that the parallel cheek marks and the obliqu lines which meet on the bridge of the nose we smeared on with a white wash.

The second day's performance was conducte along virtually identical lines with those of th preceding day, except that the stick to be swa lowed was a lightning stick (fig. 6a), and the m succeeded each other in the swallowing exhibitio until all the Nakyawimkyam had performed.[24] a sequel to the first round of performances th stick-swallowers would appear in public for second time, using an implement known as eagle stick (fig. 6b). Prior to their second a pearance they daubed specular iron over th white warrior markings which they had wo before. Again all the society members performe succeeding one another at fixed intervals; but f a grand finale the entire membership appeared a body, each man carrying a lightning stick in o hand and an eagle rod in the other.[25] These th "swallowed" in unison, using first one stick a

---

[21] On the morning of the practice dance, one Nakya member was chosen for the first afternoon's performance. He would go out secretly to cut a cedar twig about an inch in diameter and nearly two feet long. In order to make it easier to "swallow" he would peel off the bark, but one end was purposely left rough to provide a better grip for removing the stick without mishap.

[22] Elsewhere my informant said that the Momtcit never used cornmeal at all.

[23] The Momtcit men were supposed to compose and learn new songs for each of their performances, but sometimes the older men suggested songs which had been used before but which sounded new to the younger members. This was called "shaking the moss" from the old songs.

The Momtcit had certain standardized songs for use war. These included, in addition to the ones mentioned the Kokop myth on p. 155, songs to be used for maki the enemy sleepy and for making them lose their sense direction.

[24] From my informant's account I was unable to termine whether the Nakya performers came out sing accompanied by Pukonghöya or whether they danc in pairs. In either case, they succeeded each other throug out the day. There was a respite at noon during which t Momtcit members had lunch, but the Nakyawimky fasted all day.

[25] On one occasion my informant said that at t final appearance of the stick-swallowers each man carri

then the other as they faced the four cardinal directions in the customary rotation. After this display the Nakya society men returned to the kiva, to be followed in a few moments by the

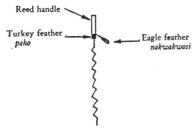

6a. Lightning-stick, one foot in length. When "swallowed" the upper *paho* remained dangling between the lips.

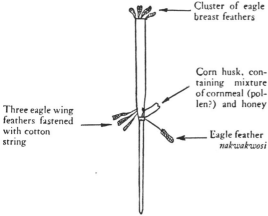

6b. Eagle-stick, about two inches round and a foot long. The lower half is made of hard wood, such as is used for battening rods. When "swallowed" the upper part protruded from the performer's mouth.

Fig. 6. Sticks "Swallowed" During the Momtcit Performance.

Momtcit. During the night, all the sticks that had been used in the ceremony were deposited secretly at the Spider Woman's shrine.

as many of each kind of stick as he chose; and that although they appeared in a body at the end, they "swallowed" in rotation rather than in unison.

Once, and once only, a Nakyawimkya "swallowed" a long, lance-like stick instead of the customary types.

[26] This narrative was obtained from the same elderly informant who supplied the details of the Momtcit observances. Because of the difficulty of getting material on Hopi war practices, the old man's story is given in full and almost in the exact form in which it was gathered regardless of a number of repetitions.

THE INITIATION OF A *REAL* WARRIOR[26]

Although membership in the Momtcit, including the Nakyawimi, automatically conferred the status of an ordinary warrior on a man, the distinction of becoming a *real* warrior (*bas kaletaka*) was reserved for those who had avowedly slain and scalped an enemy. Whether or not the *real* warriors were ever organized into a formal society with a basic fetish (*tiponi*) and an altar (*pongya*), it is impossible to say in the present state of our knowledge;[27] but there were specified rites through which all candidates had to pass before they could call themselves *real* warriors. Although it was impossible to secure a full account of the ritual the following narrative was said to contain all the important details of the procedure.

One afternoon many years ago, while the Soyal ceremony was being celebrated, a Hopi named Sikyajro happened to kill a Navaho near Yellow Rock (Sikyaowa) at the present site of New Oraibi. One of the men who was present, Tcockwatiwa of the Reed clan, had long wanted to become a *real* warrior; and there is a Hopi rule that the body of an enemy can be claimed by anyone who shouts, "I killed him!" even if he is not the actual slayer.[28] Accordingly, although there was no war going on, Tcockwatiwa cried out, "I'm the one that killed him!" Even though he later tried to back out by naming Sikyajro as the murderer, it was too late. His boast had been overheard and he had to join the *real* warriors.

A messenger was dispatched to Oraibi to fetch a drum so that the proper songs could be sung, and the men rendered the appropriate scalping chant while Tcockwatiwa performed the operation.[29] Several other songs were also sung, and it was after sundown before the men started in procession for the village, with Tcockwatiwa carrying the scalp on a pole as if it were a standard. On top of the mesa they made a complete circuit of

[27] Fewkes, 1900c, pp. 608, 609, refers to a First Mesa man named Pautiwa who is apparently the head of the Walpi Momtcit and who "is also chief of a warrior society called Kaletaka. . . ." It is hard to tell from this sort of reference whether we are dealing with two distinct societies or with one society under two names. See p. 156, footnote 13.

[28] "Actually," explained the narrator, "Kwatoko did the killing. His spirit is prayed to like Masau'u's, for power in war." Compare p. 77.

[29] A description of Hopi scalping practice is given on p. 161.

the pueblo before they entered and proceeded to Hawiovi kiva, the "home" of the *real kaletakam*.[30] The alleged slayer entered the kiva where he was to remain for four days and nights, fasting the greater part of the time, and sitting without a back rest, with his knees drawn up to the chin.[31] A circle of cornmeal—his house—was drawn around him, and it is here that the advantage of previous membership in the Momtcit becomes apparent, for the line is drawn close to toes and buttocks for those who do not belong to Momtcit, but for those who do, a little room is left for extending and flexing the legs.[32]

These events transpired on the fourth day after the Soyal.[33] The men had feasted on rabbit stew and were eager to sleep with their wives again, and most of them had already taken their bedding home from the kivas. Now they had to return once more and remain celibate for four more days on account of the *kaletaka* rites. For the first three nights the kiva groups intervisited until midnight, singing war songs that "sounded like the Coyote Dance."[34] On the third night the rites lasted until daybreak, and that morning the initiate dined on stew and *pikami* mush, whereas up to this time he had had to eat "gravy" made without meat or salt.

Towards noon, a Kokop man came to dress the *kaletaka* and to lead him from Hawiovi kiva to a shrine in the northeast. From this point the neophyte looks back and "if he is not lucky he will see his 'son'[35] (victim) coming after him as a real Masau'u." That is why it is considered dangerous to be a *real* warrior. If the slayer is lucky, however, no Masau'u will follow. In the course of a circuit of the village, the candidate must look back at four specific places, and if all goes well he is then led back to Hawiovi. Here a Spider clanswoman waits with a bowl of medicine and a clay spoon. The novice takes some of the liquid, drinks a little, rubs some over his body, and dis-

tributes the rest to the spectators. When the medicine is used up the Kokop leader (possibly the entire clan) sings "magic" songs in a low voice. Then he leads the warrior through the village streets to a special *kaletaka* stone—now missing—which used to be perched on a sort of platform of "hard, white rock." Whichever men care to do so may follow the pair to this shrine, each man carrying ashes with which to discharm himself when the spot is reached. The spectators then withdraw and the Kokop man leads the *kaletaka* to the shrine of Talautumsi (goddess of childbirth) where they bury offerings and special medicine in a secret ritual. If all is properly done, the newly-made *real* warrior is now free to go home in peace; if not, his "son," in the guise of Masau'u, is "sure to get him."

MISCELLANEOUS WAR PRACTICES

Throughout the *real* warrior initiation rites several connections with the Momtcit are apparent, but at present it is impossible to determine their exact relationship. In other war customs too the Momtcit society and its owners, the Kokop and Spider clans, play important parts, but again our data are too meager to afford a complete picture.

The Hopi claim never to have been the first to declare war and insist that they fought only in self-defence or to avenge a previous attack. Their main enemies were Apaches, Utes, and Chimwava, who were supposedly related to the Paiutes and who lived near a Mormon settlement in the north, towards Utah. The Navaho were considered negligible as enemies, and their scalps were worthless.[36]

When preparing to fight warriors wore their ordinary clothes with the addition of caps made from mountain lion or wildcat skins to which eagle feathers were attached. The chief weapons were the bow (*aouta*) and arrow (*hohu*), stone

---

[30] Note that Hawiovi is not the same kiva in which the Momtcit is held. Nevertheless, the Kokop and Spider clans play leading parts in both sets of rites.

[31] This posture is the same as that taken by novices in the Wuwutcim, and it is highly probable that the latter ceremony imitates parts of the ancient war ritual.

A series of war practices somewhat similar to those here described may be found in Voth, 1905b, p. 57.

[32] Tcockwatiwa was entitled to the easier position because he was already a member of the stick-swallowers division of the Momtcit.

[33] Perhaps there is some confusion here with the date of the Momtcit ceremony which my informant placed in

the early fall, but which Stephen records as occurring four days after the Soyal. Parsons, 1936b, p. 83.

[34] Anyone killing a coyote in January may call for a dance with his favorite aunt as partner. The words of the song narrate how the deed was done. This is an imitation of the war dance in which slayers were mentioned by name, a war whoop being issued after each deed was described. See p. 162.

[35] A scalp taker calls his trophy his "son." According to Nequatewa, 1936, p. 108, note 33, a wounded man becomes the "son" of his rescuer.

[36] On First Mesa too Navaho scalps were "worthless." Compare Parsons, 1936b, p. 98.

lub or tomahawk (*pikya-inga*), throwing-stick (*putckoho*), and spear (*lansa*).[37] Prior to their departure the fighters would make *nakwakwosi* and would pray to ancient, deceased warriors and to Masau'u, who was asked to move in spirit among the enemy and to touch them with his club so that they might be easy victims for the Hopi.[38] The men also rehearsed all songs connected with death-dealing (*ninantawi*) before making an attack. They sang "to make themselves brave," and practiced special "sleeping songs" to keep the enemy asleep while the Hopi forces approached, and "direction songs" so that the warriors would not become confused during the fighting.[39]

The Village War chief, the man who held the office of ceremonial *kaletaka* in the Soyal ceremony, generally led the men into battle. He was supposed to be dressed in the the character of Pukonghöya, and it is said that he carried no arms except a tomahawk. In all probability he was followed by the *real* warriors, after whom came the rank and file. When an enemy was felled, his assailant would begin to sing the scalping song as soon as he set to work to secure his trophy. A cut was made entirely around the head above the eyes and ears, then the hair was grasped, and as it was pulled the whole scalp peeled off.[40] A killer had to work fast as the scalping song was short and he was supposed to complete the operation before the song closed on the last word, *nina* (slayer). A piece of buckskin was also cut from the dead man's apparel, and this was later affixed to the reed which was worn in the plume cluster (*hurunkwa*) that warriors tied on their heads.[41] As a war party returned to the pueblo, the recently taken scalps were carried on poles and later brought to their homes by the owners. They were washed in yucca root (*movi*) suds, kept clean, and

"fed" from time to time. A scalp was considered to be the "son" of its taker, was kept in his house, had *paho* made for it at Soyal as if it were "a living thing," and was buried with its owner when he died.[42]

During a battle the people at home would anxiously await the returning warriors. If the fighters had taken some sheep or other loot they would generally divide it up among themselves, and on entering the village they would throw it with a discharming motion to the bystanders.[43] Returning warriors were not allowed to say that they had killed anyone, but were expected to attribute all slayings to Kwatoko or to their *wuyam*, but the *real kaletakam* did not hestitate to count their victims and often scored their tallies on the ground.[44]

On one occasion a party of fighters was returning to Oraibi from the vicinity of Bakavi when they happened to capture a Navaho boy. As they drew near the village, a messenger came running with the news that the Navaho had killed a woman that morning and had thrown her body into a wash. Because the victim, Köyangösi of the Sand clan, was a Soyal maiden, the Hopi felt that one of their "mothers" had been killed and were eager for revenge. Lomanaksa, brother of the slain woman, was ready to kill the Navaho boy on the spot, but the others asked the messenger to hurry back to the pueblo and to find out whether or not any of the other warriors had succeeded in taking any scalps that day. When the report came that no scalps had been taken, the men decided to kill the young Navaho, especially as they could then slaughter his horse and meat was very scarce at the time. Lomanaksa cried out, "Give me room!" and fired an arrow, but missed the lad's heart and wounded him slightly in the

[37] The throwing-stick was more generally used for hunting than war. The Hopi are said to have learned its use from Kisa, a god of hunting.

[38] According to Voth, 1905b, p. 59, Sotukinangwu'u was also an important war deity. On this point see Parsons, 1936b, p. 84 and footnote 4.

[39] Oraibi informants did not recall that warriors had ever prayed to the beetle (*hohoyau*) to obscure their tracks. This custom is mentioned by Stephen for First Mesa. Parsons, 1936b, p. 96.

[40] On First Mesa, only a piece the size of a man's palm was generally peeled from an enemy's skull. Parsons, 1936b, p. 98.

[41] According to Stephen, Parsons, 1936b, p. 98, buckskin taken from an enemy was used in the manufacture of bandoleers. These were purposely worn loosely so that

they came away when seized by an enemy.

[42] Several old men at Oraibi agreed that scalps were buried with their takers. I could find no knowledge of a custom of depositing scalps in a rock crevice called a scalp house, such as is mentioned by Stephen in Parsons, 1936b, p. 99.

[43] See Voth, 1905b, p. 60.

The rite described in Parsons, 1936b, p. 97, in which female relatives of warriors threw scalps onto cloud symbols, just as "ducks" are thrown in the Flute procession (p. 148), could not be established for Oraibi.

[44] Compare p. 155; and also Parsons, 1936b, p. 99, and p. 132, fig. 84.

Oraibi informants were unaware of the twenty-five day purification ceremony reported for First Mesa by Stephen. Parsons, 1936b, p. 99.

forearm. Thereupon the entire party fired a volley and the boy fell dead. At this, an old warrior called on all the younger men who had never before participated in a killing to "wipe off their *kele* markings," i.e., to remove the badges of novitiate, and all those present, regardless of age, took arrows and pretended to wipe the novice symbols from their faces.

THE HOWINA'AIYA DANCE

While all available evidence points to the conclusion that the Hopi had a horror of wanton killing,[45] and that they were rarely the aggressors in warfare, nevertheless, it seems to have been the custom for them to go regularly on the war-path each fall after the harvest was gathered. The warriors would celebrate their return by dancing with the scalps they had taken, and even in later times, when open wars were no longer fought, the custom of dancing in the fall was still retained.[46] This dance was called the Kaleti (Warrior dance) or the Market dance, Howina'aiya.

Although the Spider and Kokop clans were said to own the dance, it could be sponsored by any clansman. The proposer would choose two young men of quiet disposition to serve as *manamongwi* (girls' chiefs). While rehearsals were in progress in the kivas, the maidens would sit on the raised section and from time to time they would gather up the courage to tell the "chiefs" which men they wanted for partners. Usually, the choice fell on a paternal nephew (*imuyi*), and those who were chosen gave gifts to their aunts (*ikya'a*) on the night before the public exhibition.[47]

In former times the male performers were all *real* warriors, and all Momtcit men who were not selected for dancing were expected to serve as singers. The dance was held in the regular plaza, to the accompaniment of a drum and singing.

Several songs were rendered at intervals durin the course of the day, and two couples woul dance at a time, as in the Buffalo dance. Th boys were dressed as *kaletakam*, in kilt and sash anklets, and red moccasins. A fox pelt dangled a the loins, and a cluster of feathers was tied in th hair. Stripes of white clay were smeared acros the elbows while held at crook, across the ben knees, on the chest, back, and hair, and on th right side of the head. Mid-facial warrior marks and pairs of vertical Pukong symbols on th cheeks were daubed on in white and overlai with specular iron. Strings of beads and turquois earrings completed the costume.

The girls wore outfits comparable to those c Buffalo dancers, consisting of white moccasin with wrapped leggings, *manta*, Katcina kilt drape across the shoulders and fastened in front, and headdress with a single horn protruding from th left side and an arc-shaped bird's tail on the right A fox pelt was worn attached to the left wrist in the fashion of the female *kaletaka* in the publi dance of the the Marau society, and this wa waved up and down as the dancer gesticulated i time to the song's rhythm.

In the days when *real* warriors performed, th men would carry bows in the left hand, and in th right they would hold poles to which were tie recently taken scalps. The girls carried arrows i each hand, and as the occasion demanded, the would give them to their partners to hold wit their bows. The men danced primarily with simple prancing motion up and down, but fror time to time, the girls would raise their hands an bring the clenched right hand down forcefully o the open palm of the left as if tomahawking a enemy. This gesture was performed when th words of the song were describing how the war rior had slain a Chimwava, Ute, or Apache.[48]

---

[45] The Hopi insist that they have always lived up to the literal meaning of their name, peaceful. Until recent times there have been very few instances of murder among the Hopi, although they do admit having killed enemies in war. Chief Tawaqwaptiwa evaded all questions regarding the punishment of murderers by murmuring, "Hopi no kill."

[46] Compare Parsons, 1936b, pp. 95, 96. Stephen in Parsons, 1936b, p. 95, notes that "warriors never dance in public" lest they "cause gales of cold wind and evil disturbances in the air." This idea did not prevail at Oraibi.

Fewkes interpreted the Howina'aiya dance as a sort of Thanksgiving celebration. He considered the Hopi form to be an abbreviation of a Zuñi war dance. Fewkes, 1897b, p. 305, footnote 1.

[47] Several features of the ancient Market dance are t be found in modern "pleasure dances" such as the Buffal and the Butterfly. Compare Parsons, 1939, pp. 77, 78, passim.

Material on the Buffalo dance is given in Parson 1936b, pp. 124–130; and its relation to war practices i discussed in Titiev, 1938b, p. 107.

Brief notices of the Butterfly dance occur in Fewke 1903, p. 58; and in Fewkes, 1910, pp. 588–589. For th connection with war, see the statement of a New Orail informant on p. 87.

[48] As in the case of scalp-taking, where trophies c Navahos were considered to be worthless, the slay ing of a Navaho was never celebrated during thes dances.

After finishing their turns the men, still in costume, would mount to a designated roof-top overlooking the plaza, where their relatives had brought copious supplies of provisions and other objects of value, which were now thrown to the crowd beneath. At the same time, the parents of the girls would distribute food from a roof across the way. Sometimes, as a special gesture, a dancer would drive a live sheep or goat into the plaza, and the spectators would be invited to carve steaks from the living beast.

It was from the custom of generous gift distribution that this performance derived its name of Market dance, the presents representing booty taken from the enemy, and the bestowal of gifts being regarded as a sort of purification rite.[49]

[49] Dr. Parsons, 1936b, p. 911, footnote 1, explains this kind of gift distribution as a type of exorcism. Formerly, when warriors . . . returned, they threw away to the people whatever they had taken from the dead, 'so the dead would not come to them'." Compare Voth, 1905b, p. 60.

Note too the distribution of gifts in the public exhibitions of the women's societies, pp. 167, 169, 170.

CHAPTER XIII

WOMEN'S CEREMONIES

INTRODUCTION

ALTHOUGH the conduct of the annual cycle of ceremonies is left primarily to men, the other sex is by no means debarred from some degree of participation. Girls, as well as boys, are initiated either into the Katcina cult or the Powamu society; maidens impersonate cultus heroines in the Soyal, Flute, and Snake-Antelope observances; and women take part in the non-esoteric features of the war rituals. In addition, there are three societies—Marau, Lakon, and Oaqöl—whose membership is feminine except for a few men, usually related to the female leaders, who serve as their assistants.

In one respect it is somewhat surprising to find women in charge of regularly scheduled rites, for celibacy is invariably imposed on male religious celebrants because the "smell" of women is said to be displeasing to various supernatural powers.[1] Still, the ceremonies performed by the three feminine societies are highly regarded, even if some of the participants happen to be menstruant.[2]

Insofar as external organization is concerned, the women's rituals follow the same pattern as those of the men. They are conducted by secret societies; they are built around central fetishes which are owned by particular clans; and they consist partly of secret, kiva rites,[3] such as medicine brewing and altar building, and partly of a public spectacle which occurs on the last day of the ceremony. All three of the feminine groups hold their major celebrations in the fall, and the Lakon and Marau societies also hold winter meetings in January. According to Voth, it was customary at Oraibi for the Oaqöl to be celebrated in odd years, and for the Marau and the Lakon to be given in the even years.[4] Initiation

into these societies followed the customary scheme, and women were allowed to join as man of the groups as they chose.

THE WINTER MARAU

Although the rites performed by the three women's groups show exceedingly close resemblances to each other, the Marau ceremony stands somewhat apart from the others by virtue of the fact that it meets in its own kiva, and because it conceptually closely linked with the men's Tribe Initiation ritual, particularly, on Third Mesa, with the Wuwutcim division. The relationship between these ceremonies is described in a myth which Fewkes has recorded.

"These societies claim to have descended from no less a mythological personage than *Taiowa*, sun deity who met a maid in the underworld and drew her to him by inhalation through a flute. He took her to *Tawaki* (Sun house), and she bore him many children. To one of his sons he gave the mysteries of the *Wüwütcimtû*, and to one of his daughters those of Mamzrautu. . . ."[5] On the basis of this legend the Wuwutcim men and the Marau women regard each other as ceremonial brothers and sisters, a relationship which is borne out by many similarities in their respective observances.

The winter celebration of the Marau occurs during the January moon (*Pa-muya*) and lasts for nine days.[6] The society's standard, consisting of clusters of small hawk feathers, is set up at the outset, and the participants tie hawk plumes in their hair. The ceremony begins with a preliminary smoke[7] during which the leaders fashion numerous prayer-sticks; and eight days later the

---

[1] Compare, Parsons, 1936b, p. 709.

[2] Contrary to the almost universal fear of menstruating women in primitive societies, the Hopi are indifferent to menstrual blood. See p. 22.

[3] Although women are ordinarily greatly restricted in their use of kivas, specified ceremonial chambers are thrown open to them for the performance of their secret rituals. In fact, the Marau society at Oraibi actually had its own kiva.

[4] Voth, 1903b, p. 6.

[5] Fewkes, 1895b, p. 447. According to one of Stephen informants, Parsons, 1936b, p. 929, Taiowa is anothe name for Wuwutcim. He is the brother of Marau, an Sun is their father.

[6] In 1894 the rites began February 3; in 1898 they began on January 20. The Oraibi Marau is owned by the Lizard clan.

[7] At Oraibi the women chiefs smoked rarely or neve In fact, informants were of the opinion that the mai duties of the masculine leaders were to smoke for th

ain ritual begins.[8] On the first day there are
:ought into the kiva a number of sacred objects
cluding corn and lightning emblems, figures of
iltus ancestors, netted gourds, and various bits
f paraphernalia that are used in arranging the
tar. Among the items set out at this time are a
imber of sticks, each of which "is supposed to
present one of the dead members of the order
is is also the case with similar sticks in other
:remonies), and it is believed that the striking
f the floor announces to the deceased mem-
:rs in the nether world that a ceremony is in
:ogress."[9]

The ritual of the second and third days is much
ie same as that of the first, but on the fourth day
l the members busy themselves "making many
ikwakwosis . . . for their departed parents,
iildren and other relatives. . . . These offerings
:e carried out later in the day, and the Hopi be-
eve that the dead tie them to a string around
ieir head so that they hang down before their
ices."[10] These objects are put in a tray with
ornmeal, and the women stand about it in a semi-
.rcular formation, singing in the manner of their
ublic performance on the concluding day of the
ll celebration. The offerings for the dead are
.ter distributed in all directions.

The fifth day's rites begin soon after midnight.
"he altar is dismantled and its segments are held
a the hands of celebrants as they sing and dance.
"hroughout the day there is a general washing of
:ads among the society members, and towards
indown the women dress in motley, many of
iem wearing parts of men's costumes, and appear
a public to taunt and "song-tie" men with bawdy
erses "of a phallic or even of an obscene na-
ire."[11] The men retaliate by dousing their

taunters with water or urine, and by smearing
them with every kind of filth.[12]

Similar activities occupy the greater part of the
sixth and seventh days, and at times the women
stage burlesque Katcina dances. On the eighth
day the Marau altar is reconstructed, and the observances closely parallel those of the opening
day. That evening it is customary for a round of
night Katcina dances to be held in all the kivas.[13]
On the next day Oraibi's winter Marau ceremony
is brought to a conclusion by an all-day Katcina
dance in which the society women play little or
no part. In 1897 the Anga Katcina was represented, but in the winter of 1901 there was a performance of Palhik Katcinas, a masculine impersonation based on the Palhik girls' dance,
which Voth believed had been introduced "in
Oraibi from Mishongnovi. . . ."[14]

It is highly probable that the Oraibi termination in Voth's day was somewhat aberrant, for
Fewkes reports that the winter celebration of the
Walpi Marau for 1900 culminated with a public
dance featuring "*Palahik-tiyo* and *Palahik-mana*—
cultus hero and heroine of the society."[15] These
characters performed to the accompaniment of a
drum and a singing chorus. The female parts were
taken by relays of Marau members, and the male
rôles were enacted by various Wuwutcim men.[16]
Such a dance seems to be a far more appropriate
ending for the winter performance of the Marau
society than the ordinary Katcina dances which
Voth witnessed at Oraibi.

THE FALL OBSERVANCES OF THE MARAU SOCIETY[17]

The greater part of the fall celebration of the
Marau group is essentially along the same lines

omen. On First Mesa Stephen noted that the feminine
iiefs did their own smoking, albeit with considerable
fficulty at times. Parsons 1936b, p. 873.
[8] A round of Katcina dances generally takes place in the
.vas on the night of the preliminary smoke.
[8] The winter ritual of the Marau society has been de-
:ribed in full detail only in Voth, 1912a, on which
.is summary is based. Fewkes, 1902b, p. 494 ff., reports a
ve-day ceremony that occurred in March at Walpi,
it he gives only an incomplete account of the proceedings.
[9] Voth, 1912a, p. 23.
[10] Voth, 1912a, p. 29.
[11] Voth, 1912a, p. 32.
[12] Compare the manner in which Wuwutcim and Tao
en tease and attack Marau women during the Tribal
iitiation, p. 132. The origin of this custom is said to go
ick to the legendary sister and brother to whom Taiowa
iught their respective rites. The youth who learned the
Vuwutcim teased his sister who received the Marau

cult, calling her a nasty maid. They began to quarrel in
mock anger and poured water on each other, thus setting
the fashion for later celebrants. See Fewkes, 1895b, p. 448.
[13] The night Katcina dances which are held in the kivas
at various stages of the winter Marau form part of the
Katcina cycle. Compare p. 112, footnote 19.
[14] Voth, 1912a, p. 36.
[15] Fewkes, 1902b, p. 495.
[16] Fewkes, 1902b, pp. 496–500, gives a description of
the dance.
[17] The digest given here is a composite based on Voth,
1912a, and notes obtained in interviews with Oraibi men
and women. The description of the public dance incorporates my own observations of several performances
at Second and Third Mesas. Comparative material was
obtained from Parsons, 1936b, pp. 864–937; Fewkes and
Stephen, 1892a; and Lowie, 1925. There is also a summary of the First Mesa proceedings in Parsons, 1939,
pp. 675–680.

as the winter ceremony except that the closing day's rites are more elaborate. The same kiva is used, the altars are virtually identical and the personnel is unchanged. As in the winter ritual there is a preliminary smoke, after which the main performance continues with three days devoted primarily to esoteric altar exercises. During the fourth day prayer-objects are manufactured and food is set out for the dead, on the supposition "that the spirits of the departed come and get the food and the prayer feathers, or rather the *hikvsi* (breath, essence, soul) of those objects."[18] In conjunction with this aspect of the Marau, one of the women members of the society is dispatched to a shrine at Aponivi, which is located a few miles west of Oraibi on the direct road supposedly taken by the spirits of the deceased on their way to the home of the dead (Maski). It is said that the messenger is expected to strip off her clothes and to utter a prayer at the shrine, inviting the souls of departed Marau women to come and join in the rites of the living.[19]

From this point on the fall rites run parallel to those of the winter until, on the eighth day, preparations are begun for the public performance to be held on the morrow. Early in the morning a quantity of green farm produce is brought into the kiva, some of which is tied into a bundle. A Bow clansman prepares two sets of four reed arrows each; a rain water shield (*pavaiyokyasi*) is made, similar to that worn in the Flute ceremony, with Muyingwa depicted on it;[20] and above all, the women busy themselves with the manufacture of Marau-vahos (Marau prayer-sticks) which they carry in their hands and wave in unison as they dance. These are wooden slabs with handles, having corn tassels affixed, and painted with a great variety of corn, germination, rain, and cloud symbols. In the evening the women go to the plaza and give one public performance in which they carry ears of corn instead of their prayer-sticks. Then they return to the kiva; and soon after midnight the altar is dismantled, and there is a general head-washing. Early the next morning the village youths bring in a load of corn stalks with young ears on them, and final arrangements are made for the public exhibit which consists of a series of dances given at intervals throughout the last day.

As they get ready to appear in public, the ordinary members dress in their kiva, putting on native gowns (*manta*) and striped, ceremonial blankets (*atu'u*). They go barefooted, their faces smeared with cornmeal, and carrying corn stalks bearing young ears, as they make their way to the plaza soon after sunrise.[21] Meantime, five women who are to impersonate male characters go to the Blue Flute kiva to get into costume. They dress in men's woolen shirts, Katcina kilts, and sashes to which fox pelt "tails" are attached at the back.[22] Two are archers and carry bows and arrows and a bundle of vegetation; two are lancers and carry netted wheels and lance-like poles;[23] and the fifth carries a wand decorated with horse hair and has a fox pelt attached to her left wrist. All five wear elaborate headdresses.

When all are ready, the head woman of the Marau society leads her fellow members to the plaza in single file, where they range themselves in a wide open-horseshoe formation. Almost at once they begin to sing in low voices, waving their corn stalks (later, their Marau-vahos) in rhythm, up and down and from side to side, as they move slowly sidewise in a sinistral circuit. A few moments later, the wand-bearer comes out and takes up a position beside the society leader, but at right angles to her, so that as the other moves sideways, she goes backward. This performer moves her hands up and down in time to the singing.[24] After the dance has been going on

---

[18] Voth, 1912a, p. 55.

[19] Voth, 1912a, p. 51, footnote 1, suggests that the messenger may actually have visited a shrine nearer home which represented the original one; and Voth makes no mention of the special nature of the visit. My informants showed me the actual shrine, spoke of its location on the route to Maski, and described both the manner of the courier's approach and her invitation to the spirits of the dead. Compare the episode at the graveyard during the Tribal Initiation, p. 131 and footnote 13.

[20] Voth, 1912a, p. 59, footnote 1, equates Muyingwa, the germination god, with Alosaka who appears in the Tribal Initiation ceremonies, and with Tcowilawu who is impersonated during the Powamu rites.

[21] In subsequent appearances they carry the prayer-sticks known as Marau-vaho.

[22] It is because the women who impersonate men appear in short kilts that the Marau ceremony is popularly called "The Knee-high Dance."

[23] The paired impersonations are frequently enacted by a ceremonial mother and daughter.

[24] This performer is sometimes called a warrior (*kaletaka*). On occasion, according to Voth, 1912a, p. 68, a character called the Rabbit Mother takes the place of the wand-bearer. The latter part is played by volunteers, and sometimes a good deal of coaxing is needed before a girl will agree to appear in the abbreviated costume which exposes her thighs and legs to the scrutiny of the men.

this manner for a little while, the two archers approach from the kiva. Throwing the bundle of produce a short distance before them, they shoot their arrows towards it,[25] then move forward to pick up the bundle, toss it on and repeat their performance until they come within the circle of lancers. A few moments later the two lancers make their appearance in similar fashion, rolling their wheels and throwing their lances after them; then picking up these objects and repeating the act until they too arrive within the circle. Thereupon the lancers fetch a dish of finely ground sweet cornmeal and a bowl of water, and both lancers and archers fashion balls of *qömi* which they throw from within the line of dancers to the spectators. When the *qömi* is exhausted the archers and lancers return to the kiva, followed soon after by the wandbearer. Within a short time the song comes to a close and the Marau chief leads her group back to the kiva in single file, the youngest members bringing up the rear. The corn stalks which the women carried in the opening performance are left lying on the ground where the male spectators scramble for them. When all the performers have returned to the kiva at the conclusion of their opening dance, they are discharmed with ashes and cedar smoke and dismissed for breakfast.

Throughout the remainder of the day the society appears at irregular intervals and repeats its exhibition to the accompaniment of a different song, and on each occasion a new group of women enacts the five special parts.[26] The afternoon performances tend to be less serious than the others, and the songs frequently contain obscene references to Wuwutcim men. However, the final dance of the day is solemnly performed, and additional acts of prayer are carried out by the society's leaders before the dancers are dismissed. From a number of sources which discuss the Marau ritual at various Hopi villages, it appears that the ceremony everywhere resembles the

Oraibi version. At Walpi, for example, the major differences are the absence of lancers or Rabbit Mothers in the concluding observances, and the performance of a sort of informal Howina'aiya dance by a number of young men on the night that the Marau ceremony ends.[27] Lowie's account of the final day's activities at Mishongnovi,[28] and my own observations of the last day's performance at Chimopovy,[29] reveal no outstanding differences in the Second Mesa procedure except that there are no lancers, and the wand-bearer carries a number of sacred objects including a netted gourd and a wooden crook. A Marau dance which was witnessed by the writer at Hotevilla proved to be very sketchy owing to the small number of participants and the total absence of archers or lancers.[30]

THE INTERPRETATION OF THE MARAU CEREMONY

"Like other Hopi ceremonies," writes Dr. Parsons, "the women's ceremony of the Mamzrau presents ritual for various objects, for reproduction or fertility, for favorable weather, for war, and for cure."[31]

The fertility feature is clearly brought out in the symbolism depicted on the Marau-vaho, on the altars,[32] in prayers to germination deities, and in the initiation proceedings. When novices are being inducted a circle of cornmeal is drawn on the kiva floor, and a large ring of tied yucca stems is placed upon it. Each candidate is instructed to jump into the center of the yucca ring from the raised platform of the kiva, whereupon it is lifted waist-high and lowered again four times while prayers for fecundity are recited.[33] The rest of the initiation follows the usual lines.

War elements are involved in the impersonation of the wand-bearer, who is known as a *kaletaka*, in the enactment of lancers and archers, and in the smearing of warrior symbols on the cheeks

---

who are sure to remember any defects or eccentricities of her person when the next set of Wuwutcim songs is being composed. The fear of being taunted helps to explain the excessive bashfulness which was noted both by Stephen and Voth.

The act of shooting arrows at a bundle of farm produce is supposed to symbolize lightning striking a field.

Informants at Oraibi maintained that in ancient times the archers appeared only in the initial exhibition, and that only the lancers and the wand-bearer came out in later performances. The arrows used in the ceremony were

deposited at the shrine of the Little War Twins.

[27] Parsons, 1936b, pp. 910, 911, 928.

[28] Lowie, 1925.

[29] The dance was given on September 23, 1933.

[30] Given September 26, 1933. The Marau ceremony on Third Mesa began to shrink in importance soon after the conversion of its principal male leader to Christianity. Compare the situation at Walpi, where the woman chief turned Christian about 1907. Parsons, 1936b, p. 865.

[31] Parsons, 1936b, p. 864.

[32] See Fewkes, 1924, pp. 388, 389, figs. 3–5.

[33] Voth, 1912a, p. 52; Parsons, 1936b, p. 870.

of novices.[34] Curative aspects are stressed throughout the rites, particularly in the Walpi ceremony, for the Marau society has charge of "twisting sickness" and venereal diseases. Nevertheless, it is a little difficult to understand why Dr. Parsons "gets the impression that its curing function is the most important character of Mamzrau,"[35] for each of the Hopi rituals is credited with being able to cure a particular ailment, and the Marau exercises emphasize fertility far more than they do curing.

Perhaps the most outstanding characteristics of the Marau are its conformity to the pattern of the men's ceremonies in general, and its relationship to the Wuwutcim in particular. Some of the specific links with the latter include: the myth in which they are described as having been originated by a brother and sister; the use of chicken hawk feathers on their standards and for their novices; their exchange of bawdy songs about each other; their co-operation in the Palhik dance; their veneration of a spirit known as Twister Man;[36] and their joint control of "twisting sickness."[37] There is a slight possibility that the Marau may once have been a tribal initiation for adolescent females, comparable to the Wuwutcim for men. On the whole, the Marau is probably the most highly developed of the women's observances and sets the fashion for the Lakon and the Oaqöl.

THE LAKON RITUAL[38]

As in the case of the Marau, the greater part of the Lakon society's membership is made up of women, but the feminine leaders are generally aided by male relatives; and men seeking cures for running sores[39] may join for varying periods of time. The major emphasis of the Lakon is probably on germination, for worship of Muyingwa plays a prominent part in the rites, but other elements such as war may be found.[40]

The esoteric practices of the Lakon cult at Oraibi are held in the Hawiovi kiva, and r● closely parallel to those of the Marau for the fir● seven days. On the evening of the eighth day t● group visits one of the village springs for a bri● exercise, after which they proceed to a shrine fro● which the women members race back to t● pueblo. One runner starts out ahead with t● society's standard, which she is required to pa● on to whomever overtakes her. Very early the ne● morning the winner of the race is dressed as ● impersonation of the Lakon Maiden, the cul● heroine, who is reported to be "a facsimile of t● maid in the Snake-Antelope and Flute cer● monies."[41] Clad in full costume, and accompani● by the masculine Lakon chief, she proceeds to ● point at some distance from the town, where ● group of young men have gathered for a race. T● Lakon Maiden carries a tray as she starts to ru● and a few moments later the men set out after h● She hands the tray to the first runner that catch● up with her, and he in turn gives it to anyone w● overtakes him.

In the meantime, just as the race is about to g● under way, the Lakon group, headed by th● feminine chief, file from their kiva to the plaz● each member carrying an empty woven tra● Their costumes are like those of the Mar● women, and they assume an open-horseshoe f● mation like the latter, but they wave plaques ● rhythm in place of Marau-vaho or corn stal● and they dance in a fixed position instead ● making a sinistral circuit. No special performe● appear at the opening exhibition, and the socie● is in the midst of its performance when the winn● of the men's race arrives and deliberately forc● his way through the line as he hurries on to t● Hawiovi kiva. As soon as the women ha● finished their song, they too make their way ● the kiva for breakfast and a rest.

During the course of the day they revisit t● plaza from time to time, and on each of the● occasions they have scarcely assumed th● formation and begun to sing when two Lak●

---

[34] Parsons, 1936b, p. 873.

[35] Parsons, 1936b, p. 864.

[36] Parsons, 1936b, p. 864. "Twister Man is undoubtedly the same spirit the Wöwöchïm society deals with. . . ." It is pictured in Fewkes, 1924, plate 3, no. 1.

[37] Voth ascribes the Oraibi cure of "twisting and twitching of the face and neck," to the Horn society. Voth, 1901, p. 109, footnote †.

[38] Inasmuch as there is no published account of the Lakon on Third Mesa, this abstract is based on First Mesa procedure as described in Parsons, 1936b, pp. 830–

856; and Fewkes and Owens, 1892, pp. 105–129. Fewk● 1899b, contains additional material on the Lakon p● formances at First and Second Mesas.

The Parrot clan owns the Lakon at Oraibi.

[39] Parsons, 1936b, p. 830, suggests that the Lak● may have cured for venereal disease. Also, see Parso● 1939, p. 117, footnote *.

[40] Fewkes and Owens, 1892, p. 116, refer to a sa● painting which figures a supposed germination power w● closely resembles the Elder War Twin.

[41] Parsons, 1936b, p. 852.

Maidens come towards them. The girls are dressed to represent the heroine of their order, and each carries a large bundle of gifts on her back and holds in her hands two vari-colored corn ears with feathers attached. A male officer precedes them, carrying a little basket full of cornmeal or pollen with which he draws cloud symbols on the ground. In ritual order the girls try to throw the four ears of corn into the cloud design; first the yellow for north, then the blue for west, red for south, and white for east.[42] In this fashion, stage by stage, the Maidens approach their fellow members and ultimately move within the open circle. Thereupon the male chief returns to the kiva, and while the line of women continues to sing and dance, the Lakon girls face each other and bow, once in each of the cardinal directions.

At this point in the performance the male spectators crowd excitedly towards the dancers, shouting and clucking loudly in anticipation of the next act. Within a short time the Lakon impersonators bend over their packs, remove some of the contents, and whirling suddenly begin to scatter them far and wide in all directions. A wild struggle follows as the men scramble to retrieve the gifts, and not infrequently there is a prolonged wrangle as several spectators get partial holds on the same object and tug and sway for long periods of time until one of them gains undisputed possession. Ordinarily, the atmosphere is good-natured during these contests, and no tempers are lost even though contestants are often severely jostled and many have their clothing torn to shreds.[43]

When the Lakon Girls have flung away everything they had in their packs, they leave the plaza and return to the kiva. Then, as soon as the dancers have finished their song, they too withdraw to the kiva. The entire performance is repeated occasionally until late afternoon, different pairs of girls impersonating the Lakon Maidens at each public appearance. When the society is ready for its closing dance, a masculine chief

comes out to sprinkle the dancers and to deposit prayer-feathers and meal in the plaza shrine. When he has finished he throws the plaque in which the offerings had been kept far out over the housetops and starts back towards the kiva as the men begin to wrangle for the prize.[44] Soon after the women end their song, and the public exhibition comes to a close.

Just as the esoteric parts of the Lakon resemble those of the Marau, so too are their plaza performances alike in broad outline. In each case the society members are similarly dressed and take up similar positions as they begin their dance. Both groups sway and bob up and down as they wave various objects in unison. After the main body of performers is in action, there then arrive in each instance special actresses who represent the patronesses of their orders. These advance towards their fellow members by various stages, tossing representations of crops before them as they go. Once inside the ring of dancers they throw gifts to the crowd, then they lead the way back to the kiva. Anyone who has seen both performances would not hesitate to accept the verdict that "there is a strict parallelism in the Lalakonta and Mamzrau which is marked even in details."[45]

THE OAQÖL SOCIETY

The Hopi regard the Oaqöl in a somewhat different light from the other women's ceremonies, in that they look upon it as a recent addition to the ceremonial cycles of Walpi and Oraibi. On First Mesa it is said to have been introduced "late," and Third Mesa informants said it was brought there after the destruction of Awatovi early in the eighteenth century.[46] Voth reported that a Sand clanswoman named Kelwuhti had learned about the Oaqöl rites from an Oraibi relative who had belonged to that order during a temporary residence at Mishongnovi on Second Mesa; and that together they had made the requisite paraphernalia and had started the cult at Oraibi.[47]

[42] The colors and the directions for which they stand are always mentioned in the same order in all Hopi rites. Note the close parallel between the procession of the Lakon Maids and that of the Flute performers, p. 148.
[43] In former days, informants at Oraibi said, only baskets and trays were distributed in this fashion, but in recent years it has been the custom to throw all manner of things to the crowd. At a performance which I observed at Chimopovy in October, 1933, the gifts included candy, cigarettes, matches, and "china" dishes. All were thrown recklessly and indiscriminately. For pictures of the struggle for gifts in the Oaqöl, which shares this feature with

the Lakon, see Voth, 1903b, plates XXVI–XXVIII.
[44] At the Chimopovy performance in 1933, the society women stood on their kiva hatch after the last exhibition and threw away the baskets which they had used in the dance. Sometimes a nephew was allowed to snatch his aunt's tray.
[45] Fewkes and Owens, 1892, p. 106, footnote *.
[46] Parsons, 1925, p. 110, footnote 170; and Voth, 1903b, p. 3.
[47] Voth, 1903b, p. 3. The brief digest in this section is drawn largely from the account just cited, supplemented by Fewkes, 1901b.

Chief Tawaqwaptiwa provided the writer with a somewhat embellished version of the same tradition. According to him Kelwuhti was a witch who had managed to elude the vigilance of watchers at esoteric performances, and to overhear parts of a number of ceremonies. These she had boldly incorporated into her rites, with the result that spectators frequently recognized in the chants of the Oaqöl women songs that had been "stolen" from their own secret societies.[48] Whether or not the details of Tawaqwaptiwa's story are literally true, the Oraibi natives unquestionably regard the Oaqöl as an innovation that shows many resemblances to long-established ceremonies.

Despite its taint of reputed witchcraft the Oaqöl has a large membership,[49] and the villagers are by no means averse to its performance on their behalf. Fewkes noted that the society held a winter meeting as well as a more elaborate celebration in the fall,[50] but the Oraibi group was said to have met only in the fall. As in the case of the Marau and the Lakon, the altar ritual is concerned chiefly with germination and fertility. Muyingwa is represented on the altar and is also impersonated by some of the male officers. The initiation of novices is comparable to the Marau, in that they jump into a ring of yucca stems which is then lifted about them four times.[51] In addition, Oaqöl tyros grind corn for their ceremonial mothers during the first four days of the observances, in exchange for which the ceremonial mothers present their daughters with basket trays for use in the public dance on the last day. Men, as well as women, may join the society under special condi-

tions, particularly if they seek a cure for eruptions on top of the head, a malady which the Oaqöl is said to cure.[52]

On the ninth day of the rites there is a footrace at dawn, following which the society makes its way to the plaza. The women dress in costumes identical with those of the Lakon group, they carry similar woven trays, and they assume the same kind of a formation. Soon after they have begun to sing and sway they are approached by two distinctively garbed Oaqöl Maidens who progress by rolling a netted wheel along the ground and trying to strike it with a feathered corncob dart. On arriving within the line of dancers they unpack a bundle of gifts which they throw to the crowd. Thereupon the Oaqöl Maidens return to the kiva, leaving the others to follow as soon as their song has ended.

CONCLUSION

A comparative study of the three women's societies among the Hopi leads to the conclusion that although they are controlled by different clans and led by different sets of officers, they are nevertheless only three manifestations of one ritualistic pattern. Furthermore, that pattern is itself a reflection of the men's performances. Of the three ceremonies only the Marau has its own kiva and a clear tie with the main body of Hopi rites. There is a strong likelihood, therefore, that the Marau is the basic women's observance, and that the Lakon and the Oaqöl are hardly more than imitations of it.

[48] On First Mesa it is said that the Oaqöl program is made up of "two songs from each of the other ceremonies. . . ." Parsons, 1925, p. 110, footnote 190.

[49] Voth, 1903b, p. 5, gives a list of members drawn from 14 clans. The Oraibi women of the Greasewood clan, however, never join Oaqöl. Informants could give

no reason for this custom.

[50] Fewkes, 1901b, p. 219.

[51] Voth, 1903b, p. 11.

[52] Voth, 1903b, p. 44. Oaqöl does not cure on First Mesa, according to Parsons, 1925, p. 110, footnote 170.

CHAPTER XIV

THE SCHEME OF HOPI CEREMONIALISM

INTRODUCTION

WHENEVER informants are questioned regarding the meanings of their rites, they generally reply with the stereotyped statement, "We pray for rain, crops, and health." At first an investigator is inclined to doubt the adequacy of a single formula to explain all Hopi rituals, but the more he examines the subject the more closely the ceremonies appear to resemble each other both in manner of performance and in ultimate objectives. Dr. Parsons, in a noteworthy comment on Pueblo religion, has directed attention to "that kaleidoscope of ritual functions or patterns which is Pueblo ceremonialism. . . . Ever the same rites or functions in ever different combination."[1] Such characterization applies very aptly to Pueblo religion in general and to Hopi ceremonies in particular, for a comparative study invariably reveals a large number of identical features which are repeated over and over again in differing combinations. Thus the Soyal incorporates many aspects of the Momtcit; the Repeat Series of Night dances duplicates several portions of the Powamu; the Snake-Antelope performances resemble those of the Flute societies in numerous respects; the Marau is closely linked with the Wuwutcim; and in general, the women's ceremonies imitate each other and reflect the pattern of the men's rites. On the one hand, this state of affairs presents a bewildering intermingling of details, but on the other hand, it holds forth the hope that an insight into Hopi religion may be reached through the isolation and interpretation of those essential features which serve as common denominators throughout the rites.[2]

THE CULT OF THE DEAD

The most widely spread of the basic concepts of Hopi religion is a belief in the continuity of life after death, a notion which is "manifested again and again in the different ceremonies of the Hopi. . . ."[3] In keeping with this belief, "The modern Hopi recognize in man a double nature, corresponding to body and soul, and to the latter they . . . give the expressive name breath-body [hik'si]. . . . It is the breath-body or shade of man which passes at death through the sipapuh, or gateway, to the underworld. . . ."[4]

So strongly rooted is the Hopi faith in an afterlife that they do not consider the death of an individual to be a loss to their society. Instead, they regard a dead person as one who is merely undergoing an important change of status. It is as though the deceased were about to be re-born in the Afterworld, or as if he were to be initiated into a new order. Thus Parsons reports that the face of a corpse is "washed and covered with corn meal, as is a baby's. . . . The dead is washed like a baby . . . by his aunt and also given a new name by her, to use in the other world where he becomes like a baby. . . ."[5] Similarly, in an autobiographical account of a temporary visit to the home of the dead, the narrator describes how his head had been washed by a Kwan man soon after his arrival,[6] for headwashing is a part of the initiation proceedings in all Hopi societies.

Once they are admitted to the realm of the dead, the spirits engage on the whole "in the same pursuits they followed on earth . . . [but] it is believed that the breath-body, freed from its material double by death, has a supernatural influence. . . ."[7] It is the acquisition of supernatural power that provides the basis for the equation of the spirits of the dead with Katcinas or Clouds,[8] and since the latter bring rain, it follows that the deceased Hopi are likewise regarded as rain bringers. Hence, "the import of one of their mortuary prayers is, 'You have become a Rain god; grant us our wishes,'—that is, send us the desired rains."[9]

In all the rites, therefore, the cult of the dead plays an important part; and each ceremony employs some device for making the wants of its

[1] Parsons, 1933, p. 6.
[2] Compare Parsons, 1921b, p. 209.
[3] Voth, 1912b, p. 99. Compare p. 107.
[4] Fewkes, 1896b, pp. 161, 162.
[5] Parsons, 1925, pp. 75, 76, footnote 121. Compare Parsons, 1936b, p. 827.
[6] Titiev, 1941, p. 499.
[7] Fewkes, 1896b, p. 162.
[8] See pp. 107, 108.
[9] Fewkes, 1896b, p. 162. Compare pp. 107, 108.

celebrants known to the spirits in the other world.[10] In the Katcina performances the masked figures actually impersonate the spirits of departed tribesmen; in the Snake-Antelope and other observances sticks representing former members are set on the altars of the societies; in the Marau a messenger is dispatched to invite the dead to visit the pueblo; during the Soyal a vast number of prayer-sticks are made for the benefit of deceased relatives and friends; in the course of the Tribal Initiation a path towards the house of the dead (Maski) is made for the use of spirits returning to the village; in the Flute ceremonies women dressed like corpses pay their respects to the dead; and during the kiva rites in virtually every ceremony, communication with the other world is carried on by means of the *sipapu*.

Of all the methods of establishing contact with the dead, the preparation of prayer-offerings is by far the most common. "The prayer-feather carries the maker's desire . . . the prayer-stick calls the attention of the deity. When Cloud or Sun or other deity sees the prayer-stick, he looks for the prayer-feather and there he reads . . . what is in the Hopi maker's heart."[11] Each day the spirits are said to rise from the original *sipapu*, which is the entrance to the realm of the dead, and to look east towards the Hopi mesas. They select the best ones who are summoning them and go to visit them. Similarly, when celebrants smoke during the performance of a ceremony, the smoke goes to the San Francisco peaks where it reaches a kiva. Into this it drifts, carrying the smoker's message to the Cloud People. They recognize the supplicant, and if he is good they will send rain, but if he is evil or two-hearted (i.e., a witch) they will show their displeasure by sending a windstorm.[12]

The frequent repetition of prayers to the dead has led some students to regard this aspect of Hopi ceremonialism as a form of ancestor worship. For example, Fewkes has attempted to interpret the entire Katcina cult from such a viewpoint, but his conclusions betray a good deal of uncertainty. "In an ancestor worship of this kind," he has written, "no particular ancestral individual or named ancestor is represented; in fact, a Katcin is a generalized mythical conception which ca not be accurately identified, and is quite unlik the ancestor among the nations of the O. World. . . ."[13] As Fewkes implies, the Katcin are better described as generalized rather tha specific ancestors, i.e., as spirits of dead tribe people rather than as souls of particular ind viduals. Moreover, it can readily be demonstrate that among the Hopi the dead are venerated n because they are supposed to be capable of helpir only their living relatives,[14] but because they a supposed to control moisture and good vegetatic for all.

In this connection the Hopi believe that sin the dead can bring rain to stimulate growth, the Masau'u, the god of death, must be one of th principal "owners" of crops. This is a notion th finds expression each fall when Masau'u is in personated at harvest festivals,[15] and at the cer monial gathering of young plants during th Nevenwehe rites in the spring of years whe novices enter the Tribal Initiation societie Similarly, we find that Muyingwa, one of th most important of the vegetation deities, is pi tured as manufacturing all sorts of seeds in th lowest of the underworlds, so that the Ho evoke his help "by calling down the *sipapu* of th kiva."[16]

The Sun, also, as one of the main fertility god is closely associated with the spirits of the d ceased, for it is believed that "the dead follow th sun to the west"[17] and accompany him through opening into the Underworld. Like the spirits to the Sun rises daily and inspects the character of th prayers addressed to him. At the close of eac day the Sun brings with him the "prayer offerin that he had collected from the good people he passed over the earth in his left hand, tho gathered from the bad people in his right hand. . The good ones asked for old age, good crop rain, etc., the bad for opportunities to have inte course with women, etc."[18] The offerings of th righteous are placed on an altar, presumably receive favorable action, but those with evil i tent are thrown into the fire. The interrelationsh

---

[10] The Hopi word for prayer is *nawakina*, literally, desiring.

[11] Parsons, 1936b, p. 164.

[12] This concept was explained by different informants in two unrelated interviews. See Titiev 1943a, pp. 550, 551.

[13] Fewkes, 1923, p. 498.

[14] Exceptions are those Katcinas which serve as ancients

(*wuya*) of particular clans. These are regarded as ance tral deities by their descendants. Consult Parsons, 192 p. 77, footnote 125.

[15] See pages 185–187.

[16] Haeberlin, 1916, p. 22.

[17] Fewkes, 1923, p. 491.

[18] Voth, 1903a, p. 350.

of the dead and Katcinas, and their connection with the Sun are explained to Hopi children even prior to their Katcina initiations. According to Fewkes, youngsters are taught "to believe that from time to time family ancestors or spirits of the dead revisit the pueblos and receive prayers for the good of the tribe, after which they return to ghostly homes in the underworld, through the house of the Sun far to the west."[19]

The cult of the dead is undoubtedly one of the most essential elements in the religious mosaics of the Hopi, for it is fundamental to the structure of the Katcina cycle and plays significant parts in the Tribal Initiation and Solar ceremonies. Furthermore, in their capacity as Clouds or Katcinas the spirits of the dead are looked upon as rain bearers and are linked with the deities whose functions are to stimulate growing crops; for, as Haeberlin has pointed out, "Since the dead return to the underworld and the underworld is the place of germination, it is not surprising that . . . the deceased and especially the ancients should likewise have become associated with this idea."[20] Thus we may consider prayers to the dead as one of the common denominators in all the rituals which are concerned with rain, crops, and health.[21]

THE CONCEPT OF THE YEAR'S DUALITY

The second of the basic elements of Hopi religion is the concept of a dual division of time and space between the upper world of the living and the lower world of the dead. This is expressed in the description of the sun's journey on its daily rounds. The Hopi believe that the sun has two entrances, variously referred to as houses, homes or kivas, situated at each extremity of its course. In the morning the sun is supposed to emerge from its eastern house, and in the evening it is said to descend into its western home. During the night the sun must travel underground from west to east in order to be ready to arise at its accustomed place the next day.[22] Hence day and night are reversed in the upper and lower worlds, for while it is light above, it is dark below and vice versa.[22a] Such a situation may be diagrammed as shown in fig. 7.

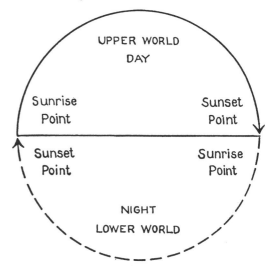

FIG. 7. THE SUN'S DAILY CYCLE.

The same principle that is used to account for the alternation of day and night is likewise employed to explain the annual shifts of winter and summer, for the Hopi believe that these too are caused by the sun's movements between the upper and the lower realms.[23] They count the seasons as extending approximately over the length of time that it takes the sun to travel from one solstice point on the horizon to the other.[24] Thus winter is regarded as beginning theoretically when the sun leaves its summer "home" (about June 21),

[19] Fewkes, 1917a, p. 226. In the same connection Fewkes, 1920, has written, "As it is supposed that human beings that have died . . . have greater powers to aid the living, . . . they are conjured from time to time to return to the village and aid their descendants or living survivors." Although Fewkes is referring particularly to the Katcina cult, identical notions find expression in many rites, especially in the Tribal Initiation and the Soyal.

[20] Haeberlin, 1916, p. 28.

[21] Compare Kennard, 1937, p. 491. "In every ceremony, the spirits of the dead are involved. . . . "

[22] Voth, 1903a, pp. 350, 351. A similar circuit is supposed to have been made by the sun even before the emergence of mankind. See Voth, 1905b, pp. 1, 9, *et passim.* In other myths, Voth, 1905b, p. 14, the sun is manufactured soon after man's Emergence.

[22a] Parsons, 1927, p. 126, describes a girl who, on being restored from the dead, turned night into day and vice versa.

[23] The use of the same principle to explain the diurnal changes of day and night and the seasonal shifts of summer and winter, affords an excellent illustration of the Pueblo tendency to reason by analogy. Parsons, 1939, pp. 88–97.

[24] Note that the sun's attainment of each of its solstice points is attended by a ceremony intended to help it begin its return journey. This custom has been fully discussed in Fewkes, 1920, p. 496.

Note too the employment of two Sun Watchers, each of whom is on duty for one half of the sun's annual cycle. Consult Titiev, 1938c, p. 40.

and is said to last until the sun arrives at its winter "home" (about December 21).[25] Conversely, the summer season extends in theory from December 21 to June 21. Once again we encounter the belief that conditions in the upper and lower worlds are reversed, for while it is winter in one sphere it is summer in the other. A simple diagram, fig. 8, illustrates this principle and at the same time shows its fundamental resemblance to the explanation of the sun's daily circuit.

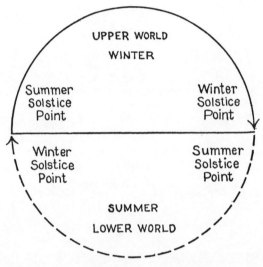

FIG. 8. THE SUN'S ANNUAL CYCLE.

The Hopi calendar is clearly built on the concept of the year's duality, for the months "are arranged approximately on the basis of summer and winter so that the first month of one season is called by the same name as the first month of the other."[26] On the whole, the theory of the calendrical system seems to be that while the upper world is experiencing a particular month of the winter season, the lower world is going through the corresponding month of the summer. Thus, when it is winter Kel-muya on earth, it is

summer Kel-muya in the Underworld, etc. At Oraibi the calendar runs according to the following pattern:[27]

WINTER		SUMMER	
Kel-muya	Nov.	Kel-muya	June
Kya-muya	Dec.	Kya-muya	July
Pa-muya	Jan.	Pa-muya	Aug.
Powa-muya	Feb.	Powa-muya	Sept.
Isu-muya	Mar.	Angok-muya	Oct.
Kwiya-muya	Apr.	Isu-muya	Oct.[28]
Hakiton-muya	May		

It is suggested, furthermore, that the two sets of months form one continuous cycle, and that events which transpire in any given month in the Underworld will be identically repeated when that month moves into position in the upper realm. As Stephen puts it, "When [Powa-muya] shines in the Above, its counterpart . . . [Summer Powa-muya] is shining in the Below, at the house of [Muyingwa]. Summer is yonder, winter is here. All vegetation is mature, fruits all ripe in the Below. When the Nashan [Summer Powamuya] shining now in the Below comes to the Above, next September, it will bring just the same harvest as that it is now shining on in the Below."[29]

One of the most significant analogies[30] based on the concept of the year's duality is the notion that death is the reverse of life; just as summer on earth is winter Below, and day Above means night in the Underworld. This explains why the Hopi depict the behavior of the god of death as the opposite of that of the living. Masau'u is supposed to sleep by day and to walk about by night; he enters a kiva with his back to the ladder and steps to the main floor from the wrong (west) side; he becomes faint from the smell of cedar smoke which the living Hopi employ to rid them from the contagion of death; and it is noteworthy that only his (Masau) Katcina may be danced publicly during the closed season when all the other Katcinas are supposed to be locked up.[31]

[25] All dates mentioned in this chapter must be regarded as approximations because the Hopi are unable to keep a strict account of time periods. Furthermore, as Fewkes, 1903, p. 19, has pointed out, the Hopi do not make a clear division of the year into seasons corresponding to our spring, summer, autumn, and winter.

[26] Titiev, 1938c, p. 39.

[27] Titiev, 1938c, p. 40. Note that the division into Winter and Summer conforms to American but not to Hopi practice. See footnote 25 on this page.

[28] Because the Hopi have been unable to fit thirteen lunar months into the two equal solar periods between

the solstices (see Titiev, 1938c), they have a good deal of difficulty in naming the months of the year, particularly at the period just prior to the winter solstice. As a result the postulated balance between the winter and summer months is perfect only in theory. Compare Kennard, 1937 p. 491, footnote 2.

[29] Parsons, 1936b, p. 239.

[30] Attention is drawn once more to the Hopi habit of thinking by analogy. Compare Parsons, 1939, p. 76.

[31] An account of a Masau'u impersonation in which h representative does many things by opposites is found "The Economic Background" in Part Three, p. 186.

Furthermore, the members of the Kwan society, whose patron deity is Masau'u, also do many things by opposites. Whereas all other officers apply chiefs' markings under their right eyes and on their left shoulders, arms, and legs, the Kwan men apply their chiefs' markings in reverse fashion. Long ago Voth called attention to another significant distinction between customary and Kwan ritual practices. He noted that in drawing cornmeal lines to represent the six directions,[32] the Kwan chief signified the Below by sprinkling meal from the northwest instead of from the southwest. "This deviation from the universal rule," wrote Voth, "I have observed several times in the ceremonies of this fraternity in the Kwan kiva, and *here only*."[33] Finally, the spirits of deceased Kwan men "cannot return to visit the living in the form of white clouds as is the privilege of most spirits. . . ."[34]

By far the most profound effect of the duality concept is exerted on the structure of the ritual calendar. This is due to the fact that life in the other world is supposed to reflect life on earth so exactly that corresponding ceremonies are performed simultaneously (with the seasons reversed) in the two spheres. "This belief that mundane ceremonies are celebrated in the underworld has gone so far that even the time when these subterranean rites occur is, they say, known to living priests, who then hold sympathetic observances. For instance, the Snake drama on earth is celebrated in August, but in the under-world it occurs in January. . . . When, in the celebration in August, the living Antelope and Snake priests gather around their altar and sing the sixteen songs . . . to bring the needed rains, the same chief, at a prescribed moment, raps on the floor in time with the song to inform [his] brother priests in the under-world that they are engaged in their devotions."[35]

As Fewkes has pointed out, "The great Hopi festivals as a rule, are complemented by lesser ceremonies, so that the same society of priests usually has two annual presentations of its rites . . about six months apart. The smaller festivals sometimes occur twice a year, also, indicating the division of the calendar into two parts."[36] At Oraibi the Snake, Flute, Marau, and Lakon societies, all of which give their major performances in the summer or fall, have brief winter meetings about six months earlier, during which they manufacture prayer-objects and conduct simple services.[37] With respect to this system a feeling seems to prevail that when the main celebration is held by the living on earth the dead co-operate with a minor meeting of the corresponding society; but half a year later, when the Underworld performers are staging their major celebration, the living hold sympathetic, abbreviated rites.[38] As Kopeli, the Snake society chief at Walpi, explained the matter to Stephen, "The prayer-sticks are made in the winter Pamüriyawû (Moisture, January, Moon) and the dance is celebrated in the summer Pamüriyawû (Moisture, August, Moon)."[39]

The open and closed seasons of the Katcina cycle likewise reflect the concept of the year's dualism. During the summer months, approximately from the time of the Soyal in mid-December until the Niman dance in midsummer, the Katcinas are supposed to be present on earth, but during the winter months the Katcinas are locked up and are "supposed to return to the underworld, 'the entrance to which is the sun house in the west'."[40]

Although the theoretical pattern of the ceremonial calendar seems to call for dual celebrations on the part of all religious societies, there are three extremely important sets of rites, the Soyal, Powamu, and Tribal Initiation, which meet only once a year. It has been suggested by Fewkes that the winter performance of the Soyal is complemented by the manufacture of prayer-offerings to the sun in July,[41] but I am unaware of any complementary rituals for the Powamu or the Tribal Initiation.

Underlying the custom of holding double sets of rites is the Hopi belief that the living and the dead can co-operate to aid each other. In his description of the Marau at Oraibi, Voth remarks, "The custom of not only informing the ancestors and friends in the other world that a ceremony is in progress here, but also of providing the means to have them share in its benefits has also been

---

[32] North, west, south, east, zenith, and nadir.
[33] Voth, 1912b, p. 116.
[34] Nequatewa, 1936, p. 104, note 10.
[35] Fewkes, 1896b, p. 162.
[36] Fewkes, 1902b, p. 494.
[37] Compare Parsons, 1936b, p. 713. Unlike the Oraibi

custom, the Lakon society of Walpi is reported to have met in the winter. Parsons, 1936b, p. 116.
[38] Fewkes, 1898a, p. 67; Fewkes, 1894c, pp. 267, 268.
[39] Parsons, 1936b, p. 713.
[40] Haeberlin, 1916, p. 30.
[41] Fewkes, 1898a, p. 67.

observed in other ceremonies."[42] Conversely, when a living man visits the home of the dead, one of the spirits says to him, " 'Make nakwakwosis for us at the Soyal ceremony. . . . We then shall work for you here, too.' "[43]

Thus we find that the concept of the year's duality is another feature which underlies the entire structure of Hopi ceremonialism. On the one hand, it throws into sharp relief the reversal of conditions between the living and the dead, but on the other hand it emphasizes the bonds between them and provides a basis for synchronous, co-operative activities between the inhabitants of the two realms.

THE CYCLE OF LIFE AND DEATH

In the light of the foregoing discussion we may now proceed to elaborate the Hopi belief in the continuity of life after death. It is not enough to show that death is considered a mere change of status or that the activities of the spirits are supposed to mirror faithfully those of the living, for the Hopi look upon life and death not as two separate and distinct stages of existence, but rather as two phases of one recurrent cycle.

Several Hopi myths plainly state that the dead merely return through the *sipapu* whence all mankind originally emerged on earth,[44] and one tale even asserts that "people who died would have been able to revive and walk around on this world four days after death,"[45] had not Coyote thrown a large stone over the *sipapu* shortly after the occurrence of the first death on earth.[46] However, Coyote's "foolish action" is believed to have barred only bodies in the flesh from free movement between the upper and the lower realms, for human spirits still retain the power to pass in and out of the nether realm through the *sipapu*. In fact, the Underworld is regarded not only as the ultimate home to which the soul of a dead person must go, but also as "the place of its [the soul's] genesis before it was embodied."[47]

The cyclic character of the soul's sojourns on earth and in the Below is clearly brought out in the statement that from the Underworld "come at birth the souls of the newly born, and to it the

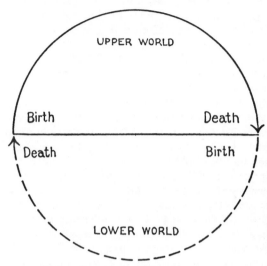

FIG. 9. THE CYCLE OF LIFE AND DEATH.[48]

shades or spirits of the dead return."[49] Furthermore, the nature of these transitions is revealed in the concepts that a person who dies on earth "becomes like a baby" in the other world,[50] and that spirits of the dead become embodied in children born on earth. In other words, death in the upper world is followed by birth in the lower world; and ultimately, the spirits of the dead are re-embodied in babies born on earth; thus making a continuous cycle such as is shown above.

The close resemblance of fig. 9 to the diagrams depicting the sun's diurnal and annual rounds, figs. 7 and 8, strongly suggests that the natives imagine a close analogy to exist between the sun's movements and the human cycle of life and death. This point was first noted by Fewkes as early as 1901. "Consider the relationship between the souls of the dead and sun and earth gods," he

[42] Voth, 1912a, p. 55, footnote 1.

[43] Voth, 1905b, p. 117. Compare Dorsey and Voth, 1901, p. 57 footnote *.

[44] Voth, 1905b, pp. 11, 12, 19, 20; and Stephen, 1929, p. 9.

[45] Stephen, 1929, p. 9.

[46] Stephen, 1929, p. 9. Parsons, 1926, p. 172, has recorded a similar explanation of death as told by a Tewa who was aware of the Hopi origin of his tale. Here Coyote says it is no good for the dead to return to earth, so he overeats, dies, and does not come back.

[47] Fewkes, 1896b, p. 162.

[48] It should be specifically noted that only three of the stages in the diagram are explicitly documented from the source material on the Hopi. The existence of the fourth stage, which is Death in the Lower World, is unquestionably implied, although it is never openly described by native informants. Its existence is postulated here only as part of an hypothesis. The life and death cycle among the Hopi is completely generalized and should never be interpreted as a belief in personal reincarnation.

[49] Fewkes, 1901c, p. 83.

[50] Parsons, 1925, pp. 75, 76, footnote 121.

wrote. "The subterranean world of which the clan ancients are denizens is the house of the sun and the earth goddess. . . . Here are generated the souls of the newly born on earth, and to this home of the Sun return the spirits of the dead."[51] The same idea has been further elaborated by Haeberlin who argues that "When one considers that 'the Hopi connects the idea of life with the east, death with the west,' that every newborn baby must be shown to the rising sun, that the dead of the Hopi travel westward, and finally that the sun in the evening descends into the underworld by way of the *sipapu* . . . it seems warranted to suppose that there is a certain parallelism in the mind of the natives between the fates of the sun and those of the individual. The sun and the individual both return through the *sipapu* to the underworld whence they came. The association is obvious and, at least as far as the Hopi are concerned, is borne out by the empirical data."[52] An interesting addition to the conclusions arrived at by Fewkes and Haeberlin appears in a myth, supposedly of Hopi origin, in which Coyote explains that " 'It is only by somebody dying every day—morning, noon and evening—that will make the sun move every day'."[53]

The complete cycle of deaths and re-births applies only to those who travel the full course of life on earth according to the Hopi pattern, and all variations or deficiencies in a person's experiences during life are supposed to affect the disposition of his soul after death. Thus the spirit of a child which has died prior to its Katcina initiation cannot return alone to the Underworld but must wait on earth to be reborn in its mother's next child or to accompany her shade to the other world when she dies.[54] Girls who are unwed or who marry illegally cannot fulfill their proper functions as rain bringers in the Below because they lack the requisite wedding garments,[55] and men who have never passed through the Tribal Initiation find that their souls must return to the general Underworld whereas the spirits of initiates have special homes reserved for them.[56] Also, the journey to the house of the dead (Maski) is painfully slow and difficult for the spirits of witches, in addition to which they face the danger of being consumed in huge ovens from which they emerge as beetles.[57]

The notion that life and death are merely two stages in a continuous cycle of events has far-reaching consequences on the structure of Hopi society. For the individual it offers a kind of immortality that helps to soften the shock of death; for social units such as the clan it provides a sense of stability based on the feeling that death cannot lessen its total membership in the two worlds; and for the pueblo or tribe as a whole it serves as a guarantee of permanence. Thanks to the operation of such a set of beliefs, the Hopi regard their dead not as outsiders who are lost to the living community, but as powerful members of society, whose sphere of activity has been changed for a time from the upper realm to the lower.

THE MEANING OF HOPI RELIGION

In its broader aspects, the religion of the Hopi can be understood only with respect to other manifestations of their culture. For about two thousand years they and their immediate ancestors have occupied a semi-arid zone, despite which, for the greater part of that time, they have relied on agriculture as their principal source of food. During many centuries they have dwelt in fairly large pueblos, but with a decentralized social organization which contained within itself an ever-present threat of collapse. Inside the towns the people lived in such close and unhygienic proximity to each other that the introduction of any contagious disease must have had terrifying consequences on the entire populace. To make matters still worse, the Hopi were never given to large scale military activity and, accordingly, they were never wholly free from the raids of predatory and warlike neighbors. Under such conditions, life was far from easy for the Hopi. Lack of rain, failure of crops, internal strife, onslaughts of disease, and enemy attacks, all combined to threaten the very existence of their society. To offset these dangers they took whatever material measures they could, but finding these inadequate to guarantee the permanence which every social group seeks, they resorted to supernatural means to give them assurance that they would not be destroyed.[58]

Against each of the perils which endangered

---

[51] Fewkes, 1901c, p. 86.
[52] Haeberlin, 1916, p. 28.
[53] Parsons, 1926, p. 171.
[54] Voth, 1912b, p. 103.

[55] See p. 38.
[56] See p. 136 and footnote 48.
[57] Titiev, 1941, p. 500; and Parsons, 1936b, pp. 826, 827.
[58] Compare Parsons, 1939, pp. x, xi.

Hopi society their ceremonial system opposed a comforting buffer. The Soyal, the Flute, the Snake-Antelope, the Powamu, the Katcina cult, and the women's societies, all combined to guarantee the control of the seasons, abundant rainfall, plentiful crops, and freedom from disease; and the Momtcit assured them of supernatural allies in war. In addition, the cult of the dead substituted for the fear of annihilation the more comforting belief in a temporary transition to another realm; and the Tribal Initiation provided close co-operation between the world of the living and the home of the dead.

Shorn of its elaborate, detailed and colorful superstructure of costumes, songs and dances, the entire complex of Hopi religious behavior stands revealed as a unified attempt to safeguard Hopi society from the danger of disintegration or dissolution. Has a prominent, leading figure died on earth? His importance is even greater now that he has taken on "a supernatural influence."[59] Is a clan in danger of extinction? There is no cause for worry, since "the social condition of life in the underworld is similar to that on this earth. . . . Those who belong to the Badger clan on earth are still members of the same clan after leaving the mortal body. In other words each earthly clan has its corresponding clan in the underworld. . . ."[60] Does disease threaten the well-being of the populace? Each secret society stands ever-ready to drive out a particular ailment which it "alone can cure."[61] Is an essential religious ceremony about to lapse?[62] There is nothing to fear, for in the Below "the different religious sodalities perform . . . much the same rites as in the upper-world. . . ."[63] Is there a threat of devastating drought? The spirits of the dead stand prepared to answer the prayers (desires) of the living by sending "rain and crops."[64]

When it is reduced to its barest essentials Hopi religion loses its distinctive flavor and turns out to be no more than a local manifestation of universally sustained religious beliefs. Everywhere primitive societies seek to guarantee their stability and permanence; and lacking material means to counteract the effects of a hostile environment or the inescapable ravages of death, they turn to the supernatural world for assurance that they will not be destroyed.[65] It is, therefore, primarily for the attainment of this goal that the entire apparatus of Hopi religion has been devised.

[59] Fewkes, 1896b, p. 162.
[60] Fewkes, 1923, p. 492.
[61] Parsons, 1936b, p. XL.
[62] Parsons, 1921b, p. 213, points out the constant danger that a ceremony may become extinct if its controlling family should die out.

[63] Fewkes, 1896b, p. 162.   [64] Voth, 1905b, p. 117.
[65] In a forthcoming study the author plans to present a large body of evidence to prove that despite an overwhelming divergence of external details, the essential principles of primitive religion are few in number and world-wide in distribution.

PART THREE

MISCELLANY

Chapter XV

THE ECONOMIC BACKGROUND

EVER SINCE the Hopi have been a pueblo-dwelling people, they have pursued an agricultural economy.[1] The problem of land ownership has, therefore, been one of the principal concerns of their social organization. Theoretically, the entire domain of each town is owned by the Village chief, and all the inhabitants hold land only at his pleasure.[2] According to a traditional account on Third Mesa, the entire Oraibi area was first entrusted by Masau'u to Matcito, the Bear clan chieftain who founded the pueblo; and it was Matcito who distributed farming plots to all the clans which joined his settlement. The contemporary pattern of ownership still reflects the traditional scheme. The Village chief is the theoretical owner of all his town's lands; these lands are divided among the clans residing in his pueblo (fig. 5); and each individual farms a specified portion of his clan's holdings.[3] In addition, there is a large piece of unassigned land, part of which may be used by any villager with the chief's consent. Under such a system land is never bartered or sold, and only rarely exchanged. Ownership is restricted to the privilege of use, but this right is so carefully recognized that if a man decides to allow some of his fields to lie fallow, no other farmer may use them without the specific permission of the owner.[4]

The actual work of farming falls almost entirely to the men.[5] An adolescent boy customarily begins to function in the economic sphere by working part of that portion of his clan's lands which his father cultivates. Then, at marriage, he begins to plant on his wife's land, particularly if it happens to be fertile. If it turns out to be poor soil, he may try to make an arrangement to continue farming with his father. This feature, coupled with the possibility that he may receive additional land as a reward for the performance of a ceremonial office,[6] gives a man a fair range of available sites for the location of his fields; a great advantage in a region where rainfall is not only very light but often irregularly and unpredictably distributed, and where the quality of a piece of ground may change from fertile to barren within a few months.

Judging from the great extent of the Oraibi domain and the deliberate attempt of the villagers to limit the size of their crops to what is considered only a fair margin of safety,[7] it would seem at first glance that there was surely enough to provide each farmer with as much ground as he cared to cultivate, but the nature of the terrain and the quality of the soil are such that not all the Oraibi holdings are equally suitable for agriculture. Accordingly, quarrels over land are by no means unusual, for the clans occupying smaller or poorer locations frequently show marked resent-

---

[1] A brief summary of Hopi economic customs is given in Stephen, 1940, p. 24.

[2] Further details on this subject occur on pp. 61–63. See too Titiev, 1934, pp. 134–142. For comparative data on Second Mesa, consult Beaglehole, E., 1937, pp. 14–18; and for First Mesa, see Forde, 1931, pp. 366–383.

The extent of the Hopi reservation is estimated at about 2,500,000 acres.

[3] In theory, only the women of a clan could hold title to land, so that a man generally farmed on the property of his wife or mother; but in practice it was not unknown for a son to inherit land from his father.

The land holdings of each clan were generally supplemented by small, irrigated gardens, conveniently located on the slopes of mesas to take advantage of natural or imposed overflow from springs (pl. I). These were owned and attended by women who grew onions, chile peppers, and other vegetables that were regarded as delicacies.

Only the Masau'u and Kokop clans had orchards specifically assigned to their use, but other clans could grow fruit trees on any free soil that was suitable. Peach trees were by far the most commonly grown. They were owned by women in terms of individual trees rather than by entire orchards. Peaches were unknown in pre-Spanish times.

[4] Some informants stated that if unfenced lands were unused by their owners for several years, they fell into the status of free territory and could be used by anyone who received the Village chief's permission.

[5] According to Hopi convention, men are regarded as the owners of their crops throughout both the growing and harvesting stages. As soon as the yield has been brought into a household, however, it becomes the property of the women who own the land on which it was grown.

[6] See p. 62 and footnote 24.

[7] Because they lack an outlet for surplus production, the Hopi try never to grow more than they can consume in one year. Corn is the only product that is grown in excess of the annual need, and every household strives to keep at least an extra year's supply on hand to forestall a famine in the event of crop failure.

ment towards those which are more favorably situated.[8] Individual jealousies are likewise prevalent, and accusations of witchcraft are freely bandied about when rain fails to fall on a particular plot of ground or when a farm is eroded by the activities of a deep-cutting stream.

The all-pervading concern of the Hopi with land problems can be fully appreciated only when one realizes how utterly dependent they are on the soil and how precarious such a dependence must always be in the face of an unfavorable environment. Not only is the presence of large deposits of alkali in itself a serious detriment to agriculture, "but when the extreme dryness of the air, the violence of the winds, the elevation of the region, and consequent cool nights, early frosts, and the heat of the sun are taken into consideration, it is a matter of surprise that plants exist at all."[9] As if that were not bad enough, the rainfall is sporadic and uneven and "the curious thing about [it] . . . is that the rains come too early and too late to be of much use to a large number of plants."[10] Thus "June is the dryest month of the year. This is particularly unfortunate since the crops require water urgently during the early growing period."[11]

Luckily for the Hopi much of the soil is very fertile if it obtains sufficient moisture, and the natural topography of the region furnishes them with a supply of water to help counteract deficiences of precipitation. Located

on the southern spurs of a large culminating plateau known as Black Mesa [the Hopi villages are so situated that thanks to a favorable] tilt of the general surface . . . they capture practically the entire surface drainage of the plateau.

In addition to the surface drainage, there is also an important southward seepage of underground water, for the surface rock on the mesa top is moderately permeable Mesa Verde sandstone which dips generally southward. This is underlain by impermeable Mancos shales, so that the imprisoned water seeps southward along the plane of contact . . . and along this line are found a large number of springs and seeps.

These two circumstances, the southward drainage of the relatively well watered Black Mesa, and the develop-

ment of a spring line along the southern edges and spurs of the mesa, are of the greatest importance in Hopi economy for the direct precipitation . . . is quite inadequate for agriculture.[12]

Besides learning to take advantage of underground seepage, the Hopi, like most of the sedentary tribes in the Southwest, early developed the technique of flood-water farming which depends largely on the choice of planting sites in such places as are most likely to be flooded in the event of rain.

The areas utilized are variable in size and location, but each is chosen so that the local rainfall may be reinforced by the overflow of water derived from higher ground. The selection of a field involves an intimate knowledge of local conditions. The field must be flooded, but the sheet of water must not attain such velocity as to wash out the crop nor carry such a load of detritus as to bury the growing plants. Such conditions require a nice balance of forces that occur only under special conditions. Shrewd observation and good judgment are necessary in the selection of fields.

The sites chosen fall obviously into two main types: gentle slopes below rock or shale escarpments, valley floors inundated by sheet floods.[13]

In Professor Kirk Bryan's opinion, the Hopi were one of the tribes that practiced flood-water farming prior to the Spanish invasion, and it is interesting to see how the principles of this method of agriculture still operate.[14] Through every large field, especially those devoted to raising corn, there runs the shallow, rather narrow bed of an ephemeral stream whose precious overflow is retained by judicious damming and artificial banking. This is a modern adaptation brought about by the accelerated erosion, which, as Dr. Bryan points out, has been going on since 1880 and has practically terminated flood-water farming in the main valleys.[15]

Not only have the Hopi learned to take advantage of local conditions in the choice of farm plots, but they have also evolved a method of planting which is best suited to their environment. They use a dibble which makes only a small hole and causes far less dangerous surface disturbance than would a plow, and they plant deeply enough to

---

[8] Some of Oraibi's deepest schisms have arisen, at least in part, from quarrels over land. See p. 75; and the account of "The Pikyas-Patki Conflict."

[9] Hough, 1898, p. 134.

[10] Hough, 1898, p. 135.

[11] Forde, 1931, p. 361.

[12] Forde, 1931, p. 360.

[13] Bryan, 1929, p. 445.

[14] An excellent treatment of this aspect of modern

Hopi farming is found in Stewart, 1940, pp. 329–335.

The entire problem of the relationship of the Hopi to their physical environment has been thoroughly treated in the recent publication by Hack, 1942.

[15] In addition to the natural process of erosion, the Hopi are losing vast quantities of arable land annually throughout the denudation of the soil by livestock. As their herds have increased in modern times the problem of erosion control has become proportionately greater.

secure some of the benefits of underground seepage and to achieve the requisite strong rooting system.

A Hopi farmer clears his field towards the close of winter, usually in February, by trampling down or removing weeds and brush either by series of small holes about a foot deep with his planting stick. The soil at the bottom of the hole is loosened to form a "bed" for the seed, and from "ten to twenty seeds are dropped in and covered with loose earth. Women occasionally help the men especially if planting is behindhand.

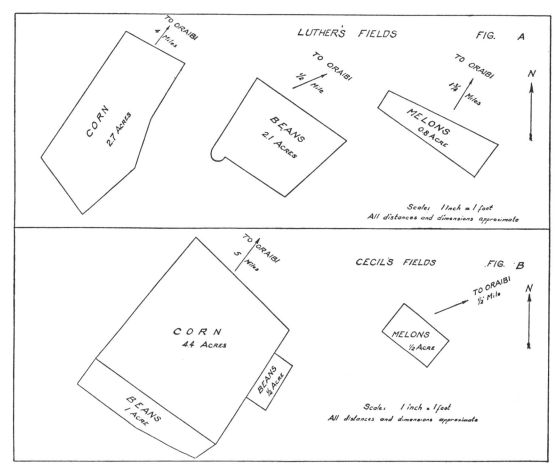

FIG. 10. FIELDS CULTIVATED BY TWO MEN.

hand, with a hoe, or in recent times, with a cultivator.[16] Then the ground is broken up "by means of the *wikya*, a stick about three feet long with a broad, fairly sharp end, which was used with a motion like that imparted to a canoe paddle, the sharp edge tearing up the ground."[17] The field is then considered ready for planting, and when the appropriate time comes, the owner digs a

They hold the bags of seed corn and drop seeds in the holes when ready. This deep planting assists in the development of the rooting system and protects the seedlings against washing out by heavy rains or flood."[18]

If the seed fails to sprout in about ten days, the hole may be re-seeded at the owner's discretion, but this rarely is done after the summer solstice.[19]

[16] Further details of Hopi farming methods may be found in Beaglehole, E., 1937, pp. 36–42; and in Hack, 1942, pp. 19–38, *et passim*.

[17] Curtis, 1922, p. 41.

[18] Forde, 1931, p. 390 ff. The next few paragraphs are based on Forde and Curtis.

[19] Data on the seeds used by the Hopi may be found in Whiting, 1937.

The corn grows like a bush and is not hilled. It is cared for by weeding, loosening the soil at the base of the plants, and scooping earth around them so that they may the better retain water.

As a rule, the holes for a given year's planting are made between those of the previous year, and several fields are devoted to corn, so that in the event that one field fails to bear, whether through lack of moisture or for other causes, the others may yield a good crop. The habit of sowing corn on several scattered sites has been developed primarily owing to the nature of the rainfall, which may water the fields in one area, while those in another location go dry. This is not a scheme for rotating crops as the Hopi generally prefer to continue sowing the same product on a piece of land that has once been found suitable, and to abandon the spot only when changing conditions make it imperative. Sometimes rows of beans may be alternated with those of corn, but more often beans are grown by themselves in smaller plots. They are planted in holes about six inches deep, and eight or ten are deposited to a hole. They generally begin to sprout in a few days. Squashes, muskmelons, watermelons, and a few gourds are other staples which may be planted either in one field or separately. (See fig. 10 for sketches of the fields cultivated by two married men during 1933.)

The choice of planting dates at Oraibi was not left entirely to individual fancy, primarily because laymen were supposed to be ignorant of the calendrical system. Instead there were two religious officers who shared the duty of watching the sun's progress from season to season.[20] One of these, the Patki chief, was in charge throughout the duration of the planting season, and it was he who made public a sort of official time schedule for sowing various crops. Although farmers were by no means compelled to follow the exact sequence suggested by the Sun Watchers, most of them felt that "it was best for people to adhere to the schedule which their ancestors had worked out."[21]

In former times, while the clan system of land tenure was universally in vogue, it was customary for each group to plant and harvest as a unit, and such activities played an important part in fostering clan solidarities. For whenever the Hopi engage in any form of communal labor, a feeling of harmony is engendered and a holiday spirit prevails.[22] This is made manifest particularly in the accounts of communal planting and harvesting on behalf of the Village chief and other high officers. It is said that when Matcito had finished apportioning land among the various clans, the people were so grateful that they promised to perform all his work for him; and in consequence the chief was formerly relieved of all farming cares, wood was hauled to his house by the villagers, and garments were woven for all the members of his family. Any public-minded individual had the right to sponsor a work project on behalf of a chief. He generally selected a time when most people were not too busy with their own affairs, and he asked the Village Crier chief to make a public announcement of the date. In keeping with the belief that Masau'u, the god of death, was the original proprietor of the earth and one of the principal owners of all Hopi crops,[23] it was customary to have someone impersonate Masau'u whenever a communal planting party went into the fields.[24]

During the harvest season too an impersonation of Masau'u was included as part of the arrangements for joint enterprises. Indeed, at Oraibi this aspect seems to have assumed the proportions of a formal ceremony, and details of the performance were planned during the winter season, months ahead of the scheduled date.[25] The responsibility for such an event was undertaken by one of the village societies, such as the Lakon,[26] and was

---

[20] This was done by observing certain fixed points on the horizon, behind which the sun seemed to rise in the course of its seasonal journey from one solstice point to the other. Twelve such points were touched by the rising sun during the planting period which ran from late in March to nearly the end of June. These points and the crops supposed to be sown when each was reached are described in Titiev, 1938c, pp. 40–42.

[21] Titiev, 1938c, p. 42.

[22] Beaglehole, E., 1937, pp. 27–32, provides comparative material from Second Mesa.

[23] Voth, 1905b, pp. 12, 13.

[24] Compare Forde, 1931, pp. 396 ff.

[25] Arrangements for harvesting parties were generally made while several secret societies were conducting their winter rites. The Hopi believe that during these ceremonies the worshippers are in correspondence with the spirit world which is enjoying summer while the living are having winter (p. 174). This is an appropriate time, then, for making arrangements to have the god of death appear on earth when the seasons shall have been reversed.

[26] The Lakon is a women's ceremony, whose public dance comes in the fall during the harvest season. See p. 168. Informants at Oraibi failed to agree on the question of whether or not the sponsoring society had to be a women's group or any unit which gave its performance in

designed to relieve either the society's own chief or one of the pueblo's officers of his harvesting duties. As soon as the decision had been reached, the head of the sponsoring group would tell the leader of the Masau'u clan that Masau'u was planning to help harvest the next season's crop. Thereupon the clan chief, realizing the proper significance of this phrase, would appoint one or two men from his own or a related clan in his phratry[27] to play the parts when the time came.

Three days before the Lakon dance, in the event that that society had assumed sponsorship of the occasion, the Masau'u impersonators would go into confinement at *the* Kokop clan house, where they would sleep or remain in concealment throughout the entire day, emerging at midnight to make gradually decreasing circuits of the village on four successive nights.[28] During this time word spreads about that "Masau'u did not wake up today," so people know what is in store. Two days before the harvest date the men go on a hunt, during which they try to kill rabbits by tossing them high in the air or in some other way which will keep the blood within the carcass. This is important because the costumes of the Masau'u actors must be covered with fresh blood. All the rabbits killed in this hunt are brought to *the* Kokop house where they are kept until needed.

After breakfast on the morning following the Lakon dance, the Village Crier chief goes to the roof of *the* Kele (Chicken Hawk) clan house from which he announces that there is to be a general harvesting (*sopkyau'ma*) on behalf of whatever official has been picked for the honor. He then tells the populace to prepare to go into the fields, and at noon he again calls out to make sure that everything is in readiness. Everyone eats hurriedly and hastens out to the designated farm. The members of the Lakon society dress in their dance costumes and go as a unit, but all others

dress as they please and go in any order they like.

As soon as all the people have left the village, the two Masau'u impersonators, accompanied by the head of the Masau'u clan, proceed to an appropriate shrine where they get into costume while the harvesting is in progress. First, the entire body is rubbed thoroughly with ashes; then an old, shabby, woman's garment (*manta*) is put on in reverse fashion, so that the right shoulder is exposed instead of the left. One strip of yucca is bound round the ankles and wrists, and another about the waist as a belt into which there is tucked on the left side an ear of black corn, which is the special property of this deity. A rabbit skin hood is made to enclose the entire head, being drawn tightly and fastened under the chin with yucca strings. Over this is poured a liberal quantity of fresh rabbit blood. A round club, about half a foot long, covered with an inverted rabbit skin and doused in blood, completes the costume.[29] Thus dressed, the two men run towards the field where the people are at work. One impersonator hides not far from the village while the other continues on until he is met by a horseman, usually of the Masau'u clan,[30] who is dispatched for the special purpose of giving him a ride. The meeting is arranged to take place out of sight of the workers, and Masau'u, jumping up behind his escort, covers himself with a blanket so that he may not be prematurely recognized.

These events are generally so timed that the actual work of harvesting is now ended, and the Lakon members are doing a dance for their colaborers. At its conclusion, the Crier chief calls out, thanking the society for its performance and ordering the men to load the corn in sacks and to begin carrying it into the pueblo. Just at this point the rider comes dashing towards the throng which, realizing his intent, begins to cry out even before Masau'u slips from the horse and, bran-

---

the fall. They did agree, however, that sponsorship was not entirely restricted to the Lakon society. Although the present description is based on Lakon responsibility for the event, the possibility of other groups taking charge must not be forgotten.

[27] In accordance with Hopi practice, all the clans in Phratry VI may claim Masau'u as one of their ancients, and any adult male from that phratry may have the right to enact the part of the god of death.

[28] The fact that Masau'u sleeps by day and walks by night is part of his customary manner of doing things by opposites. Note too that his symbol is a design of concentric circles to represent his footsteps. See Stephen, 1940, pp. 203–204.

[29] Note that the men are impersonating the *real* Masau'u and not the related Masau Katcina. Masau'u is not a masked impersonation and is an object of such great awe that only the phratry of which he is one of the *wuya* dares to be on close terms with him. However, at Walpi Masau'u was impersonated by Patki clansmen, and by a man who was either a Badger or a Snake clansman. See Parsons, 1936b, pp. 994, 1089, 1111, and 1112. The Patki men may have functioned as Masau'u impersonators by virtue of membership in the Kwan society which regards the god of death as a patron. Compare p. 137.

[30] So great is the "power" of Masau'u that only those who acknowledge him for an ancient dare to come into contact even with his impersonators.

dishing his club, darts here and there threatening to strike whomever he overtakes.[31] Then the impersonator runs to the corn which has been heaped into separate piles of black and white varieties and, with the palms of his hands, he pats the heaps to indicate his ownership of the entire crop. As this act also carries the significance of a fertility rite, all the people shout their thanks.

Immediately after, the task of sacking the corn is resumed, and although Masau'u may now and again make a sudden rush at some worker who runs off in alarm, he takes care not to disrupt the proceedings. When all is in readiness for returning to the village, the gathering lines up formally for the homeward procession. At the head stands the masculine officer of the Lakon which is sponsoring the affair, and behind him come the Village chief, the Crier chief and the War chief. Then the Lakon members take their places, followed by unmarried girls with their hair done up in butterfly wings, and in the rear come the men and boys. Before they start the Crier chief makes a speech. "Thank you, my people," he says. "You have done a good work. We will be happy going into our chief's and our mother's (chief's wife's) village with good hearts and good thoughts. Now, let us go!" At this, the Lakon officer at the head of the line makes a "path" by sprinkling cornmeal, and the homeward journey begins with everyone carrying as much corn as possible.

Meantime, Masau'u, as if tired and dejected, sits with bowed head, left elbow resting on his knee, and his chin supported in the cupped palm. Only after the procession has gone a little way does he jump up and follow. Quite often the unmarried girls are offered rides behind whichever of their nephews (imuyim) happen to be mounted,[32] and when Masau'u is observed heading for home the boys whose aunts are of the Masau'u clan will tease them, trying to get one of them to ride with the impersonator. If any girl is bold enough to accept the dare, the boy slips from the horse, the girl takes the saddle, and Masau'u jumps up behind to the great amusement of the crowd.

All this time the second impersonator has remained in hiding, but as the crowd draws near he suddenly appears, and people scatter to all sides as they try to escape the touch of his weapon. Some of the men who are armed may fire in the air to frighten the deity, and a sort of mock battle may ensue, but in a little while things quiet down and the rest of the trip is uneventful.

As soon as the village is reached, the people bring the corn to the owner's house, hasten home for a light meal, and then hurry to perform their chores before the remaining activities begin. Meantime, the Masau'us go into the Kokop house where they inhale the "steam" of various dishes; for, like the dead, they can eat only the essence (smell) of food. They then proceed to the plaza, where they again resume the dejected, thoughtful pose which Masau'u so often affects. Not long after, a member of the Masau'u clan, who has been selected for the part, dresses in the guise of a Buffalo or other non-Katcina dancer. Holding a cow bell or some similar noise-making device in such fashion that it does not betray his movements, he sneaks into the plaza and warily approaches the deities. When he gets close, he startles them with a sudden shouting and bell ringing, whereupon they jump up and make after him. As soon as they can reach him they touch him with their clubs, and he drops as if dead. Thereupon the Masau'us strip him of some of his costume and try to put on his clothes, invariably doing things by opposites so that they try to force the left moccasin on the right foot, or to wrap a headband round the ankles. Then the impersonators leave their "victim" and return to the plaza, where the same performance is repeated, as man after man of any clan comes out, usually clad in some laughter-provoking way.

When each of the Masau'us has "killed" four costumed men, the first "victim," the one from the Masau'u clan, gets up and taking some cedar bark rubs it between his palms, twists it into a little torch and ignites it. Sneaking up behind each of the Masau'us in turn, he suddenly holds the flaming cedar to their nostrils so that they must inhale some of the smoke, whereupon they drop to the ground as if slain.[33] At once the four

---

[31] To be overtaken and touched by Masau'u's club signifies the touch of death.

[32] This is another indication of the close bond of the paternal aunt with her nephew (p. 28).

[33] The Hopi use cedar smoke for purifying themselves after they have performed a burial service. It is interesting to note how the antithetical behavior of Masau'u serves to emphasize the fact that death is the opposite of life; for cedar rids men from the contagion of death, but it serves to "kill" Masau'u, the god of death.

Note too that cedar and fire are wuyam of Phratry V. See p. 49, table 1.

"victims" of each impersonator jump to their feet and, picking up the fallen deity, carry him by the legs and arms to the Hano kiva, where they place him on the ground. After a time, the Masau'us come back to life and again chase their former victims whose flight purposely takes them back to the plaza and then to *the* Kokop house. Here the costumed men pause outside, but the Masau'u actors are invited to come in by the Kokop chief who indulges with them in a ritual smoke. While this is in progress, the Kokop head woman prepares two plaques piled high with *piki*, cornmeal, and *nakwakwosi;* and when the smoking is finished, she gives one tray to each of the impersonators with prayers for good crops and long life. As the Masau'us emerge with their plaques, the dancers again shout at them, but the deities only wave their bundles with the conventional discharming motion, after which they proceed without further ado to a Masau'u shrine north of the village where they disrobe and deposit their offerings. Then they return to *the* Kokop house to be rewarded with a liberal feast of rabbit stew. For the next four days the Kokop people and the impersonators must observe a period of sex continence; and during this time, if the men who have taken the parts of Masau'u wish to smoke, they may do so only in *the* Kokop clan house. On the fifth day, all resume their normal lives.[34]

Thus did the Hopi, by the admixture of a little ceremonialism and the introduction of an element of entertainment, make their work parties into happy social activities rather than drab, prosaic affairs. No wonder it was not considered a hardship, in the old days, to relieve important officials of their farming duties.

Another joint enterprise that requires the co-operation of many people is the cleaning of a town's springs.[35] Although all the main springs of a pueblo belong to the Village chief in theory, they are freely used by the general public and their care is left entirely to the villagers. Such

cleaning and repairing as becomes necessary is carried out voluntarily on a communal basis.[36] It is usually in the spring of the year that high winds sift so much sand into the springs that it becomes imperative to clear them out. As soon as someone decides to direct the task, he requests the Village chief for permission, prepares a number of prayer-feathers, and observes ritual tabus for four days. Then he asks the town's Crier chief to call out the news and to urge the people to assemble for the work. Sometimes a number of men may add a bit of informal ceremonialism to the event by impersonating disciplinary Katcinas and mockingly acting as hard taskmasters, but as a rule there is little need for anyone to exert much pressure on the workers.[37] A festive spirit prevails among the men, and a holiday atmosphere is provided by the unmarried girls of the pueblo who bring large quantities of *somiviki* and join the laborers in a picnic when they pause for lunch.[38]

In contrast to the spirit of the communal enterprises is the routine manner in which the everyday business of farming is conducted by the average man. There is very little personal ritual associated with actual labors in the field, although at one time it was customary for a man on first clearing a piece of ground to erect a slab of stone to serve as a shrine at which he might deposit prayer-sticks, *nakwakwosi*, or other sacred objects as prayers for fertility. Again, as Forde has pointed out, special offerings might be made at appropriate spots to keep off sandstorms or to prevent a wash from cutting too deeply;[39] and during the Soyal performance in December every man was expected to place prayer-sticks in all his fields. No rites were performed at Oraibi when planting was first begun, but it is reported that on First Mesa the women would douse a farmer as he was leaving the pueblo to begin sowing his crops.[40]

At harvesting too there is little individual ritual except with regard to the sweet corn (*tawak'tci*) yield. This cereal generally matures in

[34] Another occasion when the *real* Masau'u is impersonated is in May of a year when novices are passing through their Tribal Initiation. Again there is a field party involved, this time for the purpose of picking the plant called *nevenkwivi*. The ritual is known as Nevenwehe, and is described on pp. 140, 141.
[35] The main springs at Oraibi are Lololoma's Spring and Lenva or Lenanva (Flute Spring). In addition to these, the inhabitants secure water from privately dug wells, or from natural cisterns (*patni*) on the rocky surface of the mesa. The latter are owned jointly by the women of a

clan, and inasmuch as the task of keeping them clean is a difficult one, their use is jealously guarded by the owners.
[36] Compare Beaglehole, E., 1937, pp. 30, 31.
[37] For an exception to the common rule, see p. 66.
[38] On March 18, 1934, I took part in the cleaning of the horse pond at Old Oraibi. Despite the many schisms in the village, all the men worked cheerfully side by side and everyone seemed to enjoy the whole affair.
[39] Forde, 1931, p. 396.
[40] Parsons, 1925, pp. 87, 91, 93.

early September, and it is customary for the Hopi to bake it in outdoor pit ovens situated near the field where it is grown. On these occasions each man makes up a small party consisting of his wife and two or three congenial companions; and together they camp out while the sweet corn is picked, baked, cooled, and husked. Just before the baking operation begins the farmer affixes prayer-offerings to four ears of corn which are ceremonially pushed into the pit. Then, as the remaining ears are being thrown into the heated oven, the women of the group perform a simple fertility rite by spewing water mixed with corn sprouts and tassels over the entire crop.[41]

There is virtually no ceremonialism attendant on the gathering of all other varieties of corn. As soon as the yield is brought to a household, the women spread it on the roof top to dry. Then the surplus remaining from the preceding year is shelled, and huge quantities are ground into meal. Small groups of relatives and friends frequently grind as units, the women going from house to house and dining at each home where they have worked. The monotony of their labor is spiced with incidental conversation, songs, and gossip,[42] and all the workers smear their faces with blue cornmeal so that their diligence may be readily noted.

Harvest time is a period of feasting and general joy. It is marked by informal begging expeditions (*suspala*), got up as impromptu affairs by boys or girls. Youngsters of either sex go from house to house reciting a sing-song request for muskmelons or watermelons, and after making the rounds they retire to enjoy their booty. Older boys beg for *piki* or sweet cornmeal (*tosi*), and big girls seek rabbit meat. Everyone is good-natured about it, and the housewives generally yield generous amounts of food.

As Hough has indicated, "The Hopi are practically vegetarians. There is necessarily a scarcity of animal life in the desert. Sporadically wild game appears in their dietary in the shape of an occasional rabbit, prairie dog, or rat. . . . Occasionally, a sheep or goat, meat bought of a Navaho, or a burro varies the menu of the Pueblo."[43] At the same time it must not be sup-

posed that their vegetarianism is voluntarily self-imposed, for the Hopi, especially the women, are very fond of meat. In many of the myths great emphasis is laid on the ability of men as hunters; and when, in the Underworld, it was decided to separate the sexes because they were misbehaving, the women became very wretched and "regretted the lack of flesh food. . . . '*Okiwa sikwi nawakina*' ('Alas, we want meat') was their constant cry."[44] And when at last the people were re-united, the men showed their great pleasure by giving the women gowns, girdles, corn, "and plenty of the flesh of elk, deer, bear and antelope."[45]

In the ritual too a good deal of emphasis is laid on hunting. During the Powamu season when the So'yoko, bogey Katcinas, go the rounds threatening to carry off bad children, young boys are defended by their relatives who hold them up as skillful hunters and who finally ransom the little fellows with gifts of meat (p. 218). Again, at the culmination of the Soyal ceremony, hunting prayer-sticks are distributed to men and boys who hasten to deposit them at the Antelope shrine with prayers for success in the hunt (p. 144). From such evidence it appears likely that at one stage of their cultural development the Hopi were far more dependent on game as a food supply than they are at present.

Stephen has left us a description of an old-fashioned antelope hunt which seems to have closely resembled the Plains method of driving animals into the narrowing portion of a V-shaped enclosure;[46] but in modern times the supply of antelopes has grown so small that they have become unimportant as a food source. Nowadays the rabbit is the only game to be found in the region, and the Hopi have a myth to show that a close relationship exists between the antelope, once a favorite animal with hunters, and the rabbit which has now taken its place. "Tihküyiwuqti is mother of the antelope, deer, mountain sheep and both kinds of rabbits. She gave birth to two antelopes, and the blood that issued from her during the birth she confined in a little puddle. . . . Of this blood soaked sand, she made five little pellets and formed them into five rabbits and from these all rabbits are descended."[47]

[41] A full account of these proceedings, based on observations made in 1934, occurs in Titiev, 1938a.

[42] Parties were formerly arranged on Third Mesa at which boys sang while girls took turns grinding to the music. Stephen describes such a gathering as a "Musical Grinding Party" in Parsons, 1936b, pp. 153, 154. A mythological origin is ascribed to this custom, and at

Oraibi the "female" Katcinas called Palhik grind corn i[n] time to music. See p. 125.

[43] Hough, 1898, p. 141.
[44] Stephen, 1929, p. 4.
[45] Stephen, 1929, p. 4.
[46] Parsons, 1936b, pp. 277–279.
[47] Parsons, 1936b, p. 1006.

Rabbit hunts are usually communal affairs and may be held whenever the pressure of other duties is not too great.[48] Late summer, after the crops are sown and the farm plots weeded, is looked upon as a good season for hunting. Any man, regardless of his clan affiliations, may act as the chief (*mongwi*), and as in the case of a Katcina dance sponsor, he is supposed to relieve the Village chief of his duties for the day (p. 65). Much ritual accompanies the successful performance of a hunt. When a man decides to serve as a hunting chief (*mak-mongwi*) he prepares a series of prayer-feathers for the patron deity of game animals, Tuwapongwuhti or Tihkuyiwuhti.[49] In addition, for birds of prey like Cooper's hawk (*kisa*), he makes plain *nakwakwosi*; for the Sun, in order that it may furnish good weather, he makes a *nakwakwosi* with a breath line attached; and for jack and cotton tail rabbits he makes special prayer-sticks of a smaller size than usual. From these the tip is cut off and thrown into the fire so that the flesh may cook well, and the breath line may be cut to facilitate the death of rabbits.[50] The sponsor then goes to a common crier or to the head of the Rabbit clan, and after a smoke, he asks him to announce the hunt and to give details as to date, place of assembly, and the direction to be taken during the drive. Regardless of the hunt chief's specific assertion regarding the animal to be hunted, the announcement is worded generally to include all varieties of game.

On the next day the *mak-mongwi* deposits the prayer-offerings in a cavity excavated in the sand, facing the one for the Sun towards the east and the others in the direction of the hunting ground. Within the hole the chief then builds a small fire, into which he places several pellets of rabbit dung, bits of rabbit food such as sage or grass, and cornmeal as a prayer for success and for the safety of the hunters. If the sponsor's heart is good, all will go well, but if he has evil thoughts or is a witch, accidents are liable to befall the men. The little fire is then nearly smothered, and a large bonfire kindled as a signal to the villagers that the hunt is to begin. At once the men approach, and each casts some rabbit manure on the ceremonial fire and passes his stick through the smoke. In recent times no special costume is worn, but Stephen describes an elaborate system of painting that was once in vogue for rabbit hunters on First Mesa.[51]

When all is ready the hunt chief divides the group into two parts and appoints someone to lead one division while he takes charge of the other. They start out in two wide circuits, heading in opposite directions until it is judged that they have covered a sufficiently large area. Then, at a given signal, they approach each other, cross, and begin on a smaller loop, gradually closing in until only a little territory is left in which the trapped rabbits may run about. Then the men throw their sticks at the game and the slaughter begins. The old-fashioned rabbit sticks were flat-bladed, non-returnable "boomerangs," fashioned from scrub oak and called *putcko*. Stout, straight clubs called *makmorziko*, about two feet long and one inch in diameter, were also used; and the men were adept at hurling their weapons to strike a rabbit whether it was standing still or in rapid motion.

In the past it was understood that whoever killed a rabbit outright got undisputed possession, but a series of rules covered the title to wounded beasts. Regardless of who inflicted the wound, a rabbit belonged to the person who succeeded in capturing or killing it. If a man who was temporarily without a weapon attracted the attention of another to a rabbit, the animal went directly to the one who struck the fatal blow; otherwise it was left free for its ultimate captor or slayer. In neither case did the unarmed man who first noticed it have any claim to the quarry. If a rabbit were seized by a dog, it was not automatically the property of the dog's owner, but belonged to whichever of the hunters happened to snatch it away. In the event that a jack rabbit was seen to enter a badger or a prairie dog hole, it was considered the property of the man who saw it disappear, and he might dig for it unmolested. On the other hand, if a cotton tail sought such refuge, it might be sought by anyone in the vicinity, and if it were driven to the surface, it went to whatever man could catch it. There was one difference in the customs of Second and Third Mesa that often led to disputes whenever hunters from the one place happened to join with a group from the other. When some men were mounted and the others on foot, it was the Second Mesa

---

[48] Rabbit hunting on Second Mesa is described in Beaglehole, E., 1936, pp. 11–17.

[49] These are two names for the same deity.

[50] Compare the following account of Oraibi procedure with Parsons, 1936b, pp. 1023, 1024; and with Curtis, 1922, pp. 45 ff. [51] Parsons, 1936b, p. 1023.

rule that the fellow on horseback could not dismount to chase the game. At Oraibi, however, a man might ride or run as he pleased. If, in the course of a joint hunt, an Oraibi man happened to dismount when he thought it more convenient, it never failed to evoke a storm of protest from the people of Second Mesa. In spite of rules and regulations, it sometimes happened that two men entered into a dispute concerning title to a slain rabbit. If they seemed unable to come to a decision, it was the privilege of any one of the older men who happened to be nearby to pick up the rabbit, perform a discharming motion by waving it four times round his head with his left hand, and to walk off with it. This was done to shame the disputants and to show them the futility of quarreling over one beast when there were still so many left to be slain.

From time to time throughout the day new circles were formed, and the hunt continued until the leader decided to call a halt. He then made a formal announcement to the effect that the drive was over, and after thanking the participants, he would bid them return home with happy hearts. Each man brought his game to the village and turned it over to wife, mother, sister, or paternal aunt as he desired. The recipient thanked him and laid the slain rabbits and the hunting sticks in a line on the floor. She would then proceed to "feed" them by putting a pinch of meal in the mouths of the rabbits and by sprinkling some on the sticks. This done, she would skin and clean each rabbit, place a bit of its gall on a fragment of *piki* bread, add a pinch of salt and a piece of the rabbit's fur, extend it towards the dead beast and then throw the offering into the fire. When she had thus given each of the creatures a "lunch," she would wash the stains from her hands directly over the fire in token of returning the blood that had been spilled. This rite was called "sending them home" and was performed in order that Tuwapongwuhti might have her "children" restored to her, and so consent to letting the Hopi kill all the rabbits they pleased on future hunts.[52]

There were also prescribed ways of dressing and cooking the kill. If it were a cotton tail, the ears were fastened at the back of the head very much like the hair knot worn by the old-fashioned Hopi men. If it were a jack rabbit, the ears were bound together at the front of the head. In either case, the hind feet were crossed at the back and the front legs were doubled under. Only after it was prepared in this fashion was a rabbit considered ready for the fire.

Sometimes mixed hunts were held with boys and girls alternating in the two lines as they formed constantly narrowing circles. These were called *neyangmakiwa* and were generally regarded as a sort of festivity.[53] Whenever a rabbit was slain, the nearest girls would dash madly for it, the winner carrying off the spoils. Then too if a girl succeeded in grasping a wounded rabbit or in snatching one away from a dog, she might keep it for herself. If a boy made a kill in a spot where no girls happened to be at the moment he might try to retain the rabbit for himself, but this was of little avail as the first girl to see the dead beast was allowed to snatch it from him, and if he got as far as the village unobserved, the women who had stayed at home were permitted to despoil him. In exchange for the game they received on such occasions, the girls would prepare *somiviki* and other foods, which their male relatives would carry into the fields for them. At Oraibi the mixed hunts were free of formal courtship elements, but at Second Mesa a girl might propose to a boy in conventional fashion by giving him a loaf of *qömi* instead of the ordinary refreshments.[54]

On Third Mesa there was no ceremony attached, insofar as my oldest informants could remember, to a boy's first killing of a rabbit, but on First and Second Mesas there was a brief observance of the event. "On the occasion when a boy kills his first rabbit, he is, or should be, initiated as a hunter," reports Curtis.[55] A ceremonial father is chosen who makes the boy bend over while facing in each of the four directions. Each time, the "father" makes a motion with the slain rabbit, as if drawing it from the bent-over boy to himself. For the next two days the youth eats neither meat nor salt; on the evening of the third day a rabbit hunt is announced with the novice in the rôle of sponsor; and on the morning

---

[52] Compare Beaglehole, E., 1936, p. 13.

It is hard to tell what part of the rabbit hunting ritual may be regarded as "totemic." The head of the Rabbit clan announces hunting plans and makes prayer-sticks for rabbits and game animals at Soyal; and Rabbit clansmen call their eponym "uncle," yet they freely kill and eat it.

[53] Nequatewa, 1933, p. 42. The Hopi author states that girls' adolescence rites culminate with a mixed rabbit hunt. Also compare Beaglehole, E., 1936, p. 13.

[54] Nequatewa, 1933, p. 42.

[55] Curtis, 1922, p. 46. Hunting initiation for Second Mesa is also described in Beaglehole, E., 1936, pp. 14–16

of the fourth day, ceremonial father and son bathe at daybreak in a spring, and the boy, painted like a Katcina initiate, acts as chief of the hunters during the day's activities.

Deer, mountain sheep, and antelope hunts present several variations from the manner of the rabbit drives.[56] When a party of men has arrived at the site chosen by a sponsor, they clear a level space in front of their camp and lay their guns[57] on it side by side and facing south. Then the entire party makes a series of *nakwakwosi* for Tuwapongwuhti, Hawk, Eagle, other strong birds of prey, and the Sun and the Moon. These are placed in a little plaque and smoked over in customary ceremonial fashion with the exchange of reciprocal kinship terms by the smokers as the pipe passes from man to man. A messenger is then chosen by the hunt chief to deposit the prayer-offerings at some distance from the camp, but in any direction he sees fit. He is supposed to start off while the others are talking and to keep going until their voices are inaudible. Then he stops, deposits the *nakwakwosi* on the ground, takes four places and pauses to listen. This pacing and listening is repeated four times, the messenger being careful to remember what he hears, as various sounds are considered divinatory for the success or failure of the hunt. While the courier is away, the others watch the rifles closely for auguries. If a little whirlwind (*duviphaiyan*) seems to play along the rifle barrels, it is considered especially lucky. On his return the messenger is thanked and asked to describe what he has heard, and the sponsor then determines the nature of the omens. These are supposed to be favorable if the hunt chief has a "good heart." The sound of a crow, owl, or coyote is thought to augur well for the hunters. For some reason, unknown to present-day informants, men were forbidden to shave or to pluck their whiskers while taking part in hunting expeditions.

When deer and antelope were hunted from horseback, the group would meet at a designated spot and begin a concerted drive as soon as they had raised a herd; but when the pursued animals broke formation and began to strike out in various directions, each man singled out one beast and went after it alone. Deer might be shot or clubbed, but not stabbed, and the appropriate way to kill an antelope was to catch it round the neck, somewhat in the manner of dogging a steer, and to

smother it to death. When it was deemed time for the hunters to start in pursuit of single beasts, no shouting was permitted, but each man had to signal with his hands to indicate which creature he intended to follow. Riders were not permitted to run their horses until they were definitely on the track of the animal they intended to kill.

No special ceremonies attended the skinning and cleaning of deer or antelopes, but a bit of cornmeal was generally thrown to the guts of the slain beast. The preliminary rites, however, were very similar to those described for rabbit hunts, except that antelope dung was thrown into the small ritual blaze instead of rabbit manure. It seems to have been customary at one time to let people snatch legs and other parts of a carcass being brought home by a successful hunter, until the slayer had left for his own portion only the head, skin, and breast region. Many lazy people thus found it more profitable to keep a sharp lookout for returning hunters than to take active part in the chase.

While the hunting of coyotes, *islalai*, had many features in common with other pursuits of game, it was the most distinctive of the circle drives, so much so that the name Pongovi (Circle Kiva) at Oraibi was specifically associated with the Coyote clan. Instead of being communal or open to all who cared to join, coyote hunts were generally carried on by kiva groups. When a man decided to lead a drive for coyotes, he first smoked with the head of his own kiva and informed him of his plans. If no objections were raised, the sponsor who was to act as hunt chief, *mak-mongwi*, then visited all the other kivas to smoke and announce the coming chase. If his mission were known beforehand, he was invited to enter a kiva not in the customary terms, but with a warning to be careful, "*Pasi!*" Then he seated himself west of the fireplace and north of the kiva chief who sat beside him to his right. The latter filled and lit a pipe in the usual fashion, but instead of the conventional exchange of terms of relationship, the smokers indulged in various pleasantries regarding each other's love affairs. "I hear you've been having a good time with so-and-so," a smoker would say, naming one of the other fellow's past or present mistresses; and the other would return the compliment to the vast amusement of the spectators, and sometimes to the surprise and chagrin of a husband or lover.[58]

---

[56] Compare Beaglehole, E., 1936, pp. 3–11.

[57] I could not discover what rites were performed when

men used to hunt with bows and arrows.

[58] This was not the only time that a Hopi man was liable

When the smoking was concluded, the sponsor told the kiva chief the true purpose of his mission and gave him the necessary details in regard to meeting places and the area to be covered. As soon as the leader of the hunt had gone on to the next kiva to make his announcement, the head man of the kiva just visited began to prepare the required *nakwakwosi*.

Next morning, before the men assembled, all the kiva heads together with the hunt chief deposited their offerings at the meeting ground. Then the kiva groups set out, each acting as a unit, but all combining ultimately into one large circle and closing in on each other as in a rabbit hunt. As they went the men beat two sticks together and cried out, "Ya, ya, ya!" to rout the game, but if an animal had been started before the lines had become continuous, signals were made by hand for whatever men were nearest to start in pursuit. So long as the game was within the enclosure made by the various groups, each man had to maintain his position, but if a beast broke outside the lines, it was permissible to leave the circle and to give chase. As the circle grew smaller and smaller, the hunters began to make attempts to kill their prey, and when the signal was given, everyone closed in to strike or grab as many animals as he could. Although a hunt may have been officially organized for coyotes, the Hopi were too realistic to overlook rabbits, prairie dogs, or whatever other game had been surrounded.

Rules similar to those in force on rabbit drives also prevailed on coyote hunts. Only killing a beast outright could give a man undisputed title. Wounded animals or those caught by dogs belonged to anyone who could seize or dispatch them. To this rule there was one exception; if a man's stick happened to penetrate a coyote's body, it belonged to the one who had thrown the weapon, regardless of the creature's actual slayer.

When the day's hunting was over, each group carried its booty to its own kiva, and here the carcasses were laid side by side to the north of the fireplace and facing southeast. Then the kiva

chief "fed" each coyote with cornmeal, after which he rolled a cigarette of corn husk and native tobacco and taking a few puffs, put it in turn to the mouth of each beast as in a formal smoke, addressing it as his child.[59] After this rite was finished, the men were free to take home the coyotes they had slain. Since the flesh was inedible, the animal was skinned but not cut open, and the gall offering made to rabbits was omitted. Instead, the owner made a set of *nakwakwosi*, one for each leg and one for the heart. In addition, he sometimes inserted a bit of turquoise into the mouth as a present, and he was required to draw a line with red *suta*, down the middle of the beast's forehead to the nose.[60] The hunter then took the skinned body to the edge of the mesa where he affixed a *nakwakwosi* to each leg and placed a fifth in position against the heart. After expressing thanks to the creature for having allowed itself to be slain, he prayed to it for success in future hunts and asked it to tell its parents to raise more coyotes and to send them to the Hopi. At the same time, he prayed for rain, good grass, and plentiful rabbits. Then he deposited the carcass in a crevice where it could not be reached by buzzards or crows, and went home. At some time in the future, when dances were held in Pa-muya (January), the prowess of a skillful coyote hunter might be celebrated in song, his name being mentioned as a mighty warrior.[61]

Recently, it has become more and more the fashion for men to spend a part of each winter in coyote trapping. Like the old-fashioned hunt, this pursuit too has become the object of a good deal of ritual, although the men well realize that their ancestors lacked the equipment now considered necessary for such enterprises. The man in charge of the trapping expedition is known as the hunt chief, *mak-mongwi*, and may belong to any clan or kiva. Volunteers make up the party, and no ritual attends their departure for the site chosen by the leader. Upon their arrival at the proper location, the head man urges his people to get the traps set out as soon as possible. Some beast of little value, usually an old horse, is killed and

---

to hear a shocking bit of news regarding his wife or sweetheart. At the Wuwutcim-Marau teasings too names of lovers are freely paired, and it is considered bad form to show jealousy. See p. 132.

[59] Note that in the old days a warrior always addressed an enemy scalp which he had taken as his "child" (p. 160, footnote 35).

[60] This is because warriors often marked their faces

with *suta* in similar fashion, and the coyote is thought to be a brave fighter. In fact, one of the most important warrior clans at Oraibi is the Coyote, to which the War chief belongs.

[61] Compare p. 160. This is the third trait indicating the close resemblance in Hopi opinion between a coyote hunt and war. The other two are addressing a slain animal as one's "child" and painting it with warrior markings.

cut up so that its flesh may be used as bait. Each man, carrying his traps on his back, drags off his share of the meat in a different direction, then baits and sets the traps in strategic positions so that they cannot be too readily dragged off by the captured animals.

That same night, after supper, the sponsor directs his men in the preparation of the proper prayer-offerings. First he makes a *nakwakwosi* with breath line (*hik'si*) attached, and then three without lines, all "for coyotes." After he has finished and deposited the *nakwakwosi* in a plate set before him, all the others in the party do the same. Then the leader, followed by his men, makes offerings, in order, for Tuwapongwuhti, Kisa (Cooper's hawk), other powerful birds, the Sun, and the Moon. When these are ready, the chief prepares a pipe of native tobacco and a ritual smoke is held. Next, a messenger is appointed to deposit the *nakwakwosi* with appropriate prayers in specific places designated by the leader. Coyote is to be placated; Tuwapongwuhti is asked to be generous with her "children"; Hawk is begged to bestow some of his luck and ability on the trappers; Sun is beseeched for good weather; and Moon is looked to for guidance and protection in the night. When the messenger has executed his orders, he returns and all go to bed with wishes for good dreams from the sponsor.

The next morning each man sets out to look after his traps, to secure any beast that has been caught, and to track and recover those which have dragged off their snares. If a coyote is found to be alive, the trapper is expected to stroke it gently until he can work his hand around its throat, press its head into the sand and so smother it. Most men would take the chance of being bitten rather than kill a trapped coyote in any other fashion. If a slain beast is not too heavy and not too far distant, it may be carried into camp; but if this is inconvenient, it is skinned wherever found. Prior to the skinning, the trapper smokes "with" the dead coyote and prepares *nakwakwosi* for its legs and heart. After the operation, the prayer-feathers are suitably affixed and the body disposed of with thanks and prayers for future success.

It is customary for the leader of a trapping party to spend the greater part of his time en-

couraging and helping his men rather than in the active pursuit of skins. Accordingly, he is the first one back to camp each day, so that he may welcome and thank his men when they come in. As the trappers return, they hand over the skins or dead beasts to the sponsor, who lays the day's catch by the fire and prays and smokes over it for the benefit of all, although each man retains the title to his own booty.

If it is found advisable to shift camp from time to time, the first night's ritual is not repeated, and the leader is considered free to devote himself as fully to trapping as do the others. No ceremonies mark the termination of the expedition, and no tabus are imposed on any of the members either during their stay in the field or upon their return to the village.

The recent shrinkage of the game supply has been compensated in large measure by the increase of sheep raising activities among the Hopi. Within the last fifty years almost every adult male has managed to secure a small flock, and there is scarcely a household whose members are not partners in a herd. This does not mean that there is joint ownership, for, in fact, every sheep and lamb is assigned to a specific owner, but men keep their flocks together for convenience. In this way, one sheep corral, one spring or well, and one hut built near the grazing ground, suffice for all the partners. Unlike the Navaho, Hopi women and girls never tend the flocks, and even grown boys are only seldom asked to herd.[62] This puts a heavy strain on the men, especially during the planting and harvest seasons, and it is felt that co-operation is absolutely essential if the sheep are not to be neglected. Accordingly, partnerships are formed among brothers, between fathers and sons, or with other relatives, so that each man may divide his time between his flocks and his fields. The most common schedule of labor is to have a man herd for two or more days at a stretch and to spend the intervening nights at the sheep camp. He is then off duty while the other partners take their turns at herding, and it is not too difficult for all of them to adjust their farming programs to avoid a conflict with sheep herding duties. Men who keep their flocks at some distance from the village generally have a stock of provisions at their field houses and pre-

[62] At the same time fathers take pains nowadays to train their sons to become good shepherds. Everywhere one hears men saying, "I want my boy to grow up to be a good sheep herder," a significant change of attitude from former days when farming ability was of paramount importance.

pare their own meals, but those who quarter their sheep nearby usually take a lunch of *piki* bread and water with them and eat breakfast and supper at home. Only when the sheep shearing season arrives do the women accompany their husbands or brothers into the fields to keep house while the men are busied with their tasks.

Thanks to their intelligent and increasingly careful control of breeding, the Hopi have succeeded in greatly improving their sheep both as regards numbers and in respect to strain. In this way it has recently come about that a man's economic rating sometimes depends more on his flocks than on his possession of good farming land. A young man who sold his entire share of a herd, amounting to about 100 head, for 300 dollars in cash in 1933, was branded a fool by one and all, although the sum was a fortune even in the opinion of his severest critics. And when the U. S. Government, before inaugurating a program of erosion control, suggested that the Hopi and the Navaho sell off a portion of their flocks to relieve congestion on the over-grazed ranges, the howl of protest that went up from the agricultural Hopi was even greater than that which was raised by their Navaho neighbors.

The high value imputed to sheep makes a Hopi hesitate long before he does any butchering. Rarely does he slaughter a sheep merely for the sake of adding fresh meat to his daily diet, but on special occasions he freely contributes as many head as are necessary. Naming day festivities for recently, born children, Katcina and other ceremonial dances, and especially the elaborate wedding rites—all are occasions that can be properly celebrated only with feasts which comprise flesh foods.

The utter lack of any device for refrigeration makes it impossible for Hopi housewives to keep meat fresh for any length of time. Accordingly, whatever surplus there is, is put out to dry in the sun. Sometimes it is stored away in large cuts after it has been thoroughly jerked; at other times it is pounded fine, mixed with a little fat and eaten in loosely shredded form rather than compressed into pemmican. In order to avoid reducing their herds too rapidly, some shepherds keep a few goats with their sheep and use the former as a source of meat. On the other hand, many of the

men feel that it is futile to waste care on less valuable creatures whose consumption of grass and water makes it more difficult for the sheep to thrive.

Possession of cattle has had a far less profound effect on the economy of the Hopi than has the introduction of sheep. It takes more money to buy an initial stock than the average man can afford, so that at present there are comparatively few cattle owners among the Hopi. Furthermore, the habit of turning cattle loose to graze and only occasionally rounding them up, has had a most disturbing effect on the lives of the people. Whereas sheep are constantly under supervision, cattle are not watched daily, and they readily break through fences to get at the growing crops. Thus there is a good deal of friction between the owners of cattle and the other villagers, nor is there any way for such disputes to be satisfactorily concluded. As we have previously noted, the Hopi are entirely devoid of any political mechanism for passing and enforcing laws, and no compulsion can be brought to bear on an obstinate cattle owner who refuses to pay for damages rendered by his herd.[63]

In the years that have elapsed since they were first introduced by the Spanish, horses have become a fixed part of Hopi economy. Wild mustangs are still to be seen from time to time, and an enterprising young man need never want for a steed. It is not the cost of a horse that is troublesome, but the nuisance of maintaining it is an important consideration. To buy fodder is too great an expense, so a man must turn his horses loose daily in order that they may forage for themselves. The customary procedure is to drive the horses out to a suitable pasturage and there to hobble them so that they cannot wander too far afield. However, they must be taken to a considerable distance from the village in order that they may not disturb any one's crops. When horses are being used every day, it requires a good deal of exertion on the part of the owner to drive them out each night and to round them up again the next morning. In many cases, the men of one household own horses jointly, and co-operate both in their use and in their care.

Mules are far more expensive than horses because they are stronger and hardier. Accordingly,

---

[63] Tawaqwaptiwa, Village chief of Oraibi, said that as corn was the basis of Hopi life he always favored farmers in disputes with herders. As much corn as a man could carry was regarded as fair compensation for losses.

Nowadays the Hopi are getting into the habit of reporting such difficulties to government agents, but many of them prefer to squabble indefinitely among themselves rather than appeal to white men for help.

they are preferred for the heavy work of hauling wagons while horses are broken primarily to the saddle. Nevertheless, those men who cannot afford to own enough horses and mules to be discriminating do not hesitate to use either beast in any way possible.

The growing increase in the use of wagons in the last few years has been responsible for the steady reduction of burros among the Hopi. Very little attention is paid to these homely creatures, who, though hobbled, wander freely about the village eking out a miserable existence by eating whatever garbage they are lucky enough to find in the streets or on the refuse heaps.

Owing to the fact that Hopi women are not taught how to handle horses, it falls to the men to do whatever hauling of heavy objects happens to be necessary. Wagons, sold to them by the American government on a liberal time-payment plan, have made such tasks far less wearisome than in the days when all burdens had to be packed on burros or carried in large baskets on one's own back. In spite of the easy terms offered by the government, it is only rarely that a family can afford to purchase more than one wagon for all its male membership. This is another economic feature, which, like care of horses and the herding of sheep, has the effect of enforcing cooperation among men. One of the main uses of wagons is for hauling wood to be used as fuel. In the course of time all the available timber close to the villages has been exhausted, and it has become more and more necessary to go to a considerable distance to gather wood. Until the use of wagons became practically universal, this involved a good deal of time and labor. Even now the men find it necessary to devote two days to each load, riding out some ten or fifteen miles to timber country and loading up the first day, and driving home slowly on the next. Usually, five or six trips are made during the fall to ensure a sufficient supply for the winter. If more wood is needed, supplementary trips are made whenever time and weather permit.

In addition to farming, herding, and caring for the livestock, it is the duty of a Hopi man to provide all the wearing apparel, both everyday and ceremonial, for himself and his family.[64] As a rule, the winter season with its freedom from farming tasks is utilized for this purpose. Looms are erected either in the kivas or at home, and men devote such time as they can spare from sheep herding or from the requirements of various rituals to weaving or to the making of moccasins. Apart from ordinary garments, people of either sex had to be provided in former times with special things at various stages of their lives. For a baby boy it was requisite that within about the first twenty days of his life his father, sometimes his grandfather, should make for him a little black, or black and grey striped cotton blanket called *pisalhöya*. Then at the age of eight or nine, just prior to his Katcina initiation, a lad was supposed to get a sort of G-string called *kokomvitcuna*, made of cotton and colored with black sweet corn dye. In later times these were dyed blue with indigo said to have been traded from Isleta. At one end of this garment there was a design of two concentric circles. It was first worn at the time of a Snake or Flute dance and was an indication that the boy was no longer a baby. If death should overtake a little boy, he would wear his *kokomvitcuna* as his apparel in the realm of the dead (Maski), but if he did not own one he would have to go naked in the other world. Some years after his Katcina initiation, when a youth had reached the adolescent stage, his own or his ceremonial father would make for him a *du-i-vitcuna*, a dance skirt of the type worn in Katcina dances. In addition to its ordinary uses, this garment was also supposed to comprise the wearing apparel of young men who died before attaining maturity. Not many years after this period a youth was eligible for his Tribal Initiation, during the course of which he received a garment known as *kelkwaisi*. At the conclusion of his novitiate, it could be converted to a dance kilt of the Katcina kind, and the belt, *kelkewea*, could be put to any practical purpose such as a burro cinch. In adult life, at about the age of 35 or 40, a man might make for himself a *sakwavitcuna*, a garment between a G-string and a kilt in size. It was all blue except for three parallel black stripes at the ends and two stripes at the center. It was a favorite garment to wear during the performance of daily duties; it might be used

[64] Owing to time considerations I was forced to omit many aspects of material culture from my investigations in the field. A good deal of valuable information on this topic may be found in such works as Parsons, 1936b, pp. 1181–1190; Colton, M. R. F., 1930; Colton, M. R. F., 1931; Nequatewa, 1933; Douglas, 1938; Kent, 1940; Dennis, W., and M. G., 1940, pp. 107–110; and MacLeish, 1940.

The fullest general treatment, as well as a good bibliography, is to be found in Colton, M. R. F., 1938.

during the "rehearsal" on the day before the Snake dance; and it was the most common garment supposedly worn by grown men in the other world.

For a girl there was a different series of appropriate articles of clothing, beginning with a *kwikwilhöya* in the first twenty days of her life. This was made by her father or by her grand-

Then the proud recipient wore it while observin the performance. From adolescence on, a youn woman wore the conventional garb of puebl females, the *kanelmotcapa*, or *manta*, so cut as t leave bare the left shoulder. This was the typ of garment worn throughout adult life, except fo the wedding costume. As a matter of fact, it wa customary for a bride to receive a *kanelmotcapa*

NAME	HERDING	CORN FIELDS	BEAN PATCHES	MELON PATCHES	HOUSE BUILDING	WOOD HAULING	HORSES ①	MISCELLANEOUS	NO WORK	TOTAL OF DAYS NOTED
LUTHER ②	0	10	3	9½	9½	1	0	14½	3½	51
KING	49	10	1	6	8	7	1	7	9	98
CECIL	22	9	3½	3	20	5	3½	6	10	82
ALEX ③	17	14½	0	3	0	1	9½	3	35	83
DON	22	23	0	1½	0	4	2½	5½	10½	69
TOTALS	110	66½	7½	23	37½	18	16½	36	68	383

① This does not include the routine care of horses.
② LUTHER kept no sheep.
③ ALEX was probably the laziest man in Oraibi.

CHART XI. DAILY WORK CHART COVERING THE PERIOD FROM AUG. 7–NOV. 12, 1933.

father in the event that the father was a poor weaver. It was made like a blanket and was striped across its entire surface both horizontally and vertically. Sometimes, the design was made to represent eyes, in which case the garment was known as a *poskwikwilhöya*. At the age of eight or nine a girl was supposed to receive a dress variously called *kanelkwasai*, *kanelmotcaphöya*, or *tciro*. This was made of natural black wool, with a two or three inch strip of blue along the upper border. It was worn whenever finished, and not in conjunction with any special ceremonial occasion. Not long after her Katcina initiation, an *atuhöya* would be made for a girl, usually by her grandfather, but it was not donned until the occurrence of the first dance of any kind after its completion.

and sometimes an *atu'u*, together with the mor specifically nuptial costume consisting of a larg and a small white cotton robe (*ova*), a big, fringe belt (*wukokwewe*), and a pair of white moccasin with wrapped leggings. A woman was suppose to appear in her bridal robes at the first Nima dance after her wedding, and the possession of th proper outfit was an essential to happiness in th afterlife.

All in all, coupled with the other duties that fe to a man's lot, it was no easy matter for him t keep his family supplied with clothing for dail wear as well as with the garments that carried deeper significance. In order to ascertain the pro portionate time that a Hopi devotes to such task as farming, sheep herding, care of horses an mules, and other duties, a record was kept over a period of several months in 1933–1934 of the daily activities of five adult, married males. A summary of the results is given in chart XI.

One Hopi skill, that of housebuilding, has become increasingly widespread as a corollary to a sociological change. In the days when the rule of matrilocal residence meant that a married daughter lived literally under her mother's roof, the Hopi often enlarged a dwelling but rarely built a new one. Now that daughters prefer to live in houses of their own after marriage there has been a great increase of building activity. Although some modern tools and methods have been introduced, the essential features of construction follow the old pattern described by Mindeleff.[65] The single square or rectangular room is still regarded as the essential unit, and although houses become the exclusive property of women, the men are expected to do the greater part of the heavy work.

A Hopi builder first chooses a site on a piece of unoccupied ground, usually within the pueblo's limits, marks off its dimensions, and then proceeds to gather the needed materials. Before actual construction begins, however, he is supposed to go to the Village chief who prepares four *nakwakwosi* for Masau'u and the Sun. These are placed at the four corners of the proposed structure, after which the location of the doorway is determined. Then the builder dresses the stones to be used for walls while the women prepare a mud plaster. When the walls have been built to the required height, a number of men put the main roof beams into position, and women workers finish the roof by adding layers of twigs, grass, and adobe to the big beams. Prayer-offerings are affixed to various parts of the house at this stage, and bits of food are scattered about with prayers that Masau'u may grant the inmates long life.

Mealing stones (*metates*) for grinding cornmeal, arranged in little bins, are the most important indoor furnishings today as they have been in the past, and every woman continues to require ready access to a small chamber containing an oven suitable for baking *piki*, the most essential item of Hopi diet.[66] A mother and her daughters are apt to share the same *piki* oven (*duma*), for it is no easy matter to make a new one, as the proper kind of stone must be fetched either from a place called Duma, ten or fifteen miles south of Oraibi, or from a deposit of rock at Manakavi, which lies about twelve miles southwest of the village. To begin with, a woman who desires a new *duma* must secure the services of her husband or another male relative to act as director of an expedition to the quarrying ground. If a man consents to undertake the leadership he makes *nakwakwosi* at the next Soyal to announce his responsibility and to make public the news that a quarrying expedition is being planned during the coming year. Unrelated men and women may arrange to join the party which usually sets out in the fall or spring, as the Hopi believe that unseasonable frost would result if people were to fetch stones while the crops were growing.

When the right time comes the leader tells his group the exact number of days that he will remain in charge of the work,[67] and then departs for the quarrying place ahead of the others in order to make a shrine for the reception of prayer-offerings. Each participant prepares a sacred object, and married couples, "putting their hearts together," generally manufacture a *nakwakwosi* on the night before they leave. All prayer-objects are given to the sponsor as soon as their makers arrive, and he deposits them at the shrine. Then the workers are free to hunt about until they find a suitable slab of rock, about 3 feet long, $2\frac{1}{2}$ feet wide, and 3 inches thick. A bit of cornmeal is sprinkled towards the spot where the stone lies, and it is then hewed out, loaded on a burro and brought home.[68]

Before a *duma* is ready to be installed in its *piki* house, it must be levelled off by grinding with coarse gravel or by pounding with a rock until it is smooth and even. Cotton seed is then chewed or ground to extract an oil with which the stone is carefully polished. The actual installation must be performed in secret by a skilled baker. If the owner of the new stone lacks the necessary experience, she calls on a trusted kinswoman to act for her, but if a woman has the requisite skill, she may do the work herself.[69] After the *duma* is in

[65] Mindeleff, 1891, pp. 101, ff.
[66] For First Mesa customs regarding *piki* ovens, see Parsons, 1936b, pp. 1195–1197.
[67] When his self-imposed tour of duty has expired, the leader returns to the pueblo. It is considered bad luck for anyone to quarry thereafter until a new director has assumed charge of the operations.

[68] The popular attitude towards a *duma* is that it resembles a living girl or woman in that it makes *piki* bread. Accordingly, it is not only addressed in prayer, but if a party stops to eat while conveying a stone, it must be fed too.
[69] In a case where a spiteful or jealous woman was picked, she might easily contrive to damage the new stone.

position, a fire is built under it with piñon wood as fuel. It is regulated carefully to a medium heat as excessive firing would tend to crack the stone. Once the stone is heated to the right degree a quantity of piñon sap is rubbed in thoroughly, after which an oily mixture of crushed watermelon seeds is applied and allowed to penetrate.

When the *duma* is considered ready, the woman in charge bakes a quantity of *piki*, using only white cornmeal and salt but no ashes. After this is finished, she makes the first batch of conventional blue *piki*. Throughout the baking she watches carefully for flaws and, if the batter shows a tendency to stick here or there she corrects the defect, usually by the vigorous application of more grease. A bit of the first white and blue *piki* that is baked on a new stone is torn off and fed to the fire and to the *duma*. The rest is consumed in the usual way, and the new oven is now considered fit for everyday use. Unmarried girls learn to make *piki* on their mothers' *dumas;* but after she is married, a woman likes to have one for herself, and in the course of time her husband is expected to help her secure it.

The quarrying, preparation, and installation of a new grinding stone is conducted very much along the same lines as for a *duma*. Once in place, these utensils are seldom or never removed to other quarters, and inheritance implies the right of use rather than actual possession. Such household implements are the exclusive property of women regardless of how much labor a man may have contributed to their acquirement.

Apart from the cares of motherhood and occasional tasks such as helping with house construction and repair, or weaving plaques or baskets,[70] a Hopi woman's time is devoted almost entirely to domestic tasks of which the most important is the preparation of food. To this end she must not only fetch water and chop the daily supply of wood,[71] but she must also spend hours and hours kneeling at a metate and grinding vast amounts of cornmeal which forms the base of so many Hopi foods. Of these the most widely used

is *piki*, a paper-thin "biscuit," made of a batter cornmeal and water, leavened with ashes, ar baked in crisp sheets on a hot, well greased fl stone.[72] It is then folded and rolled into "loave about one inch in diameter and about ten inch long. *Piki* may be allowed to retain the natur color of the ingredients of which it is mac (bluish-gray), or it may be tinted by the additic of various vegetable dyes. One form of white *pi* is called *avatcviki* and another, which is on rarely made, is known as *wupilangviki*. It is som what thicker than ordinary *piki*, folded in squares, and decorated with wavy lines produc by running the fingers through the batter whi it is being baked. *Piki* is generally moistened water or liquid food of any kind at one end, whic is then bitten off in the mouth; but sometimes it crumbled, salted, and toasted, and eaten as a so of "corn flake" called *piklak kutoki*.

Several foods are made of sweetened cornme to which other ingredients are sometimes added The most popular of these at present are *somivik tcukuviki*, and *tanguviki*, all of which are wrappe in corn husks, boiled, and served in little tie packets. Other preparations containing sweetene cornmeal which are regarded as old-fashioned ar are seldom seen except on occasions such as Masau Katcina dance (p. 237), are *polompikav* "doughnuts" strung on yucca fiber; *sakwavikavik* "pancakes" strung on yucca; and *hanovikavik* large "pancakes" served singly. Among the Hop every dance day is the occasion for a feast, ar virtually every home keeps a sort of open hous One of the most popular refreshments served these times is *pikami*, a mixture of cornmeal an wheat sprouts sweetened and steamed overnigh and even the poorer households generally contriv to have on hand an ample supply of *nukwivi*, stew made of boiled mutton and hominy.[74]

In addition, the more common items on th modern Hopi menu are tortillas made of cornme or white flour and served either dry or fried in deep grease such as lard;[75] beans of many varietie boiled in water to which fat has been added; chil

[70] Many years ago the women of Third Mesa used to make pottery, but in recent years this custom has been restricted to First Mesa. In fashioning basketry, Third Mesa women use the twining method but the women of Second Mesa employ the coiling technique.

[71] Although men cut and haul wood into the town (p. 195), women usually do the daily chopping. I have seen women even in the last stages of pregnancy chopping wood.

[72] The best description of *piki* baking occurs in Curtis, 1922, p. 43.

[73] The most complete list of Hopi foods and recipe may be found in Beaglehole, E., 1937, pp. 60–71.

Additional material dealing with the vegetable food primarily occurs in Fewkes, 1896c; Hough, 1898; Whi ing, 1939; and Vestal, 1940.

[74] In contrast to the feasting indulged in by spectato is the observance of food tabus on salt, meat, and fat b performers.

[75] White flour and lard are obtained at local tradin posts. They are not aboriginal foods.

peppers either baked or fried in grease; and in season, boiled or roasted squash and pumpkins, a variety of melons, and peaches. Neither goats nor cows are milked, and only the most "up-to-date" natives have learned to use dairy products. The most popular beverages, tea and coffee, have received virtually universal acceptance,[76] and have supplanted such aboriginal brews as were formerly in vogue.[77]

There is no essential difference in the foods served adults or juveniles. Even before youngsters are completely weaned they learn to sit by their elders and to dip occasionally into the common pot that is set out on the floor. Hard foods are generally moistened for them, and their coffee is usually diluted with cold water, but on the whole children are permitted to eat what they please. It is very likely that the high infant mortality of the Hopi may be due as much to improper feeding as to the utter lack of hygiene or other causes.[78]

The Hopi have long been familiar with Jimson weed, but they use it only rarely,[79] and their only commonly employed narcotic is tobacco, which is generally smoked in pipes or occasionally as cigarettes during ritual exercises.[80] Insofar as can be determined, the Hopi seem never to have indulged in the use of intoxicants. They call all spirituous liquors honakkuyi (crazy water), and only a few schoolboys have begun to acquire a taste for beer and whisky. Their chief condiments are chile, onions, and salt. Sugar is a fairly recent introduction and is known as "sweet salt" (kwangwa önga). The Hopi still prefer natural to refined salt, even where the latter is available, and in the old days the Third Mesa men used to make long, hazardous journeys annually to the vicinity of the Grand Canyon where they mined extensive salt deposits.[81] In former times, when wandering bands of nomads were apt to be encountered within a few miles

of Oraibi, it was no trivial matter to make a salt-gathering expedition, and the entire procedure was accompanied by a series of rituals by which supernatural aid was sought for the safe performance of so dangerous a mission.[82]

Although the Hopi have made a highly satisfactory adjustment to their environment in most respects, and despite the great skill and diligence with which they carry out farming operations, there are seasons when the lack of moisture makes it impossible for them to mature their crops. It is true that the custom of keeping an extra year's supply of corn on hand insures them against famine for that length of time, but should there be two or more successive years of drought, the Hopi find themselves in dire straits. It is in such emergencies that an intimate knowledge of the wild plant life in their locality stands them in good stead. As Hough has pointed out, "So close is the Hopi engrafted into his environment that there is almost no plant which he does not use in some way and no plant to which he has not given a name. It seems to be part of the education of children to familiarize them with the uses of plants."[83] Even in normal years edible tubers called dumma,[84] and the green blossoms known as "Hopi spinach" (nevenkwivi),[85] form welcome additions to the regular diet; but in times when food is scarce, these and a few other species comprise the only means of subsistence.

It is now many years, probably since 1860–1862, that the Hopi have had no famine of major proportions, but memories of the privations and suffering of that trying period are kept alive and vivid in the minds of the populace through the oft-repeated stories of the old people. So it is that despite the margin of safety brought about by their storage of excess corn, and in modern times by their flocks of sheep and goats, the Hopi never feel they are safe from the awful threat of starvation. It may even be that the ever-present

[76] Many old people who have become accustomed to drinking coffee now insist that it was known to the ancient Hopi and has always been part of the Hopi diet. On the other hand, the same people always refuse to add milk or cream because these are considered to be white men's foods.
[77] Consult Whiting, 1939, p. 20, et passim.
[78] Compare Dennis, 1940, p. 34, et passim.
[79] See Whiting, 1939, p. 89.
[80] In rituals the Hopi prefer to use a native tobacco (piiva), see Whiting, 1939, p. 90. In secular life the Hopi regard it as proper for men to smoke cigarettes freely, but pipe smoking is supposed to be correct only for old

men in their homes.
[81] Second and First Mesa men used to visit Salt Lake in New Mexico when they went for salt each year. Such an expedition was made by a group from Second Mesa as recently as 1934.
[82] See Titiev, 1937a.
[83] Hough, 1898, p. 137. However, a more recent investigator has listed a fairly large number of plants that were not generally recognized by his informants. Whiting, 1939, pp. 50, 51.
[84] Parsons, 1936b, pp. 1035, 1036, contains a description of a dumma-gathering expedition.
[85] See p. 140 and footnote 78.

dread of a food shortage has been one of the essential factors that has led them to make a virtue of humility and to decry all vanity and bragging. Thus, for instance, they customarily make a display of poverty before their gods, as when the father of the Katcinas, uncostumed and shabby, mournfully reiterates, "*Nüüookiwa*, I am poor. . . ."[86] The underlying basis for such customs seems to be dread lest a show of over-confidence inspire the deities with the notion that their help is no longer necessary.[87]

On the other hand, particularly when they are impersonating beneficial gods, the Hopi often make lavish displays of food. Presents of edibles and other gifts are distributed in great abundance among onlookers by Katcina dancers, and the clowns known as Koyemsi always make bountiful presentations among onlookers at their performances. Other clowns characteristically indulge in public displays of gluttony, gorging themselves on food provided by their paternal aunts and other relatives.[88] In the public dances of the women's societies too the performers throw many food objects to the spectators, and the men wrangle so fiercely over them that no one pays attention to the rites that are in progress.[89]

In a culture where so much thought and activity is centered on matters of food,[90] the group which functions as an economic unit must be regarded as one of the most fundamental in the society. Judged from this point of view the importance of Hopi clans and households takes on an added significance. At that stage in the cultural evolution of the Hopi when their clans first emerged, each clan probably consisted of a head woman who lived in *the* clan house with her married daughters and their offspring. Each clan owned a farming plot which was tilled jointly by the husband of the head woman, her unmarried sons, and the spouses of her married daughters. Later, when the tendency for large clans to become segmented into two or more households manifested itself (p. 46, ff.), there was very little change in the old system; for all the households within a clan still shared in the ownership of their clan's land.[91] The only difference was that the women of each household now enjoyed only the usufruct of a particular portion of the clan land, and farming was done more or less independently by the men connected with each household.

Thus does the economic system of the Hopi tend to confirm the sociological importance of the clans and their component households.

---

[86] Parsons, 1936b, p. 371.

[87] Because they are afraid that the gods will stop helping them if they admit that everything is going well, the Hopi make it a practice to belittle all their successes. For example, during the growing season in the summer of 1932 the farmers were forever lamenting the lack of rain and bemoaning the state of the crops. In 1933, however, the same men frequently referred to the *past* season as an excellent one, but expressed fears for the current one. Nevertheless, in the fall of 1933, several Hopi went so far as to admit that they had harvested exceptionally fine yields. [88] Parsons, 1936b, p. 1065 and p. 554.

[89] See p. 169 and footnote 43.

[90] Parsons, 1939, pp. 25, 26, has called attention to the fact that certain moral standards and rules of etiquette among the Pueblos are expressive of their "preoccupation with food. . . ."

[91] Land ownership by clans is discussed for First Mesa in Forde, 1931, pp. 367–371; and for Second Mesa in Beaglehole, E., 1937, pp. 14–17.

CHAPTER XVI

THE PIKYAS-PATKI CONFLICT

AS HAS BEEN demonstrated in our discussion of "The Clan-Phratry Problem," the social structure of the Hopi is made up of a number of phratries, each of which contains two or more clans. There are strong bonds uniting the people within the respective clans, but the ties between clans in the same phratry are often very weak. The outstanding example of this situation is the clash between the related Bear and Spider clans that culminated in the split of 1906, but there are other instances of strife between clans belonging to the same phratry. The Sun clan is said to have a traditional warning against the Eagle clan; and at the present time the Pikyas clan, which the Oraibi chief ranks as second to his own, is involved in a controversy with the Patki clan. The story of the latter conflict was narrated to the writer in 1934 by Frank Siemptiwa (pl. II d). Frank is now the head of the Pikyas clan, Village chief of Oraibi's permanent colony at Moenkopi, second to the Oraibi chief in the conduct of the Soyal, and impersonator of the important Aholi Katcina. Naturally, Frank's account is biased in favor of the Pikyas clan, but nevertheless it serves to show how ceremonial privileges and their concomitant titles to land may become a source of bitter dissensions among relatives.[1]

A good number of years ago, a Patki man named Siwinimptiwa began to tell his clanmates that they should be rated higher than the Pikyas people and that, by virtue of the ceremonies which they possessed, they were entitled to a good sized plot of ground. On the other hand, he claimed, the Pikyas people at Oraibi were the descendants of an original Tewa strain from Hano, which meant that they were not true Hopi and were entitled only to a small patch of ground. Thus was brought about the fulfillment of a long-standing prophecy which warned the Pikyas group to beware of the Patki and to have few dealings with them.[2]

According to the Pikyas version, the trouble between the two units began during a temporary failure in the Pikyas succession. Owing to the fact that the last Pikyas officer in the Soyal had died while all the other masculine members of the clan were too young to take his place, the related Patki clan had been asked to choose one of their men to succeed the deceased Pikyas official.[3] In those days, owing to the ever-present danger of enemy attacks, it was customary for the head woman of a clan to learn all the ceremonial lore of her group, so that she could train a successor in the event that an officer were suddenly killed. In the course of time, therefore, when some of the young Pikyas boys had grown up and had entered the Soyal ceremony, their head woman taught one of them the duties of the Pikyas chief in that ritual. When the young man assumed office, his clan claimed the plot of ground that had been given over to the use of the incumbent. To this the Patki people objected, laying permanent claim to the rewards which they had temporarily enjoyed. In fact, they went so far as to insist that the disputed territory was part of their ancestral holdings. Thus for many years there were constant contentions between the two peoples.

At the time that Lololoma, uncle and predecessor of the present chief, was ruling Oraibi with the help of his older brother, the heads of the two factions met at his house to discuss their respective claims. Nothing came of this meeting, so some time later the leaders on both sides held another conference with Lololoma, this time on the actual site of the land under dispute. It happened that two brothers from the Coyote clan were on opposite sides in the argument, one having married a Patki woman and the other a Pikyas,[4] and they grew so angry and so heated in their talk that the chief became offended and brought the issue to a close.

---

[1] Compare p. 61 and footnote 22.

[2] One must not place too much reliance on such supposed forecasts of danger, as the Hopi are very much inclined to "prophesying" both present and past situations.

[3] When a succession to office fails within a clan, the Hopi commonly seek a successor from another clan in the same phratry.

[4] It is to be expected that men would side with their wives' groups in land disputes because all married men cultivate farms on their wives' clans' property. This is one of the important ties that binds men to their marital household units, and helps crosscut clan lines. Compare p. 43.

"You've been telling me that your ancestors told you about having a large piece of land," said Lololoma to the Patki representatives. "You know that I'm the head chief here, and yet I don't have as much ground as you are claiming. I don't think that you own as much as you are asking for."

Hereupon he pointed out the holdings allotted to the various officers in the Soyal and other important ceremonies and showed that by comparison the Patki claims were excessive. (See fig. 5.) "Now I've had enough of such talk," continued the chief. "You Patki people have talked so strongly (angrily) that I think I'll be on the Pikyas side as they are my real helpers. Now it's up to you to decide what you are going to do."

(It was Lololoma's idea, so my informant explained, that if people claimed land falsely they would be punished with death, that is, from the gods.)

"All right," said Siwinimptiwa, the Patki leader, "we'll listen to your words. We'll give up *all* our claims to land. We're through!"

At first the Patkis planned to make a settlement at the spot where their undisputed land lay and to have no further dealings with the pueblo of Oraibi. This notion was never carried out, but the Patki leaders recruited a following and moved to Moenkopi. Lololoma promptly sent a warning to the Pikyas chief of that village to be on his guard against further trouble, but after a short time the Patki faction moved off to Monavi, west of Moenkopi, where they hoped to start a rival town. However, not all their clan relatives joined them, so after a while the disgruntled Patki people began to drift back to Moenkopi. Siwinimptiwa lost more and more of his following until it became impossible for him to make new plans for an exodus. After his death, some of those who had sided with him continued to make trouble for the Pikyas people, and it is this element that is the source of the present dissensions at Moenkopi.

Chapter XVII

ADOLESCENCE RITES FOR GIRLS

ON THIRD MESA a ceremony called *poli-inteveplaluwa* was formerly performed annually for unmarried girls ranging in age from about 16 to 20. It was in no way connected with the start of the menstrual cycle, nor do the people of Oraibi seem to recall that any ritual was ever attendant upon menstruation.[1]

At some time in June, prior to the date of the Niman Katcina dance, a group of eligible girls would arrange for the ceremony by telling their paternal aunts that they were ready to grind corn. The true significance of this statement was readily understood, of course, and it was soon arranged that the rite should be performed at the house of some one of the aunts concerned. Here all the girls would gather one evening, and after grinding a little corn, they would go to bed. For the next four days the girls devoted themselves almost exclusively to the task of corn grinding. From early morning to night they worked quietly and without the accompaniment of song, in a chamber from which the sun was excluded by draping rabbit skin rugs over doors and windows. The young women had to abstain from fatty foods, meat and salt (the customary food tabus in all Hopi rituals); they might not peep from the windows; and except for a beverage of sweet cornmeal and water taken at noon, they could not drink any liquids throughout the day. Each evening the group was visited by their paternal aunts who brought fresh supplies of corn to be ground and who carried away the meal that had been made that day. In exchange for this the aunts brought to their nieces the choicest foods that could be prepared without breaking the dietary tabus.

In charge of the ceremony there was usually a girl who had already been through the rites and was in a position to know the requirements. She was generally assisted by two trustworthy boys who were picked to help her supervise the candidates and to see that they observed all the regulations imposed on them. All three served without reward.

On the third day the male directors organized a rabbit hunt in order to secure meat for a stew to be prepared as part of a feast when the ceremony was concluded on the morrow. The next day the girls stopped grinding and devoted themselves to the baking of fresh *piki* bread. That afternoon there occurred the culmination of the entire ritual when the girls had their hair put up in butterfly wings (*poli-inta*) by the director of the ceremony.[2] Ordinarily, a Katcina dance was held on this day, and after an elaborate feast the girls showed themselves in the plaza in their new coiffure, which is worn on all ceremonial occasions until marriage.

At Oraibi the emphasis of the adolescence ritual was laid not on the physiological aspect, but on the social fact that such girls were now ready to be married. Indeed, if a girl already had a lover, she would usually arrange for her wedding to take place as soon as possible after the termination of the rites. It was because this custom was looked upon as a preliminary to marriage that all parents insisted on their daughters going through it. The difficult corn grinding and the preparation of *piki* had the effect of proclaiming that girls who had met this test were good housekeepers and were capable of performing the tasks required of a bride.

This ceremony was also a regular feature at Second Mesa where it appears to have closely resembled the Oraibi performance.[3] Edmund Nequatewa refers to it as a " 'test ceremony' of grinding corn"[4] which shows that in motivation it resembles Third Mesa procedure. The Hopi author makes no mention of a rabbit hunt held in conjunction with the rites, but speaks of a joint hunt for boys and girls which took place soon after their conclusion, during which the girls might make proposals of marriage by dint of *qömi* gifts.

It is at First Mesa that the greatest conceptual

---

[1] Beaglehole, E., and P., 1935, pp. 45, 46, provides comparative data.

[2] Stephen, 1940, pp. 26–27, gives an excellent account of this style of hair-dressing.

[3] Beaglehole, E., and P., 1935, pp. 44, 45.

[4] Nequatewa, 1933, p. 42. I was told that the people of Chimopovy retain this custom, although the butterfly wing coiffure is rarely worn.

divergence from the Oraibi performance is found. As Stephen describes it the rite is a definite adolescence ceremony directly attendant on a girl's first menstruation;[5] but there are several identical features, such as the exclusion of the sun with a rabbit skin blanket, the same food tabus, corn grinding in the company of other girls at the home of a paternal aunt, and the culmination in the butterfly wing hair-dressing. Apart from th connection with first menses, there is anothe special feature at First Mesa, in that the candida is treated like a ceremonial novice to the exter that she may not scratch herself by hand, bu must use a special object called a *nahazrih* which serves first as a standard and later as prayer-stick.[6]

[5] Parsons, 1936b, pp. 139–143.

[6] An interesting commentary on the errors into which one may fall through ignorance of the kinship system is found in Stephen's description of this rite. In speaking of the head scratcher, he says in one place that it was made by the girl's grandfather. Later he corrects himself, ascribing the manufacture of the article to the husband of the pate nal aunt at whose house the ceremony is being held. O viously, the confusion arose because Stephen was unawa of the fact that the husband of a paternal aunt is calle by the same term as that employed for the grandfathe *ikwa'a*. (See p. 29.)

Chapter XVIII

A FEW SEX PRACTICES

THERE seems to be some correlation between the scatological habits of the Hopi and their attitude towards sex. They exhibit so much indifference towards bodily excretions of all sorts that there is an attendant carelessness regarding the organs involved. Toilet facilities are completely wanting, and but little trouble is taken to conceal the performance of the natural offices. Men and boys especially, urinate at will in the presence of the other sex, and women may often be observed in the act. The old-fashioned manner of dress too betrayed a disregard for the concealment of private parts of the body. The dress of the women, so cut that the left shoulder was bare, permitted the breast to be exposed; and the breech clout for men was worn in such fashion "that a man's penis was barely covered" and in some instances was actually disclosed.[1] This does not mean that the Hopi were exhibitionists; it simply indicates that they considered such things as much a matter of fact as any other part of their daily behavior. A similar indifference is found in some of their place names. "Horse Vulva," "Clitoris Spring," "Girl's Breast Point," and "Feces Kiva" are used as freely as the name of Oraibi.

To a person brought up in such a community, things of the body arouse none of the shame that they do in other cultures.[2] Accordingly, sex actions, as such, are not regarded as reprehensible, and youthful love affairs are lightly treated as perfectly natural occurrences. Yet, the Hopi are by no means devoid of a sense of modesty, and young girls tend to be exceedingly coy. It is more than likely, however, that the bashfulness displayed by Hopi maidens grows out of a dread of publicity rather than from any other cause, for in a pueblo secrecy is almost impossible, and eavesdropping and gossip are freely indulged in by one and all. Men who brag of their conquests and those who gaze at women in public are very much despised. In fact, girls in the Marau ceremony who may be called upon to don the short kilt worn by one of the performers often exhibit a painful sense of shame because they are publicly exposed to the stares of the men.[3] Women who frankly enjoy watching the obscenities of the clowns may refuse to witness their performance at any village other than their own, because they feel that it is indecent.

Although sexual indulgence, provided it does not offend the restrictions imposed by Hopi custom, is considered a perfectly natural act, there is some scorn shown for individuals who lack restraint. The word crazy (*honakti*) is often used in the sense of licentious, but at the same time offenders are neither punished nor debarred from any of the village activities. In former times there seem to have been many cases of homosexuality, and other aberrations have also been reported, but these are not very frequent at present.[4]

One convention that marks the sex habits of the Hopi is the idea that for every favor a woman grants she is entitled to some form of payment. This applies as well to a boy's *dumaiya* partners[5] as to adulterous women or out-and-out prostitutes. Nevertheless, there is almost as much distinction made between a girl who takes presents from a lover, and a prostitute, as there is in our society. Married men sometimes employ panders to help them meet sweethearts in secret places, but this seems ridiculous in view of the fact that the news soon spreads throughout the village.

Some men, not necessarily witches, are said to have hypnotic power which they can exert to bring unwilling girls to them. This is said to be very dangerous as a girl may become permanently insane if she is not properly restored to her normal state; but although the men who are suspected of practicing this form of allurement are despised and feared, they are not run out of the village.[6] The hypnotist (*duskyavu*) sings certain magical songs which force the girl to come to him and to respond to his wishes. They may be learned from unscrupulous medicine men or from witches. In one case I was told of two men who rubbed their bodies with a secret medicine, sang the necessary songs to entrap the girls whom they desired, and awaited their coming in a hidden spot.

---

[1] Parsons, 1936b, p. 410, footnote 1.

[2] Compare Beaglehole, E., and P., 1935, pp. 39–41.

[3] Cf. Parsons, 1936b, p. 910, *et passim*.

[4] Compare Beaglehole, E., and P., 1935, p. 65.

[5] See p. 31.

[6] Compare Beaglehole, E. and P., 1935, p. 63.

Soon the girls arrived, but before the plotters could enjoy them, someone happened to pass by and the spell was broken. At this the girls, who "didn't know what they were doing," came to their senses, and realizing their situation, burst into tears and ran away.

Although continence for varying periods of time is prescribed for participants in every important ceremony, there are cases reported of the violation of this tabu; and one man, crippled since birth, is said to have been born in that condition as the result of an affair between his mother and a man who was still wearing his Katcina dancing costume.[7] It is said that the "smell" of women is displeasing to the clouds, and hence no rain will fall if people have intercourse during the performance of sacred rituals.[8]

Contraceptive medicines, emmenagogues, and aphrodisiacs are all reported, but I was unable to secure direct evidence of their use. Most of the supposed instances of their employment were highly improbable, but I cite one such story because it incorporates several of the sex practices here mentioned.

An old man from the village of Bakavi is supposed to have related this story just prior to his death. The adventure is said to have occurred when he was already old and feeble, and spending the greater part of his time in the kiva to which he belonged. One day, as he was about to descend into the kiva, a young woman who lived just across the way invited him to dine with her. The old man willingly accepted, and in the course of the meal the girl put some sort of a medicine into the mouth of her guest.

"Perhaps it's poison," thought the poor fellow, but he was too near the point of natural death to be much concerned. To his surprise, far from growing weaker, he soon found a glow pervading him that was very pleasant. Then the girl shut the door of her house, and spreading a sheepskin on the floor invited him to lie down beside her. There she removed his clothes and applied more of the medicine to his body.[9] Soon the old man found himself sexually stimulated to such an extent that he stayed with his hostess for twenty-four hours and was still desirous all night long after he had left her.

The next morning he returned to his normal condition and gradually became alarmed at the possibility that he had fallen into the clutches of a witch. At this he decided that he had better pay her for his affair, so that she should bear him no grudge. Accordingly, he told his son the whole story and ended with a request for money, but the son thought that he was merely trying to extort a few dollars for some other purpose, so he refused his help. Sorrowfully, the frightened old man went to plead with one of his maternal nephews, who proved more obliging and gave him two dollars which he carried off to his mistress. The girl took the money, and from that time on the old man lived in peace for the rest of his natural life.

---

[7] Parsons, 1925, p. 101, speaks of a bad Powamu chief who while "engaged in ceremony . . . had relations with women. If Powamu chief does this, the people will have rheumatism and be crippled."

[8] In depositions made to government officials by Christian Hopi there are numerous references made to irregular sex affairs during the performance of ceremonies.

[9] The particular aphrodisiac used by this woman was supposed to be a plant that grows near Flagstaff where the greater part of Hopi medicines are said to be found. It comes in two varieties, the red being more potent than the white. Some claim that it grows in the form of the male sexual organs and that if prodded with a stick it gives off a sort of liquid discharge. I was unable to secure either the English or the Hopi name of this plant.

Chapter XIX

THE RISE OF HOTEVILLA[1]

IN STRIKING contrast to Oraibi's disintegration is Hotevilla's steady growth and progressive integration. Under the combined leadership of Lomahongyoma (Spider) and Yokioma (Kokop) 298 Conservative men and women had formed the original settlement at Hotevilla on the evening of September 7, 1906, with very little more equipment than they could carry on their backs. A day or so later their numbers were reduced through the action of the United States Government agents who arrested or took off to school several of the leading men. Within a few weeks a difference of opinion between Lomahongyoma and Yokioma led the former to withdraw from Hotevilla with about 60 followers, who ultimately founded Bakavi. The actual work of building the village of Hotevilla was thus left to about 200 people. These were united by a common zeal for the retention of the old Hopi way of life and were guided by a leader who was endowed with the necessary courage and stamina to cling to his principles and to fight for their preservation against all odds.

During the winter of 1906, the Hotevilla settlers suffered miserably. They were short-handed; they had not had time enough to build adequate shelters before cold weather came; and their food supply was pitifully low. Many died before spring, but the survivors lost none of their determination; and with the coming of milder weather they built good houses, staked out new farms, and planted their first crops.[2] When these had been harvested and the material welfare of the pueblo had begun to be assured, the Conservatives turned their thoughts to the resumption of their rituals. New kivas were constructed and new shrines were erected and dedicated. Sacred objects which had been carried to Hotevilla by their expelled owners were now brought into use again, and duplicate fetishes were shamelessly manufactured to take the place of those that had remained in the possession of the Friendlies at Oraibi. Men who had served as leaders of major ceremonies resumed their duties, and new officers were chosen or appointed as needed. Within two years of its inception, Hotevilla's cycle of rituals was well under way, and in a surprisingly short time her calendar was virtually complete, and her performances became the best executed and the best attended on Third Mesa. So rapidly did the religious life of Hotevilla develop in the very years when Oraibi's ceremonies were progressively declining, that some of the chiefs in the parent village voluntarily turned their fetishes and altars over to Hotevilla leaders.

Perhaps the best way to gain an insight into Hotevilla's development is through a study of its kivas and their associated ceremonies.[3] The first religious structure built in the new pueblo was erected by Poliwuhioma of the Spider clan, a nephew of the Conservative leader, Lomahongyoma. Poliwuhioma named his kiva Sakwalenvi[4] after his clan's kiva at Oraibi which had housed Lomahongyoma's Soyal and which had served as Chief kiva for the Hostile faction. It was only fitting, therefore, that Sakwalenvi at Hotevilla should have been dedicated to the same ends. In this kiva Poliwuhioma acted as chief of the Soyal, although he had been only a common member of that ceremony at Oraibi. Since the original Soyal materials had never fallen into the hands of the Conservatives, Poliwuhioma used the substitute paraphernalia that had been devised by his uncle in 1897.[5]

In Sakwalenvi too the Blue Flute society began to stage its winter meetings, as it had done at

---

[1] This topic was first studied by Dr. Leslie A. White and his field party at Oraibi in 1932. It was subsequently expanded and elaborated by the present writer.

[2] To avoid conflict, the Hotevilla settlers chose land which had never been cultivated before.

[3] My principal informant on Hotevilla ceremonialism was a man who had lived at Hotevilla until his marriage to an Oraibi woman. His material was checked by an informant who was already a middle-aged man in 1906, and others. For the location of Hotevilla kivas, see fig. 11.

[4] Although officially named Sakwalenvi, this kiva was also known as Tcocovi. This name means "Place of the Bluebird" and is probably a reference to the members of the Bluebird clan who had come from Second Mesa to help the Oraibi Hostiles at the time of the split (pp. 83, 84). In any event, members of the Spider clan have a right to use Bluebird names as these clans are regarded as belonging to the same phratry.

[5] Lomahongyoma probably took his Soyal materials to Bakavi, but soon gave them to his nephew at Hotevilla.

Oraibi. This ceremony was traditionally owned by the Spider clan; so the Hotevilla celebrants had the advantage of using the orthodox fetishes which they had transported to their new home. Lomahongyoma apparently did not take the Blue Flute paraphernalia with him when he returned to Oraibi, and they came into the possession of Qöyayamptiwa of the Water Coyote clan. While he was a resident of Oraibi, Qöyayamptiwa had never belonged to the Blue Flute, but during a a serious illness at Hotevilla he had vowed that upon his recovery he would undertake the duties of the Blue Flute chief. To this office he could rightfully lay claim because he was married to Lomahongyoma's niece, Talahongsi (Spider), who had been in the Blue Flute since early girlhood.[6] The society's biennial summer performances, which by tradition are not held in kivas, are celebrated at Hotevilla from the home of Sikyanimka, Qöyayamptiwa's sister's daughter.

The Al (Horn) kiva was the second one finished in Hotevilla. It was built by Sikyaheptiwa (Patki)[7] whose wife was a Spider clanswoman named Puhukwapnim. The original builder died not long after the kiva was finished, and it was repaired by Sakhöyoma[8] (Sun), who had been an Al society member at Oraibi, and who now became chief of the kiva which housed that ceremony. The story of the disposition of the Al materials is somewhat involved. Long ago, Qötcventiwa (Bow) had been chief of the rites at Oraibi and had had charge of all the fetishes. He decided to "rest" for a few years and gave the chieftainship to his nephew, Tanakhongniwa, who went insane and died prior to 1906. Then Nasiwaitiwa, younger brother of Qötcventiwa, took over the leadership, and at the time of the split he kept the altar materials at Oraibi. There they remained even after the ceremony had been allowed to lapse, until Duwaletstiwa, a Christianized

nephew of Nasiwaitiwa, removed the Al paraphernalia from *the* Bow clan house and burned them before the eyes of the local missionary at New Oraibi. Soon after this *auto da fe*, the former Al chief, Qötcventiwa, who had gone to Hotevilla with the Conservatives, decided to establish the ceremony there by using a few things that had been saved from the flames and making replicas of the parts that had been destroyed. Before he died, however, Qötcventiwa seems to have reached the conclusion that leadership in this ceremony involved too much responsibility, for he asked his sons not to become Al chiefs.[9] When they obeyed his wishes, leadership of the rite passed to Piphongva, a Gray Badger, who had been a common member of the society, but whose wife was in the same phratry as Bow which owns the ceremony.[10]

Not only did the Al kiva play host to the society of the same name, but it also became the home of the Antelope society. At the time of the split the Antelope chief was Duvengötiwa, of the Spider clan, and as his people had owned the ceremony he took the genuine materials for its performance to Hotevilla. At his death, the office was transmitted in customary fashion to his sister's son, Nasiwisioma, who remained active until his mind was made uneasy by his wife's infidelity. He then resigned and handed the position to his maternal uncle, Kiachongniwa, who still acts in the capacity of Antelope leader. Both Nasiwisioma and Kiachongniwa had been only ordinary members of the Antelope society at Oraibi.[11]

A third ceremony which performed its esoteric rites in the Al kiva was the Lakon. Its former leaders, Kuwanyamka and her brother Lomanaksu of the Parrot clan, had left their sacred objects at Oraibi, although they had been among the Hostiles who were driven out of the village.[12] At Hotevilla their nephew, Nahongvi'ima,[13] act

---

[6] The shift of Blue Flute chieftainship from traditional Spider ownership to Water Coyote is an example of the process of substitution which Dr. Parsons discusses in Parsons, 1939, pp. 1144–1149. Many other instances occur in this chapter.

[7] The Al kiva at Oraibi was controlled by the Bow clan.

[8] Sakhöyoma was married to Kiaro of the Sand clan, who assumed Hotevilla's Marau leadership.

[9] This would have been an irregular form of transmission, as sons do not inherit their father's offices.

[10] Piphongva's wife was Tcocwisnim (Greasewood). Her father was a Spider and she had been in Lomahongyoma's Blue Flute ceremony at Oraibi. It is interesting to note how many Spiders and people related to Spiders took

ceremonial offices at Hotevilla.

[11] Note how the Antelope chieftainship passed from hand to hand within an original household group. Duvengötiwa, Nasiwisioma, and Kiachongniwa all came from the same natal household as well as from the same lineage and clan.

[12] Attention has already been called to the apparent contradiction in the case of Lomanaksu, who performed the Lakon as a Progressive but who went to Hotevilla as a Conservative. It may be that there was a lapse of several years between the two events. See p. 81, footnote 11 and p. 83 and footnote 128.

[13] Nahongvi'ima's wife, Duvenumsi (Le clan), was the daughter of a Spider clansman, Duvewuhioma, who was Lomahongyoma's brother.

as nominal chief, although he is said to erect no altars and to conduct no complete set of rites. Instead, when the appropriate times for Lakon celebrations occur, he merely makes prayer-sticks and deposits them at the proper shrines.

The third religious structure to have been completed at Hotevilla was the Tao (Singers') kiva, whose builder was a Kokop clansman named Lomahongvi. According to Oraibi custom, the Tao kiva should have been controlled by the Parrot clan, but Lomahongvi took over this function because he had been a Tao kiva member at the parent village and because his ceremonial father was in the Rabbit clan, which is related to Parrot. At Lomahongvi's death, charge of the kiva fell to his brother's son, Qöyahongva (Sand), whose wife Sonwaisi belonged to the Rabbit clan.[14] Within this kiva was lodged the Tao society. At Oraibi its chief Masawistiwa (Katcina) had been a Progressive and had retained his fetishes at home. The office was filled at Hotevilla, therefore, by a former ordinary member of the ceremony, Qöyahongva, who was also the Tao kiva chief. As he lacked the original materials he was forced to rely on makeshift altars and fetishes.

The very important Powamu society also chose the Tao kiva as its base. Inasmuch as the Powamu chief Qömahöniwa (Real Badger) had been a Progressive, he held his ritual properties at Oraibi and there transmitted them to Siletstiwa, his nephew.[15] However, the Conservatives had been using duplicate materials under Napkuiva's (Rabbit) guidance long before they had moved to Hotevilla,[16] so Napkuiva merely moved his version of the Powamu to the latter pueblo. The chieftainship then passed to Kiacwaitiwa (Real Badger), a Hotevilla medicine man, who served four years and then handed the office to his maternal uncle, Qötcvuyauoma. He also kept it for four years and then transmitted it to Nakwatiwa, his younger brother. Four years later Nakwatiwa returned the chieftainship to Qötcvuyauoma, who held office until he went blind. He was then suc-

ceeded by Sakhongva (Gray Badger), who is the present Powamu chief at Hotevilla.

One of the women's ceremonies, the Marau, also makes use of the Tao kiva. The religious objects used by this society had remained at Oraibi in 1906, where they were in the hands of the chieftess Qötcnumsi (Lizard) and her brother, Kuwanvikwaiya. When the latter became Oraibi's first convert to Christianity, his sister lost interest in the ceremony and voluntarily transferred it to Hotevilla, where Kiaro (Sand) became the woman leader, and Puhunimptiwa (Lizard) served as male chief.[17]

It was Puhunimptiwa too who was responsible for the erection of the Tcu (Snake) kiva, fourth of Hotevilla's new kivas. He became leader both of the kiva and of the Snake society. At first he did not have the use of the traditional materials for the Snake rites which had remained at Oraibi. There the Snake chief had been Masangöntiwa (Snake), a Hostile, but his successor, Kuktiwa (Snake), had been a Friendly. Not long before the split, Kuktiwa "rested" and allowed Sikyahongniwa (Lizard), uncle of Puhunimptiwa, to act in his stead. In 1906 Sikyahongniwa and Puhunimptiwa went to Hotevilla, but they did not remove the Snake paraphernalia. These were used at Oraibi by a new Friendly chief, Duveyamptiwa (Snake clan), who served until 1912. He then became upset over the loose conduct of his son[18] and gave up the ceremony. Puhunimptiwa thereupon requested the use of the traditional materials, and when Duveyamptiwa complied, Puhunimptiwa became Hotevilla's Snake chief and served in that capacity until his death a few years ago.

Kwan kiva was the fifth to be built. It was put up by Nakwaheptiwa of the Sand clan for the use of the Kwan society, of which he became the chief.[19] He was forced to use duplicate fetishes because the originals had been retained by Oraibi's Kwan leader, Lomaleohtiwa (Masau'u). In due time Lomaleohtiwa handed his office to his nephew, Homer Nakwahongniwa, but Homer

---

[14] This is another example of Hopi substitution.

[15] Siletstiwa lives at Moenkopi, but regularly returns to Oraibi for the Powamu performance.

[16] See p. 83 and footnote 126.

[17] After his removal to Hotevilla, Puhunimptiwa became one of the most dynamic religious leaders in the town. He served as chief of the Snake and the Marau societies, and he became a secondary leader in the Blue Flute. He also acted as a father of the Hotevilla Katcinas. Puhunimptiwa was allied to both of Hotevilla's leading clans, as one of his daughters was married to a Spider and

another to a Kokop.

[18] The son was Arthur Puhukwaptiwa (Sun), who had three wives and several mistresses in quick succession.

[19] Traditionally, the Kwan kiva chieftainship and the leadership of the Kwan society belong to the clans in Phratry VI, which include Masau'u and Kokop. However, Nakwaheptiwa had been a common member of the Kwan society and had had a Masau'u man for his ceremonial father. Furthermore, he had important connections at Hotevilla, as one of his daughters, Tcocyamka (Greasewood), was married to Lomahöyoma, a Spider.

moved to New Oraibi, became a clerk in Mr. Lorenzo Hubbell's trading post, and lost all desire to perform his ceremony. At Nakwaheptiwa's request he gave him the Kwan materials for the use of that society at Hotevilla.

Sand clan[20] to provide a home for the Wuwutcim society. Until Hawiovi was erected, the Wuwutcim had been sharing the Sakwalenvi kiva with several other societies. The Wuwutcim is supposed to use a vulva-shaped piece of watermelon

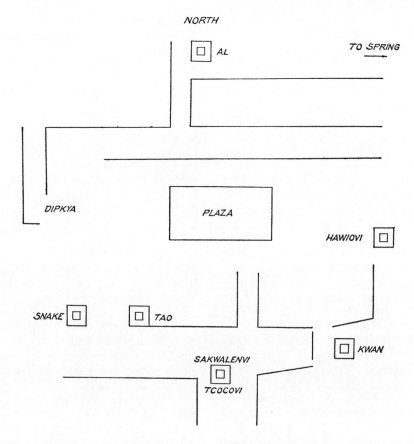

FIG. 11. HOTEVILLA KIVAS.

(Dipkya is the spot where the final Katcina song of the yearly open season is rendered during the Homegoing dance. See p. 233).

The sixth and last of Hotevilla's kivas was Hawiovi, which was put up by Qöyahöniwa of the

as its main altar and has only a few associated fetishes, but these had been retained in Oraibi by

[20] In accordance with Oraibi tradition, the Hawiovi kiva and the Wuwutcim ceremony pertain to Chicken Hawk and the other clans in Phratry IX. Qöyahöniwa had

a double tie with this phratry as his father was Hongniw (Chicken Hawk) and his wife was Talahepnim of the re lated Squash clan.

Talasnöntiwa (Chicken Hawk), who was on the Progressive side in the split. When he decided to withdraw from active participation, he gave his paraphernalia to his nephew Horace, but Horace never employed them, as he had settled at New Oraibi and had gone to work for Lorenzo Hubbell. Some informants believe that Horace was influenced in his behavior by his Christian uncle, Talasnimptiwa. At the present time, while Horace has not been converted, he nevertheless keeps his Wuwutcim fetishes unused in *the* Chicken Hawk house at Old Oraibi. The Hotevilla Wuwutcim is thus forced to rely on duplicate materials. The first chief, Duveletstiwa (Squash), was succeeded when he died by Qöyahöniwa, his sister's husband, who built Hawiovi kiva soon after he had become leader of the Wuwutcim.

All in all, it took Hotevilla, with its unified Conservative background, only about half a dozen years to establish a nearly complete cycle of ceremonies. Of all the rites that had ever been performed at Oraibi in its heyday, only the Gray Flute, the Momtcit, and the Oaqöl were missing.[21] In their new surroundings the Hotevilla rituals conformed as nearly as circumstances permitted to Oraibi models, and every effort was made to employ orthodox fetishes, to meet in properly-named kivas, and to select chiefs from the traditional proprietary clans. Within a very short time Hotevilla, rather than Oraibi, became the acknowledged religious center of Third Mesa, and the Oraibi populace, including chief Tawaqwaptiwa, formed the habit of attending Hotevilla's ceremonies as spectators.[22]

In its formative years Hotevilla was generally untroubled by political problems. After Lomahongyoma's early withdrawal from the scene, Yokioma acted as the undisputed Village chief, and it was not until he died in 1929 that the problem of his successor became a major issue. For nearly a decade there were three claimants to the Village chief's office. The weakest of these was Qötchongva, a Sun clansman, who based his claim on the fact that he was the son of Yokioma. Inasmuch as this is contrary to the Hopi system of inheritance, he had few supporters. The second contender, Pongyayauoma (Kokop), had a somewhat better case because he was Yokioma's sister's son, and many villagers felt that the pueblo's chieftainship should be retained in Yokioma's lineage. However, others argued that the Village chief's position was not to be treated as a separate entity, but was to be linked with possession of the Soyal ceremony. This attitude accords most nearly to Oraibi belief,[23] and as a consequence, Hotevilla's Soyal leader, Poliwuhioma, the Spider clan nephew of Lomahongyoma, is gaining more and more adherents and is now looked upon as Village chief by virtually the entire pueblo.[24]

---

[21] The Gray Flute seems to have been so completely in the hands of Progressives that their rivals apparently made no effort to take over or to duplicate this ceremony. The Momtcit had lapsed long ago with the conclusion of active warfare, and the Oaqöl was known as a miscellaneous assortment of bits taken from other rites.

[22] On nearly every religious festive occasion practically the entire population of Oraibi makes its way to Hotevilla.

Now that the old antagonisms have lost much of their bitterness, there is a good deal of visiting among related families, and in 1932 Tawaqwaptiwa was able to brag on his return from a Hotevilla dance that he had, "Eight times eat." [23] See p. 63.

[24] The selection of a chief was a matter of frequent discussion, and when a consensus was finally reached it was without any formal administrative action.

CHAPTER XX

THE CEREMONIAL CYCLE AT BAKAVI

WHEN Kuwannimptiwa and Lomahongyoma led their followers to Bakavi after their second expulsion from Oraibi, in October 1907, they had with them the traditional ritual paraphernalia for the Oraibi Blue Flute ceremony, and they may have had duplicate materials for the Soyal. Both sets of religious properties belonged to Lomahongyoma, but he was too broken by the

was called Sakwalenvi after Lomahongyoma's old kiva at Oraibi.[2] Its builder was Talaswaitiwa (Water Coyote), who had formerly served as War chief in the Snake and the Blue Flute societies.[3] By his participation as an officer in the latter, Talaswaitiwa was closely tied to Lomahongyoma, and by virtue of his marriage to Tawanumsi (Lizard), a phratry sister of Kuwan-

TABLE 10. CLAN AND CEREMONIAL GROUPS AT BAKAVI IN 1907.*

Phratry	Clan	Total Men	Total Women	Wuwutcim Tcu	Wuwutcim Sakwalenvi	Wuwutcim Hawiovi	Snake	Antelope	Blue Flute	Powamu	Momtcit	Kwan	Al	Tao	Marau	Oaqöl	Lakon
															(Women)		
I	Rabbit	1	1														
	Parrot	2	0						1	1			1				
II	Bear	0	1														
	Spider	2	1		2			1	2**		2						
III	Sand	2	0		1							1					
	Snake	1	0	1			1					1					
	Lizard	4	5				3	0†							2	1	
IV	Eagle	2	0		2			1			1						
V	Greasewood	1	5												1	3	1
	Reed	3	6	1				1	1			1			5	3	2
VI	Real Coyote	2	0	1			1					1			2	2	3
	Water Coyote	8	5	1	1	3	3		5					1			
VII	Real Badger	1	0														
	Gray Badger	7	2		1					5‡		1	2	3			
	Navaho Badger	1	0	1					1	1							
VIII	Pikyas	0	1														
	Patki	1	0										1				
	Totals	38	27	5	7	3	8	3	10	7	3	5	4	4	10	9	6

* Ceremonial ties refer to affiliations while resident at Oraibi.
** One Spider woman was also in Blue Flute.
† One Lizard woman was in the Antelope Society.
‡ A Gray Badger woman was in the Powamu.

turn of events to employ them regularly and soon turned them over to more virile leaders at Hotevilla.[1] Accordingly, when the inhabitants of Bakavi attempted to establish a cycle of ceremonies, they had to manufacture all the required objects.

The first step was the building of a kiva which

nimptiwa, he was related to Bakavi's Village chief. All but two of the ceremonies performed at Bakavi made use of Sakwalenvi. In this kiva were held the Soyal, the Wuwutcim, the Tao, and the Powamu rites. One man took it upon himself to serve as chief of the Soyal and the Wuwutcim societies.[4] He was Polingyauoma, of the Parrot

[1] Informants disagree as to whether Lomahongyoma took his fetishes and altars away from Hotevilla during his sojourn at Oraibi or left them there when he tried to return to Oraibi. In either case they soon passed into the possession of Hotevilla men.
[2] Note that at Hotevilla too the first of the new kivas was called Sakwalenvi. Until Lomahongyoma's rebellion

this had been the Chief kiva at Oraibi.
[3] The ceremonial affiliations of Bakavi's populace in 1907 are listed in table 10.
[4] There is some doubt as to whether Polingyauoma actually took over the leadership of the Wuwutcim, and it is possible that this ceremony was not performed at Bakavi.

clan, who had been a member at Oraibi of the Al, Blue Flute, and Powamu ceremonies, and who also was known as a medicine man. Inasmuch as Polingyauoma had never been in the Oraibi Soyal even as a common participant, the news of his assumption of the leadership aroused a good deal of resentment at Oraibi, especially on the part of Tawaqwaptiwa. The Powamu rites were conducted by a Gray Badger man, Nasikwaptiwa, whose wife Qöqötca (Lizard) was a phratry sister to the Bakavi Village chief. Nasikwaptiwa belonged to the phratry that traditionally controlled the Powamu, but he had not been an officer in the rites at Oraibi. Informants were uncertain regarding the performance of the Tao and could not agree on who was supposed to conduct it.

Bakavi's second kiva was called Kwan and was devoted exclusively to the ceremony of the same name. Its builder was Talaswuhioma (Gray Badger), who had been a common member of the Kwan society at Old Oraibi but who acted as its chief at Bakavi.

The last of the active ceremonies, the Al, did not use a kiva but met at the house of Nasi-wunka, a Lizard woman from Kuwannimptiwa's phratry. The rites were led by Polingyauoma, who also headed the Soyal, and Talashöyoma (Gray Badger), both of whom had been common members of the society at the parent pueblo.

Until 1934, Bakavi's ceremonial cycle was quite fragmentary in comparison with the full calendar established at Hotevilla. In spite of their proximity the two towns do not co-operate in each other's rites, although Bakavi men sometimes join in Hotevilla's Katcina dances, against the wishes of many Hotevilla residents. There is a possibility that Bakavi will attempt a more ambitious program in the future, and there is some talk that chief Kuwannimptiwa will take over the leadership of the Soyal in accordance with the customary practice on Third Mesa, where the Village and Soyal chieftainships go together, but in all likelihood Bakavi's program of rites will not expand because of paucity of adult men and the lack of traditional officers and paraphernalia.

CHAPTER XXI

A QÖQÖQLOM KATCINA PERFORMANCE AT ORAIBI[1]

IN THE afternoon of the day when the Soyal ceremony culminates in a pueblo-wide distribution of prayer-sticks, it is customary for the Hopi on Third Mesa to stage a Qöqöqlom performance. This is the first Katcina dance of the year to be performed by a whole group. Its purpose is to open all the kivas for the use of Katcinas, thus completing the work of the solitary Soyal Katcina and making a graphic announcement of the fact that the Katcina season, closed since the last Niman ritual in July, is now open again.[2]

The 1933 Qöqöqlom was sponsored by Hawiovi kiva,[3] and the father of the Katcinas was Siletstiwa, a Badger clansman who is the head of the Powamu ceremony and in charge of the Katcina cycle for the first half of the open season.[4] As only one song was to be used throughout the performance, only a brief rehearsal was held in the officiating kiva. The participants were volunteers from various clans and kivas, as the only qualification is initiation into the Katcina cult.

When everything was ready the performers went with their equipment to Qowawaima, the shrine where all Katcina dances begin. The men ranged their masks in a row beside them, went through a final practice, then donned their masks and walked in a single file towards the village. On the outskirts of the inhabited zone they were met by Siletstiwa, who sprinkled a cornmeal path as he led them to an open space near the Tao kiva.[5] Here they lined up in two ranks, with seven male Katcinas standing side by side in front, and three "female" impersonators ranged behind them.[6] The masks worn by the male Qöqöqlom were black, with eye openings and other designs painted in blue.[7] The costumes were

an odd mixture of shabby Hopi and American clothes, the only semblance of uniformity being a "collar" of cloth or fur. Despite their motley appearance, the male Katcinas wore regulation turtle rattles and carried the usual gourd rattles, but the wearing of such garments as overcoats interfered with the use of fox pelts as "tails."[8] In his left hand each man carried a large sack of sacred cornmeal and a long stick bound with rabbit fur at one end.

The "women" Katcinas too were dressed in unorthodox, miscellaneous fashion. Two had on Koyemsi masks, and the third wore the mask of a "female" Hemis Katcina. All three were dressed in odd bits of women's ceremonial costumes which they had borrowed from relatives. They carried woven trays full of cornmeal, into which a number of prayer-feathers had been set.

As soon as the Katcinas were ready to dance at their first stopping place near the Tao kiva, two men left the line and went through the ceremony of opening the kiva. First they sprinkled liberal quantities of meal down the hatch, then they drew broad lines leading away from the kiva opening towards the four cardinal points. Their actions at this time were somewhat exaggerated and fanciful but not necessarily comic. While they were still busy with their duties, the father of the Katcinas gave the command for the others to begin singing and dancing.[9] In contrast to the unusual attire of these Katcinas, their performance was along orthodox lines.

When they had concluded their song the Katcinas were led to a second stopping place. This was in front of the Hawiovi kiva, which one man was delegated to open. While this dance was

---

[1] The performance to be described here was witnessed by the writer on December 20, 1933.

[2] Compare p. 111.

[3] The sponsorship of the Qöqöqlom rotates annually together with that of the Niman. This device gives unity to the management of the Katcina cycle, for it means that the same kiva has charge of the first and the last group dances of the season.

[4] Although it is customary to have the Powamu chief serve as father of the Katcinas for the first dance of the year, inasmuch as he is in charge of all the Katcinas at the time, I was told that if he were unavailable, any Powamu

man might be asked to serve in that capacity.

[5] Ordinarily, Katcinas are led to the main dance plaza but on this occasion they perform near the kivas. In 193 they "opened" the Tao kiva although it had been unuse for many years.

[6] Male Katcinas usually stand in single file formatio with the "females" in a parallel row beside them.

[7] See Earle and Kennard, 1938, plate III.

[8] See Dorsey and Voth, 1901, plate XXXI.

[9] When the two men who were opening the kiva ha finished, they merely resumed their places in the danc group and continued with the others.

going on, several of the more important women of the village came out and sprinkled all the dancers. From here the group moved into the main dance plaza of the pueblo, where they repeated their song twice, facing in different directions as they sang. One of the Qöqöqlom dropped out of the line to open the Tawaovi kiva near which, although it is the Chief kiva, no performance was given. The Katcinas then proceeded to the Powamu kiva, where the last dance of the day was performed. When this was over, the father of the Katcinas remained in place and the three "women" dancers also retained their positions, but all the male Katcinas went up to the raised section surrounding the kiva hatch. This they circled four times, sprinkling liberal amounts of meal in the rites of opening, and now and again indulging in antics which resembled the behavior of Hopi clowns. As they went round and round the hatch, the Katcinas threw large handfuls of meal into the air, into one another's faces, or hard against the buttocks of their fellow dancers. Some pretended to lean so far over the kiva entrance that they almost fell in, and others kicked and mauled each other about.

Having finished their activities at the Powamu kiva, the male dancers proceeded to the Marau kiva which is near by. As they went, each man sprinkled a broad meal line leading from Powamu kiva to the other. En route, some acted lame, others marched with high prancing motions, and a few stopped to indulge in various buffooneries to amuse the bystanders. All the spectators, the "women" dancers, and the father of the Katcinas, remained behind and did not try to follow the men. When the Marau kiva had been opened, the Qöqöqlom went off towards the southeast, back to Qowawaima, where they performed a secret rite including the deposit of the sticks tipped with fur, as prayers for luck in the four-day rabbit hunt which was scheduled to begin on the morrow.

One by one the men straggled back to the dance line and began to divest themselves of their turtle and gourd rattles. These they gave as "gifts" to the father of the Katcinas, who wrapped them in a blanket and later carried them back to the kiva where each reclaimed his possessions.

Before they got into line for the closing act of the ceremony, some of the Qöqöqlom put on a show to amuse the crowd. Two men took off their rattles and made it known, in pantomime, that they meant to run a race, the winner to keep the other's rattles. Each made a comic attempt to "warm up," and each called on another Katcina to serve as his manager and to act as starter and timer. A starting line was drawn, but just before the race began one of the competitors decided to take off his coat, so throwing a stone squarely at the back of his manager, he motioned his desire, only to have his request refused. At last, after more comic byplay, the starting signal was given, and as the men approached the finish line they converged on each other and collided so that it was impossible to pick a winner. A free-for-all developed with both sides claiming the victory. Finally, the father of the Katcinas intervened as peacemaker and placed the two sets of rattles with those that he had already received from the other performers. Then all the Katcinas resumed their places in line.

On this occasion they did not repeat their song or dance, but received the customary dismissal with meal and prayer-feathers from the father of the Katcinas. Afterwards, they filed off to a shrine where they deposited their offerings and unmasked. As they were going out of the village towards their shrine, a masculine Katcina put his arm lovingly round the shoulders of one of the "females," and while yet within full view of the bystanders, performed the jumping movement that always stands for copulation. After that the line of Katcinas was soon lost to sight without event.

Chapter XXII

THE SO'YOKO KATCINA

INTRODUCTORY

ON ALL the Hopi mesas there are a number of bogey Katcinas who have the dual function of disciplining children and of ridding the fields of mice and helping prepare them for the spring planting. The best known of these Katcinas are the So'yoko and Natacka. In former times they used to be impersonated annually in conjunction with the Powamu ceremony, but with the collapse of Oraibi's ritual calendar, the So'yoko performance came to be given independently at irregular intervals.[1] An interesting myth "explains" the nature and function of the So'yoko Katcina on Third Mesa.

THE SO'YOKO MYTH AT ORAIBI[2]

Once upon a time there lived so large a population at Oraibi that the number of children was very great. The youngsters grew bold and mischievous, snatching food from each other and constantly squabbling and fighting. Thereupon certain witches, such as the men from Kwitavi,[3] decided to cut down the increase of children. One day their chief told his kiva mates to gather a vast amount of piñon gum. At a secret meeting they fashioned the gum into large blocks, covered them with a wedding garment (ova), and sang magic songs over them. Just as they were finishing the last song, they noticed movements under the ova, and lifting it up, they disclosed a gigantic couple, a male and female So'yoko.[4]

"It's pretty hot," said the giants. "Yes," was the reply, "it is hot." "What can we do for you?" asked the So'yokos. "Well, we've got a lot of children here," replied the kiva leader, "and they are getting out of control. We would like to get rid of some of them, so we want you to snatch and eat them for your food." He then asked the giants to live at Mungyaovi (Porcupine Point), and to raid Oraibi for children before sunrise each

day until the population had been considerabl[y] reduced.

For a long time the So'yokos lived at Mung[yaovi], getting along very well and raising thre[e] children of their own. Each morning the mal[e] would go out with a carrying basket (hoapu) while his wife stayed home to cook. He would ap[p]roach Oraibi mesa until he came upon som[e] children, whereupon he would snatch up two o[f] them, put them into his basket, and return home. At last the people, alarmed by the regular dis[-] appearance of youngsters, kept watch and soo[n] discovered that So'yoko was the culprit. Th[e] Village chief of Oraibi worried and worried abou[t] the matter, and finally decided to seek help fro[m] the Little War Twins who are the guardians o[f] the Hopi.

Accordingly, he prepared two sets of bows an[d] arrows, fashioned a couple of balls out of buck[-]skin, and made two shinny sticks. Early the nex[t] day he took four prayer-feathers, and before sun[-]rise he set out for Pu'kongowacpi, the home of th[e] Little War Twins. When he arrived they wer[e] in the midst of a fast and furious game of shinny while their grandmother, the Spider Woman, wa[s] busy about the fire. The Oraibi chief entered th[e] kiva-like residence, but the Twins were so take[n] up with their game that they were not aware o[f] his presence until their grandmother, strikin[g] them a backhand blow with a stick, called thei[r] attention to the stranger's presence. "Our grand[-]mother is too mean," they shouted angrily at first but soon they quieted down, and looking at th[e] objects carried by the chief, whispered that the[y] wished he might have brought the things for them. The Spider Woman scolded them for their im[-]pudence, and then bustled about preparing thei[r] favorite food, hurucuki,[5] and a rabbit stew, afte[r] which she invited the stranger to join them.

Then the grandmother spoke. "I know you ar[e] the Village chief of Oraibi," she said, "and tha[t]

---

[1] See p. 118.

[2] Compare the version recorded by Voth, 1905b, p. 86 ff., and compare Parsons and Beals, 1934, table one.

[3] The literal meaning of Kwitavi is Feces Kiva. This name was applied to Katcina kiva at Oraibi, whose members were suspected of witchcraft. It is frequently used in tales dealing with evil behavior. See Titiev, 1939a, p. 93

and footnote 10.

[4] These Katcinas are sometimes known as Sanaiso'yok because they were fashioned from piñon gum. Their crea[-]tion follows a typical pattern of Hopi mythology.

[5] Hurucuki is made of a mixture of blue and white corn meal, boiled in water and eaten as a sort of dumpling. I[t] is considered especially good with meat courses.

nething is troubling you. Speak out and tell us at is the matter." "Well," said the chief, ings are in a bad condition at my village be- se Sanaiso'yoko has been carrying off our ldren, two at a time, and we can't get rid of n. I thought that as you are the defenders of people you might be able to help me." To this grandmother replied, "I know that the vitavis are the ones who made the So'yokos out piñon gum. Now you had better hustle up as se giants have three children already and may n have more. I know that we are supposed to your protectors and I agree that we ought to p you out, but it's up to the Twins to say at's in their minds." At once the older spoke and said, "I think it is our duty to help him, besides, he might give us something for a ward." Hardly had Spider Woman finished re- aching him for his greed than the younger in earned a reprimand for bragging, "I can pe him out myself no matter how fierce he is." In the end it was agreed that the War Twins uld lend their help to the Oraibi people; so ly the next day they proceeded to the village, ying shinny all the way as they went and con- uing their game as long as they saw no signs their opponent. They did not notice the ap- ach of So'yoko, who came up behind them, ched out a long arm, and deposited them in basket. Thanks to a powerful medicine en them by their grandmother, the Twins had fear and laughed and jested as the giant carried m rapidly towards his dwelling. After a time older brother told So'yoko that he needed to ve his bowels, but the giant wouldn't stop and d him to go right ahead in the basket. A few nutes later he gave the same reply to the unger Twin who wanted to urinate.[6]

It did not take So'yoko long to get home, and ce there he joined his family at breakfast with- inviting the Twins, and then told them to pare to go into the oven, to which the brothers lied that they were ready at any time. As soon the walls of the oven were white hot So'yoko ew in one of the Twins, who immediately wed and spat about some of his medicine and n began to urinate against the walls to cool m off. A moment later the other brother was own in, and the So'yoko woman promptly be-

gan plastering the opening to the oven so that the victims might steam and bake to a turn.[7] The Twins felt no alarm because instead of keeping hot the oven was getting cooler and cooler, so they spent their time in jesting as to which of them would make the tastier morsel. During the night the brothers lifted the cover and crawled out of the oven. Then they started a fresh fire, and when the walls were sufficiently hot, they seized the three children of their enemies and having thrown them into the flames, they replaced and re- plastered the cover so that it did not appear to have been disturbed. In the beds of the children they put three stumps under the blankets so that they would not seem to be missing.

Early the next morning the wife of So'yoko pre- pared a batch of *hurucuki* and then got ready to take out the roasted Twins. First she drew one child up by a leg, and commenting on the suc- culent flavor, removed the rest of the meat from the oven and called on her husband to wake the children for breakfast.[8] As the youngsters seemed to be sleeping soundly, So'yoko suggested that they dine later and joined his wife at her repast. "So'yoko man and So'yoko woman," cried out the older Twin from his hiding place, "you are feast- ing on your own children and not on us." The giants looked about in great bewilderment, but even as they sat there wondering, Pu'kong re- peated his taunt. Hurriedly, So'yoko rushed to his children's beds and pulling back the covers dis- covered the stumps. At this he began to cry, un- able to understand how the Twins had escaped and how his own offspring had been substituted for them in the oven.

Just then the Little War Twins revealed them- selves. "Are you the ones who threw my children into the fire?" asked So'yoko. "Yes," replied the brothers, "we are the ones who did it." "Then," stormed the angry giant, "it is time for us to have a fight, and I think that I can easily beat you. You move off a bit and I'll stay here and then we can have it out." Hardly had the Twins taken up their position than So'yoko seized two curved rabbit sticks and hurled one speedily at the older brother. Pu'kong ducked nimbly, and the stick continuing on struck a cedar tree with such force that it burst into flames. Then the giant hurled his second stick with lower aim at the younger

---

For some unexplained reason, there is a reference to ecation or urination in virtually every myth connected h Spider Woman which I gathered at Oraibi.

Children are often told that So'yoko dwells in fire, and when a fire crackles it is said to be the voice of So'yoko.

[8] The narrator made no effort to account for the dis- crepancy between the two victims which So'yoko woman put into the fire and the three which she drew out.

Twin, but he leaped into the air and the stick hit a second tree. Quickly the brothers retrieved the weapons, and returning to their places they said, "Now it is our turn. You are done and we are going to end your life right here." With that the older Twin threw one stick at the giant's knees causing him to tumble to the ground, and the younger brother promptly threw the other at So'yoko's neck, immediately decapitating him. Then they seized his mate, and dragging her to the edge of the mesa, threw her to her death on the rocks below.

Having destroyed their enemies, the brothers returned to the house of the So'yokos and entering the store-room, removed all the loot that the giants had taken from the children they had kidnapped and eaten. These things the Twins carried back to Oraibi, where they deposited them in the plaza and called on the villagers to pick out whatever belonged to them. The Oraibi chief was overjoyed at the response his plea for help had brought from the Twins, and he gladly gave them the gifts he had made for them. Then the brothers set out for their grandmother's home again, "and I think they are still living there."[9]

THE SO'YOKO RITES AT ORAIBI[10]

The So'yoko rites at Oraibi follow the myth only in a general sense, for many details of the ceremony differ from those of the narrative. On Third Mesa any father may ask the So'yoko group to appear, and any kiva may undertake the impersonations.[11] The ceremony begins with ritual smoking and prayers for rain, crops, and health in keeping with the customary Hopi formula. That night one of the kiva members dresses as Hahai'i Wuhti, mother of the Katcinas, and another puts on the Kwikwilyuka Katcina outfit. Carrying a basket of shelled sweet corn they make the rounds of the kivas to announce the coming performance, Hahai'i's words and actions being mimicked by Kwikwilyuka who mocks whomever he likes.[12]

As soon as the various rôles have been assigned to members of the officiating kiva, the parents of uninitiated children begin secretly to relate to the So'yoko impersonators all the naughty deeds,

saucy words, or stubborn actions for which th want their offspring reprimanded. Each your ster's misdeeds must be remembered correctly, a good deal of the efficacy of the performance pends on giving the child the feeling that bogeys have an intimate knowledge of his cc duct. Next day the Hahai'i and the Kwikwilyu dress outside the village so that they may appe in costume as if coming from the San Francis mountains, where all the Katcinas are said dwell. Parents warn their children that son thing unusual is going to happen this day a take pains that they shall be present when Katcinas arrive. At each house Hahai'i lea some sweet corn and warns little girls to gri diligently, so that they may have a good rans for the So'yoko when he tries to carry them Where there are boys in a house, Kwikwilyu leaves tiny horsehair snares, advising the lit fellows to trap mice, bats, and small birds offerings to the giants who are soon to con Incidentally, he relieves the seriousness of situation by imitating everyone in sight. Fr then on the village is alive with bustling pare eager to provide things which So'yoko may cept as substitutes for their children. The you girls help their mothers to grind large quantit of baked sweet corn (tosi), and to prepare ot foods known to appeal to giants. At the sa time the boys are busy trapping small game stringing the carcasses on sticks, while th fathers kill sheep and stuff the hides with r or deck them with horns to resemble mount sheep.

Early on the morning of the fourth day word goes out that the giants are coming, soon the group appears.[13] Each Katcina makes call peculiar to it, and these, added to the fie looking masks, the dread of anticipation, and weapons brandished by the performers, enough to frighten all but the very boldest children. When they reach a house the So'yo recites a list of the child's misdeeds and threate to put him into the basket (hoapu) which carries on his back. At this one of his relativ begins to argue in the child's defence, a good d of attention being paid to the dialogue by

---

[9] This is the conventional ending for all stories dealing with the War Twins.

[10] I am greatly indebted to Mrs. Charis Denison Crockett for putting at my disposal her notes on the Oraibi So'yoko. For a First Mesa comparison, see Steward, 1931, pp. 69–71.

[11] According to Voth, 1901, p. 118, the So'yoko u to be given at Oraibi on the morning of the Bean da day.

[12] This Katcina often behaves like a clown.

[13] For pictures of So'yoko groups, consult Fewk 1923, plates 2, 7.

ctators, who are quick to judge the qualities
 the speeches made by Katcina and defender
ke. If it is a boy whose home is being visited,
 is urged to offer his recently trapped game to
 So'yokos, who pass it from hand to hand and
ally reject it as worthless, much to the lads
rm. Sometimes, one or another of the per-
mers makes a gesture as if to grab the lad,
t the rules forbid that he actually be touched.
eantime the defending kinsman is busy relating
 boy's good points, arguing that he is a good
nter, that he is quick to learn the duties of a
eepherder, and that he does not deserve to be
rried off. At last some of the meat that has been
epared in advance is offered to the Katcinas
o examine it carefully and agree to accept the
nsom. When a girl's house is visited the pro-
dure is only slightly varied. She too hears her
d behavior described and is relieved to have a
nswoman speak up in her behalf, saying that
 is a diligent housekeeper and not lazy when
is necessary to grind corn. Then she offers a
ap of baked sweet cornmeal, which the ac-
mpanying Hehea Katcinas promptly seize and
te.[14] If they pronounce it good, the ransom
accepted, the food is loaded into the carrying
skets, and the group moves off to the next
use.

When the bogeys have made the rounds of the
lage they come at last to their home kiva,
ere there may be heard the sound of singing
d dancing going on inside. The Heheas peep
wn the hatch, and throwing their lariats at the
ummer, pretend to have roped him successfully
d so seem to haul him out of the kiva. An argu-
nt then ensues, the drummer claiming that the
tcinas have interfered with a dance rehearsal
d the Katcinas threatening to carry him off to
 San Francisco mountains. Then the Heheas
ntinue to make repeated casts into the kiva
til they have brought out all the remaining
mbers. These are usually in costume for an
masked dance such as the Buffalo or Butter-
.[15] The So'yoko Katcinas then ask to see the
nce which they had overheard being rehearsed
the kiva, and as the performance begins, the

bogeys begin to show more and more interest
until finally they fall into line and dance with
many comic antics. When the performance is
over, the kiva men ask for a reward, and the
happy So'yokos give them not only all the food
that they have just collected, but also all the
ornaments that they are wearing. Then the unmasked dancers invite the Katcinas into the kiva
to receive prayer-offerings.[16] Once out of sight
of the public, all the members of the kiva enjoy
a feast of the good things which have been offered
as ransoms for naughty children. To explain the
disappearance of the So'yokos after their entrance
to the kiva, uninitiated youngsters are told that
the giants have returned to their homes by an
underground passage.

THE ORAIBI SO'YOKO IN 1911

The last performance of the So'yoko Katcina
at Oraibi was held in the early spring of 1911,
at the request of Piqösa of the Badger clan, who
wanted to discipline his son, Dupki of the Pikyas
clan. In order to conceal his own share in the
proceedings from the child, Piqösa asked Tanakyestiwa, husband of his wife's sister, to sponsor the performance. This was highly appropriate in that the latter was of the Coyote clan
in whose custody the So'yoko masks are kept.[17]
Inasmuch as Tanakyestiwa belonged to Tawaovi
kiva, it was that unit which staged the performance. Tanakyestiwa selected two of the
tallest of his kiva mates, Don Talayesva and his
brother Ira Puhuwaitiwa (Sun clansmen), to impersonate Natacka Katcinas. Don selected one
variant known as Nunuvina, and Ira chose another known as Wihajruma. Kuwanwaitiwa of
the Rabbit clan and Duvehöyoma of the Bear clan
appeared as older brothers of the So'yoko, characters who serve as the main speakers for the
entire group of bogeys. The mother of So'yoko
was played by Qömawuhioma of the Rabbit
clan; and the Heheas were Claude Tawanimp-
tiwa of the Rabbit clan, and Pierce.

The first house visited was that of Piqösa, who
had asked for the performance, but who had not
taken part in order that he might be on hand to

---

4 It is for this reason that these Katcinas are called
heatosisona (Hehea-sweet-cornmeal-seeking).

5 Although these dances ordinarily require performers
both sexes, the men from the kiva take all the parts at
 time.

6 In spite of the fact that the So'yoko ceremony is
posed to bring beneficial results, the natives say that

cold and windy weather always follows a So'yoko appearance.

17 It may be significant that Tanakyestiwa's nickname
was Atosle, one of the impersonations that the Hopi associate with So'yoko. This name corresponds to the Zuñi
bogey called Atoshle. See Parsons, 1939, pp. 51, 52, *et
passim*.

defend his son. Then the group went to the home of Siontiwa, a Masau'u boy whose father, Sikyayestiwa of the Greasewood clan, spoke up for him and offered sheepmeat which he pretended was deer. The group then called on Lilly, a Rabbit girl, whose maternal grandfather, Humi-höniwa (Lizard) shielded her from the giants; but Lilly was not badly intimidated and threatened to report the So'yokos to the principal of the day school. The next girl too was defended by her maternal grandfather. It was Delia of the Sun clan, on whose behalf Duvenimptiwa of the Sand clan argued with the Katcinas. As no other houses had asked for a visit, the performance terminated after this call.

The Oraibi So'yoko is said to be fiercer than that of the other villages, because here the bogeys are permitted to feign seizure of children and to be more harsh in rejecting the preliminary offers of ransom. Even at Oraibi, however, it was absolutely forbidden to touch a child for fear that the "power" of the So'yoko might do the child permanent harm. In fact, I was told of a youngster, long ago, who defied the bogeys to such an extent that they actually had to put him into their baskets and carry him off for a short distance, finally getting rid of him at a shrine. Not long after the lad died, and it was agreed that his death had been due to his coming into too close contact with the Katcina's "power."[18]

SO'YOKO PERFORMANCES ON SECOND MESA[19]

During the evening of the fourth day preceding the appearance of the bogey group, there comes to the village a man impersonating the So'yok-mana (So'yoko girl), who goes from house to house telling the inmates that the giants are coming in four days and warning the boys to trap small game and the girls to grind corn so that they may ransom themselves. On the morning of the performance So'yok-mana appears again to warn the children to be ready with their gifts. The group consists of: a So'yoko male and female, each with a large carrying basket on the back; a We'e'e Katcina in a blue mask and carrying a long black and white ringed pole without snare; two Natackas with fierce, bulging eyes and huge

black bills fashioned from large gourds, each with a bow in the left hand and a saw or a large knife in the right hand; two Masau Katcinas in regulation attire but with striped woolen blankets substituting for the woven rabbit skin garments they are supposed to wear; and eight or ten Koyemsi, two of whom are equipped with lariats.

As they come to a house, the Koyemsi do all the arguing and bargaining, taste the sweet corn-meal and accept or reject the proffered gifts, and sometimes seem to consult the So'yokos who stand in their midst. The two Natackas remain somewhat in back of the main group, uttering their weird cry and maintaining a constant prancing motion forward and back. Once in a while one of the Natackas brandishes his knife or scrapes his saw along the ground, but on the whole their appearance rather than their behavior is supposed to inspire fear. Unlike Third Mesa performers, they do not threaten to snatch children. The Masau Katcinas mingle with the Koyemsi and carry large sacks into which they put most of the food that is collected, and the We'e'e merely stands to one side making no play of any sort with his pole, although it was said that he is supposed to threaten to wreck the house if he deems the ransom insufficient.

In addition to the dispute between the Katcinas and the relatives of a little boy, and apart from the fierce rejection of his timidly proffered stick on which are strung the tiny carcasses of mice or birds, there is generally introduced an added feature. Sometimes the boy, stark naked, is doused with water and made to take a run by himself; and sometimes he is made to run a mock race with one of the Katcinas, the little fellow dashing madly to win in the hope that it will help save his life. With girls too the Katcinas sometimes indulge in a little by-play. On one occasion someone produced a piece of chalk, drew a hop Scotch game, and challenged the performers fierce bogeys and all, to play against the little girl. As they make the rounds, the Koyemsi who carry ropes try to lasso any bystander who comes too close, the idea being that anyone who is caught must pay a forfeit for his release. So liberal are the quantities of food received that the Koyemsi and the Masau Katcinas are generally kept busy mak

[18] Dr. Parsons has called my attention to a similar story prevalent at Zuñi to explain why Atoshle no longer carries children away in her basket.

[19] The following description is based primarily on personal observations which were made in company

with Dr. Eggan at Mishongnovi on February 17, 1934 It is supplemented by Dr. Eggan's notes on a Shipaulov performance (which he has very kindly permitted me t use), and also by interviews regarding Chimopovy pro cedure.

ng side trips to their home kiva with the booty that overflows their sacks and burden baskets.

At each kiva a bit of ritual is performed. As the group clusters about the hatch the kiva chief emerges, naked except for G-string. With a great deal of satisfaction the Katcinas submit him to a bath in cold water, while he, to set a good example to the village youngsters, makes exclamations of delight even though he be shivering with the cold. Then the kiva leader sets out for a brisk run, after which he re-enters the kiva and soon emerges again carrying a pipe, cornmeal and *nakwakwosi*. He smokes over each performer, sometimes letting the Masau Katcinas take a few puffs too, and then presents them with the meal and prayer-feathers that form the customary reward of Katcinas.

At about three-thirty in the afternoon at the Mishongnovi performance of 1934, the bogeys had completed the circuit of the village and had arrived at last in front of their home kiva, within which could be heard the beating of a drum. As with the other kiva heads, the chief was doused and made to run. On his return the Koyemsi requested that he let his kiva mates perform for their benefit, but the leader argued that it was only a rehearsal and that the performers were not yet dressed in costume. The Koyemsi insisted and finally suggested that their sister, the So'yok-mana, take a part. After a long debate the So'yok-mana agreed to enter the kiva, whereupon all the Katcinas began to strip off their adornments for her use. They then decided to bet that their sister would outshine the other dancers, so they removed a good part of their costumes and paraphernalia, which, with the food that they had with them, was taken into the kiva where the stakes were presumably being held. In a short time the drummer came out of the kiva, followed by the singers who were dressed in everyday clothes but each of whom had a smear of white clay daubed on his cheeks. Then came four men who were to dance a sort of Apache war dance.[20] Two were dressed as warriors and carried revolvers and plaques for shields; and two, dressed as maidens in conventional dance costumes, carried arrows with the metal points down.

With them there came the So'yokmana, bearing her crook in the left hand and a big knife in her right, and accompanied by a man in miscellaneous garb including fringed leggings and a straw hat, who carried a rifle. While the set of four dancers was executing a lively step with marching, counter marching, and backward movements, the So'yok-mana and "her" partner carried on a burlesque by pausing a whole beat too late, continuing forward long after the rest had reversed, and generally tangling with the other performers. It was the So'yok-mana who was the main offender, and her partner achieved many comic effects by rushing her into the proper position immediately after she had made a glaring error in the routine of the dance.

As the dance drew to a close all the masked impersonators who had been watching the performance quietly suddenly began to fidget and gradually to close in on the dancers. All at once they made a grab for the two "women" dancers, and hugging them from all sides, pretended to copulate with them. As if in retaliation, the singers began to crowd the So'yok-mana, and all at once a free-for-all developed with the kiva men stripping the Katcinas of the greater part of their costumes, a ludicrous effect being presented by the nearly naked men who still wore their huge bogey masks. In the end the Katcinas appeared to be routed, and hastening to the edge of the mesa, they scampered down to the lower level and out of the village while their opponents fired now and again into the air.

Thus, in vivid and dramatic fashion, does the Second Mesa performance explain the disappearance of the bogeys. In view of the general resemblance of the Oraibi conclusion, except for the manner in which the Katcinas make their exit, I am inclined to believe that at one time the Third Mesa ending also included the dispersal of the maskers after a simulated sex bout, but that for some reason or other this was toned down at Oraibi. As performed on Second Mesa, the element of sex license and the routing of the Katcinas for their misdeeds serve to link the So'yoko performance very closely to similar exhibitions on the part of clown groups.

[20] Practically the same costumes, painting, and steps were observed by the writer at a Hotevilla performance of what purported to be a Comanche dance on February 10, 1934.

CHAPTER XXIII

THE ORAIBI PATCAVA CEREMONY[1]

IN THE years when novices have been admitted to the Tribal Initiation societies, the Powamu chief may decide to extend his ceremony by holding a performance known as the Patcava. In anticipation of the event each man plants two "crops" of beans in his kiva instead of one. The earlier, which is dedicated to the Patcava *manam* (maidens), generally consists of Lima beans because they have prettier blossoms. When these plants are a few inches high, the Powamu chief orders a second planting in the usual manner associated with his rites (p. 144).

The kivas most closely concerned in the Patcava rites are the Chief kiva and the four which conduct Tribal Initiation ceremonies—Hawiovi, which houses the Wuwutcim proper, and Al, Tao, and Kwan which put on the observances for which they are named.[2] The head of each of the participating kivas selects a girl, usually a niece or a daughter, preferably unmarried, to act as a Patcava *mana* for his group. During the ceremony

these maidens must refrain from sexual indulgence and must not eat salt, fat, or meat. They are carefully supervised to prevent any violation of these restrictions. All of the recently inducted Tribal Initiation men are expected to sleep in the kivas and to observe the same tabus, and each kiva head picks one initiate from his kiva to serve as a partner to the Patcava *mana*.[3] These men are entrusted with the care of the special Patcava "crops" in their respective kivas. They must exercise every precaution to prevent damaging the stalks and it is their duty to water the plants, and to rotate them from time to time so that all sides get equal amounts of heat.

On the evening of the first of the last four days of the Powamu celebration, the day following the Katcina initiation, the opening rite of the Patcava takes place. Just as night falls, a He'e'e Katcina impersonator,[4] a member of the Powamu society, unmasked but carefully muffled in a blanket, makes his way to the shrine on Oraibi

---

[1] The present account was obtained at Oraibi in 1934. It is a composite of data secured from several informants all of whom had participated in the Oraibi performance of 1913, on which this description is based. It was the last complete Patcava that was ever held at Oraibi.

The only existing account of the Patcava at Oraibi is the brief summary that appears in Voth, 1901, pp. 122–125. Insofar as essential elements are concerned, there is a close correspondence between Voth's report and the present one.

A partial description of this ceremony on First Mesa is given by Steward, 1931, pp. 74–79.

[2] In 1913 the membership of the Chief kiva (Tawaovi) was so large that it was divided into two parts, each of which staged an independent Powamu night dance. In the same way, two Wuwutcim initiates from the Chief kiva were named as partners to the Patcava maidens who were chosen to represent the two halves of the group. To all intents and purposes, the Chief kiva functioned as two kivas with a common home.

[3] A study of the Patcava personnel throws much light on ceremonial and sociological inter-relationships. The following list deals with the special performers in the 1913 observance:

TAWAOVI: Don (Sun clan, single) and Sikwapnim (Patki clan, married).

Herbert (Coyote, single) and Posyongnönsi (Masau'u, single).

The head of this kiva, the Chief kiva, was Talaskwaptiwa of the Sun clan. Don was his own great nephew, and Herbert was the ceremonial son of the Village chief's

clan (Bear). Sikwapnim was married to the nephew of the Village chief, and Posyongnönsi was the real granddaughter of the chief.

HAWIOVI: Ira (Sun, single) and Alice (Pikyas, single).

This kiva was in charge of Lomanimptiwa of the Bow clan. No reasons were advanced for the choice of Ira and Alice, but it may be significant that Ira was the great nephew of the Chief kiva leader, and Alice was the niece of the Pikyas chief who plays the important part of Aholi in the Powamu rites, and who is second only to the Village chief.

AL KIVA: Luther (Sand, single) and Sikyaletsnim (Greasewood, married).

Nasiwaitiwa of the Bow clan, the head of this kiva, was forced to name Luther who had been the only Al initiate in 1912. Sikyaletsnim was picked because she was a younger woman from a clan in the same phratry as Nasiwaitiwa hence, his niece.

TAO KIVA: Frank Jenkins (Patki, married) and Sikyamönim (Katcina, single).

The kiva head, Masawistiwa of the Katcina clan, had to pick Frank because there were no other initiates from this kiva. Sikyamönim was a true niece of the kiva chief Masawistiwa.

KWAN KIVA: Mark (Rabbit, married) and Etta (Masau'u single).

Lomaleotiwa (Masau'u), kiva chief, chose Mark because he was his ceremonial son, and Etta because she was his own niece.

[4] An He'e'e is illustrated in Voth, 1901, plate LXVIIa.

rock at the west edge of the village. Here he is joined by a number of other Katcinas, many of them of watchman or guardian types which are permitted to carry weapons. These personators are volunteers and may represent any Katcina they choose. They wear their masks tilted on top of their heads in order that they may have less obstructed vision in the dark, and uninitiated children are prevented from approaching too closely. While the others wait at the foot of the rock, He'e'e sings a secret song at Oraibi shrine, after which she enters the village with her "brood" all about her, each Katcina uttering his special cry.[5] Four times around the participating kivas He'e'e leads her "children" before she returns to Oraibi rock. She then climbs alone to the shrine to deposit prayer-offerings, but the other Katcinas remain below and divest themselves of rattles, bells, or other noise-making devices in order that they may return to their kivas without attracting the attention of the uninitiated.

Soon after sunset on the following day, He'e'e again appears at the Oraibi rock shrine, where she meets her "children" and repeats the previous day's performance. Before sunrise the next morning, at about the same time that Hahai'i is getting ready to appear in the village,[6] the He'e'e impersonator climbs to the top of Pumpkin Hill (Patangwocdöka), a short distance east of Oraibi. At the first light of day he sings a special song four times, then undresses and returns in civilian garb for breakfast. Thrice he revisits this shrine

and repeats the same performance, timing his last appearance so that it comes just before the noon hour. On this occasion, instead of disrobing, He'e'e proceeds in full costume towards the north, to a shrine called Waltca (Gap). Here the Hototo Katcinas are supposed to dwell, and two impersonators are awaiting He'e'e's arrival.[7] These follow her as she proceeds to Putatukyaovi[8] where the Suhunsomtaka Katcina joins the party. From here He'e'e leads the way to a shrine where a Palakwai Katcina is waiting,[9] then turns westward and heads towards Oraibi. At Katcinwala (Katcina Gap), near a spot sacred to the water serpent Palulokong,[10] a whole crowd of assorted Katcinas join the procession and accompany He'e'e into the village. She leads the way to the Chief kiva which the group circles four times before making a four-fold circuit of the other kivas as on the two preceding nights.[11] When they reach the Powamu kiva, the He'e'e takes her "children" down to a lunch of bean sprout stew (harukwivi), provided by the members of that kiva.[12] As soon as they have finished eating, the Katcinas continue their rounds of the kivas until they have completed four sinistral and four dextral circuits. On the final round the Katcinas enter their own kivas as soon as they are reached, so that by the time the He'e'e arrives at the last kiva, the Powamu, she is attended only by impersonators who belong to that unit, and when they descend into the kiva the He'e'e rites are over for the day.[13]

[5] Katcina processions without singing or dancing are known as qöqötinumya.
[6] This occurs early in the morning of the day that the Bean dance is to be performed (p. 117). Although Voth makes no mention of the daybreak rites, he gives a brief account of the noon activities. Nevertheless, he does not differentiate the Patcava from the Powamu at this point. See Voth, 1901, p. 117.
[7] The Hototo are male Katcinas, supposedly of an ancient type. They occur in two varieties, one featuring a bill and the other a mask with teeth indicated. The former is pictured in Fewkes, 1903, plate XXXVII. Also, see Voth, 1901, plate LVIIIb. Fewkes gives the name as Hotote.
[8] Putatukyaovi means "Spiral Mesa," and is marked by a pictograph representing concentric circles. This is the symbol of Masau'u, and it may be significant that the Katcina who lives here is described as a "warrior lady." She wears "horns" fashioned from grass at either side of her head. See Voth, 1901, plate LVIIId.
[9] The Palakwai Katcina represents a Red-tailed hawk. He is pictured in Fewkes, 1903, plate XV. Also, see Voth, 1901, plate LVIIIe.
[10] The Palulokong is described on p. 121 ff. Although

the serpent plays no part in the proceedings here described, it is important to note at this point that the narrator called the Palulokong ceremony to mind in the midst of a description of the Patcava. There are many resemblances between the Patcava ceremony and Palulokong rites.
[11] It should be noted that the three Katcinas whom He'e'e meets at special shrines before she gathers a miscellaneous group at Katcinwala, Hototo, Suhunsomtaka, and Palakwai, are among those Katcinas who are specifically named in the narrative of Katcina wanderings which the Powamu chief, in the character of Muyingwa, relates to the novices who are being initiated into his ceremony. See Voth, 1901, pp. 99, 100. Evidently, the movements of the He'e'e Katcina during the Patcava comprise a dramatization of at least one part of the Powamu chief's recital.
[12] Note the skillful timing of this performance. The Katcinas enter the village and dine on bean sprout stew at the time when all the natives are feasting on the same dish.
[13] The men who had been chosen to be the partners of the Patcava maidens are forbidden to appear with the group led by He'e'e.

While this activity is drawing to a close, the Patcava maidens are getting ready for their first appearance They meet at a shrine called Boki (Dog-house), north of the village. Each girl is dressed in the ceremonial costume prescribed for women, consisting of *manta, atu'u,* white moccasins with attached leggings, the hair fashioned in large butterfly wings, and masked in the fashion of Hemis Katcina "girls." They are led by four Mon (Chief) Katcinas[14] and a Hahai'i Wuhti impersonator. As soon as the He'e'e performance has been terminated, the Powamu chief leads the Patcava group into the village. The girls are supposed to be on their way to Duwanasavi (see p. 120) to harvest the bean crop with which they are to appear on the morrow. Near the Wiklavi kiva the procession comes to a halt while the Mon Katcinas sing a secret song, very long and extremely "important," about plants which grow, ripen, and are harvested. Then the group moves on to the dance plaza where the song is repeated, after which they go to the Sakwalenvi kiva for a third and final rendition. At the close of the singing the Powamu chief dismisses the Mon Katcinas and the Hahai'i Wuhti with meal and feathers. No offerings are given to the Patcava *manam* who are scheduled to appear again next day, and the Powamu chief leads them out of sight of the populace to the Katcina shrine known as Qowawaima.[15] The girls are now permitted to get into everyday clothes and to resume their normal occupations. That night they attend the Bean dance in which their partners, who have not been allowed to participate in the He'e'e rites, are allowed to join.

In ordinary years the Powamu ceremony concludes with the Bean dance, but in Tribal Initiation years an added Patcava observance takes place on the following day. Early in the forenoon the Patcava girls go to the kivas which they are to represent, bearing with them special trays[16] full of baked sweet cornmeal which they have prepared. They then go to Qowawaima to dress again in the ceremonial garb worn by the "female" Hemis Katcinas, and to await their partners. Meanwhile, practically all the men in the village, except four men especially singled out for other functions by the kiva heads, dress in Katcina costumes, a great variety of types being represented at the option of the impersonators. The partners of the Patcava maidens also dress in the Katcina outfits which they have chosen, but for the time being they do not mask and do not take immediate part in the activities. Within the Powamu kiva, the He'e'e Katcina[17] gets into costume and emerges at the head of those Katcinas who had descended with her at the close of the previous day's circumambulating. As a rule, more Katcinas join her on this occasion than were with her on the day before. As He'e'e visits the other kivas she picks up more and more of her "children" until a veritable horde of Katcinas is rambling about the village in her wake, and a confusing babble arises as all the impersonators call out and hoot and perform characteristic antics.

While He'e'e is leading her brood around the kivas, a messenger sent by the Powamu chief arrives from Qowawaima to tell her to hurry. Three times he comes and goes, and on his fourth appearance he brings word that it is now time to harvest the crops. At this He'e'e waves aloft her quiver and arrows, as a signal for the Katcinas to run about blocking the view of the spectators and forcing them to withdraw indoors. All non-participants are herded into the nearest houses, whether their own or those of strangers. Children especially are warned not to look out, and windows and doorways are blanketed. In order that they may be the better obeyed the Katcinas feign anger, and those who carry whips do not hesitate to use them on anyone caught peeping out. When the streets are free of profane observers, He'e'e climbs to the roof of *the* Kele (Chicken Hawk) clan house,[18] where she sings her song and overlooks the proceedings. The other Katcinas rush into their kivas to help the four uncostumed men "harvest" the crops sacred to the Patcava girls. In addition to plucking the plants, the attendants

[14] Only Badger clansmen, or those related to Badgers, may play the part of Mon Katcinas.

[15] Qowawaima is a spot near the southern edge of Third Mesa and about two or three hundred yards from the village of Oraibi. It is particularly sacred to the Katcinas and is the home of Eototo and Aholi. At this place the Katcinas assemble before starting an all-day dance, to pray, to put on the masks, and to hold a final rehearsal before filing into the dance plaza within the pueblo. There are similarly named shrines at other Hopi towns.

[16] These trays are sacred and are used only for the Patcava, being secretly stored away at other times. The kiva chiefs keep them in repair.

[17] Owing to the strenuous nature of the He'e'e impersonation, it was customary to have a different man play this part on the last day, while the previous performer rested. The Powamu chief chose both actors.

[18] *The* Kele clan house is chosen, because the Kele clan owns the Wuwutcim ceremony, in honor of whose novices the Patcava is celebrated.

also tie a separate bundle of sprouts to a grease-wood stick, and to this is attached a bunch of "string-beans," fashioned from a dough made of the sweet cornmeal furnished by the Patcava *manam* and suitably colored. At this point the partners of the Patcava maidens put the finishing touches on their costumes, pick up their masks, and hasten to Qowawaima. When the special bean crops are "harvested," they are put on the sacred trays together with the greasewood sticks, the imitation "string-beans," bits of the spruce brought from Kisiwu, and vari-colored ears of corn. Then the kiva heads, each one aided by his four special assistants, carry the loaded trays to Qowawaima. The Katcinas now proceed to the same spot, He'e'e waiting till all of them are on their way before she leaves *the* Kele roof and re-joins her brood.[19] As soon as the people, by dint of cautious glances at various intervals, have determined that the Katcinas have all withdrawn from the village, they emerge again into the streets and patiently await the resumption of the spectacle.

Upon reaching Qowawaima, the Katcinas find the Village chief, in his Eototo costume, awaiting the arrival of the Powamu chief who has gone off to a secret shrine to perform a private ritual with the Patcava girls. When this is over, the Powamu chief leads the maidens to Qowawaima, as if they had just come from Duwanasavi, to which they were supposed to have been on their way at the end of the preceding day's rites. Going up to Eototo, the Powamu leader asks four times for the right to enter Oraibi, and requests permission to show what he can do.[20] Eototo finally gives his consent, and a line of march is formed

for the procession into the village. Before starting out the more experienced men instruct the Pat-cava girls and their partners how best to carry the heavily laden trays. The maidens are sup-posed to carry their loads as far as possible, but if they tire they may be relieved by their escorts.[21]

When all is ready the Powamu chief takes the lead,[22] and close behind him there come delegates acting for the Village chief, the Crier chief, the War chief, the Village chief in the guise of Eo-toto, the Pikyas head as Aholi, and He'e'e. Then follow the Patcava *manam* with their partners at their right hands, the two couples representing the Chief kiva at the head. The general assembly of Katcinas brings up the rear, straggling in and out of the line and keeping up a continuous din.[23]

Soon after the procession has started on its way, the Crier chief announces a short halt in order to afford the girls a breathing space before the more arduous part of their journey begins, and then the march is resumed. Without stopping again, the Powamu chief leads the way to the special "cistern" that was "opened" by the Eototo and Aholi Katcinas on the preceding morn-ing.[24] Here a rite of "closing" is performed, and a lid is actually put over the opening. Then the celebrants march four times around the spot, after which they move on to the Powamu kiva nearby and begin to circle it four times. On the third round, all the Katcinas, including the part-ners of the Patcava girls but excluding Eototo and Aholi, begin to strip off their bells and rattles as they go. At the end of the fourth trip around the kiva, the maidens hand over their loaded trays to their partners, who carry them on a fifth cir-cuit. As this draws to a close, and while most of

[19] An "unofficial" but very amusing comment was brought into the description at this point. My informant remarked that whereas the Katcinas had not eaten for some time, many of them were apt to visit the outdoor cooking pits and to help themselves to *pikami* while the owners were restrained from watching.

[20] This is a dramatization of the arrival of the Badger clan at Oraibi in the time of Matcito, who is represented in this instance by Eototo. The ceremony which the Badgers offered to teach the Hopi in exchange for a home was the Powamu, including the Patcava; and the maidens bearing the crops are supposed to symbolize the manner in which these ceremonies will bring copious harvests to the Hopi.

[21] The girls do not like to ask for help, as the people claim that those with good hearts will have no difficulty, but those who are bad or who have violated the tabus—especially that of sex—will find the loads too heavy for them.

[22] The Powamu chief takes precedence over the Village chief's representative at this point, because while a cere-mony is in progress, its leader is supposed to serve as Village chief *pro tempore*. Compare p. 65.

[23] The noise which the Katcinas make at this time has an utilitarian motive. It is the duty of the escorting Kat-cinas to ask their partners, from time to time, whether they want help with their loads. Inasmuch as the Katcinas are not supposed to speak, the incessant din kept up by the procession makes whispered questions inaudible to the bystanders.

[24] See p. 117. The Bow clansman who dug the "cistern" on the day before impersonates the Saviki, one of the Bow clan's ancestral Katcinas, during the Patcava. At the latter rites he carries a bundle of black sweet corn as he marches in the procession, and at the time the "cistern" (*patni*) is being closed he distributes it among the spectators. Quite often, as a jest, he feigns to offer an ear to one person, then whirls rapidly about and throws it to someone else.

the participants are facing east, the Crier chief suddenly calls out, "*Um utimo tupkyaya'a!*" (Hide, i.e., cover up your children's heads). At once, all uninitiated children are blindfolded in one manner or another, and with all possible speed, the Katcinas hurry to descend into their kivas. Two of the four uncostumed attendants from each kiva grasp the loaded trays borne by their kiva mate, and hasten with it to the home of the Patcava girl who is allowed to keep the contents as a reward for her services. The other two helpers aid their Patcava *mana* to unmask speedily, then take her by the arms and rush her out of sight into their kiva. The village officers too take refuge in their respective kivas, and only the Eototo and Aholi make their dignified way slowly, and in full view of the spectators, to the Chief kiva.

When the uninitiated children are permitted to look about them again, they are amazed to find that the great crowd of Katcinas whom they had just been watching has completely disappeared, and the grown-ups tell them that the Katcinas all flew away.[25]

In the kivas the Katcinas undress, and the Patcava girls too take off their costumes, wrap them in blankets, and change into civilian clothes before going home. All the participants are expected to observe the ritual tabus for four more days before they may resume their normal lives.

The Patcava girls are considered to have acted as "mothers" of the entire village, and to have "fed" the people with the "crops" which they brought with them. In exchange, the men from each kiva sow and tend a special plot of corn for their Patcava *mana* at the next planting, and when it ripens the crop is harvested and brought to her house. The partners of the Patcava maidens are expected to take the leading rôles in arranging this reward for their ritual companions.

[25] In the 1913 observance, an amusing incident occurred at this stage of the proceedings. John Lansa, then a young man, now the husband of the Oraibi chief's adopted daughter, was playing the part of a Kove Katcina. When the time came for the performers to make their hasty exit, John happened to be next to a group of men from Tawaovi kiva, and in the excitement he followed them into their kiva instead of going to the Kwan kiva where he belonged. As soon as he realized his error, he burst out of Tawaovi and scurried for the Kwan kiva, but it was too late; the eyes of the children had been uncovered, and they plainly saw the bewildered Katcina during his solitary dash for cover. The grown-ups immediately grasped what had happened, and to prevent being asked embarrassing questions, they passed off the incident by remarking sadly, though inwardly all were laughing over John's plight, "Alas, that poor Katcina, he has no wings!"

CHAPTER XXIV

THE NIMAN KATCINA DANCE[1]

ALTHOUGH the day long Katcina performances of the spring and summer are conducted with a minimum of formality, the closing
dance of the year is carried out according to the
regular pattern of such formal ceremonies as the
Soyal or the Snake-Antelope. Inasmuch as a
Niman (Homegoing dance) must be given soon
after each summer solstice as the final act of the
open Katcina season, its sponsorship cannot be
left to chance, but must be anticipated in advance.
It was customary at Oraibi, therefore, to have the
responsibility rotate annually from kiva to kiva
in a fixed order,[2] the heads of the kivas being required to serve as sponsors whenever their turns
came. A sponsor would begin by selecting an assistant from among the members of his group, and
together they would pick the men who were to
serve as fathers of the Katcinas, song leaders of
the male and "female" impersonators, and gatherers of sacred spruce from the shrine at Kisiwu.

The first step in the Niman procedure, an announcement of the coming ceremony, occurs towards the close of the preceding Soyal, about six
months before the dance is to be held.[3] On one
of the four nights that the Soyal men are resting
in their kiva at the close of their rites, the newly-
appointed officers for the forthcoming Niman
meet with the Katcina and Powamu chiefs for
a ritual smoke in the sponsor's kiva. All wear
their hair loose and are naked except for G-
strings. The kiva chief picks his biggest pipe,
fills it with native tobacco, lights it, puffs a few

times, and passes it to the man on his left who
smokes a little before they exchange reciprocal
terms of relationship.[4] Then, after smoking a
few moments in silence, the second man passes
the pipe to the officer on his left, and the same
procedure is followed until the pipe reaches the
last man who must smoke it out before handing
it back directly to the kiva chief.

While the ritual smoke is in progress, the ordinary members of the kiva and various other men
drop in from time to time. All of these must have
passed through their Tribal Initiation, or they
would not be eligible to participate in the evening's rites.[5] Each man brings with him his
Katcina costume and puts the skirt and sash in
any convenient spot, but deposits his turtle shell
and gourd rattles north of the fireplace. Here
there are already set out two small plaques containing cornmeal, a number of *nakwakwosi*, two
"mother" ears of corn, and a mask of the type
that has been chosen for the Niman by the sponsor.[6] Having disposed of their burdens, the men
smoke informally and chat quietly so as not to disturb the officers.

When the formal smoke is concluded the kiva
head begins to speak. After naming the men
whom he has chosen for special functions during
the Homegoing dance, i.e., the very men with
whom he has just been smoking, he makes the
first official announcement of the Niman:

"In mid-summer, when the sun reaches its
summer home, these Katcinas, our friends, are

---

[1] Reasonably complete accounts of the Niman Katcina
dance have been published only for First Mesa. The best
sources are Parsons, 1936b, pp. 493–569, *et passim;* and
Fewkes, 1892a, pp. 69–94, *et passim.*

Since the Niman has never been described for Third
Mesa, the present account is given as fully as possible.
All the material was obtained from Oraibi informants who
had participated in these exercises in the years prior to
1906.

[2] Informants in 1933–1934 were unable to recall the order
in which kiva sponsorship had formerly rotated at Oraibi,
but at Hotevilla the kiva sequence was Al, Tcu, Sakwalenvi, Kwan, and Hawiovi.

[3] The writer was present throughout the announcement
proceedings of December 23, 1933.

[4] The officers who participate in the ritual smoke must
sit in prescribed order. The kiva chief sits at the southwest

corner of the fireplace and the others are ranged in an arc
on his left. His assistant sits immediately next to him, followed by the Katcina chief, the Powamu chief, the fathers
of the Katcinas, the song leader of the men, the song leader
of the "women," the head of the spruce gatherers, and the
remaining members of the spruce-gathering expedition.

[5] Although membership in the Tribal Initiation is not
prerequisite for Katcina activities, it is required on this
occasion because the performance is linked with the Soyal,
a ceremony conducted exclusively by those who have
passed through the Tribal Initiation.

[6] According to Stephen, Parsons, 1936b, p. 494, the
Niman sponsorship at Walpi rotates annually among five
kivas, all of which have specific Katcina types which they
must impersonate when their turns come. At Oraibi the
head of the sponsoring kiva has an unlimited choice of
Katcina types.

to be put up and to dance. From now on we people must not be mean to each other, so that we may have a good life and so that all people may have a good life with us."

The kiva chief's assistant and the Katcina and Powamu heads repeat the speech verbatim; then the men chosen to be fathers of the Katcinas and dance leaders repeat the same words, after making brief prefatory remarks expressing thanks for the honor of having been picked as officers.

When the announcements are finished, the sponsor begins to sing one of the songs which he has had composed for the coming Niman. Sometimes he has taught it to his kiva mates in advance, and sometimes they now hear it for the first time, but in a little while the entire assemblage picks up the tune and prepares to rehearse it in dance formation. A bowl of whitewash (*duma*) is brought out, and all but the fathers of the Katcinas and the Katcina and the Powamu chiefs begin to dress and paint. Each man puts on a G-string, kilt and sash, loosens his hair, and takes off his shirt, shoes, and stockings. Then he crooks his left elbow and smears a stripe of white clay wash so that it includes both the upper and the lower arm, repeats the process with his right elbow, runs a smear across his sternum and another across the corresponding part of the back, whitens the entire face, and bends each knee so that with a single motion he stripes both thigh and calf. Next, he ties his turtle-shell rattle below his right knee, puts on a number of strings of beads, affixes a *nakwakwosi* to his hair, and after picking up his gourd rattle in the right hand, seeks out his place in the dance line. It is interesting to see how readily the men agree on their positions in the dancing column, although the places nearest the leader in the center are the most prized. No one decides who shall impersonate males or "females," yet, there is rarely a disproportion between the two types. Youngsters and old men generally choose places at the front or rear of the line, and the order is based entirely on singing and dancing ability without regard to size or age.

As soon as everyone is in position, the father of the Katcinas makes the customary speech, urging the men to sing with happy hearts, and as he begins to sprinkle the dancers with meal, he calls on the leader to begin. So fixed are the steps for the various types of Katcina impersonations, and so well do the songs adhere to the pattern, that no coaching is necessary even at the outset, and having learned the song the men dance to it so readily that a white observer looks on in amazement.[7]

After one or two rehearsals in costume, the Katcinas give an "official" rendition in the sponsoring kiva before they start on a round of the other kivas.[8] At this time, the fathers of the Katcinas, the head of the Katcina clan, and the Powamu chief, all sprinkle the dancers. Then, when the men have finished and departed for another kiva, the fathers of the Katcinas remain behind to smoke, and the Katcina and Powamu heads go off to the Powamu kiva.

The dance group does not keep in formation as it goes to the next kiva. At the hatch the leader shakes his rattle, the inmates call out, "Yungya'a (Come in)!" and the Katcinas enter, line up, and dance and sing in customary fashion, while the kiva chief, whether or not he is a Powamu initiate, serves as father.[9] As the men file out after the dance is ended the sponsor, who is purposely last in line, pauses by the ladder and, with his left hand resting on a rung at shoulder height, repeats the announcement of the Niman which he had made in his own kiva. The hearers reply with thanks, and the sponsor hurries out to rejoin the Katcinas, who are already on their way to another kiva. The same procedure is followed in all the kivas in the village, after which the dancers return to the sponsor's kiva and the formal announcement of the forthcoming Niman is regarded as complete.

It is generally spring before Niman affairs demand attention again. No major rites are performed at this time of the year, and apart from the occasional presentation of a Katcina dance there is nothing to prevent the men from devoting their spare time to the memorizing of the round of songs to be given at the Homegoing dance. If a man has a good deal of wool to be spun, he may propose to hold a spinning bee at which Niman songs may be rehearsed. If so, he informs the dance sponsor of his plans, and on the date set the latter walks down all the streets in the village calling out the time and place of the meeting as he goes. The men congregate in the morning and sing and spin until noon, when the proposer

---

[7] Compare p. 127 and footnote 106.

[8] For these performances the Katcinas do not mask. However, in each kiva which they visit the men recognize the impersonation by the song and dance.

[9] This is one of the few occasions on which a non-Powamu man may serve as a father of the Katcinas.

rewards them with a feast at his house. During the afternoon there is no gathering, but that evening the Niman sponsor again walks through the pueblo with the request that all men go to his kiva. Inasmuch as these practices must be kept secret from the uninitiated, nothing more definite is said, but it is understood that only those who are planning to participate will gather at the officiating kiva.[10] This time, the steps and the tunes are rehearsed and the Katcina and Powamu chiefs, as well as the fathers of the Katcinas, sprinkle the dancers. At the close of the evening's practice, the men return home but the officers remain and smoke informally before they leave the kiva.

Similar rehearsals are held from time to time until the day of the Niman draws near. The actual date of the performance is determined by the Sun Watcher, who announces when the sun is in its summer home (summer solstice point). The following morning the chiefs of the Blue and Gray Flute societies go to the respective houses that contain their ritual objects in order to make prayer-offerings.[11] Four days later the Niman rites begin.

To initiate the proceedings the Katcina chief and the Powamu leader meet in the main Katcina clan house at sunrise to make prayer-sticks and to smoke and pray. Meantime, the wife of the Village chief prepares a feast of stew and folded white *piki* at her house, and late in the afternoon the chief, the Crier chief (Tca'akmongwi), the War chief (Kaletaka), the Katcina and Powamu chiefs, all assemble to make prayer-objects and to discuss final plans for the Niman before they enjoy their feast and disperse.

Before sunrise the next morning, the Crier chief goes to the home of the Village chief and takes the tray of prayer-offerings to the top of *the* Kele clan house, where he deposits them at his special shrine. Then he faces north and makes an announcement, speaking in a low tone for the most part, and deliberately making himself in-

audible during the secret parts of his message to the clouds. "You, living in the North, loom up," says the Tca'akmongwi. Then comes a whispered phrase, after which he continues, "From now on in sixteen days, these Katcinas, our friends, are to be put up as we have planned. So you people must be kind to each other and help each other with happy hearts." This announcement he repeats in each of the four cardinal directions. Soon after, the Katcina and the Powamu leaders take the offerings which they had manufactured prior to the meeting at the house of the Village chief, and these they deposit at Katcina shrines west and north of the pueblo. For the next sixteen days the Niman sponsor and the Katcina chief keep count of the days by making a series of scratches on the walls of their houses.

Nothing of special interest occurs until the ninth day, when the Katcina and Powamu heads and the fathers of the Katcinas go into retreat in the Powamu kiva. From now on the rites in that kiva are open only to members of the Powamu society, while concurrently, in the officiating kiva, the sponsor continues to look after various details connected with the Homegoing performance. During the next three days the Powamu kiva is the scene of a good deal of ritual devoted to prayer-stick-making, the laying out of sand paintings, the erection of altars, and the singing of many sacred songs.[12]

Immediately after breakfast on the thirteenth day, the Katcina chief, the Powamu chief, and the fathers of the Katcinas make prayer-sticks for the spruce gatherers who are about to visit Kisiwu, a shrine about 60 miles northeast of Oraibi. At the same time, in his own kiva, the Niman sponsor, aided by his helper and the dance leaders, likewise prepares a number of offerings. The Katcina chief brings the *pahos* made in the Powamu kiva over to the sponsoring kiva, and here the two sets are put into a sack together with a pipe, some Hopi tobacco, and sacred cornmeal,

---

[10] Compare Parsons, 1936b, p. 495.

[11] The Blue Flute ordinarily met at *the* Spider clan house as it was controlled by the Spider clan, but the Gray Flute, although it was owned by the Patki clan, was accustomed to meeting in *the* Kele clan house. This feature was unexplained by Oraibi informants.

The two societies met independently and made prayer-sticks that were placed in plaques and smoked over. Then they sang the same songs that they used in their biennial summer performances, accompanying them with flutes

and dentalium shell rattles. No costumes were worn, the participants being naked except for breech clouts. Early in the afternoon a good runner was dispatched to deposit the offerings at a shrine located at the summer solstice point. This is one of the rituals which provides definite evidence of the solstitial nature of the Flute rites. Compare pp. 149 and 153.

[12] Fewkes, 1892a, pp. 69 ff., gives details of Niman altar construction and related rituals as performed on First Mesa.

which are turned over to the director of the spruce fetching party.[13] He also receives some *nakwakwosi* which are carried separately, and when all is ready he starts to leave the kiva, but pauses by the ladder to tell the assemblage to be happy and good while awaiting his return.

The pickers leave the village and travel east for about half a mile. Here their leader deposits a road-marker (*putavi*)[14] of the Katcina chief's making. About a mile farther on, the party pauses again while their head man puts down seven *nakwakwosi* for the sun, one from each of the Niman officers. After traveling on a short distance the director calls a halt and gives each man a prayer-feather made by the Katcina chief, to tie in his hair. When they have gone about two and a half miles from Oraibi, the leader dismounts while the others continue on. Alone he goes to the side of the road, draws from his bundle two prayer-sticks made by the Katcina and Powamu chiefs, and puts them down together with a road-marker which the former had prepared. After sprinkling the offerings with cornmeal, the leader hastens to catch up with his comrades. Other sacred objects are deposited at Patuwi, about nine miles east of the pueblo at Tusyopdöka (Hard Rock Point) some three miles farther on, and at Wikwaptcomo which is quite near their destination. At these points the road-markers of the Katcina chief, the Powamu chief, and the Niman sponsor, respectively, are placed beside the path.

It is usually just before sundown that the party arrives at Kisiwu. Instead of proceeding to the spring at once, they make camp for the night a short distance off. Being tired from traveling, they go to sleep early and arise before sunrise to begin the day's activities. About 100 yards from Kisiwu they strip to their G-strings and loosen their hair. Their director then distributes among them all the remaining prayer-offerings except those which were separately carried. Then they proceed in single file, led by their chief, who carries a pipe, native tobacco, a whistle made of the ulna of an eagle, and the netted gourd (*mongwikuru*) and "bull-roarer" (*tovokinpi*) belonging to the Katcina chief. As they approach very near to the spring, the group pauses while the chief blows the whistle and whirls the "bull-roarer." At this they take four

steps and the same performance is repeated. A third and a fourth time they follow this procedure, and at the last one they find themselves right at the spring. "We are here!" cries out the leader to the Katcinas who dwell in the sacred spring, "We have come with happy hearts!"

After these preliminaries the men remove the logs which surround the water-hole, and picking a spot that is relatively dry, they set out a number of prayer-sticks in a row. Then they squat down for a formal smoke, at the close of which the head man begins to fill the netted gourd that he had brought along. Four times he dips an eagle feather (taken from the bird's leg) into the spring and runs whatever water he has scooped up into the container; then he dips it into the spring and lets it fill up. Once full, a *mongwikuru* must not be allowed to rest on the ground, but must be suspended from some object at all times until it has served its purpose. The explanation for this custom rests on the belief that the gourd full of water from a holy place represents rain, and if the *mongwikuru* is put down anywhere it will bring premature precipitation to that spot without benefiting the people at home for whom it is intended.

As soon as the gourd has been filled, the men leave the spring and go back to their camp to dress. Somewhat later, they return for a careful inspection of the row of *pahos*. If a prayer-stick has fallen, or if a feather seems to have been damaged, the omens are bad; but if all are in position it is a good sign, and if some of the offerings have accumulated dew (moisture), the auspices are particularly favorable. Once more the group returns to its base, takes a light lunch of water and *piki*, and begins to gather spruce. First, the leader cuts a little shrub, considered male, while an assistant cuts another which represents a female. These two are regarded as brother and sister to each other and are to be used as shrines in the plaza while the Niman is being performed. Into each hole caused by their removal, some of the *nakwakwosi* which were separately carried are deposited as payment, and the special shrubs are sacked and carried apart from the rest of the spruce.

The party now sets about the task of picking young and blooming plants to be attached to the dance kilts (*vitcuna*) of the Katcinas, and a large

---

[13] Spruce-gathering journeys were once held in conjunction with almost every important ceremony at Oraibi.

[14] A road-marker consists of a string with an eagle feather attached. It is generally placed with the string extending in the direction to be traversed. Cornmeal is sprinkled on it when it is deposited.

amount of spruce in any condition to be used as "collars." In picking these, unlike the procedure for securing the "brother and sister," no knife may be used, and payment is made in a lump by depositing the rest of the special prayer-feathers at the base of any flourishing spruce tree. When all the sacks are full and there is no more gathering to be done, the group prepares to set out at once on the return journey. No particular order is observed, but at each of the places where he has put down road-markers, the leader stops to examine the condition of his offerings, to set aright those which have become awry, and to turn the road-markers about so that they face towards home.

The expedition tries to get as near Oraibi as it can before dark, as the next day is *totokya* (the day before the dance is held), and they are expected in the village soon after sunrise. Just outside the northeastern corner of the pueblo, the party stops to unload, and the sacks of spruce are secreted in any convenient outbuilding that happens to be empty. The leader breaks off a few twigs, keeps some, and gives the rest to one of his assistants. Then the chief gatherer, carrying the full *mongwikuru* and other ritual objects, makes his way to the Powamu kiva while the other men proceed to the Niman sponsor's kiva. In each of these chambers a formal smoke is held by the dance officers who are connected with one kiva or the other, and a detailed, circumstantial account of the journey is related, the head man speaking in the Powamu kiva, and the helper who was given the twigs of spruce reciting a similar account in the sponsoring kiva. Although the avowed purpose of these speeches is to reveal all the omens observed on the trip, the very bad signs are generally omitted because they might cause grief; and people with "bad" (unhappy) hearts are unfit to conduct a ceremony. After the speech-making, the gatherers go home to rest and eat.

On this day the dancers are very busy finishing their costumes and preparing dolls or other things to be distributed at the dance. According to Stephen, a very important rite occurs in the morning, when the head women ("mothers") of each clan come down into the kiva with their chiefs' sticks and make prayer-sticks under the supervision of various men with whom they then engage in a brief smoke.[15] Soon after supper all the participants in the Niman assemble at the officiating kiva. Only the Powamu chief is absent, as from now on he must maintain a long, solitary vigil, smoking and praying all night in the Powamu kiva. In the other kiva, the activities begin with a complete dance rehearsal, followed by a ritual smoke for officers while the dancers sit about and look on. By now it is after midnight; the spruce gatherers are dispatched to bring the loaded sacks from their cache; and upon their return the entire group leaves the kiva and moves on to the dance plaza. All the dancers wear only breech clouts, but those who are to impersonate male Katcinas affix their turtle-shell rattles and carry their gourd rattles. They line up in the customary manner and go through one full performance, using the song which is to be publicly rendered next day on their first appearance after the noon rest.

Meanwhile the Katcina chief is busy erecting the "brother" spruce shrine, while the fathers of the Katcinas put up the "sister" shrub. Aided by the Niman sponsor and his helper, these officers dig little holes in front of the Katcina shrine (*pahoki*) at the northwest corner of the dance plaza. Into these they deposit prayer-feathers and meal before inserting the trees in such manner that they will stand erect. Then they affix *nakwakwosi* here and there to the branches and complete their operations by sprinkling cornmeal paths from the shrines to the southeast, the Hopi path of life. After this the Niman sponsor and his assistant withdraw to their kiva to smoke and pray, while the Katcina chief and the fathers of the Katcinas take up their positions and carry out the duties which they are to fulfill during the dance. The Katcina chief stands at the head of the line, to the left and somewhat in front of the first dancer. From time to time he leaves his place to sprinkle the dancers and to speak to them in a low voice before the fathers of the Katcinas also sprinkle the men and call aloud to them.

When the night rehearsal in the plaza is concluded, the dancers are led to their customary resting place and dismissed. By now it is nearly dawn, and the men hurry to the sponsoring kiva to attach spruce "collars" to the bases of their masks, and to tie or sew bits of spruce to their

---

[15] Parsons, 1936b, p. 523. Very likely, similar rites were carried on at Oraibi, but my informants considered such esoteric matters too sacred to be disclosed.

Throughout Stephen's works there are scattered references to women taking part in ritual smokes. On Third Mesa, however, all informants agreed that the women never smoked, but had male members connected with their ceremonies do all the smoking for them.

dance kilts. Then they paint up, take their masks, and go out to Qowawaima, where they finish putting on their complete costumes and practice their opening song while the masks are ranged beside them in a row.[16] The Katcina chief and the fathers of the Katcinas do not remain with the men after the plaza rites are over, but join the Powamu chief in his kiva. They then emerge while the Katcinas are rehearsing at Qowawaima

along. As they enter the plaza to begin the day's dancing, many of the Katcinas carry a variety of gifts which they distribute before shifting from the first to the second position. At this stage, the chief of the sponsoring kiva and his assistant both leave the kiva and go to their homes to get their heads washed, then eat breakfast at about the same time that the dancers are breaking their fast at their resting place (*katcin nunuspa*)

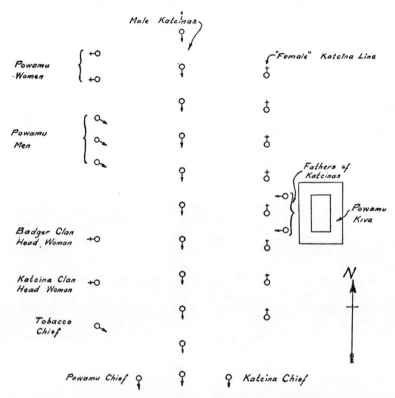

FIG. 12. FINAL POSITION OF NIMAN KATCINA DANCE.

and await the coming of the dancers, the Katcina chief standing a short distance from Qowawaima and the fathers somewhat nearer the village.

As soon as the last practice is concluded, the dancers assume their masks and start for the plaza in dance formation. When they reach the spot where the Katcina chief is waiting, he takes the lead and sprinkles a meal path as he goes. Soon they approach the waiting fathers of the Katcinas, who fall into line behind the Katcina chief and who also sprinkle meal as they walk

during the first recess of the day. Although the Powamu chief does not come out of his kiva, he too eats at the same time as the others.[17]

After breakfast the Niman sponsor and his helper go into their kiva, pick up a few pipes and some native tobacco, and go to the Katcina resting ground where they sit in a special place and smoke and pray throughout the day, offering a pipe to any visitor who cares to join them. At each interval between dances, the men unmask and range their masks, facing southeast, in a line

[16] Parsons, 1936b, p. 530, footnote 3, contains several additional points on the last night's practice which First Mesa informants revealed to Dr. Parsons. It may be that similar rites were held at Third Mesa but not described to me

[17] Eating at the same time as the celebrants of a rite is an expression of communion with them.

before the smokers. At noon the Katcina chief and the fathers of the Katcinas lead the dancers only part way towards the place of rest, and then go to dine with the Powamu chief. The sponsor and his aide, who have been forbidden to drink water throughout the forenoon, dine with the Katcinas. Soon after lunch the Katcina chief and the fathers again await the coming of the dancers as they did before the opening dance of the day, and the performance continues throughout the afternoon.

When the last of the dances is starting, the head of the officiating kiva goes with his helper to put away their smoking outfits, after which they are free to go to the plaza as spectators. At about the same time, the head women of the Katcina and Badger clans (the two clans which control the Katcina cult), the Soyal Tobacco chief, who is usually the head of the Rabbit clan which is in the same phratry as the Katcina clan, and any Powamu initiate who cares to do so, generally enter the Powamu kiva to await the coming of the dancers, for the routine of the concluding dance in the Niman is somewhat different from that of all other plaza performances. After the concluding song has been sung in the first two of the customary three positions, the Katcina chief and the fathers of the Katcinas pull up their respective "brother" and "sister" tree shrines, and carry them along as they lead the Katcinas to a dancing spot just west of the Powamu kiva (*dipkya*)[18] for the final rendition of the last song.

While the dance is in progress, the trees are carried into the Powamu kiva, and almost at once the people who have been waiting there come out to bless the Katcinas in various ways. The Katcina chief, followed by the fathers of the Katcinas, goes down the line sprinkling each performer with cornmeal. Then the Powamu chief asperges each dancer with medicine water; the Tobacco chief blows a puff of smoke at each man; and after him comes the "mother" of the Katcina clan, who carries concealed under her ceremonial blanket (*atu'u*) the Katcina *tiponi* which is used at Katcina initiations and in the Niman observances that precede the dance. Without displaying the *tiponi*, she makes a motion with it under her garment towards every man in the line as she passes him. The Badger clan "mother" does the same with the *tiponi* that was

[18] This is the same place where the first Katcina group of the season, the Qöqöqlom, holds the last dance of its performance. See fig. 11.

used at the Powamu initiation and in the preliminary Niman rites. As they conclude their blessings, and while the dance is still going on, the Powamu chief, the Tobacco chief, and the two "mothers" re-enter the kiva to leave their sacred objects. Then the Powamu chief distributes prayer-sticks and prayer-feathers which have been made during the last few days to the officers and ordinary Powamu members who are in the kiva, and all come out again, the Powamu chief standing at the right hand of the first dancer, in a position analogous to that of the Katcina chief on his left.

When it comes time to sprinkle the men as they begin the concluding verse and chorus of the entire performance, many people take part. One after another, the following serve as sprinklers: Katcina chief, fathers of the Katcinas, Powamu leader, Tobacco chief, clan "mothers," any Powamu member. Each person on finishing takes up a specific position. (See fig. 12.)

When the song ends, the distribution of prayer-offerings begins. First the Katcina chief gives prayer-sticks, prayer-feathers, and cornmeal to the men at the head of the line until he runs out of sticks, whereupon he gives the remaining dancers only feathers and meal. The fathers of the Katcinas give *nakwakwosi* and meal to the first few men, then continue with prayer-sticks for those who have not yet received any; and when their supply runs out, they distribute only meal and feathers. Each succeeding official does the same, until at the close, every performer has at least one prayer-stick and several sets of feathers and meal. When the offerings have been given out, the distributors again assume their positions as in fig. 12.

It is now time for the Katcinas to be dismissed to their homes. Before they are led out of the village for the last time of the season, the fathers of the Katcinas make a farewell speech. It is a solemn occasion, and all the adults listen attentively while the men speak.

"Now we have finished the day. This morning I told you that we were to have a good time here for this one day, but at the sunset you must go home to your parents as I promised you. Now the time has come, the sun has reached its place and I am tired, and you too may be tired.

"When you go home and get to your parents and sisters and the rest of your relatives who are waiting for you, tell them all the words that I am going to tell you. Tell them that they should not wait, but let them come at once and bring rain to our fields. We may have just a few crops in our fields, but when you bring the rain they will grow up and become strong. Then if you will bring some more rain on them we will have more corn, and more beans, and more watermelons, and all the rest of our crops. When harvest time comes we will have plenty of crops to gather, so we will have plenty of food for the whole winter.

"So now, this will be all. Now go back home happily, but do not forget us. Come to visit us as rain. That is all."[19]

At the close of the speech, the Katcina chief leads the Katcinas out of the village, all the other officers remaining in position and sprinkling the men with meal as they go by. Led by their chief the Katcinas leave the pueblo limits, file past Oraibi rock, clamber down the mesa and make their way to a shrine called Katcin Kiva, which has a small opening with a lid over it. The Katcina chief removes the cover and stands aside. Then each dancer steps up and drops in his prayer-feathers and cornmeal, but not his prayer-stick. When all have finished, the Katcina chief restores the lid and goes back to the village to join the group in the Powamu kiva.

After a performer has deposited his offerings, he unmasks and hurries to a spot nearby, where some female relative—a wife, sister, or mother—has brought his civilian clothes and two blankets. Each man takes off his costume, washes off the paint, and puts on everyday apparel. Then he carefully strips his mask of its feathers and places it in one blanket, while all the rest of his paraphernalia, including his prayer-stick, are wrapped in the other blanket and carried home for him by his female attendant.[20]

From Katcin Kiva the dancers, each carrying his mask concealed, return to the officiating kiva where they find the sponsor and his helper wait-ing for them. When all have assembled, the masks are ranged close to and parallel with the northern banquette, facing north. The kiva head and his assistant smoke pipes informally with the leaders of the dance and whatever other men may care to join them, and after the smoke the performers are free to return home.[21] Simultaneously, in the Powamu kiva, those who had remained to sprinkle the Katcinas as they filed out of the village at the close of the dance, await the return of the Katcina chief from Katcin Kiva. When he makes his entry they begin to break pieces from the spruce tree shrines which had been left there when the dancers were quitting the plaza. As soon as everyone has a share the group disperses and the Katcina chief and the fathers of the Katcinas carry home the "brother" and the "sister" spruces.[22]

Very early on the morning following the Niman dance the final rites pertaining to the seasonal departure of the Katcinas take place. While sacred songs are being sung within the Powamu kiva, four pairs of Katcinas appear outside and circle the kiva.[23] Then Eototo and a "female" impersonation of the type performed the day before take up a station at the north of the kiva. At the west, in the costumes worn on the preceding day, stand a male and a "female" Katcina, both impersonated by Parrot clansmen. On the south, two Eagle[24] clansmen form a Katcina couple, and at the east, there is a Badger pair.

Soon the Katcina chief climbs up the ladder until his head is about on a level with the hatchway. From this position he throws meal upwards in the four directions. Then, in ritual order, north, west, south, and east, the male Katcinas hand annulets into the kiva. Again the Katcina chief sprinkles meal upwards and, in order, the same men pour water from *mongwikurus* into a bowl which he holds up.[25] Once more meal is thrown, and this time the "female" impersonators make discharm-

---

[19] This speech is formalized, not improvised, and is repeated each year. If there are two Katcina fathers, each makes the same speech. The closing phrase indicates the identity of Katcinas with clouds. Literally, it goes, "*Um itamu poptaiyani yoyangwu'u akwai,*" "You us visit (come to see) raining with." Compare the literal translation by Kennard in Earle and Kennard, 1938, pp. 37, 38.

[20] Despite the effort expended in gathering spruce, it is discarded at the time the men undress. Spectators frequently snatch bits of spruce from the dancers as they are leaving the plaza.

[21] The customary ritual tabus against salt, meat, fats, and sexual activity are observed for the next four days by all participants. The Niman sponsor and his assistant sleep in their kiva during this time.

[22] Those who have acquired bits of spruce, prayer-offerings, or the tree "shrines," take them to their fields the next day and deposit them with prayers for good crops.

[23] For comparative material regarding First Mesa procedure at this stage in the rites, see Parsons, 1936b, pp 535 ff.; and for Second Mesa see Fewkes, 1892a, pp 99 ff.

[24] In former times, it was said, the Turkey clan which is now extinct used to take the part performed by Eagle clansmen.

[25] Compare the rites at Powamu kiva on the morning of the Bean dance, p. 118.

ing motions with sprigs of greasewood which they carry, and then toss them down the kiva hatch. Next, the Katcina chief, still standing on the ladder, holds up a *paho* so that it is just protruding out of the kiva. Eototo reaches for it but it is withdrawn rapidly until, after three ritual feints, he is allowed to grasp it.[26] The same procedure is followed with the other Katcinas and then the Katcina chief emerges, followed by the Tobacco chief and members of the Powamu society. The former blows smoke on each impersonator, and the latter sprinkles them with meal as they march four times around the kiva. On completing the circuit, the Katcina chief leads them out of the village to Katcin Kiva as on the preceding day, and into the open shrine they put their prayer-sticks and other sacred objects. When the Katcina chief replaces the lid he is performing the ultimate act of the Homegoing ceremony, and from that moment on no more Katcinas may be impersonated until next winter.[27] Later in the day all the captive eagles in the pueblo, except those whose quills are still soft, are ceremonially

strangled and buried.[28]

Three days later the officers who have just conducted the Niman rites assemble in the officiating kiva before daybreak. After a formal smoke, the sponsor takes one of the masks which had been left near the north banquette at the close of the dance, wraps it in a blanket, and carries it to the kiva which succeeds his own in the fixed cycle of Niman responsibility. There he puts the mask north of the fireplace and engages in a smoke with the kiva head who is to succeed him. Then the retiring leader makes a brief announcement. "Next year," he says to his smoking partner, "You are to put on the Niman dance with —— (naming a member of the latter's kiva)[29] to help you."

After the visitor has taken his departure, the newly-named sponsor carries home the mask, regardless of its owner, and keeps it concealed until the Katcina season opens again, when the man to whom it belongs may claim it. The other masks which have been left in the last officiating kiva are called for at their owners' convenience.

[26] The four-fold ritual feint is discussed in Parsons, 1939, pp. 368, 369.
[27] The one exception to this rule is the Masau Katcina which is described in detail in the following chapter.

[28] For information regarding this custom, consult Voth, 1912b, pp. 105–109.
[29] This contradicts a previous statement by the same informant, to the effect that the Niman sponsor picks his own assistant, p. 227.

Chapter XXV

MASAU KATCINA DANCE AT HOTEVILLA

LATE in October 1933, many people at Oraibi began to speak of a Katcina dance that was soon to be held at Hotevilla. As I well knew that it was the time when the Katcinas were supposed to be "locked up," I thought that I was being teased, but soon it became evident that a masked dance was actually being rehearsed. As I later found out, there was a young woman resident at Hotevilla who, during pregnancy, had vowed that in the event of a successful confinement she would ask for a Masau Katcina dance, since this Katcina is not "locked up" with all the others after the Homegoing dance but may appear out of season. The relation of the name to the "real" Masau'u, whose chief characteristic is to do things by opposites, made it likely that all sorts of innovations might be expected from the associated Katcina, and it was with a good deal of anticipation that I went to Hotevilla on November 11, 1933, to see the performance of this unique Katcina.

Instead of approaching from the conventional Katcina shrine, which is somewhat south and east of the plaza, the dancers came from the northwest;[1] but having reached the actual dancing ground they entered from the customary northeast opening. They were preceded by Puhunimptiwa, who often served at Hotevilla in the rôle of father of the Katcinas, and who sprinkled a cornmeal path for them to follow.

Apart from the divergence in the direction of their approach, and apart from the fact that they did not rest between numbers at the shrine generally used by Katcinas, the outward conduct of the dancers did not vary in any essential detail from an ordinary performance. There were twenty-one men and four "women" impersonators. The men wore their dance kilts not about the waist, as is customary, but draped about the neck and across the shoulders and fastened in front under the chin somewhat like a hood. Each had on an old-fashioned rabbit skin robe, arranged about

the body in such fashion that it bulged at the stomach but hung straight down from there to below the knees. This robe was secured about the waist with a woman's belt, from which at the small of the back there dangled a Katcina fox pelt. Although they wore moccasins, all the men were barelegged except for the usual turtle shell rattle worn below the right knee. Just above the elbow of the left arm there was a band from which were suspended one or two feathers, and a bow guard was worn about the left wrist. Each man carried a conventional gourd rattle in his right hand, but in place of spruce in the left hand he held a sprig of cottonwood (de've) in the morning dances, and Hopi "spinach" (nevenkwivi), or other foods in the noon dances. Each mask was surmounted by three upward protruding twigs of a plant called siwi, to which were affixed several nakwakwosi. Fastened to the top of the mask was the customary cluster of feathers with several bright colored plumes in front. The sides and top of the mask proper were painted in red, blue-green, and white solid circles to indicate vari-colored clouds. The eye holes were painted black and had only little horizontal slits for vision. A hollow effect was achieved by encircling them with rings of reddish-brown stained cornhusks, twisted and shaped into the form of a doughnut. A similar ring encircled the mouth, within which there hung suspended by nearly invisible strings, three teeth, two upper and one lower, made of large squash seeds, or shaped from bits of white wood. A grotesque appearance like that of a death's head was thus achieved, in keeping with Masau'u's character as the god of death. Each dancer wore a sheep horn suspended from the neck but dangling almost as low as the waist.[2] (See pl. II e.) This was referred to as a "necklace," but I could not gather its significance.[3]

The "women" wore the regulation manta, choosing garments that were old and soiled; and draped across the shoulders, the small white

---

[1] The Masau Katcinas approached from the northwest because that is the direction where the home of the dead (Maski) is located.

[2] See Fewkes, 1903, p. 76.

[3] There appears to be a certain connection in Hopi

belief between Masau'u and mountain-sheep, for a shrine dedicated to the latter is said to be located near Grand Canyon, in the vicinity of the home of the dead over which Masau'u presides. See Titiev, 1937a, p. 249.

mantle with a red and blue striped base that is called *atu-höya*. In the early morning dances one of the "women" wore white, wrapped leggings and moccasins, and the other three had on the regular sort, but in later appearances all the "women" were barefooted and barelegged, with the legs whitened with clay. The hair was combed straight back across the top of the head and fashioned into little "butterfly wings" at the sides. It was dusted with a dirty greyish-brown earth to give an aged effect. The face mask worn by the "women" consisted of a gray woven band some four or five inches wide and stretching from ear to ear across the eyes, nose, and part of the mouth. Into this were set tiny red "doughnuts" to serve as eyes and mouth. A row of feathers hanging from the lower border of the mask completed the concealment of the face. A sprig of greasewood carried in the left hand, and a gourd resonator, sheep's scapula, and notched stick in the right, made up the remainder of the outfit of the Masau Katcina "women."[4]

In its organization the dance very closely resembles that of the Hemis Katcina. Once in the plaza, the performers line up in a double column with the "women" at the left hand of the men and spaced about at the middle of the men's file. As in the Hemis, the Masau dance opens with the performers silent but stamping rhythmically with the right foot for a few beats. Then, in rotation, and starting with the man at the head of the line, each dancer does a left about face without breaking time. As it comes the leader's turn to face about, his position being in the center of the line, he begins to sing, and thenceforth all take up the tune and sing and stamp in unison. From time to time the dancers face about one way or the other while the father shouts directions or approval, and occasionally sprinkles each Katcina with sacred meal. When the first measure is concluded, the father spreads blankets on which the Katcina

"women" kneel while they play their instruments.[5] During this part of the dance the men stand close together, side by side, facing the "women" and holding their gourd rattles about shoulder high. At a given signal, after the father has again sprinkled all the performers, another portion of the dance routine begins with a fast and loud shaking of rattles in time to the stamping of the men and the scraping of the "women." Then the tempo slows down and singing starts as the rattling becomes subdued. On the exact beat when this part is concluded the "women" cease scraping, pick up their instruments, resume their positions at the left side of the men, and stamp and turn in unison with the other dancers, while the father hurriedly removes the blankets from under their feet.

All this is a replica of the performance of a Hemis Katcina dance except, of course, that the songs differ. Immediately after the noon rest, however, the Masau dancers began to give evidence of their comic nature.[6] On their first appearance after lunching, the Katcinas entered the plaza carrying not the customary gifts for distribution among the spectators, but cooked foods in pottery bowls or trays, and many old-fashioned Hopi delicacies, mostly variations on a cornmeal base.[7] They also brought in parched and popped corn, melons, *piki* bread in various colors, and baked sweet corn. A laugh arose whenever a Katcina appeared bearing a roasted sheep's head, and one dancer aroused huge merriment when he solemnly disclosed a prairie dog roasted whole.

Not only did the gifts themselves cause a good deal of laughter, but the manner in which they were presented was often very comic. One dancer, in particular, gave a capital performance in pantomime. Singling one of his maternal nephews out of the crowd, he held towards him a pottery bowl full of some sort of stew. As the young man reached for it, the Katcina withdrew

---

[4] The rhythm-keeping device, which has most inappropriately been called a "Hopi fiddle," is played by resting a notched stick on an inverted gourd and rubbing it up and down with the edge of a sheep's scapula. The stick is called *jrukunpi*, the gourd *putcikyapi*, the scapula *sokyatci*, and the act of playing is *jrukunta*.

[5] In spite of the shabby dress of the Masau "females" they are accorded the regular courtesy extended to "women" Katcinas of having the father spread blankets for them so that they need not kneel on the bare ground.

[6] The natives generally describe the Masau as "a funny Katcina." Compare the custom of clown performances beginning after noon. In this case, though, I later discov-

ered that before breakfast there had been a burlesque performance of a Butterfly dance.

[7] Some of the more unusual foods, many of which are now rarely or never made are: *polompikavi*—of sweetened blue cornmeal dough, shaped like doughnuts, strung on yucca; *sakwavikaviki*—of sweetened cornmeal dough, pancake shaped, and strung on yucca; *hanovikaviki*—of sweetened cornmeal dough, large pancakes, served singly; *wupilangviki*—square *piki*, thicker than usual and with wavy line designs made by running the fingers through the batter while baking; *koletviki*—of cornmeal dough, shaped like a potato and steamed; *qötutpe*—roasted sheep or goat head; *dukyatpe*—roasted prairie dog.

and so gradually "lured" him into the midst of the plaza. There, in full view of all the spectators, the Katcina made his nephew kneel down and eat, admonishing him severely when he seemed to hesitate. At last, when the youth was fairly started on his meal, the Katcina warned him not to dare to leave until he had finished every bit. This done, the righteous uncle returned to his place in the dance line, moving with high, proud steps and a lofty toss of the head.

The first of the afternoon dance performances began in conventional fashion, but after a measure or two the Katcinas, men and "women" alike, took up a semi-circular position, and bowing up and down from the hips, fell into the stance, rhythm, and tune of the Marau dancers.[8] The men waved their rattles and the "women" their gourds in the same manner that the Marau performers manipulate their prayer-sticks. Suddenly one of the men broke out of line and moving to one end of the semi-circle, he detached his fox pelt and holding it before him, proceeded to give an excellent imitation of the manner in which the "dancing *kaletaka*" performs during the Marau. To make their burlesque more realistic, some of the Masau dancers tossed out a few balls of *qömi*, which the Marau women throw to the spectators at their dances. All at once, every dancer resumed his normal position and manner, and the dance proceeded quite seriously to its close.

When, after the customary rest period, the Katcinas re-entered the plaza for their second afternoon dance, they were seen to have with them yucca trays such as the Lakon women carry. At a given point in the midst of their performance, the whole line of Masau Katcinas rushed pell-mell toward the middle of the plaza where they

[8] See p. 166.

had left their gifts, and, having chosen to burlesque this particular aspect of the Lakon performance, they began to throw presents to the assembled crowd. The spectators, quickly getting into the spirit of the thing, promptly began to make the peculiar call with which they try to attract the attention of the Lakon women, and immediately began to wrangle for presents exactly as they do during the Lakon.[9] Not content merely with throwing gifts about, the Katcinas would bow up and down as Lakon distributers must do, and rushing into the crowd, they would feign to throw in one direction, then turn suddenly and let go in the opposite direction as hard as they could. When all their gifts were gone, the regular Masau Katcina formation was resumed and the dance was soon brought to a normal close.

In all the disorder and confusion attendant on these burlesques I noted one thing especially—each song began and ended in orthodox fashion. No matter what was soon to follow, the men sang and rattled, and the "women" knelt and scraped, if only for a few moments, before they broke ranks to mock the women's societies; so that in each individual dance of the day's series every phase of the customary routine was at least touched upon. Furthermore, taking the Masau performance as a whole, the forenoon dances were formal, except for the Butterfly burlesque soon after sunrise, and the concluding dance of the day was performed according to conventional standards. Thus, in spite of the eccentricities of the Masau Katcina, the normal dance pattern was preserved by restricting the comic interludes for the most part to a central portion not only of a particular dance but also of the entire day's activities.

[9] Compare p. 169.

PART FOUR

APPENDIX

1. MAJOR CEREMONIES AT ORAIBI

Name	Controlling Clan	Home Kiva	Associated Ailment[1]
Wuwutcim	Chicken Hawk	Hawiovi	Twisting sickness
Singers	Parrot	Tao	?
Al	Bow	Nasavi	Lightning shock
Kwan	Kwan[2]	Kwan	Loss of weight[3]
Soyal	Bear	Tawaovi[4]	Ear-ache
Powamu	Badger	Hotcitcivi[5]	Rheumatism
Blue Flute	Spider	Sakwalenvi	?
Gray Flute	Patki	Hawiovi	?
Snake	Snake	Tcu	Snakebite and abdominal swellings
Antelope	Spider	Nasavi	Epilepsy (?)[6]
Marau	Lizard	Marau	Facial sores[7]
Oaqöl	Sand	Hawiovi	Head eruptions
Lakon	Parrot	Hawiovi	Running sores
Momtcit	Spider, Kokop	Wiklavi	Sore throat[8]

[1] For comparative material consult Parsons, 1933, pp. 9–16; and Parsons, 1936b, p. XL, *et passim*.

[2] Informants were not agreed on the exact clan which owned the Kwan society, but all agreed that it was controlled by a clan in Phratry VI.

[3] Loss of weight here implies that the body is wasting away to a skeleton.

[4] Tawaovi is the present name of a kiva formerly known as Pongovi. The Soyal was housed here after Uncle Joe drove it out of Sakwalenvi. See p. 80.

[5] Although the official name of this kiva is Hotcitcivi, it is popularly known as the Powamu kiva.

[6] The symptoms of this ailment were described as shaking and foaming at the mouth.

[7] According to Voth, 1901, p. 109, footnote 2, the Marau ceremony cures for deafness.

[8] Voth, 1901, p. 109, footnote 2, reports that the Momtit cures for soreness in the bronchial tubes.

2. CHIEFS OF CEREMONIES AT ORAIBI PRIOR TO 1900[1]

1. Soyal

Nakwaiyamptiwa (Bear)—Wuwutcim at Sakwalenvi[2]

Talaiyauoma (Squash, but son of a Bear man)—Wuwutcim at Sakwalenvi

Kuyingwu (Water Coyote, but married to Bear)—Wuwutcim at Sakwalenvi, Momtcit

Sakhongyoma (Bear)—Wuwutcim at Sakwalenvi, Momtcit

Lololoma (Bear)—Wuwutcim at Sakwalenvi, Momtcit

Talaskwaptiwa (Sun, but married to Bear)—Wuwutcim at Sakwalenvi

2. Wuwutcim[3]

(a) Hawiovi [main] branch
   Kuwanletstiwa (Kele)
   Qötchongniwa (Kele)
   Talasnöngtiwa (Kele)
   Kwani (Kele)
(b) Hano kiva branch
   Namitnauoma (Squash)
(c) Sakwalenvi branch
   Lomahongyoma (Spider)—Blue Flute, Momtcit
(d) Tcu kiva branch
   Masangöntiwa (Snake)—Snake

3. Tao

Talangakyoma (Katcina)—Powamu
Masawistiwa (Katcina)—Powamu

4. Al

Sikyapyaya (Cedar, but son of a Bow man)—Nakyawimi
Qötcventiwa (Bow)

5. Kwan

Kelwistiwa (Masau'u)—later switched to Wuwutcim for cure
Masaletstiwa (Masau'u)
Na'sastiwa (Reed, but son of a Masau'u man)

6. Powamu

Tawahevi'ima (Badger)—Al
Si'ima (Badger)—Tao, Momtcit
Qömahöniwa (Badger)—Al, Gray Flute

7. Snake

Tawai'ima (Snake)
Kuktiwa (Snake)—Wuwutcim at Sakwalenvi
Sikyahongniwa (Lizard)—Wuwutcim at Tcu, Nakyawimi
Masangöntiwa (Lizard)—Wuwutcim at Sakwalenvi

8. Antelope

Masaiyamptiwa (Spider)—Wuwutcim at Sakwalenvi, Blue Flute
Nuvasi'ima (Spider)—Tao
Duvengötiwa (Spider)—Al

9. Blue Flute

Masaiyamptiwa (Spider)—Wuwutcim at Sakwalenvi, Antelope
Lomayestiwa (Spider)—Wuwutcim at Sakwalenvi
Lomahongyoma (Spider)—Wuwutcim at Sakwalenvi, Momtcit

10. Gray Flute

Tuvi (Siva'ap)—Wuwutcim at Hawiovi, Momtcit
Kelyamptiwa (Pikyas)—Wuwutcim at Hawiovi
Lomahongva (Patki)—Wuwutcim at Hawiovi

11. Marau

(a) Women Officers
   Tangakwainim (Lizard)
   Qöyavenka (Lizard)—Oaqöl
   Qötcnumsi (Lizard)—Oaqöl

(b) Male Officers
   Wuwupa (Lizard, son of Tangakwainim)—Wuwutcim at Hawiovi

---

[1] This list is based on information supplied by my oldest informant. The officers in each ceremony are given in chronological order as he remembered them. Compare the lists in tables 4 and 5.

[2] In this list the personal name of the officer is given first, and this is followed by his clan's name in parentheses. The names given after the dash refer to his other ceremonial affiliations. These data are often incomplete owing to lapses in my informant's memory, but no attempt was made to supplement his material from other sources.

[3] The Wuwutcim was so popular at Oraibi that it required the use of four kivas to accommodate all the members.

Kuwanvikwaiya (Lizard, son of Tangakwai-nim)—Wuwutcim at Hawiovi

Humihöniwa (Lizard, Kuwanvikwaiya's broth-er)—Wuwutcim at Hano, Momtcit

Nawini'ima (Lizard, Kuwanvikwaiya's broth-er)—Kwan

12. Oaqöl

(a) Women Officers

Kelwuhti (Sand)

Tcocnumsi (Sand)[4]

Humiyaunim (Sand)

Qöyangösi (Sand)

(b) Male Officers

Masatöniwa (Sand)—Wuwutcim at Hawiovi, Blue Flute

Homikni (Lizard)—Wuwutcim at Hawiovi, Momtcit

Qöyahongniwa (Rabbit, but son of Lizard man)—Al, but switched to Wuwutcim for cure, Powamu, Gray Flute

Kelnimptiwa (Sand)—Wuwutcim at Hawiovi, Powamu

13. Lakon

(a) Women Officers

Qöyangnaisi (Parrot)

Nuvawuhti (Parrot)—Marau

Huminimsi (Crow-Parrot)—Marau, Oaqöl

Sakyamka (Crow-Parrot)—Marau

(b) Male Officers

Hoventiwa (Parrot)

Naksu (Parrot)—Wuwutcim at Sakwalenvi

Tawaletstiwa (Badger, son of Naksu)—Wu-wutcim at Sakwalenvi, Nakya, Powamu

14. Momtcit

Talai'ima (Spider)—Wuwutcim at Sakwalenvi

Lomayamptiwa (Kokop)—Wuwutcim at Sak-walenvi, Blue Flute

Lomahongyoma (Spider)—Blue Flute

Humiwai'ima (Spider)—Wuwutcim at Sak-walenvi, Antelope, Blue Flute

15. Nakyawimi[5]

Tcotcungu (Cedar)—Al, Masau'u impersonator

Mokyatiwa (Rabbit)—Al, Antelope, Blue Flute, Masau'u impersonator

16. Paiyatamu[6]

Qötcvuhtima (Pikyas, son of Eagle man [?])—Wuwutcim at Hano

Qöyapela (Eagle)—Tao, Momtcit

17. Yaya[7]

Duvengna (Greasewood)—Wuwutcim at Sak-walenvi, Tca'akmongwi in Soyal

Sikyahongniwa (Lizard, but son of a Greasewood man)—Wuwutcim at Hawiovi, Snake, Nakya

Talasnöntiwa (Kele)—Wuwutcim at Hawiovi, Snake

Tcoti'ima (Kokop)—Wuwutcim at Hawiovi

---

[4] For some time after the death of Tcocnumsi the Oaqöl ceremony lapsed, but as bad weather followed, Sakhongyoma, acting Village chief, decided that the ob-servance was too important to be omitted and ordered it resumed, Humiyaunim assuming the leadership. This is one of the rare instances where a Village chief exerted his authority in dealing with a ceremony other than the Soyal which he controls.

[5] Although my informant tried to differentiate the per-sonnel of the Momtcit from the Nakyawimi, he often got the two confused.

[6] The Paiyatamu, a clown society owned by the Eagle clan, formerly met at Hano kiva. It has not been active for many years.

[7] The Yaya, a curing society owned by the Greasewood clan, has long been extinct at Oraibi. It used to meet in Hotcitcivi kiva. A brief account of its exercises may be found in Parsons, 1936b, pp. 1007–1010, *et passim*.

3. THE RITUAL CALENDAR AT ORAIBI[1]

Name of Ceremony	Month	Determination of Date	Announcement
Tribal Initiation	Nov.	Observation of Sun[2]	Crier chief
Soyal Katcina	Nov.	Day after Tribal Initiation	None
Soyal	Dec.	Sixteen days after Soyal Katcina	Crier chief
Mastop Katcina	Dec.	Eighth day of Soyal	None
Qöqöqlom Katcina	Dec.	Ninth day of Soyal	None
Niman Announcement	Dec.	Third day after Soyal	None
Night Kiva Dances	Jan.	Voluntary after Soyal	None
Winter Offerings (Flute or Snake, and Lakon)	Jan.	Moon after Soyal (?)	None
Powalawu	Feb.	First sight of February moon	Powamu chief
Powamu	Feb.	Eight days after Powalawu	None
Repeat Series	Feb.	About 16 days after Powamu	Katcina chief
Winter Offerings (Marau)	Feb.[3]	?	None
Nevenwehe	May	Sun at Wukomuzriuyipi[4]	Crier chief
Summer Offerings (Flute)	July	Morning after the sun reaches Tawatkiata[5]	None
Niman	July	Sixteen days after sun reaches Tawatkiata	Crier chief
Flute or Snake-Antelope	Aug.	Sixteen days after August moon appears	Crier Chief
Marau and Lakon	Sept.	?	?
Oaqöl	Oct.	?	?
Momtcit	Oct.	?	?

[1] Cf. Parsons, 1933, pp. 58–61; Parsons, 1936b, p. 1040, *et passim;* Nequatewa, 1931, pp. 1–4; and Fewkes, 1903, pp. 21–23.

[2] On Third Mesa the start of the Tribal Initiation is said to have been announced when the Sun Watcher noted that the sun had risen at a point known as Dingapi. On First Mesa it was said to have begun after sunset observations by Singers' chief. See p. 131, footnote 8.

[3] This date was given as late February or March. At this time too the season for outdoor Katcina dances begins.

[4] See Titiev, 1938c, pp. 39, 40.

[5] Titiev, 1938c, pp. 39, 40.

4. ORAIBI KIVAS PRIOR TO 1900

. **Sakwalenvi**[1] (Blue Flute kiva), owned by pider clan. It was headed by Lomahongyoma Spider) and his brother Qötcata (Spider).

. **Hawiovi** (Going-down kiva), owned by the Bow and Sand clans. It was headed by Masa'to Sand, but son of a Bow man).

. **Tao** (Singers' kiva), owned by the Parrot lan. It was headed by Talangakyoma (Katcina) nd his nephew Lomanaksu (Katcina).

. **Nasavi** (Middle-place kiva), owned by the Bow clan. It was headed by Qötcventiwa (Bow), who was succeeded by his nephew Tangakhong-iwa (Bow), who was followed by his brother Nasiwaitiwa (Bow).

. **Kwan** (Agave kiva), owned by the Cedar lan.[2] It was headed by Duhikya (Cedar), fol-owed by his brother's son Tangakwai'ima (Badg-r, but married to a Kokop woman), who was ucceeded by Na'sastiwa (Greasewood, but the on of a Kokop man), who was then followed by Lomaleohtiwa (Masau'u).

. **Hotcitcivi** (Zig-zag kiva), owned by the Badger clan. It was headed by Si'ima (Badger), who was followed by his brother Qömahöniwa (Badger), who was succeeded by his nephew Siletstiwa (Badger).

. **Tcu** (Rattlesnake kiva), owned by the Snake clan.[3] It was headed by Masangöntiwa (Snake), whose successor was Nuvakwahu (Sand), who was followed by Sikyahongniwa (Lizard), who was succeeded by Duveyamptiwa (Snake).

8. **Hano** kiva,[4] owned by the Squash clan. It was headed by Namitnauoma (Squash), who was succeeded by his mother's sister's son Talasnimptiwa (Squash).

9. **Wiklavi** (Fold-of-fat kiva), owned by the Spider (?) clan. It was headed by Humiwai'ima (Spider).

10. **Marau** kiva, owned by the Lizard clan. It was headed by Kuwanvikwaiya (Lizard), who was followed by his nephew Humihöniwa (Lizard).

11. **Pongovi** (Circle kiva),[5] owned by the Coyote clan. It was headed by Kuyingwu (Water Coyote).

12. **Katcin** (Katcina kiva),[6] owned by the Katcina clan. It was headed by Singötiwa (Katcina) and Pongyawisioma (Katcina).

13. **Is** (Coyote kiva), owned by the Coyote clan. It was headed by Ko'sili (Coyote), who was succeeded by Qömawuhioma (Coyote).

In addition to the kivas listed above, Oraibi informants in other contexts referred to Kiacsuc (Parrot-tail kiva), a "common" kiva that was supposed to have been built by the Hostiles at the time that Oraibi was the scene of two rival ceremonial cycles (p. 83).

At one time or another too mention was made of a Blue-jay, a Hemis, and a Pakovi (Place-where-water-settles) kiva, but informants were unable to give any details concerning them.

[1] This was the Chief kiva until Lololoma moved to Pongovi. See p. 80.

[2] Once again we note that the exact clan concerned here s indeterminate, but leadership pertained to Phratry VI.

[3] Snake, Sand, and Lizard are often confused in Phratry III.

[4] From number 8 down, all the kivas, except 10, were known as "common" kivas. This means that they housed none of the major ceremonies.

[5] For data on the later history of this kiva, see p. 80, footnote 109.

[6] This kiva was nicknamed Kwitavi (Feces kiva).

5. KIVAS AND THEIR ASSOCIATED SHRINES[1]

1. Sakwalenvi Kiva and Nuvatukyaovi (Snow-mountain-peaks-place, i.e., the San Francisco mountains).

Long ago, it was said, Katcina dancers from Sakwalenvi always fetched spruce from the San Francisco mountains instead of at other shrines. Accordingly, when it was their turn to sponsor the Homegoing dance, their messengers were sent to the San Francisco mountains for spruce, instead of to Kisiwu.

2. Hawiovi and Kisiwu (Shade-throwing-place).

A spring located at Kisiwu, regarded as one of the main homes of Katcinas. Many cattails (*wipu*) grow here, and it is to this place that expeditions are sent to fetch spruce for the Niman. Tcowilawu, the Katcina ancient of the Badger clan who is impersonated in the Powamu ceremony (p. 115), resides at Kisiwu.

3. Tao kiva and Duwanasavi (Center-of-the-earth).

Duwanasavi is the home of the germination god known as Muyingwa. He is sometimes described as the husband of Talautumsi, goddess of fecundity.[2]

4. Nasavi and the shrine of Alosaka.

Alosaka is known as the main home of the Al society. It is said to be located near the San Francisco mountains. To this place go the spirits of deceased Al men, and it is here that the founder of the cult is supposed to dwell. On the third night of the Tribal Initiation ceremony, the spirits of Al men are supposed to return from Alosaka for a visit to the pueblo. No Katcinas live at this shrine.

5. Kwan kiva and Kwanivi shrine.

Instead of going to the general home of the dead (Maski), the souls of deceased Kwan men are said to go to Kwanivi. They are looked upo[n] as defenders of the people and are expected to re[-] turn to the village during the Tribal Initiation[.]

6. Hotcitcivi and the shrine called Oraibi.

A rocky formation on the western edge o[f] Third Mesa is called Oraibi and is reputed to b[e] the town's eponym. It serves as a Katcin[a] shrine, and is said to have been in existence eve[n] prior to the founding of Oraibi by Matcito.

7. Tcu kiva and Owakovi (Place-of-coal?)

In the Snake legend, when Tiyo and his wif[e] were driven out of Oraibi[4] they were supposed t[o] have taken shelter at Owakovi, thus convertin[g] it into a Snake society shrine.

8. Marau kiva and Homolovi.

Homolovi is a shrine situated among a cluste[r] of ruins near Winslow, Arizona. An Oraibi stor[y] tells how Matcito had trouble with the Katcina[s] in ancient times, so that for many years no dance[s] were held. At last it happened that a boy chase[d] a rabbit behind Homolovi rock, and when he fo[l-] lowed it he saw a Hemis Katcina girl sittin[g] there. She explained that she had taken the for[m] of a rabbit in order to attract his attention, an[d] she told him to announce that the Katcinas woul[d] come in four days to dance at his village. Th[e] boy told his chief, and all the people were over[-] joyed, especially the younger ones who had neve[r] seen a Katcina. On the fourth day the Katcina[s] were heard practicing in the plaza before dawn[,] and after daybreak they danced until sunset. I[n] memory of this event a Katcina shrine was buil[t] at Homolovi.[5]

9. Pongovi and Tokonavi.

A local shrine near Oraibi is said to be name[d] for a sacred spot on Navaho mountain where [a] large, shallow cave shelters a spring. High above[n]

[1] A ritual bond exists between most of the major ceremonies, the kivas in which they are held, and particular shrines. Many of the latter are supposedly situated at distant points, but these generally have local representations near the pueblo. Sometimes the distant shrine is visited, but more often celebrants resort to the local substitute. In all likelihood shrines located on earth have counterparts in the lower world. On this point see Voth, 1912a, p. 79, footnote 1.

[2] Sometimes Muyingwa is said to be the brother o[f] Talautumsi.

[3] According to Nequatewa, 1936, p. 104, footnote 10[,] Kwan spirits may not revisit a pueblo.

[4] See p. 153.

[5] This story is supposed to deal with *real* Katcinas, an[d] not with Katcina impersonators.

on the face of a steep cliff, there is a Katcina pictograph. Ruined houses nearby are believed to represent a former habitation site of the Hopi. Tokonavi shrine is regarded as one of the most important homes of Katcinas.

In considering the relationship of ceremonies to kivas and shrines, it is important to note the distinction made between the Wuwutcim and the other branches of the Tribal Initiation. Whereas the kivas housing the Al, Kwan, and Tao are all connected with special homes (shrines) to which their members resort after death, the two principal kivas of the Wuwutcim —Sakwalenvi and Hawiovi[6]—are associated with two of the best known Katcina shrines, San Francisco mountains and Kisiwu.

[6] Sakwalenvi and Hawiovi are the most important of the Wuwutcim kivas because the former was Chief kiva, and within the latter were performed the most esoteric rites of the entire cult.

6. STATEMENT AND AGREEMENT[1]

Oraibi, Ariz., Sept. 8, 1906.

1. The friendly Oraibis and friendly Shimo-pivis do not want the unfriendly Hopis to come back into either the village of Oraibi or Shimo-pivi.

2. If the unfriendlies will go off to a place agreed upon and build themselves a village and make themselves fields, then;

3. The friendly Hopis of Oraibi and Shimo-pivi will let the unfriendlies come back either to Oraibi or Shimopivi, three unfriendlies at a time, and take from Oraibi and Shimopivi any property—horses, cattle, sheep, burros, turkeys, chickens, or implements, tools, utensils, house-hold goods, or crops of corn, melons or beans or any other property belonging exclusively to the unfriendly Indians; but such unfriendly Indians shall not enter either Oraibi or Shimopivi, not for more than one day, without the consent of the first Chief at this time, Sept. 8, 1906, of the village—or if he be away, then of such chief as may be in the village,—and such unfriendly Hopi will leave the village at sundown.

4. All Hopis, both friendly and unfriendly agree that, in order that the unfriendly Indians may have lands for farms and pasture, and water, for themselves and their flocks and herds, they will exchange lands, fields and pastures with each other; both parties submitting their propositions to the Superintendent or Agent and abiding by his decision.

5. The friendly Hopis agree that they will not go into the new village of the unfriendlies in groups of more than three at a time, and then not without the consent of the Chief or assistant Chief of the village, and that they will leave at sundown.

6. Both Friendlies and Unfriendlies agree that if any Hopi comes into their village from any other Hopi village and so conducts himself or her-self, or indulges in such expressions as to disturb the peace, quiet and happiness of anyone in the village he or she shall be asked to go away and if he or she does not do so the Chief or assistant Chief of the village will order him or her to do so and if this is disobeyed the Chief of the village will direct one or more men to arrest the in-truder and take him or her to the Superintendent or Agent at Keam's Canyon.

2.

1. I, the Superintendent, knowing that the two parties cannot live together in the same village in peace and harmony do, on condition that those who are now in camp and outside of all Hopi vil-lages will select a place reasonably removed from all other Hopi villages, hereby promise that, with the consent of the Indian Office, I will, at all times and under all circumstances, counsel, aid and assist the unfriendlies just as I would and do other Indians on the reservation, and to exactly the same extent I would and do other Indians whose conduct in general is that of those so re-moving and removed.

2. That I will go further along these lines, with the consent of the Indian Office, and will give first aid and assistance to those removing and removed by issuing to them first such tools, implements and utensils as may be in the Govern-ment storerooms, that may be useful in building the houses, storerooms, corrals and kivas of the new village, and in developing and storing water for the people of this new village till their supplies may be equal to the average of those of the older villages.

I further promise that, with the consent of the Indian Office, I will make such expenditure of money in employing the people of the new village to work in developing springs, storing water, building roads and trails and furnishing such ma-terial as may be needed for making windows and doors for their buildings, and whatever may be necessary for rendering their springs and reser-voirs useful, efficient, and sanitary.

3. That I will visit the new village from time to time, as in my judgment it needs and demands, as I do the other villages.

---

[1] This document was signed by Chief Tawaqwaptiwa and a group of his followers on the day following the ex-pulsion of the Hostiles from Oraibi, at the request of the Indian Agent at Keam's Canyon. It was designed to give the defeated party a safe opportunity to remove some of their belongings from their former residences. The present copy was made from an original loaned to me in 1934 by Tawaqwaptiwa.

4. That so far as the school work among the Indians is concerned I will deal with the people of the new village as I do with the people of the other villages, as circumstances and conditions will permit, or as I may be ordered or directed to do by the Commissioner of Indian Affairs.

5. I further promise that as soon as the Hopis now in camp outside of all Hopi villages shall have selected a site for the new village I will call from the other villages a number of Hopi men, and with a number of men from among the excluded go to the site and look it over and try to so arrange all matters as to avoid future friction among a people who should live together in peace and harmony.

(Signed)

THEO. G. LEMMON, Supt.

TAWAQUAPTIWA—chief of Friendlies
Ho-mi-hong-ni-o-ma
Na-qui-es-ti-wa
Lo-ma-es-ni-wa } for Friendlies
Ta-las-mayn-yi-wa
To-vey-es-ti-wa.

Witnesses to all signatures
Lillian Durgin
Elizabeth Stanly

Interpreters interpreting and signing
Lahpoo
Frank Jenkins

7. LETTER FROM SHERMAN INSTITUTE

While Chief Tawaqwaptiwa was attending Sherman Institute soon after the split of 1906, Lomahongyoma (Uncle Joe), his main opponent, returned to Oraibi with a party of Hostiles who had recently been driven out of the town.[1] Tawaqwaptiwa was in favor of expelling his enemies again, but officials of the United States Government were anxious to have both sides make peace. A document stipulating terms of agreement was drawn up and presented to Tawaqwaptiwa to sign. At first he flatly refused, whereupon Mr. Perry, a government agent, somehow connected with the military branch of service, and Mr. Harwood Hall, superintendent of the Sherman Indian School, who had jointly compiled the paper in question, threatened to deprive Tawaqwaptiwa of his chieftainship. When the latter remained obdurate, however, they changed their tactics and coaxed and wheedled him into signing.[2] Frank Siemptiwa, the chief's lieutenant and head of the Moenkopi colony, who stubbornly continued urging Tawaqwaptiwa not to sign the document, was sent out of the room before the chief capitulated.

[1] See p. 93.
[2] The account of the signing of the document was given me by Tawaqwaptiwa. It obviously reflects his view of the controversy.

The following transcript was made from a copy in Tawaqwaptiwa's possession in 1934:

DEPARTMENT OF THE INTERIOR,
UNITED STATES INDIAN SERVICE,

Sherman Institute, Riverside, Calif.,
February 23, 1907.

My People at Oraibi, Arizona:

I want my people to live peaceably with the Hostiles who have returned to the village and who have put their children in school. I want them to be permitted to stay in the village.

I want my people to obey Mr. Martin, the teacher, and the judges, and to do as the Superintendent at Keam's Canyon desires them to do.

I want my people to let the old Judge,[3] all Friendlies and all Hostiles [cultivat]e[4] their own fields and raise corn to live on.

I want my people to have no trouble with returned Hostiles over the ceremonies, but I think Uncle Joe had better stay out of the Flute ceremony. My people should talk these matters over with the teacher and Superintendent and have no trouble.

I want my people to obey the Government and do. . . . [The rest is missing.]

[3] This refers to Qöyangainiwa, of the Badger clan, who had been appointed a native Judge at some time prior to 1906.
[4] A defect in the original letter mars this word.

8. AN INTER-PUEBLO COUNCIL OF CHIEFS

In August 1933, Chief Tawaqwaptiwa of Oraibi went to the village of Mishongnovi on Second Mesa to watch the Snake dance. While there he was invited to attend a conference for the purpose of discussing the poor state of the crops and the lack of rain. A young Bear clansman, David Sakwaiwisa of Mishongnovi, was the first to speak about it to the Oraibi chief.[1]

"It's up to us, the Bear people, to look after our people and to pull them through," remarked David.

"That's true," replied Tawaqwaptiwa, "it is our duty as chiefs to pull our people through, but somehow we don't seem to have good luck. There is something between us that is not right."

It was at this point that David suggested a consultation, and the chief agreed to attend, though not without misgivings lest some of the other speakers be witches and offer evil advice. However, Tawaqwaptiwa followed David to his mother's house where he found assembled Lomanakyoma of the Pikyas clan, father of David and the first Mishongnovi man to turn Christian; Talaheptiwa, Village chief at Chimopovy, and Yoyohongnova, his nephew; Frank Masakwaptiwa, Village chief of Shipaulovi; Qötcnimptiwa of the Sun clan, an important Soyal officer at Chimopovy; Duwangötiwa, Soyal officer at Shipaulovi; and Talaswuhiyoma, the Wuwutcim chief at Mishongnovi.[2]

Upon Tawaqwaptiwa's entrance he was joyfully greeted by Lomanakyoma. "I want to talk to you about our lives," he said. "We need rain and our crops are in bad shape. I've been trying to think from whom we could get help. We raise these crops so that we can live on them but we have no food and that is why I want to talk to you."

"Well, it's the same way at my place," responded the Oraibi leader, "we haven't had any good luck with our crops. It's the same way at Moenkopi where they have irrigation, but cool rain helps the crops better. I look everywhere but I can't find help any place and it's pretty bad. I don't know how to lead my children on the good road."[3]

"Yes, that's true," agreed Lomanakyoma. "I looked everywhere for help and I decided to call on you, the head chief of Oraibi. Maybe I can get help from you."

"I guess your old uncles told you that when you can't get help anywhere you ought to look to the Oraibi chief," said Tawaqwaptiwa,[4] "but on my part I find no one from whom I can get help. We are far gone. That is why I just sit still; I fail to get help from anyone. I'm not as important as the old chiefs who could always, somehow, get a good sized rain for their children.

"My ancestors told me, and you all know it, that some day we were going to reach such a condition. You [pointing to Masakwaptiwa] are a chief at Shipaulovi, and you [indicating Talaheptiwa] at Chimopovy, and all of you have been told these things. Every ruler knows how he can lead the people on the good road and this is an important thing; it's our life. And now we are scattered, we've got too many *mongwis* (chiefs).[5]

"Now I know what you are after. If you really mean it, I've got to tell you some important things. I'm a ruler at Oraibi—I'm a bad *mongwi* as I have heard. This famine is mine, this sickness is mine, all these bad things are mine, yet, you look to me for help."[6]

"Yes, that is true," said Talaswuhiyoma. "I'm like you. These Mishongnovi people look on me

---

[1] Chief Tawaqwaptiwa was the informant who described the inter-pueblo council to me. His narrative is here reproduced as fully as possible, and the direct quotations are presented as they occur in my field notes.

[2] It should be remembered that this gathering was not definitely arranged and that the men who participated do not comprise any regularly constituted body of officers.

[3] Note the air of humility that runs throughout Tawaqwaptiwa's talk. It is not true that the Moenkopi crops failed that year. Compare p. 200 and footnote 87.

[4] Despite his pose of humility, the Oraibi chief never fails to emphasize the great importance of his position.

[5] Reference is made here to the schisms on Third Mesa

which led to the founding of new pueblos at Hotevilla and Bakavi, at each of which non-traditional Village chiefs assumed office.

[6] The interpreter, Don Talayesva, explained that the chief's words were not to be taken literally, but were full of hidden meanings, "just like a poem."

Once again the speaker adopts an air of humility as he tells of the charges levelled against him by his opponents, especially, although this is not explicitly stated, by those who have accepted Christianity. The fact that the man in whose house the meeting is being held is a converted Christian is completely disregarded. The Hopi see nothing incongruous in such situations.

the same way as your people look on you. All these bad things they put on my back [attribute to me]. All these bad things, they say, are mine. Now we are gathered to talk about this subject. Our great-grandfathers lived well but now we have branched off from their road by taking the wrong side and following the bad road. I've been told by my ancestors the same thing that you all know, and now we have reached the time of trouble. It looks as if our people will starve. We are cowards and we don't want to starve, so we look everywhere for help but I don't think we'll get it anywhere, Isohi! (Alas!)[7]

"Now let us who are present here look at ourselves and take pity on ourselves and on our people.[8] By doing this we might get help somewhere. This bad path we are on won't do; it isn't worth anything. I love you and all my people; let's all live."

"Yes, my uncle," said Frank Masakwaptiwa in his reply to Tawaqwaptiwa's words, "your speech is all true. I am like you, too, and all these *mongwis* (chiefs) in the villages around here get the blame for the bad things. We *mongwis* have been told by our ancestors how to lead the people right but now there are too many *mongwis* who try to lead the people instead of us—and we are nothing. That is why things are bad, that is why we can't get back on the good road. Instead of blaming us they ought to look at themselves. They hardly listen to us who are their true governors.[9] On account of misbehaviour we get this punishment. Now we get this punishment. Now we have no luck and we don't get rain when we dance. Let us take pity on ourselves."

It was now the turn of Talaheptiwa, the chief of Chimopovy. "Well," he began, "I've been listening to all these speakers, especially to the first one (Tawaqwaptiwa), when he said that we get all the blame for bad things. I'm like that myself, and in this way we have trouble getting on the good road. Now we must decide what we can do.

This sort of living won't do, we can't get along with such bad luck. Let's all take pity on ourselves and push each other forward [on the good path] and help each other."

Several other men then spoke in turn, each repeating the substance of what the other speakers had said. At last Tawaqwaptiwa spoke again.

"I've never spoken to the Mishongnovi people since I've been chief at Oraibi," he began. "Three years ago I spoke to the people of Chimopovy about the crops that were eaten by the cattle from First Mesa. At that time I told them that we've got to mind our food. It is our life and everyone has to look after his stock so there won't be any trouble about the cattle eating the crops. However, it doesn't seem that they thought my talk is good, and now our minds are not together but are all tangled up.[10] Maybe some of you are willing to let the cattle eat the crops and so you keep still, but that isn't right. I am only one, so it's up to all of you to decide what you want to do.

"I don't know how to bring rain, I don't know how to make my prayers reach the four directions, I don't know how to make the crops grow—I've no power to do these things."

Just then the Snake dancers were seen entering the plaza; so the conference broke up, and the men hurried out to watch the proceedings.

The Oraibi chief decided "to make some use of this talk and to keep it in his heart." Sure enough, the next day it rained, and there were intermittent showers on the two following days. The next morning, while Tawaqwaptiwa was on his way to the Snake dance at Walpi, he noticed that rain had covered the Oraibi valley but that none had fallen at Second Mesa.[11] At this he thanked the Cloud People because he realized that his talk had been worth something, but at the same time he felt that the Second Mesa people had not meant what they had said and that they had spoken only with their tongues and not with their hearts.[12]

---

[7] There is an indication here that the Hopi people are accusing their leaders of being witches and deliberately leading them astray. Compare Parsons, 1939, p. 154; and Titiev, 1943a. The punishment for witchcraft is death.

[8] It is said that if a witch "takes pity on himself," and seeks to avoid punishment, he may do so by good deeds. The speaker is not denying the possibility that he may be a witch; he is only seeking to avoid the consequences. The Hopi believe that people are sometimes transformed into witches without being aware of what has happened. On this point, consult Beaglehole, E. and P., 1935, p. 5.

[9] I was present one day when Masakwaptiwa, Village chief of Shipaulovi, was complaining bitterly about the con-

tending factions in his pueblo. "I remember that when you people had your troubles in 1906," he said to Tawaqwaptiwa, "I was laughing at the way your people behaved. Now it is the same way here at Shipaulovi."

Every Hopi pueblo, I was told, is now divided into factions, and the question of upstart chiefs is a vital issue.

[10] It should be recalled that harmony must prevail among all suppliants if they wish their prayers to be answered. See pp. 64 and 67.

[11] Compare the passage in Parsons, 1936b, p. 437, footnote 1.

[12] This is an excellent example of the suspicious attitude which each Hopi pueblo has towards the others.

9. THE YELLOW QÖQÖQLOM AT CHIMOPOVY[1]

On the morning when the Bean dance is to be performed at Chimopovy, there appear in the village two Yellow Qöqöqlom Katcinas. They bring gifts of bean sprouts, turtle rattles, bows and arrows, plaques, and dolls, which they distribute primarily to children. As they are allowed to speak, they make it known that these good things were sent by the Chief (Mon) Katcinas, known as Ahul, who live with many of their subject Katcinas at the spring called Kisiwu. When all the gifts have been handed out, the Yellow Qöqöqlom proceed to the Chief kiva. Here they promise to return in the evening with many other Katcinas and to bring with them numerous benefits such as food and rain. Then a cornmeal path is made for them in the direction of Kisiwu, and as they start out they agree to re-appear soon after sundown.

At twilight all the people who can possibly crowd in hasten to await the Yellow Qöqöqlom at Chief kiva. In a little while the voices of the Katcinas can be heard coming nearer and nearer, and soon the older of the two shakes his rattle down the hatch.

"Yungya'a!" (Come in!) shouts the Chief. "Is everyone present?" asks the Katcina. "Yes, we are all waiting for you," cries the Chief.

Thereupon, while the spectators continue to call out invitations and welcomes, the Katcinas enter with huge bundles of sweet corn, watermelon, and other good foods. They deposit their burdens north of the fireplace, and then the kiva chief says to them, "This morning you were here and made us all happy by giving gifts to our children. When you promised to return in the evening, we told you to have your sisters make fresh piki for us and to ask your brothers to bake lots of sweet corn for you to bring when you came back. I am glad to see that you have brought the things we wanted and that you have kept your promise. Now we should like to have you tell us the story of your journey here."

"Yes," replies the Katcina, "we were here this morning and we are happy to bring the things you want. When we got back to Kisiwu we told our chiefs, Ahul, Eototo, and Kuzrua, about your

requests, and they decided that as we were very strong we ought to go hunting for some game while the other men baked sweet corn and the women made piki."

Fig. 13. Yellow Qöqöqlom Katcina
at Chimopovy.

[1] This account was given to me by Oraibi informants who had seen the performance at Chimopovy and who claimed that it was also given at Shipaulovi. It was never a part of the Third Mesa Powamu, and I do not know whether it was performed at First Mesa. For a rough, native sketch of this Katcina, see fig. 13.

From here on the older Katcina narrates the various episodes of the return trip to Chimopovy, while the younger mutters something from time to time, and now and again accompanies in pantomime his brother's account of their adventures.

"As you know," the Yellow Qöqöqlom continues, "the days are now so short that we had to hurry. Luckily we soon spied some game, and shooting together we each brought down a buck.[2] You see, my brother is a poor runner [here the other Katcina protests violently], or else we would have caught up with our kill much sooner."

The speaker then goes on to tell, in spite of constant denials from his companion, that his buck was better, that his dexterity in skinning it was the greater, and that the clumsiness of the younger brother was all that made them late.

When they got back to Kisiwu they were told by Eototo that they would have to hurry, as all the other Katcinas were already on their way to Chimopovy, and that they had better hasten to overtake them, as they were supposed to lead the others into the village. In spite of the urge for speed, however, they stopped to eat the lunch of melon and baked sweet corn that their chief, Eototo, set before them. [At this point in the recital they gluttonously consume big pieces of melon, seeds and all, and an ear or so of corn. At each stage of the story where eating is mentioned, they actually eat the food indicated with all the haste called for by the narrative.]

Having finished their lunch the brothers hurriedly picked up their bundles and set out on the run to overtake the other Katcinas. All went well until they came to a running wash. After several false tries the older Katcina succeeded in safely leaping across the stream; but when, at last, the younger got up his courage to jump, he landed in midstream and was being rapidly carried off by the current when his brother waded in and rescued him. Unfortunately, the younger Qöqöqlom had swallowed so much muddy water that precious time was lost while he received first aid. So many rivulets issued from the half-drowned Katcina that many fields were irrigated by the contents of his stomach. However, the delay had made them late once more, so when the younger brother had recovered the two set out again on the run. Soon they got to Munpa [another Kat-

cina home] where they found their grandparents picking beans.

"My, but you are late," said the grandparents. "We've heard that this is the night that the Hopi are having the Powamu dance at Chimopovy, and you'll have to hustle if you want to get there on time. But have a bite to eat before you go."

The Katcinas then eat some fresh squash, seeds and all, and the story continues. At the next Katcina home, Bakiovi, the Yellow Qöqöqlom hurried in and found no one present, but happening to see some movement in one corner they discovered their grandparents in the act of intercourse.

"My grandfather spoke with some difficulty," continues the narrator, "but he chided us for being so far behind the others and then set some melon before us which we gobbled hastily [suiting the action to the words] on the run."

At each stopping place the same procedure was repeated. At Wikyaiovi their grandparents gave them peaches; at Wunakovi they got corn and *piki;* and at each point they picked up more and more gifts to bring to the Chimopovy people. At last the adventurers arrived at Pikyanivi, a shrine not far from the village, where their grandparents fed them with *somiviki* and sent sweet corn as a gift for the Hopi. As they came rushing out, they finally came in sight of the Katcinas who had preceded them. Then they stopped, late though they were, drew a starting line, and engaged in a footrace to see which would be the first to overtake their brothers and sisters. Of course the older brother triumphed, and then they continued on to the Tokonavi shrine where more Katcinas were waiting to join the group on the way to Chimopovy.

"Don't stop here," said these Katcinas. "You're supposed to be the first to arrive, and here we are nearly all dressed and ready to set out for the Chief kiva. You'd better hurry if you want to get there ahead of us."

"Then we ran just as fast as we could," concludes the older brother, "and now it is pretty nearly time for the others to be here. Listen!"

At this moment there can be heard the cries of a number of Katcinas who, having arrived at the kiva, are waiting their turn to be admitted. Before the other Katcinas are invited to enter,

---

[2] Note that a so-called Kokle Katcina, pictured in Fewkes, 1903, plate XXXIV, has the same sort of a mask as the Qöqöqlom, and carries a slain buck across his shoulders.

however, the people cry out asking the Yellow Qöqöqloms if they know how to sing and dance. On their replying that they do, they are urged to exhibit their talents; and putting on a comic dance they excuse their awkwardness on the grounds that they are nervous in front of so many people. As they dance they accompany their actions with a little song. The burden of this song is concerned with the gluttonous devouring of a fat antelope and resulting flatulence.

At the conclusion they hurriedly distribute the gifts they have brought, and as the cries of the waiting Katcinas become more and more insistent, the kiva chief gives the Yellow Qöqöqloms a quantity of sacred meal and prayer-feathers. Then they leave the kiva just as the others, led by the Chief Katcinas, Ahul, Kuzrua, and Kokosochöya, begin to come down the ladder. These "mixed" Katcinas now give a dance for the spectators, at the close of which they are thanked, dismissed in conventional fashion, and sent back to their home at Kisiwu. After their departure, the Powamu Katcinas arrive to perform the Bean dance which lasts almost till dawn.

BIBLIOGRAPHY

BIBLIOGRAPHY

ATKINS, J. D. C.
1886. Annual report of the commissioner of Indian affairs. Washington.

BANDELIER, A. F.
1892. The "Montezuma" of the Pueblo Indians. American Anthropologist, old series, vol. 5, no. 4. Washington.

BARTLETT, K.
1934. Spanish contacts with the Hopi. Museum of Northern Arizona, Museum Notes, vol. 6, no. 12. Flagstaff.
1936. Hopi history, no. 2. Museum of Northern Arizona, Museum Notes, vol. 8, no. 7. Flagstaff.

BEAGLEHOLE, E.
1936. Hopi hunting and hunting ritual. Yale University Publications in Anthropology, no. 4. New Haven.
1937. Notes on Hopi economic life. Yale University Publications in Anthropology, no. 15. New Haven.

BEAGLEHOLE, P.
1935. Census data from two Hopi villages. American Anthropologist, vol. 37, no. 1. Menasha.

BEAGLEHOLE, E., AND P.
1935. Hopi of the Second Mesa. American Anthropological Association, Memoirs, no. 44. Menasha.

BLOOM, L. B.
1931. A campaign against the Moqui Pueblos. New Mexico Historical Review, vol. 6, no. 2. Albuquerque.

BOURKE, J. G.
1884. The snake-dance of the Moquis of Arizona. New York.

BREW, J. O.
1937. The first two seasons at Awatovi. American Antiquity, vol. 3, no. 2. Menasha.

BRYAN, K.
1929. Flood-water farming. Geographical Review, vol. 19, no. 3. New York.
1941. Pre-Columbian agriculture in the Southwest, as conditioned by periods of alluviation. Annals of the Association of American Geographers, vol. 31, no. 4. New York.

COLTON, H. S.
1934. A brief survey of Hopi common law. Museum of Northern Arizona, Museum Notes, vol. 7, no. 6. Flagstaff.

COLTON, M. R. F.
1930. The Hopi craftsman. Museum of Northern Arizona, Museum Notes, vol. 3, no. 1. Flagstaff.
1931. Technique of the major Hopi crafts. Museum of Northern Arizona, Museum Notes, vol. 3, no. 12. Flagstaff.
1938. The arts and crafts of the Hopi Indians. Museum of Northern Arizona, Museum Notes, vol. 11, no. 1. Flagstaff.

COLTON, M. R. F., AND H. S.
1931. Petroglyphs, the record of a great adventure. American Anthropologist, vol. 33, no. 1. Menasha.

CRANE, L.
1926. Indians of the enchanted desert. Boston.

CROTHERS, W. D.
1872. Annual report of the commissioner of Indian Affairs. Washington.

CURTIS, E. S.
1922. The North American Indian. Vol. 12. Seattle.

CUSHING, F. H.
1923. Origin myth from Oraibi. Journal of American Folk-Lore, vol. 36, no. 140. Lancaster.

DENNIS, W.
1940. The Hopi child. New York.

DENNIS, W., AND M. G.
1940. Cradles and cradling practices of the Pueblo Indians. American Anthropologist, vol. 42, no. 1. Menasha.

DONALDSON, T.
1893. Moqui Pueblo Indians of Arizona. Extra Census Bulletin of 11th Census of the United States. U. S. Census Printing Office. Washington.

DORSEY, G. A., AND VOTH, H. R.
1901. The Oraibi soyal ceremony. Field Columbian Museum, Anthropological Series, vol. 3, no. 1. Chicago.

1902. The Mishongnovi ceremonies of the snake and antelope fraternities. Field Columbian Museum, Anthropological Series, vol. 3, no. 3. Chicago.

Douglas, F. H.
1938. Notes on Hopi brocading. Museum of Northern Arizona, Museum Notes, vol. 11, no. 4. Flagstaff.

Earle, E., and Kennard, E. A.
1938. Hopi kachinas. New York.

Eggan, F.
1933. The kinship system and social organization of the western Pueblos. Unpublished doctoral dissertation in the University of Chicago Library.

Fewkes, J. W.
1891. The meaning of the Moki snake dance. Journal of American Folk-Lore, vol. 4, no. 13. Boston and New York.
1892a. A few summer ceremonials at the Tusayan Pueblos. Journal of American Archaeology and Ethnology, vol. 2. Boston.
1892b. A few Tusayan pictographs. American Anthropologist, old series, vol. 5, no. 1. Washington.
1893. A-wá-to-bi: An archaeological verification of a Tusayan legend. American Anthropologist, old series, vol. 6, no. 4. Washington.
1894a. The kinship of the Tusayan villagers. American Anthropologist, old series, vol. 7, no. 4. Washington.
1894b. The snake ceremonials at Walpi. Journal of American Ethnology and Archaeology, vol. 4. Boston.
1894c. The Walpi flute observance. Journal of American Folk-Lore, vol. 7, no. 27. Boston and New York.
1894d. On certain personages who appear in a Tusayan ceremony. American Anthropologist, old series, vol. 7, no. 1. Washington.
1895a. The Oraibi flute altar. Journal of American Folk-Lore, vol. 8, no. 31. Boston and New York.
1895b. The Tusayan new-fire ceremony. Boston Society of Natural History, Proceedings, vol. 26. Boston.
1896a. The Micoñinovi flute altars. Journal of American Folk-Lore, vol. 9, no. 35. Boston and New York.
1896b. The prehistoric culture of Tusayan.

American Anthropologist, old series, vol. 9, no. 5. Washington.
1896c. A contribution to ethnobotany. American Anthropologist, old series, vol. 9, no. 1. Washington.
1897a. The sacrificial element in Hopi worship. Journal of American Folk-Lore, vol. 10, no. 38. Boston and New York.
1897b. Tusayan katcinas. Bureau of American Ethnology, 15th Annual Report. Washington.
1897c. Tusayan snake ceremonies. Bureau of American Ethnology, 16th Annual Report. Washington.
1897d. Morphology of Tusayan altars. American Anthropologist, old series, vol. 10, no. 5. Washington.
1898a. The winter solstice ceremony at Walpi. American Anthropologist, old series, vol. 11, nos. 3 and 4. Washington.
1898b. The growth of the Hopi ritual. Journal of American Folk-Lore, vol. 11, no. 42. Boston and New York.
1899a. The Alosaka cult of the Hopi Indians. American Anthropologist, vol. 1, no. 3. New York.
1899b. Hopi basket dances. Journal of American Folk-Lore, vol. 12, no. 45. Boston and New York.
1899c. The winter solstice altars at Hano Pueblo. American Anthropologist, vol. 1, no. 2. New York.
1900a. The new-fire ceremony at Walpi. American Anthropologist, vol. 2, no. 1. New York.
1900b. Tusayan flute and snake ceremonies. Bureau of American Ethnology, 19th Annual Report, pt. 2. Washington.
1900c. Tusayan migration traditions. Bureau of American Ethnology, 19th Annual Report, pt. 2. Washington.
1900d. A theatrical performance at Walpi. Washington Academy of Sciences, Proceedings, vol. 2, no. 33. Washington.
1901a. The lesser new-fire ceremony at Walpi. American Anthropologist, vol. 3, no. 3. New York.
1901b. The Owakülti altar at Sichomovi Pueblo. American Anthropologist, vol. 3, no. 2. New York.
1901c. An interpretation of katcina worship.

Journal of American Folk-Lore, vol. 14, no. 53. Boston.

1902a. Sky-god personations in Hopi worship. Journal of American Folk-Lore, vol. 15, no. 56. Boston and New York.

1902b. Minor Hopi festivals. American Anthropologist, vol. 4, no. 3. New York.

1903. Hopi katcinas. Bureau of American Ethnology, 21st Annual Report. Washington.

1906a. Hopi shrines near the east Mesa, Arizona. American Anthropologist, vol. 8, no. 2. Lancaster.

1906b. Hopi ceremonial frames from Cañon de Chelly, Arizona. American Anthropologist, vol. 8, no. 4. Lancaster.

1907. Hopi. Bureau of American Ethnology, Bulletin 30, pt. 1. Washington.

1910. The butterfly in Hopi myth and ritual. American Anthropologist, vol. 12, no. 4. Washington.

1917a. A religious ceremony of the Hopi Indians. Scientific American Supplement, vol. 83. New York.

1917b. The Pueblo culture and its relationships. Second Pan-American Scientific Congress, Proceedings, sec. 1, vol. 1. Washington.

1920. Sun worship of the Hopi Indians. Smithsonian Institution. Annual Report for 1918. Washington.

1923. Ancestor worship of the Hopi Indians. Smithsonian Institution, Annual Report for 1921. Washington.

1924. The use of idols in Hopi worship. Smithsonian Institution for 1922, Annual Report. Washington.

1927. The katcina altars in Hopi worship. Smithsonian Institution. Annual Report for 1926. Washington.

FEWKES, J. W., AND OWENS, J. G.

1892. The Lā-lā-kōn-ta: a Tusayan dance. American Anthropologist, old series, vol. 5, no. 2. Washington.

FEWKES, J. W., AND STEPHEN, A. M.

1892a. The Mamzrauti: a Tusayan ceremony. American Anthropologist, old series, vol. 5, no. 3. Washington.

1892b. The Nā-ac-nai-ya: a Tusayan initiation ceremony. Journal of American Folk-Lore, vol. 5, no. 18. Boston and New York.

1893. The Pa-lü-lü-koñ-ti: a Tusayan cere-

mony. Journal of American Folk-Lore, vol. 6, no. 23. Boston and New York.

FORDE, C. D.

1931. Hopi agriculture and land ownership. Journal of the Royal Anthropological Institute, vol. 61. London.

FORREST, E. R.

1929. Missions and pueblos of the old southwest. Cleveland.

GOLDENWEISER, A. A.

1937. Anthropology. New York.

GUTHE, C. E.

1925. Pueblo pottery making. New Haven.

HACK, J. T.

1942. The changing physical environment of the Hopi Indians of Arizona. Peabody Museum Papers, vol. xxxv, no. 1. Cambridge.

HACKETT, C. W.

1911. The revolt of the Pueblo Indians of New Mexico in 1680. Texas State Historical Association, Quarterly, vol. 15, no. 2. Austin.

HAEBERLIN, H. K.

1916. The idea of fertilization in the culture of the Pueblo Indians. American Anthropological Association, Memoirs, vol. 3, no. 1. Lancaster.

HARGRAVE, L. L.

1930. Shungopovi. Museum of Northern Arizona, Museum Notes, vol. 2, no. 10. Flagstaff.

1932. Oraibi: a brief history of the oldest inhabited town in the United States. Museum of Northern Arizona, Museum Notes, vol. 4, no. 7. Flagstaff.

HODGE, F. W.

1910. Oraibi. Bureau of American Ethnology, Bulletin 30, pt. 2. Washington.

HOUGH, W.

1898. Environmental interrelations in Arizona. American Anthropologist, old series, vol. 11, no. 5. Washington.

1917. The Sio Shalako at the First Mesa. American Anthropologist, vol. 19, no. 3. (Commentary by J. W. Fewkes.) Lancaster.

KENNARD, E. A.

1937. Hopi reactions to death. American Anthropologist, vol. 39, no. 3. Menasha.

KENT, K. P.

1940. The braiding of a Hopi wedding sash. Plateau, vol. 12, no. 3. Flagstaff.

KIDDER, A. V.
1924. An introduction to the study of south-western archaeology. New Haven.
KROEBER, A. L.
1917. Zuñi kin and clan. American Museum of Natural History, Anthropological Papers, vol. 18, pt. 2. New York.
LEUPP, F. E.
1906. Annual report of the commissioner of Indian affairs. Washington.
1907. Annual report of the commissioner of Indian affairs. Washington.
LINTON, R.
1936. The study of man. New York.
LOWIE, R. H.
1915. Exogamy and systems of relationship. American Anthropologist, vol. 17, no. 2. Menasha.
1919. Family and sib. American Anthropologist, vol. 21, no. 1. Menasha.
1920. Primitive society. New York.
1925. A women's ceremony among the Hopi. Natural History, vol. 25. New York.
1929a. Hopi kinship. American Museum of Natural History, Anthropological Papers, vol. 30, pt. 7. New York.
1929b. Notes on Hopi clans. American Museum of Natural History, Anthropological Papers, vol. 30, pt. 6. New York.
1934. An introduction to cultural anthropology. New York.
1937. Relationship terms. Encyclopaedia Britannica, 14th Edition, vol. 19. New York and Chicago.
LUMMIS, C. F.
1892. Social status of Pueblo women. American Anthropologist, old series, vol. 5, no. 4. Washington.
LUXAN, D. P. DE
1929. Expedition into New Mexico made by Antonio de Espejo, 1582–1583. Translated by G. P. Hammond and A. Rey. The Quivara Society. Los Angeles.
MACLEISH, K.
1940. Notes on Hopi belt-weaving of Moenkopi. American Anthropologist, vol. 42, no. 2. Menasha.
MATTHEWS, W.
1902. Myths of gestation and parturition. American Anthropologist, vol. 4, no. 4. New York.

MENDELIEFF, K.
1886. An Indian snake-dance. Science, old series, vol. 7, no. 174. New York.
MINDELEFF, C.
1900. Localization of Tusayan clans. Bureau of American Ethnology, 19th Annual Report, pt. 2. Washington.
MINDELEFF, V.
1891. A study of Pueblo architecture, Tusayan and Cibola. Bureau of American Ethnology, 8th Annual Report. Washington.
MORGAN, L. H.
1909. Ancient society. Chicago.
MURDOCK, G. P.
1934. Our primitive contemporaries. New York.
NEQUATEWA, E.
1931. Hopi hopiwime. Museum of Northern Arizona, Museum Notes, vol. 3, no. 9. Flagstaff.
1933. Hopi courtship and marriage. Museum of Northern Arizona, Museum Notes, vol. 5, no. 9. Flagstaff.
1936. Truth of a Hopi. Museum of Northern Arizona, Bulletin no. 8 (M. R. F. Colton, Ed.). Flagstaff.
1938. Dr. Fewkes and Masauwu. Museum of Northern Arizona, Museum Notes, vol. 11, no. 2. Flagstaff.
OWENS, J. G.
1892. Natal ceremonies of the Hopi Indians. Journal of American Ethnology and Archaeology, vol. 2, no. 2. Boston.
PARSONS, E. C.
1921a. Getting married on First Mesa, Arizona. Scientific Monthly, vol. 13, no. 3. Utica.
1921b. The Pueblo Indian clan in folk-lore. Journal of American Folk-Lore, vol. 34, no. 132. Lancaster.
1921c. Hopi mothers and children. Man, vol. 21, no. 58. London.
1922. Contributions to Hopi history. American Anthropologist, vol. 24, no. 3. Menasha.
1923a. The Hopi buffalo dance. Man, vol. 23, no. 12. London.
1923b. The Hopi Wöwöchim ceremony in 1920. American Anthropologist, vol. 25, no. 2. Menasha.
1923c. Laguna genealogies. American Museum of Natural History, Anthropological Papers, vol. 19, pt. 5. New York.

1925. A Pueblo Indian journal. American Anthropological Association, Memoirs, no. 32. Menasha.

1926. Tewa tales. American Folk-Lore Society, Memoirs, vol. 19. New York.

1927. Witchcraft among the Pueblos: Indian or Spanish? Man, vol. 27, nos. 70, 80. London.

1933. Hopi and Zuñi ceremonialism. American Anthropological Association, Memoirs, no. 39. Menasha.

1936a. The house-clan complex of the Pueblos. Essays in Anthropology presented to A. L. Kroeber. Berkeley.

1936b. Hopi journal of Alexander M. Stephen. Columbia University Contributions to Anthropology, vol. 23 (E. C. Parsons, Ed.). New York.

1937. Naming practises in Arizona. American Anthropologist, vol. 39, no. 3. Menasha.

1939. Pueblo Indian religion. Chicago.

1940. A pre-Spanish record of Hopi ceremonies. American Anthropologist, vol. 42, no. 3. Menasha.

PARSONS, E. C., AND BEALS, R. L.
1934. The sacred clowns of the Pueblo and Mayo-Yaqui Indians. American Anthropologist, vol. 36, no. 4. Menasha.

PRUDDEN, T. M.
1903. The prehistoric ruins of the San Juan watershed. American Anthropologist, vol. 5, no. 2. Lancaster.

1914. The circular kivas of small ruins in the San Juan watershed. American Anthropologist, vol. 16, no. 1. Lancaster.

ROBERTS, F. H. H.
1930. Early Pueblo ruins in southwestern Colorado. Bureau of American Ethnology, Bulletin 96. Washington.

1932. The village of the great kivas. Bureau of American Ethnology, Bulletin 111. Washington.

SCHOLES, F. V.
1936. Church and state in New Mexico, 1610–1650. New Mexico Historical Review, vol. 11, no. 1. Albuquerque.

1937. Troublous times in New Mexico, 1659–1670. New Mexico Historical Review, vol. 12, no. 2. Albuquerque.

SIMMONS, L. W. (editor)
1942. Sun chief. New Haven.

SOLBERG, O.
1906. Über die Bahos der Hopi. Archiv für Anthropologie, new series, vol. 4. Braunschweig.

STEPHEN, A. M.
1929. Hopi tales. Journal of American Folk-Lore, vol. 42, no. 163 (E. C. Parsons, Ed.). New York.

1939–1940. Hopi Indians of Arizona. The Masterkey, vol. 13, no. 6; vol. 14, no. 1; vol. 14, no. 3; vol. 14, no. 4; vol. 14, no. 5; vol. 14, no. 6. Los Angeles.

STEWARD, J. H.
1931. Notes on Hopi ceremonies in their initiatory form. American Anthropologist, vol. 33, no. 1. Menasha.

1937. Ecological aspects of southwestern society. Anthropos, vol. 32, nos. 1 and 2. Vienna.

STEWART, G. R.
1940. Conservation in Pueblo agriculture. Scientific Monthly, vol. 51, no. 4. Lancaster.

STRONG, W. D.
1927. An analysis of southwestern society. American Anthropologist, vol. 29, no. 1. Menasha.

SULLIVAN, J. H.
1884. Moquis Indians. American Antiquarian, vol. 6, no. 2. Chicago.

THOMAS, A. B.
1932. Forgotten frontiers. Norman.

TITIEV, M.
1934. The social organization of the Hopi Indians. Unpublished doctoral dissertation in Harvard University Library. Cambridge.

1937a. A Hopi salt expedition. American Anthropologist, vol. 39, no. 2. Menasha.

1937b. The use of kinship terms in Hopi ritual. Museum of Northern Arizona, Museum Notes, vol. 10, no. 3. Flagstaff.

1938a. The Hopi method of baking sweet corn. Michigan Academy of Science, Arts, and Letters, Papers, vol. 23, pt. 4 (1937). Ann Arbor.

1938b. The problem of cross-cousin marriage among the Hopi. American Anthropologist, vol. 40, no. 1. Menasha.

1938c. Dates of planting at Oraibi. Museum of Northern Arizona, Museum Notes, vol. 11, no. 5. Flagstaff.

1939a. The story of Kokopele. American Anthropologist, vol. 41, no. 1. Menasha.

1939b. Hopi racing customs at Oraibi, Arizona. Michigan Academy of Science, Arts, and Letters, Papers, vol. 24, pt 4 (1938). Ann Arbor.

1941. A Hopi visit to the afterworld. Michigan Academy of Science, Arts, and Letters, Papers, vol. 26, pt. 4 (1940). Ann Arbor.

1943a. Notes on Hopi witchcraft. Michigan Academy of Science, Arts, and Letters, Papers, vol. 28, pt. 4 (1942). Ann Arbor.

1943b. Hopi snake handling. Scientific Monthly, vol. 57, no. 1. Lancaster.

1943c. The influence of common residence on the unilateral classification of kindred. American Anthropologist, vol. 45, no. 4. Menasha.

TOZZER, A. M.

1928. Social origins and social continuities. New York.

VESTAL, P. A.

1940. Notes on a collection of plants from the Hopi Indian region. Harvard University, Botanical Museum Leaflets, vol. 8, no. 8. Cambridge.

VICTOR, F. F.

1871. The river of the west. Hartford.

VOTH, H. R.

1900. Oraibi marriage customs. American Anthropologist, vol. 2, no. 2. New York.

1901. The Oraibi Powamu ceremony. Field Columbian Museum, Anthropological Series, vol. 3, no. 2. Chicago.

1903a. The Oraibi summer snake ceremony. Field Columbian Museum, Anthropological Series, vol. 3, no. 4. Chicago.

1903b. The Oraibi oaqöl ceremony. Field Columbian Museum, Anthropological Series, vol. 6, no. 1. Chicago.

1905a. Oraibi natal customs and ceremonies. Field Columbian Museum, Anthropological Series, vol. 6, no. 2. Chicago.

1905b. The traditions of the Hopi. Field Columbian Museum, Anthropological Series, vol. 8. Chicago.

1912a. The Oraibi marau ceremony. Field Columbian Museum, Anthropological Series, vol. 11, no. 1. Chicago.

1912b. Brief miscellaneous Hopi papers. Field Columbian Museum, Anthropological Series, vol. 11, no. 2. Chicago.

1915. Hopi proper names. Field Columbian Museum, Anthropological Series, vol. 6, no. 3. Chicago.

WALLIS, W. D.

1936. Folk tales from Shumopovi, Second Mesa. Journal of American Folk-Lore, vol. 49, nos. 191–192. Lancaster.

WHITING, A. F.

1937. Hopi Indian agriculture—II. Museum of Northern Arizona, Museum Notes, vol. 10, no. 5. Flagstaff.

1939. Ethnobotany of the Hopi. Museum of Northern Arizona, Bulletin 15. Flagstaff.

WINSHIP, G. P.

1896. The Coronado expedition, 1540–1542. Bureau of American Ethnology, 14th Annual Report, pt. 1. Washington.

TOPICAL INDEX AND GLOSSARY OF NATIVE TERMS

TOPICAL INDEX AND GLOSSARY OF NATIVE TERMS[1]

---

[1] Compare the much more extensive glossary prepared by Parsons and Whorf, and published in Parsons, 1936b, pp. 1198-1326. This glossary should be consulted by anyone interested in the phonetic transcription of Hopi terms.

wupilangviki (square *piki*, decorated with design of wavy lines)

wuvata (see Whip)

wungwa (clan member, used only in the singular)

Wuwutcim society (see also Tribal Initiation), 64 footnote 34, 125, 130 and footnote 1, 133–134, 136 footnote 48, 138, 142, 164, 165 and footnote 12, 167, 168, 191 footnote 58, 211

wuya (clan symbol, clan ancestor or clan ancient)

yalaha (specular iron)

Yapa (Mocking Bird), 138

yonga (cactus)

Yungya'a (entering, the first day of a ceremony)

PLATES

NOTES ON PLATES

The Pueblo of Old Oraibi. The last cluster of buildings at the left has been erected since 1906.

PLATE I.
The Pueblo of Hotevilla. An air view of the village founded by the Conservative faction which was driven out of Oraibi during the split of 1906. Note the small terraced gardens in the central foreground and the peach orchards in the background.

PLATE II.
a. A Mud Fight at Old Oraibi. During the marriage rites of a nephew, his paternal aunts attack his mother. At the left, two aunts are shown throwing the groom's mother to the ground.

b. Climax of the Mud Fight. The groom's mother, her hands tied, lies prostrate on the ground. One aunt is doing a mock war dance around her body, brandishing scissors in one hand and a lock of the victim's hair in the other.

c. Chief Tawaqwaptiwa of Oraibi. Tawaqwaptiwa was leader of the Friendly faction in the split of 1906. This photograph was taken in front of his house in August, 1932. Note the fox pelt which serves as the "tail" of a Katcina dancer's costume.

d. Frank Siemptiwa. Siemptiwa is regarded as the Oraibi chief's lieutenant, serving as leader of the Moenkopi colony. This picture was taken in December, 1933.

e. The Masau Katcina. A photograph based on an exceptionally accurate painting of the little known Katcina which is associated with Masau'u, the god of death. The impersonation of the Mausau Katcina is the only masked representation that may be given during the closed portion of the Katcina cycle.

PLATE III.
a. Soyal Pahos. A cluster of prayer-sticks deposited by their owners at the close of the Soyal ceremony in 1933. They are made of slender willow stems to which turkey feathers are attached by strings of native spun cotton thread.

b. The Shrine of Talautumsi. A shrine situated on the mesa top, south of Oraibi pueblo. The image of Talautumsi, which plays an important part in the Tribal Initiation ceremonies, is lodged within the walled-up area.

c. The Shrine of Sowika. This rock is supposedly the dwelling place of Sowika, patron deity of children. It faces the eastern edge of Old Oraibi, and parents bring sick children here at sunrise. Holding a mixture of cornmeal and water in the mouth, the parent sucks at the child's joints and the affected parts, and then spews the moistened meal against the cup-like depressions at the base of the shrine. This procedure is repeated four times.

PLATE IV.
a. Archaeology in the making at Old Oraibi. This section of the village was abandoned during the split of 1906. The remains of the Kwan kiva are seen in the foreground.

b. The Snake Shrine at Oraibi. Located west of the village on the mesa top. The pottery vessels in which the reptiles have been kept are thrown here at the conclusion of the Snake-Antelope rites.

c. The Shrine of Matcito. Situated at the foot of the western stairway to Oraibi, this shrine is supposed to represent the first home of Matcito, legendary founder of the pueblo. The holes are said to show where the roof beams rested.

I. The Pueblo of Hotevilla.

II. a. A MUD FIGHT AT OLD ORAIBI. b. CLIMAX OF THE MUD FIGHT. c. CHIEF TAWAQWAPTIWA

b

c

a

III. a. Soyal Pahos. b. The Shrine of Talautumsi. c. The Shrine of Sowika.

a

b

c

IV. a. ARCHAEOLOGY IN THE MAKING AT OLD ORAIBI. b. THE SNAKE
SHRINE AT ORAIBI. c. THE SHRINE OF MATCITO.

Old Oraibi
A Study of the Hopi Indians of Third Mesa

Mischa Titiev
Foreword by Richard I. Ford

According to their own mythology, the Hopis emerged into the present world through an opening in the earth, or *sipapu*. Archaeological evidence indicates that at the very least they are direct descendants of the earliest Southwest peoples.

Located in present-day northern Arizona, the Hopi Villages are grouped along three peninsular extensions of Black Mesa, known as First, Second, and Third Mesas. At the foot of Third Mesa lies the town of New Oraibi; at the summit are the pueblos of Bakavi, Hotevilla, and Old Oraibi.

Long considered an ethnographic classic, *Old Oraibi* is as detailed a picture of Hopi religion as can be shown by an outsider. First published in 1944, it considers lifeways in the old pueblo of Oraibi, the only Third Mesa town until the famous 1906 split between Traditionals and Progressives. In addition to a full description of the social organization of Oraibi and the events surrounding the schism, Mischa Titiev offers a lively portrait of Hopi ceremonialism, katcinas, and the ritual cycle.

A sensitive portrayal of one of America's most fascinating cultures as it existed a century ago.

Mischa Titiev (1901–1978) was professor of anthropology at the University of Michigan.

University of New Mexico Press.

ISBN 0-8263-1344-2

90000

9 780826 313447